To dearest D...
 on his birthday
 March 13th, 1960.
From Gladys.

THE MEMOIRS OF

SIR ANTHONY EDEN

FULL CIRCLE

THE MEMOIRS OF

THE RT. HON.

SIR ANTHONY EDEN

K.G., P.C., M.C.

——

FULL CIRCLE

CASSELL · LONDON

CASSELL & COMPANY LTD
35 Red Lion Square · London WC1
and at
MELBOURNE · SYDNEY · TORONTO · CAPE TOWN
JOHANNESBURG · AUCKLAND

———

© The Times Publishing Co. Ltd., 1960
First published 1960

Made and Printed by Offset in Great Britain
by William Clowes and Sons Ltd, London and Beccles
F.1159

FOREWORD

I began to think of writing a book about my years in office after my operation in the spring of 1957. My first intention was to proceed with it in the accepted order of time, from the early nineteen-thirties until the present day.

This method had the advantage that the lessons of the 'thirties and their application to the 'fifties, which are the themes of my memoirs, could be more easily displayed. It imposed a limitation, however, which I considered decisive. At least four years must elapse before my account of the more recent period could be presented. I thought that I should not wait so long. This book will expose wounds; by doing so it could help to heal them.

The years during which I held responsibility for the conduct of my country's foreign policy fell into two periods. The first was from 1935 until 1945, with a break of eighteen months from February 1938 until the early autumn of the following year, due to my resignation from Mr. Chamberlain's Government. I returned to Cabinet office, in company with Mr. Churchill, on the outbreak of war on September 3rd and became Foreign Secretary again towards the end of 1940.

The second period dates from the autumn of 1951 until January 1957, during the whole of which time I was either Foreign Secretary or Prime Minister. It is with this latter period that this volume deals, but the policies which I upheld and pursued during that time were based on my earlier experiences. In giving effect to them I found myself, from time to time, in disagreement with other opinions held in my own country and in allied countries. This has been a cause of regret to me.

So much of my life has been spent in the conduct or execution of foreign policy that I feel I should set down these events as they presented themselves to me. The reflections and decisions I record in this volume are those which I formed at the time. I hope that this account and my reasoning, as well as the experiences I lived through, may be of service to others.

My material has consisted of the personal minutes which I wrote, often to Sir Winston Churchill as Prime Minister when I was Foreign Secretary, or to other colleagues when I was Prime Minister myself. Another source used has been the notes dictated to form the messages sent home when I was engaged upon a mission abroad, or sent abroad either to our embassies or to the statesmen of other lands. Yet another source has been the occasional notes jotted down at the moment and intended to be the basis for a fuller record when opportunity offered. But it is all the thought of the time on the action of the time set down at the time.

I considered that such an account could be useful because, though the pattern of world politics may be modified and its contours appear from time to time smoother or more menacing, nothing can change man's need to take counsel with all who have pursued the endless adventure.

ANTHONY EDEN

Fyfield Manor,
   Pewsey, Wiltshire

September, 1959

ACKNOWLEDGMENTS

I wish to express my thanks to Mr. Alan Hodge for his help in the preparation of Books Two and Three of this volume, and to Mr. Bryan Cartledge for his help in respect of Book One. I would also like to thank Lord Furneaux and Mrs. B. W. Scott for their assistance on a number of chapters in the same Book. I am grateful to Mr. Robert Blake for both general and detailed advice at many stages of the work. Miss Edwards, my secretary, has typed the volume and facilitated its production.

The official documents printed in this volume are Crown Copyright, which is legally vested in the Controller of Her Majesty's Stationery Office, and I am obliged for permission to reproduce them.

CONTENTS

BOOK ONE

Foreign Secretary

BOOK TWO

Prime Minister

BOOK THREE

Suez

MAPS

BOOK ONE

Foreign Secretary

I

I TAKE OVER
October – November 1951

The end of Allied unity – Russian aims – Bevin at the Foreign Office – The United States and Europe – Marshall Aid – The Berlin airlift – Communism in China – Afro-Asian nationalism – I become Foreign Secretary

My world began in war. It has been spent in war, its preparation and its aftermath. On this account, my confidence in what could be done to create an international order in the years after the last war was sharply salted by experience. So was that of others who were conscious of the cravings of Soviet power. Hopes were as fervent, but more prudent than after the first world war.

In the spring of 1945, I led a strong British delegation, which included Attlee, Halifax and Salisbury, to the San Francisco Conference. The American delegation under Edward Stettinius co-operated with us in complete loyalty, and we were sustained by Commonwealth statesmen like Jan Smuts and Mackenzie King. Yet, near the end of our work on the United Nations Charter, when the moment came for Attlee and me to return to take part in the British general election, I felt a growing presentiment at the way events in Europe would work out. During the conference, the Prime Minister and I had exchanged telegrams of foreboding as the Russian mood and methods became increasingly disquieting.

Historically and geographically there were reasons enough why Russia should be our ally in peace as in war. Three great conflicts had proved that necessity: the Napoleonic war and the first and second world wars. In the wake of the first two we had drifted apart, to the detriment of both countries. Towards the end of the last war Mr. Svernik, then chairman of the Soviet Trade Unions and later President of the Soviet Union, was my guest at a luncheon at the Foreign Office.

I spoke to him on this theme, suggesting that we should avoid repeating our error. He appeared sincerely eager to agree, and no doubt he was, on terms. Ideology and Soviet ambitions got in the way, so allied unity in war crumbled at the first touch of peace.

One cause could have held us together, the determination to prevent Germany from ever again threatening the peace. With a France dismembered by the occupation and an America which could become disinterested, this might have been a powerful enough motive. But Hitler's final frenzy had brought too complete a destruction upon Germany. Russia saw no need to seek a Western ally, still less to pay a price for one, though she would at all times accept compliance.

For the communists, the cease-fire was only a moment to take stock. War was to them an event, at most a phase, in their onward march. The Soviets were not stopped by it, they did not pause for it and they never questioned their faith. It is this automatism that is so disconcerting to the West and which the West has not yet learnt to meet and overcome. In the Soviet mind the collapse of the capitalist world is only a question of time and opportunity, to which they are always ready to give a prod.

There were indications of trouble to come, well before Potsdam. Moscow resisted the establishment of a democratic and representative Polish Government and relentlessly pushed their Polish puppet administration to make growing demands upon the West. I had wished to raise the Polish issue much earlier in the war and I asked Mr. Cordell Hull, the American Secretary of State, during our visit to Moscow in 1943, to make plain our position together. I encouraged him all I could to join with me in this, but though our relations were always excellent, he held firmly to the position that he had no authority for such action. Perhaps this reluctance did not matter as much as I then thought. Even if the best of agreements had been obtained at the earliest of moments, the Soviets would scarcely have heeded them in the hour of victory. The Russians were then too conscious of their strength to respect any check but greater force. Eleven years later, events in Hungary showed this conduct to be unchanged.

The day I went to hand in my seals at Buckingham Palace, after my party's defeat at the general election of 1945, I had a brief conversation with Ernest Bevin in one of the adjoining rooms. He had just been appointed Foreign Secretary, I think considerably to his surprise. Hurriedly, between the ceremonies of surrendering and receiving seals, we discussed the actual position at Potsdam in respect of Russian-

Polish demands. I repeated to him what he knew already, my strong aversion to agreeing to any concession for the Poles beyond the line of the Oder and the eastern Neisse. I repeated, as I had often done to them and to the Russians, that in their own interest I was sure they would be unwise to claim land so far to the west. They would only lay up trouble thereby for the future. Bevin listened and said that he would do his best, which he did, but he could not prevail.

Ernest Bevin and I had been good colleagues during our years in the War Cabinet and often discussed foreign affairs together. At that time I was closer to him than to any other member of his party, and the friendship between us lasted until his death. The period 1945–50 in British foreign policy was dominated by his personality, and it was fortunate for our country and for Europe that this was so.

Bevin was shrewd and he soon saw that the problem of his term of office would be how to withstand the growing Soviet appetite. At the close of the war our country was in no mood to be alerted to this new danger and it took a man of stature and sincere conviction, first to discover the extent of the danger for himself, and then to lead his people to share his judgment. This Bevin did and it is his enduring memorial. His principal difficulty lay in his own party, where, throughout his period as Foreign Secretary, there was an active minority which was cool to his policies or hostile to them. Fortunately Bevin possessed the authority in the Labour Party, and above all in the Trade Union movement, to dominate his critics.

The last time I saw him was in the House of Commons after his resignation. He had taken this hardly and expressed resentment. He gave me his account of events and I felt deep sympathy for him, but the man was very ill, past bearing the burdens of his office, yet bravely not wishing to admit it. There was stature about Bevin. I have never felt it more strongly than that day when he knew that his work was over and his powers were visibly in decline.

Though my handling of some events would have been different from his, I was in agreement with the aims of his foreign policy and with most that he did, and we met quite frequently. He would invite me to his room in the House of Commons where we discussed events informally. In Parliament I usually followed him in debate and I would publicly have agreed with him more, if I had not been anxious to embarrass him less.

Early in the life of the Labour Government, Mr. Oliver Stanley commented in the House of Commons on the continuity of our foreign

5

policy, referring to Mr. Bevin's speech in a debate on the United Nations Charter:

> We were told in the election from the platforms of hon. Members opposite, that their return would create a new world.... Well, we have now had a fortnight of the new world and certainly in the new world there are still some familiar speeches. The right hon. Gentleman, the Foreign Secretary, in that splendid speech he made on Monday, which was acclaimed in all parts of the House, made me wonder whether in his spare time—if he ever has any spare time now—he had not been dipping into that brilliant old play, 'The Importance Of Being Anthony'.

These immediate post-war years would have presented the Western nations, and the Labour Government in the United Kingdom in particular, with infinitely greater difficulties if the Soviets had played their hand with skill. They were improvident and careless. They squandered their goodwill, and there was then so much of it that it almost seemed as if they did not care. I was perplexed at this aspect of Soviet policy, for I knew Stalin to be a prudent if ruthless man. Perhaps the answer is to be found in this conversation. In Moscow one evening during the war, Mr. Churchill and I were invited after our work to supper in Stalin's flat. In the course of conversation we spoke of the diplomatic methods of a number of countries. We came last to Russia, and Stalin remarked, 'Perhaps we Russians are not as simple as you think.' I replied that we had never thought them that, but rather as skilful and therefore formidable. Stalin rejoined that the truth probably lay between the two, that they were neither as simple as some thought nor as skilful as others believed.

Whatever the motive for post-war contempt of the opinion of others, the consequences were made plain with brutality. In language and in action the Soviets showed a disregard for the engagements they had entered into at Yalta and Potsdam and elsewhere. The countries of eastern Europe, which they had occupied and where they had promised to hold free elections, were taken into political bondage. Not content with this, their ambition moved westward.

I do not believe that there was any alternative policy, short of fellow-travelling, which would have enabled Britain to establish relations with the Kremlin in those years. Happily for Europe we were not left alone. In the United States were statesmen of wisdom, authority and courage who wrought a revolutionary change in their country's traditional policies. There was to be no repetition of the withdrawal into isolation as after the first world war. On the contrary, the United States lent of its extensive resources to restore Europe's industrial and commercial life. Europe today is economically flourishing and shows many signs of recovering her ancient leadership. This is largely due to the efforts of her own peoples, but the help of the United States was indispensable and it was freely given.

The capital crisis for the Western allies came when Russia tried to blockade Berlin. The airlift was the splendid answer, brilliantly executed. In those days Bevin asked me if, to demonstrate national unity in this policy, I would go to Berlin and make a speech there. I did so with alacrity and still recall the earnest, eager faces of the Berliners. They showed a glowing courage amid their shattered city.

The defeat of the attempt to blockade Berlin shaped future events in Europe. What General Marshall had done economically, General Eisenhower did militarily. N.A.T.O. was built and strengthened by stages which, however slow, solidified Western defence. On N.A.T.O's immediate front the position improved. On its southern flank it became through the years more dangerous, and is so today, because there has been no Western unity on policies there.

At the other end of the world, revolutionary changes had overturned the scene since I had left the Foreign Office in 1945. All China had fallen under communist control. Few had foreseen it, not even the Russians. It may be that there were sometimes doubts in the Kremlin as to the future consequences of these great events, a rival pope in Peking might not always be convenient. But if the Soviet leaders ever had such thoughts, they did not express them. For the immediate future, the success of the Chinese Communists in defeating Chiang Kai-shek supported by the United States, appeared to Moscow as an enticing development. A whole new field of subversion and troublemaking was opened up for communist exploitation.

The Korean war had been raging for over a year when I came back into office. A new danger confronted the world on the periphery of East and South-East Asia, where a rapidly deteriorating position in French Indo-China pointed peril for us all. Communism has been most successful where it has been able, as in China, to harness national forces, and least successful where it has come into direct conflict with an ancient faith and freedom firmly held, as in Hungary and Tibet.

The third great change which had occurred since 1945, the rise of

Afro-Asian nationalism, is less easy to define. Its various manifestations still create their problems. The desire for self-government, to form a state upon a common sentiment of nationality, these ambitions have long been a political force in history. They dominated Europe in the nineteenth and early twentieth centuries. Complicated by questions of 'colonialism', they dominate the Middle East today; they will dominate Africa tomorrow.

I believe it right to encourage, and where possible to guide, these national aspirations. I certainly tried to do so in many parts of the world, both as Foreign Secretary and Prime Minister. But it does not seem to me that sympathy towards these countries should license those who lead them. They still have to observe that respect for engagements upon which international confidence depends. There is a tendency to favour these new states, which is natural enough, and is encouraged by a very human wish to raise the standard of life of their people. All the same, this warm-heartedness can have dangerous consequences, when any one of these states has designs upon its neighbours. Nor is it good policy to speak and act feebly towards them from fear that, if rebuked or restrained, they or a dictator who leads them will turn to communist powers or be replaced by communist rivals. When we insist upon the observance of international engagements, we are not doing so on behalf of the nation whose direct interests may be affected, but on behalf of ourselves. Once indulge uncontrolled appetites, and it is only a matter of time and of whose turn comes next.

During these immediately post-war years Mr. Attlee presided over an administration of many talents and a triumphant majority. Men like Cripps, Bevin and Morrison were personalities to give strength to any Government. One weakness was that all of them had served strenuously in the war years. This, combined with the rigours of the offices they held, took a toll of their health. In its last years, without Cripps and Bevin, the Labour Government was but a shadow of its former self. Its message also was exhausted. Nationalization had been extensively applied to coal and railways, gas, electricity, and iron and steel. There was no enthusiasm for more among a public which was sure that it had had enough, and suspected that it had had a surfeit. Two marginal general elections followed. In 1950 the Labour Government had a majority of six votes in the House of Commons and eighteen months later we won an overall majority of seventeen seats on a small minority of votes.

★   ★   ★   ★   ★

8

At Mr. Churchill's invitation I became Foreign Secretary once again and had to translate my convictions into action without delay. For the present we were out of Abadan and the Iranian oilfields and had a crisis in Egypt on our hands, with mounting tension in Europe.

The relations between Russia and the Western powers were vituperative and bad. Meetings of the United Nations were often the occasion of slanging matches, never of negotiation. This was not only a disagreeable state of affairs, it was also dangerous. It was not that I minded abuse as such, but that indulgence in this habit was absorbing energies on both sides of the Iron Curtain which ought to be more intelligently used. I thought I must make an immediate effort to try to put a stop to name-calling.

I thought, also, that at the various meetings with the Russians and in discussions among themselves, the Western powers had attempted too ambitious a programme. They were for ever trying to table proposals to resolve all the major differences between East and West. This was a natural legacy of the war conferences, but the method was not getting us anywhere. It is not always prudent to start with a package proposal; it can be useful to lead up to one by agreeing the ingredients. I thought we should drop ambitious plans and meetings to handle them and choose detailed topics and work them out one by one.

Within a few days of my return to the Foreign Office I was due to attend the sixth session of the General Assembly of the United Nations, meeting exceptionally in Paris. I decided to use this opportunity for something more than a speech of general support and good intentions, and to set the course which I proposed to follow as Foreign Secretary.

To this assembly Britain, France and the United States had submitted proposals with regard to disarmament. The preliminary work upon these had been admirably done, so far as our country was concerned, under the authority of the previous Labour Government, and I was in full agreement with them. They were presented by Mr. Acheson on behalf of the three countries. Mr. Vyshinsky's speech of rejection was exceptionally virulent even by his standard of polemics. It made a bad impression on the delegates and I decided to reply the next day:

> On Wednesday last, three of the powers represented at this assembly, the United States, France and ourselves, put before you certain proposals for disarmament. One might surely have expected, remembering the hopes which were placed in the United Nations in the early days, that these proposals would have been

welcomed, or at least considered on their merits. Yet, within a few hours, they were denounced by the representative of the Soviet Union in a speech which certainly did not err on the side of moderation. Mr. Vyshinsky's cataract of abuse did not anger me, but it saddened me, as I think it must have saddened and discouraged the millions throughout the world who read or heard of it.

In my view, the peoples of our countries do not expect their leaders to shout abuse at one another, but rather to make contacts and try to reach understanding for peace. The most fantastic of all the charges levelled against us last Thursday was that we are warmongers. Let me assure this audience—need I do it?—that everyone in Britain, the people, Parliament and Government, deeply desires peace. And is not that natural enough? We have suffered too much, as individuals and as a nation. We had six years of war. For more than a year of that war, the countries of the Commonwealth and Empire stood alone, alone in the fight against Hitler's aggression, whilst those who are now calling us warmongers had a pact with Hitler.

I then explained our disarmament proposals, outlined our programme and described the tasks which faced the General Assembly if it was to work constructively for peace:

In the first place, Korea. The United Nations, which took up the challenge of aggression, is ready and waiting to make another great effort and help to bring about the pacification and unification of this unfortunate country, once an armistice has been concluded. Thereafter, the United Nations will be called upon to play its part in the great task of restoring the shattered economy and the devastated homeland of these long-suffering victims of aggression.

In the second place, Germany. Can we not accept the German Federal Chancellor's request? We are asked to agree to a commission to determine whether conditions in the Federal Republic of Germany, in Berlin and in the Soviet zone of Germany make it possible to hold genuinely free elections by secret ballot throughout these areas. That has formed the subject of the joint note which we have addressed to the Secretary-General. Would not this proposal do something to reduce the tension that exists today in Europe? Would it not help to bring back unity and confidence to the heart of Europe? Would we not thus bring nearer the day when a free Germany could play her part in peaceful association with a free Europe?

Then there is the issue of Austria, which has waited for so long. Can we not sign that treaty? Can we not bring to that small country evidence that the great powers can agree on this one issue, and relieve them of the burden of occupation? Cannot the Austrians be allowed at last to live and let live?

And why cannot Italy be brought into full membership of our organization? This nation, with its freely-elected Government and its ancient glorious traditions, should be represented here. Why does the veto have to be used to prevent it? Why does it frighten anyone? Surely this is a matter on which we should be able to agree without damage to anyone's interests.

I ended my speech:

On both fronts, political and economic, let us grasp definite and limited problems, and work for their practical solution. That is the real road to peace. That is the way to make a fresh start . . . . Preparation, conference and agreement: starting from small issues and working to the great. A steady pursuit, with a fixed determination and with real good will.

In the last few minutes of my speech I had a strange experience. I suddenly felt a tremor go through the audience, which had hitherto been receptive. The Assembly was not unkindly but it appeared distracted. As I left the platform I discovered that a black cat was strolling across the stage, out of sight from the raised platform where I had been speaking. Its leisurely and indifferent demeanour intrigued the delegates and was generally conceded as a good luck sign, though I discovered that black cats have a different significance in some countries.

My speech had one consequence. Mr. Vyshinsky attempted a somewhat embarrassed reply, forgoing for once the abuse and adopting a milder tone. The matter was as uncompromising as before.

In the chapters which follow I shall describe how I attempted to give effect to the step-by-step approach which I had outlined to the Assembly. I shall not describe chronologically my work at the Foreign Office between 1951-1955. I have instead chosen certain of the more important problems which came before me and dealt with them separately. Such treatment has the advantage that it is easier to follow, but it also carries the dangers of selection and over-simplification. It will be remembered that the events which I now describe were never seen in isolation at the time, but were constantly entangled with a dozen other problems which were vexing us simultaneously. None of them can be understood in isolation from the others.

II

KOREAN CEASE-FIRE
October 1951 – July 1953

*Armistice talks – Prisoners – Danger of communist attack –
Retaliation against Chinese bases – Anglo-American agree-
ment – Japanese Peace Treaty – A communist 'smear' – President
Rhee – Indian resolution on prisoners – Intransigence of Mr.
Vyshinsky – My discussion with M. Ruegger – President Rhee's
right and left – Armistice signed*

The United States, compounded of many elements, spread over
a vast territory, facing two contrasting oceans, can express a
national will, given leadership and the occasion. In the Korean
crisis, Mr. Truman gave the lead and the response was firm. Over
Quemoy and the Matsus, national opinion at a later time as effectively
imposed restraint. It remains true that the executive has larger authority
in the United States than in the European democracies with their
smaller areas.

At the time of my return to the Foreign Office, the United States
forces had been fighting in Korea for a year. Despite varying and
vehemently expressed opinions by the lobbies, the policy which the
United States Government was pursuing had national support.
Throughout the fighting a determination that the aggressor should not
get away with it had never varied. For this a heavy price was bravely
paid, in young American life and countless treasure. The Government's
declared purpose was to secure a workable armistice. I felt that they
meant this and that they had no taste for war on the Chinese mainland.
They understood the danger of that tar baby.

In this year exasperation with Chinese intervention had grown, but
it did not provoke a national demand to take the war to the Chinese
mainland, however fervently some might advocate this course.

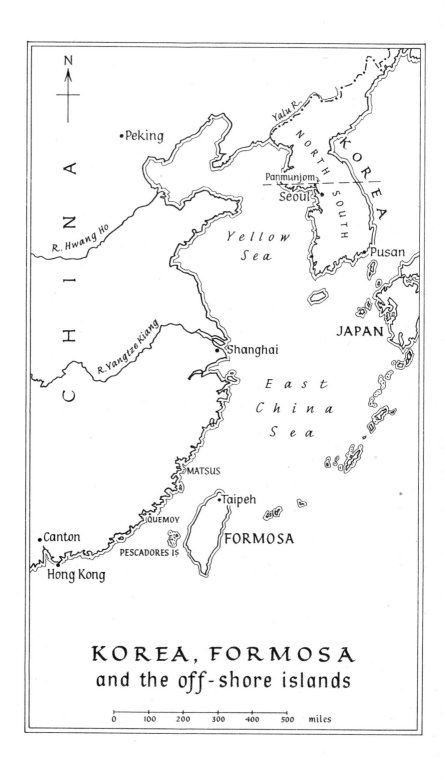

KOREA, FORMOSA
and the off-shore islands

0 100 200 300 400 500 miles

Whether American opinion would become more militant depended on Chinese Communist actions. If the Chinese increased their scale of intervention, the American mood would stiffen, but not otherwise. I was sure that the Truman Administration was as sincere in seeking an armistice as it had been determined to act in repelling invasion. In this I judged that they represented American opinion.

During the autumn of 1951, the Korean armistice talks pursued their jerky progress. The demarcation line between communist and United Nations forces looked like being agreed, though the problem of the exchange of prisoners was more stubborn. I did not like anything I could learn about the fate of our prisoners of war and those of the other United Nations forces. General MacArthur had issued a public statement in the early days of the fighting, declaring that the United Nations forces under his command would abide by the Geneva Conventions for prisoners of war and sick and wounded. He and his successor, General Ridgway, had consistently adhered to this promise. The International Red Cross had been given full facilities in South Korea, but all efforts to get the same treatment in North Korea had failed. The Chinese and North Korean authorities had not furnished regular lists of the prisoners they had taken, nor had United Nations prisoners received food or parcels from the Red Cross.

I supported the determination of the United Nations command that we could not agree to a cease-fire which left the fate of our prisoners in suspense. The position was about as unsatisfactory as it could be. As I put it to the House of Commons, 'We have not even had contact with our prisoners, we do not even know where they are. We do not know how many there are. The Red Cross have never been allowed to see them. All this must be cleared up before we can agree to an armistice.' It was going to take some time to do. M. Ruegger, President of the International Committee of the Red Cross, was a personal friend of mine. He had made a special visit to Peking earlier in the year to try to assist the victims of the war in Korea. I resolved to have a talk with him as soon as opportunity offered.

In the military sphere I thought the most disturbing portent was the growing communist air strength in Korea. The Far East command estimated that the enemy could dispose of over a thousand first-line combat aircraft, but that was not the worst of the story, as it appeared to me. More than half this number, mainly jets, were based on Manchurian airfields and were consequently immune, though they were close enough to attack United Nations front-line positions. Nothing was more remarkable in the record of this warfare than the restraint shown by the American high command of the United Nations forces and the pilots in the squadrons, the majority also American, in allowing the communist forces the use of these Manchurian airfields, without ever pursuing the enemy home to their nests. The communists had a Tom Tiddler's ground where they could not be touched and from which they could mount a powerful offensive.

I was impressed by General Ridgway's handling of his command, and of the armistice negotiations. He seemed to me a fine soldier and a painstaking negotiator. He was more at home in the field than later in the political atmosphere of N.A.T.O., and he cannot be blamed for doing his own job best.

Progress in the armistice talks brought the Americans face to face with a real practical problem. Confidence could be felt in an armistice agreement only if there were adequate methods of supervision applying to both sides. With our knowledge of the communists and their deep suspicion of anything in the nature of inspection of their activities, it hardly seemed possible that effective arrangements for supervision could be agreed. The Americans were no more anxious than we to contemplate the wrecking of the negotiations on such an issue, yet there was no denying its significance to the security of our forces.

We discussed this at a meeting held at the American Embassy during the N.A.T.O. Conference in Paris in November 1951, when Mr. Acheson was accompanied by General Bradley and others, and representatives of our Chiefs of Staff were with me. Mr. Acheson was candid in his exposition, as was his wont, and General Bradley explained that, while we must press for the fullest inspection, all must admit that the communists would never agree to such methods. If this were so, we must take their good intentions to a certain extent on trust and let it be known that, if they should violate the armistice, no holds would be barred. I was sharply conscious of this dilemma and felt sympathy with the attitude of the Americans. They had to think not only of the security of their agreement, but of the security of their forces. So, on a smaller scale, had we.

That night I sent a personal report to the Prime Minister as follows:

The Americans want an armistice and are prepared in order to get one to accept arrangements for supervision which they fear will be unsatisfactory. But they feel bound to take precautions against infringement of the armistice in the form of a major attack by the communists, which they might not be able to foresee owing to inadequate supervision arrangements. Even so, like us, they doubt whether the communists will break the armistice, since they believe that the Chinese have had enough.

Finally, the Americans left me in no doubt that the United States would rise in its wrath if there was a major attack. They clearly feel that the American Administration could not hold that position against the clamour of public opinion.

I promised Acheson that I would let him and his colleagues know our considered views as soon as possible. What they seek is to assure Ridgway that if he cannot get satisfactory terms on supervision he is to work for an armistice none the less, keeping at the back of his mind that if the communists broke the armistice by a major attack, drastic measures against China would be taken. We also need to give the United States Government in the near future our reaction to the proposal that, immediately after the conclusion of an armistice, there should be an announcement in general terms of the serious consequences which must flow from a major infringement.

Meantime I suggest that Chiefs of Staff might be instructed to examine and report:

(a) on the actions that would be desirable (if the occasion should arise) against the communist air force and their bases north of the Yalu; and

(b) on the implications of naval blockade.

★　★　★　★　★

On my return to London I discussed the American proposals with the Prime Minister and the Chiefs of Staff. The danger was not imaginary. The communists seemed to be building up their forces under cover of the armistice talks and, if no effective supervision were possible, they might launch another attack on the United Nations forces. The Government agreed that General Ridgway should be authorized to conclude an armistice even though he was not completely satisfied about arrangements for supervising it. As soon as it was concluded, as many of the countries as possible who were contributing to the United Nations forces in Korea would issue a statement in general terms, warning the communists that any serious breach might make it impossible to confine hostilities to Korea.

The United States authorities contemplated two retaliatory measures: a naval blockade of China, and the bombing of Chinese airfields, bases and junctions north of the Yalu River. We informed them that we were unable to support a naval blockade, which could not be effective, but favoured the bombing plan, should the armistice terms be broken. No general air attack on Chinese towns was contemplated.

We discussed the terms of the warning with our allies. On December 16th, the United States Ambassador came to tell me that the State Department now thought that they could find a formula for the terms of a warning to the Chinese and North Koreans. This would be within the framework of the revised draft which we had proposed, and would declare our attitude in the event of a breach by them of any armistice concluded in Korea.

Mr. Gifford said that the United States Government thought that a warning statement ought to be issued, even if agreement was reached in the armistice talks about supervision, since there could be no confidence that such arrangements would be effective. They therefore did not share our view that, in certain circumstances, no warning would be required. I said that we were giving thought to this point, but it had not been the original form of the American suggestion. The Ambassador assented. He said finally that the United States Government realized that it was not possible for us to agree in advance on the minimum steps which might be taken, in the event of a major breach of the armistice. This matter would have to be hammered out if such an event occurred. Meanwhile it was understood that we were not committed to the steps which they had proposed, while they themselves still held to their proposals. This need not prevent us from issuing the warning.

The Labour Government had agreed in principle that, should the Chinese launch a major attack from beyond the Yalu River, the United Nations forces would retaliate by bombing the communist airfields in Manchuria. They had, however, insisted that they should be consulted before this was done. We held to this position, and we worked out methods to ensure that the time lag between attack and retaliation should be as small as possible. The final form of words which the two Governments accepted was a sensible compromise which ran, 'should aggression be committed again in Korea, the consequences would be so grave that it would, in all probability, not be possible to confine hostilities within the frontiers of Korea.'

When the Prime Minister and I visited the United States in January 1952, for talks with Mr. Truman and Mr. Acheson, the only commitment we entered into was to despatch the warning message after the armistice was signed. The Americans described to us the action which they would wish to take against airfields north of the Yalu River in the event of any breach, but Mr. Acheson was careful to say that this was a matter on which we should no doubt want to consult our colleagues and have further discussions.

Another talk which I had with Mr. Acheson and Mr. Dulles during this visit, on January 10th, concerned a divergence of view between us which went back some little time. Mr. Truman had appointed Mr. Dulles as his special representative, with the rank of Ambassador, in order to negotiate the Japanese peace treaty, thus expressing the spirit of bipartisanship. The Labour Government, when in power, had always insisted, rightly I thought, that Japan's attitude towards the two Chinese Governments should be entirely her own concern. Mr. Herbert Morrison, who was then Foreign Secretary, and Mr. Dulles had, after discussion, agreed in June 1951 that neither would bring any pressure to bear on the Japanese one way or the other.

I shared these views, and held them all the more strongly for trade reasons. It was clear that if Japan was to have an outlet for her resurgent export trade, the Chinese mainland was the natural one. I thought it important that she should not be deprived of this by being led to adopt an inflexibly hostile attitude towards the Chinese People's Republic. If she did, she would regret it later, when her full sovereignty and independence had been restored by the ratification of the peace treaty.

When I discussed the matter with Mr. Acheson and Mr. Dulles, they explained to me the domestic political difficulties which the Administration faced on this issue. If Japan did not indicate that she intended to recognize Chiang Kai-shek's regime, then the 'China lobby' might be able to prevent ratification of the peace treaty by the Senate. I replied that I fully understood their position, but that the view of His Majesty's Government had not changed. Mr. Dulles had mentioned a communication he had received from Mr. Yoshida, the Japanese Prime Minister, and hinted that it might be necessary to use this during the Senate's debate on ratification. I was not shown the text, or informed that there was any immediate intention to make it public. I made it clear, however, that I must not be regarded as having acquiesced in the development which had taken place.

In view of this, I was surprised when a few days later the United States and Japanese Governments simultaneously published a letter from Mr. Yoshida to Mr. Dulles clearly stating the Japanese intention to recognize the Nationalist regime in Formosa as the Government of China. Neither date nor announcement had been agreed with me. Its publication so soon after my visit to Washington was embarrassing, and could give the impression that I had agreed to its contents. Mr. Morrison, understandably, felt that the move was contrary to the spirit of his agreement with Mr. Dulles; and matters were not improved when an article in an American newspaper alleged, falsely, that he had known of the Japanese intention all along.

Through our Ambassador in Washington, I expressed to Mr. Acheson my surprise at the timing and manner of publication of the letter. In reply, Mr. Acheson conveyed his strong regret at what had occurred, and assured me that the fact that it might be seen in relation to my discussion with him was unintentional. He promised to re-state the position which I had always taken if he were questioned about the British attitude. This terminated an unnecessary misunderstanding.

★ ★ ★ ★ ★

On my journey home I reflected on the plight of the unhappy Koreans. Geographically their country had some resemblance to the Low Countries of Europe in the pre-atomic days. It was a cockpit round which surged the great powers, Russia, China, Japan, the United States. Now it was being fought over because communist aggression had been resisted in the Far East. This could only be of limited comfort in many Korean homes, destroyed by war. The Koreans were not the first to learn that, while freedom is precious, 'liberation' is a high price to pay for it.

Fighting continued, and the extraordinary episode of the bacteria began. The Chinese Government suddenly opened a campaign of great violence against the Americans for the alleged use of germ warfare. They claimed to possess plenty of evidence in the form of unexploded canisters with various kinds of insects crawling out. The Indian Ambassador in Peking wisely counselled neutral inquiry by the International Red Cross. The Chinese replied that members of the international investigation team would only convey to the United Nations any military information which they were thus in a position to acquire. This seemed to me a suspiciously weak objection.

Mr. Acheson at once proposed an investigation by the International Red Cross and supported an offer of help to victims by the World Health Organization. The Chinese Government refused any form of international investigation into its charges. The whole affair appeared as a curious and unsavoury manœuvre. It is likely enough that the heavy bombardment and the ravages of war in North Korea dislocated such health services as the country had previously known, and that an epidemic broke out. Knowing of this horror, communist propaganda may have decided to use it to smear the Americans.

A command, in effect American, over the forces of many different nations, in fighting which caused casualties and bereavement in American homes more often than in ours, could be an international irritant. In Britain, Parliament was at times restive and critical. I thought that Mr. Acheson dealt with these moody manifestations very patiently. He never forgot what was due to an ally and worked in the spirit of an equal partnership, even though the United States carried so much the heavier load. I never held anything back, because I was sure that to conceal points of difference would only encourage them to ferment. On one occasion I showed him a telegram from Mr. Selwyn Lloyd, the Minister of State, giving an account of feeling in the House of Commons with regard to Korea. After reading the telegram, Mr. Acheson said: 'In fact, you would like us to make fewer mistakes, and to keep you better informed when we do make them'. He went on to welcome the visit of Lord Alexander, then Minister of Defence, with Mr. Lloyd to Korea. 'I understand', he said, 'the anxieties which the British public must be feeling, and I hope that this will do something to dispel them.'

President Rhee's uninhibited actions also caused embarrassment to his United Nations defenders, martial law and the arrest of members of the Korean Assembly appearing incongruous in a cause championed by democracies. He was the only man able to lead the independent, brave and contrary Koreans, but the wider consequences of his deeds did not concern him. His conduct strained relations with the United States, to whom he owed so much and acknowledged so little. President Rhee was courageous and sinewy as well as remarkably astute. His interlocutors seldom had much effect upon him. He tenaciously held sway, and still does.

★　　★　　★　　★　　★

I arrived in New York for the seventh session of the General Assembly of the United Nations on November 8th, 1952, and found allied policies on Korea in a twisted tangle. This was not so much anybody's fault as everybody's fate.

The Democratic Administration of the United States had been defeated in the election that month. The Republicans had not yet taken over, with the result that the American delegation was in the unenviable position of caretaker. Mr. Acheson led the delegation; the President-elect, General Eisenhower, was also in New York. The repatriation of prisoners of war was still unsettled and was the principal obstacle to an armistice. The Indian delegation was about to table a resolution on this subject and the Americans were troubled by what was known of its terms.

I had much sympathy with the American position. A fortnight before, twenty-one powers, including the United Kingdom, the United States and most of the countries with combatant troops in Korea, had tabled a draft resolution calling upon the Chinese Government and the North Korean authorities to agree to an armistice. This was to be based on the principle of no forced repatriation. The President of the Assembly was asked to transmit the resolution to the communist authorities and to report on the result of his action.

My first contact with the Americans was at luncheon at Sir Gladwyn Jebb's house on the day after my arrival, when Mr. Acheson made plain the importance they attached to maintaining the neutral support which they had gained for the principle of no forced repatriation. He was impressed by the dangers of ambiguity. I shared these opinions, but I was also anxious to use the Indian resolution, if I could. At the best, it might secure agreement; at the worst, it could show up the intransigence of the communists. As originally drafted, the resolution was not sufficiently specific that prisoners who refused repatriation should be freed. Mr. Lovett, United States Minister of Defence, later remarked that the proposals 'herded the prisoners into a compound with only one exit—to the North.' This would have to be altered.

M. Schuman, the French Foreign Minister, joined us after luncheon, and we agreed to continue our discussion after we had heard Mr. Vyshinsky's speech, due on the morrow. This proved unhelpful and uncompromising. He insisted that all prisoners of war must be repatriated, and urged the Assembly to adopt a resolution which the Soviet delegation tabled on the same day. I thought that his speech had reduced the prospects of an early armistice.

I decided to speak before the General Assembly on the next day and to state the four principles which I thought should govern the repatriation of prisoners of war. These were:

First: that every prisoner of war has the right, on the conclusion of an armistice, to be released.

Second: that every prisoner of war has the right to be speedily
repatriated.

Third: that there is a duty on the detaining side to provide
facilities for such repatriation.

Fourth: that the detaining side has no right to use force in the
disposal of prisoners of war.

In other words, after an armistice, a prisoner of war may not be either
forcibly detained or forcibly repatriated. These suggested principles
found wide support in the Assembly.

Later that day we had another meeting with the American delegation. They recognized the value of Asiatic support for our principles,
if we could get it, provided that it was clearly expressed. The United
States Government would be prepared, in deference to our views, to
support the resolution on the lines of the draft, combining the four
principles I had set out and the Indian resolution's proposals for a
repatriation commission. I thought that this was quite as far as we could
expect Mr. Acheson to go. It was now for us to see whether the Indian
resolution could be amended sufficiently to meet this requirement.

Several days of negotiation followed. Mr. Menon had naturally to
get approval from Delhi for any modifications of substance to his text
which he might be willing to make. His own speech in the Assembly
had been restrained and constructive, but this resolution was not a
matter which concerned a few countries alone. The twenty-one nations
who sponsored the earlier joint resolution had each to study it and
express a view. Meetings were arranged, while I had a number of
telephone conversations and a luncheon with General Eisenhower,
during which I explained my purpose. The attitude of the President-
elect had to be guarded at this stage, but I found him helpful.

Even so, negotiation was far from smooth. There was suspicion of
the Indian motive and irritation at the American constitution, which
compelled the interregnum. There were reports in the press of Anglo-
American divergencies and I had to issue a public statement correcting
the suggestion that we were abandoning the principle of repatriation
without force. International discussions taking place over many days
in a great city where interest is keen must be expected to suffer such
incidents. All the same, I was by no means confident of the outcome,
when the communists settled the matter by their intransigence.

On November 24th Mr. Vyshinsky intervened unexpectedly in the first committee debate to make a bitter and scornful attack on the Indian resolution. This confirmed the impression I had gained from his earlier speech that the chances of securing an armistice were slight. It had another consequence. It gave Mr. Acheson an opening which he used most skilfully. He warmly commended the Indian initiative and expressed agreement with the intention of the resolution. The next day Mr. Lloyd and I saw Mr. Krishna Menon and a further narrowing of the gap between the Indian and American views resulted. When I left for London that afternoon, I felt sure that a satisfactory text would be agreed.

On December 3rd the General Assembly endorsed the Indian resolution by 55 votes to 5, the minority being the communist bloc. The United States delegation gave its full support to the Indian initiative. It also gave an undertaking that the United States Government, as responsible for the unified command in Korea, would exert every effort to carry out the proposal. There is no doubt that this vote had an important influence on the course of the negotiations for the armistice. The result would not have been attained unless the American delegation had been prepared to study and accept another point of view than its own. Out of this grew an understanding of the purpose of its allies on an issue admittedly of more importance to the United States than to them. This was not weakness, but the statesmanship which draws friends, and the United States did not lose by it. Diplomatic tales do not always have such happy endings.

I continued to be much preoccupied with the position of our prisoners of war. I took the opportunity of a visit to London by M. Ruegger in the first days of 1953, to invite him to luncheon, when we had a long talk over this vexing question. We canvassed many possibilities. M. Ruegger had just returned from Peking, where he had found Mr. Chou En-lai unhelpful about suggested supervision by the Red Cross in North Korea. He thought, however, that Chou En-lai might be interested in the 'establishment of safety zones' for the protection of sick and wounded. This seemed to me important and hopeful.

Our main discussion was concerned with the possibility of positive action at once. I suggested that an appeal by M. Ruegger to the President of the General Assembly of the United Nations, then in session, should be held in reserve, and that I should make an immediate approach to the United Nations command on the question of the sick and wounded. We both thought this the best method of resolving the deadlock. At this discussion M. Ruegger and I were troubled about the indoctrination of prisoners. He said that his committee were meeting in Geneva on January 8th and promised that after consulting them he would put his ideas on paper. I said that I would gladly study them. This discussion had some important consequences, for it set us on the approach which led to the first exchange of prisoners of war, the sick and wounded. After that opening, though progress was slow, it was continuous.

Another subject which greatly troubled me was the continued imprisonment of Captain Vyvyan Holt, who had been our Minister in Korea, together with certain members of his staff and other civilians, some of them priests. There was no justification in international law for their treatment, but we had no direct contact with the North Koreans and no means of putting effective pressure upon them to secure their release. I had tried every means at our disposal to effect some result, including approaches to other communist powers, all without avail. One week-end in February, I decided that I would make another attempt through the Soviet Ambassador, who was now Mr. Gromyko. I thought that I had noticed some recent indications of a desire on the part of the Soviet Government for some improvement in our relations. This might be turned to good account, but I was not sanguine. I therefore asked Mr. Gromyko to call at the Foreign Office, and told him that I wished to enlist the good offices of his Government in regard to the detention of Captain Holt and other British subjects in North Korea. I gave him an *aide-mémoire* setting out the facts and pointed out that these people, who were civilians, had been detained for a very long time. Though the Soviet Government had maintained that this was not a matter of direct concern to them, they had been good enough on one or two occasions to transmit messages and I appealed to Mr. Gromyko to do what he could to secure the release of these unfortunate people.

The Ambassador said that his Government had always taken the attitude that they had no responsibility in this matter and, so far as he knew, the position had not changed. I said, in reply, that I was aware of this; but we had no means of direct contact with the North Koreans and it was for this reason that I was asking the Soviet Government to use their influence with them to have these civilians released.

At the end of the interview, Mr. Gromyko accepted the *aide-mémoire* and promised to transmit it to Moscow. He said that he could not forecast what action his Government would take. But this time to my surprise and delight, the oracle worked. The Russians got into touch with the North Korean Government and, some six weeks later, our Head of Chancery in Moscow was summoned to the Ministry of Foreign Affairs and informed that the Soviet Government had ascertained that a number of British subjects were interned in North Korea. There followed a list. This information had been obtained from the North Korean authorities, we were told, as a result of the assurance the Soviet Chargé d'Affaires had given Mr. Lloyd on March 19th.

★ ★ ★ ★ ★

When I next visited the United Nations in March 1953, I reaffirmed the four principles and upheld the Indian resolution. The communists' efforts to divide the world on this issue had not succeeded. After consultation with our allies, I added this paragraph:

The offers we made at Panmunjom and the resolution of last December remain open. It still lies within the power of those who began this conflict to agree to an armistice on fair conditions. The opportunity and the responsibility are theirs.

A move by the communist front was, in fact, very near. In a broadcast early in April, Mr. Molotov announced on behalf of the Korean Peoples' Army that it 'consents to the exchange of sick and injured prisoners in conformity with the provisions of Article 109 of the Geneva Convention, referring to the period of hostilities.' He was quoting a letter from the supreme commander of the Korean People's Army, which added that such an exchange of sick and injured war prisoners should lead to a smooth settlement of the entire problem of war prisoners, and thereby to the achievement of an armistice in Korea. I heard of this broadcast with relief, fortified a few days later by a telegram from our Ambassador in Tokyo telling me that the North Korean radio had announced the release of our interned civilians.

As a result of Mr. Molotov's statement, the possibility of a resumption of armistice talks was canvassed. There was, however, one important complication. Such an event was greeted in South Korea with disapproval, at least in official circles. Condemnation of any settlement which left Korea still divided was overwhelming and violently expressed. The exchange of the sick and injured prisoners went forward just the same, as I had hoped. Agreement on the terms of the armistice grew nearer.

The Korean President had, however, one or two cards he could play. In June a total of eight camps, containing a population of 35,000 anti-communist North Korean prisoners, joined in a simultaneous break-out. There were few American guards, 27,000 prisoners escaped, a thousand were recaptured, and a few killed and injured. About 9,000 prisoners remained in captivity. This was a right and left for President Rhee. A right at the communists who were alarmed and indignant at so spectacular a desertion; a left at the Americans who were nominally in charge of the camps and correspondingly embarrassed in the negotiations. Delhi reported to London that the Chinese Government were in a state of intense agitation over these happenings in South Korea. It was not lost on them that the number of escaped Koreans tallied with the total which the Americans claimed had refused repatriation. We were able to assure the Indian Government that we knew it was untrue that the Americans had connived at these escapes. The Indians were helpful in reassuring Peking and the denials carried conviction. All the same, President Rhee's action nearly succeeded in its purpose. He received a stern rebuke from General Mark Clark, commander of the United Nations forces. On instructions from London, our Minister in Korea joined in the remonstrance. It is doubtful if President Rhee was much affected; he knew what he was about.

The armistice was signed on the morning of July 27th. Thus ended an ordeal marked by brave endurance in physical conditions of stark danger, suffering and discomfort. The United States bore the heaviest loss in life and wealth, both actually and proportionally. No just man will question the spirit of that sacrifice which bore no selfish taint.

One unwelcome duty remained. We thought it necessary to clear up with the United States Government the question of our obligations in the event of any other initiative by President Rhee. In a note dated July 28th we made it plain that if President Rhee broke the armistice and marched north, we should not be committed to take part as we would be by a communist breach of the armistice. The State Department agreed.

Arrangements for a political conference moved more slowly. Membership, as well as motives and policy, created endless difficulties which Lord Salisbury, acting as Foreign Secretary during my illness, helped to smooth out by exchanges with Delhi, Washington and Moscow.

Meanwhile the release of prisoners of war under Indian supervision had been carried through reasonably well, with only minor incidents. Even the machinery for supervising the armistice terms appeared to be working satisfactorily. By mid-September the clearing of mines and hazards from the zone was almost complete. All this was confirmation that the armistice would hold. At the end of the month our Minister, Mr. Graham, had a conversation with President Rhee, in which he had been less categorical than Mr. Graham had expected about conditions for the political conference. This also seemed an encouraging augury.

Chinese preparations to integrate Korea into the Manchurian economy gave President Rhee justification for his belief that if Korea were not united soon, it would not be for years to come. The communists were building strong defences along the frontiers, and no one was ready to face the casualties involved in an assault upon them. Even if an attack was successful, the new Korean frontier line would be more exposed and vulnerable than the present one. In other words, the partition of Korea, however indefensible from some points of view, might be the only means of reaching an acceptable *status quo* between the communists and the free world.

The fighting in Korea achieved a balance of power, recognized and respected as such. Had the United States not acted to halt the northern irruption, the decision would have gone to the communists by default. Further attempts must have followed, on a larger scale and bearing more imminent danger of world conflict. That was the lesson of Europe in the 'thirties. It was also the lesson of the Middle East in the 'fifties. Thanks to the decision of President Truman and those who upheld him, the worst Korean tragedy was averted. The warning was clear, the invasion was stayed, the balance restored.

III

THE PANGS OF E.D.C.
October 1951 – June 1953

*Britain and Europe – The Russian threat – The Pleven Plan –
My memorandum to Mr. Churchill – Our visit to Washington – Discussions with M. Schuman – Death of King George VI –
Dr. Adenauer in London – Netherlands and E.D.C. – We
prepare treaty with E.D.C. – Soviet opposition – Signing of the
treaties – The Council of Europe – The death of Stalin – My
illness and recovery*

The United Kingdom's relations with Europe became an issue of
foreign policy soon after the end of the war. Our attitude towards Europe and the 'European idea' was in these years a
constant target for criticism by our allies, who complained that our
practice fell short of our precepts. It is true that we continuously encouraged closer co-operation and unity between the continental powers,
but we did so from the reserve position that we would not accept a
sovereign European authority, from which our Commonwealth ties
precluded us. Others found this attitude patronizing and irritating.

Perhaps as a result of our island tradition, we have a different instinct and outlook on constitutional questions from our European
neighbours. We have no written constitution and this is not due merely
to obstinacy or to suspicion of legal form. It is because, as a people,
we like to proceed by trial and error. We prefer to see how a principle
works in practice before we enshrine it, if we ever do so.

The federal movement in Europe has a long history. In 1946 Mr.
Winston Churchill revived its prospects in a speech at Zürich, when he
declared that 'we must build a kind of United States of Europe'. In
1949, a conference of European statesmen was held at The Hague and
the Council of Europe was founded. Its Consultative Assembly at

Strasbourg was to be the forum for the discussion of European problems. Many hoped that it would be the forerunner of a European federal parliament. Speaking to the Assembly on August 11th, 1950, Mr. Churchill gave the first concrete expression to the idea of a European army:

> We should now send a message of confidence and courage from the House of Europe to the whole world. Not only should we re-affirm, as we have been asked to do, our allegiance to the United Nations, but we should make a gesture of practical and constructive guidance by declaring ourselves in favour of the immediate creation of a European army under a unified command, and in which we should bear a worthy and honourable part.

I think that this speech may have been misunderstood at the time. It raised hopes that Great Britain would be willing to merge her forces with those of the European powers to an extent which Mr. Churchill certainly did not contemplate. The character of the European army, its composition and organization, was to give much trouble in the next few years, but Britain's relationship to it was only part of the controversy. It was less explosive than German rearmament.

The war over, the victorious Western powers disarmed and most of them went home. The Russians stayed, almost at full strength, and made that strength felt. The Soviet attempt to blockade Berlin forced the lesson home. In such conditions the absence of a German army to defend German territory was a critical weakness in the pattern of Western European defence. In 1950, N.A.T.O., still in the process of formation, could only muster fourteen divisions with which to confront one hundred and seventy-five Soviet divisions, not so gently poised in Eastern Europe. But at this time memories of two world wars were still too vivid for such a disturbing European reality to be accepted. A momentous event at the other side of the world changed many values; the Korean war broke out in July. Communism was on the march in the East and Europe became starkly aware of her weakness.

Military preparations for the defence of the West were rushed forward. In September a fateful meeting of the North Atlantic Council was held in New York, when the United States Government called for an immediate decision in favour of German rearmament. They made it clear that if the European members of N.A.T.O. continued to flinch from this issue, the United States might not take part in an integrated

European command. This faced France with a most unwelcome choice. French opinion hated the idea of the rearmament of Germany and successive French Governments had committed themselves against it. Somehow means must be found to meet the American demand, which was too serious to be shrugged off. This had to be done while avoiding the dangers, equally vivid for many, of a German national army.

The Pleven Plan for a European Defence Community was the resulting compromise. Hastily and ingeniously concocted by M. Monnet and his associates, the proposals which later became the E.D.C. were presented to the French Assembly by M. Pleven on October 25th, 1950, and were accepted. The Pleven Plan called for the creation of a European army, into which national contingents would be integrated at the level of the smallest possible unit. This meant that there would be no German army, but German battalions distributed amongst European brigades. The whole scheme was European. The force would be under a European Minister of Defence, responsible to a European Assembly. There would be a European Defence Council of Ministers and a common European defence budget.

A conference on E.D.C. was called to meet in Paris in February 1951. The Labour Government were convinced that the United Kingdom could not accept these French proposals and Mr. Bevin feared that they would delay the building up of adequate forces in Western Europe. These fears proved justified, at least so far as the German contingents were concerned. But whatever its limitations, the plan for E.D.C. had one arresting consequence. It marked the first development of better Franco-German relations, which might still change the face of Europe.

The French showed skill and determination at this Paris conference, which reached agreement on the major features of the Pleven Plan by the end of July. A parallel meeting was being held in Bonn, to discuss an alternative plan, favoured by the United States and the United Kingdom Governments, for a direct German contribution to N.A.T.O. It failed, and the European army became the only road by which German contingents could take their place in the line. On September 14th in Washington, Mr. Herbert Morrison, the Foreign Secretary, joined Mr. Acheson and M. Schuman in a declaration of support for E.D.C. They also stated that:

The Government of the United Kingdom desire to establish

the closest possible association with the European Continental Community at all stages of its development.

This was the position when I returned to the Foreign Office on October 27th, 1951. I had no quarrel with the conception of a European Defence Community. On the contrary, I liked the idea, for I have never thought that my country need have any apprehension on account of a closer union between the nations of continental Europe. We have suffered too much from the lack of it, and the trend these days should be towards larger units. My reservation arose from other causes. I feared that the plan, imaginative as it was, might fail for just that reason. It seemed to attempt too much, to ask more of the nations concerned than they could freely give and then the outcome might be disillusion, leaving Europe in disarray. On the other hand I was prepared to admit that I could be wrong in this judgment, which might be the result of our English preference for taking our changes in doses rather than at a gulp. This was the temper in which I approached E.D.C.

We had two decisions to take. The first was whether in practice we could join an army forming part of a European federation; I agreed with our predecessors that we could not. The second was what the practical effect of our decision would be on the progress of E.D.C.

At the end of November I went to Rome for a meeting of the North Atlantic Council. Here I learnt that the Americans now shared our view that the United Kingdom could serve the alliance better by remaining outside the European army. The following is the text of a personal message which I sent to the Prime Minister describing my first important interview on this subject:

I met General Eisenhower on the morning of November 27th. The General volunteered his opinion on the question whether any offer on our part to participate in the European army would be decisive for the success of the project. He said that he was convinced that such an offer now would be a mistake. Later I had an opportunity to probe this subject further with him. He confirmed that this was a definite conclusion which had not been lightly arrived at. He thought we should do all in our power to encourage the European army, but, if we were to offer to enter it at this stage, we should further complicate the budgetary and other technical arrangements and would delay rather than hasten a final solution. Moreover, in his view, we and the United States could be more effective as elements supporting the European army within the Atlantic Organization. As the European army developed it was his thought that maybe we and the Americans could be drawn into reserve. We should be there and available if needed, but it might be no bad thing if the Europeans could stand on their own.

All this was looking into a fairly distant future. As to the present, of course, there was no doubt that, in his mind, we should help from without rather than participate from within.

This conversation was important. The United States Government had previously been inclined to favour our entry into the Defence Community. It was now clear that the policy which we preferred could be pursued in full accord with them. When I addressed a press conference in Rome on November 28th at the close of the N.A.T.O. meeting, I thought it best to make our position definite. I said that British units and formations would not participate in a European army, but that there might be some other form of association. My words, and a cautious speech which Sir David Maxwell-Fyfe made on the same day at Strasbourg, gave rise to much disappointment among the E.D.C. countries. The view was too easily taken that words like 'association' and 'close relations' meant nothing, and were mere camouflage for Great Britain's intention to turn her back on Europe for good. I had expected this, but I thought it better to make plain at once what we could not do, so that we might agree on what we could do.

On December 1st, I summarized the position as I saw it in a personal minute to the Prime Minister:

> Thank you for letting me see the proof of your note on United Europe.
>
> Here are some comments:
>
> 1. At present there is only one plan under discussion for a European army.
>
> 2. This is the so-called Pleven Plan. This has made technical progress, but it is in political trouble over fundamental questions of sovereignty. This plan does not permit national armies to exist in participating countries, except for overseas garrisons. Its purpose, at least in French and Italian minds, is to pave the way for federation. I have never thought it possible that we could join such an army.

3. The late Government made clear its attitude to the army, and to the Schuman Plan, in a joint statement by the Foreign Secretaries of France, the United States and the United Kingdom, at Washington in September.

I quoted this in the House in my speech in the foreign affairs debate, and it was generally approved. Schuman was also fully satisfied with it as a statement of our position, when I discussed it with him in Paris before the debate.

4. Now that the Pleven Plan is running into trouble in the countries that put it forward, we are being made the whipping boy.

5. That appears to be Strasbourg's only activity at this time.

6. It is possible that the Pleven Plan will fail, though it has the backing of General Eisenhower. If so, we shall be back again with the problem of Germany's part in Western defence.

7. Opposition to a German national army is strong, not only in France; Adenauer has never advocated it.

8. Even more important is the reaction of Russia, who would view the creation of a German national army and her admission to N.A.T.O. which must follow, as a major threat.

Conclusion:

(a) We should support the Pleven Plan, though we cannot be members of it. This is what the Americans are doing, and it is the course Eisenhower wants us to take.

(b) If the Pleven Plan does collapse, we should try to work out a more modest scheme with our allies, based upon the technical military arrangements agreed upon, but without elaborate political superstructure.

(c) Any move for (b) will require careful timing. If we move too soon, the Pleven Plan will collapse, and we shall be told we have killed it.

(d) We should have more of a chance to play our part if Strasbourg did not keep shaking the table and summoning me.

(e) The Foreign Office has been set to work to examine above thoughts, and prepare a short paper for you.

When Mr. Churchill and I visited Paris in mid-December, we did all we could to assure the French Government of our determination to help the Paris Conference to succeed. The talks went well and the joint communiqué which we issued at the end of our discussions on December 18th stated that:

> His Majesty's Government will associate themselves as closely as possible with the European Defence Community in all stages of its military and political development.
>
> The United Kingdom Forces under the direction of the Supreme Allied Commander in Europe will be linked with those of the European Defence Community for training, supply and operations by land, sea and air.

The French were pleased with this statement, and thought that it would help them in their E.D.C. negotiations. Before I left Paris, M. Schuman told me that the first reactions of the French press had been favourable.

★ ★ ★ ★ ★

Mr. Churchill and I visited Washington in January 1952, for talks with President Truman and Mr. Acheson. My first meeting with Mr. Truman was on the sad occasion of President Roosevelt's funeral service at the White House. This introduction was at Mrs. Roosevelt's thoughtful initiative. I liked him immediately. Greatness was thrust upon Truman, but he never let his knowledge of this daunt his courage or his power of decision. He served the world well.

These talks gave us a useful opportunity to discuss the progress of E.D.C. and the attitude of the United Kingdom towards it. At a meeting on January 8th, the Prime Minister reaffirmed our support for the formation of a European army, although he did not personally approve the details of the Pleven Plan. He thought that the system had been too much dictated by current European views on federation; but in view of the need for German help in defending Western Europe, he was ready to do anything which might assist in the creation of a European army, short of British participation.

Mr. Acheson confirmed that the Americans had no wish to urge the United Kingdom to join E.D.C. He hoped, however, that we would try to dispel the fears which were causing the Benelux countries, particularly the Netherlands, to shy away from full acceptance of the Pleven Plan. It was not true, said Mr. Acheson, that the United States would lose interest in Europe once E.D.C. had been created; supplies of American equipment to the Netherlands would not be reduced if she

35

became a partner in the Defence Community. I said that we would certainly help in trying to allay these fears. I pointed out that the Dutch, like the British, were a seafaring people and attached importance to their membership of a North Atlantic organization. It might therefore be helpful to emphasize that the Atlantic community was going to last and that E.D.C. was simply a closer union within the wider grouping.

The Administration understood, but large sections of the American press were still blaming the United Kingdom for delays in the E.D.C. negotiations. Even well-informed newspapers were suggesting, quite wrongly, that General Eisenhower wanted us to join the European army and that the negotiations in Paris were foundering because of our recalcitrance. This was causing irritation, and would soon cause friction between us.

On January 11th, Columbia University paid me the compliment of awarding me an honorary degree and invited me to deliver the Gabriel Silver lecture. I took the opportunity to make a statement of our position:

The American and British peoples should each understand the strong points in the other's national character. If you drive a nation to adopt procedures which run counter to its instincts, you weaken and may destroy the motive force of its action.

This is something you would not wish to do—or any of us would wish to do—to an ally on whose effective co-operation we depend.

You will realize that I am speaking of the frequent suggestions that the United Kingdom should join a federation on the continent of Europe. This is something which we know, in our bones, we cannot do.

We know that if we were to attempt it, we should relax the springs of our action in the Western democratic cause and in the Atlantic association which is the expression of that cause. For Britain's story and her interests lie far beyond the continent of Europe. Our thoughts move across the seas to the many communities in which our people play their part, in every corner of the world. These are our family ties. That is our life: without it we should be no more than some millions of people living on an island off the coast of Europe, in which nobody wants to take any particular interest.

But does this mean that we are turning our backs on Europe? Certainly not. I would remind you of a few facts.

Apart from our contribution to the United Nations in Korea and our duties in Malaya: apart from the substantial strength which we have to keep in the Middle East in the general interest, we have the largest armoured force on the continent of Europe of any of the Atlantic powers. And we have undertaken to keep it there, with our other formations, as long as they are required for the purposes of our common defence.

Is this to abandon Europe?

We have played a leading part in the reconstruction of the economy of Europe. We have promised our full support to all European efforts to achieve greater unity. Our position on all this is well understood by our European friends. When the Prime Minister and I were in Paris, shortly before we came to you, we had talks with the French Government on these matters, and the statement which we issued jointly then showed how thoroughly we are agreed. I do not think there should be any more misunderstandings.

On my return from America, I had to work out the actual form of the United Kingdom's association with E.D.C. M. Schuman had invited me to go to Paris on February 1st to discuss the results of my Washington visit. The French Government were not in a strong parliamentary position, and I knew that they would like to announce that we had made some practical suggestions to help them. Already more deputies disliked E.D.C. than would admit it, while open critics blamed Britain's attitude.

M. Schuman has a gentle manner and a natural charm which makes him a pleasant colleague at all times. But this is not the whole man. The mind is quick, and the statesman much more tenacious than he seems. As this account will show, M. Schuman has a quiet persistence which he made rewarding. He was always coming back to get a little more of what he wanted, and he usually did.

My colleagues in the Cabinet had already approved a number of practical suggestions and agreed that these should be embodied in a declaration, to be made public at a moment of my choosing. When I spoke to M. Schuman on February 1st, I told him that I was prepared to make a statement to the House of Commons which would embody the following points:

(i) We wish to establish close political and military links with the Community by whatever methods are agreed to be most appropriate.

(ii) United Kingdom forces on the continent would, subject only to the requirements of SACEUR*, operate as closely as possible with the E.D.C. forces and be linked with them as far as possible in matters of training, administration and supply.

(iii) Arrangements could be made to accept individuals, units and formations of the E.D.C. for training with British formations in Germany and elsewhere and to lend British officers and units, where this is administratively possible, to the E.D.C. formations.

(iv) His Majesty's Government consider that co-operation between the Air Forces of the United Kingdom and the European Defence Community should prove to be a particularly profitable field of action.

(v) His Majesty's Government are resolved to maintain armed forces on the continent of Europe for as long as is necessary, having regard to the requirements of the European Defence Community as well as to their obligations to the North Atlantic Treaty and their special responsibilities in Germany.

I explained to M. Schuman that, with regard to paragraph (i), we thought that it might be useful if British representatives were to sit with some organizations of the E.D.C. such as the Council of Ministers, perhaps as observers. On paragraph (ii) I said that in practice it would be difficult to realize a close integration between British and E.D.C. army units. Our formations on the continent were chiefly armoured divisions, which did not lend themselves to this treatment. As between air forces, opportunities seemed much greater. M. Schuman seemed to like these ideas. He said that the French were not at all anxious to allow German air forces to operate on their own, and the more closely these could be tied in the better.

When we continued our discussion the next day, it was soon clear that my offer did not satisfy the French Government. M. Schuman proposed that we should declare our readiness to conclude a formal treaty with the Defence Community for mutual aid in the event of aggression. I told him that it was doubtful whether we could accept this. We already had the N.A.T.O. commitment and I was not convinced that a further engagement was necessary. But I agreed to

* Supreme Allied Commander, Europe.

38

incorporate in my statement various minor alterations in wording to help the French Government.

★　★　★　★　★

Shortly after my return from Paris, the whole world was saddened by the death of His Majesty the King. The news was broken to me by the Prime Minister who telephoned, opening the conversation with with the words, 'Imagine what is the worst thing that could happen to us.'

It was my unusual experience to serve as Foreign Secretary under four Sovereigns. My office entailed frequent attendance upon King George VI during the many audiences accorded to foreign representatives, which preceded his coronation in 1937. Envoys came from all over the world, sometimes bringing decorations and gifts. I grew to respect King George then; these ceremonies would have been an ordeal to any man. For a King who had come so unexpectedly to the throne at such relatively short notice, they were especially exacting. Yet he played his part manfully, without apparent weariness or the slightest impatience. Though I often had conversations with him, I never grew to know King George VI at all closely until the moment of my resignation in 1938. On that occasion, when I came to hand in my seals, His Majesty proved himself a most sympathetic and understanding listener. He questioned me and I gave him a full explanation of my action. I do not suggest that he agreed, but the circumstances of our meeting for some reason removed all restraint and we had a man to man talk, which I much valued and which gave me encouragement in what was inevitably an unhappy hour. The Sovereign reads Foreign Office and other telegrams of importance and has full and impartial knowledge of all that passes, though constitutionally careful in expressing an opinion. Having read the same documents, it is sometimes comforting to find one has independently reached the same conclusions.

I had one experience in common with King George. We were both of the generation of the first world war. He had served at Jutland where my younger brother was killed, while I was at Ypres. Perhaps it was this that made our attitude towards those older and younger than ourselves much the same. I felt his death as that of a personal friend.

I was a guest at Sandringham only a few weeks before the King died. By a sad coincidence, I had been at the same house sixteen years earlier, just before his father's last illness, to receive my seals of office as Foreign Secretary.

39

The Prime Minister invited the Leader of the Opposition, Lord Woolton and myself to go down to the airport to meet the Queen returning from Africa, the first stop on the Empire journey she had set out to fulfil. The sight of that young figure in black coming through the door of the aircraft, standing there poised for a second before descending the gangway to the duties which lay before her, is a poignant memory.

★   ★   ★   ★   ★

In the second week of February the French Assembly debated E.D.C. It was soon apparent that its request for a formal treaty relationship with us had a dual motive. M. Schuman had already expressed to me his desire for a pact against outside aggression. The French were now thinking in terms of another contingency, secession or misbehaviour by one of the members of E.D.C. itself. The United Kingdom was to be asked for an undertaking to help the Defence Community in such an event. Fears of a resurgent Germany were still a powerful force in France. I understood this mood well enough, but I thought it a little incongruous to try to build a new community in such a spirit.

If such fear of Germany persisted, it could not be met in E.D.C; N.A.T.O. was the place for this. There we and the United States could give E.D.C. any help they needed and Germany would be in company of her own stature or larger. But it would merely have caused indignation or alarm to have suggested this solution then. Therefore I kept these thoughts to myself and, to help the French Government, prepared for the discussion of a treaty between the United Kingdom and E.D.C.

In mid-February the council of N.A.T.O. was due to meet in Lisbon. I wanted to make sure of unity between the principal allies before the event and on February 13th Mr. Acheson arrived in London. He dined with me that evening and we discussed what we could do to help the French. We agreed that a joint declaration guaranteeing our support for E.D.C. in the event of threats to the organization, from inside or out, would be more suitable than a treaty. Mr. Acheson told me that the United States had already been considering a new 'Monroe Doctrine' for Europe, which would amount to a promise that if one European country threatened the peace, the others could count on American support. This was admirable good sense and our declaration would serve this purpose.

On the following day the French Foreign Minister came to London and we put our proposal before him. M. Schuman told us that he was most grateful for this suggestion, which would help him very much. He said that there were people in France who thought that, once the European Defence Community had been brought into existence, the Americans would want to withdraw from Europe. The proposed declaration would correct this impression. Mr. Acheson replied that the impression was quite false. The Americans, so far from wishing to quit Europe, wished to stay. M. Schuman told me that if France could be assured of the political presence of the United Kingdom in a way which would not leave his country face to face with Germany, he thought that French opinion would be satisfied.

Anglo-American and French drafts of a declaration were then prepared and we each appointed representatives to work upon them. We thought that the best time to issue the declaration would be the occasion of the signing of the final E.D.C. treaty. In the meantime, in the statement which we issued at the end of the tripartite talks in London, we gave a hint that we had some helpful ideas. Then we prepared to welcome the next visitor.

When Dr. Adenauer joined us in London on February 18th, we showed him draft proposals for negotiating some of the obstacles which were holding us up. Discussions were under way in Bonn about the new status of the German Federal Republic. A principal difficulty was how to convoke joint meetings of the N.A.T.O. and E.D.C. Councils, for Dr. Adenauer wished to be sure that this procedure did not discriminate against Germany. We agreed on a formula which I proposed. This laid down the conditions in which a joint meeting of the councils could automatically be convened. Any of the members of N.A.T.O. or E.D.C. could then summon it. This concluded a good meeting of the three Western Foreign Secretaries. I was able to report to the House of Commons: 'The European atmosphere, heavily charged a fortnight ago, has been lightened, and the way is clear for concrete agreements.'

During the meeting of the North Atlantic Council at Lisbon, I told the Benelux Foreign Ministers and the Italian Prime Minister, Signor De Gasperi, of the declaration of support for E.D.C. which we were preparing. They were pleased to hear it. During these years I had several occasions to hold discussions with De Gasperi. He was a wise and tolerant man; every meeting increased my regard for him. I was happy to have the opportunity to contribute with him to rebuilding Anglo-Italian relations after the war. I took all the more pleasure in this, since I had been compelled to oppose the policies of the Fascist era, which had such unhappy consequences for Italy.

At luncheon at our Embassy on February 22nd, M. Schuman and M. Faure, then Prime Minister, told us that there was now no urgency, from the French point of view, to make the declaration public. I was sorry, but not surprised, to hear from the French Ministers that at some later date the United Kingdom would once again be formally invited to join the Defence Community. French parliamentary opinion, they said, would insist on this gesture. I reflected that our relations with the Continental powers would be easier if they did not so often force us into the position of having to say 'no'. Formal invitations and formal refusals did not help those of us who wanted to go as far as possible to meet them.

Shortly after the Lisbon meeting, the Paris Conference ran into serious trouble. The Germans wanted the E.D.C. treaty to contain a clause which would commit E.D.C. forces automatically to resist an attack on any member of the Community. The Netherlands were not prepared to accept this, because the North Atlantic Treaty did not contain a similar provision. They were unwilling to commit themselves, as a member of E.D.C., to any action which would not involve a commitment by the United Kingdom, for they feared that they might find themselves fighting for a German interest without United Kingdom forces by their side. As a result of this disagreement, which brought negotiations to a standstill, the Paris Conference proposed·on March 14th that the United Kingdom should be asked to enter into a treaty relationship with E.D.C.

Mr. Schuman had already told my Parliamentary Under-Secretary, Mr. Nutting, that the proposed Anglo-American guarantee to E.D.C. would no longer be enough to ensure ratification of the E.D.C. treaty by the French Assembly. He said that the French would look to us for 'something special', a gesture which would fulfil our special relationship with France.

I realized that if the entire E.D.C. project was to be saved from a breakdown, for which we would be blamed, Her Majesty's Government would have to make a positive response to these approaches. I flew to Paris on March 19th to find out how best we could help, inviting Dr. Stikker, the Netherlands Foreign Minister, to dine with me that evening at the British Embassy. I knew and liked him. He was a direct man and I was sure that I would get from him a forthright account of his dilemma. Dr. Stikker told me that, unless his Government could be certain that Great Britain would be equally involved, with the Netherlands, in any 'automatic' military commitments to which the E.D.C. treaty might give rise, the Netherlands Parliament would never agree to enter the Defence Community on the proposed terms. It was for this reason that the Dutch and the French had agreed to ask Her Majesty's Government to extend to E.D.C. the provisions of the Brussels Treaty.*

I explained to Dr. Stikker that this was a difficult business for us. It was natural that we should conclude the Brussels Treaty with our closest European friends and allies. To extend it to Italy and Germany, because they were members of E.D.C., and for the forty-five years which the treaty had to run, was quite a different proposition. I added that in practice it was inconceivable, despite the absence of an automatic commitment under the North Atlantic Treaty, that the United States and N.A.T.O. as a whole would not react to an attack on a country in Europe. I agreed to study the matter further and to talk the question over with the French Foreign Minister on the following day.

When I saw M. Schuman at the Quai d'Orsay, I repeated the view which I had put to Dr. Stikker. It was well known, I said, that the reason why the North Atlantic Treaty had been drafted so as to exclude 'automatic' commitments was that the United States were constitutionally unable to commit themselves automatically to go to war. I hoped, therefore, that it would be possible for the E.D.C. countries to settle this point satisfactorily between themselves. My hope was not really very strong. Once again I heard the cry that for parliamentary reasons, it was essential for Her Majesty's Government to enter into some form of treaty commitment with the European Defence Community.

I explained our objections to extending the Brussels Treaty in order to guarantee another organization, and that we also felt some difficulty about committing ourselves for fifty years. Our inclination was to hold to the period of the North Atlantic Treaty, which might come to an end seventeen years hence. I did not then foresee how useful the Brussels Treaty was to be to me later in another context. I undertook to consider a declaration or agreement which would include Germany

* This treaty was signed on March 17th, 1948, by the Governments of the United Kingdom, France, Belgium, the Netherlands and Luxembourg. It was to last for fifty years and pledged the signatories to give all military and other aid in their power to any of their number who was subjected to an armed attack in Europe. The treaty set up permanent consultative machinery and provided also for social and economic co-operation.

and Italy, to last as long as the North Atlantic Treaty remained in force. M. Schuman said that he thought that a commitment on these lines would be helpful.

Finally, I added that we were constantly being asked to declare our relationship with E.D.C. and we were trying to respond helpfully. The proposal which I had referred to was the absolute limit to which my country could go. Was there a danger that we should be asked to go further and join E.D.C ? If so, I must make it absolutely plain once more that we could not and would not do this. M. Schuman replied that he had been thinking of arranging for a French parliamentary delegation to come to London just before ratification, to invite Her Majesty's Government to join the Community. I said that we should greatly prefer an approach through normal diplomatic channels instead of a public invitation, and M. Schuman accepted this. Three weeks later, when we had announced our intention to conclude a treaty with E.D.C., M. Schuman agreed to regard the approach as having already been made at our meeting.

★　★　★　★　★

After my talks in Paris, I was sure that the European Defence Community would not be established unless we responded to the French proposal. We had to make yet another effort to meet our ally's needs. On returning to London, I explained the position to my colleagues. They accepted that Her Majesty's Government should offer at once to conclude a formal treaty with E.D.C. By its terms each party would be obliged to give military assistance to the other, if either were the object of an armed attack in Europe. This mutual undertaking would last for as long as the United Kingdom remained a member of N.A.T.O.

When Sir Oliver Harvey, our Ambassador in Paris, told the French Foreign Minister of the terms of our offer on April 5th, all seemed set fair. Our draft text of the treaty was put before the steering committee of the Paris Conference on April 8th, and General Eisenhower was kind enough to send me a message on the meeting, telling me of the round of very cordial speeches which followed our offer.

I now cherished a cautious hope that the Paris negotiations could once again move forward, this time to a final conclusion. With every day that passed, I became more aware of the need to get the E.D.C. treaty completed and signed. A determined, if clumsy, diplomatic campaign was being maintained by the Soviet Union to paralyse the negotiations. This was not having much effect, but it was an international irritant and we should be better without it. I was confident that it would die down once the treaty was signed. Russian diplomacy is adept at accepting realities. The Soviets' campaign was complicated by their equivocal position in East Germany. Moscow knew that if Germany remained divided, it could not prevent the Federal Republic joining the Western defensive organization, nor halt West German rearmament. The Russians feared these things. But they dared not offer to end the division of Germany in the only way which could attract West German opinion, by genuinely free elections.

In an attempt to confuse the issue, the Soviet Government tried to distract German attention from E.D.C. by raising hopes of German reunification and a peace treaty. As part of this delaying action, they handed a note on March 10th to the representatives of the United States, France and the United Kingdom. In this they proposed that the four powers should 'discuss without delay the question of a peace treaty with Germany', and should 'examine the question of the conditions favouring the speediest formation of an all-German Government expressing the will of the German people.'

M. Schuman, Mr. Acheson and I were agreed as to the effect of a four-power conference on Germany at this stage. It would slow up progress on E.D.C., and postpone the integration of Western European defence. The Soviet purpose was a little too blatant. At the same time, it was important not to dash any German hopes, even faint ones, which this initiative might arouse. In a few days, we had our reply ready. This stated that discussion of a peace treaty could only follow the creation of an all-German Government by free elections. Free elections could not be held until a United Nations Commission had been able to ascertain, in the Soviet zone as well as in the Federal Republic and Berlin, that adequate safeguards existed for the political liberties of the individual. The sooner this work could begin, we implied, the better.

What I referred to at the time as the 'battle of the notes' continued all through April and May, and on the whole the Russians got the worst of it. The Soviet Government refused to allow the United Nations Commission of investigation to operate in the Eastern zone of Germany. They were evasive when we offered to discuss some other form of impartial commission. They would not accept that an all-German Government must be freely elected to prepare for the negotiations; nor would they admit that this Government, once established, must itself be free to take its own decisions about alliances and foreign policy. The Soviet note delivered on May 24th, just as the E.D.C. treaty was going to be signed, fell back, rather desperately, on abuse of the European Community and 'the aggressive North Atlantic bloc'.

Though the tone of the Soviet Government's notes became increasingly uncompromising, I was anxious to keep the correspondence open, for there was always a hope that it might be possible in time to hold a four-power conference on the German problem on terms we could accept. Meanwhile, there was complete allied agreement to press ahead with plans to make Western Europe militarily strong. I believed that when the Russians saw that they were not getting anywhere by threats, there was a chance that they might be willing to negotiate in earnest. We had to show that we could not be blustered out of our intentions.

On May 21st, I flew from London to take part in the final negotiations on the German contractual agreement and the treaty between ourselves and E.D.C. On my way to Bonn, I called at Paris to see if all was ready for the signing of the final agreements between the E.D.C. powers, which had been initialled on May 9th. I found the French in considerable uncertainty and disarray. From a long talk with M. Schuman, I concluded that the French Cabinet had still failed to reach a definite decision about E.D.C. It looked to me as if, even at this stage, they might baulk at signing the treaty, and I reported accordingly to London. M. Schuman and I discussed the possible reactions of the Soviet Union to the signature of the German contract and the E.D.C. treaty. We agreed that, while persisting with our own plans, we should make every effort to draw the Russians into declaring their intentions for Europe. We should make it clear that we were always ready to talk. Dr. Adenauer's political position in Germany was at this time vulnerable, and there was no need to add to his difficulties by translating firmness into rigidity.

In Bonn, I was joined by Mr. Acheson. When M. Schuman arrived and spoke to us on May 24th, it emerged that the French Government were now fastening on the wording of the tripartite declaration, which was to accompany the signature of the E.D.C. treaty, as a pretext for further delay. After two days of urgent discussions and much telephoning between Bonn and Paris, we overcame this obstacle, and the contractual agreement with Germany was finally signed on May 26th.

I found it a strange experience. After two world wars which had filled my life, I was signing with a German in Germany a document which gave the greater part of the country a control of its affairs once again.

We moved on to Paris, where Mr. Acheson and I were present on the morrow at the signing of the E.D.C. treaty in the Salon de l'Horloge of the Quai d'Orsay. On the same day the Governments of France, the United States and the United Kingdom issued their tripartite declaration. This had been strengthened at the last minute as a result of French misgivings, and the Anglo-American undertaking now read:

> Accordingly, if any action from whatever quarter threatens the integrity or unity of the Community, the two Governments will regard this as a threat to their own security. They will act in accordance with Article 4 of the North Atlantic Treaty.

This assurance was intended to allay French fears that Germany might at a later stage secede from E.D.C. and set up her own national army.

All was signed and sealed, but far from delivered. The Parliaments had yet to have their say, and in France the tide of opinion was turning against the federal idea which had inspired the Pleven Plan. There were many second thoughts. Some felt that E.D.C. conflicted with the imperial conception of Union Française, and with the independent destiny of France as a great power in her own right. Others were made queasy by the permanent dilemma of French policy: whether Russia or Germany was more to be feared. If Russia, then the rearmament of Germany was a risk that must be taken. If Germany, then the revival of a Franco-Russian entente was an alluring vision. From this emerged a period of hesitation and requests. Their confidence sapped by the steady drain of the Indo-China war, the French were tempted to postpone a final decision until Russian intentions had been fully tested.

★   ★   ★   ★   ★

During the summer of 1952, while the E.D.C. treaty was beginning its long and eventually fruitless quest for ratification, another European organization came into being. This was the European Coal and Steel Community, which by June had been approved by all its six member-countries. I thought that this event might provide an opportunity for the Council of Europe. Our seat on the Council was useful to us as a point of contact with European developments and I did not want to see it neglected while the military and coal and steel organizations became the focus of European attention and activity. If we were to maintain close links with Europe, its Council should have something specific to do. I suggested that it would have a more promising future if it were remodelled to serve the Coal and Steel Community, the Defence Community, and any future organizations of the kind there might be. By using the Council, countries could establish close relations with the European Community in its various activities. As European organizations grew, their institutions and functions were likely to multiply in an unwieldy manner. I thought that the Council of Europe could be useful to guide and check this tendency.

These were the ideas which lay behind the proposals I put to the Committee of Ministers of the Council of Europe in March. They were dubbed by the press 'the Eden Plan', the first of many such. But this time the name had not been earned, the contents being the result of much hard work by Mr. Anthony Nutting and members of the Foreign Office.

On May 23rd, the Committee of Ministers unanimously approved the principles of our plan. The Assembly's debate at the end of May went well for us, as I reported in a message to my colleagues:

> Our stock in Strasbourg now stands high. This is due to our initiative in launching proposals which have been accepted as proof of our willingness to establish close political, as well as technical links with the European Communities.

In September, I attended the new session of the Consultative Assembly on my way to Yugoslavia, and told them that our suggestions were designed to meet a situation of fact. They were not intended to be a rigid or sensational plan. Their purpose was simply to help reconcile the aim of the six powers, which was to create a supranational community, with the need to keep Europe united.

A resolution, embodying the United Kingdom proposals, was adopted by the Consultative Assembly on September 30th by 102 votes to nil, with one abstention. Two years later, the failure of E.D.C. robbed the plan of much of its purpose. But it has provided effective contact between the European Coal and Steel Community and the Council of Europe, by means of simultaneous sessions in Strasbourg. The need to keep Europe united remains an imperative for statesmanship to realize.

*　　*　　*　　*　　*

During the next six months, world leadership changed. On November 4th, in a landslide Republican victory, General Eisenhower became President-elect of the United States. The Republicans owed their first presidential success for twenty-four years very largely to the personality and record of their candidate. His many friends in Europe, while taking no sides in American politics, were happy in the election of a soldier to whom Europe owed so much. General Eisenhower's recent work as commander of N.A.T.O's forces had further enhanced his reputation.

Shortly after his inauguration, President Eisenhower invited me, with Mr. Butler, the Chancellor of the Exchequer, to come to Washington to discuss international and economic matters. I welcomed this opportunity to get on terms with the new American Administration, to which I wanted to explain our position about Iran and Egypt. We also wished to discuss with the United States Government the outcome of the Commonwealth Economic Conference, over which I had presided. At the end of 1952 this conference had worked out means of expanding world trade and of extending to other countries the methods of payment in use between its members. I wanted to learn the American attitude to this Commonwealth plan for another reason. I had recently become Chairman of the Organization for European Economic Co-operation, and its Council was to meet after our return from Washington.

Since 1948 O.E.E.C. had played a leading part in rebuilding the economy of Western Europe. In its early years the organization owed much to the initiative and interest of Sir Stafford Cripps. Since then, its sixteen member countries have worked out an effective system, reaching agreement on specific economic problems without surrendering sovereignty. A chief architect of O.E.E.C's success at this time was its Secretary-General, M. Robert Marjolin. If the Chancellor of the Exchequer and I could get some help from the new American Administration in broadening world trade, this would encourage O.E.E.C. Unfortunately, our discussions at Washington on this topic, though agreeable in temper, were barren in results.

As we approached New York on March 2nd, the ship's wireless told us that Marshal Stalin had suffered a stroke and was dangerously ill. Three days later, it was announced from Moscow that Stalin had died. I did not share the optimism of those who saw in this event an easement of the world's problems. The permanent challenge of communism transcends personalities, however powerful. But whatever the aftermath, March 5th marked the end of an era. My mind was crowded with memories. I thought of an incident in my first meeting with Stalin in 1935, when at a point in our talks he walked across to a map of the world and pointed to Britain, remarking: 'It is strange that so much should depend upon one small island.' I remembered also the hours I had spent in discussion with Stalin in Moscow in the dark month of December 1941. The Germans were almost near enough for the sound of their guns to reach us. The diplomatic corps and much of the administration had withdrawn to Kuibyshev, but Stalin remained. He steadied and saved his country then.

For a quarter of a century, Stalin ruled a vast empire in the manner of an eastern despot, made more terrible and more effective by a modern technique of persuasion and repression. Ruthlessly, he had driven his country into the front rank of the world's industrial powers. Against all expectation, he had mobilized the heroism of the Russian people, and urged them to the untold sacrifices which made possible the defeat of the German invader. The victory won, he gave no pause. His armies remained to hold in subjection the territories through which they had advanced to the west. He extracted from his exhausted countrymen their last ounce of strength to rebuild their devastated land, and to prepare for the next stage of communism's aggrandisement. However malign its purpose, the scale of Stalin's achievement was stupendous, dwarfed only by its cost in human suffering. My hope was that the Soviet peoples would now be allowed to give less tortured expression to their greatness. With this went the sober knowledge that, while a third of the world remained under totalitarian communist rule, the free democracies could never drop their guard.

Although the death of Stalin brought some modification in the technique of Moscow's foreign policy, its real character was not changed. On April 16th President Eisenhower appealed to the new leaders of the Soviet Union to give tangible evidence of a desire for peace, which could lead to a world-wide reduction in armaments. 'We care only', he said, 'for sincerity of peaceful purpose, attested by deeds. The opportunities for such deeds are many.' The Soviet reply lacked the hectoring abuse which had been commonplace in Stalin's time, but its attitude to the specific problems named by the President yielded nothing. On German reunification, Moscow called for a peace treaty followed by the withdrawal of occupation forces. There was no mention of free elections. Similarly, an Austrian peace treaty seemed as far away as ever. The new Soviet ruling committee, headed by Malenkov, wanted to lower the international temperature, and therefore abandoned much that was uselessly provocative in Stalinist policy; but the 'cold war' was their policy and it persisted.

★   ★   ★   ★   ★

For some time, I had been suffering from internal pains which had been variously diagnosed. These were acute when I attempted long journeys, especially by air, and I had sometimes to give myself injections to relieve the sharpest spasms. The previous summer I had also had an attack of jaundice.

Early in April 1953, I was due to pay an official visit to Turkey. A few days before, my wife was insistent that I should call in another opinion and Sir Horace Evans was asked to see me. An X-ray examination showed gall-stones and Sir Horace insisted on an immediate operation. The visit to Turkey was cancelled, and the Prime Minister took over my duties at the Foreign Office. I entered a nursing home that afternoon, feeling that the streets in their April sunlight looked astonishingly gloomy. My gall bladder was removed, but the operation did not go well. The fever was high and I lost strength. Jaundice recurred and a second operation was decided upon. There was no real improvement and my condition grew worse.

By chance, Dr. Cattell, a famous Boston surgeon who has made a life study of this particular operation, came to London at this time to lecture. On Sir Horace Evans' invitation, he came round to see me. Having examined me, he was forthright. He asked me whether I wished him to tell me the exact position as he saw it. I said 'Yes'. He continued that I would never recover unless I underwent a third operation. He was confident that he could perform this successfully if I would go to Boston. Some discussion followed as to whether Dr. Cattell could operate in London. He explained that he was prepared to do this if we insisted, but that, naturally, he thought the chances would be better if I would go to Boston, where all the facilities with which he was familiar were to hand. I agreed, for despite some protests, I do not consider that medicine or the arts have national frontiers. Sir Horace Evans and Dr. Cattell waited upon the Prime Minister and the matter was arranged. I was removed by ambulance to Chequers, where I spent a few weeks trying to regain my strength.

Early in June we drove slowly from Chequers to London Airport, where the Governor-General of Canada had kindly sent his aeroplane, fitted with a comfortable bed, to convey me across the Atlantic. The aeroplane landed on a remote corner of the airfield and only the Prime Minister and Lady Churchill were allowed to see us off. My son, who was at that time A.D.C. to the Governor-General in Canada, met us at the airport in Boston. We drove to the New England Baptist Hospital and, after two days to recover from the exhaustion of the journey, the operation was successfully performed. My strength gradually returned.

While I was counting the days to my removal to Newport, where Mr. and Mrs. John Ryan had generously lent us their house in which to convalesce, I received a letter from the Prime Minister which was downcast in tone. This was so strange an event that I was less surprised when a message reached me from Downing Street to say that the Prime Minister was seriously ill. I was kept fully informed and the sad business was revealed. Sir Winston had suffered a stroke, but he had been determined to hold on at least until I could return to work. When he could speak, he told Mr. Butler and Lord Salisbury of his determination and they upheld him in it. Lord Salisbury took over the Foreign Office and Mr. Butler assumed authority for home affairs.

The Prime Minister's plan for a Bermuda Conference to prepare for a 'summit' meeting had to be suspended. But Lord Salisbury, by a visit to Washington for discussions with Mr. Dulles and M. Bidault, kept alive the possibility of a four-power conference, which our allies wished should be concerned with Germany. Their wish was realized six months later, in Berlin.

IV

THE BERLIN CONFERENCE
June 1953 – February 1954

Plans for four-power meeting – 'Agonizing reappraisal' – French scepticism –My views on Russia and Germany – Berlin Conference –Mr. Dulles– The Russians and free elections – The 'Eden Plan' for Germany – Uncompromising attitude of Russia – Deadlock over Austria – Dangers of German neutralization

On June 17th, 1953, anti-Soviet demonstrations suddenly broke out in East Berlin and in several towns of the Eastern zone of Germany. These riots followed signs of unrest in Czechoslovakia and showed how thin was the communist crust in these occupied lands. Despite the hopes of freedom these risings inspired, Soviet policy was not, for the moment, toughened in Eastern Germany; some internal political concessions continued to be granted. It looked as if Mr. Malenkov and his colleagues needed a pause to consolidate their power in the Kremlin. The dismissal of Beria as Minister of State Security revealed internal rivalry. In these conditions the possibility that Moscow might be ready for some form of agreement in central Europe was slight, but just worth exploring.

Lord Salisbury's conversations in Washington showed that there were other arguments for a fresh approach to the Soviet Government. M. Bidault declared that his Government could not hope to secure the ratification of E.D.C. until a further attempt had been made to reach a European settlement by negotiation. France was not prepared to make the sacrifice of sovereignty involved in E.D.C. until she had final proof of Russian intransigence. Dr. Adenauer, in a letter to Mr. Dulles, also declared himself strongly in favour of a new effort to discover Russia's intentions by bringing her to the conference table. The three Ministers decided, in the words of their communiqué, 'to propose a meeting in the early autumn of the Foreign Secretaries of France, the United Kingdom, the United States and the U.S.S.R. to discuss directly the first steps which should lead to a satisfactory solution of the German problem, namely, the organization of free elections and the establishment of a free all-German Government.'

The Soviet Government blocked this invitation in a note they handed to our Ambassador in Moscow on August 4th. They would only agree to a conference which would include communist China and discuss the problems of the world at large. The Western proposal for all-German free elections was flatly rejected:

> The Soviet Government consider that such a proposal not only cannot contribute to the unification of Germany and the creation of an all-German democratic Government and the conclusion of a peace treaty with Germany, but that it involves leaving Germany divided into western and eastern parts, the conclusion of a peace treaty being dragged on as before.

Feeling that something more was needed to influence the forthcoming elections in the Federal German Republic, Moscow proposed, a few days later, that a peace conference on Germany should assemble within six months. Meanwhile, a provisional all-German Government should be formed, as the precondition for holding free elections. This was a specious request, for a project which the Soviets knew could not be realized. As if to dot the i's and cross the t's of their refusal, they declined to attend a meeting to discuss the conclusion of an Austrian peace treaty. The West replied with an invitation to salubrious Lugano, and the Soviets countered with an offer of two conferences instead of one.

I spent some weeks convalescing in the Mediterranean, and cruising in H.M.S. *Surprise*. When I returned to the Foreign Office on October 5th, this mammoth correspondence was heaped upon my desk. On October 16th Mr. Dulles and M. Bidault arrived in London for discussions. We decided to persist in inviting the Soviet Government to a conference. We said that it would be better if we four met, instead of sending each other notes. Then things slowly began to move, until at the end of November the Russians accepted our proposal for a four-power conference, with a condition. This was that they would ask for a five-power meeting, including China, when the four met. I thought we could handle that.

This Soviet reply added a useful item for the Bermuda Conference.

Sir Winston Churchill and I arrived on the island on December 2nd. Mr. Dulles, M. Bidault and I soon met to discuss our reply to the Russians. We had to settle details of time and place. Mr. Dulles considered that time was now a vital factor and not just a matter of convenience. The United States, he said, was prepared to accept a four-power meeting, on the assumption that it could be held in the near future and that we would be able to extricate ourselves from it quickly, if it became clear that the Russians intended to accomplish nothing and were merely taking part in it for propaganda purposes. It was virtually certain, Mr. Dulles said, that the only result which the Russians hoped to achieve at this meeting was to delay our present plans for strengthening the position of the West, both in E.D.C. and in N.A.T.O. The conference must not be allowed to delay the ratification of E.D.C.

Mr. Dulles told us that the United States Congress was in a mood in which, unless there was some positive action towards European unity in the next two or three months, its foreign aid appropriations would be so rigid and so qualified that there would be very serious repercussions on the N.A.T.O. programme. The four-power meeting should therefore start as soon as possible and, if it became clear that no satisfactory solutions would be reached, it should be ended in time for French parliamentary action to be taken on E.D.C. during February. Mr. Dulles concluded with the statement that he could not take the responsibility for saying that Congress would continue their firm and loyal support of N.A.T.O., or pursue the creation of a strong economic and military body on the continent of Europe, if this situation were to drag on much longer. If this time-table could not be adopted, he was afraid that the Soviet manœuvre would have achieved its purpose of bringing about disunity between us.

This was the first I had heard of the possible 'reappraisal' of American policy towards Europe. Mr. Dulles was to speak forcefully, or brutally as the French thought, about this in Paris a few days later. I saw the strength of the argument for an early date and I would have preferred it. But having worked so long for this meeting, I did not want to rush my fences at the end. I thought that having asked for the meeting and the Russians having accepted, we had at least to give time enough for serious business. At a later discussion January 4th, 1954, was suggested. The French Government were in a difficult position; the election of a new President of the Republic was in the offing and this might mean a change of Government during January. M. Laniel consequently favoured this early date, to which we all agreed. For place, we accepted the Russian suggestion of Berlin.

Immediately after my return from Bermuda, I flew to Paris for a meeting of the North Atlantic Council. There I had a long talk with Dr. Adenauer on December 13th, and we discussed the idea which I had raised at Bermuda for some form of security declaration which would help to allay Russian fears of a resurgent Germany. Its purpose was to emphasize the purely defensive nature of the Federal Republic's association with E.D.C. The Chancellor confirmed that his Government would be willing in principle to issue such a declaration, although he had some criticism of the draft we had prepared. I said that I did not think we should offer this security declaration on a plate to the Russians. It was important to wait and see what progress was made with other matters at the four-power conference. If the Russians showed interest in security, we could say that we had certain ideas, and then we could develop them in the light of the general progress of the conference. We would use them only after consultation with the Federal German Government.

Dr. Adenauer was apprehensive that public opinion in Europe might form too sanguine a view of Soviet statements or of the prospects of the conference. I agreed that we had a double task; not to seem reluctant to negotiate, but at the same time not to mislead our peoples regarding the prospects of success. The Russians were behaving more intelligently since Stalin's death. They now had a new slogan, 'Europe for the Europeans', the idea being that they themselves were Europeans, while the Americans were not. The Chancellor went on to say, as he had done before, that it was Germany's urgent wish that the United Kingdom should come as close as possible to E.D.C. and to Europe. There were two main reasons for this. First, Europe could not do without Great Britain's experience, character and way of life, and secondly, the French must not be allowed to think that Germany was striving for hegemony through E.D.C.

I replied that we would come as close as we could. We kept coming closer. There was a genuine difficulty for our people, however, about actually joining any European federation. Dr. Adenauer entirely understood and accepted this. He did not expect us to join E.D.C., but he wanted the French to feel calm and secure and he needed British advice and help. There was to his mind a grave, though perhaps remote, danger which should be remembered. The German people after their collapse in 1945 had been led to build up their hope and faith in a united Europe. If this were to fail, there would be a dangerous psychological vacuum. I then told the Chancellor that all the Ministers at Bermuda had felt that the choice lay between E.D.C. and complete confusion. After some discussion of the Saar, our meeting ended. I was encouraged by this conversation, which showed that co-operation with the Federal German Government at the Berlin Conference would present few problems.

Three days later, I had an important conversation with Mr. Dulles. What he told me on this occasion was much in my mind throughout the following year, and particularly after the failure of E.D.C. On the evening before he came to see me, Mr. Dulles had spoken at a press conference of the 'agonizing reappraisal' of American foreign policy, which would have to take place if France failed to ratify E.D.C. His speech had raised a storm of angry comment in the French press. It was eagerly seized upon by all those who found Europe's military dependence upon the United States irksome, and its tone had given rise to concern even amongst America's closest friends. Mr. Dulles now told me that it was no accident that he had spoken so strongly about the implications of any failure to ratify E.D.C. His longer statement in the N.A.T.O. Council the previous day had been carefully gone over by the President, and he would have liked to publish it, but M. Bidault had objected. The United States Government felt that it was essential to give French public opinion a jolt. The French, he said, did not seem to be aware of the very grave consequences upon American policy if the hopes of a European arrangement, which would unite France and Germany, were to be dashed. He had been speaking to M. Jean Monnet and had reached the conclusion that it was probably not possible to find a French Government which could put through E.D.C. and govern France, since the majorities required for these two purposes were different. This was clever, but I was not sure it was true, for I was beginning to question whether any French Government could put through E.D.C. Mr. Dulles continued that it might be necessary to work for a French Government which could take office solely for the purpose of putting through E.D.C. That was one reason why he had thought it necessary to give a jolt now, rather than wait until nearer the ratification debates.

Mr. Dulles then told me that he thought we, by which he apparently meant the United States and Britain, were approaching a parting of the ways with regard to American policy. If things went wrong, the United States might swing over to a policy of western hemispheric

defence, with the emphasis on the Far East. This might not be immediately apparent, but once the trend started, it would be hard to stop.
Already there was mounting pressure for such a change. Moreover,
he was afraid that if E.D.C. were not ratified in the spring, the Germans
would become disillusioned with the European idea, and would press
strongly to be released from the present allied restrictions. It would
be difficult to avoid pressure to separate the Bonn agreements from
E.D.C. Mr. Dulles pointed out that the consequences of a swing
of American policy towards hemispheric defence were of obvious
concern to Great Britain. He hoped, therefore, that I might find an
occasion to underline the warnings which he had issued in his statement, and make some appeal to France.

I told Mr. Dulles that I feared it must be regarded as doubtful whether
E.D.C. would go through. The French as a whole seemed impervious either to cajolery or to the prospects of dire alternatives. I had
therefore been wondering whether we could not strengthen N.A.T.O.
obligations and machinery, and thus control Germany ourselves within
N.A.T.O. This would surely be better than a peripheral or hemispheric
strategy. I added that these thoughts should of course be kept strictly
to ourselves, as we must give no hint to the French that there was
an acceptable alternative to E.D.C.

During the months which followed, the French were inclined to
dismiss Mr. Dulles' threat of 'reappraisal' as bluff. After my talk with
him, I was not so sure, although I did not like the method. It was much
in our interest that the Americans should keep their N.A.T.O. commitment to help defend the European continent. It would be reckless to
regard this as a natural right, or to assume that it could never be withdrawn. There were many in Europe, including the United Kingdom,
who were reluctant to recognize this unpleasant possibility. I did my
best to remind them of it.

On my return from Paris, I set to work with my advisers in the
Foreign Office on our plans for the Berlin Conference. Good prelimin-
ary work had already been done by a working group of American,
French and British officials, in which our own delegation was led by
Sir Frank Roberts. After studying their findings, which were extremely
thorough and included a detailed plan for the organization of free all-
German elections, I wrote down my own thoughts on the prospects:

Soviet objectives in Europe:
    For the Soviet Government, the principal obstacle to their plans

in Europe is the presence of American troops and American influence on the continent. The military and political strength of the United States in Europe will be consolidated if Germany is drawn into the Western system and raises forces to assist in Western defence. Soviet policy in Europe has thus two main purposes:

(i) to obtain American withdrawal from Europe, thus fatally weakening the Western alliance;

(ii) to prevent the resurgence of a strong *united* Germany integrated with the West.

Western objectives in Europe:

The most important requirement for the Western powers, on the other hand, is to reach agreement on the reunification of Germany as a free, democratic state looking towards the West and able and willing to associate itself with the West in E.D.C., etc. When we originally proposed a meeting of Foreign Secretaries at the time of the Washington talks, it was our intention that E.D.C. would be in existence before the opening of any conference. Our task should then have been to reach satisfactory arrangements with the Russians in the light of this *fait accompli*. But the hesitations of the French Parliament, which may be partly ascribed to the Soviet Union's less intransigent international behaviour, have prevented this.

Handling of the German problem at Berlin:

The main positive Western objectives in Berlin will be to make progress towards a German peace treaty and to conclude the Austrian treaty. An important negative objective will be to ensure that French ratification of the E.D.C. treaty is not further delayed by the Berlin Conference. We must avoid creating the impression that we (and more particularly the Americans) are in such a hurry to get on with E.D.C. that we are not aiming at serious negotiations on Germany and Austria. We must therefore establish the position that we, unlike the Russians, have a practical plan for German reunification, which would produce a representative all-German Government with which alone a peace treaty can be negotiated. This must be based on free, all-German elections as the essential first step.

We should then be able to counter the Soviet thesis that a peace treaty should be negotiated without delay, but with an unrepresentative provisional all-German Government selected from the existing Federal Government and the discredited Soviet zone regime. The subsequent organization of elections would be left entirely to these two groups of Germans, without any outside supervision. This Soviet approach is designed (*a*) to build up the waning prestige of its puppets in the Soviet zone and (*b*) to create an unrepresentative all-German Government, including Soviet zone communists, which would be prevented from aligning Germany with the West and would be under increasingly strong Russian influence. The Western approach has the support of all the major parties in the Federal Republic and in Berlin, who regard the Soviet alternative as completely unacceptable.

We must also resist any Soviet proposals aiming at German neutralization or at a return to four-power control of Germany. In short, we must adhere firmly to the principles (i) that an all-German Government with which we can negotiate a peace treaty can only emerge from free elections, and (ii) that this all-German Government must be able to choose its own international associations provided that they are not inconsistent with the United Nations Charter. This policy is in line with that pursued by the three Western Governments at the last four-power ministerial meeting with the Soviet Government in 1949, and with the provisions of the Bonn Conventions which I signed in 1952. On these principles there can be no compromise.

I doubted whether Molotov would be empowered to reach any agreement about Germany which included free elections. He should be able to agree with us on Austria, since we were accepting Soviet amendments to the Austrian State Treaty. But in planning our tactics, we had to be prepared for a negative all along the line. Consequently, I wished that, before we allowed the Russians to entangle us in an endless wrangle about the agenda, we should take the initiative by bringing forward a complete plan for German reunification, preceded by free elections. If the conference broke down later, we would at least have made our position clear to the world, and have fixed the responsibility for the failure. Our whole argument was based on the freedom of a government of a united Germany to take its own decisions. This also we had to declare without equivocation in our plan. It was not, after all, our fault if the result of freedom of choice would be to align Germany with us.

The other two items on the Berlin agenda would be Austria and the Russian proposal for a five-power conference. We could not accept that an Austrian agreement should be dependent upon progress towards a German peace treaty. I had an open mind about a five-power conference. I knew that our position, and that of the French, was likely to be less rigid than the American; it was important that we should maintain a united front. Above all, we had to ensure that discussion of this Russian proposal did not monopolize the conference to the exclusion of its true purpose. I concluded my reflections as follows:

> This analysis may seem rather sombre. But I do not wish to minimize the difficulties and dangers of this meeting, desirable though it is. Even if we do not succeed in our immediate objectives, we should be able to give and receive some assurance regarding our own and Soviet intentions, and it is probably in the Soviet as well as in the Western interest to maintain contact and to avoid any aggravation of the cold war after Berlin. But this must not be allowed to prevent the West from completing its own security system rapidly, through the ratification of the Bonn and E.D.C. treaties. Above all, Western unity must survive the conference unimpaired.

All this I explained to the Prime Minister and my colleagues, who gave me the fullest support both before and throughout the conference. A foreign secretary in any democratic country is wise to tell his countrymen in advance what he is trying to do, though this is not easy if he is to avoid showing his hand. In a broadcast a week before I left for Berlin, I asked the nation not to expect too much. Disillusionment and exasperation could only do harm. I concluded with a warning I thought necessary in view of communist attacks on N.A.T.O:

> And let me make one thing clear. We cannot jettison our own security any more than we ask the Russians to jettison theirs. We cannot abandon our defensive arrangements as a condition of agreement.

A tiresome argument with the Russians about which building to use provided a discouraging prelude for our conference. It is usually prudent to be conciliatory on matters of secondary importance, though in dealing with the Russians these can add up to quite a bill. We gave way to the extent of meeting alternately in our sector and theirs. This worked quite well, and I was intrigued by the contrasting impressions of the Soviet and the Western zones, the bleakness of the former and the hopes of the latter. The Western Foreign Secretaries arrived in Berlin a few days before the conference was due to open, for a final discussion of plans and tactics. Accordingly I left London on January 22nd.

I have never kept a regular diary, and I did not do so during the Conference. I did, however, make an occasional note before going to bed. Here is the note which I made for that day:

> Motored to airport quite comfortably after various alarms— none of them serious. Good-bye sadly to Clarissa. A pleasant flight, with beauty queens to tend us, until twenty minutes from Berlin, when we flew into heavy cloud and fog. I didn't enjoy it, and was glad when we emerged over the roofs of Berlin. Guard of honour and other ceremonies on arrival. Press broke ranks and it was rather a scramble at the finish.

The preliminary meetings between Mr. Dulles, M. Bidault and my-self confirmed the complete agreement between us on the problems of the conference. Only on the Korean issue was there some difference of opinion. India had proposed that a committee of the General Assembly should discuss a Korean political settlement in the United Nations. Now there was a Russian proposal for a five-power conference, at which Korea would be on the agenda. Mr. Dulles did not like either of these methods. My notes continue:

> *Saturday, January 23rd*: First meeting at French H.Q. in morning. It passed pleasantly and successfully. Bidault in good form in chair. This was followed by excellent luncheon, served on a beautiful modern French table-cloth. Further meeting *chez nous* which also went well, so that virtually all the preparations are now completed and we are agreed. Foster dined in the evening, and we had about an hour alone afterwards. I am troubled about U.N. Assembly meetings. Americans are resisting because of their suspicion of India, but I doubt if the tactics are wise. Wouldn't it be less troublesome in the end to have a short meeting now, especially if Panmunjom can crawl forward meanwhile? Anyway, we are not agreed, which is dangerous.

Sunday, January 24th: To church in morning. Enjoyed the service, which was well done. A walk by the lake with Tony and Evelyn* afterwards, when I canvassed with them that we need not so rigidly oppose a five-power meeting. It was better, I argued—or could be—than an Assembly committee. Work on telegrams in p.m. Bidault came to dinner. A useful talk. He was unhappy about Far East assembly problem. Agreed we three might have to meet.†

That night, I sent a short telegram to the Prime Minister:

Preliminary moves have gone as well as could be expected. There is close unity between us and the Americans and French. Russians have made a few tentative approaches, and so I am asking a small party of bears to dinner later this week. We have made all arrangements for keeping in touch with Adenauer, so the stage is set. Weather cold and fine. Berliners are very friendly.

Anthony.

I had some dealings with Mr. Dulles over the Japanese Peace Treaty, but the Berlin Conference was the first occasion when I negotiated with him as a partner. We were able to keep closely in step with each other and with M. Bidault, with good results, I think, for our countries. My later experience was not so fortunate. My relations had always been cordial and often intimate with the four earlier American Secretaries of State whom I had known as colleagues. We differed sometimes of course, but misunderstandings were rare, soon recognized to be such between us and in due course resolved. My difficulty in working with Mr. Dulles was to determine what he really meant and in consequence the significance to be attached to his words and actions. I know that I was not alone in this, but the consequences were unfortunate for Britain, the weaker partner.

Mr. Dulles had made a prolonged study of international affairs, though he had little practical experience of them, and his knowledge, especially of the legal aspects of our problems, was extensive. Sometimes I would take action which I believed would bring our policy into line with that of the United States, as for instance in the matter of

---

* Mr. Anthony Nutting, M.P., Parliamentary Under-Secretary of State for Foreign Affairs, and Mr. Evelyn Shuckburgh, my Principal Private Secretary at the Foreign Office.

† See Chapter V, p. 88.

the Users' Club during the Suez dispute, only to find that the policy had not the significance it had been declared to have. Almost as baffling, though not finally so unfortunate, was Mr. Dulles' sudden and undiscussed incursion to Bonn in the midst of my tour of the Western capitals. Nor could I understand the prolonged coolness of American policy towards the Baghdad Pact in its most critical period, when the inspiration for the unity of the northern tier certainly seemed to us to have been shared by Washington. There was often, no doubt, sufficient cause for what appeared to us these sudden shifts of policy in the leading nation of the West. A preacher in a world of politics, it sometimes seemed as if Mr. Dulles had little regard for the consequence of his words, as demonstrated by the outburst against colonialism and the virtual declaration of neutrality in another critical phase of the Suez dispute. The lesson may be that allies should subordinate their interests more closely to the opinions of their stronger partner, but an alliance does not gather strength that way.

The first formal session of the Berlin Conference opened on January 25th. No procedural difficulties arose and M. Bidault and I made preliminary statements covering the Western approach to the conference. Both our speeches were unpolemical and Mr. Molotov seemed receptive to my references to our former collaboration with him, and to our desire to provide for the security of all countries, including the Soviet Union. I concluded by speaking of the need to bring about free elections in Germany, and so enable a Government to be set up with whom we could make a peace treaty. I said we would have a definite plan to put forward, and indicated its general outlines. Molotov's speech, although it was not aggressive in tone, repeated all the familiar Soviet themes. He concluded by proposing the following agenda for our meeting:

(1) Measures for reducing international tension and convening a five-power conference.
(2) The German question and the problem of achieving European security.
(3) The Austrian State Treaty.

At the end of the day, I made this note:

A morning in bed at work on my speech. It was rather a hurried affair, but didn't come out too badly. Luncheon at home and then a few turns round the garden. It had been snowing intermittently, but, as the sun came out, it was quite pleasant. I prefer this sharp cold climate here to the soggy relaxing damp of Bonn.

To the Allied building, which seems well suited to its purpose, except that I found it difficult to stand up on the polished linoleum of the corridors. Opening was much as expected. Molotov produced nothing new. The same old gramophone record with scarcely a variant. Austria the only faint suggestion of one. Some jibes at the Americans which they resented. Bidault spoke very well, and my smaller piece was adequate. Molotov rather surprised us by asking for an adjournment when I had finished. His personal attitude was friendly.

I watched them march out when all was over, like a platoon. I was standing aside waiting for Tony. One or two broke ranks to shake hands. Rather an inhuman platoon.

On the following day, Mr. Dulles asked to see M. Bidault and myself to discuss our attitude to Molotov's proposed agenda. We agreed that we must try to avoid a prolonged wrangle about it and get down to discussion of Germany and Austria. We therefore decided to accept the Russian order of discussion. As I noted that evening: 'By accepting Soviet agenda we have saved much haggling and gained world good will. We shall need it.'

In all, we discussed the German problem at thirteen meetings of the Berlin Conference. Much of our time was spent listening to lengthy and identical repetitions of the Soviet case. Mr. Molotov never allowed our treatment of this part of the agenda to proceed from declamation to negotiation. It was soon apparent that he was determined to use the conference as a platform from which he could launch attacks on E.D.C. and N.A.T.O.

On January 27th, Mr. Molotov came to dine with me, and I was able to sound out his views on Germany. I explained that we were quite as anxious as the Soviet Government to prevent any revival of the German danger. We were convinced that the best, and indeed the only method yet suggested from any quarter was E.D.C. I then developed all the arguments for E.D.C; that there would be only twelve German divisions, that they would be under the control of obviously peace-loving countries such as France and Holland and also ourselves, that Germany's armaments production would be under international control, that these twelve divisions, with only a tactical air force and with no navy or atomic weapons, would absorb a contribution from the German economy as great as Hitler's 1939 forces, and that they would not be under the control of a German national government. I pointed out that if, despite these safeguards, Germany were to attack the Soviet Union, we would be at the side of the Soviet Union in accordance with the Anglo-Soviet Treaty. Surely this was the best way to prevent the dangers we both feared. But if this was not enough, I went on, we had offered to consider with the Soviet Union what further security arrangements could be made.

Molotov commented rather acidly that pieces of paper were not sufficient security against the revival of the German army. He then expressed considerable scepticism about E.D.C. He thought we were under illusions about future developments in Germany. He was very critical of Adenauer, whom he described more than once as an enemy of the Soviet Union. He added that Adenauer's successors were likely to be even more aggressive and dangerous. E.D.C., said Molotov, was an organization without the Soviet Union and directed against her. Of course, the Soviet Union was strong enough to defend herself against Adenauer, but surely we were agreed that our objective should be to avoid any war at all, by an agreement between the Soviet Union, the United Kingdom and France to prevent any revival of German militarism. We had proposed free elections, he continued, but Hitler had come to power as a result of elections which were free. He agreed that there should be free elections in Germany, but that the four occupying powers should surely agree beforehand upon the kind of government they wished to result from free elections.

This last remark, I thought, revealed too much of Soviet thinking. The Russians had been convinced that Mr. Churchill and I would come back to the Potsdam Conference. They made no concealment of their opinion in advance and were much astonished when the results of the 1945 election were known. One of my Foreign Office friends who had seen the Soviet leaders that day, commented in a message to me: 'One result is quite certain. Uncle Joe is more than ever convinced that free elections are a great mistake.'

At this later meeting in Berlin, I said to Molotov that I had not heard of any Soviet alternative to E.D.C., other than the proposal in one of the Soviet notes for a German national army. Surely, I continued, this would enable the Germans to develop their strength independently, and to play off the Western powers against the Soviet Union as Molotov had feared. We must all face the fact that Germany would be rearmed; and indeed, the Soviet Union had begun to rearm Eastern Germany. Molotov commented that this was not a very serious rearmament, to which I retorted that there was not a single German soldier in West Germany. Molotov's only positive contribution was to say that it all depended upon the kind of German Government which controlled the future German army, and to repeat his criticisms of Dr. Adenauer. I pointed out once more that the whole virtue of E.D.C. was that the limited German force would not be under the control of any German Government but of an international organization composed of obviously non-aggressive countries, with whom we would be closely associated.

Before turning to these specific subjects, I proposed to Mr. Molotov, and he agreed, that we must try to re-establish the climate in which we had discussed our common problems in the war years. He suggested more than once that after many years of lack of contact, he was rather out of touch with our point of view. He certainly revealed this, in what was a rather difficult though not unfriendly conversation, in which I had to take all the initiative. My main object was to persuade him that we had not come to Berlin only to oppose the Soviet Union.

On January 30th, we had our first discussion of the German question. Molotov proposed that representatives from the Federal Republic and the East German regime should be invited to attend. We had expected this request and Dulles, as chairman, refused to accept it, on the grounds that the East German regime were not legitimate representatives of the German people. I pointed out, in support of this refusal, that it was precisely in order to establish legitimate representatives of the German people that I had repeatedly urged the holding of free and all-German elections.

After lengthy argument over this demand, Molotov proposed during a recess that we should continue the discussion in closed session the next day. I said that I could not accept this proposal. It would have prevented me from taking the initiative with Western and German opinion by presenting our plan for German reunification. I had agreed with my Western colleagues that I should do this at the earliest opportunity. When the session resumed, Bidault gave me a lead-in by saying that whereas in Austria there was a single Government recognized by all four powers, in Germany there was not; the first thing, therefore, was to bring about a union of Germany. I took this opportunity, though not strictly in order, to set out the main points in the Western plan. These were:

I. Free elections throughout Germany.

II. The convocation of a National Assembly resulting from those elections.

III. The drafting of a constitution and the preparation of peace treaty negotiations.

IV. The adoption of the constitution and the formation of an all-German Government responsible for the negotiation of the peace treaty.

V. The signature and entry into force of the peace treaty.

I elaborated each of these points in some detail, and Western policy was now on record for all to see. This became known as the 'Eden Plan'. For the moment Molotov contented himself with a mild remark to the effect that Bidault and I had perhaps taken advantage of the indulgence of the chair, and with that we adjourned.

All conferences involve entertainment between delegations, which can be a tedious business. Molotov asked us to the Soviet entertainment which was very well done and included a lovely ballet. The result was an enjoyable evening.

The three Western Foreign Secretaries resolved that they would not compete in rival entertainment, but combine. This arrangement would also have the advantage of reducing the number of parties. We discussed how we should allot the entertainment, and I proposed that the French should be responsible for the food and wine, the Americans for the speeches and the British for the band. This was carried unanimously. The French did their part as only they can, and Mr. Dulles fulfilled his share admirably. As for the band, which should always be provided at international entertainments where language difficulties can make conversation sluggish, I secured the help of the Royal Irish Fusiliers, an exceptionally fine battalion of this regiment then forming part of the garrison in Berlin. Their band appeared in gay uniform and lent colour as well as sound to the proceedings. They also intrigued Mr. Molotov mightily. A little way through dinner, he asked me to explain how the band of the Royal Irish Fusiliers could be playing at a dinner at which the British Foreign Secretary was a host. 'Ireland', he said, 'is neutral. How can her soldiers belong to the British Army?' I answered that these Irishmen were volunteers, either from Northern or Southern Ireland or even, maybe, from London. The tradition of the Irish regiments, which had always formed a splendid part of the British

Army, continued proudly. Molotov still looked dissatisfied so I introduced him to the band-master after dinner.

Despite the compliments he paid the band-master, Mr. Molotov evidently found this association baffling and rather sinister. A few nights later when dining with me, he raised the whole business all over again and worried at it, like a dog at a bone. 'Mr. Molotov', said the interpreter, 'recalls that you spoke to him about the Irish regiment. He still does not wholly understand the position. He does not think it right that a small country, which is neutral, should have regiments in the army of another country.' I repeated my explanation, but I do not think it carried any more conviction than at the first delivery.

At our meeting on January 31st, Molotov gave us his preliminary comments on the Western proposals. He disclosed two main lines of argument from which, throughout the rest of the conference, he never budged. The first of these was that as a result of making free elections the first stage of our plan for reunification, the arrangements for the elections would be left in the hands of the occupying powers. This, he said, showed distrust of the Germans. Secondly, and more important, Molotov insisted that the all-German Government which would emerge from our plan would not be free in external affairs, since it would be bound by the engagements which had been 'imposed' on the Federal Government in the Bonn and Paris Agreements. E.D.C., he added, would untie the hands of the German militarists and would restore a regular German army.

At successive meetings, our discussion revolved continuously around these two points. Against all the evidence and despite our repeated assurances, Molotov professed to believe that the Western plan for reunification was a device for compelling a unified Germany to adhere to Western defensive organizations which were hostile to the Soviet Union. In reiterating this, he lost no opportunity to attack the policy of the United States in Europe. In order to underline the unreality of this argument, Mr. Dulles proposed on February 4th, and I agreed, that the clause in the Western plan which emphasized the freedom of an all-German Government in external commitments should be altered to read as follows: 'the all-German Government shall have authority to assume *or reject* the international rights and obligations of the Federal Government and the Soviet zone of Germany'. Even this, with our explicit assurance that a unified Germany would choose for itself whether or not to join E.D.C., made no impression. Molotov argued in one breath that we were not prepared to give real freedom to

Germany, and in the next that we were giving free rein to German militarism.

Stranger still was the Soviet position revealed by Mr. Molotov when he produced his own proposals. These were modified versions of earlier draft peace treaties which the Russians had put forward in 1952 and again in 1953. Two of their salient points were plausible enough, that all foreign troops were to be withdrawn from German territory, all foreign bases being liquidated; and that Germany should undertake not to enter any coalition or military alliance directed against her former enemies. The third point made nonsense of the whole Soviet position. It proposed that Germany should have her own national army, thus creating the very dangers which Molotov had told me he feared. If paper restrictions were, as Molotov argued with me, of no avail when dealing with Germans now, they would hardly be more valuable when Germany had a national army.

On free elections, Molotov continued to insist that the formation of a provisional Government drawn from the Federal and East German régimes should precede their organization. Of our own plan, we heard little or nothing. After studiously ignoring it for five sessions, Mr. Molotov rejected it flatly on February 4th. It was then clear that the Soviet Union was determined to block the reunification of Germany, except on terms which would have deprived the German people of their freedom indefinitely and would have dismantled the Western alliance.

I dined again with Molotov on the evening before he rejected the Western plan, and sent to London this personal account of our conversation:

Although Molotov had had a rather hard day at the conference and had shown some signs of strain, he was as always a courteous host and his general attitude, although reserved on questions of substance, was as friendly as at our first dinner last week. Once again, however, I had to make all the running. He raised no particular subjects himself and seemed to prefer a listening rôle, although many of his reactions were interesting.

At dinner we talked about old times and exchanged the usual toasts on Anglo-Soviet friendship, etc. The main point of interest which emerged concerned today's quadripartite meeting. Molotov clearly thought he had been successful in inducing Mr. Dulles and M. Bidault to chase all the hares he had raised in his speech yesterday. He tried to argue that, in insisting upon taking the problem of all-German elections first, I was overlooking the wider issues of European security.

After dinner, we once again spoke in a smaller circle. I said we really must produce some results from this conference (he did not dissent) and asked Molotov what he thought the prospects were. I mentioned the Far East, and he said he hoped something might be done there. I then mentioned Austria, and he said that this might indeed be possible. He immediately added that there should be some agreement on Germany without, however, suggesting what this should be or how it should be brought about. He said good-humouredly that my plan was an ultimatum. I denied this, and urged him to comment upon it and to suggest any improvements. This immediately brought us back to the whole question of European security. I at once reminded him of the Anglo-Soviet alliance, which we had toasted at dinner, and said that he knew as well as I did that neither the British people nor our allies would ever join in an attack against the Soviet Union. If Germany did so, we would be at the side of the Soviet Union. I repeated the arguments why N.A.T.O. and E.D.C. could only be defensive, and explained why Germany, even if she wished to do so, could not, given the present world balance of power and our plans for the future of Germany, resort again to aggression. When I once again pointed out that the German contribution to E.D.C. would only be twelve divisions, Molotov retorted that nevertheless we apparently could not do without them.

Molotov was quite ready to admit our own good intentions, and indeed paid several compliments to the peaceful character and the political wisdom of the British people. But he came out more strongly than at our first dinner against E.D.C. and N.A.T.O. His theme was that these organizations did not include the U.S.S.R., and were directed against her. I reminded him that the Soviet Union had built up a military and political bloc in eastern Europe long before N.A.T.O. or E.D.C. had been thought of. He laughingly asked me whether I was referring to Yugoslavia, with whom the Soviet Union still had a treaty. In more serious mood, he assured me with every appearance of sincerity that the Soviet Union's treaties with Poland and Czechoslovakia, etc., were directed only against a renewal of German aggression, and that there were no open or secret clauses conflicting with this. I retorted that N.A.T.O. and E.D.C. were equally defensive and concerned only with aggression in general. Molotov commented that this was a riddle.

This naturally led us on to a discussion of American intentions. I had previously told Molotov that he was very wrong in regarding the Americans as a bellicose people. I had added that he was equally wrong in fearing American bases, and in handing over, as he had in his last speech, many purely British bases, such as Aden, to the Americans. I told him that he must know as well as I did that no bases on British territory would ever be used for aggression against the Soviet Union—indeed, they could not be used at all without the express consent of Her Majesty's Government. Whatever Molotov might say in public, he must realize that the United Kingdom, and indeed the other nations in N.A.T.O., retained their complete independence. Molotov readily agreed that United Kingdom policy was entirely independent.

I said that he must also realize from his wartime contacts with General Eisenhower that President Eisenhower was a wise and peace-loving man. Molotov agreed, and said that soldiers knew what war was like. Mr. Dulles had also figured in our previous conversation. Molotov did not speak of him with any bitterness. Indeed, he described his speech today as defensive in character.

During our N.A.T.O. discussion, Molotov insisted that the last word in regard to starting a war rested with an American commander-in-chief. I denied this, and insisted upon the political control by the different N.A.T.O. Governments, reminding him that N.A.T.O. generals were under quite as good control as Soviet generals. I asked him whether he would be happier if the N.A.T.O. commander-in-chief were not an American, but got no answer.

On E.D.C. in particular, Molotov's opposition was more uncompromising than in our previous conversation, but this was no doubt inevitable, given the present stage of the quadripartite conversations. He certainly did not respond to my repeated suggestion that he should tell me what better way there was to keep German militarism in check.

We concluded once again on the note that candid conversations of this kind were helpful, and that we should try to meet again in the same way during the conference. Mr. Malik told me as I left that Molotov had welcomed the way I had spoken. I wish I could believe that it had done any good. I do feel, however, that I may have done some good in bringing home to him that our own

Western intentions in general are not aggressive, and also in showing him that we are firmly attached to N.A.T.O. and E.D.C. and
that he cannot expect to drive wedges between the Western
democracies. It is clearly one of Molotov's main purposes in
Berlin to detach us or the French, or both, from our American
allies.

The Prime Minister had suggested to me that I might use my conversations at Berlin to try to probe into the unknown quantities of
personal relationships within the Kremlin. We knew little of the new
team. On February 3rd, I sent this personal message to Sir Winston:

> I have tried in my two dinner conversations with Molotov to
> penetrate a little his relations with Malenkov, having in mind our
> conversation. I must confess that I have not got very far. He has
> never once volunteered a reference to Malenkov himself, and when
> I have done so, though perfectly correct in his comments, he has
> shown no particular enthusiasm. I do not mean to suggest by this
> that his relations with Malenkov are other than good, but it may
> be that they are less close personal friends than we know that
> Molotov and Stalin were.
> Alternatively, it may be that Molotov regards foreign affairs
> as his own field, and does not like suggestions from any quarter
> that Malenkov should be brought into them directly or publicly.
> He clearly has a very free hand and has never even hinted in any
> of our talks, private or public, at the need for a reference home. I
> suppose he could be regarded now as the elder statesman of the
> Kremlin.
> Hayter*, who has now many contacts with the Russians, agrees
> with the above, especially the second paragraph, which he believes
> to be the correct explanation.

In the days that followed, it became obvious that so far as the German question was concerned we could get no further. However much
the form of the various Soviet proposals changed, their substance
remained the same. On February 11th, I sent a message to London
giving my conclusions:

> Yesterday was by far the worst day in discussions here, in that

* Sir William Hayter, Her Majesty's Ambassador in Moscow.

Molotov showed his hand more unashamedly. It is now perfectly evident that the objective of the Soviet attack is not merely E.D.C., but N.A.T.O. and the whole Western defence system. As I mentioned before I left London, they plan to entice all Europe under the slogan: 'Europe for the Europeans'. The so-called European Security Pact would in my judgment result in the free countries of Western Europe enjoying the same independence and security as Hungary, Poland, etc.

I do not think we can do any good by discussing Soviet demands for the abolition of N.A.T.O. in public, and I am more than ever convinced that the sooner this conference ends its discussion of the German side of our affairs the better. I will do my best to this end.

Our discussions on the Austrian State Treaty were equally fruitless. The Western powers had made it clear that they were ready to proceed to the signing of the treaty, on the basis of the original draft proposed by the Soviet Government. During the conference, however, Molotov introduced a series of amendments which showed his determination that the treaty should not be signed. They were unacceptable to the Austrian delegation, who attended this part of our deliberations headed by their Foreign Minister, Dr. Figl, as they were to us. Molotov proposed, for example, that occupation troops should remain in Austria until a peace treaty had been signed with Germany, on the fantastic pretext that militaristic forces in Germany were preparing a second *Anschluss*. I pointed out to Molotov that, since the Soviet Government were doing their best to hold up a peace treaty with Germany, this was a demand for the indefinite occupation of Austrian territory. The Russians also insisted that Austria should be subject to the same restrictions in her alliances as they wished to impose upon Germany in their draft peace treaty. Dr. Figl's assurance that Austria would not enter into any military alliance made no impression on Molotov, for whom E.D.C. was again the bogey. I felt the deepest sympathy with the Austrians during these sessions, which were most unpleasant to sit through. Molotov behaved with a callous brutality, and although the little Austrian delegation took their punishment bravely, they were much dejected. It was exasperating not to be able to do more for them, but they were to have their reward later.

On February 19th, we assembled in an atmosphere of gloom for the final meeting of the conference. In my closing statement on behalf of the United Kingdom delegation, I said that we had come to Berlin with the hope of making progress with the reunification of Germany and concluding a state treaty with Austria. I did not see how it was possible, I went on, for any permanent system of security to be established for Europe, or on a wider basis, so long as these two problems remained unsolved. I hoped that the Soviet Union would themselves one day accept that view. Meanwhile, I trusted that our High Commissioners would be able to make some useful progress, in the interests of the German people, on some of the matters we had referred to them. Equally, I said, in the case of Austria, failure had been a great disappointment to the Austrian people and to their friends elsewhere. On the other hand, the decision to call a conference on the Far East* had broken the deadlock that had existed for so many months, and opened the way for a settlement on Korea. I also welcomed the prospect which the agreement held for an eventual settlement in Indo-China.

Mr. Molotov, as chairman, had the last word. He ended, as he had begun, in a controversial tone which was clearly intended for *Pravda* rather than for those around the table.

The only worthwhile result of the Berlin Conference was incidental; it called the Geneva Conference into being. But the problem of a divided Germany remained, as it remains to this day. On my return to London, when I reported to the House of Commons on the conference, I thought it necessary to deal with a deceptively attractive solution to the German question, which still has its adherents, neutralization:

> I have told the House briefly of our plan which we submitted, and which we regard as the best way of bringing a united Germany back into the European family. Now I want to say a few words to the House on what I regard as the worst way, and that is the so-called neutralization of Germany. I am convinced that German neutralization is both a dangerous and an unrealistic concept, and I will say why.
>
> A united Germany will be a country of about seventy million people, with wide and rich industrial resources. Does anybody seriously suggest that in this modern world such a country could remain neutral and completely isolated from her neighbours? . . . In my view, such a Germany would be bound to gravitate to one side or the other, and, as a result, she would inevitably find herself playing off the East against the West to the danger of us all and,

* See Chapter V, p. 89.

most of all, to the danger of the German people themselves. Such a solution, I think, would encourage, indeed make inevitable, the rebirth of German militarism and repeat the tragic story of the between-the-war years.

As I told the House then, a neutral Germany with an army of her own, such as the Russians proposed, was equally dangerous. The only safeguard against the misuse of her forces would be a system of control imposed from outside, such as that which was created at Potsdam. When I wound up the debate for the Government, I posed the dilemma:

Is Germany to be neutral and disarmed?... If so, who will keep Germany disarmed? Or is Germany to be neutral and armed? If so, who will keep Germany neutral?

V

WAR IN INDO-CHINA
October 1951 – April 1954

*The communist rebellion – General de Lattre – Aid to France –
French complaints – Cambodia and Laos – Success of Vietminh –
Five-power conference – Possibility of partition – American
anxieties – Conversations with Mr. Dulles in London – The
battle of Dien Bien Phu – General Navarre's appeal for help –
Views of Mr. Dulles and Admiral Radford – An emergency –We
refuse military intervention*

The restoration of peace in Indo-China was the most dangerous
and acute of the problems with which I had to deal during my
last four years as Foreign Secretary. The long series of diplomatic
exchanges with our French and American allies, the discussions at
Berlin and the final negotiations at Geneva in 1954, involved the
security of the non-communist world in South-East Asia. They frequently revealed differences between the three Western powers; these
had to be overcome and France helped to find a solution of her difficulties. Our campaign against the communist guerillas in Malaya, then
in a critical phase, gave us a close interest in the Indo-Chinese vortex.
It affected our Asian partners in the Commonwealth, particularly
India, quite as much. For this reason, my aim was to secure the participation of these Asian countries in any settlement we might reach,
or at least their benevolence towards it. If I was to do this, I had to take
their Governments completely into my confidence and show them
every phase of our negotiations and progress.

As its name implies, Indo-China is the meeting-place of two civiliza-
tions. The ancient Hindu temples of Angkor, in Cambodia, contrast
with the predominantly Chinese culture of Annam and Tongking. The
line of demarcation has ebbed and flowed; the political reality has not

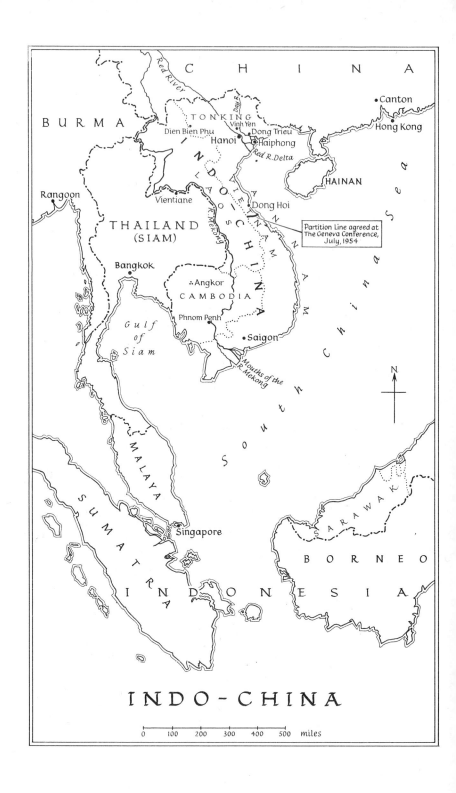

Red River

C H I N A

•Canton

BURMA

TONKING

Vinh Yen

Dien Bien Phu   Dong Trieu

Day R.

Hong Kong

Hanoi   Haiphong

Red R. Delta

HAINAN

Rangoon

Vientiane

Dong Hoi

THAILAND
(SIAM)

Partition Line agreed at
The Geneva Conference,
July, 1954

Bangkok

∴Angkor

CAMBODIA

Phnom Penh

Saigon

Gulf
of
Siam

Mouths of the
R. Mekong

N

MALAYA

South China Sea

SARAWAK

Singapore

BORNEO

SUMATRA

INDONESIA

INDO-CHINA

0   100   200   300   400   500   miles

changed. China and India confront one another in these disputed lands as surely as in Tibet, if less obviously. This was the underlying truth in Vietnam, Laos and Cambodia. The immediate dilemma was different and sharper.

The United Kingdom's only previous intervention in Indo-Chinese affairs had been in 1945, when, in accordance with the Potsdam Agreements, an Anglo-Indian force under General Gracey occupied the southern half of the country until the French were able to resume control. At this time Ho Chi Minh, a Moscow-trained communist and veteran leader of the Vietnamese nationalist movement, had taken advantage of the Japanese collapse and Emperor Bao Dai's abdication to install himself and his Vietminh Party at the head of a provisional government of Vietnam. The negotiations which dragged on throughout 1946 between this self-styled 'President' of Vietnam, who had established himself strongly in the north, and the French Government, failed to produce agreement between them, either on existing differences, or on the future status of Vietnam. At the end of the year, Ho Chi Minh's party resorted to violence with an atrocious massacre of French civilians in Hanoi. Eight bitter years of war followed.

The triumph of the communist revolution in China and the arrival of Chinese troops on the Indo-Chinese frontier at the end of 1949 disagreeably transformed the situation. In Indo-China, as in Korea, the communists could now play Tom Tiddler. The Vietminh rebels could find refuge, equipment, money and training facilities across the Chinese border; with this assistance, they built up their strength from disorganized guerilla bands to an army highly skilled in Indo-Chinese warfare, supported by numerous irregulars. For some time, their high command proved more than a match for the French.

If the French were to succeed in Vietnam, they had to unite the country against the communists and to transform lethargy into enthusiasm. Indo-China had no tradition of unity, and there was little in common between the rich south and the overpopulated north. The loyalties felt by the ordinary Vietnamese peasant were to his village, or to the leaders of his sect. The lack of common feeling extended to differences within the south and the north. Cao Dai and Hoa Hao sects maintained their private armies, independent of both sides. It would be unfair to look on this disunity as a purely Vietnamese characteristic, for most new Asian states have experienced the same symptoms. India, Indonesia and Burma were able to preserve some unity, as the demands for independence grew, because they had strong leaders backed by deep nationalist feelings. This was not true of Vietnam, where the communists had been able to absorb most of the nationalist movement. During the war, they had taken a prominent part in the resistance. Moderate nationalists were consequently forced to choose between a government which, though communist, stood for independence, or a return of colonial rule.

In 1949, the French made an attempt to resolve this dilemma with the 'Bao Dai experiment'. They invited the ex-Emperor to be the head of a new Associated State of Vietnam and hoped, by recognizing its independence within the French Union, to break the communist monopoly of Vietnamese national aspirations. Grants of independence within the Union were later made to the Associated States of Cambodia and Laos. Despite this, Vietnamese distrust of the French remained Ho Chi Minh's strongest ally. French plans for independence came too late and appeared to be squeezed out of them. Even after the Pau Agreements of 1950, France retained powers so extensive that the Vietminh could label Bao Dai a French puppet. The transfer of local authority from French to native officials was still made with obvious reluctance. In the last years of French rule, there were more French officials in Indo-China than there had been British serving in all India at any period of our rule.

The new Head of State was neither a popular nor an inspiring figure. He preferred the casino to the council chamber and the antics of his corrupt and transient Ministers in Saigon did not appeal to moderate nationalist opinion. M. Letourneau, the able and courageous Minister for the Associated States, admitted that if he had been creating Bao Dai he would have made him somewhat different, but the choice lay between him and Ho Chi Minh. There was no third force in Vietnam.

It was with this in mind that the United Kingdom, together with the United States and twenty-five Western nations, guardedly recognized Vietnam in 1950 as an Associated State of the French Union. This did little to help the new Vietnamese regime, for the communist bloc had anticipated the move and recognized Ho Chi Minh's rebels as a Government. It had one important sequel; the United States Government were now able to help the French with arms and money, without bolstering colonialism.

Meanwhile, during 1950 the military picture had grown steadily darker. French forces had been compelled to withdraw from their network of isolated posts into the strong perimeter around the Tongking delta. This withdrawal, apart from the blow to morale, caused the French heavy losses in men, equipment and authority. At the end of the year, French women and children were evacuated from Tongking. It was in this situation that France's most able soldier, General de Lattre de Tassigny, arrived to take over the dual post of High Commissioner and Commander-in-Chief.

I knew General de Lattre and admired his vivid personality. He had a remarkable gift for rekindling and holding the confidence of the troops he led. In this he bore a likeness to Field-Marshal Montgomery. I had a graphic account of his inspection of British troops in this country from one of those present. He quickly impressed every soldier on parade with his knowledge of all that concerned the regiment's traditions, including its affiliations overseas, as well as with the conditions of service. Men in the ranks are not easily impressed by generals, least of all by foreign ones, but General de Lattre left on these soldiers of another land an indelible memory of a combative and decisive leader. His new appointment was a brilliant success; although he was to spend only eight months in Indo-China, he achieved startling results. The French troops regained the initiative and the mobility, so essential in this type of warfare. The heavy defeats which were inflicted on the Vietminh at Vinh Yen, Dong Trieu and on the Day River, and the progress made towards clearing the interior of the delta region, revitalized French confidence. After a few months of General de Lattre's leadership, no one spoke of losing Hanoi or Tongking. Paradoxically, during the first year of her independence, Indo-China was dominated by a Frenchman as never before.

★   ★   ★   ★   ★

Despite this record of success, it seemed to me, when I returned to the Foreign Office in the autumn of 1951, that the chances of winning the war in Indo-China were still slender. At the beginning of the next year they were further diminished by the tragic death of General de Lattre de Tassigny after a long illness in Paris. Though many times defeated, the rebel forces had grown in size and matured in quality. As long as the Vietminh could find refuge in China, they could never be completely rounded up and destroyed. Though Chinese Communist manpower was not being used, there was disturbing evidence of increasing material and technical help during the spring. Guerilla units were creeping back into the Red River delta, from which they had been expelled with so much trouble during the previous summer. I thought that even to contain the Vietminh would be a costly and lasting commitment. To ensure a victorious solution, a much more vigorous effort was called for, including a reinforcement of several divisions from France. This was not to be expected under the volunteer system which governed recruiting for Indo-China. Whereas our National Servicemen went to fight in the Malayan jungle and in the forests of Kenya, in France the obligation was limited to national territory.

In my view, the best hope for France was a general settlement in South-East Asia which would include a cease-fire; an armistice in Korea must be followed by negotiations in Indo-China. This was in the best interests of the French and it seemed to me the outcome to work for, distasteful as it must be to French feelings. Two years were to pass before it could be realized.

During the early months of 1952, the reports which I received from our Ambassador in Paris, Sir Oliver Harvey, showed that the French mood was pessimistic and confused. There was a unanimous desire to finish the war, and senior officers of the French General Staff were already admitting privately that evacuation would be inevitable in the end. The problem was to compel Ho Chi Minh to negotiate terms which would enable the French to make a respectable withdrawal. This could only be done if the military situation were substantially improved. There was a growing feeling in Paris, partly inspired by rumours of impending Chinese military intervention in Indo-China, that Great Britain and the United States should give more help. The French complained that they could not be expected to defend the interests of the free world in Indo-China single-handed and at the same time make the contribution to European defence which was being demanded of them. Underlying this argument was the fear that, owing to her commitments in Indo-China, France would find herself militarily inferior to a rearmed Western Germany in the proposed European army.

These were the views with which the French Government confronted Mr. Dean Acheson and myself when we flew to Paris at the end of May for three-power discussions on the problems of Europe and South-East Asia. On the 26th, before the formal discussions opened, I had a long talk with Mr. Acheson at the British Embassy. He told me of the United States' determination to do everything possible to strengthen the French hand in Indo-China. On the wider question of the possibility of a Chinese invasion, the United States Government considered that it would be disastrous to the position of the Western powers if South-East Asia were lost without a struggle. On the other hand, the Americans were determined to do nothing in that area which would provoke a third world war. Their present thinking was that deterrent action was the best course. At an appropriate moment there might have to be some form of warning to the Chinese. If the warning were ignored, Mr. Acheson believed that a blockade of the Chinese coast and the dislocation of her communications would have to be considered. I agreed generally with Mr. Acheson's approach, though I personally thought it unlikely that China would enter the war, and said so. The present state of affairs suited China very well and she would have nothing to gain by internationalizing the conflict. I told Mr. Acheson that Her Majesty's Government were strongly opposed to any course of action in South-East Asia which would be likely to result in a war with China. We both agreed that although possible means of deterring China should be examined, any provocative action must at all costs be avoided.

On May 30th, Mr. Acheson and I had a long and difficult conference with the French Prime Minister, M. Pinay, and the principal members of his Government. M. Pleven, the Minister of Defence, took the lead in presenting the French case, which confirmed our Ambassador's warning, and made depressing hearing. Mr. Acheson remained sympathetic but firm. There was no doubt, he said, that France's effort in Indo-China was in the general interest. He pointed out, however, that the United States was already bearing a third of the cost. The French Ministers repeatedly argued that if further aid was not forthcoming, there would be grave parliamentary difficulties in France. These would prejudice the ratification of E.D.C. and the continuation of French efforts in Indo-China.

There need be no end to pressure of this kind and, when the conference was over, I took M. Pleven to one side and told him that the only effect of France's attitude would be to exasperate her best friends. I have been a Francophile all my life, and I had every sympathy with the French position, but, as I told M. Pleven, the French argument that Indo-China made it impossible for France to build up an army in Europe would not carry conviction in the United Kingdom. British opinion, I said, would be more impressed when France increased her National Service to two years as we had done, and called up her reserves for training. M. Pleven was inclined to suggest that the British should do more. I replied that we had a larger army in Europe than the French, despite our commitments in Malaya and in the Suez Canal zone, where we had seventy thousand troops. M. Pleven commented, somewhat ruefully, that the arguments I had used to him about the French army were those which he heard at frequent intervals from Field-Marshal Montgomery.

As we were driving away from the conference, Dean Acheson told me, more in sorrow than in anger, that if further aid were approved by Congress, the United States would be bearing about half the cost of the Indo-China war, yet to hear the French talk, one would think that his Government were only supplying them with the odd revolver or two. I reflected that if the French really wanted American aid, they were going about it in the worst possible way.

When we held a further three-power meeting in London at the end of June, I learnt that I had been wrong in doubting the French method. Mr. Acheson told me, before the talks began, that his Government had agreed to increase their aid to the French in Indo-China by $150 million during the coming fiscal year. This was an increase of 40 per cent., and generous by any standards.

During the formal discussions which followed, M. Schuman proposed the creation of a permanent military organization to study the situation in South-East Asia and plan the measures which could be taken for the defence not only of Indo-China but of the whole region. I was in favour of this plan, which was the genesis of S.E.A.T.O.

The year ended, as it had begun, in stalemate. The implications of the Indo-China problem now extended far beyond South-East Asia. In view of the French anxiety to maintain military parity with Germany, the fate of E.D.C. was in part dependent upon its solution. As Sir Oliver Harvey reported at the time, Indo-China had become the key to European problems. France knew that she had no future in Indo-China, whatever the military outcome. A respectable departure would have been welcomed by every shade of French opinion; the problem was to find a solution which would not damage the French reputation in North Africa and throughout the French Union. If the French were to be able to vacate Indo-China without handing the country over to the communists, they would have seriously to weaken the Vietminh before they left. Military success had to precede negotiation. If it was to be achieved, the despondency which prevailed in Paris would have to be dispelled, and we had to help to do it.

★　　★　　★　　★　　★

France entered the New Year with new ministers and old policies.

M. Letourneau, with whom our relations were always most cordial, retained his post as Minister for the Associated States in M. Mayer's Government, and continued to battle tirelessly with the responsibilities of that office. He told Sir Oliver Harvey that the policy of the new Government towards Indo-China would remain the same as that of its predecessor, and that there could be no question of negotiations with Ho Chi Minh, since even to talk of this had a damaging effect on Vietnamese morale.

In February 1953 the French Government made new plans to equip and train Vietnamese forces to replace their own. They decided to create fifty-four new light battalions of Vietnamese troops; their rôle was to be like that of Wingate's Chindits, to live off the country, to maintain contact with the enemy, to disperse if attacked by powerful forces, and to concentrate against weak points. It was an ambitious project, though its effects could not be felt for one, or probably two, years. Meanwhile, the Vietminh were striking back and, on April 20th, they invaded Laos for the first time. The forces involved were comparatively small, but victory would give the rebels contact with sympathizers in Thailand and would be disastrous for French authority and leadership. In this crisis the Laotian Crown Prince displayed courage and resolution, and the way in which the whole country rallied to his support exposed the bogus character of the Vietminh's 'Government of Free Laos'.

During my illness in the spring and summer of 1953, I watched developments in Indo-China with increased foreboding. The devaluation of the local currency in May, carried out from Paris without consultation even with the Commissioner-General, proved a costly deed in politics. All classes in Indo-China were furious, some for business and some for sentimental reasons. The devaluation caused heavy financial loss in all three countries and, being a proof of French economic domination, outraged national pride.

On June 14th, while in hospital in Boston, I learned of an incident which was typical of Indo-Chinese politics. The King of Cambodia crossed the Thai frontier into voluntary exile, taking with him some extreme nationalists, among them two brigands happily named Oum and Ouch. He left full powers in the hands of his Prime Minister. The King's gesture, which lasted for only a week, paid off, for, when it came to negotiating with the French Government shortly afterwards, the King pitched his terms high and, after acrimonious argument, got them. The judiciary and police passed immediately into Cambodian hands, and negotiations were set in train for the transfer of further powers. Unhappily, each French concession to the Associated States appeared to be made from weakness, and only whetted the political appetite it was intended to satisfy.

If Cambodia was clever and Vietnam cold, Laos was polite and moderate, being quick to learn the dangers of administrative indigestion. I liked the Laotians. In all my dealings with them I found them a sincere and simple people, asking only to be left alone. On one occasion one of their ministers, having discussed with me the business of the Geneva Conference, showed signs of wishing to unburden his mind on some other topic. I asked him what was troubling him. The communists who would infiltrate homeward to Laos after the armistice, he said. Some had gone quite far afield and joined Vietminh forces, others were in the northern provinces. The country had suffered, in the north in particular, with damage to roads and bridges, and a number could be given work on these and other forms of public undertakings in the country. But there would be some leaders whom it would be difficult to employ and he thought of putting them into the Government, where he could watch them. I thought this original but dangerous, and told him so.

In the summer of 1953, a new treaty was signed between France and Laos, by which the French provided military equipment, training facilities and a military mission, under the authority of the Laotian Government. The two countries were to exchange diplomatic representatives on an equal basis. All this was sensible and Laotian spirits were further raised by French military successes against the Vietminh invader during the summer, but I was warned that the Vietminh would be in a position to launch another formidable attack by 1954. In fact, it came in December 1953, following a peace offer which Ho Chi Minh had made only two weeks earlier, as a weakening preliminary.

The new offensive was no doubt intended to show the ineffectiveness of the French guarantee to Laos in the recently concluded treaty. It may not have succeeded in this purpose, but it did serve to arouse concern for the future of the French military position. This concern, and fears of Chinese intervention, were becoming particularly acute in the United States. On December 29th Mr. Dulles told a press conference that in the event of an invasion of Indo-China, the American reaction 'would not necessarily be confined to the particular theatre chosen by the communists for their operations'. On January 12th, 1954, after proclaiming the doctrine of instant retaliation, Mr. Dulles gave warning that Chinese intervention would have 'grave consequences which might not be confined to Indo-China'. These admonitions did not seem to me on the mark. I did not believe that any Chinese intervention was imminent; there was no need for it. The Vietminh were doing well enough as it was. More practically, the view was already being canvassed in the American press that the United States should step in to help the French with sea and air power before the military situation deteriorated further.

The French had no wish at the time for direct American military intervention; large Chinese ground forces were too near at hand. At the same time, I did not believe that the French would be able to hold the Tongking delta indefinitely. And at the beginning of 1954 my thoughts began to turn to the possibility of some form of partition as a solution which might bring hostilities to an end and effect a settlement which would hold. My chief concern was for Malaya. I wanted to ensure an effective barrier as far to the north of that country as possible. I thought it possible that the Western powers might guarantee Laos and Cambodia and part of Vietnam. More important still, I hoped that matters might be so contrived that India, and perhaps some other eastern nations, would join in the guarantee. This would buttress the agreement. I was convinced that the longer negotiation was delayed, the more difficult the situation would become for the French.

The Berlin Conference, at the end of January 1954, provided me with an opportunity to develop this idea. Mr. Molotov had proposed that the conference should discuss, in addition to the German question and the Austrian State Treaty, the convening of a five-power conference, including China, to 'seek measures for reducing tension in international relations'. It seemed to me that this was the chance we needed. In a message to London from Berlin I urged favourable reflection upon the possibility of a five-power conference, provided that the Americans could be brought to consider it. I liked this much better than a debate at the United Nations:

At least we should be dealing with principals and not with nations anxious to talk but unwilling to bear much burden. We should also resolve in this way the question of Russia's status, which has been an obstacle at Panmunjom, for clearly she would be a principal of any five-power meeting. We should be able to put the Russians in an embarrassing situation if we could present them with acceptable terms for a five-power conference and they still resisted any kind of progress with Germany and Austria.

Of course a dominant factor in all this is the American attitude. They are at present strongly opposed to the idea of a five-power conference with China, mainly, I understand, because they are not prepared to admit the right of communist China to be one of the great powers dealing with world problems. It seems to me that their objection might be less if the conference were specifically limited to the Far East. Mr. Dulles admits that non-recognition is no obstacle to meeting the Chinese and, in fact, the Americans are meeting them at Panmunjom.

I was encouraged by a telegram from the Prime Minister, in which he expressed the Cabinet's warm approval of my views and hoped that I would be able to persuade Mr. Dulles of their wisdom. Mr. Dulles confirmed the American reservations in a private talk with Bidault and myself on January 26th. While remaining firmly opposed to a five-power conference with a world-wide agenda, he told us that he had no objection to discussing 'appropriate questions' with the Chinese Communists, although he doubted whether Indo-China came under this heading. I thought that there was a gleam of hope here.

There were indications that Molotov might eventually agree to limit the agenda of the proposed conference to Far Eastern questions. On the 28th Mr. Dulles, M. Bidault and I had a useful meeting, when Dulles clearly accepted the force of the argument I had strongly urged, that we could not afford to appear completely negative in the face of the Soviet initiative. I sent a message to the Foreign Office as a result of this meeting:

We shall now get to work with the Americans and the French on producing a practical proposal to put forward here at the appropriate time. I think we may be making progress on this difficult subject. But no doubt we shall meet with plenty of snags yet, even if we don't strike a rock.

The snags were not slow to appear, and it took two weeks of hard negotiation in restricted sessions and private talks to bring us within sight of agreement. The various draft proposals produced by the United States delegation were, it seemed to me, too barbed to stand a chance of acceptance. I had to urge them to eliminate clauses which merely arraigned the Chinese. In this I was helped by M. Bidault, and by February 11th Mr. Dulles, who worked earnestly to accommodate our point of view, had come as far to meet us as the state of American opinion with regard to China would allow. All four Foreign Secretaries drew nearer to agreement on the major issue, namely that representatives of the United States, France, the United Kingdom, the Soviet Union, the Chinese People's Republic and the two Korean Governments, should meet to discuss Korea and possibly Indo-China.

The principal question which still divided us, a crucial one for the United States, was whether China was to be accorded the status of a 'convening power' or not. In view of the impact on Vietnamese morale, the French were as anxious as the Americans that this should not happen. Bidault, like Dulles, desired that the four powers at Berlin should issue invitations to all the other participants in the proposed conference, including China; Molotov still stood firm for a five-power conference of which China was to be a full member from the start.

Although I understood the political significance of this point, it was exasperating to be baulked at this stage by an issue apparently of procedure. There was a real danger that the negotiations might break down. The problem, as I expressed it in a telegram to the Prime Minister on February 13th, was 'to find something which will meet the bear without parting us from the eagle'. Two days later, we found it; the United Kingdom delegation put forward a draft resolution which omitted any distinction between convenors and convened. All were lumped together. For forty-eight hours we continued to study texts. Then at a meeting on February 17th, when I happened to be in the chair, Molotov came across the line by proposing an amendment to my text, without even mentioning his own. I felt that we were home. After examination, Molotov's amendments, which were minor, were accepted and the resolution was adopted by the Berlin Conference the next day. The Geneva Conference had become a reality; it was to assemble on April 26th.

I realized how small this result was so far, but at least it gave the French something to hold on for, and us something to work for. We now had to enlist as much help as we could on our side for a long tug of war. This conviction was to guide my policy during the next two months.

★ ★ ★ ★ ★

While we were negotiating in Berlin, the fighting in the Tongking delta during February 1954 was brave and grim. On one occasion the Vietminh, after crawling through drainage pipes, entered an airstrip and destroyed five Dakotas and vast quantities of petrol. These spectacular incidents were frequent and guerilla warfare was taking a steady toll of life on both sides. In view of the political uncertainty in France, I was impressed by the reports which reached me of the confidence of the French troops and their commanders throughout the delta. This was remarkable when one remembers that these troops had been exposed, in the south delta for instance, to almost continuous action over a period of months. Exceptional personal courage was shown, and French military morale in Indo-China was consistently higher than civilian morale in Paris.

It was essential that the French should hold their ground militarily, in order that their bargaining position at Geneva should not be weakened. But I did not consider it to be in the best interests of France that the scale of the fighting should be increased, or that she should be encouraged to expend her straitened resources in trying to force a military decision. The Americans took a different view. On February 8th, our Ambassador was told at the State Department that the United States Government were perturbed by the fact that the French were aiming not to win the war, but to get into a position from which they could negotiate.

At this time Mr. Bedell Smith, the American Under-Secretary of State, was reappraising the situation with a small group invited by the President to consider the Indo-China problem. He told our Ambassador that there was no intention of sending American troops into Indo-China; the President would not do it even if he had the power. Yet the American Ambassador in Saigon had succinctly remarked that 'the French would not be allowed to skedaddle unless China gave absolute guarantees'. I did not see how this dual purpose was to be realized.

On the other hand, I was not very happy about the proposal which Mr. Nehru made on February 22nd, that there should be a cease-fire in Indo-China before the Geneva Conference met. The Indian High Commissioner, Mr. Kher, came to see me, to ask me for my views on this. I told him that in a conflict of this character, where there was no continuous fighting line as there had been in Korea, it would be difficult to arrange a cease-fire without leaving the peoples of the Associated States at the mercy of the Vietminh. In a war not of fronts but of manœuvre and infiltration, a cease-fire would enable the Vietminh, by clandestine movement and in civilian disguise, to establish themselves in any part of Vietnam and Laos not immediately under Franco-

Vietnamese control. This had to be guarded against. It could only be done if the armistice agreement had the political backing of real authority; but I emphasized that we should welcome an exchange of views with the Indian Government on a problem which was of such great importance to both of us.

It was clear to me that any negotiated settlement was bound to produce either a communist share in the government of most of Indo-China, or complete communist control of part of the country, and I thought that the latter alternative was preferable. Although I had every sympathy with the American view that both these solutions were disagreeable, I thought it unrealistic to expect that a victor's terms could be imposed upon an undefeated enemy. There were some indications of a greater willingness in Vietnam to face partition. There was no love lost between north and south. We felt that the distress at amputation might prove more apparent than real.

On March 29th, in a speech to the Overseas Press Club of America, Mr. Dulles said that the imposition of the communist system on South-East Asia 'should not be passively accepted but should be met by united action. This might involve serious risks, but these risks are far less than those that will face us in a few years from now if we dare not be resolute today.' I had no objection to strong American words, but I wanted to be sure that they meant what they appeared to say. We had been told that the United States was not prepared to intervene in Indo-China in the only effective way, on land. It was important not to encourage the French by the offer of lesser means which could not succeed. It was necessary to make our own position clear. On April 1st I sent a message to our Ambassador in Washington:

> Your recent reports indicate that the United States Government, while rejecting (rightly in our view) intervention by United States forces as means of defeating the Vietminh, nevertheless hope that victory can still be achieved by Franco-Vietnamese forces, given sufficient pressure, material aid and possible political and technical advice from United States. Her Majesty's Ambassador at Paris, however, has made it clear that such a policy is becoming increasingly unacceptable to the French.
>
> We fully share United States desire to see Indo-China preserved from communism and agree that, so long as there is any hope of success, the French should be urged to maintain their present effort. But after earnest study of military and political factors, we feel it

would be unrealistic not to face the possibility that the conditions for a favourable solution in Indo-China may no longer exist. Failure to consider this possibility now is likely to increase the difficulty of reaching tripartite agreement should we be forced at Geneva to accept a policy of compromise with the communists in Indo-China.

Sir Roger Makins communicated these views to Mr. Dulles and Mr. Bedell Smith. He added that if it came to negotiation, we considered partition to be the least damaging solution. To this Mr. Bedell Smith replied that the United States had carefully studied the partition solution, but had decided that it would only be a temporary palliative and would lead to communist domination of South-East Asia. They had consequently rejected the plan. Mr. Dulles then told our Ambassador that the best hope was to compel China to desist from aid to the Vietminh by the threat of military action. He said that we possessed a military superiority in the area now which we might not have in a few years' time. So if a warning was not heeded, we should now be in a position to put our threats into effect. Military action involved risks, but the risk of letting Indo-China go was greater. The United States was thinking in terms of a joint warning, by several countries, of naval and air action against the China coast; it would not threaten the landing of American troops. On April 6th, the United States Ambassador in London, Mr. Aldrich, came round to see me to discuss the position. A long talk with him enabled me to understand better some of the American cares. He handed me a memorandum which, among other things, showed American concern about any Chinese share in deciding who should attend the Indo-China part of the Geneva Conference. This was reasonable enough, in view of the state of American opinion.

Meanwhile, the position of the besieged French garrison at Dien Bien Phu had deteriorated further. The American Government now approached the French and ourselves with a new proposal. This was to the effect that all the countries concerned should issue, before Geneva, a solemn declaration of their readiness to take concerted action under Article 51 of the United Nations Charter against continued interference by China in the Indo-China war. We were informed that the proposed warning would carry with it the threat of naval and air action against the Chinese coast and of active intervention in Indo-China itself. This *ad hoc* coalition, comprising the United States, France, the United Kingdom, Australia, New Zealand, Thailand, the Philippines and the three Associated States of Indo-China, would simultaneously set about organizing the collective defence of South-East Asia.

Reports from Paris indicated that this idea had met with a lukewarm reception there. On April 5th, President Eisenhower sent a message to Sir Winston Churchill urging him to fall in with the American plan and suggesting that Mr. Dulles might fly to London within a few days to discuss his proposal. This offer was accepted, but at the same time I warned Sir Roger Makins in Washington that he should say nothing at this stage which might commit us to the joint action proposed.

We were now faced with a decision of major importance. I was determined that we would not be hustled into injudicious military decisions. I welcomed the American proposal for the organization of collective defence in South-East Asia, since this would contribute to the security of Malaya and Hong Kong and would remove the anomaly of our exclusion from the A.N.Z.U.S. Pact, to which the United States, Australia and New Zealand were parties. But I felt that to form and proclaim a defensive coalition, before we went to the conference table, would be unlikely to help us militarily and would harm us politically, by frightening off important potential allies. By the beginning of May, the rains would be starting in Indo-China and extensive campaigning by either side would be impossible for several months. Since the complete collapse of the French military effort before then was improbable, I did not think that concern for the immediate military situation should be the guiding factor in our policy. In a summary of the position which I made shortly before Mr. Dulles' visit, I set down my views as follows:

The United States proposal assumes that the threat of retaliation against China would cause her to withdraw aid from the Vietminh. This seems to me a fundamental weakness. There is a distinction between warning China that some specified further action will entail retaliation, which might be an effective deterrent, and calling upon her to desist from action in which she is already engaged. I cannot see what threat would be sufficiently potent to make China swallow so humiliating a rebuff as the abandonment of the Vietminh without any face-saving concession in return. If I am right in this view, the joint warning to China would have no effect, and the coalition would then have to withdraw ignominiously or else embark on warlike action against China.

Neither blockade nor the bombing of China's internal and

external communications, which the United States Government appear to have in mind, were considered by our Chiefs of Staff to be militarily effective when these were discussed in connection with Korea. They would, however, give China every excuse for invoking the Sino-Soviet Treaty, and might lead to a world war. Nor should we commit British forces to operations in Indo-China. The time to consider a warning to China may come later. If, for instance, a negotiated settlement of the Indo-China problem were to be reached at Geneva, possibly on a basis of partition, a warning to China that further communist encroachment in Indo-China would entail retaliation, and possibly even war, would be far more likely both to deter China and to be acceptable to British (and French) public opinion. It does not seem that the Americans have yet formed any clear conception of the military operations which they propose should be conducted against China if threats fail to produce the desired result. Nor have they weighed the consequences of this policy. On the other hand, the proposal to organize collective security in South-East Asia is in itself attractive; and there is advantage in expressing our views to the Americans whilst their own ideas are still not fully formed.

My colleagues entirely shared the opinions I had formed. Doubts as to the wisdom of the current trend in American policy were increased by the effects it was producing on Indian opinion. In measuring our chances of success at Geneva, I felt strongly that the outcome would depend to a considerable extent upon the position taken up by India and other Eastern nations with an interest in a settlement. I knew that China would be reluctant, at this stage at any rate, to align India against her, and would make considerable efforts to conciliate Asian opinion in general. India had an abiding interest in the outcome of the conference and could play a considerable part at Geneva behind the scenes. Nobody could tell what the future would hold, but it was essential not to alienate India by our actions in a part of the world which concerned her closely. For those reasons, I was disturbed to hear from our High Commissioner in Delhi that Mr. Dulles' recent speeches had created the worst possible impression there. In India there was widespread suspicion that the United States was determined that nothing should come out of the Geneva Conference. This, and the hostility which had been aroused in France by Senator Knowland's threat of a possible delay of American foreign aid to N.A.T.O.

countries, provided additional reasons for dissuading the United States Government from pushing ahead too fast with these proposals.

★　★　★　★　★

Mr. Dulles arrived in London on April 11th for talks which took place informally that evening and formally on the two succeeding days. I was relieved to find that the United States Government had modified their plan for a warning declaration threatening the use of force. A draft of such a warning was produced outside the meetings for us to look at, but it was not brought forward at the formal discussions.

Our first conversation took place on the evening of the 11th, after dinner at the American Embassy. Mr. Denis Allen, Assistant Under-Secretary of State at the Foreign Office, was with me. At my invitation, Mr. Dulles gave us a long explanation of the background to his Government's proposals on Indo-China. The United States Government, he said, had come to the conclusion that the French could no longer deal with the situation, either politically or militarily, on their own resources alone. If the French position in Indo-China collapsed, the consequences would be extremely grave. Not only Thailand, but also Malaya, Burma and Indonesia would be exposed to eventual absorption by communism. The battle at Dien Bien Phu had reached a crucial phase and American military authorities did not rate the French chances of victory highly. For these reasons, Mr. Dulles went on, the United States Chiefs of Staff had suggested three weeks ago that American naval and air forces should intervene in the Indo-China war. He told us that some aircraft-carriers had already been moved from Manila towards the Indo-China coast. On reflection, Mr. Dulles had considered that the United States should not act alone in this matter and that before a decision to intervene were taken, two conditions should be met. First, there must be some assurance that the French Government were willing to grant the Associated States real independence within the French Union, so as to provide the necessary political basis for effective resistance. Second, the United States Government must ascertain whether their allies, especially the United Kingdom, Australia and New Zealand, took an equally grave view of the situation. For these reasons, although he no longer had in mind a warning declaration specifically directed against China, Mr. Dulles wanted to see the formation of an *ad hoc* coalition which might develop into a South-East Asia defence organization. He thought that this in itself would deter China from further interference in Indo-China, and would strengthen our position at Geneva by giving evidence of our solidarity.

We were already aware of the pessimistic view which the Americans took of our ability to defend Malaya in the event of a French collapse in Indo-China, and I therefore began my reply with some observations on that topic. I said that Her Majesty's Government had every intention of continuing to hold the position in Malaya. Although a deterioration of the situation in Indo-China would certainly make our task many times more difficult, we were determined to do our utmost to cope with it. I added that the security position in Malaya was improving.

I then went on to distinguish between the two aspects of Mr. Dulles' proposals; the long-term issue of collective security in South-East Asia, and the more immediate question of 'united action' in Indo-China. On the first point, I told Mr. Dulles that we welcomed the idea of an organization for collective defence in South-East Asia, but that it would require the most careful thought and study, particularly on the question of membership. I emphasized that on no account should India and the other Asian Commonwealth countries be deliberately excluded. The other question was that of Indo-China itself, where fighting was in progress and where we were committed to a discussion with the Soviet and Chinese Governments at Geneva. If there was to be any question of Allied intervention, military or otherwise, or of any warning announcement before Geneva, that would require extremely careful consideration. It was doubtful whether the situation in Indo-China could be solved by purely military means and we must at least see what proposals, if any, the communists had to make at Geneva. Accordingly, I told Mr. Dulles that, in my view, the communiqué which would be issued after his visits to London and Paris should not go beyond a warning that we would not allow the work of the Geneva Conference to be prejudiced by communist military action. I was not convinced that any immediate mention should be made of any decision concerning collective security in South-East Asia, if that were agreed upon.

We had some further discussion and Mr. Dulles concluded with pessimistic comments about France. He wondered whether France was not, by a process of historical evolution, inevitably ceasing to be a great power. I declined to be drawn into direct comment on these observations and said that we, with our experience in Malaya, could understand the difficulties with which the French were confronted in Indo-China, where even if the military situation developed favourably, they would be faced with a long-term guerilla problem even more serious than Malaya at its worst.

Our formal talks on April 12th and 13th added little to this initial conversation. I said that I could agree to no more than to engage in preliminary discussions on the possibility of forming a mutual security system in South-East Asia. On the question of intervention, Mr. Dulles was convinced that Indo-China was the place for such action, should it become necessary, provided that two requirements could be met. First, an unequivocal declaration by the French Government of independence for the Associated States and secondly, the placing of the conflict on an international basis. This, he said, with the addition of outside air and naval support, would create the possibility of victory. Mr. Dulles added that he was confident that Congress would authorize the President to use United States air and naval forces, and possibly even land forces. I was not convinced by the assertion which Mr. Dulles then made, that the situation in Indo-China was analogous to the Japanese invasion of Manchuria in 1931 and to Hitler's reoccupation of the Rhineland. I explained that the British Chiefs of Staff did not believe that Allied intervention could be limited to the air and the sea. I told Mr. Dulles that British public opinion, with the Geneva Conference in prospect, would be firmly opposed to any present commitment to become involved in war in Indo-China.

It was also becoming obvious that difficulties lay ahead on the subject of the membership of the proposed security system in South-East Asia. I repeatedly emphasized that although India and other Asian countries might well choose to remain outside such an arrangement, they should nevertheless be given every opportunity to participate and should be kept fully informed. If they could not be with us, we must not put them against us. Mr. Dulles, on the other hand, hoped that any indication that India might be invited to join would be avoided. He explained that if there was any question of extending the security arrangements westwards to include India, there would be a 'strong demand' in the United States to extend it eastwards as well, to include Nationalist China and Japan. He therefore suggested that the controversial issues of India on the one hand, and Formosa on the other, should be avoided, and that the discussions should be limited in the first instance to South-East Asia proper. I did not like this balancing of India against Formosa. The two did not seem to me comparable. However, we reached no final decision on this matter. Our joint announcement after the talks merely stated that:

. . . we are ready to take part, with the other countries principally concerned, in an examination of the possibility of establishing a collective defence, within the framework of the Charter of the United Nations, to assure the peace, security and freedom of South-East Asia and the Western Pacific.

Our minute of the conference then contains the following paragraph, which had relevance to subsequent events:

It was agreed that in any statement to the House of Commons, Mr. Eden should explain that the whole question of membership was a matter for further consideration and that it would be discussed with the Government of India as with the Government of Pakistan and others.

In the event, the subject of the composition of the proposed security pact was not raised in the House, but had the appropriate supplementary question been put, I would have replied in the agreed terms.

Within three days of the conclusion of the London talks, however, it appeared that Mr. Dulles had taken steps to settle the question of membership in advance, on his own terms. On April 16th, Sir Roger Makins reported that Mr. Dulles would be convening a meeting on the 20th, in Washington, of the Ambassadors of the United Kingdom, Australia, New Zealand, France, the Philippines, Thailand and the three Associated States. Its object was to set up an informal working group to study the collective defence of South-East Asia. The State Department had also repeated its warning that any attempt to include India would be countered by the inclusion of Formosa. This was an extremely serious matter. Quite apart from the timing of such a meeting, it was clear to me that it would attract wide publicity, and the countries invited would be regarded as already constituting the proposed organization. I could not possibly accept this. Not only had India been given no opportunity to express her views, but Burma, too, was closely concerned and there had been no time for proper consultation with either the Indian or the Burmese Governments. To hold a mass meeting at this stage would be insulting to them both and consequently harmful in its effects on the Geneva Conference. I instructed Sir Roger Makins to put these views to Mr. Dulles and to tell him that the United Kingdom could not participate in such a meeting, which was entirely contrary to the spirit of our agreement in London. I concluded a message restating our position with these words:

Americans may think the time past when they need consider the feelings or difficulties of their allies. It is the conviction that this tendency becomes more pronounced every week that is creating mounting difficulties for anyone in this country who wants to maintain close Anglo-American relations. We, at least, have constantly to bear in mind all our Commonwealth partners, even if the United States does not like some of them; and I must ask you to keep close watch on this aspect of our affairs, and not hesitate to press it on the United States.

It emerged that it was too late to cancel the meeting altogether since, as I had feared, it had already been publicized in the American press; but, as a result of Sir Roger's representations in Washington, Mr. Dulles agreed to convert it into a general briefing conference on the coming negotiations at Geneva. With this we had to be content, although I was still unhappy about the impression which the Washington 'get-together' might create.

★ ★ ★ ★ ★

A number of Asian powers were due to meet in Colombo on the same day as the Geneva Conference opened. These were India, Pakistan, Ceylon, Burma and Indonesia. On April 22nd I met Mr. Dulles again in Paris, where we were both to attend a N.A.T.O. Council meeting. I took the opportunity to repeat my wish that we should avoid taking any action which might lead the Governments represented at Colombo to come out publicly against our security proposals. I told Mr. Dulles that I had been in touch with the Asian countries concerned, and I thought that I had so far persuaded them to refrain from any unfavourable expression of opinion. But I considered it very important that we should not issue any list of countries to be invited to join the proposed security system, until we had been able to see more clearly the trend of Asian opinion. Mr. Dulles, however, still adhered to his idea of launching S.E.A.T.O. with a small nucleus of members, and of doing this at the earliest possible moment. He thought that this might help to rouse the French from their defeatism. I was sure that if we took this action, India and other uncommitted states would pronounce against it, with unfortunate consequences for our efforts at Geneva.

Before we were able to discuss this matter further, it was suddenly overshadowed by an issue of even greater urgency. On the evening of April 23rd, we were assembled in the Quai d'Orsay for an official dinner, which was being given by the French Government for the N.A.T.O. powers, when Mr. Dulles drew me aside. Then he told me that a telegram had arrived from General Navarre to the French Government, to the effect that only a powerful air-strike by the United States in the next seventy-two hours could save the situation at Dien Bien Phu.

The battle of Dien Bien Phu had begun on March 13th. The French high command had always hoped for a pitched battle of this kind, and General Navarre had been confident that he would be able to inflict such heavy losses on the enemy that the Vietminh's back would be broken. Things did not work out that way. The French were heavily outnumbered. In their perimeter they had at the outset about six thousand men, including troops of the finest quality from the Foreign Legion, and they were surrounded by about thirty thousand Vietminh, well supplied with artillery and anti-aircraft guns. The Vietminh strength in artillery took the French by surprise; they had not antici-pated that it could be brought up in such force and carried piece by piece by coolies. The fighting was fierce and bitter. The defenders were seriously handicapped by bad weather and the Vietminh showed a reckless disregard for their heavy casualties.

By the time that General Navarre's request for American support was received, the garrison at Dien Bien Phu was surrounded and half the airstrip was in enemy hands. Guns and mortars on the neighbour-ing hills were firing into the fortress. Enemy forces were at this stage estimated at forty thousand and the French at about twelve thousand. Air supplies had enabled the French to maintain twelve days' food and four days' ammunition, a slender reserve. The French Air Force had heavy commitments on supply duties and had to give close tactical support to the garrison. They could not effectively interrupt the flow of Vietminh supplies from the Chinese border to their main depot, north-east of Dien Bien Phu. It was the bombing of this depot, dis-persed over a wide area eight miles square, which General Navarre now wished to see undertaken by the Americans. The French Air Force could then concentrate on attacking the enemy strong points in the Dien Bien Phu area. The French General Staff argued that bombing by an outside force, apart from the material damage it would cause, would have a considerable effect on the morale of troops in the fortress and on French and native forces in Indo-China generally. They told our General Staff that the Americans had offered sixty B-29 aircraft, which would operate from Manila. Each sortie could drop approximately four hundred and fifty tons of bombs and would operate from twenty thousand feet. We were also told by the French that a United States Air Force general and ten officers had visited Dien Bien Phu to study conditions and discuss the general situation.

When Mr. Dulles told me of General Navarre's request for help we had a brief conversation amid the expectant diners. I described it in a personal message to the Prime Minister later that night in these words:

I said that I found it hard to believe that any intervention from fleet carriers at this stage could have such an effect on the situation. Pleven had just told me that it was not true that the best French troops were all locked up in Dien Bien Phu. There were one hundred thousand troops in the Tongking delta, of whom the greater part were French Union forces. I feared that intervention could not save Dien Bien Phu and it might have far-reaching consequences. At this point Gruenther* came up and said that he had never known the French morale at so low an ebb. Could we do anything to revive it? He feared that a collapse in Indo-China would be followed by the fall of the Government here, and its successor might be neutralist. Dulles repeated his thesis about the vacuum created by the collapse of France as a world power. He appeared to share my doubts as to whether intervention by air would be decisive, but said that if I felt able to stand with him he was prepared to recommend the President to ask Congress for 'war powers'. (I am not sure that this is the right technical phrase, but this was its effect, for it would give the President special powers of the widest character to move armed forces.)

Dulles then read me extracts from a telegram from the President which expressed concern at the military news from Indo-China and also contained phrases which seemed to imply that we were somewhat indifferent in the matter. I said that this was certainly not so, but that I frankly did not believe that conditions in Indo-China could be remedied by outside intervention alone at this hour, even if help were immediately available. It was all too reminiscent of the French demand for our last R.A.F. squadrons in 1940. On the other hand, if the Americans were ready to discuss with us on a military basis the possibility of coming to the help of Thailand in the event of a total collapse in Indo-China, I was prepared to recommend this to you. Dulles agreed. I think it

* General Gruenther, then Supreme Allied Commander, Europe.

would be valuable to offer such secret talks between us two in Washington. If French morale is really crumpling and they are going to pack up in Indo-China, it is worth considering a joint Anglo-American guarantee of the Thai frontier, and this, in their present mood, I believe that the Americans might give.

At the conclusion of our talk I told Dulles that I trusted that no action would be taken in response to the French appeal without consultation with us. It might have far-reaching consequences for us all, and we must have an opportunity to consider these in advance. Dulles reassured me on this point.

I am fairly hardened to crises, but I went to bed that night a troubled man. I did not believe that anything less than intervention on a Korean scale, if that, would have any effect in Indo-China. If there were such intervention, I could not tell where its consequences would stop. We might well find ourselves involved in the wrong war against the wrong man in the wrong place.

On the following day, April 24th, I discussed the situation further with Mr. Dulles and Admiral Radford, the chairman of the American Joint Chiefs of Staff Committee. Mr. Dulles began by saying he was now convinced that there was no chance of keeping the French in the fight unless they knew 'that we would do what we can within the President's constitutional powers to join them in the fight'. The French had said that it would not be enough if we were to assure them that we would join them in defending the rest of Indo-China, in the event of the fall of Dien Bien Phu. Unless we participated, by an air-strike, in the battle for the fortress itself, that would be 'their last battle'. Mr. Dulles wished to make it plain that there was no possibility of United States participation in the Dien Bien Phu battle, because the President had not the power to act with such speed and because it was perfectly clear that no intervention could now save the fortress, where the situation was desperate. I asked Mr. Dulles what measures he had in mind. Admiral Radford replied that there must be some military effort to assist the French without delay. He suggested that British participation might take the form of sending R.A.F. units into Tongking from Malaya or Hong Kong. He also enquired whether we had not an aircraft-carrier in the area. Neither he nor Mr. Dulles gave any more explicit account of the joint military action they contemplated. Admiral Radford went on to say that he thought it most likely that when Dien Bien Phu fell, the whole military situation in Indo-China would get out of control within a few days. There might be riots in Saigon and Hanoi, and the whole population might turn against the French. The only way he saw of preventing this was to demonstrate that France now had powerful allies in the fight.

In reply to this, I said that the French had not painted anything like so desperate a picture to us. On the contrary, the French Government's line with Her Majesty's Ambassador that morning had been that the situation at Dien Bien Phu was very bad, but that they would fight on elsewhere if it fell. I asked Admiral Radford if he really thought that air intervention by the United States and the United Kingdom could decisively alter the situation. Had the Americans considered the effect on world opinion and how the Chinese would react? I said that I assumed they had not forgotten the Russo-Chinese alliance. It was possible that if we went into Indo-China we should find ourselves fighting Vietnam as well as Vietminh, and in addition heading for a world war. Admiral Radford replied that he had never thought that the Chinese would intervene in Indo-China, nor had they the necessary resources available. If they attempted air action, we could eliminate this by bombing the Chinese airfields, which were very vulnerable. At the end of our meeting, I told Mr. Dulles that he was confronting British opinion with about as difficult a decision as it would be possible to find. I would at once consult my colleagues.

I thought it necessary to clear up the discrepancy between the American account of the French Government's opinion and that which the French had given us. Accordingly, later that afternoon Mr. Dulles and I conferred with M. Bidault at the Quai d'Orsay. Dulles began by telling Bidault that if the French could give an assurance that they would continue the struggle after the fall of Dien Bien Phu, the United States would at once set about organizing the defence of the entire region. I noticed that Dulles' remarks clearly implied that the London communiqué had in some way already committed the United Kingdom to armed action in Indo-China. I interrupted to point out that this was not so and Bidault at once agreed. Bidault did not give a direct answer to Dulles' question, and merely emphasized the catastrophic results of the fall of Dien Bien Phu. Mr. Dulles then produced the draft of a letter, which the United Kingdom delegation was allowed to glance at briefly, and handed it to M. Bidault with the offer to send it to him formally if it would be helpful. So far as we could make out, the sense of the letter seemed to be that although it was unfortunately now too late for American support to be provided at Dien Bien

Phu, the United States was nevertheless prepared, if France and the other allies so desired, to move armed forces into Indo-China and thus internationalize the struggle and protect South-East Asia as a whole. M. Bidault hesitated for several minutes. He then announced that he was prepared for Mr. Dulles to send him the letter officially. When the meeting was over I at once sent a telegram to the Foreign Office:

> It is now quite clear that we shall have to take a decision of first-class importance, namely whether to tell the Americans that we are prepared to go along with their plan or not. It seems essential that I should discuss this with my colleagues and I am, therefore, returning to London tonight.

Shortly after this, Maurice Schumann rang me up to say that both Laniel and Bidault were now strongly in favour of my returning to London, and hoped that I would urge my colleagues to agree to proceeding on the lines desired by Dulles. During the course of the evening, however, the French appeared to have second thoughts. Denis Allen sent me a message after my departure from Paris to say that Bidault was, on reflection, far from enthusiastic about the American proposals. If Dulles pressed the matter, it was probable that Bidault would advise Laniel not to accept American intervention.

★　　★　　★　　★　　★

From London Airport, I drove to Chequers to give the Prime Minister a full report on the situation. As happened so often in the years we worked together, I found that Sir Winston and I, though physically separated by hundreds of miles, had formed exactly the same conclusion. We agreed that it now seemed inevitable that the French garrison at Dien Bien Phu would be overwhelmed or compelled to surrender. I said that Mr. Dulles and Admiral Radford evidently feared that this would promptly be followed by the collapse of all French resistance throughout Indo-China and, in order to avert it, favoured some dramatic gesture of Anglo-American intervention in Indo-China. They now recognized that this could no longer save Dien Bien Phu, but still wanted to rally French and Vietnamese morale and to prevent a general disintegration. Congress would be more likely to approve such action if intervention were to be on an Anglo-American basis. The Americans had therefore proposed that the United States and the United Kingdom Governments should give the French a joint assurance that they would join in the defence of Indo-China, and that, as an earnest of this, they should be given immediate military assistance, including token British participation. I told the Prime Minister that I disagreed both with the American belief that such intervention could be effective and with the view that it could be limited to the use of air forces. I doubted whether intervention would have any substantial effect in rallying public opinion in Indo-China, and I was certain that it would not be welcomed by nationalist opinion in South-East Asia generally. Militarily, I did not believe that the limited measures contemplated by the United States could achieve substantial results; no military aid could be effective unless it included ground troops. Sir Winston summed up the position by saying that what we were being asked to do was to assist in misleading Congress into approving a military operation, which would in itself be ineffective, and might well bring the world to the verge of a major war.

We agreed that we must therefore decline to give any undertaking of military assistance to the French in Indo-China. It now seemed inevitable that large parts of the country would fall under communist control, and the best hope of a lasting solution lay in some form of partition. Sir Winston and I both thought that our aim should be to strengthen the negotiating position of the French at Geneva, and we did not consider that this would be achieved by hasty and limited military action. On the contrary, it would be preferable to keep the Chinese guessing as to what form of action France's allies intended eventually to pursue. I then showed the Prime Minister the directive which I had prepared in advance for the emergency Cabinet meeting which was to take place in a few hours. It read as follows:

1. We do not regard the London communiqué as committing us to join in immediate discussions on the possibility of Allied intervention in the Indo-China war.

2. We are not prepared to give any undertaking now, in advance of the Geneva Conference, concerning United Kingdom military action in Indo-China.

3. But we shall give all possible diplomatic support to the French delegation at Geneva in efforts to reach an honourable settlement.

4. We can give an assurance now that if a settlement is reached at Geneva, we shall join in guaranteeing that settlement and in setting up a collective defence in South-East Asia, as foreshadowed in the London communiqué, to make that joint guarantee effective.

5. We hope that any Geneva settlement will make it possible for

the joint guarantee to apply to at least the greater part of Indo-China.

6. If no such settlement is reached, we shall be prepared at that time to consider with our allies the action to be taken jointly in the situation then existing.

7. But we cannot give any assurance now about possible action on the part of the United Kingdom in the event of failure to reach agreement at Geneva for the cessation of hostilities in Indo-China.

8. We shall be ready to join with the United States Government now in studying measures to ensure the defence of Thailand and the rest of South-East Asia, including Malaya, in the event of all or part of Indo-China being lost.

The Prime Minister approved this directive, and when the Cabinet met at 11 a.m. on Sunday, April 25th, it was unanimously endorsed by my colleagues.

While the Cabinet was in session, other moves were being made. During the afternoon, the French Ambassador, M. Massigli, came to tell me that Mr. Dulles' letter had been delivered to the French Government. He also informed me that the United States Government were now proposing that an immediate declaration should be made on behalf of the Governments of the United States, the United Kingdom, France, the Philippines and the Associated States, proclaiming their common will to check the expansion of communism in South-East Asia and to use 'eventual military means' for this purpose. Once President Eisenhower had been assured that the United Kingdom would participate in this declaration, he would be prepared to seek Congressional approval for intervention. United States naval aircraft would go into action at Dien Bien Phu on April 28th. The French Government had been urged by the Americans to persuade us to agree to this course.

This was a new development and the Cabinet met once more in emergency session at 4 p.m. on the same afternoon to discuss it. I was surprised at the American tactic of approaching us on a major issue by way of the French, instead of through our own Ambassador in Washington, who had not been consulted in any way. If the United Kingdom acceded to this latest American proposal, we should be supporting direct United States intervention in the Indo-China war and, probably, later American action against the Chinese mainland. Her Majesty's Government consequently decided to reject the American proposal, and I was asked to inform Mr. Dulles and M. Bidault of our decision, on my way to Geneva.

VI

THE GENEVA CONFERENCE
April – July 1954

The ambushes of diplomacy – Dulles and Bedell Smith – Commonwealth opinions – Jean Chauvel – Delays – Soviet Ministers to dinner – My staff at Geneva – The conference opens – Slow progress – A typical day – Chou En-lai – A slight advance – A threat of force – Mendès France – A visit to Washington – Guatemala – Back to Geneva – A settlement reached – A summing up – S.E.A.T.O.

My wife and I flew that evening to Geneva and I broke my journey briefly at Orly airport, where M. Bidault was waiting. I informed him of the Government's decision concerning the American proposals for intervention in Indo-China. He was not surprised by this, although he was gravely perturbed by other aspects of the situation, especially by the fact that there had been a leakage to the American press on the current differences between the Western allies.

As we flew on I thought of the many occasions when I had visited Geneva before the war, in the days of the League of Nations, and of the international conferences I had experienced in this city. There was the crisis when King Alexander of Yugoslavia and M. Barthou were murdered in Marseilles, when war seemed near and I had to face my first critical international responsibility in handling the dispute at the request of the Council of the League. Then there was the Italian invasion of Abyssinia, the murder of Dollfuss, Hitler's growing power, and the gathering menace of war. I was back again after seventeen years, and I should need good fortune if we were to stop this dispute being the first in a chain of events leading to another catastrophe.

Our Royal Air Force machine ran into some stormy weather near the airport, which put a stop to these reflections. We were greeted by

the Swiss with their traditional courtesy. They seemed glad to be playing their part as hosts again for the work we had to do. We drove to
the hotel which the British Foreign Secretary has always used, and
were lodged in the rooms I had known so many years before, looking
out over the Lake of Geneva. M. Beñes had always occupied the floor
beneath me when I had been here before. Now we had other foreign
missions as neighbours, with the Chinese predominating.

In the modern age there are many contrivances for overlooking or
overhearing the proceedings of others. Peeping Toms and flapping ears
have gadgets never thought of when I was in Geneva before. I was
soon warned of this and told that if I proposed to hold meetings in my
sitting-room, as I had always done, I must expect our discussions to be
overheard. It was suggested that as a precaution I should accompany
my talks with some 'noises off', such as beating on the tables, which
could confuse any would-be listeners. The only trouble was that while
I was attentive to this advice at first, I was apt to forget it when I became absorbed in the discussion. As a result we must have been easy to
hear in the more important moments and only inaudible when it did
not matter.

We were rescued from all this embarrassment by the generosity of a
Swiss friend, M. Pictet, who lent us his villa, Le Reposoir. This was
beautiful and secluded, yet within easy reach of the city. We moved
there, glad to be free of these new ambushes of diplomacy. I told
Sir Winston what I was up to and received the following thoughtful
endorsement of an aspect I had not considered: 'Any expense necessary
for your security will of course be met by H.M.G.'

The issue of intervention continued to dog us during the opening
stages of the conference. As soon as I arrived in Geneva, Mr. Dulles
came to see me to learn the British attitude to the United States proposal. I told him once more that if a settlement were achieved at the
conference, the United Kingdom would be prepared to join in guaranteeing it. If the conference failed, we would be ready to examine the
situation afresh, but we were not willing to take part in armed intervention now.

The Americans continued to believe that some action must be taken
outside the conference. They wished to encourage the French to keep
fighting and prevent a steady communist advance in South-East Asia.
On April 30th, Mr. Dulles and I once more discussed the proposed
South-East Asia pact. I said that there was no question of our weakening in our willingness to examine such a proposal. On the other hand,

we really must know before we began the talks what we both had in mind and, in particular, whether the proposal implied a commitment to military action in Indo-China. As I had several times explained, Mr. Dulles knew we could not agree to this. He replied that he did not think anybody was advocating military intervention in Indo-China, though he understood that perhaps some remarks of Admiral Radford, whom he was inclined to criticize, had caused us to draw back in our attitude towards the pact. Admiral Radford, he said, was not the spokesman of the United States. Only the President and himself could express their Government's opinion. At this point I handed to Mr. Dulles a memorandum setting out my views on the whole question of South-East Asian defence, which read as follows:

1. Communism in Asia cannot be checked by military means alone. The problem is as much political as military; if any military combination is to be effective, it must enjoy the widest possible measure of Asian support.

2. We should aim to get the support of Burma as well as Thailand, as the immediate neighbours of Indo-China. But Burma will not come in unless the project commands some sympathy from other Asian countries, particularly the Asian members of the Commonwealth.

3. If we cannot win the active support of all the Asian countries of the area, it is important that we should, at the very least, secure their benevolent neutrality.

4. To secure this widely-based Asian support, we must prepare the ground carefully for what is, in any case, intended to be a lasting defensive organization, not a hastily contrived expedient to meet the present crisis.

5. This does not mean that we desire to delay. On the contrary, we have already been actively using our influence, particularly with the Asian members of the Commonwealth, with encouraging results. Pakistan and Ceylon have already promised not to oppose a South-Eastern collective defence on the lines we envisage, and we have succeeded in diverting Mr. Nehru from his original intention of condemning it root and branch. We have thus averted the danger that the Asian Prime Ministers at Colombo would unite in condemning our project, and have grounds for hoping for the actual support of some of them.

6. Mr. Nehru's latest statement shows that his ideas have

moved closer to our own. With persistence, we may even secure his endorsement of the kind of negotiated settlement in Indo-China that would be acceptable to us.

7. While we do not believe that a French collapse in Indo-China could come about as rapidly as the Americans appear to envisage, this danger reinforces the need to lay the foundations of a wider and viable defence organization for South-East Asia.

8. We propose therefore that the United States and the United Kingdom should begin an immediate and secret joint examination of the political and military problems in creating a collective defence for South-East Asia, namely:

(a) nature and purpose;
(b) membership;
(c) commitments.

We then spoke of the Colombo Conference. I said that from the reports that had reached me so far, matters had not gone too badly. If this proved to be so, I was sure that our reserve in not announcing the names of the proposed members of the defence pact, in advance of the Colombo Conference, would have paid a dividend. It might even be that some of these countries would now be prepared to associate themselves in some way with our pact. If so, that would be a considerable gain, and would be a reply to the Chinese communist cry of 'Asia for the Asians'.

One of Mr. Dulles' reasons for wishing to push ahead with the organization of South-East Asian defence more quickly than we considered wise, was M. Bidault's evident depression about the position of France at the conference. When we three held a short meeting on the afternoon of the 30th, M. Bidault said that, as far as these negotiations were concerned, 'he had hardly a card in his hand, perhaps just a two of clubs and a three of diamonds'. In his view it was no good to talk about partition. It was certainly not a possible policy for the French, in the light of their responsibilities to the three Associated States. Equally, a cease-fire was impossible, because the two sides were so inextricably mingled everywhere that the result would be a massacre. Probably the best course was to work for an armistice, which would allow some disentanglement of the forces. I had every sympathy with M. Bidault and, after he had gone, Mr. Dulles asked me to consider whether there was not something we could do to help the French. If we started now to have talks in Washington about the South-East Asia pact, would not that hearten the French and show that we were preparing against all eventualities? I said that the difficulties appeared to me to be the same. If we were not preparing to go to the help of the French in Indo-China, I found it hard to see how pretending that we might be going to do so would really help anybody. If the talks were to be public, we should at once be asked whether we were going to intervene in Indo-China, which we could not do. If we admitted this, we would not help the French. The best I thought we could do was to create doubt as to our intentions if the talks broke down, or if no arrangement was arrived at. This might be some help, but it would require very careful wording. We agreed to think the matter over.

★   ★   ★   ★   ★

The arrival of Mr. Bedell Smith at Geneva on May 1st, to take over the leadership of the United States delegation, did something to lift the pall which was beginning to descend on the discussions between the three Western allies. I had known Mr. Bedell Smith since our wartime association, when I was my country's Foreign Secretary and he was General Eisenhower's Chief of Staff. I had attended conferences with him and seen him at work, and from the first I liked him. He could feel strongly, yet was always understanding. He was forthright, but a friend. The three powers held a meeting on the morning of May 1st, which he attended, accompanying Mr. Dulles. At the end of our discussions, as I was leaving, Bedell Smith greeted me warmly and said that he was most anxious for a full talk at the earliest possible moment, so that we could co-ordinate our policies. I said that, although conditions were difficult, I felt sure that we could soon work out a common line. Bedell Smith said emphatically that of course we could, and that I was not to pay any attention to a number of foolish things which were being said in the United States at the present time. The warmth with which he spoke meant much to me and, as I telegraphed to London, I was encouraged by the prospect which his co-operation opened up.

The value of Mr. Bedell Smith's understanding attitude was apparent at an exceptionally difficult discussion which Lord Reading and I had with the American delegation after dinner that evening. It brought to a head the differences between our American allies and ourselves, which had been building up since January. I record it as I reported it in a message to London that night:

After some discussion as to the reasons for the present mutual hostility between the United States and China, in spite of the close relations which had existed between them in the past, the conversation turned to the situation in Indo-China and we were subjected to a prolonged, and at moments somewhat heated, onslaught upon our attitude. Only Mr. Bedell Smith seemed to have any real comprehension of the reasons which had led us to take up our present position. Mr. Dulles began by saying that the situation was very disturbing. In the past we had always been in accord on our policy at conferences; now we were in complete disarray. I said that we were not in any disarray as regards Korea, but as regards Indo-China I simply did not know what it was that we were being asked to do. If it were that we should intervene with armed forces, I could only say that I had already explained fully the reasons why any such action was impossible and that anyhow I was unable to discover what steps we were being asked to take and what result was expected to follow.

Mr. Dulles then said that it was his impression that we were not prepared in any circumstances to back them up in action in Indo-China. He asked the direct question whether that was so and went on to say that he was not asking us for any material assistance, but only for our moral support in any action that they might take. I said that this was quite a new approach. I asked what sort of action they had in mind and he replied that that had not yet been decided. Mr. Bedell Smith intervened at this point to say that he agreed neither with the United States nor the British Chiefs of Staff. The former were too optimistic and the latter too pessimistic. Dien Bien Phu had become a symbol, but it was no longer possible to save it. He thought, however, that though it would be quite impossible to attempt to stop a communist advance on the border of Malaya, it was possible to find a position from which Thailand, Burma and Malaya could be defended. One of the difficulties was that they had never been able to sit down with the French over a map and examine the military possibilities of the situation.

I said that we must really see where we were going. If the Americans went into the Indo-China war, the Chinese themselves would inevitably step up their participation. The next stage would be that the Americans and the Chinese would be fighting each other and that was in all probability the beginning of the third world war.

Meanwhile Mr. Robertson,* whose approach to these questions is so emotional as to be impervious to argument or indeed to facts, was keeping up a sort of 'theme song' to the effect that there were in Indo-China some three hundred thousand men who were anxious to fight against the Vietminh and were looking to us for support and encouragement. I said that if they were so anxious to fight I could not understand why they did not do so. The Americans had put in nine times more supplies of material than the Chinese, and plenty must be available for their use. I had no faith in this eagerness of the Vietnamese to fight for Bao Dai.

Our American hosts then introduced the topic of the training of Vietnamese forces to defend their own country. Whatever the attractions of this scheme, they admitted that it would take perhaps two years to finish. The problem was what would happen meanwhile. When Lord Reading asked Mr. Dulles what he thought about this, he replied that they would have to hold some sort of bridgehead, as had been done in Korea until the Inchon landings could be carried out. Lord Reading commented that this meant that things would remain on the boil for several years to come, and Mr. Dulles replied that this would be a very good thing.

There was then some discursive and divergent discussion as to the resemblance of the Indo-China conflict to that in Korea. This did not advance us very much and I was not sorry when we broke up. As I reported to London that night, I was disturbed by this conversation because it showed clearly that the Americans were deeply aggrieved by our refusal to support them in such military measures as they might think advisable and that, except for Mr. Bedell Smith, they could not understand why we were holding aloof. At the same time they had no plans of their own, but were searching about for some expedient which would serve to restore, or at least to hold the situation.

The first session of the conference on Indo-China was only a few days away and we had still failed to reach agreement on Western policy, but I was determined that we should not endorse a bad policy for the sake of unity. On May 2nd, I reported to London:

My view is that we cannot give the Americans the moral support they seek for their plans as at present conceived. It still seems that they have not worked out their ideas at all clearly and we must

* The United States Assistant Secretary of State for Far Eastern Affairs.

know exactly what it is they propose to do and under what authority they intend to proceed. . . . I am conscious of the effect of our differences over this question upon Anglo-American relations. But I am sure our only wise course is to follow a consistent line. This means we must refuse, pending the outcome of negotiations here, not only to allow ourselves to be drawn into the Indo-China war, but also to promise our moral support for measures of which we do not yet know the full scope. On the other hand, we can continue to assure the Americans, as we have done already, that we are eager to work with them in building a collective defence with the widest possible Asian support, to guarantee and support whatever settlement can be achieved in Indo-China and to assure the security of the rest of the area.

I discussed these views of mine fully with my Commonwealth colleagues at Geneva, Lester Pearson of Canada, Richard Casey of Australia and Clifton Webb of New Zealand. I was encouraged to find that we were all in agreement.

I had also been maintaining close contact with the Prime Ministers of India, Pakistan and Ceylon. I had received a message from Mr. Nehru on May 5th, in which he said that although he could make no commitments until the pattern which emerged from Geneva could be seen more clearly, India would be glad to assist in promoting and maintaining a settlement in Indo-China. This was good news.

During these preliminaries to the conference, the French delegation were carrying a load of troubles. M. Bidault came to dine with me on May 4th to discuss our joint position in the coming session on Indo-China. He was accompanied by M. Jean Chauvel, one of the many able and devoted civil servants who have kept the machinery of French government working during the frequent political changes of recent years. Their abilities cushioned the consequences of these changes, the importance of which the foreign critic is inclined to exaggerate. M. Chauvel was in his element in this emergency. An excellent war record influenced General de Gaulle to place him at the head of the Quai d'Orsay. After some years at the United Nations, he was now Ambassador in Berne, and could be seconded to give his time to the negotiations at Geneva. M. Chauvel has a quick and lucid mind, and saw clearly where France's true interests lay. He never stepped outside the strict limits of his authority, but within these he guided the discussion relentlessly to the vital decisions. I respected his sense of purpose and his firmness in maintaining it. If, as a result of these negotiations, his country was spared the worst calamities, a large share of the credit should go to Jean Chauvel.

On this occasion, both Bidault and Chauvel were so pre-occupied with the political situation in France and with the possibility of the Government's defeat, that neither had much attention left with which to face the immediate problems of the conference. My task was to persuade them to decide upon a policy and to help them into a position from which negotiations could begin. In addition, the representatives of the Associated States had so far failed to appear at Geneva. Bao Dai was being flushed out of Cannes by the Vietnamese Foreign Minister and so far there was no Laotian or Cambodian present. I said that it was intolerable that the entire work of the conference should be held up while these representatives were being collected. Our failure to be ready to negotiate was giving Molotov and Chou En-lai ammunition which they would be sure to use. Bidault readily agreed and said that he would be prepared to meet Molotov without the Indo-Chinese, if necessary.

Two days later, Mr. Bedell Smith and I went to see M. Bidault. I knew that his position, trying to agree on a policy with his colleagues in Paris at such a time, was not an easy one. I thought that it would help him if I told him where we stood, so I said that, for ourselves, we were prepared to support the French strongly, if they were able to clear their policy, concert it with us and present it at the first meeting. Bedell Smith firmly endorsed my view and, after some talk and telephoning, Bidault finally agreed to have concrete proposals ready in time for a plenary session of the conference on May 9th. I felt the deepest sympathy for Bidault during these agonizing days. News of the fall of Dien Bien Phu had just arrived and he was dreading the receipt of instructions from Paris which would amount to virtual surrender in Indo-China as a whole.

The opening of the conference's formal discussion on Indo-China had also been delayed by differences between ourselves and the communists on the question of who was to be represented at the conference table. Molotov demanded that a Vietminh delegation should participate in the talks. It was not possible to resist this, but Bidault and I agreed that, in accepting it, we should require communist co-operation in the evacuation of wounded from Dien Bien Phu. Molotov and Chou En-lai refused to agree on the basis of a formal bargain but later, on May 10th, after some talk behind the scenes, an unofficial arrangement was reached. When Vietminh participation was accepted, the Vietminh delegate made an announcement expressing his willingness to authorize the evacuation of seriously wounded prisoners from both sides.

I foresaw that the communists would also demand the admission to the conference of representatives of the so-called 'Free Laotian' (Pathet Lao) and 'Free Cambodian' (Khmer Issarak) Governments. This had to be firmly resisted. The move was made at the first plenary session which the conference devoted to Indo-China, on May 9th. We made it plain that this was not a question on which we could compromise. But I did not expect that Molotov and Chou En-lai would sabotage the entire conference by pressing the issue, stubborn as the exchanges were. In the event, they gradually dropped it.

Procedural problems did not seriously hinder the opening of our formal discussions on Indo-China, as I had feared that they might. Mr. Molotov was helpful in our preliminary talks and I began to think that he was genuinely anxious that the conference should succeed. Chou En-lai's attitude, to begin with at any rate, was entirely different. He was cold and bitterly anti-American, and my first interview with him at our villa was rigid and disagreeable. We sat grimly exchanging sharp acerbities It was on this occasion that he brusquely rejected my proposal of a truce for the evacuation of wounded at Dien Bien Phu.

★　　★　　★　　★　　★

On May 5th, Molotov and Gromyko came to dine with me. Molotov was in an unusually relaxed mood and we talked freely about the film of Her Majesty's Coronation, the development of the Commonwealth and the workings of the French Chamber of Deputies. On the subject of the conference itself, he was also amenable and, throughout that evening, did not attempt to score so much as a debating point. This was a transformation from Berlin, prompted, I thought, by worry over the situation in Indo-China. Molotov suggested that he and I should alternate in taking the chair at the sessions of the conference. He said that it was the only possibility, unless the heads of the nine delegations were to preside in turn, which clearly would not work. I knew that the French and the Americans would accept this, so I agreed.

The proposal fitted Mr. Molotov's theme that the conference depended to a large extent upon the two of us, the implication being that we both had allies whose views on the situation in Indo-China might be more extreme than our own. At one point I said that this was the most difficult conference in which I had ever taken part, and Molotov said that he shared my opinion. I thought it essential that we should get on with the Indo-China talks, as I was afraid of the consequences if matters were allowed to drift. I said that I did not think Korea was so urgent. After all, there was no fighting there and matters could be allowed to remain for the time being in their present state, if we could not agree on further steps. But the Indo-China situation had very dangerous possibilities. Molotov fully agreed. It seemed to me, I said, that the first thing to work for was an armistice, which was not the same as a cease-fire. If we could get the fighting stopped through an accepted armistice, we should then have a chance to sort out the position under less pressure. Molotov again agreed, but said that conditions must be attached to the armistice, though he thought that these could be devised. I did my best to explain to him the background to the strong views which the Americans held on China. He listened attentively, and told me that in the past the Soviet Union had also thought well of Chiang Kai-shek. They had considered that, in the course of time, Mao Tse-tung would probably establish himself in power, but they had not expected this to happen so quickly. Now that Chiang Kai-shek had lost his hold, it was useless to try to build him up again. The Americans, said Molotov, must be brought to face the truth of the situation. He added with a frosty smile that he had observed that Mr. Dulles had succeeded during his stay in Geneva in never once acknowledging Mr. Chou En-lai's existence.

Towards the end of our conversation, I said that I would speak very frankly. If the Indo-China situation was not effectively handled here at Geneva, there was a real danger that the supporters of each side would go on increasing the degree of their participation, until finally there was a clash between them. If that happened, I continued, it might well be the beginning of the third world war. Molotov fully agreed with this assessment. When he and Gromyko had left, I recorded this impression of our conversation in a message to London:

It is too soon to put this evening into its proper perspective. We shall be able to form a more accurate judgment when the discussions on Indo-China are actually in progress. It may of course have been no more than an extremely subtle and adroit exercise in 'wedge-driving', but we all formed the impression that there was more substance to it than that.

I was fortunate in my staff at Geneva. It was small, but could not have been bettered in the Foreign Office of any country. Sir Harold Caccia and Mr. Denis Allen, who led it, both had first-hand knowledge of the Far East. Sir Harold was tough and persistent in negotiation, cool in hours of crisis. I knew him well, for he had been my Private Secretary when I resigned as Foreign Secretary in 1938. Mr. Allen had a perfect command of his facts on all occasions and was immensely resourceful. Near the end of the conference Sir Anthony Rumbold took over from Mr. Shuckburgh, who had been my Principal Private Secretary since my return to the Foreign Office three years before. These four men are certain to play leading parts in the conduct of their country's diplomacy.

The formal session began on May 9th. Before the final settlement was reached on July 21st, we discussed Indo-China at eight plenary and eighteen restricted sessions. During much of this period the Korean Conference was also in session, and Molotov or I had often to act as chairman there. We made no real progress over Korea, but these meetings and their preparation made heavy demands upon our strength and time. As is usual at international conferences, much of the real work was done in informal talks which took place daily, away from the conference table. The course of the negotiations was frequently influenced, as a rule adversely, by diplomatic events far away from Geneva. It quickly became clear to me that we should make little progress if we continued to discuss Indo-China in plenary sessions, which merely provided a stage for the striking of attitudes by both sides. On May 13th, I accordingly suggested to Bedell Smith and Bidault that we should continue our talks in restricted sessions, consisting of the heads of all nine delegations with only two or three advisers apiece. No account of the proceedings would be given to the press. This proposal was agreed upon, and on the following day Molotov and Chou En-lai also accepted it.

Although we quickly reached agreement on the principle that we should work for a military armistice in Indo-China before discussing the details of a political settlement, the negotiations soon snarled on the issue of Laos and Cambodia. Chou En-lai, and to a lesser degree Molotov, refused to acknowledge that the situation in these two Associated States was different in kind from that in Vietnam, and insisted on a blanket settlement for Indo-China as a whole. There was a plan behind this. The military situation might compel us to make concessions to the communists in Vietnam, and they wanted these to apply to Laos and Cambodia as well. We had at all costs to prevent this. The civil war in Vietnam on the one hand, and the direct invasion by the Vietminh of Laos and Cambodia on the other, could not be dealt with on the same basis.

I was concerned at this time by developments outside Geneva which, it seemed to me, might endanger our admittedly slender chances of making progress in negotiation. On May 15th I was surprised to find reports in the Swiss morning papers of Franco-American discussions on the possibility of military intervention by the United States in Indo-China. That this issue should have been resurrected at such a moment was startling. I at once asked Mr. Bedell Smith if there was any truth in these reports, and he told me he knew nothing about the matter. When M. Bidault came to see me later in the morning, I asked him if he could confirm the rumours, and he gave me a vague denial which largely reassured me. However, at the end of our meeting, M. de Margerie, his principal adviser on that occasion, led me to the window and said that he had a document which he had been instructed by M. Bidault to read to me. This contained the conditions for United States intervention in Indo-China. I commented: 'Then what the newspapers said is true.' 'Certainly,' Margerie replied, 'very much so.' He gave me the conditions, which were for intervention either after the failure of Geneva, or earlier if the French so desired, and he emphasized that the American preference had been clearly expressed for the earlier date.

Later in the day, the *New York Herald Tribune* arrived, giving the full details of the Franco-American negotiations. This was a relief, as it enabled me to raise the matter with Bedell Smith without disclosing that I already had information from the French. Bedell Smith exploded with indignation, and deplored Washington's inability to keep any discussions secret. I pointed out that, for us, the seriousness of the situation lay not only in the matter of the announcement, but in the fact that we had received no prior intimation whatever of these conversations. Bedell Smith said at once that it was intolerable that we should get information of this kind from a newspaper and that of course we should have been told. The United Kingdom Government were to have been informed, once French acceptance of the conditions was known. He emphasized that the matter was not nearly so serious as the newspapers had made it look. All that was contemplated, he said, was American assistance with the training of troops. Whatever the nature of the intended action, it was clear that the publicity given to these talks could do grave damage, and Bedell Smith and I agreed to limit it as best we could.

I told the Australian, New Zealand and Canadian delegates what had happened, and sent a reassuring telegram to Mr. Nehru. I was relieved when M. Bidault informed me, two days later, that France would make no request for intervention while the conference was still in session. Nevertheless, the episode had its dangers. It was not that I minded 'noises off'. They could be helpful, but only under certain very definite conditions. I reported to the Prime Minister:

> I myself fear that this new talk of intervention will have weakened what chances remain of agreement at this conference. The Chinese, and to a lesser extent the Russians, have all along suspected that the Americans intend to intervene in Indo-China whatever arrangements we try to arrive at here. The Chinese also believe that the Americans plan hostilities against them. These reports could help to convince them that they are right, and I do not accept the United States argument that the threat of intervention will incline them to compromise.

My pessimism appeared at first to be justified. We were making no progress in our attempt to segregate the problems of Laos and Cambodia from that of Vietnam, and two restricted sessions devoted to the subject failed to bring us nearer to agreement. I was nevertheless flabbergasted when the American delegation showed to Bidault and myself, on May 19th, a prepared statement proposing that we should now bring the restricted sessions to an end and go back into plenary session. I said that we could not possibly do this after so short a time. It had taken us three weeks to get into secret session and now we were to go out in two days. We must, I thought, give the experiment a full and fair trial. M. Bidault commented simply that a proposal such as the Americans had put forward would immediately bring his Government down. It was decided that the restricted sessions should continue.

★ ★ ★ ★ ★

In view of the uncertain attitude of the Americans towards the negotiations and the obvious difficulties of the French position, it fell to me to undertake much of the exploratory personal diplomacy which had to be done if we were to make any progress. Here is a typical day of which I took a note:

Thursday, May 20th.

A very heavy day of negotiations. Chou En-lai arrived at 11 and we had an hour's discussion. It might have been even longer if I had not thought that he had had enough. He states his case with little acceptance of any other, and is very hard to shake. However, I hope that the exercise was worth while. Went from there to report to Bidault and Bedell Smith, who did not seem to consider the results too bad. Further meeting with them in the evening when we reviewed possibilities afresh. I suggested we might consider dealing first with the proposals in the French and Vietminh text, and then examine their application to the individual countries later, thus reserving the position of Laos and Cambodia. The French favoured two or three committees, but from what Chou En-lai told me in the morning, I doubt whether the communists will take this and anyhow it is not very practical.

Dined with Molotov, who made the evening as easy as he could. He clearly thinks he and I have a special task in this conference to try and facilitate agreement. He remarked that he read in the papers that we and the U.S. were having differences, and he did not believe that. I said he was right not to, because allies often have to argue their respective points of view. Molotov said: 'That is right, we have to do that amongst ourselves, too', and he emphasized to me once again that China was very much her own master in these matters. After dinner we had a talk on the conference deadlock and he produced a proposal very similar to that which I had been discussing with the Americans and French earlier. I did not commit myself, but undertook to put it to my allies. He said that he would do the same to his.

Nothing occurred to make me modify my original impression that Molotov was genuinely anxious to reach a settlement. In our frequent private conversations he often came forward with some helpful suggestion or concession, which enabled the work of the conference to move forward. Our partnership as joint chairmen worked smoothly. Chou En-lai's intentions were less easy to fathom, and it took me some time to achieve any kind of personal contact. My second interview with him was not much better than the first, but at its close an incident occurred which may have helped at least to ease personal relations. The Chinese were housed in a very fine villa, on a larger scale and more splendid than ours. The room in which we held our meeting displayed some beautiful pieces of Chinese porcelain. After we had finished our firm exchanges and as I rose to go, I walked towards these and said how lovely they were. Chou En-lai seemed pleased and we discussed the pieces. A number of them had been brought from the Chinese Legation at Berne for the occasion; others, if I understood correctly, from China itself. Whether or not Chou En-lai felt any deep interest in the porcelain himself, I could not tell, but I thought it a mark in his favour that he understood the importance which his country's art could have for his visitors. We went into other rooms to look at more examples and I greatly enjoyed these relaxed few minutes. There were not many during the conference.

Soon after this, I invited Chou En-lai and some of his colleagues to dine with me. I did not intend to discuss the immediate events of the conference, but to talk over the past. It was always possible that in doing this we should find incidents and occasions where our sympathies had coincided. I did not for a moment suppose that I could in the slightest degree modify any one of Chou En-lai's opinions, any more than he could modify mine. On the other hand, I thought that it might help to remove any additional surface causes of friction between us. One of the questions I had to probe was whether the Chinese Government were prepared to come to an arrangement at all. The French could still hold on in Indo-China, but at any moment some major disaster might overcome them and no choice be left but an ignominious exodus. While the French armies were still in being, we had a certain bargaining factor, weak though it was. With every month that passed, this counted for less. I felt that the Chinese might yet be constrained to come to an arrangement which would spare their enemy humiliation, allow a free life to some part of Vietnam and give Laos and Cambodia the reality of independence. If we could not reach agreement soon, the military position would deteriorate and it would then become evident to the world that the Chinese had no need to bargain. The Chinese themselves probably knew this already, but they might also be wise enough to reckon that it was not good politics to drive an enemy to despair. They could now agree to terms without loss of face. In a few months' time, nothing but capitulation would suffice. The question was whether the Chinese saw matters in this light. I had to find out.

There was one factor which I thought might tell in our favour. The Chinese had been diverted from their internal problems by the Korean war. The communist revolution was still incomplete at the time of

Geneva, and they were anxious to finish it. It was possible that their desire to push ahead with land reform and the nationalization of the commercial life of their country, might give them some interest in reaching a settlement on Indo-China.

Our dinner went off well. I refrained from discussing the work of the conference and Chou En-lai did the same. We spoke of our experiences and events in the Far East and Europe which had led to the second world war. He told me of the hardships which the Chinese people had suffered. He reminisced on his experiences during the Long March of 1934, when the Chinese Red Army had covered six thousand miles on foot over some of the most formidable terrain in Asia. His fellow guests all took part and we passed an evening which was both an agreeable and a necessary exercise. When I twitted him with not having a representative in London, he expressed a willingness to send one. Mr. Chou En-lai is poised and firm in negotiation. He works for the fine point, even by the standards of his country. But I felt that patience might pay dividends.

I decided to persevere at our next meeting with my plan for what I called the 'protective pad'. Many countries had an interest in this and, if I could once get the conception established, the position might hold, perhaps for years. For ourselves and for the United States, there was advantage in this barrier of states which we could prop up with Western help. With time, they might grow to understand enough of the free way of life to wish to hold to it. It would be best if communism could be held at arm's length, clear of Cambodia and Laos, and halted as far north as possible in Vietnam.

I was less certain that the scheme would be welcome to the communist states, but even they had something to gain from an immediate arrangement of this kind. They had considerable territories to absorb. While the population of some areas might be in the majority communist, there were also racial problems of which the Chinese were well aware. The population of Indo-China had never affected the Chinese. Though this was no barrier to the spread of communism, it was a motive for not rushing things. Another argument was the possible American reaction, and the general consciousness of the peril of world conflict.

This was the first international meeting at which I was sharply conscious of the deterrent power of the hydrogen bomb. I was grateful for it. I do not believe that we should have got through the Geneva Conference and avoided a major war without it. Its effect was least on

United States policy. This was natural, since America could not at that time be reached by bombs from Soviet Russia, and the Chinese had none anyway. The Chinese came next. They probably count life cheaper than any other people on earth. To them, though the nuclear threat was grave, it was not decisive.

The same was not true either of Soviet Russia or of ourselves, for we were sharply conscious of what the spread of an Indo-China conflict must mean. Soviet Russia would have the grim choice of leaving her ally to her fate, and half the communist world to its destruction, or plunging herself into the abyss of nuclear conflict. We can argue as to which would have been her choice, had she been compelled to make it. It was certain that she would at least consider a compromise arrangement to avoid it. If we could bring about a situation where the communists believed that there was a balance of advantage to them in arranging a girdle of neutral states, we might have the ingredients of a settlement.

It was important that I should not overplay my hand about the dangers of world war. If I were to cry 'Wolf! Wolf!' too frequently and too loudly, I would suffer the fate of all alarmists in diplomacy and not be believed. I had to describe the situation sombrely and try to convince the communist nations of the sincerity of my convictions. In this I had an ally, India. That country also had a concern in limiting the onward rush of communist forces. Although Delhi might discount the danger, the protective pad could help. India did not wish to see Burma and Thailand passing under communist control. I had also to convince the actual protagonists in the fight. This was to prove a long and wearisome business.

★   ★   ★   ★   ★

It was now that the work of the conference did, in fact, begin to move forward. In the first place, we managed to by-pass, for the time being, the issue of separate treatment for Laos and Cambodia. Chou En-lai and the Vietminh delegate were persuaded, with some help from Molotov, to agree to the conclusion of separate armistice agreements for each of the three Associated States. We had no objection to the principles on which these agreements would be based forming the subject of a single negotiation. I made these notes of the discussions:

Thursday, May 27th.
    Called on Chou En-lai at 10.30. He was in a much easier mood

than in our earlier conversations. Think our talk about Laos and
Cambodia may have been useful. French and Americans at the
Reposoir at 11.30. Rather good meeting. French produced their
own text and were anxious to push this instead of the British one
on which we had been working. At the very end they said they
would accept either. I went to see Molotov, but failed to agree my
text with him. He wanted too many changes.

There followed a bad afternoon in restricted session. The net
result is at least three texts and much confusion. I suggested an
adjournment in which we might try to sort them out, but we
failed. The experts are to meet tomorrow, but nothing will come
of this.

Friday, May 28th.

As we expected, the experts' meeting brought no results. If anything they went backwards. Saw Krishna Menon in the morning
and found myself in broad agreement with him over what we
want.

Denis [Allen] came back to luncheon, and we discussed new
formula which is his brainwave, and might be acceptable to get
the staff talks started. Presided over a Korean session, and then
asked Bidault and Bedell Smith to meet me, when I showed them
our new formula. After some discussion, during which American
lawyer made every kind of difficulty, Bidault and Bedell Smith
both approved it. Both said they could take it, though neither
expected that the Russians would accept it. Only amendment they
would allow was addition of the word 'simultaneous' [the Russians
were likely to demand a single cease-fire for all three fronts].

Since Molotov was away at Berne, I went round to see him after
dinner. He thought new draft was a fair attempt at a compromise,
and that it might be acceptable. He asked for the word 'simultaneous' and for other changes which I could not give him. I
explained to him that no important amendment of the text was
possible. He said he would do his best.

This was the text of the United Kingdom proposal, which the conference accepted on May 29th:

> In order to facilitate the early and simultaneous cessation of
> hostilities it is proposed that:
> (a) Representatives of the two commands should meet

immediately in Geneva and contacts should also be established on the spot.

(b) They should study the dispositions of forces to be made upon the cessation of hostilities, beginning with the question of regrouping areas in Vietnam.

(c) They should report their findings and recommendations to the conference as soon as possible.

This was a significant but by no means spectacular advance. We had established a sub-conference of military commanders to work out an armistice agreement. We had created a new tool, but this did not of itself bring substantial agreement any nearer. Here is the note which I made for the day:

Saturday, May 29th.
Early telephone message from the Russians that Chinese would accept the text. Difficult morning, however. Harold Caccia saw Americans and French about it. Both accepted the text. Had trouble over the Thailand application [for a United Nations Commission]. Saw Krishna before lunch. Iranian Ambassador came to lunch, when we discussed oil. Molotov arrived at 2.30, when we discussed texts and plans.

Afternoon meeting became exceptionally troublesome. French started off with a reasonable speech, accepting my text. Vietminh then delivered their worst speech so far, most of which was entirely unconnected with our document. I feared the worst. However Molotov stepped in with a firm reminder that we were discussing my text, and an implied rebuke to Vietminh. There were some reservations by Cambodia, and acceptance by Chou En-lai. Finally a very far-reaching American reservation. It surprised me, since there had been no hint of it last night. Finally we adjourned to try to fix a date for the first meeting of the staff talks.

On resumption all this was agreed, except that right at the end Bedell Smith suddenly said he wanted to make his reservations public. This naturally started off a chain reaction, everybody saying they wanted to do the same, and Chou En-lai suggesting jovially that we might all hold press conferences. I said that it might be better in the circumstances not to publish my text, but simply to say that we had agreed to begin the staff talks between the two sides, announcing dates, and this was accepted. Back exhausted and not very pleased with what should have been a relatively happy day. Late news from Paris that French and Americans have agreed some plan apparently for intervention in Indo-China. Gladwyn [Jebb] imagined that I was aware of this, but I am not, so telephoned for information.

Bedell Smith's action indicated that Washington must once again be losing patience with our negotiations. He had given me no prior notice, which was unlike him, and so had presumably received new instructions. As I reported to London at the time, the Americans seemed deeply apprehensive of reaching any agreement, however innocuous, with the communists. Their delegation had recently been expressing concern about the contacts which they believed to be taking place between the French and Vietminh delegations, and seemed to fear that they would make a deal of their own. I saw no reason to worry about this. There were signs, too, that the bogey of intervention was once again with us. Sir Gladwyn Jebb reported from Paris on May 31st that the United States had practically reached agreement with France on the conditions for intervention, should the conference fail. Bidault confirmed to me on the same day that, if no agreement were to be reached at Geneva, American help was contemplated to the extent of three divisions. He added that he regarded this as distant thunder which might help the conference. I saw the force of this, and I could not complain of what might happen if the conference failed. At the same time, I had to make it clear to Bidault that the policy of Her Majesty's Government had not changed since our conversation at Orly airport, and that there could be no question of any commitment by us to participate in intervention. M. Bidault replied that he perfectly understood this.

The conference had now reached deadlock on the question of the composition of the international commission which was to supervise the armistice arrangements. This commission was to consist of a small number of neutral nations. Molotov and Chou En-lai were pressing for the inclusion of Poland and Czechoslovakia, in addition to India and one or two other Asian countries. We could not accept two communist states, and my own proposal was that the supervisory authority should be made up of the five Colombo powers, who were both Asian and neutral. This was rejected by the communists. During the first two weeks of June, session after session passed in mutual recrimination and endless argument over the question of whether or not a communist nation could be regarded as neutral. Moreover, although we had at last brought the two sides together to discuss the military aspects of an armistice in Vietnam, we were still no nearer to agreement on the problem of Laos and Cambodia.

I told a plenary session of the conference on June 10th that 'the United Kingdom delegation is ready to resolve these differences but, if the different positions remain as they are today, it will be the duty of the conference to admit to the world its failure.' French reluctance, American apprehension, Chinese suspicion and maybe ambition, were combining to bring the conference to a standstill. My own position was becoming increasingly embarrassing. As I pointed out to Bedell Smith and Bidault, I was continually producing proposals, because if I did not we stuck fast. On the other hand, we were constantly being criticized for doing so, particularly in the American press. I was conscious that time was not on our side. Since neither the Americans nor the French had established any contacts with the communist representatives, I had been compelled to adopt the rôle of intermediary between the Western powers and the communists. My activities in this respect were open to every kind of misrepresentation. I was concerned about their effect on Anglo-American relations. On the other hand, I was encouraged by the close accord maintained throughout the conference between ourselves and the other members of the Commonwealth, including those, like Mr. Nehru, who were not represented at Geneva. They sent me messages of thanks and encouragement. I needed them, for I began to feel that we should never make effective headway. I had never known a conference of this kind. The parties would not make direct contact and we were in constant danger of one or another backing out of the door.

In negotiations of this character, long periods of deadlock are worth enduring while there is any chance that informal talks can uncover fresh possibilities of agreement. On June 15th, the conference seemed nearer to breakdown than it had ever been. Bedell Smith showed me a telegram from President Eisenhower advising him to do everything in his power to bring the conference to an end as rapidly as possible, on the grounds that the communists were only spinning things out to suit their own military purposes. This implied that to keep hostilities going would help the French and their allies. I was sure that the reverse was the truth.

On that same evening Molotov asked to see me and produced some minor concessions on the issue of the supervisory commission, which at least indicated that he still had an interest in reaching agreement. Chou En-lai's visit on the following day to talk about Laos and Cambodia was more encouraging. He told me that he thought he could persuade the Vietminh to withdraw from these two countries, and that China would recognize their royal governments, provided that there were no American bases in the territory. I received a strong impression that he wanted a settlement and I accordingly urged Georges Bidault to have a talk with him and to discuss this new offer. I told Bidault of my conviction that there might be a chance of a settlement as the outcome of this talk, and begged him to go into it with the utmost seriousness and determination.

My hopes were justified. On June 17th, after Bidault's successful interview with Chou En-lai, Jean Chauvel was hard at work drafting a proposal which would set in motion two further sets of military staff talks, on Laos and Cambodia. If accepted, this would result in armistice talks being begun on all three fronts in Indo-China. M. Chauvel urged me to stay on in Geneva until these groups were constituted and had started their work. I agreed, and persuaded the Americans to do the same. However, Mr. Robertson, deputising for Mr. Bedell Smith at our restricted session on the 18th, at the last moment launched a violent and wholly unexpected attack on the Chinese proposals which the French were working on. This did not fit in with anything the Americans had told me, nor with Bedell Smith's description of the Chinese offer at an earlier session. I feared that this might wreck things. Fortunately, Cambodia and Laos were not perturbed and made friendly statements. The French redraft of the Chinese text was finally agreed to by the conference on the following day. That evening in a personal message to the Prime Ministers of India, Pakistan and Ceylon, I summarized the position we had reached as follows:

As you will see from the communiqué issued today and from the account of our meeting which will be reaching you in the normal way, the conference reached agreement this evening on a proposal enabling representatives of the two commands to begin military discussions on the questions relating to the cessation of hostilities in Laos and Cambodia. This agreement follows fairly closely the general lines of that reached three weeks ago in respect of Vietnam. Like that agreement, it will enable direct contact to be established between the two sides which we hope will be fruitful. As Mr.

Chou En-lai said in the course of a conversation I had with him this morning, it should be easier to reach agreement on the arrangements for supervision once the terms of a military settlement have been worked out for each of the three States.

You will have gathered from the information we have made available that there has been a perceptible relaxation on the question of the withdrawal of Vietminh battalions from Laos and Cambodia. This, coupled with an accommodating attitude on the part of the French, Laotian and Cambodian delegations, has helped to bring about the present agreement.

I shall be leaving Geneva tomorrow, as will also Mr. Bedell Smith and Mr. Molotov. I understand that Mr. Chou En-lai will also be leaving shortly. Meanwhile, as stated in the communiqué, the work of the conference will continue and the military representatives have been asked to report to it within twenty-one days. When these reports are received we shall all be able to consider the position that has been reached and decide whether it seems desirable for the Ministers to return. The understanding is that if the work of the committees is sufficiently advanced, the Heads of Delegations will come back.

On my way home to London on June 20th, I stopped in Paris to have luncheon with the new Prime Minister of France, M. Mendès France, who had been voted into power by a large majority two days earlier. In his investiture speech to the Assembly, Mendès France had courageously undertaken to achieve a settlement in Indo-China by July 20th. He told me that in view of the difficulties presented by the American and Vietnamese attitudes, he was not optimistic about his chances of fulfilling this pledge. I gave him my own assessment of the situation at Geneva in the same terms which I later used to my colleagues in London. I urged Mendès France to have an early meeting with Chou En-lai, and also, if he felt able to do so, with the representative of the Vietminh. He agreed to do this. M. Mendès France had an intensive driving power and a ruthlessness which was necessary for the straits we were in. He was the man for the short lap.

* * * * *

On arrival in London, I told my colleagues of the limited success which we had so far achieved at Geneva. We had won one of our main points, which was to establish that Laos and Cambodia must be treated differently from Vietnam. We had also enabled armistice talks to begin in each of the three Associated States. I told them that we were still very far from the end of the road. The Chinese might even have difficulty in restraining the Vietminh, who were in a position to demand a high price. Ho Chi Minh might seek to strengthen his position by launching a major onslaught on Hanoi while the conference was still in session. I thought that I should warn against this and in my report to the House of Commons on June 23rd, I concluded with these words:

> Final agreement at Geneva will not depend upon us and our allies and associates alone. It should be clear to all that the hopes of agreement would be jeopardized if active military operations in Indo-China were to be intensified while negotiations for an armistice are proceeding at Geneva. If this reminder is needed, I hope that it may be heeded. If it is, then I think there is a chance —I do not put it higher than that—there is a chance that, with continued patience, these long and difficult negotiations will produce an acceptable result. Any agreement reached must, of course, do more than simply bring the fighting to an end, urgent though that is. It must pay regard to the wishes of the peoples of Indo-China and to the legitimate rights of France. Such an agreement, if we can get it, will provide a basis upon which to build the security of South-East Asia. But it will do much more than that; it will greatly strengthen peace throughout the world.

Sir Winston Churchill and I flew to Washington on the 24th. Our main purpose, as I saw it, was to persuade the United States Government at least to give the French a chance of reaching a settlement at Geneva within the next few weeks. This implied that there must not be, before the conference was over, any publicized meeting to plan and proclaim an anti-communist alliance in South-East Asia. We should make it plain once more that we could not commit ourselves to any form of 'united action' in the area, before the results of Geneva were known.

My first conversation with Dulles at the State Department was encouraging. He now accepted that nothing short of intervention with ground forces could restore the situation in Indo-China, and also seemed ready to countenance the partition of Vietnam, but he stressed that partition would only be effective if the French could be persuaded to abandon their stranglehold on the Vietnamese economy. Otherwise, the non-communist regime would be vulnerable to subversion from within. I accepted the force of this. Dulles asked me what was behind my idea of a dual system of guarantees. I then explained my plan.

I told him that my ideas had arisen partly out of the discussions at Geneva. If an acceptable settlement could be reached, there had been talk of guaranteeing it. I favoured this, but I added that a guarantee to be implemented only by collective action would be unacceptable. No one would then act unless all acted. This was the communist idea and it amounted to giving them a veto on action. Some other system of the Locarno type would be much better, so that, if the settlement were broken, guarantors could act without waiting for unanimity. In addition to this, I thought that there should be a collective defence agreement, which would be limited to those powers willing to undertake specific commitments for military action, in the event of renewed communist aggression. I told Dulles that the United Kingdom was willing to examine the possibilities of this latter arrangement at once. I also tried to impress upon him the importance of United States participation in guaranteeing an Indo-China settlement. He replied that there was little chance of this. It would be difficult, he said, to persuade Congress to guarantee, in effect, the communist domination of North Vietnam. We agreed, however, that it would be useful to inform M. Mendès France, before he entered into final negotiations, of the minimum terms which the United States and the United Kingdom would feel able to accept. A committee of State Department and Foreign Office officials at once set to work to prepare a draft of these. A study group was also set up which prepared the way for S.E.A.T.O.

During a further conversation with Mr. Dulles on June 29th, we agreed on the text of a joint communication to the French Government, stating the willingness of the United States and the United Kingdom to respect an armistice agreement on Indo-China which:

1. Preserves the integrity and independence of Laos and Cambodia and assures the withdrawal of Vietminh forces therefrom.

2. Preserves at least the southern half of Vietnam, and if possible an enclave in the delta; in this connection we would be unwilling to see the line of division of responsibility drawn further south than a line running generally west from Dong Hoi.

3. Does not impose on Laos, Cambodia, or retained Vietnam any restrictions materially impairing their capacity to maintain stable non-communist regimes; and especially restrictions impairing their right to maintain adequate forces for internal security, to import arms and to employ foreign advisers.

4. Does not contain political provisions which would risk loss of the retained area to communist control.

5. Does not exclude the possibility of the ultimate reunification of Vietnam by peaceful means.

6. Provides for the peaceful and humane transfer, under international supervision, of those people desiring to be moved from one zone to another of Vietnam; and

7. Provides effective machinery for international supervision of the agreement.

My use of the word 'Locarno' to describe a possible type of defensive arrangement in South-East Asia had raised a storm of outraged protest in the United States. In many American minds, Locarno was associated with appeasement and the 'bad old days'. This was a confusion. Locarno had nothing to do with Munich in either time or temper. The thought behind the Locarno Pact, that of a reciprocal defensive arrangement in which each member gives guarantees, was a good one and might well be applied to our problems in South-East Asia. I had to persuade the Americans that Locarno was not a dirty word. After our talks, I was satisfied that the American Administration not only understood what it meant, but seemed to like the idea.

★　　★　　★　　★　　★

Before leaving England, the Prime Minister and I had read a report from Washington of a meeting between Mr. Dulles and some leading American journalists. According to an account which our Embassy thought reliable, the Secretary of State had declared his conviction that American policy in the Middle East, as well as in Asia, had been badly handicapped by a tendency to support British and French 'colonial' views. He was reported to have spoken of his determination to talk bluntly about the Middle East, and of his aim to 'shift policies'. Sir Winston and I heard nothing of these misgivings during our talks in Washington. Perhaps they were overshadowed by events in Guatemala, which suddenly became prominent in the world's headlines, after previous rumblings.

Since 1952, the left-wing regime of President Arbenz of Guatemala had fallen increasingly under communist influence. Relations with the United States had steadily deteriorated and the United Fruit Company became the focus of anti-American feeling in the country. Guatemala was weak in arms, and the United States Government watched and worried over President Arbenz's attempt to build up his arsenal. In their view, the situation in Guatemala was a threat to the security of other central American republics, and above all to the Panama Canal, seven hundred miles away. We had also an interest in Guatemala's intentions, because of the Guatemalan claim to the neighbouring territories of British Honduras. They had threatened to take the colony by force in 1948, and since then had sponsored a violent propaganda campaign designed to incite the people of British Honduras to revolution. Like the United States, we had therefore placed an embargo on the delivery of arms to Guatemala.

In May 1954, American anxiety was sharpened by the arrival in Guatemala of the Swedish freighter S.S. *Alfhem*, with a cargo which was said to include two thousand tons of arms from behind the Iron Curtain. Sir Roger Makins, our Ambassador in Washington, was told by Mr. Dulles that the United States Navy had been ordered to establish what amounted to a blockade of the Guatemalan coast. Any suspicious vessels were to be searched for arms, with the permission of the Governments concerned if there was time to obtain it, and Mr. Dulles asked for our co-operation. He said that, whatever the law might be and the formal view we might take, he hoped that we would in practice agree to whatever action was necessary in order to prevent further arms reaching Guatemala.

I thought this a strange way of phrasing a request from one democratic Government to another, but it was clear that American concern was genuine and deeply felt. It seemed to me that their fears of a communist 'build-up' in Guatemala were probably exaggerated, and our reports were that the supplies were mainly, if not entirely, small arms. All the same, I considered that, within legal limits, we should do all we could to assist our American ally. I instructed our Ambassador to inform the United States Government that we would do our best to help, though we were not convinced that these Guatemalan purchases were in fact as dangerous as they appeared to believe. The chance of arms being exported direct from the United Kingdom to Guatemala was remote; our arms embargo had been in operation for several years and the control was efficient. We would certainly do what we could to discourage and prevent British shipowners or agents or merchants from having anything to do with this sort of trade to Guatemala.

On the other hand, we could not possibly acquiesce in forcible action against British ships on the high seas. The rule of law still obtained in this country, and it was of great importance to us as a maritime nation that it should also obtain on the high seas.

Despite this representation, Mr. Dulles still did not exclude the possibility of the United States Navy taking action against a British ship without our permission. I therefore again emphasized the deplorable consequences that any such step would have for Anglo-American relations, and asked Sir Roger Makins to seek an assurance that nothing of the sort would be done. Mr. Dulles felt unable to give this assurance. The Americans, he said, would do their utmost to avoid an incident; but if they were faced with a situation in which a consignment of arms was going to Guatemala in a British ship, and they were in the last resort faced with the unpleasant alternative of letting the consignment through or stopping the ship, he could not give an assurance that they would not stop the ship. He went on to remark that in the cold war conditions of today, the rules applicable in the past no longer seemed to him to meet the situation and required to be revised or flexibly applied.

This was worrying. Anglo-American solidarity was of overriding importance to us and to the West as a whole. I believed that even if we did not entirely see eye to eye with the United States Government in their treatment of the Guatemalan situation, we had an obligation as their principal ally to go as far as we could to help them. At the same time, I certainly could not accept the principle which seemed to under-lie the American request for a right of search. I decided to do what I could to help matters by a public statement, and on June 18th authorized the following:

> Her Majesty's Government strongly disapprove of the sale of arms to Guatemala, and for several years have been refusing licences for the export of any arms to that country. They will, of course, continue this refusal.
>
> In fact, very few British ships sail to Guatemalan ports, but the British Government will co-operate to the fullest extent possible under British and international law in seeking to prevent British ships from carrying arms to Guatemala.

There is no general power of search on the high seas in peace-time. The British Government, however, have certain powers under Defence Regulations and otherwise to detain or requisition in certain circumstances. The Commander-in-Chief, West Indies, is being instructed to take appropriate action where practicable if the carriage of arms by British ships should be suspected.

This was accepted as reasonable on both sides of the Atlantic, and we were over our first obstacle.

While Sir Winston and I were on the high seas on our way to the United States, fighting began in Guatemala. On June 17th the country was invaded from Honduras by about two hundred volunteers under Colonel Castillo Armas, an exiled Guatemalan officer. Though Honduras kept protesting innocence, the arms and the incursion by land and air originated from there. It was a modest affair, but as the Guatemalan Government had no aircraft, the one or two operated by the insurgents seemed formidable. American sympathies were openly with Colonel Armas. But even if the invasion was encouraged from without, the Government's failure to rally the people to their standard was an indictment of their rule.

As soon as the invasion took place, Guatemala appealed to the United Nations, and declared that she was the victim of external aggression by Honduras and Nicaragua. The aim of the United States Government was to keep the question out of the United Nations and to refer it to the Organization of American States. There, as the Caracas Conference of March that year had shown, Guatemala was likely to be in a minority. When the matter came up on the Security Council, Brazil and Colombia duly proposed that the Organization of American States should deal with the matter. This was vetoed by the Soviet Union. The position of the United Kingdom and France was therefore capital, and the United States wanted us to support their action.

The crucial vote, on whether to adopt an agenda which included the Guatemalan appeal, was due to take place in the Security Council on the day of our arrival in Washington, June 25th. Mr. Dulles raised the matter with me as we drove from the airport to the White House. I hurriedly informed myself of the business and, after consultation with the Prime Minister, I met Mr. Dulles at the State Department to discuss the situation. I said that the solution I would prefer was that the agenda should be adopted, the Council should be immediately informed of the decision by the Organization of American States to send observers

and then, after any speeches, the Council should be adjourned by a procedural vote which would not be subject to veto. Mr. Dulles replied
that he was opposed to the inscription of the item on the agenda. If
this happened we should be in danger of losing control of the proceedings, since any member of the Council might propose a resolution
without warning, as the French representative had done on a previous
occasion. I then said that in these circumstances I was prepared to instruct the United Kingdom representative as follows:

After Mr. Lodge had objected to the inscription of the item on the
agenda and the debate had started, Sir Pierson Dixon* would indicate
that he could not vote against a complaint of this sort being received
on the agenda, but that in the circumstances he would abstain, since a
strong regional organization existed which could deal with such a
matter, and was already taking action. Sir Pierson Dixon would have
to make it clear that the Security Council was not disinteresting itself
in the matter, and also that the Organization of American States would
report to the Security Council the result of their efforts.

Mr. Dulles said that this procedure would be agreeable to him. In
his view the Guatemalan Government were violating the provisions
of the Charter because they had not made an attempt to settle the dispute first through the regional organization, of which they were
members and which was prepared to take action. He quite agreed that
any state was able to bring a dispute to the attention of the Security
Council, and this had been done in this case. He also agreed that the
jurisdiction of the Security Council could not be ousted. But there was
a question of interpretation and a question of judgment involved. In his
view, since the regional organization was able and willing to deal with
the dispute, they should be allowed to do so, and the Security Council
should wait to see whether their action was successful. I said that I
would instruct Sir Pierson Dixon as proposed, and Mr. Dulles said he
would telephone Mr. Cabot Lodge.

The outcome of all this was that on that same evening the adoption
of the agenda which included the Guatemalan complaint was rejected
by 5 votes to 4, both the United Kingdom and France abstaining.
The effect of the Anglo-French abstentions was equivalent to a vote
against, since the seven votes required to place an item on the agenda
were not, as a result, forthcoming. A few days later, the Organization
of American States sent a fact-finding commission to Guatemala, but
in the meantime President Arbenz's regime had been overthrown by

* Permanent Representative of the United Kingdom at the United Nations.

Colonel Armas. A mutual aid pact was signed between the new Guatemalan Government and the United States.

Though there was no need to shed tears over the fall of a Government with communist leanings, whose record was cruel, I was not entirely happy about these proceedings, nor was opinion at home. Yet our motives were clear enough. Her Majesty's Government agreed to co-operate with the United States Government, or at least not to oppose them, taking the view that first priority must be given to the solidarity of the Anglo-American alliance. If allies are to act in concert only when their views are identical, alliances have no meaning.

      ★   ★   ★   ★   ★

The Prime Minister and I then paid a short and very agreeable visit to Canada, before returning to England by sea. The Canadian Government had been consistently helpful throughout the Indo-China negotiations, and I was glad to be able to thank them personally for their co-operation. Later they were to give us further help by accepting to serve on the supervisory commission.

I returned to Geneva for the last phase of the conference on July 12th. The atmosphere was taut. Only eight days remained of the month which M. Mendès France had allowed himself for the conclusion of an agreement. Whatever happened, it was clearly going to be what Wellington called 'a damned nice run thing'. The auguries were not encouraging. During the absence of the principal delegates, the meetings between the military representatives of the high commands had made little progress. The Vietminh were being intransigent. The problems of the composition and functions of the supervisory commission still remained, and we could expect prolonged haggling over the demarcation line in Vietnam. I held conversations with Mr. Molotov and Mr. Chou En-lai in turn, immediately after my arrival. As a result of these, I reckoned that we had an even chance of agreement, provided that we could persuade the Americans to join us in a final all-out diplomatic effort. With this thought in mind, I flew to Paris the next day for discussions with M. Mendès France and with Mr. Dulles, who had just arrived from America.

M. Mendès France's main purpose in these conversations, which he pursued with drive and skill, was to dispel Mr. Dulles' suspicion that there would inevitably be some departure by France from the seven points on which we had agreed in Washington. He described to us his negotiations with the Vietminh on the question of the demarcation line in Vietnam, and effectively demonstrated that at no point had his position diverged from the minimum terms which had been defined by the Americans and ourselves. He said that it would be of the greatest help to him if Mr. Dulles would come on to Geneva and give France full backing there; success or failure might depend on this. I did all I could to support Mendès France and to reinforce his request. I told Dulles that we were on a knife-edge, with an even chance of getting the sort of agreement we all wanted. His decision might well decide the issue.

Our combined arguments at first produced no impression. Mr. Dulles told us that after discussion with the President, it had been agreed that he should not return to Geneva. He reiterated his fears that, in the event, France would be compelled to depart from the seven points, and the United States would then have to dissociate herself from the resulting agreement. He said that even if the settlement adhered to the seven points faithfully, the United States still could not guarantee it. American public opinion would never tolerate 'the guaranteeing of the subjection of millions of Vietnamese to communist rule'. Dulles concluded by saying that he did not want to put himself in the position of having to say 'no' in public. To this Mendès France replied that the United States would not escape the dilemma by refusing to appear at Geneva. Since they were already represented at the conference, they would have to make a decision in any case. He repeatedly emphasized that Dulles' suspicions about a departure from the 'seven points' were wholly unjustified; it was precisely because he wished to secure them that he was anxious for Dulles to come to Geneva. In the end, Mr. Dulles told us that he would give us his final answer on the following day. M. Mendès France's courage and persistence were rewarded.

On the following morning Mr. Dulles and I first met together and had some discussion on the kind of documents which might be exchanged, based on drafts which he had prepared of a joint 'position paper'. It was decided that this should be reduced to one document setting out the attitudes of the United States and French Governments, and that I should express in a separate letter my general agreement. A conference followed at the Quai d'Orsay, where Mr. Dulles announced that Mr. Bedell Smith would be returning to Geneva in the very near future to share in the work of the conference. The documents were put into shape, signed and exchanged after luncheon at the American Embassy. At that meeting the scene was one of friendly confusion, papers and luncheons and ladies all over the place. However, this all disentangled itself in time and Mendès France and I got away for a reasonable flight to Geneva. I was grateful for the reception I received in Paris from the crowds who were coming and going for the *Quatorze Juillet* celebrations. They were extremely friendly, and many of them called out '*merci !*'

The first few days after my return to Geneva from Paris passed in a flurry of meetings between the various Heads of Delegations, often as many as five in one day. The military sub-committees and delegation staffs had been working feverishly and an immense number of draft agreements had accumulated, both military and political. We had to agree and shape these into a comprehensive settlement. In the military talks, the French and Laotians had already achieved one significant success. The two bases which France was entitled by treaty to maintain in Laos were to be excepted from the general withdrawal of foreign troops from Laotian territory. M. Mendès France and I had repeatedly urged this point in our talks with Chou En-lai, and he and the Vietminh now accepted it. This meant that the invading Vietminh would be withdrawn from the northern provinces, while, with French help, the Laotians should be able to build up effective forces to deal with any recurrence of trouble. This was the best I had hoped to get, but there were still major differences to overcome. On the question of the demarcation line, Mendès France held fast to the 18th parallel, while the Vietminh moved from the 13th to the 16th and stuck there. The communists insisted that elections should be held in Vietnam during 1955 at the latest, whereas the French maintained, I thought rightly, that it would take at least two years for the country to be restored to a condition in which elections would be possible.

We still had to reach agreement on the composition of the supervisory commission. I had a crucial meeting with Chou En-lai when he came to see me on July 17th. He placed a sinister interpretation on the tripartite talks in Paris a few days before, and argued that we were going to split South-East Asia in two with an anti-communist alliance. He was particularly insistent that the three Associated States must be independent, sovereign and neutral. I could reassure him on some of this. I said that there was nothing new about the proposed defensive agreement in South-East Asia, which I had myself been advocating for years. It would merely form a counterpart to the Soviet-Chinese alliance, and I added that so far as I knew there was no intention that the Associated States should be members. The greater success there was at the conference, I said, the less need was there to fear that such a pact would split South-East Asia. Chou En-lai replied, with characteristic subtlety, that the smaller the apparent danger of South-East Asia being split, the better the conference was likely to succeed.

I was still so uncertain of the outcome that I thought it prudent to prepare for the possibility that the conference might fail, even at this late stage. If this happened, the countries of the Commonwealth and of South and South-East Asia, together with the United States and France, would, I hoped, make an immediate declaration of their intention to work together to ensure their common defence. It was true that we should need a defensive organization for South-East Asia and the South-West Pacific, whether agreement was reached at Geneva or not. But if the conference failed, the need would be immediate. Accordingly, I sent a message to Australia, New Zealand and the five Colombo powers, warning them of the alternatives. If we reached a settlement, I asked them to associate themselves with it in some form as soon as possible. In particular, if the Asian powers would act promptly in this way, the settlement would have its best chance of useful life. If we did not agree at the conference, I hoped they would join us in collective defence.

The first indication that the conference might at last be on the verge of success came on the afternoon of July 18th, when Chou En-lai proposed to me that the supervisory commission should consist of India, Canada and Poland. After all the argument, this was a definite step towards us and the proposal was accepted by all three Western powers. From that moment the tangled ends of the negotiations began to sort themselves out. On the afternoon of the 20th, after frantic activity at all levels, M. Mendès France and the Vietminh delegate were able to announce that they had reached agreement on a demarcation line, which was to be a river just south of the 17th parallel. M. Mendès France had also persuaded the Vietminh to agree that elections should not be held until July 1956. By nine o'clock that evening, the armistice agreements for both Vietnam and Laos were almost complete. The Cambodians skilfully held out till last, when we were exhausted. Molotov and I, as joint chairmen, together with Mendès France, held a long meeting with them and the Vietminh. It was a gruelling session. At two o'clock on the morning of the 21st, after hard bargaining and some surprising last-minute concessions by Molotov, we succeeded in resolving the remaining differences between them. As we were concluding our meeting, news arrived that the armistice agreements for Laos and Vietnam had been signed by military representatives of the two commands. The Cambodian agreement followed shortly after noon. The pattern of the final settlement was now complete.

I had already been warned by Bedell Smith that the United States Government could not associate themselves with the final declaration. The most they could do was to issue a declaration taking note of what had been decided and undertaking not to disturb the settlement. Since Dulles had been at least as responsible as ourselves for calling the Geneva Conference, this did not seem to me reasonable. I also feared that it might lead to serious difficulties at our final meeting, for the Chinese had indicated that they would insist upon signature of the final declaration by all the delegations. I thought that I had better have this out with Molotov before the meeting. I went to see him and we eventually agreed that, in order to eliminate the problem of signature, the declaration should have a heading in which all the participating countries would be listed.

At 3 p.m. on July 21st, I took the chair at the final plenary session of the conference. After the various declarations had been read, I made my closing statement as chairman. I said that we had now come to the end of our work, which for a number of reasons had been both prolonged and intricate. The result was not completely satisfactory, but we had stopped an eight-year war and reduced international tension at a point of instant danger to world peace. This achievement was well worth while. All now depended on the spirit in which the agreements were carried out.

★ ★ ★ ★ ★

The origins of the Indo-China conflict were confused, arising from the uncertain conditions which followed the war and Japanese conquest. A large part of the world regarded it as a colonial war and the communist leaders skilfully exploited this situation to pose as liberators from colonialism. There was never a national determination against Vietminh in Indo-China comparable to that in Malaya which enabled the jungle war to be won. There was no clear-cut breach of a treaty or international engagement which had to be respected in the world's interest, as there was later when the Suez Canal was seized in defiance of engagements recently renewed, the greatest international waterway passing under the control of one state. In these conditions a massive intervention in the conflict by France's allies could not have been justified, a limited one would have only made matters worse. The terms finally agreed still seem to me about the best bargain France and the Associated States could have made.

I had shared the anxieties of the Cambodians and Laotians, now relieved but wary. The Vietnamese had saved more of their country than had at one time seemed possible. I said good-bye to Mendès France who, as I had telegraphed to the Prime Minister, 'had fought his corner brilliantly', and to the two communist leaders, who had been doughty opponents. I drove down on my last journey to Geneva airport with Bedell Smith, a splendid friend throughout. As I flew home, I was naturally relieved that my faith in the negotiations had to some extent been justified and that we had managed to stop the fighting on acceptable terms, though I knew that the problems of Indo-China were by no means over. I hoped that France would be able to overcome the agonizing memories of recent calamities, and would use her unrivalled experience of the country to help the Vietnamese to acquire equal status among the free nations of South-East Asia. Laos and Cambodia, I believed, had the will to live, and Vietnam the means. In the months ahead the United States would be playing a greater part in all their destinies. I hoped that she would do so in such a way that her generous assistance would not be resented. My own country would still have its share of responsibility in assisting these events, and in ensuring the future security of a troubled region. That security is still under menace, as has been shown by the ruthless occupation of Tibet by Chinese military power. Tibet in 1959 is the Albania of Good Friday, 1939.

★   ★   ★   ★   ★

We had now to organize collective defence in South-East Asia. The study group we had set up in Washington to prepare the scheme for our decision worked hard, and on July 17th submitted its recommendations to the United States Government and ourselves. Mr. Robert Scott, our Minister in Washington and one of the ablest members of our Foreign Service, represented us in the group. As a result of his explanations, the Americans accepted our wish first to approach the Governments of the five Colombo powers. Accordingly, on July 30th I sent a message to the Prime Ministers of India, Pakistan, Ceylon, Burma and Indonesia asking for their consideration of our proposal to convene a meeting in September to discuss possible measures of collective defence for South-East Asia and the South-West Pacific. It was subsequently decided to hold this meeting at Manila. I told them:

Your participation would do much to determine the nature and policies of the projected organization. I have always hoped to see the Asian powers play a leading rôle in the defence of South-East Asia. The area is of such importance and its peace is as yet so insecure, that we feel it vital to safeguard its peaceful development and ensure its stability.

Even if you feel that you must stand aside, therefore, I am sure you will understand why we, for our part, shall feel it right to go ahead with such countries as are willing to join with us. Though we should still do our best to take account of your views, our task would be far more difficult without your participation, at least in some form.

In the meantime, there was encouraging news from Colombo. On behalf of the five Colombo powers, Sir John Kotelawala, Prime Minister of Ceylon, issued a declaration on August 3rd concerning the Geneva settlement. In it, the Governments of these countries expressed their 'deep satisfaction' at the agreements which had been reached, and extended to them 'their firm support'. I thought this was valuable. It would give the settlement a better chance to survive.

The later response from the Colombo powers to my suggestion that they might participate, if only as observers, in the coming Manila Conference, was much as we had expected. Pakistan agreed to attend. Ceylon, Burma and Indonesia followed India's lead, and informed us that they could not accept our invitation, on the grounds that to do so would be to depart from their Governments' declared policy of neutrality and 'non-alignment'.

Despite this reservation, it was clear that our policy of bringing the Asian powers into the picture at an early stage had been fruitful. Even if we had not enlisted their positive support for S.E.A.T.O., at least they understood what we were about, and had no ill feelings towards our action. Malcolm MacDonald reported at this time from his observation post as our Commissioner-General in South-East Asia that nothing in United Kingdom policy had been more admirable than the close contact, throughout the Geneva and subsequent negotiations, with the Colombo powers. It had made a most friendly impression in Asia, given many Asian leaders a clear understanding of our motives and aims, increased our influence throughout Asia, and prevented a much worse division of opinion than existed between the West and Asia.

The defeat of E.D.C. in the French Assembly at the end of August compelled me to devote all my time to European affairs, and as a result I was unable to attend the conference which assembled at Manila on September 6th. Lord Reading most ably represented the United Kingdom in these discussions, which were completed by the signing of the South-East Asia Collective Defence Treaty and the Pacific Charter on September 8th.

Having missed Manila, I was particularly glad to be able to attend the first S.E.A.T.O. Council meeting at Bangkok, in February 1955. I had been anxious to call in at the capitals of some of the countries which had helped me during the Geneva Conference, and this gave me my chance. I was also able to spend a few days in Malaya to see for myself how our campaign there was making headway. Our three days of talks at Bangkok were devoted to setting up the permanent structure of the South-East Asia Treaty Organization. We divided it into three areas of activity; defence against aggression, protection from subversion, and the development of economic, social and cultural welfare. I expected that the third sphere would prove to be the most important.

I have pleasant memories of that conference. In the tropical heat, the greatest charm of the building in which we met was that it was open to the heavens; when the discussion became torpid, the flitting birds provided a pleasant diversion. Co-operation between the delegates was easy as well as effective, and I thought the results substantial.

VII

ROUND-UP
August – October 1954

France rejects E.D.C. – A talk with Dr. Adenauer – The Brussels Treaty – Germany and N.A.T.O. – My tour of the capitals – Brussels – Bonn – Rome – An embarrassing intervention – Paris – Views of M. Mendès France – Talks with Mr. Dulles – Preparation for a London Conference – The British offer – The Saar – Ratification of Paris Agreements

During the summer of 1954, it became obvious that a decision on E.D.C. could not be postponed much longer. The plan, for all its merits, was becoming something of an entangling impediment. While it existed no German military contribution was possible, because the Bonn Conventions for restoring German sovereignty were tied to it.

When Sir Winston Churchill and I visited Washington in June, the E.D.C. treaty had been ratified by all its members save Italy and France. Italian ratification was expected within a few weeks. The outcome in France was still uncertain, and a parliamentary majority for E.D.C. was as elusive as ever. Pinay, Mayer and Laniel had each failed to find enough support in the Chamber and had put off the decisive day. I hoped that success at Geneva might strengthen Mendès France sufficiently to enable him to carry through ratification before the summer recess. But there were some fierce opponents and more half-hearted advocates of E.D.C. in his Government. Socialist and M.R.P. supporters of the scheme would not join him.

In these conditions, the Prime Minister and I agreed with the Americans that we must take preliminary steps to free the Bonn Conventions from dependence on the fate of E.D.C. Dr. Adenauer's position in Germany was being weakened by the continued failure of his policy to show results. The fact that it was not his fault made no difference. We considered that the Federal Republic must be free to form the alliances of her choice, and to do so her sovereignty must be restored to her. The Russians would continue to do what they could to tempt Germany away from the West and we must not furnish pretexts for them.

At the end of July, the French Ambassador in London, M. Massigli, informed me that Mendès France was convinced that there was no majority in the Assembly for E.D.C. as it stood. Therefore he proposed to discuss with the other E.D.C. powers certain amendments to the treaty. These were to be introduced into the text after its ratification by France. If the other five countries would accept his suggested changes, he would then invite the Assembly to ratify the treaty, on the understanding that they would be incorporated afterwards.

Early in August, my wife and I left for a brief holiday in southern Austria, where we had taken an old castle near the Wörthesee from some English friends. While we relaxed and bathed, international difficulties continued to mount. I was not surprised when, on the evening of August 18th, a messenger from France arrived, breasting the battlements with a letter from Mendès France. In this he told me of his intention to meet his fellow E.D.C. representatives in Brussels on the following day. He did not underestimate the difficulties which faced him, or the exasperation caused by previous French delays. He added that the first reactions to his proposals from the countries concerned gave him no grounds for optimism, although he would do all he could. Whatever the outcome of the Brussels Conference, he thought it important that France and the United Kingdom should reach early agreement on questions affecting the cohesion of Europe. He told me that Sir Winston Churchill had accepted his suggestion that he should fly straight from Brussels to England for a meeting, and had invited him to Chartwell. I telegraphed to the Prime Minister:

> If agreement is not reached at Brussels, Chartwell meeting may assume more formidable proportions and take longer. I have asked the Foreign Office to keep me posted of Brussels progress, and if required I can always fly back by R.A.F. plane from here. Meanwhile I will await events.

The Brussels talks ended in failure, as they were almost bound to do. The French amendments extended the right of secession from the treaty and discriminated openly against Germany. The five powers went as far as they could to meet the French position, but the gulf could not be bridged and France was left in a minority of one. It is not reasonable to blame the other E.D.C. powers for refusing to emasculate a treaty in which they believed, but without a united majority at home there was little more that Mendès France could do, even if he would. I decided to fly home.

On August 23rd, I sent the following account of the Chartwell meeting in a personal message to Mr. Dulles:

At our meeting with Mendès France today, the Prime Minister and I impressed upon him with all the force at our command the grave dangers which France and the whole Western world would incur if the French Assembly refused to ratify the E.D.C. treaty. The Brussels Conference had shown that France was isolated from her European partners and she would be altogether isolated if the French Chamber continued to refuse a decision on the German defence contribution. We urged Mendès France strongly to put all his authority behind the E.D.C. treaty, with the Spaak interpretations, as much the best solution for France. He said that he would put the issue to the vote next week, but he was quite definite that it would be rejected and that his Cabinet would not agree to make the vote a question of confidence. He agreed, however, that the attempt must be made, although the strength of his advocacy is uncertain.

We urged Mendès France to make it clear to the Assembly that, if they rejected E.D.C., some other solution of the German problem must be found, with or without France, without delay. He did not dissent, and was ready to consider German entry into N.A.T.O., with or without some smaller grouping within N.A.T.O. He said he was ready as a first step to give Germany her political sovereignty without any delay and to announce this in the debate. A simple solution to the problem of German rearmament must then be found within two months.

We warned him of the difficulties of finding and bringing into force any such solution which Germany and everyone else concerned could accept in so short a time. We concluded on the note that he must try to persuade France to accept the E.D.C. as much the best way out, but that if this were impossible the Germans must receive their political equality immediately and be included within some acceptable defence framework, preferably N.A.T.O., shortly thereafter. We impressed upon him, in particular, that we intended to work in close agreement with the United States Government, and that we had a debt of honour to Adenauer and those European countries who had ratified E.D.C.

Mendès France argued strongly against a meeting of the United States, the United Kingdom, Germany and Benelux. Though we did not tell Mendès France so, we also see difficulties about such a meeting and think that the other countries concerned must be expected to do so. In any event, nothing of the kind can take place until after the French vote next week. We are giving urgent thought to some alternative procedure which would meet your objective, and I will telegraph to you again very soon.

A week later, after two days of bitter and emotional debate in which M. Mendès France was more referee than advocate, the French Assembly passed the crucial motion to 'move to other business' by 319 votes to 264, with 43 abstentions. E.D.C. was dead. So long as there had been the faintest hope that it could be saved, I had not been willing to hold any formal discussion of possible alternatives, for to do so would have strengthened the hand of the opponents of E.D.C. in France. I had also been against exercising pressure upon France, for I was convinced that this would drive hesitant moderates to join the opponents of German rearmament in any form. On the day before the vote, the United States Government suggested that we should hold an eight-power conference excluding France. One of the objects of this meeting was to emphasize French isolation. I thought this a bad plan, for, whether we considered French action right or wrong, we needed France, and I saw no cause to stand her like a naughty girl in the corner. The idea was dropped.

All the same, the problem was urgent, and we should have to move fast if Western European unity was to be saved. Some months earlier I had asked my skilled advisers at the Foreign Office to work on this problem, and at the end of August I considered their findings. There was no easy way through. One alternative was a diluted E.D.C., within the framework of N.A.T.O., to which the United Kingdom would belong. The French could be expected to like this, but there was not much in it for other E.D.C. powers. The dilution would make the mixture rather thin for them. I preferred to bring Germany into N.A.T.O., under the various safeguards which had been devised for her entry into E.D.C. This solution would be likely to run into trouble in France, although Mendès France had optimistically told us at Chartwell that the French Assembly would find it hard to take a second entirely negative decision. We would have to devise safeguards which were effective but not blatant, otherwise we should lose German opinion. The Germans could not be offered less now than in 1951, when E.D.C. was first conceived. Despite these complications, I thought that the entry of Germany into N.A.T.O. must be faced. My colleagues authorized me to discuss this with the German Chancellor and with the Americans.

*   *   *   *   *

Dr. Adenauer's response to our approaches further increased my respect for his qualities of statesmanship. He believed in the unity of Europe, and the defeat of E.D.C. destroyed a plan which he had made his own. He had waited long for it, but when Sir Frederick Hoyer Millar, our High Commissioner in Germany, went to see him on September 2nd to get a reaction to our ideas, the Chancellor's attitude was reasonable and sympathetic. He agreed with us that German membership of N.A.T.O. was better than a diluted E.D.C. He was ready to accept safeguards, as long as these did not discriminate against Germany. The German Government, he told us, would be prepared voluntarily to undertake to limit its armed forces. I thought that this offer would help to make a N.A.T.O. solution more acceptable to the French.

Satisfied that Bonn would contribute something, I now had to consider how to steer events towards the N.A.T.O. solution. I decided to plan for a nine-power conference in London, to which we would invite the six E.D.C. powers, the United States and Canada. I proposed to assemble this within the next two weeks, and that it should reach agreement on the problem of bringing Germany into Western defence. We would then lay its decisions before a full meeting of the N.A.T.O. Council later in the autumn. First replies from the Governments invited were favourable, although Mr. Dulles expressed doubts as to whether the necessary diplomatic preparations for such a conference could be completed in time to give it a chance of success. He was anxious, he said, to avoid any repetition of the disharmony of the Brussels meeting in August. I was aware of this risk, but I strongly believed that the dangers of delay outweighed it.

I went for the week-end of September 5th to our Wiltshire cottage, and while there an idea came to me that it might do some good if I made a tour of the six European capitals before our conference. At least this would show willing, and we might get rid of some vexing problems that way. But even if I made this journey, I had not enough to propose on behalf of Her Majesty's Government to make sure of success. A diplomatic traveller must have a full quiver. I wanted some new ingredient. In the bath on Sunday morning, it suddenly occurred to me that I might use the Brussels Treaty to do the job. At the Foreign Office a few days before, there had happened to be some discussion of the treaty in another context, and I expect that this put the idea into my head.

The Brussels Treaty, signed in 1946, had been directed principally against a revival of German aggression. If we could bring Germany and Italy into it and make the whole arrangement mutual, we should have a new political framework for Europe, without discrimination. The Brussels Treaty could be transformed into a mutual defence pact, of the Locarno type, which would cover all Western Europe. There would be other advantages. The supranational features of E.D.C. would go, and the United Kingdom could then be a full member, sharing from within instead of buttressing from without. The Brussels Treaty lasted longer than N.A.T.O., for fifty years as against twenty. In its new form, it could provide a focus for those in all countries, including Western Germany, who cherished the vision of a united Europe. Finally, I had been troubled by the conviction that if Germany came into N.A.T.O. we should be asked to increase our military contribution on the continent. This would not be popular at home, but it would be more acceptable if it were made within the context of a revived Western Union.

On my return to London, I sent this minute to the Prime Minister:

We may now expect Adenauer's reply on Tuesday. On the assumption that it is not entirely out of line with our ideas of Germany in N.A.T.O. on certain conditions offered or shared, we should, I think, consider whether we can do anything further to prepare for the eight or nine-power conference.

My own feeling is that it would be helpful if I could take a rapid tour of the European capitals concerned, in advance of the conference, in the following order:

Brussels (for the three Benelux powers)

Bonn
Rome
Paris.

There are, of course, always certain risks in such a venture, but the advantages seem to me to outweigh them. The journey would enable me to establish contact in each of the capitals with men whom I know, and I would hope to get some impressions which would be of value to us before and at the conference. Furthermore, by travelling in this order and visiting Paris last, I should have a formidable body of opinion behind me, supposing we are all agreed upon the general line for handling this problem, i.e. that Germany must be brought along into the N.A.T.O. family as proposed.

Paris would no doubt be the most difficult capital, but I might be able to dispel some of the illusions there, which could be helpful in advance of the meeting.

I do not ask for a final decision on this until we have had Adenauer's reply on Tuesday. But I am asking the Foreign Office to prepare the necessary telegrams and time-table so that the messages can be despatched on Tuesday. I hope you will agree.

The Prime Minister did agree. I also discussed the transformation of the Brussels Treaty with him and one or two principal colleagues, and they liked the idea.

When we received Dr. Adenauer's final reply on September 7th, it appeared that, although the Chancellor was in full agreement with our general aim, he shared Mr. Dulles' fear that an immediate nine-power conference might fail for lack of preparation. He was inclined to favour a plenary meeting of the N.A.T.O. Council, preceded by personal discussions. He thought, however, that it would be entirely appropriate for the United Kingdom to take the initiative and to act as a kind of 'honest broker' in exploring the ground on behalf of N.A.T.O. as a whole. This accorded well with my own ideas. On September 8th I received a warm message of encouragement from M. Mendès France, welcoming my proposed tour. Others followed in the same sense.

Before I left for the first stop of my journey, Brussels, the French Ambassador gave me some indications of his Government's latest views, which were not entirely discouraging. He began by saying that the admission of Germany into N.A.T.O., with nothing but some conditions which Germany might offer, would have no chance in the French Chamber. I pulled a long face at this, whereupon M. Massigli said: 'Wait, there is more.' The French Government, he continued, had further considered whether there was any way in which the situation might be eased, particularly from the political angle. Their preliminary conclusion was that the Brussels Treaty might be the best instrument for this purpose. The treaty might be reshaped to include Germany and Italy, and some military arrangements might be made under it, which could conceivably include a European commander-in-chief. I replied that while I was prepared to consider any proposals, I was not enamoured of the idea of building any kind of military structure under the Brussels Treaty. I was firmly convinced that the admission of Germany into N.A.T.O. was the right way to handle the military aspect. This conversation showed me that although my visit to Paris would certainly be my toughest assignment, there was at least some common ground which might lead to agreement with the French. Much would depend upon the extent of the support which I could muster in other capitals.

★   ★   ★   ★   ★

I took with me only one senior Foreign Office adviser, Sir Frank Roberts, whose information was infallible and whose energy was inexhaustible. I kept some notes of the journey every evening, on which to base my telegrams and reports home. That night I wrote:

Saturday, September 11th.
   Woke up at seven, finished my box and wrote to W [Sir Winston] and Harold [Macmillan].
·   C came to see me off. Also all six Ambassadors; quite a party. Good flight. Spaak met me. Drove to Embassy, and after wash and brush-up, to Spaak's for luncheon. An excellent meal—note *jambon des Ardennes*. After luncheon Spaak, Beyen, Bech and I with two advisers apiece retired to Spaak's study, and talked there for three and a half hours. It went very well. They were delighted with the idea of a modified Brussels pact to include Germany and Italy. There was much comment on political situations in Germany and France, on Adenauer and MF. They all rate the former highly while maintaining their fears of the Germans. They are all at least suspicious of the latter. There is also pessimism as to whether France would accept anything like the proposals I had in mind.

Spaak was the saddest at the loss of E.D.C. and I felt very sorry for him. After these talks I went back with Bech to Embassy and for a short walk with him in the Park. This was pleasant. He was less critical of MF than Beyen. They all dislike MF's entourage, and think their counsel *néfaste*.

Dinner at Embassy which was well done. It is a beautiful house with some lovely 18th century fittings, decoration and panelling. My room was charming.

After dinner more talk and *mise au point* of what we had agreed.

The Benelux Ministers approved the procedure I had suggested. They thought that a nine-power conference was an essential preliminary to a full N.A.T.O. meeting, and hoped both would take place in London. They authorized me to put our general ideas to the German Chancellor with their full support. Before going to bed, I telegraphed to London:

> I found all three Benelux Ministers fully aware of the realities of the international situation and, in particular, of the dangers of Germany slipping over to the Russians, and of America retreating to the peripheral defence of 'fortress America', on which I had spoken to them. They are anxious that I should do my best to bring these dangers home to Paris, where they were, in their opinion, discounted.
>
> I think today's talks provided a very hopeful basis for our further and more difficult meetings. There is unanimity between us and the Benelux countries in our assessment of the situation and in our plans for dealing with it.

Not for the first time I had found excellent encouragement from our Benelux allies. These countries are firm and understanding friends, wisely led and ably represented.

From Brussels I flew to Bonn, where the Chancellor was my host at luncheon. I told him that the Benelux powers were anxious to find some constructive way out of the present difficulties. They had been disturbed and hurt by the experience of the Brussels Conference in August. The Chancellor agreed that those events had been unfortunate and we discussed the present French temper. Dr. Adenauer shared my fears that the French might not realize the dangers inherent in the 'agonizing reappraisal' of American policy, of which Mr. Dulles had warned us several months before. Maybe they thought that the Americans were bluffing; if so, they might be wrong. We agreed that if I was able to make the French understand the risks they were running, and if we could produce some thoughts which would assist M. Mendès France, then I might succeed in Paris.

I used this opening to put forward my proposal about the Brussels Treaty. The Chancellor was deeply interested, particularly in its possibilities for creating a focus for European policies. He told me that it was still true that the youth of Germany believed in the European idea. They must be given justification for that faith, or they might turn to 'bad thoughts'. I replied that this was one of the motives which had led me to put forward this idea. The Chancellor said that an important feature of the Brussels Treaty was Britain's participation. He attached the greatest importance to this. In fact, as things were, he did not want to be left alone with France. We then adjourned for an hour so that Dr. Adenauer could consider my proposal.

When we resumed our talks, the Chancellor began with a long and critical summary of German historical events from 1848 to 1939. He used this to explain, without excusing, the German failure to build up a firm a democratic structure. It was, he said, the task of the Federal Government to do so. Fortunately, Nazi ideas had, for all practical purposes, disappeared. Germany was, however, placed geographically between the East and the West and the division of the country encouraged honest as well as dishonest Germans to look east. The European idea, which had a great appeal to German youth, remained the only certain way to confirm German association with the West and to strengthen German democracy. Our joint European problems should be considered against this background, since the consequences for Europe as well as for Germany would be disastrous if Germany fell within the Soviet orbit, either directly or gradually via neutralization.

The Chancellor said he would not waste any words on the meeting with Mendès France or the French decision. It was no use now trying to revive E.D.C., or something like it, although such a community might be possible later on. The entry of Germany into N.A.T.O. was the right solution. In so far as this meant a German national army he was prepared to accept self-imposed limitations and would also be prepared to put this army into an integrated army, if this became possible later. The German goal remained an European organization, and Germany was as anxious as France that the United Kingdom should be associated with it. Referring to safeguards, the Chancellor said that one of his main reasons for preferring the N.A.T.O. solution at this stage was that S.H.A.P.E. could ensure that all the N.A.T.O. countries did as much as they should, but that no one did more. He attached the greatest importance to maintaining the United Kingdom's undertaking of automatic assistance to the E.D.C. and vice versa, which was not part of the N.A.T.O. treaty. Finally, he said that he now thought that our purposes could best be realized through my plan for German entry into N.A.T.O. on the one hand, and the expansion of the Brussels Treaty to include Germany and Italy, on the other.

I thanked the Chancellor for his picture of the German scene and said I thought there were two problems before us: first, a closer German political association with the West; and secondly, the German defence contribution. Her Majesty's Government thought the first even more important than the second. The Brussels Treaty proposal would, I believed, help to solve our difficulties about joining any supranational organization. It would also meet two conditions to which the Chancellor had attached importance; automatic assurances of assistance, and continuing political consultation. I thought the position of Italy was also most important and I hoped that our proposal would help the Italian Government in their internal difficulties.

Dr. Adenauer added that the more he thought over our plans, the happier he was. He expected that the French would agree, since the important points for most Frenchmen were that the British should participate on a footing of equality with them, and that France should not be left alone with Germany. He also thought that Mendès France would personally welcome our plan as the only way out of his parliamentary difficulties; it would enable him to turn to the economic problems which primarily interested him. The Chancellor declared that he now favoured the proposed London conference of the nine powers, and considered that it should be held as soon as possible after I had completed my European tour.

A further short talk with Dr. Adenauer before I left for Rome on the following day ended a most satisfactory visit. I suggested that if all went well with my talks in Rome and Paris, we ought to aim at having the conference in London a few days after my return there. Adenauer agreed. Subsequently, in conversation with German officials, the dates of September 22nd or 23rd were mentioned. Adenauer, in accepting this, commented 'the sooner the better'. The Chancellor, who saw me off at the airport and presented me with an old print of the Rhineland, had been forthcoming and helpful throughout. Our personal relations were, and remained, excellent. I telegraphed the news of our progress to the Foreign Ministers of the Benelux countries. I added that, although Dr. Adenauer had been surprisingly optimistic about the French accepting our suggestion, I still felt, with them, that Paris would prove very difficult.

★　★　★　★　★

Arriving in Rome that evening, tired from my journey, I was refreshed by a quiet and enjoyable dinner with our Ambassador, Sir Ashley Clarke, and his charming wife. The British Embassy had formerly been the German one. Its rooms are large and gloomy and for me had baleful memories of the Gestapo; but the grounds are extensive and agreeable and include a swimming pool. My first talk on the following morning with the Italian Foreign Minister, Signor Piccioni, sustained my hopes for our plan. He told me that the Italian Government welcomed the initiative which I had taken in making this tour. They were conscious that the consolidation of Europe and a military contribution by Germany were both urgent tasks and that an alternative to E.D.C. must be found without delay. I said that Her Majesty's Government attached much importance to the contribution which Italy could make. The object of my journey was to see whether Europe could do something for itself. I told Signor Piccioni of our proposal for German entry into N.A.T.O. and for an expansion of the Brussels Treaty. I added that it had been warmly welcomed by the Benelux powers and by Dr. Adenauer, who were all agreed that there should be a meeting in London as soon as possible, if the idea found favour with the Italians and the French. The remodelling of the Brussels Treaty without the inclusion of Italy would not be satisfactory for Anglo-Italian relations.

Signor Piccioni replied that he accepted these ideas unreservedly as a basis for discussion. The more the United Kingdom engaged itself in assisting a solution, the easier it would be to find one. The best way to prevent a new isolationism in America was to compose the Franco-German quarrel. The consolidation of Europe with the association of the United Kingdom, he went on, would weaken neutralist tendencies in Italy, which unfortunately had a pro-Russian complexion. Signor Piccioni then referred to the Coal and Steel Community, the O.E.E.C. and the Council of Europe. He thought these should all be strengthened and wondered if a connection could be established between them and the new treaty. I agreed that this could be considered, and mentioned the provision for regular consultation and the economic clauses which were already in the Brussels Treaty.

We then discussed possible French reactions to my plan. Signor Piccioni asked me whether, if the French rejected it, we would be prepared to go ahead. I told him that the mood of the Benelux Governments was to do so and leave the French to come along later, and that this seemed to be Dr. Adenauer's thought also. The French could not be allowed to frustrate our plans indefinitely and I would certainly tell them this. Unfortunately the issues had never been explained to the French people by their public men. The French had probably convinced themselves that American talk of reappraisal was bluff. This was dangerous, for in fact the geographical position of France might become less important as new methods of warfare developed. Signor Piccioni agreed with this and said that the Italian Government would use their influence in the sense we wished.

When I discussed the situation later in the day with the Italian Prime Minister, Signor Scelba, he confirmed that his Government would do everything they could to help with the French. I spent two hours with the Prime Minister, a great part of our discussion being devoted to Trieste, usefully as I thought. My note for that day concluded:

> Late for dinner. Excellent meal. Everybody relaxed and friendly, Italian Cabinet nearly all there. Liked Saragat.

The entry for the following day is longer. September 15th began with a shock from Washington:

> Pleasant swim in the pool with Ashley at 7.30 and discussion of the present situation over breakfast in the sunshine. The Italians have helped us greatly, but Trieste troubles me. We must get that settled.
>
> Just before starting for the airport, secretary from the U.S. Embassy arrived with message from Dulles, asking for immediate reply. He proposes to fly today (U.S. time) to Bonn and on Friday morning to London. Can I receive him Friday? His reasons for visiting Bonn seem to be singularly unconvincing. There is also a long rigmarole of criticism of Brussels Treaty because it is not supranational. I was inclined to try to dissuade him from visiting Bonn without Paris, but Ashley and Frank [Roberts] were against this, so I contented myself with short reply that I would be glad to see him in London, and a reply to his criticism.

I thought that Dulles' intervention was unhappily timed. I was on the verge of the most delicate phase of my negotiations and I had kept the Americans fully informed at each stage of my journey. My chances of success in Paris would depend largely upon preserving the pattern of unanimity which had been built up during my talks in Brussels, Bonn and Rome. Dulles made it clear in his message to me that he was critical of the plan for expanding the Brussels Treaty, and that he would regard any solution which did not provide for the creation of a supranational institution as 'makeshift'. In view of this, I was apprehensive of the consequences of Dulles' sudden visit to Adenauer, which had been decided on without prior consultation with London or with me. My conversations up to this point had confirmed my opinion that this was not the moment to try for another supranational solution. Any attempt to persuade the E.D.C. powers to hold out for it would only result in continued failure to agree, with consequent dangers to Western unity.

There was no time to argue all this, as I was leaving for the airport. I was still uncertain as to the real purpose of the Secretary of State's journey, and it was evident from our Ambassador's report that Bonn was also perplexed. On the other hand, it was some comfort that Mr. Dulles appeared to accept a meeting in London as I had been urging. I replied:

> I received your message just as I was on the point of leaving Rome. I shall be glad to see you in London on whatever day would suit you. The dates September 27th and 28th which you suggest for the preliminary nine-power conference should, I think, prove possible.
>
> We too had hoped that E.D.C. would be passed. But every country now agrees that as things are, there is no present possibility of reviving the supranational idea. We must encourage other forms of European unity.

I hoped that Dulles' talks with the German Chancellor, which were already arousing a great deal of speculation in the German newspapers, would convince him that the United Kingdom plan offered the best chance of a realistic solution.

My notes for the day continue:

> Flew off to Paris. Reasonable flight, bumpy at end. Met by

Mendès France and a disordered horde of journalists and photographers when we arrived about 3.30.

To Embassy for talk with Gladwyn [Jebb] and Tony [Nutting]. Some rather fierce talk about what we should offer the French in addition. I was against anything at this stage and was rather unpleasant about it, goaded by my fatigue and Tony's assurance that the Chiefs of Staff were willing.

Meeting with MF tough and unsuccessful. Had half an hour in advance alone, when he complained about Foster. He showed signs of wishing to continue to talk alone of result of my tour, but I showed I would rather give account myself in conference. However, MF showed no willingness to agree to Germany in N.A.T.O., and after an hour of this I said I would go home to think matters over.

In interval before dinner saw U.S. Chargé, told him what MF had said, and suggested Foster make an effort to come here. Returned to Hôtel Matignon before dinner. Still no progress. Dinner therefore in rather a gloomy atmosphere.

Afterwards more argument in which the only daylight was that French were willing to operate any military aspects of Brussels Pact through N.A.T.O. Did all I could to impress upon MF the real dangers of the situation. French negative policy would result in driving Germany into arms of Russia and U.S. into 'fortress America'. He accepted all this, but he has some fellow-travelling advisers.

Broke up after midnight without having made much headway, except that I hope to make Mendès France understand that everyone else wanted Germany in N.A.T.O. as soon as possible, and he was likely to find himself alone.

My discussions with M. Mendès France had been involved and long. He agreed that the Brussels Treaty would be a good point of departure, but he was worried about the safeguards and controls which could be devised to allay French fears of German rearmament. I told him that it was clear that these safeguards could not now be so tight as those which had resulted from E.D.C., and that they would have to give the appearance of being non-discriminatory. I thought that they should be organized through a strengthening of the N.A.T.O. machinery. The other powers agreed, Mendès France did not. He wanted the safeguards to be made part and parcel of the Brussels Treaty by the addition of military clauses. The question of German entry into

N.A.T.O., he said, should only be considered after these safeguards had been established.

This seemed to me to be all wrong. I told Mendès France that Germany would not be likely to consider entering the Brussels Treaty or giving voluntary safeguards if she were only to be admitted to N.A.T.O. after a probationary period. This was a fence which we must jump. The treaty could not simply be a cage for the Germans. The French proposal would mean that there would be two organizations with conflicting tasks, the Brussels Pact to control and limit armaments and their use, N.A.T.O. to organize the maximum effort for the defence of Europe. I said that if safeguards had to be worked out and accepted, as a precondition to the discussion of German entry into N.A.T.O., all hope of bringing Germany into the Western European system would have to be abandoned. With this our argument ended.

On the following morning I addressed a meeting of the permanent N.A.T.O. Council. Somewhat unexpectedly, the French Prime Minister arrived to take the chair. My notes for the day continued:

MF asked to speak to me in the Palais de Chaillot alone afterwards. We sat on the sofa by the window and he told me that he had spent a nearly sleepless night and that he had concluded that the arguments I had put to him about German entry into N.A.T.O. were decisive. He accepted them and the fact that Germany must come in. But then I must help him. We must make the utmost that we could of the Brussels Treaty. We must put as many as possible of the assurances into it and so forth, otherwise he would have no chance of getting his majority. He was quite ready to take on an even chance or worse, but not to go into action when his chance was zero. I told him that he knew that I would help all I could, but that all I had told him last night was true. Unhappily the 'Chamber' had never been told it. He admitted this and we agreed to meet after luncheon.

This is the first break in the clouds and I was cheered accordingly.

At a later meeting that day, Mendès France and I had some further discussion of safeguards. I suggested that it would be fair to say that France accepted that Germany should enter N.A.T.O. at the same time as the Brussels Treaty was expanded. France wanted to start off by putting all or most of the controls and safeguards into the Brussels

Treaty, and the rest into N.A.T.O. Others preferred to approach the problem from the opposite point of view. We were willing to consider the French thesis sympathetically and to do our best to induce the others to do likewise. Her Majesty's Government could not, however, be expected to endorse and recommend it against their better judgment. This statement of the position was later drafted more fully and accepted on both sides.

★　★　★　★　★

I returned to London well content with our progress so far. At least the way was now open for the nine-power conference in London at the end of September, with a fair chance of success, provided that the American attitude could be softened. I reported in these terms to my colleagues immediately after my return, and they fully approved the outline of the settlement which was now taking shape.

I then drove out to London Airport to meet Mr. Dulles who, on arrival, introduced a most generous passage into his comments to the press. He spoke of the 'brilliant and statesmanlike British initiative'. Our conversation in the car was not so cheerful, as a note which I wrote at the time shows:

> Cabinet at H. of C. at 10.30. Saw W [Sir Winston] for a moment beforehand and showed him text of what MF had agreed to. Nothing of note until my departure to meet Dulles. On our drive back D spoke gloomily of outlook, complained that Brussels pact had no supranational features. That this was what had interested U.S. Told me Hoover's appointment had delighted Senate because they assumed he shared his father's views (though he added that he didn't entirely). Alleged that Democratic senators were now as much in favour of reducing overseas commitments as Republicans, etc. He also professed to believe that Adenauer was worried about Brussels because it had no supranational features. I retorted that he had not said so to me and that if Europe wanted to build something supranational later no doubt they could, on this basis or another. We certainly would not discourage them. But after the vote in the French Chamber the time was clearly not ripe. I also told him of regret in France that he was not going there on this visit. He said he would probably send Livy Merchant★. I said that would be most helpful.

★ Mr. Livingstone Merchant, then a senior official at the State Department and always helpful to Western understanding.

At our formal meeting that afternoon, I explained to Mr. Dulles that I had undertaken my tour of the European capitals because of the urgency of finding a solution to fill the gap left by the collapse of E.D.C. The ideas I had outlined were:

(a) German entry into N.A.T.O. with safeguards over German rearmament of a non-discriminatory character, and the concentration of all military arrangements within the N.A.T.O. framework;

(b) The expansion of the Brussels Treaty for use as a political instrument to keep alive the idea of European unity.

In Brussels, Bonn and Rome I had found a hundred per cent. agreement with these ideas. In Paris, the discussions had been more difficult. I then explained the position of M. Mendès France. I concluded by asking Mr. Dulles whether he agreed that a nine-power conference could now profitably be held and whether he thought that there was anything further we could do to prepare for it.

Mr. Dulles prefaced his remarks by saying that his earlier description of the United Kingdom initiative as brilliant and statesmanlike had not been empty words. But he must emphasize the difficulties with which he was faced through the collapse of E.D.C. The idea of a United States of Europe had great appeal in his country and this had been reflected in Congressional resolutions and legislation. The rejection of E.D.C. had come as a great shock and would be used by opponents of foreign aid and by the isolationists. The American Chiefs of Staff were still engaged on their strategic reappraisal and had not yet reached their conclusions. The tendency was reflected by the withdrawal of American land forces from the area of Korea and Japan and unwillingness to build up land power in South-East Asia. The presence of American troops in Germany was an exception and it was doubtful how long that exception could be maintained in face of Congressional pressure. It was really immaterial whether a N.A.T.O. plus Brussels solution was better or worse than E.D.C. Congress had been 'sold' on the latter as the means of uniting Europe, which would then be capable of standing on its own feet without American help. In the new conditions, the future for foreign appropriations was highly doubtful and, though he and the President were determined to salvage as much as possible, we must assume that continued American participation in Europe, on the present scale and in the present form, was impossible and that some reduction was inevitable. He added that the assurances given in the President's declaration of April had only secured Congressional approval with the greatest difficulty in the context of E.D.C. We certainly should not rely upon them being repeated for the plan now under consideration.

I remarked that this was a grave and worrying statement, because continued American support was crucial. I hoped, therefore, that American opinion could be brought to realize that our present plan for German entry into N.A.T.O. and the Brussels Treaty provided the best means of strengthening the West.

Mr. Dulles acknowledged that he saw no better alternative, but repeated that American policy was under reappraisal, that he could not prejudge the outcome and accordingly would not be in a position to make any commitments on behalf of the United States at a conference later this month or indeed, very likely, until after the elections in November. He subsequently qualified this by saying that the United States Government could agree to the restoration of German sovereignty and the admission of Germany to N.A.T.O., but could not accept any new commitments about the American forces in Germany. He would of course do his best.

We ended by discussing Mr. Dulles' criticisms of the Brussels Treaty plan. He emphasized the importance of keeping alive the idea of real integration in Europe. Dr. Adenauer had expressed qualms that it might be difficult to make further progress in that direction through the Brussels Treaty organization, because of British membership, and he, Mr. Dulles, hoped that some means could be devised which would enable the others to go ahead if they so desired, without the United Kingdom, in fields extending further than Brussels. I told him that the United Kingdom would certainly not stand in the way of any integration desired by her fellow members of the pact. Mr. Dulles finally said that he would attend the conference in London on September 28th; I at once despatched invitations to the nine Governments concerned.

I knew that even if Mr. Dulles threw the full weight of American support behind our plan, the conference would not easily reach agreement. Mendès France was in search of a majority. He understood that France could not be the odd man out in Europe a second time. Therefore he would want to make sure. This meant that he was likely to come to the conference asking for more, and I thought we should be wise to have something in reserve. This could best take the form of a practical move on our part, to show our friends in Europe that we were in earnest. I accordingly prepared the following note of the position that would confront us at the conference and sent it to the Prime Minister:

> The problem will be to reconcile:
> (i) the German desire for rapid restoration of sovereignty and membership of the North Atlantic Treaty Organization (N.A.T.O.);
> (ii) French reluctance to admit either, until elaborate safeguards have been agreed, notably a complicated and probably unworkable system for the control of armament manufacture on the Continent; and
> (iii) American reluctance or inability to repeat the undertakings they gave in connection with the European Defence Community (E.D.C.) about maintaining American military strength in Europe.
> M. Mendès France may press the conference to agree to this or that unnecessary or dangerous proposal, on the grounds that without it he will not get a favourable vote from the French Assembly. We cannot allow our discussions to be conducted on this basis. The task of the conference must be to produce a workable plan designed to meet legitimate French requirements, but not to attempt tortuous gymnastics in order to get a majority for M. Mendès France.
> If we produce a workable plan, the Americans are unlikely to allow it to fail through the lack of the essential American support. If, however, we are to do this it will be necessary for the French to face some unpleasant realities. They will have to accept German sovereignty and German membership of N.A.T.O., and withdraw or drastically reduce their safeguard proposals. If they are to do this, they must be given some striking *quid pro quo*. The assurance most likely to strike French opinion is the continued presence of British troops in France. The undertakings on this subject given in the context of the E.D.C. treaty are set out in an annex.
> In my opinion, the key to the success of the conference will be a new commitment by the United Kingdom to maintain our present forces on the continent, and not to withdraw them against the wishes of the majority of the enlarged Brussels Treaty powers. This would not give France a veto, but we should no longer be

able to withdraw our forces at our sole discretion, and would have to obtain the consent of the majority of the seven expanded Brussels Treaty partners, who should take their decision in knowledge of the Supreme Allied Commander, Europe's (SACEUR's) views. It would be necessary to provide for certain exceptions to the general rule: an overseas emergency so acute that there was no time to go through the process of consultation, or balance of payments difficulties which made it financially impossible for us to maintain the strength of our forces on the continent.

I realize that this would be an unprecedented commitment for the United Kingdom, but the hard fact is that it is impossible to organize an effective defence system in Western Europe, which in turn is essential for the security of the United Kingdom, without a major British contribution. This situation will persist for many years to come. By recognizing this fact and giving the new commitment, we may succeed in bringing in the Germans and the French together, and keeping the Americans in Europe. If we do not, the conference may fail and the Atlantic alliance fall to pieces.

I therefore propose that we should give a new British undertaking at an appropriate stage during the conference. It will be most important meantime to keep it secret. This undertaking would be:

(i) to maintain on the continent the effective strength of the British forces now assigned to SACEUR, i.e. our four divisions and the Tactical Air Force, or whatever SACEUR regards as equivalent fighting capacity; and

(ii) not to withdraw those forces against the wishes of a majority of the Brussels Treaty powers, who should take their decision in the knowledge of SACEUR's views.

This undertaking would be subject to the understanding that an acute overseas emergency might oblige us to short-circuit this procedure and that, if the maintenance of our forces on the continent of Europe throws at any time too heavy a strain on the external finances of the United Kingdom, it will be open to the United Kingdom to ask that the financial conditions on which the formations are maintained should be reviewed by the North Atlantic Council.

A.E.

September 27th, 1954.

I thought that Cabinet discussion of the position was unnecessary at
this juncture; it could come later at the appropriate moment, if any
of my colleagues so desired. I explained this in a manuscript message
to the Prime Minister in which I wrote:

> I do not expect that moment to be before the middle of the
> week; it might be later. But I cannot be sure and I would like
> to have my hands free.
> The last lines, dealing with finance, have been proposed by
> Treasury at the official level and seem to me well chosen.
> We have discussed these ideas in Cabinet before and I hope
> it will be possible to avoid summoning one. I don't want other
> parties at the conference to think we have some master solution.
> They have got to do some work themselves.   A.E.

The Prime Minister, I now think quite rightly, replied that this raised
some very grave points which should have formal Cabinet consideration and decision, and suggested that when I came nearer the moment
of action we should discuss the timing in relation to the whole decision.
This we did.

★　　★　　★　　★　　★

On the following day, Ministers from the six European powers, the
United States and Canada, assembled in London for the nine-power
conference. The opening sessions, and the private conversations which
I had with the delegates, convinced me that the British offer which I
had proposed would be needed, if the conference was to succeed. In
particular, Adenauer and Lester Pearson, the Canadian Secretary of
State for External Affairs, appealed to me for a lead in this direction.
Late that night, my colleagues met to consider our decisions.

Though I was only asking that we should continue our present
practice, the commitment was a grave one, on account of its duration.
It was not surprising, therefore, that some doubts were vigorously
expressed, despite which my colleagues gave me the authority for
which I asked. It was now necessary to make the best use of it. I decided
to take Mr. Dulles into my confidence and to set the stage as best we
could between us. As host Foreign Secretary, I was in the chair throughout the conference and I arranged with Mr. Dulles that, at a given
moment, he would make his statement recommending in this new
context the renewal of the American pledge to E.D.C. I would then

follow up with Her Majesty's Government's offer. All this worked out well.

Mr. Dulles said:

> If, out of the elements of the situation with which we are dealing, if by using the Brussels Treaty as a nucleus, it is possible to find in this new pattern a continuing hope of unity among the countries of Europe that are represented here, and if the hopes that were tied into the European Defence Community treaty can reasonably be transferred into the arrangements which will be the outgrowth of this meeting, then I would certainly be disposed to recommend to the President that he should renew a pledge comparable to that which was offered in connection with the European Defence Community treaty. . . . In reason, you can count on us.

Having thanked Mr. Dulles for his statement, I said that I was conscious that my own country had a part to play. I then gave the assurance which Her Majesty's Government had authorized, to maintain on the mainland of Europe four United Kingdom divisions and the Tactical Air Force for so long as the majority of the Brussels Treaty powers desired it:

> My colleagues will realize that what I have announced is for us a very formidable step to take. You all know that ours is above all an island story. We are still an island people in thought and tradition, whatever the modern facts of weapons and strategy may compel. And it has been not without considerable reflection that the Government which I represent here has decided that this statement could be made to you this afternoon. I want only to add this: we are making it in the same spirit as Mr. Dulles spoke just now, because we hope that by doing so we shall make a contribution to enable this conference to succeed, and re-create confidence on this European continent and make it possible for us to show an example of unity to the world.

The reaction was immediate. All understood the real meaning of what I had said. Britain would hold her military place in Europe, to keep the peace. It was not our numbers that mattered, but our presence. Here, in the context of the 'fifties, was the flag for which Foch had asked so many years before. It would fly in Europe now, to keep closed the conflicts of the century, and the cost would not be dear.

From this point on, the conference moved rapidly forward. Only M. Mendès France, with his sights set on retaining a majority in the French Assembly, was reluctant to match the concessions of the other delegates with some of his own. In this he was probably wise, for he had a fickle Chamber to deal with. In addition to the American and British declarations, other countries made contributions of great importance. The Benelux powers renounced the right to manufacture atomic, bacteriological or chemical weapons. The Germans renounced not only this, but also the right to manufacture guided missiles, large naval vessels and bombers. Mendès France, however, clung tenaciously to his plan for an arms pool to achieve the co-ordinated production and standardization of European armaments, under the aegis of the Brussels Treaty organization. The scheme had obvious attractions, but raised endless practical difficulties. In particular, the Americans would naturally be reluctant to channel all their supplies through the new Brussels Treaty structure. Under pressure, the French eventually agreed not to make acceptance of their plan a precondition of their agreement to the other proposals before the conference; instead, a working group was set up to consider it. On the question of safeguards and armaments control, the conference agreed to a modified version of the scheme which Mendès France had put to me in Paris. An agency for the control of armaments was to be set up as part of the Brussels machinery, which would ascertain by inspection that the agreed levels of armaments were not being exceeded.

My colleagues sent me many kindly messages at the conclusion of the conference. To these I replied, sending the following in particular to Mr. Dulles:

> Thank you so much for your message. I cannot tell you how much I have valued your unwavering support during this critical week. I believe, like you, that we have made an historic step forwards. Without you it would have been quite impossible. Warmest regards.

On October 20th I flew to Paris to take part in the final shaping and signature of the Paris Agreements which gave effect to the decisions of our conference and transformed them into formal instruments. The expanded Brussels Treaty organization was renamed Western European Union, and its headquarters were set up in London. The occupation regime in Germany was brought to an end as soon as the practical arrangements could be made. The German Federal Republic was invited to become a member of N.A.T.O., while Western European Union was accepted by the North Atlantic Council as part of the N.A.T.O. defence system. Finally, W.E.U. provided a framework for agreement on a most vexatious European problem, the Saar.

In 1947 the Saar was detached from occupied Germany and included in the French economic and monetary system. Its final status had to be decided when a peace treaty with Germany was eventually concluded. With the establishment of the German Federal Republic and the growth of the German 'economic miracle', the Saarlanders began to chafe under the economic bonds which tied them to France. In Germany, some were quick to seize upon the issue, comparing it to the loss of the east German territories. The French argued that the coal and steel production of the Saar was essential to them, if they were to maintain parity with Germany in the European Coal and Steel Community. This was true, but despite concessions from the French Government relaxing their economic control, the Saar again became the focus of bitterness in Franco-German relations. The success of the conference in London provided a stimulus for its settlement in direct negotiations between Dr. Adenauer and M. Mendès France.

I was only involved in this at second remove, the final negotiations taking place late one evening at the British Embassy in Paris, where I was staying. I left Dr. Adenauer and M. Mendès France closeted with their advisers in the beautiful library which Duff Cooper had given the Embassy. After they had been there some hours, I became troubled at the delay and asked that discreet inquiries should be made as to how they were getting on. I learnt that they had finished some time before and had tip-toed from the Embassy, thinking that we had already gone to bed. So ended, I hoped for good, disputes about a territory with which I had first been concerned twenty years before by advocating the despatch of British troops to supervise the voting in the Saar.*

It remained for the Paris Agreements to be ratified by all concerned. Our own vote in the House of Commons was overwhelming, 264 to 4, the official Opposition being divided on the issue and deciding to abstain. For the other countries, save France, the parliamentary position presented no problems. In Paris, the end was dramatic. At 5 a.m. on

* The sequel was less happy. Thanks to a vehement campaign by the formerly banned pro-German parties in the Saar, the Saarlanders rejected the European Statute in October 1955. After prolonged negotiation, in which France secured important economic concessions, the Saar was reunited with Germany at the end of the following year.

Christmas Eve the National Assembly rejected Article 1 of the bill authorizing ratification of the Paris Agreements by 280 votes to 258. This article governed the establishment of the Western European Union and the entry of Germany into N.A.T.O. Mendès France then put the question of confidence on the reversal of this decision. That vote was to be taken a few days later.

The defeat was a serious event and there were at once suggestions for vigorous allied declarations, preferably by the President and the Prime Minister, to make clear the consequences. I thought it essential to state our position firmly, but better not in such a way as to provoke French resentment, as a high-level pronouncement would do. Therefore, I prepared a Foreign Office statement, which we put out that evening:

> The Paris Treaties are still under discussion in the French Chamber, and there is to be a further vote on Monday. It is clear that what is at stake is the unity of the Western allies.
>
> The rejection of the Paris Agreements would not mean that German rearmament would not take place. The issue is not whether the German Federal Republic will rearm, but how.
>
> The United Kingdom commitment, offered at the London Conference, to maintain British forces on the continent of Europe, depends on the ratification of the Paris Agreements by all parties.

This warning made its contribution to the majority which M. Mendès France won. Deputies had been reluctant to believe that there could not be further concessions and yet another conference. Now the 'brutality', as some named it, of the British statement put the position beyond argument. Some brilliant speeches, notably by M. Mollet and M. Mendès France, came to the rescue and December 29th gave a favourable vote.

As we saw the New Year in with this good news, I felt we had reason to be satisfied with our work during the preceding months. Germany was now a sovereign partner in the defence of Europe, and the damage to European unity caused by the failure of E.D.C. had been mended. Russia's attempt to exploit the crisis had failed. We could now be sure that future negotiations with the Soviet Union could be conducted from a base of political and military strength.

I told four thousand Conservatives at our Party Conference in October how I justified our military share in the defence of Europe:

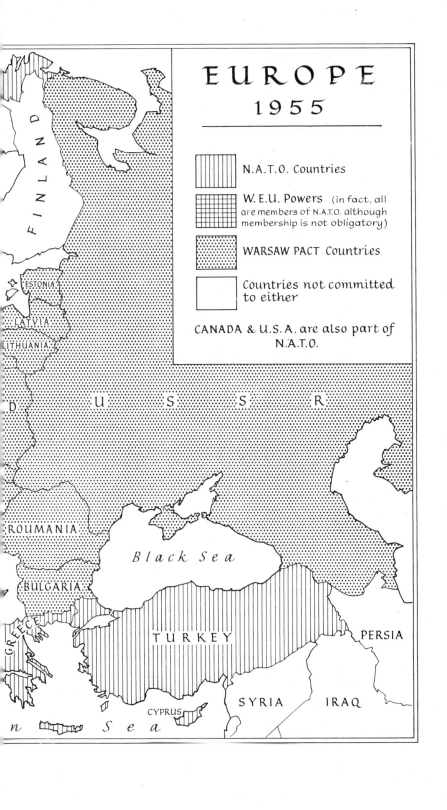

EUROPE
1955

N.A.T.O. Countries

W.E.U. Powers (in fact, all are members of N.A.T.O. although membership is not obligatory)

WARSAW PACT Countries

Countries not committed to either

CANADA & U.S.A. are also part of N.A.T.O.

FINLAND

ESTONIA

LATVIA

LITHUANIA

D

U   S   S   R

ROUMANIA

BULGARIA

GREECE

Black Sea

TURKEY

PERSIA

CYPRUS

SYRIA

IRAQ

n   S e a

It is not the first time even in our lives that British forces have been stationed on the continent of Europe. They have been there for the last ten years. Within our own memory they have fought two bloody wars on those battlefields. What is different about this pledge is that it is given to prevent a war and not to win a war.

★　★　★　★　★

The Paris Agreements have surpassed our hopes in some respects and fallen short of them in others. Franco-German relations are, at present, a happier chapter. Long may it so continue. It would be foolish in the extreme for our country to be other than gratified at closer understanding between Paris and Bonn. The failure to realize this earlier in the century has shadowed two generations. On the other hand, the United Kingdom's relations with France and Germany are not as close and cordial as they have been and should be. To perfect these should be the principal task of Western statesmanship.

When we had finished our task in Paris, I hoped that Western European Union would take its place as a leading authority in the new Europe. The responsibility for standardizing armaments, with which it is entrusted, is important though difficult to discharge. But I intended it to have also a wider scope. It has not worked out that way and of recent years little effort has been made to use the possibilities of W.E.U. In part this may be due to the fact that six countries have gone their own economic ways, though this should have made the political importance of the union all the greater. Certainly it would be of advantage to peace if the nations who are its members could meet regularly and informally, as its machinery allows, and concert their policies closely. Between them they command a wealth of wisdom and experience; it is a pity that it is not collectively at the disposal of the world.

VIII

ADRIATIC DIPLOMACY
September 1952 – October 1954

A talk with President Roosevelt – The history of Trieste – The Italian Peace Treaty – The tripartite declaration of 1948 – Tito breaks with Moscow – My visit to Tito in 1952 – An impression of Djilas – Tito returns the visit – Attitude of De Gasperi – Italian relations with Yugoslavia – Our reasons for action – The Anglo-American declaration of October 1953 – Diplomacy goes underground – Dr. Velebit and Signor Brosio – A successful solution

During 1942 I flew to the United States and spent a short but pleasurable visit at the White House. President Roosevelt was vividly interested in the post-war world and even at that date his mind was active with a variety of plans for the future, in peace as we hoped. I shall always remember the freshness and vigour of those conversations with that remarkable man. We spoke, amongst other things, of President Wilson's vision, of his contribution to the creation of the League of Nations and of the aftermath of his failure. We discussed his aims and methods, where ours might be the same and where they might differ. I remarked that I hoped we should not attempt to pursue one of Wilson's objectives a second time, for he had not given diplomacy its scope. I hoped we might reach open covenants secretly arrived at. The President laughed and agreed. In the post-war years, the method applied to the Trieste settlement corresponded most nearly to the description I had given the President.

Trieste presented us with a problem which was always vexing and sometimes volcanic. Like so many of Europe's trouble spots, its origins go back far into history. For about fifteen hundred years a race of Slavs has been settled on both sides of the Julian Alps, their presence creating

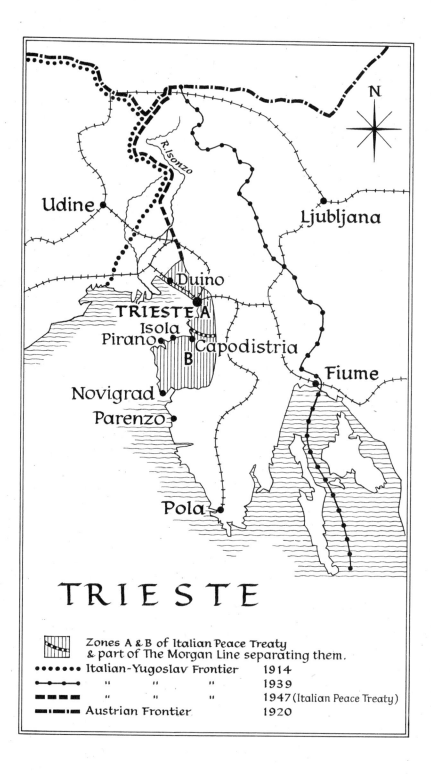

TRIESTE

Zones A & B of Italian Peace Treaty
& part of The Morgan Line separating them.
•••••••• Italian-Yugoslav Frontier   1914
•—•—•—•   "   "   "   1939
▬ ▬ ▬ ▬   "   "   "   1947 (Italian Peace Treaty)
▬•▬•▬ Austrian Frontier   1920

a persistent minority problem. In 1915 Italy entered the first world war on the side of the Allies, in return for a promise of frontier adjustments which included the whole of the Istrian peninsula, exclusive of Fiume and the Isonzo valley. Thus half a million Slovenes were placed under Italian rule. Their position was unenviable when the Fascists came to power. Not surprisingly, after the second world war every Slovene was determined to mend this state of affairs if he could.

In the peninsula which juts southward from the eastern side of the head of the Adriatic and includes Trieste as its only great port and city, Italians, Slovenes and Croats are so inextricably mingled that the drawing of an accurate racial map is a cartographer's nightmare. It is roughly true to describe Trieste and the coastal towns as predominantly Italian, while the peasantry of the hinterland is either Slovene or Croat. Cavour admitted this as long ago as 1860. In the total area the South Slavs are in a clear majority, but these considerations did not stop either Italy or Yugoslavia from claiming the whole. In nationalist controversy, everything depends upon where in the past you begin. The Italians claimed to be the heirs of the vanished republic of Venice, which once ruled the whole peninsula. In the eighteenth and nineteenth centuries it was mainly under the control of the Habsburgs whose mercantile policy gave life to the port of Trieste. Both Italy and Yugoslavia had strong claims in the area which looked like giving plenty of trouble as the second world war neared its end.

In May 1945 New Zealand troops entered Trieste to find that Yugoslav forces had got there first. A subsequent military agreement between General Morgan and General Jovanović resulted in British, reinforced later by American, forces occupying Trieste itself, together with a narrow corridor running from south of the port northward to the Austrian frontier. The rest of the territory was occupied by Yugoslav troops. The so-called 'Morgan line' was intended only as a temporary boundary, but all efforts to establish a permanent, agreed Italo-Yugoslav frontier failed. It was typical of this period that a four-power commission, set up in 1946 to determine a division which would leave minimum populations under alien rule, was only able to offer four different solutions and to suggest four different boundary lines.

At last, in 1947, the Italian Peace Treaty produced an apparent compromise. There was to be a free territory of Trieste, stretching from Duino in the north to Novigrad in the south and extending to a maximum depth from the coast of about ten miles. Its integrity was to be guaranteed by the Security Council, and a governor was to be appointed, with the concurrence of the allied powers. The area east of the new boundary was to go to the Yugoslavs, who were in an overwhelming majority there.

Until the allies nominated a governor, the free territory of Trieste was to be divided into two zones. Zone A, the northern half, which included Trieste itself, was to be administered by the United Kingdom and the U.S.A; Zone B, the southern half, was to be administered by Yugoslavia. These arrangements, like so many that are intended to be provisional, gradually lapsed into semi-permanency. The allies were never able to agree upon a governor, every Western nomination being vetoed by Russia, and every Russian nomination by the West. The Yugoslavs made little pretence from the start that their occupation of Zone B was temporary, and showed every sign of intending to incorporate it in due course into their own country.

The year 1948 was a critical one in the history of the cold war. Communist power was thrusting and obtruding itself in many lands. One by one the satellite countries shed all appearance of being ruled by coalition governments and communist domination became starkly revealed. At the beginning of the year, Yugoslavia still seemed firmly bound to Moscow. Certainly the Western powers had no cause to conciliate South Slav sentiment, or to placate a country whose subversive activities on the frontiers of Greece had become notorious.

There seemed also a danger that the Communist Party of Italy, one of the strongest and best organized in the West, might win the general election which was due in April. The party had, however, one great weakness. Rigidly obedient to the line laid down by Moscow, the Italian communist leader, Togliatti, could not appeal to national sentiment over the question of Trieste. The Western powers thought this the moment to raise that question in a form calculated to embarrass communists everywhere. Accordingly, on March 20th the United Kingdom, France and the United States proposed a drastic revision of the Italian Peace Treaty. They suggested that the whole of the free territory of Trieste, including Zone B, should go to Italy. As expected, the tripartite declaration was highly popular in Italy and contributed to a sweeping victory won by the Christian Democrats a month later. Juridically it did not mean so much, because any revision required the agreement of Soviet Russia, which would not be forthcoming. Later events cast doubts on the wisdom of this Western initiative. In the most tangled diplomatic problems it seldom pays to snatch a short-term advantage, especially if this limits the area of manœuvre, as in this instance.

When I became the Foreign Secretary the legal position was exactly the same as it had been after the ratification of the treaty four years earlier. There was still no governor and there was an effective partition of the free territory, with some ten thousand troops, half British and half American, occupying Zone A. But one important new development had occurred since the tripartite declaration. At the end of June 1948, the Yugoslav Communist Party was expelled from the Cominform, to the accompaniment of scorching anathemas from the Kremlin. Mr. Khrushchev has told us that Stalin expected the early fall of Marshal Tito as a result of this excommunication. He probably did, but nothing of the kind happened. Neither economic blockade, nor taint of heresy deflected the Yugoslav dictator. He continued to defy Moscow and purged with ruthless efficiency any in his Government who still hankered after the Kremlin brand of communism. Stalin's fury showed that he understood the full meaning of this bold and successful revolt.

The changed policy of Yugoslavia influenced the problem of Trieste. Marshal Tito could not be expected to align himself at all readily with the West. He had to be able to repudiate accusations of servility to the imperial powers. But the swing was sufficient to show that he might in time co-operate with the nations he had hitherto been denouncing with such venom. In November 1951 Tito took what seemed to me a decisive step by signing an agreement accepting military aid from the United States. It then became all the more important to remove the cause of dissension between Yugoslavia and Italy, now happily one of the principal powers in the N.A.T.O. alliance. A more prosaic consideration also influenced me; the cost and trouble of maintaining the allied occupation of Zone A could not be endured indefinitely, while we received little for our pains but abuse from both sides. We were locking up five thousand soldiers in an unrewarding occupation. Something must be done about this; so far at least Washington and London were agreed.

We made little headway with negotiation during the first year after my return to office. Both sides gave out unyielding public declarations. Each claimed the whole of the free territory and the arguments were equally irrefutable, on their own unprovable assumptions. The various secret proposals put forward did not seem to me to hold much promise. Despite much diplomatic activity we were, at the end of it all, as far away from a solution as ever.

In September 1952, with the full support of Mr. Acheson, I decided to pay a visit to Belgrade and there to discuss Trieste and other problems personally with Marshal Tito. I flew via Strasbourg, where an engagement to speak to the Consultative Assembly of the Council of Europe gave me a chance to talk with the Italian Prime Minister, Signor De Gasperi. I always found this statesman a sympathetic colleague with whom it was a pleasure to work, but I was not surprised when this time he had little help to give me. He told me that Italy could accept neither the indefinite continuance of the existing situation, nor an Italo-Yugoslav condominium in the free territory, which was one of Tito's recent suggestions. Both proposals were politically impossible for him, he said. I asked whether a division on zonal lines, Zone A to Italy, Zone B to Yugoslavia, with certain adjustments, would be acceptable. On this he was cautious and non-committal, though he did not rule it out as a solution. I promised that I would not make concessions in Belgrade and I hoped that, for his part, the Prime Minister would do his best to keep the diplomatic temperature down. He did.

On September 17th I flew to Belgrade. I looked forward to the experience, for I was the first Foreign Secretary of a leading Western power to visit Yugoslavia since Marshal Tito's breach with the Kremlin, indeed since the end of the war. The Marshal chose this moment to reveal what had hitherto been a closely guarded secret, his marriage to Jovanka Budislavljević, a twenty-eight year old major in the Yugoslav Army. They had been married since the beginning of the year, but only a few of Tito's intimate friends were informed at the time. The outside world learned the news by reading the name of Mme. Jovanka Broz after the name of Marshal Josip Broz Tito upon the invitation cards to the reception given for me at the White Palace. Madame Tito was charming and my only chagrin at the discovery was that I had not brought my wife with me. I had thought that I was heading for a widower's court.

I had my first meeting with Marshal Tito before the luncheon at which he was host on September 18th. We discussed our problems for an hour before and after the meal, which ended with speeches of goodwill. The day after our first meeting he broke what had been his invariable rule since the breach with Stalin, by accepting an invitation to a luncheon given by our Ambassador, Sir Ivo Mallet, at the British Embassy. I was able to return his friendliness by giving him an invitation from Mr. Churchill to visit England at an early date.

Before the end of my stay I had further conversations with Marshal Tito at the lakeside resort of Bled in the Slovenian mountains and a delightful interlude at Dubrovnik, rarely surpassed for a combination of scenery, climate and architecture.

On the question of Trieste one important fact emerged. Marshal Tito still claimed that either the matter should be shelved or that a condominium should be accepted as a compromise. But he and Mr. Kardelj, the Foreign Minister, both agreed that they would acquiesce in the permanency of the present division between zones, provided that it was pressed upon them by others. Tito would not, and could not, volunteer this solution and he made it clear, despite my arguments, that he would refuse any modification of the boundary which favoured the reasonable Italian claim to the coastal towns of Capodistria, Isola and Pirano, a few miles south of Trieste. Stiffened by the Slovene Minister, who was present at some of our talks, Tito was firm on this, until we reached the point where further persistence on my part would have exasperated rather than convinced him. On September 23rd I left for Austria, feeling that the visit had been worth while; even on Trieste I was not entirely disappointed.

I met all the leading Yugoslav Ministers and thought highly of Kardelj, but the man who intrigued me most as a personality was Milovan Djilas. He sat next to me at the luncheon at the British Embassy and we were soon deep in discussion of the rival merits of free enterprise and state socialism in their various forms. I expounded my views on a property-owning democracy and he countered with a description of the co-operative socialist state which he hoped Yugoslavia would build. He did not talk like the average communist, by rote, but possessed an original mind and was exceptionally informed on all questions of political economy. He cross-questioned me about a book compiled by my great-grandfather, *The State of the Poor*, with which he showed himself completely familiar. This book is in the nature of an anthology of the conditions of the 'labouring classes' in England at the end of the eighteenth century. Sir Frederick Eden spent much time and money in collating his facts, which he set out in the first survey of its kind attempted in this country. Djilas reminded me that Karl Marx had praised the book and I assured him that in my country even a Tory politician could survive that.

As I listened to Djilas, he seemed to me a genuine egalitarian and lover of liberty and I wondered how he would be able to reconcile his faith and enthusiasms with the rigid communist creed. I saw him once or twice afterwards on official occasions, but never with an opportunity for any serious talk, and I was sad, but not surprised, when I learnt of his later imprisonment for deviation from the communist path. He is a man I shall always respect.

These discussions with the Yugoslavs convinced me that if there was ever to be a solution of the Trieste problem, it would have to be imposed, after being carefully prepared. Neither side could take the political risk of accepting a proposal from the other. But if the United States and the United Kingdom were to declare that they regarded the zonal boundary as permanent and hand over the administration of Zone A to Italy, there was a chance that the shock would eventually produce a reluctant agreement between the two protagonists. For the success of such a policy two conditions were indispensable: it must have the full backing of the United States and ourselves and it must be presented as final. The Italians must not be given the impression that they were acquiring Zone A as a stepping stone to further gains in Zone B.

There seemed little chance of these conditions being fulfilled for the time being. The Americans did not dissent from my view that division along existing zonal lines was probably the right answer. On the other hand they were unwilling to press it upon De Gasperi. The forthcoming Italian elections and the desirability of persuading Italy to join E.D.C. were among the reasons for this reluctance. Naturally enough, De Gasperi, aware of his bargaining strength, had no intention of voluntarily limiting his demands to Zone A. He promptly staked his claim to Capodistria and the coastal towns. This, as I well knew, Tito would not concede and we had no means of forcing him. I was not surprised when an independent American approach made in Rome at the end of the year proved to be a failure.

In March 1953 Tito paid a return visit to England. It went easily and none of the disasters which had been freely predicted in fact occurred. The problem of Trieste was only discussed in general terms, for the situation had not altered since my talks in Yugoslavia six months earlier.

While I was undergoing my several surgical operations in the late spring and early summer of 1953, the prospects for Trieste underwent some changes also. At the elections, Signor De Gasperi's Coalition fared less well than expected. As a result, his place was taken by Signor Pella at the head of a Christian Democrat Government which only commanded a minority of seats in the Chamber. The new Prime Minister was under even greater pressure than his predecessor to take some initiative about Trieste and at the end of August made a favourable public reference to the tripartite declaration of 1948, which had awarded both zones to Italy. The Yugoslav press hinted that this speech was a good reason for their own Government to reconsider the whole question of Trieste. These hints were taken in Italy as a threat to annex Zone B, and Pella answered by moving troops to the frontier of the free territory. These events, and the recurring crises they expressed, convinced Lord Salisbury and his advisers at the Foreign Office that continuing inaction on our part was dangerous. Meanwhile, the United States Government had come to share our point of view. On September 14th the American Ambassador handed Lord Salisbury proposals from Washington, advocating almost the same plan which we had put forward at the end of the year before. It was suggested that our two Governments should inform Yugoslavia and Italy, without further consultation with either of them, that the present situation could not continue and that we had therefore decided to withdraw our troops and to hand over the administration of Zone A to Italy. Although this solution would be imposed, it would be put forward with every intention of being final. If each country, as a result, annexed one zone, the United States and the United Kingdom would not object, provided that Italy gave assurances for free port facilities in Trieste and both countries gave guarantees of fair treatment for minorities. These undertakings, and any adjustments in the boundary line which might be agreed, could be dealt with in later negotiation between the two countries.

The one point on which London was not in full agreement with Washington was the extent to which a public declaration should be made that the solution was final. Her Majesty's Government considered that they must not give the Italian Government a pretext for continuing to maintain their claim on Zone B, for they knew that Tito would only accept partition by zones if this were a final settlement. The United States Government were unwilling to be so explicit. The most that Mr. Dulles was prepared to say was, 'The two Governments hope that the measures being taken will lead to a final peaceful solution.' This was a serious weakening of the proposals, but the United States Government had come some way to meet us and Her Majesty's Government made ready to put out a joint statement in step with their ally.

This was the position when I returned to the Foreign Office on October 5th. That morning Lord Salisbury and I fully discussed the stage which events had reached and I endorsed what he had done. We

were both conscious of the risks. I could not be sure that a solution
which I knew that Tito would have taken at the end of 1952, would
be acceptable in Belgrade a year later. Slovene opinion had been active
against concessions and so had the pressure of those who did not want
to see agreement between Yugoslavia and the West. As for Italy, our
agreement would be popular because it would place her in Zone A on
an equality with Yugoslavia in Zone B. The danger was a public declaration by the Italian Government that they regarded Zone A as merely
the first instalment. We did our best to avert this by representations of
our own in Rome. But the lack of finality in the Anglo-American
declaration remained the weak point. Against this, the situation was
deteriorating so fast that we should soon be faced with a threat to the
peace of Europe. I agreed that the risk must be taken and that we must
declare our proposals in both capitals. So did my colleagues when the
decision was put to them that same day.

On October 8th we announced the plan. The Italian Prime Minister
interpreted it to mean that Italy was not being asked to forgo her
claims on Zone B, and said so publicly. Yugoslavia instantly entered a
formal protest, closed the frontier, called up reservists, moved warships and drew the attention of the United Nations to the situation.
The Italians responded by reinforcing their troops in the positions they
had taken up at the end of August. In a short time there were nearly
fifty thousand soldiers on the frontier. Tito announced that he would
consider the arrival of Italian troops in Zone A as an act of aggression.
The British Embassy in Belgrade was damaged by mobs, on the walls
in Italy appeared the inscription *Porco Eden*. The Trieste cauldron
bubbled more menacingly than before and I was its most denounced
ingredient.

It looked as if the only effect of our action had been to make matters
worse and when Parliament debated Trieste this was, quite naturally,
vehemently pointed out to us. Mr. Noel-Baker accused us of 'criminal
ambiguity' in the language of our declaration. Mr. Dalton described it
as 'a gross exhibition of incompetence'.

All this did not matter very much and I was quite unrepentant about
our action. I explained to the House:

> We had concluded from our previous contacts that there was
> no chance of getting our solution, or any solution, accepted in
> advance by negotiation without vigorous intervention on our
> part. I am quite sure that judgment was correct . . . .

I said that we wanted a solution of the Trieste problem 'within the next few months' and stated my conviction that we should succeed. I had cause for my confidence, for out of all this hubbub had come one wise suggestion. The Yugoslav Government proposed that there should be direct talks between the American, British, Italian and Yugoslav Governments. This was precisely what I wanted, but to have the best chance, the suggestion had had to come from one of the protagonists, and be tolerated by the other. Plenty of conferences and troubles followed. There were many discussions between the French Government, the United States Government and ourselves, and the three Foreign Secretaries met without much advancing matters. In November there were anti-British riots in Trieste. Outwardly we were in as much trouble as ever, but in fact we were over the hump once direct talks had been proposed by one of the parties. We had yet to get agreement about how to hold them, and they must be secret. We had to go underground.

The United States Government now came along with a four-phase plan. The first phase was for an approach to Tito. I did not like this, as I felt sure it would cause irritation and mean delay. The second phase was based on a proposal of mine for a secret unconditional meeting of the Ambassadors concerned. I thought that this approach should be made to both sides and not just to the Italians alone. The third phase was for an approach by our two Governments to Yugoslavia to work out a solution in secret. If that failed, we had to be prepared to fulfil our decision of October 8th. I told Mr. Holmes, the experienced American Minister in London, who handled this stage of our discussions, that I could not commit Her Majesty's Government to this last step at present, particularly as I thought that the chances of a settlement had improved since October. But we both agreed that the negotiations must be carried on in London where there was a chance of preserving secrecy. This decision proved of capital importance.

Early in the New Year, 1954, the two Governments informed Rome that we proposed to start discussions with Yugoslavia and, on February 2nd, the first meeting was discreetly held. Her Majesty's Government were represented by Mr. Harrison of the Foreign Office and the United States Government by Mr. Thompson, their Ambassador in Vienna. These two officers continued to handle these very complex negotiations for a period of nearly eight months. Despite their skilled diplomacy, they could not have succeeded without the help of the two Ambassadors in London, Dr. Velebit for Yugoslavia and Signor Brosio for Italy. The former had taken an active part with the partisans and was a personal friend of Marshal Tito. He had not been brought up in diplomacy but he showed every aptitude for it. Though formally presenting his country's requirements, he never forgot that its need was a settlement. He was also a very likeable man.

The Italian Ambassador, Signor Brosio, was supple and highly skilled at his profession as well as a man of much personal charm. He was one of the most popular ambassadors that even Italy has sent us. The two men were well matched. Neither ever missed a point but both understood that agreement had to be reached. How to do this in a form which each of their countries could accept, they had to determine. In the end they did, but only because they were able to carry through their work in the utmost secrecy.

Our purpose was to persuade Yugoslavia to accept a frontier corresponding as closely as possible to the zonal boundaries. We had not much power of manœuvre, because we could not present to the Italians anything that appeared less favourable than our proposals of October 8th. The Yugoslavs required much persuasion, but we could sweeten the pill. One of the sweets was financial and here the United States Government were generous and wise. They offered $20 million, to which the Chancellor of the Exchequer added £2 million from us, this to help pay for the construction of a new port at St. Nicola in Zone B south of Trieste and for other necessities.

I kept in close touch with every phase of this negotiation and Mr. Harrison saw me frequently. Sometimes I would intervene with one Ambassador or the other, but mainly the work was done in the diplomatic closet. By the end of May we had been able to agree a memorandum, which was initialled by the Yugoslav Ambassador and the British and American negotiators. This dealt with all such questions as minorities, finance and the free port. As to territory, Yugoslavia in effect accepted something very near to the solution which they had rejected and Italy had accepted during the previous October.

Next we had to persuade the Italians that this arrangement was also worth their while. Not surprisingly, their response was unenthusiastic. Signor Scelba had succeeded Signor Pella as Prime Minister at the end of February, and I had had a number of discussions with him on European matters, when I found him a firm but fair man to work with. He had also a lively awareness that the question of Trieste could easily bring him down. So, throughout the summer, proposals and counterproposals went to and fro between London and Rome, London and Belgrade, London and Washington.

It was then our turn to call in Signor Brosio's help. This he gave, journeying to Rome and bringing us the results. We had soon regulated everything except the vexed territorial question and even that was narrowing down. The last stages became very stubborn, however, and argument raged fiercely around an area of about two square miles. I feared that this was going to become symbolic and that we should be deadlocked. I invited the Yugoslav Ambassador to see me at the end of July and asked him to press his Government for a small territorial concession. Reasonably, he inquired in reply whether this would be the last. I said that he could always make it conditional on the settlement of all other matters.

Through August and September the argument continued and at times I thought the agreement would founder on this small patch of land. During September I made my flight round the Western European capitals, following the collapse of E.D.C. While I was in Rome I spent more than two hours with the Italian Prime Minister, Signor Scelba, discussing almost entirely the subject of Trieste. The talk was good, but I understood the restricted limits which penned him.

Tito also had not much room to manœuvre. Nor had we. But Yugoslavia was at this time very short of wheat. Mr. Robert Murphy was therefore sent to Belgrade by the United States Government, with authority to offer wheat to the Yugoslavs. This injected a mood of reasonableness and made possible a minute adjustment of territorial exchanges, Yugoslavia at one point dropping back a couple of hundred yards without asking for any compensation. On such small matters can international agreement sometimes depend. We were therefore able to offer the Italians alternatives, either the line we had agreed with the Yugoslavs on May 31st, or that same line with two small variants. This, we thought, should do the trick. It did. On the 23rd the Italian Ambassador informed us of his Government's willingness to accept one of the alternatives, the Lazaretto wedge at one end of the line, in return for a rockpile at the other.

The documents were duly initialled in London on October 5th and the handover to the Italians in Zone A proceeded without incident. The boundary commission finished its task, adjusting the demarcation line without acrimony. Allied Military Government came to an end on October 26th.

The problem of Trieste had been solved. It had poisoned relations between Italy and Yugoslavia for nearly a decade; it had been costly to the allies in men, money and temper. The solution was a classic example of the true function of diplomacy, an open agreement secretly arrived at. I do not believe that it could have been reached if we had not taken our initiative of October 8th, 1953, which won so much reproach and contumely. Peace is not just something that happens. At times it is necessary to take risks and even to increase the immediate danger to win a lasting agreement. Trieste was one of those occasions.

IX

OIL
October 1951 – March 1955

Oxford – Oriental languages – Oil agreement of 1933 – Post-war history of Iran – Dr. Musaddiq – Iranian oil nationalized – My discussions with Mr. Acheson – Views of the Iranian Ambassador in London – Obduracy of Musaddiq – The Shah – The Churchill-Truman proposals – Diplomatic break with Iran – Discussions with the United States – The fall of Musaddiq – Relations with Iran restored – The settlement – The Baghdad Pact

My interest in the Middle East was in part the result of my early introduction to foreign languages and literature. During my younger years from about the age of four, I spent much of my childhood abroad. My father believed that we should learn foreign languages early in life. Thus began sojourns on the continent of Europe, chiefly in France and Germany, which lasted spasmodically for several years. I learnt French and German and spoke French for a while more easily than my own language. The German I neglected when I had to learn Greek to get into Eton. I had preferred Greek to Latin, but abandoned both for the first world war.

The fighting over, I was tempted to stay in the army. The multiplicity of generals in my regiment was, however, a discouragement; my own brigadier being the thirty-ninth in succession. I would have been content in the army if I could always have had work like a brigade-major's, or the command of a company. Obviously that could not be. Also, after four years of soldiering, I felt a need for education of another kind.

Among civil callings, the Foreign Office was favourite. On the advice of a friend of my sister, Sir George Clerk, later our Ambassador in Paris, I decided to read Oriental languages. I next considered which to choose. A Durham neighbour, General Surtees, had spent part of a distinguished military career in Turkey. I used to drive over to his beautiful home at Mainsforth and began to learn the language with him. It was soon evident that to know Turkish it was useful to know some Persian and some Arabic. Persian is the Italian of the East and appealed to me most. Oxford Schools then required two languages, so I decided to make Persian my main language and Arabic my secondary one.

I went up to Oxford at the age of twenty-two. I enjoyed my years at Christ Church; the metamorphosis from a brigade-major to an under-graduate appeared alarming, but it was all made easy. The intellectual douche was refreshing.

The university meant other pleasures too. Limited travel was possible on my gratuity, and a few weeks after leaving the army my brother and I were in Venice. At the *Biennale* that year a memorial exhibition of Cézanne's paintings was being held. My father had inducted me at an early age into the marvels of the Impressionists and if I did not understand, at least I felt the beauty of Manet and Degas. But this was something different, showing me a new vision. It seemed a reve-lation, which may seem strange to those who now see a natural succession from the Impressionists to Cézanne. The last meant much more to me at that time.

Up at Oxford some friends and I founded a small art society which we called The Uffizi, one of the many mushroom growths that Oxford digests so easily. We invited lecturers to talk to us according to our tastes. I wanted someone to speak or read a paper to us about Cézanne and I decided to approach Mr. George Moore. He was a life-long friend of my father, to whom he had dedicated his *Modern Painting*.

My embassage was fascinating but unsuccessful. George Moore talked to me of his pictures and told me how they represented the period he loved. He had not, he felt, enough sympathy to write of Cézanne. He showed proper surprise at my choice of reading at Oxford. 'Persian, most interesting. I have found it so difficult to learn English. In all my life only one man has known English really well, George Meredith. Poor George, and what a use he made of it.'

My Schools were hard work. The set books gave too much time to the antique; they have been wisely modernized since. We had to read Darius' inscriptions at Behistun and understand the cuneiform in which they are cut. A Zoroastrian religious work came next in date, an intriguing but formidable book to master, before embarking on the *Shâhnâme*, Persia's epic book of kings, written before the language underwent its Arabic infusion. For glorious reward there followed the odes of Hâfiz; for penance Akhlâk-i-Jalâli, a medieval philosophic treatise of brain-twisting intricacy. Hâfiz has never been satisfactorily translated, though many have tried, including FitzGerald, who was successful with a secondary poet, Omar Khayyâm. Miss Gertrude Bell has fared the best, but the greatest poets are really untranslatable.

My tutor in Persian, Richard Paget Dewhurst, was a former Indian judge and a man of prodigious learning among Eastern languages. I would often attend upon him for my lecture in his lodgings and there find him correcting, in his spare time, the proofs of the higher examination papers at some Indian University. He took extreme pains with his pupil in Persian.

Oxford has taught Arabic since the seventeenth century with the endowment of Archbishop Laud, an unexpected association. Professor Margoliouth, who held the chair while I was up at Oxford, was an Arabist and Orientalist of wide renown. He is said to have addressed Baghdad University in Arabic so pure as to be almost unintelligible to his audience. They were as impressed as we might be if we were harangued in the language of Wycliffe, and only a little more enlightened. Margoliouth had a reputation for severity, but he treated me with much kindness and his lectures were a delight, even if his learning was often deeper than I could fathom. I read with him the Qurân and an agreeable Arab historian of the early caliphs. A medieval commentary on the Qurân I found less acceptable, having no taste for theological discourse or controversy.

    ★   ★   ★   ★   ★

I was Under-Secretary at the Foreign Office in 1933, when the Persian Government denounced the Anglo-Persian Oil Company's concession. In the absence of the Prime Minister, Mr. Ramsay MacDonald, and the Foreign Secretary, Sir John Simon, I advised an immediate appeal to the Council of the League, fortified in my recommendation by the experienced advice of Sir William Malkin, a much loved man with a brilliant record as legal adviser at the Foreign Office. Mr. Baldwin was temporarily in charge of the Government and endorsed this proposal. On his return, I saw the Foreign Secretary and the conversation ran something like this :

'I understand that you advised the Government to take this case to the Council of the League.'

'I did.'

'No doubt you will have satisfied yourself as to the strength of our case before doing so?'

'I thought we had a good case, and Will Malkin thinks so too.'

'I shall be interested to hear your reasons. I am not, of course, yet familiar with the details. I have, however, some slight experience of the law and, from what I know, I should certainly not have recommended this course.'

There followed a lengthy catechism of Sir William Malkin and myself, towards the end of which even that most patient of men was exasperated. I was indignant. A few days later Sir John Simon opened his brief with a brilliant defence of our case at Geneva. It was only then that I realized that I had merely been subjected to an exploratory cross-examination, enabling him to establish the facts. I took part in the negotiations which followed in that year, culminating in a new agreement between the company and the Government of Persia. Sir John Cadman most ably represented the company.

In later years I paid a number of visits to Iran, as it became in 1935, and to its oilfields in war and peace. The last of these visits was in 1948. I had, therefore, some first-hand knowledge of the problem with which I was soon to deal: how to recover our national position and a British company's oil concession in Iran.

★　★　★　★　★

It had taken some tough negotiation at Yalta, and subsequently, to bring about an agreed withdrawal of allied forces, Russian and Western, from Iran after the war. When they had gone, the country suffered from a succession of weak Governments, temporarily sustained by wayward deputies. Their programmes were admirable, their performance pitiable.

After an unhappy interlude, the Shah, without consulting Parliament, appointed General Razmara as Prime Minister in June 1950. A strong nationalist, Razmara had been trained at St. Cyr and had spent all his life as a soldier. His intentions were excellent. He proposed to decentralize the administration and to get more revenue by ratifying the supplementary agreement with the oil company. This agreement had been signed in the summer of 1949, but successive Governments made no attempt to explain or define its terms in public, although they were more generous than those of any other oil company in the Middle East. Defamatory tales concerning it ran from mouth to ear and Iranians are good at story-telling.

Into this state of affairs erupted Dr. Musaddiq. His National Front won a number of seats in Tehran and he became the spokesman of an elemental nationalism. In June 1950 he was appointed chairman of the Parliamentary Commission which eight months later proposed nationalizing the oil industry.

General Razmara, as Prime Minister, had had another and still bolder objective, to secure some honesty in public life. This was about the last thing Parliament wanted. Hitherto Prime Ministers had obtained parliamentary majorities by means which the members enjoyed. Dr. Musaddiq did not share such greedy appetites. His aim was rather to make an emotional issue of the oil agreement, which it was only too easy to do, given the uninformed state of public opinion. The Iranians knew that ever larger sums were paid by the company to the British Government in taxation. They also knew that the 1933 agreement provided for increasing payments to the Iranian Government, as tonnage increased and the dividends paid by the company grew. Dividend limitation, which the company accepted at the Treasury's behest, prevented this happening in full and fomented suspicion. The Iranians could not comprehend a company voluntarily limiting its dividend. All they saw was that, as a result, they did not get as much money as they thought they were entitled to. I understood their feelings, for it must seem to them disingenuous that His Majesty's Government, as a large shareholder, should take increasing sums in taxation, and refuse the increased dividends from which the Iranian Government would have benefited.

I felt sufficiently concerned about this on my return from Iran in 1948 to ask to see the Chancellor of the Exchequer. I told Sir Stafford Cripps that I feared trouble must arise if dividend limitation were continued in this instance. It should be possible to make an exception for the company, whose dividends influenced the receipts of a foreign government. The Chancellor expressed regret, but replied that an exception was impossible.

The company was aware of the danger too and warned the Government at home. They, perhaps, fell in too readily with the Prime Minister of Iran's request that no announcement should be made of the considerable financial help the company was affording his Government privately. Nor did the people of Iran know soon enough that the company had been trying to persuade General Razmara to reopen discussion on a fifty-fifty profit-sharing basis, or that the unratified supplementary agreement made future provision to compensate for dividend limitation.

So all was made ready for a Musaddiq victory. The campaign for nationalization was pursued with abandon. The Prime Minister was summoned by Parliament to state whether nationalization was practicable or not. He referred the question to a panel of Iranian experts, all of whom reported unfavourably. On March 3rd, 1951, General Razmara presented these reports and their contents were broadcast over the Tehran wireless. Four days later he was assassinated.

A week afterwards, a resolution nationalizing the oil industry was approved by both Houses of the Iranian Parliament. On April 28th, Dr. Musaddiq became Prime Minister and on May 1st the nationalization law was passed. The Iranian people, he declared, were opening 'a hidden treasure upon which lies a dragon'.

These events caused disquiet outside Iran. His Majesty's Government took up the issue of nationalization and referred to the provisions for arbitration in the 1933 agreement. A few weeks later, the company formally notified the Government of Iran that it requested arbitration in accordance with the 1933 agreement and had appointed an arbitrator, but the Government of Iran ignored this, so the company applied to the President of the International Court of Justice at the Hague to appoint a sole arbitrator. On the same day, His Majesty's Government instituted proceedings before the Court against the Government of Iran. They argued that a British company had been treated in a manner not in accordance with the principles of international law. Further exchanges followed between the Government of Iran and the company, whose staff were given a week in which to declare whether they wished to enter the service of the nationalized company. All refused.

Similar behaviour marked the shipment of oil. The Iranian authorities refused to clear tankers, unless the master first signed a declaration that the cargo was the property of the nationalized Iranian Oil Company. The masters refused and, by the end of June, all shipments of oil from Abadan ceased.

In July, the International Court suggested that certain provisional measures should be taken, pending their final decision. His Majesty's Government accepted these, but the Government of Iran said that the order was unwarranted interference in the internal affairs of the country. Matters grew steadily worse. President Truman then took a hand by suggesting that Mr. Averell Harriman should visit Tehran for discussions on the oil dispute. This he did and, after lengthy talks, a formula resulted. A British Government mission joined in the parleys but no progress was made, because the Government of Iran insisted on the literal application of its nationalization law. The negotiators went home.

A few weeks later, the Iranian Government ordered all the British staff of the company to leave the country within a week. Britain retorted by submitting the dispute to the Security Council. Musaddiq travelled to New York to attend the meeting in person, but no significant result was achieved before the time limit expired. His Majesty's Government had moved land forces and a cruiser to the vicinity of Abadan where the fate of the largest oil refinery in the world was at stake. The temptation to intervene to reclaim this stolen property must have been strong, but pressure from the United States was vigorous against any such action. The British staff was instructed to withdraw.

A fortnight later, the Security Council concluded its discussion by adjourning the debate on the United Kingdom complaint until the Hague Court had pronounced upon its competence in the oil dispute. Here was a dismal failure to measure up to events. Fortified by the success of his theft, Musaddiq, at the invitation of the United States Government, extended his journey to Washington. There he held discussions, which also brought no result. Breaches of international engagements were not then as frequent as they have since unhappily become. It was not surprising that these events had their repercussions elsewhere.

Egypt had been entirely quiet since the war. In 1945 I had favoured a plan by which British forces would have been withdrawn from the great cities of Egypt as soon as the war was over, and concentrated mainly in Cyrenaica and Tripoli. Smaller forces, capable of reinforcement by air if necessary, would have been stationed on the Suez Canal. Unfortunately, we had not, at that time, reached a settlement as to the future of Cyrenaica, though Marshal Stalin had made it clear that he had not the least objection to any military agreements we might make in North Africa. Mr. Churchill felt strongly that we should make no territorial gains from the war, and the plan, which involved treaty making, was not brought into effect for some years. This was a misfortune.

Now, as a result of events in Iran, Egypt became ebullient. The troubles fomented on the Shatt al Arab, festered on the Nile. There were riotings and shootings and attacks upon our troops. In October,

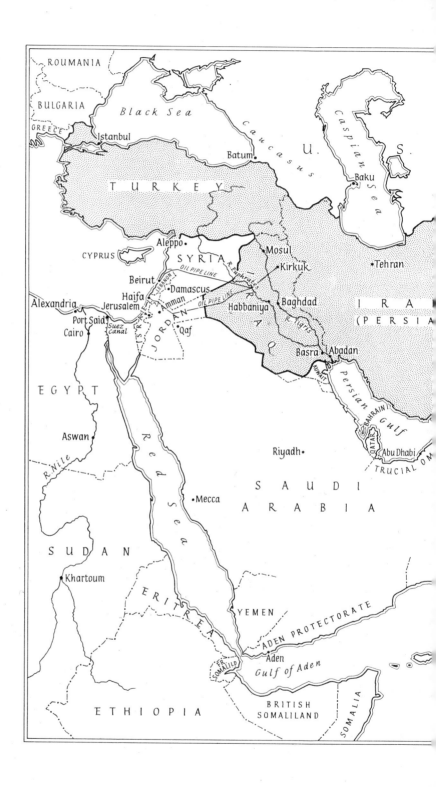

R.

Kabul

FGHANISTAN

PAKISTAN

THE MIDDLE EAST

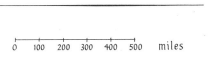

Countries of the Baghdad Pact shown thus:

0   100   200   300   400   500   miles

N

abian

ea

the Labour Government, as one of its last acts, increased the garrison of Egypt by two brigades.

★   ★   ★   ★   ★

This was the lowering prospect I contemplated on the day I took over at the Foreign Office. We were out of Iran; we had lost Abadan; our authority throughout the Middle East had been violently shaken; the outbreaks in Egypt foreshadowed further upheavals. I had to consider how this situation was to be met. I was sure that we must first deal with the source of our recent trouble, the oil problem.

In Britain, though there was indignation at the loss of Abadan, there was not at any time any strong feeling against Iran. This was in part due to the success with which the oil industry closed the gap in production caused by the loss of Abadan oil. The British people did not suffer directly and had difficulty in taking Musaddiq seriously. He was the first real bit of meat to come the way of the cartoonists since the war. 'Old Mossy', with his pyjamas and iron bedstead, became a familiar figure.

Our interest was not confined to oil. We had a real concern in the country's prosperity. If Musaddiq's policies were to prevail, the oil industry would be ruined and with it any possibility of material progress in Iran. A backward and corrupt agricultural state would move deeper into poverty, with calculable consequences. On the other hand, if a settlement were to be reached, it must be based on certain fixed principles. Just to come to terms at any price with Musaddiq, lest worse befall and he be replaced by communism, would be a policy of despair. I could not accept this, nor did I believe that the only choice in Iran lay between Musaddiq and communism.

This opinion would have to be firmly explained to the United States Government, with whom I proposed to seek common ground on which we could stand. I was concerned by the extent to which Musaddiq was being aided in the oil dispute by a United States policy of 'neutrality'. The Government of Iran argued publicly that the United States was supporting them. If this current were allowed to swell, it would sweep all away.

I decided to arrange an early discussion with Mr. Acheson. Fortunately, the occasion was at hand in the shape of a meeting of the United Nations Assembly in Paris. In preparation for this, I drew up certain principles on which our minimum requirements could be founded. I proposed to hand these to Mr. Acheson in Paris.

There were four of these principles:

1. There must be fair compensation for loss caused by nationalization of concessionary rights and property, to be agreed between the two parties or, in default, settled by arbitration.

The amount of compensation could not be settled unilaterally. Unless it were accepted that the question of compensation must be settled by some independent judicial authority, no British or American interest in foreign countries could be safeguarded against breach of contract. The effect of this on foreign investment, in itself desirable for the country concerned, would be disastrous.

2. It is not enough when nationalization occurs that there should be the acceptance of the principle of fair compensation; it is necessary, as Mr. Harriman publicly stated, that there must be security for payment of effective compensation.

In this instance compensation could, in effect, only be paid in the form of oil, therefore the industry had to be restarted with efficient management and an assured future.

3. Iran should not by reason of her unilateral action secure, overall, more favourable terms than concessionary Governments which have respected their contracts.

This was evidently in the interests of the United States and ourselves and of all countries who had a part in similar agreements.

4. His Majesty's Government cannot negotiate on a basis of discrimination involving the exclusion of its own nationals.

This was a British interest upon which Parliament rightly insisted. It was also something more. If such discrimination were permitted against one power, it could clearly be extended to others.

The whole issue was so complicated that I felt I could not handle it effectively by frequent references to the Cabinet. I decided to ask the Prime Minister to let me set up a small committee of the colleagues principally concerned. I would report the results of our work to him and to the Cabinet from time to time. Mr. Churchill approved and the group worked with me over several years until the settlement was reached. Lord Leathers, then Minister of Co-ordination for Transport and Power, with his wide business experience, was of special help to me at all our meetings. There were continuous consultations between us and the company at every stage. For, despite its large shareholding, the Government's chief concern was for the sanctity of contracts, the company had to consider the interests of its shareholders also.

I flew to Paris on November 4th for my first negotiations with the American Secretary of State. Dean Acheson has a remarkable intellectual brilliance. His mind never dawdles. Despite a natural courtesy, his gifts can edge him to intolerance. He does not suffer fools gladly, which suffering is a large part of diplomacy. Yet Mr. Acheson is above all a loyal colleague. I would never hesitate to go tiger-hunting with him. If there were occasional squalls in our dealings, our relations usually gained from them.

Acheson was born in Canada and does not look like a typical citizen of the United States. This was thought to have injured him politically. I cannot tell, but a consequence was that we were sometimes mistaken for each other. On one occasion I was travelling alone by aeroplane from New York to Washington, when a United States Naval officer passed me a note which read: 'You are either Dean Acheson or Anthony Eden. Whichever you are, will you autograph my book?'

Though trenchant in his form of expression, Acheson was scrupulously fair-minded. I remember an occasion at the State Department when we went through a long session on Iran with our advisers. I had not been happy at the opinions we were being given and asked a number of questions of the Secretary of State and his advisers. The replies did not comfort me and I left the meeting perplexed. The next day, the Secretary of State remarked to me: 'You did not like some of the answers we gave to your questions yesterday. You may like to know what happened after you left. I said to my people, "I do not know what effect your answers had on Mr. Eden, but they certainly did not convince me. I think you had better go away and do some re-thinking about them."' I was relieved, and said so. I also thought that this was typical of the American character. No people are sterner self critics.

We had five discussions on Iran, lasting many hours, during my ten days in Paris. Their outcome was a good example of how allies should work over differences. Mr. Acheson was accompanied by Mr. Harriman and other advisers and sometimes also by Mr. Walter Gifford, the United States Ambassador in London. Sir Pierson Dixon was with me.

We began with sharply differing views on the future of Iran. Musaddiq was still in the United States when our discussions opened, and the American Government were anxious to complete an agreement with him if this were possible. They thought that they had reduced his terms. The question which seemed to them now to arise was whether they should do their best to support Musaddiq, financially and otherwise, in order to keep a stable Government in Iran, or whether they must sit back and watch the country go to pieces. It seemed to the United States a reckless policy to allow the situation to deteriorate, as they considered it would if Musaddiq were left without any help.

Our reading of the situation was different. I did not accept the argument that the only alternative to Musaddiq was communist rule. I thought that if Musaddiq fell, his place might well be taken by a more reasonable Government with which it should be possible to conclude a satisfactory agreement. I knew that the country was possessed of an elasticity and resilience which appearances did not suggest. Iranians have always been good at coming again.

As a result of his authoritarian methods, Musaddiq was frequently at odds with his Parliament. As early as September, Mr. Middleton, our Chargé d'Affaires at Tehran, was telling us how the Prime Minister, 'being unable to deliver a speech in the Majlis, was obliged to make it in the street to a crowd of passers-by, whom he described as the real Majlis.' When the Majlis continued to criticize him, he took to packing the public galleries with his supporters and organizing demonstrations outside. But these devices were not enough to restore his authority, or to silence criticism.

We could not agree to the latest American proposal which appeared to involve excluding British technicians from Iran and handing over a very valuable British asset. Nor could we accept the principle of confiscation without compensation. In my view, no agreement would be better than a bad one.

The United States Government had another anxiety, that we should not be able to prevent the production and sale of the oil in Iran without our agreement. Despite the present lack of facilities, Musaddiq might eventually be able to sell a considerable quantity. I did not believe that this would happen because the oil would be stolen and we had a Hague Court decision behind us to prevent it being sold.

In order to clarify our differences in the technical as well as in the political spheres, I suggested that I should arrange for such discussions to be held in Paris at once. This was welcomed by Mr. Acheson and they took place at our Embassy three evenings later. On one of the intervening evenings, we had another useful talk over the political issues in which our American friends explained their difficulties with Musaddiq, who was still in Washington and was said to be in a negotiating mood. Against this, the situation in Iran was described as becoming very critical. Musaddiq had authorized the application of martial law in Tehran. I repeated my arguments and reaffirmed my conviction that communism was not the only alternative to Musaddiq.

On the evening of November 7th our two advisers arrived from London, bringing with them instructions which had the approval of the Prime Minister and the Cabinet. They were in accordance with the views I had expressed before leaving London. We explained our objections to the United States proposals and, after some discussion of these, we were asked what alternative solution we would think practicable and acceptable. I then put forward our proposal for American participation. The Americans were properly reluctant to appear in the rôle of securing commercial interests for themselves. Mr. Harriman thought, however, that if this proposal had been made the previous summer, it might have influenced Iranian thinking and have led to a more satisfactory situation. So did I, though I did not say so.

In my own examination of this question, I noted how much we had suffered from the failure of our two countries to agree. I told the American negotiators that throughout this business Musaddiq had played off the United States against the United Kingdom. This must be stopped. I believed that the participation of American interests was the only way. We continued our discussions on the next day, our advisers meeting in the morning, and the Ministers in the evening for more than three hours. I gave the Americans the statement of principles which I had drawn up in London and it was agreed that there was no object in encouraging Musaddiq to stay longer in Washington. We discussed the problem of the announcement to be issued on his departure.

These meetings showed a useful improvement in work together, at least to the extent of understanding our differences. The final discussions in this series took place on November 14th. We both admitted our divergent points of view about the future of Iran. In other respects we were drawing closer. We decided that it might be wiser not to issue any immediate British statement. We agreed that we would pursue, with the United States, the idea of an arrangement through the International Bank. At Mr. Harriman's suggestion I undertook to look again at some letters he had written to Dr. Musaddiq.

Outwardly it might seem that we had not made much progress, but I felt that there was a gleam of hope, especially if the Americans could be persuaded that we were right about possible alternatives to communism in Iran. I knew that the United States Ambassador took the view that the United States ought not to obtrude their views too much in a matter where large British interests were at stake.

I have always been fortunate in the American Ambassadors with whom I have had to work. At this time, Walter Gifford was United States Ambassador at the Court of St. James's, where he and Mrs. Gifford were admirable representatives. Mr. Gifford had no previous training in the diplomatic service. He came from a brilliant career with American Telephone and Telegraph. To rise from office boy to head of one of the largest companies in the world is the kind of dynamism we admire most in the United States.

No man could have had such a record without the corresponding gifts. Walter Gifford was wise enough to feel his way cautiously. He carefully consolidated every position gained and, by his third year, was proving himself an outstanding Ambassador. Gifford's background, with its wide experience of men and affairs, taught him how to handle the British. He soon won our respect, and affection followed. I remember after one argument in which I took part, very senior American representatives being present, Walter Gifford broke in when the altercation became rather warm, with the curt observation: 'This is a British business, and now we have had our say I think we should do better to let them get on with the job as they think fit.' We were surprised and sorry to say good-bye to the Giffords. So were all who cared for the tough reality of Anglo-American relations.

I realized what a tussle lay ahead, both to align Anglo-American opinion and to persuade the Iranians where their true interests lay, but I felt that we had made a beginning which might check the 'long, dismal, drawling tides of drift and surrender'.

★   ★   ★   ★   ★

On my return, I decided to test my convictions about the internal situation with the Iranian Ambassador in London, who was a friend of many years' standing. After some general discussion of prospects, including intervention by the International Bank, the Ambassador remarked that he had now the impression that 'Dr. Musaddiq's position was not as strong as it had been'. He clearly did not think this was bad news, because in the discussion he mentioned that unfortunately the present Iranian Prime Minister was essentially negative in character. I told the Ambassador that I was sincerely anxious to bring about a settlement of all our differences but of course, for this to be realized I must have some help. The Ambassador said he knew well what my feelings were and he also appeared to approve our recent attitude. When I said I thought it was no good trying to rush matters, and recalled the Persian proverb that patience is from God and haste is from the Devil, His Excellency fully agreed.

I asked him whether I was right in thinking that there was no real hostility among the Iranian people. Personally, I could not believe that there was, however much ferment there might be among certain sections of the community. The Ambassador said he was sure that this judgment was right, and that if only we could surmount these immediate problems, all would be well again. I said that I hoped the Iranians would have noticed our agreement with the Sheikh of Kuwait. It seemed a great misfortune that Iran was not enjoying a like increase in revenues. The Ambassador groaned sympathetically and repeated his assurance that his own personal help would be available at any time.

The N.A.T.O. meeting in Lisbon in February provided the opportunity for another useful talk with Mr. Acheson. Our policies were now more closely aligned. In reply to a request for financial aid, the Iranian Government had been told that they would receive no help from the United States unless and until they reached agreement with us. This was straight talking. Clearly it imposed upon us an obligation not to refuse any reasonable offer. I was able to assure Mr. Acheson that we had no intention of doing so, but no offer of any kind had come our way from the Iranians. Anglo-American relations further improved as a result of the appointment of Mr. Loy Henderson, an experienced career diplomat, as United States Ambassador in Tehran. Henderson was an able official. He never allowed himself to be played off against us by Musaddiq. We admired his industry without which the agreement of 1954 could not have been reached.

I found one other source of comfort in those early weeks of 1952. Reports from British Consuls, who were now being withdrawn from their posts on Musaddiq's demand, were encouraging in one important aspect. They all agreed that recent manifestations of anti-British feeling were largely artificial, and confirmed the judgment of the Iranian Ambassador in London. If the present Government were replaced by one which did not whip up anti-foreign sentiment for its own purposes, opinion would soon change.

We battled on through much the same conditions during 1952. The International Bank was helpful. After consultation with us, its representatives visited Iran to get information about the condition of the oilfields. A mission arrived in February with a plan for restarting the industry. They put it to Musaddiq, but he would have none of it. The talks were resumed early in March, only to be broken off after a few days. 1 was not unduly perturbed by these developments; they were part of the process of educating the world in the unreasonableness of Musaddiq.

When its turn came, the International Court did not help a settlement. The British Government asked for their good offices, whereupon Musaddiq made a journey to The Hague at the end of May to plead his cause. He crept out of Iran quietly, for fear of assassination. The argument continued after he had left The Hague until, towards the end of July, the Court decided, by a majority vote, that they had no jurisdiction.

At this time, I set out my views in general terms in a message to Mr. Middleton, who was in charge of our Embassy at Tehran and was handling his explosive responsibility most skilfully:

> We are ready at any time to negotiate a settlement, but, in order that there may be negotiations it is essential that there should be two parties who are prepared to negotiate. Hitherto the Iranian Government has done nothing but strike attitudes. Any Iranian Government which genuinely desires a settlement must be prepared to face facts. A great effort will be necessary if any substantial quantity of Iranian oil is to be sold in world markets which have done without it for nearly a year, and it is primarily up to the Iranians to create conditions which will make Iranian oil attractive. As regards ourselves, friendly Iranians can be assured that it gives us no pleasure to see Iran in the mess into which she has got herself, and if she genuinely tries to seek a way out she will meet with no ill-will or vindictiveness on our part. On the contrary we have always wished our two countries to work sincerely together for their mutual advantage. That is still our purpose.

However, no amount of guidance, wise or otherwise, had any effect. Interviews with Musaddiq, whether in bed or out of it, affable or corrosive, did not advance us one jot.

In this same July there came a lively interlude. Dr. Musaddiq had insisted on full powers, which the Iranian Parliament was then reluctant to give. The Shah refused to agree to his Prime Minister's demand for virtual control of the armed forces and Musaddiq resigned. Qavam-es-Saltaneh, an ingenious and experienced former Prime Minister, succeeded him, but had to resign after rioting in Tehran, in which the Communist Party took a hand and many lives were lost. The Shah did not feel able to support him. In five days Musaddiq was in office again, this time with a subservient Parliament. He was aided by the coincidence in timing of the Hague Court's verdict, hailed as a personal victory. Yet it was the Communist Party which had probably gained most and the Prime Minister soon found the rabble-rousers eager to claim authority. As an alternative to communism, Musaddiq had become incongruous.

The Shah of Iran has the qualities of a good constitutional ruler. He is highly intelligent and well informed. His reforming zeal has frequently tilted against corruption, which still bedevils too much administration in Iran. Unfortunately, the demands on the Shah are exacting and he has sometimes to take and hold decisions in the face of the squalls of popular opinion. He finds this more difficult, and during Musaddiq's later period of power his authority fell to a low ebb. With the return of a less extreme and eccentric administration, the Shah's position strengthened. Respect for the Crown is widespread, if not very deep, in Iran. The nation would gain if it were firmer, and the Shah's work for his country has earned this.

After the Iranian rebuff to the International Bank, I pondered whether there was any other initiative I could take. We had to keep trying to reach a settlement in our own interest, and to keep world opinion favourable. I thought that we should do all we could to find a new basis for arbitration. This seemed the most likely course to make agreement possible and I advocated it to my colleagues.

I proposed that if acceptable terms of reference could be found, the Anglo-Iranian Oil Company should try to arrange for the movement of oil from Iran, as soon as agreement on arbitration was reached. At the same time, we would be prepared to relax some of the restrictions which we were imposing on trade with Iran. I also suggested that, if the United States agreed to this new attempt, we should suggest to them that it should be an Anglo-American one.

The Government endorsed this course and I approached Washington accordingly. The United States Government were favourable. Making good use of these proposals, Mr. Churchill invited Mr. Truman to join him in a joint approach to the Iranian Prime Minister. Mr. Truman agreed and, at the end of August, they sent a message giving details of the action which the two Governments were prepared to take and which they 'sincerely hope will meet with your approval and result in a satisfactory solution'. The text of the proposals was as follows:

1. There shall be submitted to the International Court of Justice the question of compensation to be paid in respect of the nationalization of the enterprise of the Anglo-Iranian Oil Company in Iran, having regard to the legal position of the parties existing immediately prior to nationalization and to all claims and counter-claims of both parties.

2. Suitable representatives shall be appointed to represent the Iranian Government and the Anglo-Iranian Oil Company in negotiations for making arrangements for the flow of oil from Iran to world markets.

3. If the Iranian Government agree to the proposals in the foregoing two paragraphs, it is understood that:

(a) Representatives of the A.I.O.C. will seek arrangements for the movement of oil already stored in Iran, and as agreements are reached upon price, and as physical conditions of loading permit, appropriate payment will be made for such quantities of oil as can be moved;

(b) Her Majesty's Government will relax restrictions on exports to Iran and on Iran's use of sterling; and

(c) The United States Government will make an immediate grant of $10 million to the Iranian Government to assist in their budgetary problem.

The Churchill-Truman message unfortunately had no good effect on its recipient. The gloomy accounts which arrived from Tehran did not fortify confidence in the success of our initiative. Musaddiq's megalomania was described as verging on mental instability. Never very amenable to reason, lately it had been necessary to humour him like a fractious child. Graver still, his principal motive was described as 'spite against the Americans and ourselves'. He would stop at nothing to vent his dislike, even though this meant alliance with the communists. He used the first interview with the two Ambassadors to demand money in threatening terms, saying that he would give the United Kingdom one week in which to reply to a note he had sent them on August 7th, which had included a request for £50 million.

In a later interview about this same message from the President and the Prime Minister, Musaddiq described it as evil, and remarked to the United States Ambassador that the Iranians were not donkeys and could no longer be deceived by professions of friendliness. The joint record of these conversations with our two Ambassadors is an admirable exercise in persuasive diplomacy. It was in vain. Musaddiq counter-attacked vigorously. Within a few days the press was clamouring to break off relations with Britain. By the end of October he had succeeded and the last member of the British staff had left. The final report was: 'The general state of the country remains confused and disordered.'

I was saddened by all this. There could be no question of yielding to Musaddiq's terms. I knew that the Iranian Prime Minister was under pressure from his extremists. I had informed my colleagues about this and had also warned them that he might break off diplomatic relations with us. The United Kingdom Government remained absolutely firm in standing by the Anglo-American proposals. We were convinced that to attempt to put forward new suggestions would weaken our position and offer Musaddiq further opportunities for blackmail. I was much influenced by another consideration, which the United States Government did not share with me. I was now certain that the longer Musaddiq stayed in power, the stronger the Communist Party would grow in Iran. It was an international interest not to give him comfort.

Even as late as October, the United States Government held opinions on the Iranian political future which differed from ours. We were told that we did not attach, so far as they could see, any importance to keeping Musaddiq in office. Yet, from the point of view of the security of Iran and of general security, a change from Musaddiq, in the American judgment, could only be a change for the worse. It was very much to the credit of the President and Mr. Acheson that, despite these firmly held opinions and the natural desire to make progress with a vexing and much debated international topic in an election year, they never took an initiative which we would have considered highly damaging to our interests. Only a few days before leaving, our Chargé d'Affaires had reported to me: 'If the idea that the Americans are working against us and are supporting Dr. Musaddiq and the National Front could be eradicated from the Iranian mind, this would be the greatest single blow that could be dealt to Dr. Musaddiq.' Without doubt the restraint shown by these American statesmen made possible the agreement of two years later.

Dr. Musaddiq's position at the New Year, 1953, appeared to be even stronger than in July. He had dissolved the Senate, intimidated the Shah and extorted full power from the Majlis. But his success was due to dictatorial methods which had provoked opposition from some of his most effective supporters. Kashani, who as Speaker of the Majlis had led the extreme nationalists, now formed an alliance with the conservative opposition. In the middle of February, Musaddiq launched a violent attack on the court through every organ of his propaganda machine. After a stormy interview on the 24th, the Shah appeared to yield to his threat of resignation and agreed to leave Iran temporarily. On the 28th, Kashani, who heard of this, was unwilling to allow Musaddiq such a complete victory, and organized royalist demonstrations in Tehran. The mob, under the leadership of retired army officers, flushed Musaddiq from his house and forced him to flee in his pyjamas. Only the support of the security forces and counter-demonstrations by the communists saved the Prime Minister. All demonstrations were then banned and troops and tanks patrolled the streets of the capital, while the Shah stayed in the Palace. The Prime Minister broadcast accusations against the court for interfering in the country's affairs, and attacked it for conspiring with the Opposition and the press, against the Government. The Shah's Minister of Court immediately answered him back; the dispute simmered on.

In the intervals between these alarums we continued our attempts to bring about an oil settlement. In January we were at work in London, with American representatives, on joint proposals. I telegraphed to Mr. Churchill, who was resting in Jamaica:

> After protracted negotiations, we have reached what we regard as satisfactory arrangements with the Americans about the proposals to be put to Musaddiq. They have been endorsed by the Cabinet and the company and they contain no disagreeable departures from our previous plan. If accepted, they should give us a satisfactory outcome both financially and politically to this long and troublesome business. Americans propose to put them to Musaddiq tomorrow. No one can tell, of course, what he will do. I will keep you posted.
>
> Do hope you are not in fog as we are.

These package proposals were handed to the Iranian Prime Minister on January 15th. They contained three elements: impartial arbitration on claims and counter-claims, the opening of commercial negotiations and United States financial aid to Iran. The United States Ambassador began the discussions by enduring a seven-hour interview with Musaddiq. The terms of reference for arbitration invited the Hague Court to set up a tribunal. This was to determine the sum required to provide fair compensation to the A.I.O.C. for the loss of its enterprise in Iran. For that purpose, they instructed the tribunal to employ the principles applied in determining compensation under any United Kingdom nationalization law which the company might specify. The company could, if they wished, require the court to apply the principles of the Coal Mines Nationalization Act of 1946, under which the loss of future profits was taken into account.

Dr. Musaddiq had repeatedly confirmed to Mr. Henderson his acceptance of the principles of the Coal Mines Nationalization Act, but in an interview on January 29th he went back on this undertaking. He offered arbitration only on 'property and establishments of the oil company in Iran', excluding future profits. Mr. Henderson firmly reminded the Prime Minister of four previous conversations. In answer to questions put by the Ambassador, he had stated that a United Kingdom nationalization law would be agreeable to him, even though the British law selected would provide for payment to former owners of compensation for loss of future profits. It was on the basis of this understanding that the present conversations had been inaugurated. Musaddiq reneged on this and said that he did not remember making any such statement.

I found this disappointing but not altogether unexpected. It was solely because Musaddiq had agreed to these arrangements for compensation that we had been able to put forward our proposals. We were now dealing with a Republican United States Administration. Naturally enough, they were eager to take a new initiative. On the other hand, I was not prepared to depart from the principles of our January proposals, so painfully elaborated. While doing what we could to meet the United States on presentation and tactics, we had to hold fast on essentials. The State Department was worried by the possible economic consequences of a failure to reach agreement with Iran. They feared that these would be even more dangerous than the repercussions of a bad agreement. I did not share this view, and in a telegram to our Ambassador in Washington I said:

Even if Iranian oil were to appear in world markets on an increasing scale, it is still our strong view, and that of A.I.O.C., that this is a risk that must be faced, rather than make a bad agreement which would unsettle other producing countries and certainly have serious repercussions on British and American companies' investments over wide areas of the world. The State Department are making much of this balance of risks which is essentially one for the oil industry to weigh. There is no evidence that the United States companies have been consulted. You should, therefore, give the State Department the above assessment which we have made after most careful consideration and, unless you see objection, suggest that the views of United States companies should be sought.

As regards Musaddiq's latest conversation with Henderson, it seems clear that, if he really means what he says, his present attitude offers no prospect whatever of any settlement. It merely serves to illustrate how necessary it is when dealing with Musaddiq to stand firm and not cast about to meet each veering mood or allow ourselves to abandon points of principle in the face of blackmail . . . .

The Americans wished to limit compensation to a maximum period of twenty years, which they thought might help to allay Iranian fears. I agreed to this and to a number of their suggestions on tactics. As a result, on February 20th we went into action together once again. We made no more progress than on earlier occasions. In the course of numerous conversations with the United States Ambassador, Musaddiq constantly shifted his position and was consistent only in his refusal to face up to our proposals. On March 20th, after twisting and spinning for several days, the Prime Minister eventually announced his refusal to accept the proposals for an oil settlement handed to him by the United States Ambassador a month before.

By then I was back from the United States where I had been with Mr. Butler mainly to discuss economic matters. The visit had lasted nine days, during which I held a number of conversations with President Eisenhower and Mr. Dulles. Once again I found the American Government eager for a further effort at negotiation with Iran. The following is the text of the personal message which I sent to the Prime Minister about this part of our discussions:

At my conversation with the President, Mr. Dulles was present for part of the time and the Ambassador throughout. The President began with an affectionate reference to yourself and then plunged at once into a discussion on the Middle East. He was extremely worried about the position in Iran. He said that as a result of Henderson's intervention in favour of the Shah, his position with Musaddiq had been much weakened and that there was a definite possibility that he might be given his passports. He seemed to feel that a rupture of relations between the United States and Iran would be intolerable and must be prevented at any price. He thought that in any case it might be necessary to recall Henderson and send another United States representative who was less compromised. He himself made the point that it would be undesirable to make any settlement with Iran which would undermine the agreements with other oil-producing countries, but while recognizing this, he seemed ready to bring pressure to bear on American oil companies and to go to considerable lengths to keep Musaddiq in power, since he regarded him as the only hope for the West in Iran. Mr. Dulles said that he was certain that Musaddiq would turn down the latest Anglo-American offer and the President remarked that, in this event, he would like to send to Iran a man in whom the Iranians had confidence, with authority to make the best arrangement he could to get the oil flowing again. He had in mind Mr. Alton Jones, who was his personal friend and had his unreserved confidence. He said the American people would never be brought to understand the need to make sacrifices in the Middle East and that the consequences of an extension of Russian control of Iran, which he regarded as a distinct possibility, would either involve the loss of the Middle East oil supplies or the threat of another world war. I suggested that Russian control of Iran, if it was ever achieved, would not necessarily involve the control of other Middle Eastern oil supplies, and that they could not benefit from Iranian oil resources but only deny them to the West where they were not needed any longer. The President said that his experts had told him that a pipeline could be built from Abadan to the Caucasus in a matter of a couple of years. I several times emphasized the effect on other countries of a bad agreement with Iran. While the President accepted this, he seemed obsessed by the fear of a communist Iran. Musaddiq has evidently again scared the Americans.

We canvassed a number of possibilities. Dulles reasonably accepted that, if our proposals of February 20th were rejected, we should let the whole question of the oil issue be suspended. The United States would then wish to take minor measures to keep Musaddiq afloat. In our discussion it transpired that this might include sending to the Abadan refinery American technicians and a small amount of machinery which the Iranians needed. I said at once that I must emphasize in the strongest possible terms the deplorable effect on Anglo-American relations which the presence of Americans working in stolen British property would cause. As our discussions proceeded this was generally accepted, the more so since it was evident that the major oil companies were unanimously opposed to any proposal to send technicians. There was, however, the continuing fear that Musaddiq would link himself to Russia, to which I replied that his policy was rather to play off the great powers one against the other.

In the end I was satisfied that we were nearer agreement. The situation in Iran was certainly gloomy, but I thought we should be better occupied looking for alternatives to Musaddiq rather than trying to buy him off. In our last talks we were agreed about this and also that we should both stand on the February 20th proposals. I telegraphed to the Prime Minister:

> The difficulty of this situation remains that the Americans are perpetually eager to do something. The President repeated this several times. I reminded him that in response to American pressure we had modified our terms over and over again for an Iranian settlement. For my part I had many times felt in the last two years that if we could just stay put for a while the chances of settlement would be improved.

Mr. Bedell Smith was deft and ingenious in these discussions. Mr. Winthrop Aldrich, who was in Washington for these conversations, also helped us with counsel and knowledge of the oil industry.

After my operation in April, I could take little part in these affairs, though I heard of Musaddiq's weakening authority. At the end of June he had succeeded in ousting Kashani from the presidency of the Majlis. This victory was gained at the price of open enmity with the Chamber. The Prime Minister's domination of the Iranian press and radio, his dissolution of the Senate and his intimidation of the court, had combined to leave the Majlis as the only place where criticism of his policy could be voiced. The Opposition, encouraged by a public withdrawal of support by President Eisenhower, tabled interpolations against the Government for July 14th. Dr. Musaddiq refused to attend and, in reply, launched a referendum asking the Iranian people to choose between himself and the Majlis. Since the Government was unhampered by any scruples and was receiving the full support of the communists, the majority in favour of Musaddiq was enormous. Armed with 'the expressed will of the people', on August 14th he called upon the Shah to dissolve the Majlis. The following evening a royalist *coup d'état* attempted to set up General Zahedi as Prime Minister, but bad planning and indiscretion led to its failure and the Shah's flight to Baghdad.

Dr. Musaddiq immediately dissolved the Majlis on his own authority. Anti-royalist demonstrations were organized and the army was forbidden to pray for the Shah. Still unwilling to become completely dependent on the communists, on August 18th the Prime Minister ordered the police to break up their demonstrations. Throughout 1953, every political success of the Government had narrowed the basis on which it rested. The campaign against the Shah had disgusted the army, its suppression had lost Musaddiq the support of the communists. On August 19th a renewal of royalist demonstrations was unopposed by the two forces which could have controlled them. By that evening Musaddiq and his Ministers were in hiding, and General Zahedi was able to invite the Shah to return to an enthusiastic welcome in Tehran.

The news of Musaddiq's fall from power reached me during my convalescence, when my wife and I, with my son, were cruising the Mediterranean between Greek islands. I slept happily that night.

Early in September, reports reached the Foreign Office that the State Department had been holding meetings with the American oil companies. At these, it was alleged, the State Department pressed for the formation of an all-American company to buy out the Anglo-Iranian. This idea was not to the liking of the American oil companies. The Foreign Office rightly expressed its concern that the State Department should apparently be discussing with these companies plans which were so different from the joint proposals we had agreed. This was followed up in a few days by a comprehensive memorandum in which the Foreign Office held closely to the joint proposals.

*　*　*　*　*

I returned to work after my long absence and took charge of the Foreign Office on October 5th. Lord Salisbury had conducted our affairs admirably for six months. After a talk with him and with the Minister of State, Mr. Selwyn Lloyd, who had just returned from U.N.O., I decided that my most immediate task in the Middle East was to restore diplomatic relations with Iran. Mr. Loy Henderson had been loyal in his representation of our interests. I was sure, however, that he would agree that it was urgent to get an oil settlement and that we could only hope to do this if the United Kingdom Government were directly represented in Tehran.

Accordingly, I sent off two telegrams. The first was a personal message to Mr. Entezam, then Iran's representative at the United Nations:

As soon as I got back to the Foreign Office the Minister of State told me of your recent talk with him. Would you please convey to the Shah and the Prime Minister my thanks for this initiative. I feel that the best way to begin this new phase is for us to resume diplomatic relations. We are ready to do this and I am sure that everything will be easier when we are in direct touch. Perhaps you could ask your Government to consider this. Meanwhile either the Minister of State, or, if he has not returned to New York, Sir Gladwyn Jebb, will be ready to discuss the matter further with you.

The second telegram was to our Ambassador in Washington in the following terms:

Please give Mr. Dulles the following message from me:
I have just got back and at once looked into recent correspondence about Iran. The first thing that struck me was the admirable way in which Henderson had handled matters, and I should be very glad if you could let him know how grateful I am for the part he has played.

I am no less grateful for the study which your people in the State Department have given to the problem, and for your readiness to send Hoover out to Tehran. I entirely agree that in everyone's interests, and particularly in Iran's, we must try to solve the oil question as soon as possible, always provided of course that this can be done without detriment to other vital interests. But I feel strongly that our immediate aim should be to re-establish diplomatic relations. You will not misunderstand me, I am sure, if I say that negotiations through intermediaries, however trusted and well-briefed, can be no completely satisfactory substitute for direct contact. Sooner or later we should have to come into the talks, and from all points of view it would in my opinion be preferable for us to be in them from the start. In any case, on general political grounds it is foolish for this estrangement between us and Iran to go on any longer.

While therefore I gladly accept the suggestion that Hoover should go to Tehran, I should like to see his purpose defined as follows:

In co-operation with Henderson—

(a) to make clear that we want to re-establish relations as soon as possible and shall be ready to do so whenever the Iranians are;

(b) to assess the political situation in its relation to the oil problem, having discussions for this purpose with the Shah and General Zahedi; and

(c) to explain to them the problems involved in putting Iranian oil back on the market, and to try to elicit what ideas the Iranians themselves have about a possible settlement.

I hope you will be able to agree to that definition. Meanwhile, the latest proposal is being considered urgently and we will let you have our comments as soon as possible. I very much hope Hoover will not leave until you have them. We should much like to see him here both on his way out and on his return.

As soon as the House of Commons met, I expressed the hope in Parliament that a new chapter had opened in Iran. There was a new Government there, I told the House, and to them, and to the people of Iran, Her Majesty's Government wished to extend once more the hand of friendship. The Government of Iran were aware that we were ready to resume diplomatic relations; if this could be done, I concluded, it would then be easier to discuss together the complex problems of Iranian oil.

The Swiss Government were looking after our interests in Tehran and I asked them to make sure that these words reached the ears of the Iranian Foreign Minister. They produced a response in the form of a communiqué issued by him. So we moved steadily towards a resumption of relations. I decided that we could best inaugurate the event in a joint statement by the two Governments. With Mr. Henderson's help, we worked this out and in the first days of December the Swiss

Minister told me that the Iranians had accepted the form of words which I had suggested. On December 5th the announcement was made. The two Governments had decided 'to resume diplomatic relations and to exchange Ambassadors without delay'. The Swiss Minister said that the news was received with relief in Tehran. I was also glad of the event and grateful to those, American and Swiss, who had helped to bring it about.

I had given thought to the choice of a Chargé d'Affaires. Mr. Denis Wright was a young member of the Foreign Service who had acute intelligence and a considerable knowledge of economic matters, including the problems of the oil industry. I was sure that he was our man. We armed him with formidable instructions and, what was more useful, with authority to offer the Iranians some railway equipment, of which they stood in urgent need, as speedily and cheaply as possible. Wright had some difficult opening days and attempts were made to enmesh him in the political intrigues of the Iranian capital. He proved equal to wiles and warnings, and his appointment was an outstanding success. We entered the New Year with relations restored, but the oil settlement still to make.

The detailed negotiations which followed fell into three phases. The negotiations which concerned Her Majesty's Government and the Anglo-Iranian Oil Company; the form of consortium, if any, which we could accept; the essential requirements of the company, including compensation. Apart from all questions of Anglo-American relations, there were strong arguments for giving the big American oil companies a share in marketing Iranian oil. They had world-wide production and marketing interests and could adjust their programmes to make room for Iranian oil. This would be indispensable when Iranian oil began to flow again. The same considerations applied to Royal Dutch Shell and French interests, which shared in the Iraq Petroleum Company. We felt it essential that A.I.O.C. should have by far the larger share of the consortium, something not much short of half. The other companies, including Royal Dutch Shell which was forty per cent. British, would buy their interest in the consortium.

The representatives of the group would negotiate an agreement with the Iranian Government to manage production and marketing on terms similar to other Middle East oil agreements. Satisfactory arrangements would have to be made in regard to the currency in which payments were made to the Iranians. These were our conditions for negotiation evolved with Sir William Fraser, chairman of the A.I.O.C., and approved by Her Majesty's Government. They were not greatly altered in the subsequent discussions.

The second phase concerned the oil companies, with the British and American Governments being kept closely informed. Negotiations for forming the consortium were inevitably extremely complex. There were differences of opinion about the probable financial results of various schemes. It had to be decided how much A.I.O.C. should receive from the other companies in return for surrendering a proportion of their interest in Iran's oil. The oil companies sorted out these questions among themselves with remarkable rapidity, considering their tangled character. Those joining the consortium agreed to pay £32 million, initially, plus a levy on their exports to a total of £182 million which should be reached in twenty years.

The third phase was negotiation with the Iranian Government, who had been helped meanwhile with an advance of $22 million by the United States. It was a political necessity to meet Iran's requirements in respect of sovereignty, while giving the consortium the control they considered essential for their operations. Careful account was taken of Iranian interests. The National Iranian Oil Company was to continue to operate outside the area reserved for the consortium, while taking over some activities within it, and it was represented on the board of the operating and refining companies. The fixed assets in the consortium's area were to be the property of the National Iranian Oil Company, but were to be freely used and adapted by the consortium as long as the agreement lasted.

The companies' interests were equally well guarded. They were given sufficient control of oil operations inside their area. In the event of a quarrel between the two parties, an automatic and elaborate system of arbitration was set up. But the consortium's best security was its own strength and the example of Musaddiq's failure. Compensation was the final difficulty. The Iranian Government agreed to pay £25 million to the company, spread over ten years, in settlement of all claims. They also accepted sterling as the currency for all transactions in return for an understanding regarding its limited convertibility. In the final stages the Shah played a decisive part by preventing the endless delays in ratification which could have killed the agreement.

At the end of July, the British Government approved the final proposals, which were indeed a remarkable improvement on what might have been expected three years before, when we were out of Abadan with only an indefinite prospect of ever returning there. On the Iranian side, full credit must be given to the courage and tireless energy of their brilliant Finance Minister, Dr. Amini. The three negotiators on behalf of the consortium, Mr. Page for the American companies, Mr. Snow for the English, and Mr. Loudon for the Dutch, showed remarkable patience and ingenuity.

On Friday, December 17th, I wrote this note:

> It is a strange thing about this year that though many people have written about the problems which we have, we hope, solved: Western European Union, Egypt, Indo-China, Iran, Arabia (Buraimi), very few have given much credit to Iran, which was, I believe, the toughest of all. Three senior officials helped me in turn, Makins, Dixon and Caccia. All excellent.

The agreement has worked well. The oil has flowed and been absorbed at a greater rate than was originally provided for. During 1955 the revenue accruing to Iran was about £31,600,000, a remarkable result in so short a time. It can be said of this agreement, as of few international instruments in our time, that it has thoroughly justified itself from the point of view of each participant. I have mentioned only some of those to whom credit is due. The list would not be complete without reference to Anglo-American co-operation in Tehran. This we owed once again to Mr. Loy Henderson, and to our Ambassador, Sir Roger Stevens, who had joined him and quickly established his authority as our representative.

$$\star \quad \star \quad \star \quad \star \quad \star$$

This settlement would mean economic recovery for Iran. There remained the unsolved problem of defence for the Middle East as a whole. If the Anglo-Egyptian Treaty worked in an emergency, this would enable us to defend Egypt and the canal zone, but, for a while at least, the vital northern area would be left exposed. It was the policy of Her Majesty's Government to build up an alliance which would be effective to protect this. We had been disappointed by the Egyptian Government's refusal to enter into the plans which the Labour Government had worked out. Some other approach must be found, and the United States Government thought so too.

I was therefore delighted to hear at the end of 1954 that Nuri es-Said, the Prime Minister of Iraq, was working on a plan to strengthen the Arab League pact, by the inclusion of Turkey and with the help of the

United Kingdom and the United States. He arranged meetings with the Turkish Prime Minister, Mr. Menderes, and with Colonel Nasser to discuss this idea. Nasser was strongly opposed, but Turkey was as firm in support. Mr. Menderes visited Baghdad in January 1955, and before he left, the two Prime Ministers announced their intention of concluding a pact of mutual co-operation, which would be open to other states with interests in the area. This agreement was signed on February 24th.

I thought that we should give full support to this initiative, even though the Egyptian Government were putting pressure on the Iraqis to withdraw. It was possible that the pact could grow into a N.A.T.O. for the Middle East. There seemed a chance that Pakistan, which had signed a mutual defence agreement with Turkey in April 1954, would join, as might also Iran and Jordan.

There was another reason why we should support, and maybe join, the pact. The Anglo-Iraqi Treaty of 1930 would expire in 1957 and we had to take account of nationalist feeling, even in the most friendly countries. It was important to get rid of any taint of patron and pupil. An attempt by the Labour Government to negotiate a new treaty had ended in riots and disappointment. I was sure that the defence arrangements between ourselves and Iraq, which advantaged us both, would be better placed in a wider agreement between equals.

I explained my views to my colleagues and told them that the Iraqi Government had expressed the hope that we would accede to the pact as soon as possible. I asked for their consent to open negotiations for this purpose and they agreed, understanding that the whole Middle East, including the Persian Gulf, required to be defended on the frontiers of Iraq and that this could only be done in co-operation with local forces. It was true that by acceding to the pact we would undertake obligations to co-operate with Turkey and Iraq for their security and defence, but we had such obligations already, under N.A.T.O. and under the Anglo-Iraqi Treaty. I believed that we should be much better placed to fulfil them as part of an agreement in which Turkey and Iraq were helping each other, rather than by separate engagements with each.

It was also true that if we came into the pact we would assume some obligations to Iraq to help her with military equipment, but this was not a new obligation either. Ever since the Iraqis had become a nation, they had looked for such material help and many of their officers had been trained with the British Services.

Discussions concerning the pact figured in conversations I held in Cairo and in Baghdad on my way to and from the S.E.A.T.O. conference in Bangkok. I spent a night in Cairo on the outward journey, when Colonel Nasser came to dinner at our Embassy and we had some discussion in which Sir Ralph Stevenson, our Ambassador, and Field-Marshal Sir John Harding, the C.I.G.S., took part. Sir John gave an excellent strategic appraisal with which Nasser entirely agreed. Nasser declared that his interest and sympathy were with the West, but he argued that the Turco-Iraqi pact, by its bad timing and unfortunate content, had seriously set back the development of effective collaboration with the West by the Arab States.

I was familiar with this plea; it is never the right time for some. We used every argument we could to persuade Nasser at least to restrain his criticisms and, if the agreement were reasonable in terms, to cease his opposition. I do not think, however, that we made much impression. Colonel Nasser, whom I thought a fine man physically, was friendly throughout our talks. He referred repeatedly to the great improvement in Anglo-Egyptian relations, to the importance which his Government attached to this improvement and to his hopes for its continuance in the future. Nasser was not, however, open to conviction on the Turco-Iraqi enterprise. I commented on this in my report to London at the time, adding: 'No doubt jealousy plays a part in this and a frustrated desire to lead the Arab world.' Before our talks began we were photographed together. As the flashlights went off, he seized my hand and held it.

I also broke my journey outward at Karachi, where I was the guest of the Governor-General, Mr. Ghulam Muhammad, a friend of many years' standing. His strength was at that time unhappily failing. I found a steady approach in Pakistan to the problems which still divided the country from its neighbours, Kashmir being politically the most explosive.

I made a stop on my return journey from Bangkok at Delhi, where my visit, with Mr. Nehru as host, was wholly delightful. My wife and I stayed in his house and enjoyed the easy informality of an all too brief stay. This was only my second visit to Delhi. On the previous one I had been at the Viceroy's house as the guest of Mr. Rajagopalacharya. I reflected how nearly I had succeeded Lord Linlithgow as Viceroy, when Mr. Churchill had asked me to take the post in 1943.

Parliament was in session while we were in Delhi and Mr. Nehru invited me to address the Members of both Houses, as I had done once before. This time the task was made more formidable by a beautifully phrased introduction from India's Vice-President, Mr. Radhakrishnan. Few Englishmen could match his eloquence. I certainly could not and felt rather like a little boy stumbling across a ploughed field after a leveret has shown its swift, light paces.

At the time some by-elections, as we should call them, were then taking place in one of the provinces. The reports of the Chief Whip and the comments of Members of Parliament seemed a very close parallel to our own habits and experiences.

Of all the experiments in government which have been attempted since the beginning of time, I believe that this Indian venture into parliamentary government is the most exciting. A vast sub-continent is attempting to apply to its tens and hundreds of millions a system of free democracy which has been slowly evolved over the centuries in this small island. It is a brave thing to try to do and is so far remarkably successful. The Indian venture is not a pale imitation of our practice at home, but a magnified and multiplied reproduction on a scale we have never dreamt of. If it succeeds, its influence on Asia is incalculable for good. Whatever the outcome, we must honour those who attempt it.

On the last lap of the journey home I stopped for an evening in Baghdad. I found from a talk with the Prime Minister that plans for a new defence agreement between us, together with our adherence to the Baghdad Pact, had made good progress. My wife and I dined with King Faisal that night, when the Crown Prince and the Prime Minister were also present. It was a friendly evening and afterwards we had some discussion of a tentative draft of the new agreement which the Prime Minister had produced. I saw that we were only separated by points of detail.

At dinner that evening there were some cornflowers on the table. I knew that the King had enjoyed his years at Harrow and I asked him if they were a reminder of these. Smilingly he gave me one and asked me if I would carry it home to another old Harrovian, Sir Winston Churchill. I duly discharged my responsibility.

On arrival in London I presented my report to my colleagues and they agreed that we should negotiate the defence agreement with Iraq on the lines I suggested and join the Baghdad Pact. On March 30th I informed the House of Commons of our decision:

It has been our aim to forge a new association with Iraq, which would bring our relations into line with those which already exist with Turkey and our other partners in N.A.T.O. The agreement which we have now reached with the Iraqi Government carries out that aim. It is based on the concept of co-operation between equal partners, which it has been our purpose to establish generally in our relations with Middle Eastern countries.

Mr. Morrison described the agreement as 'an achievement of considerable importance', but reserved his opinion on it. In the debate which followed on April 4th, the Opposition as a whole took a non-committal line. Their main objection to the pact was its effect on Israel. I was conscious of this, but I was sure that if it could bring new security to the Middle East, Israel would benefit also. In any event, no alliance to which we were a party could be described as being directed against Israel. The House did not divide and on the next day the United Kingdom formally became a member of the Baghdad Pact. In September Pakistan and in November Iran also joined, giving the pact a frontier stretching from the Mediterranean to the Himalayas.

X

THE NILE
October 1951 – October 1954

The Wafd – Nahas Pasha – Anglo-Egyptian Treaty denounced – Egypt and the Sudan – Riots in Cairo – Fall of Nahas – American views on Sudan – Military revolt and General Neguib – King Farouk abdicates – Changes in Middle East strategy – Sudanese self-government – Anglo-American discussions – Arms to Egypt – Nasser gains power – Anglo-Egyptian Treaty

Egypt in the 'thirties and 'forties has been described as a three-legged stool, the King, the Wafd and the British. The three legs might be uneven in length, the stool might rock and tilt, but somehow it contrived to stay up. Mussolini's ambitions in the Mediterranean had encouraged acceptance of the British by the Egyptians. Better the devil you know.

In 1936 an Anglo-Egyptian Treaty was arduously negotiated in Cairo by our High Commissioner and later Ambassador, Sir Miles Lampson, and signed by me in London with representatives of all Egyptian political parties, a total of thirteen. This multitude of signatures was an unusual but necessary precaution, though criticized at the time by the Opposition at home as being undemocratic. The procedure shared responsibility and made it difficult for any Egyptian party to evade the agreement later. The occasion of the signing of this treaty was the only time that I appeared on a set of postage stamps, and they were Egyptian.

A considerable party came to London for the event, including the wives of several of the representatives. Some of these had never left Cairo before and I arranged a special luncheon party for them. Thinking I might add to their entertainment by giving them unusual fare, I arranged for grouse to be sent down from Yorkshire for the meal, it being then mid-August. Afterwards I asked how the luncheon had gone off and received the reply, 'I am sorry, but it was not a success; the ladies complained of being given old crows to eat.'

The 1936 treaty gave the Egyptian Government increased authority and served us well in the war years. For some time afterwards the three-legged system continued to function. Even in the opening months of 1951, the casual observer felt no concern. The Wafd had recently been re-elected with a large majority. Its Prime Minister, Nahas Pasha, who had signed the 1936 treaty, had many years of leadership to sustain him. But the decay was there. The economic situation was deteriorating and the Government's inefficiency was blatant. Corruption was frequently practised and more frequently rumoured, with Madame Nahas and the Minister of the Interior as commonly canvassed offenders. The Prime Minister was senile and there was no effective Opposition. Even by Egyptian standards, this was a dismal and discreditable state of the nation.

It would be a mistake to regard the Wafd as commanding national support in the same sense as a political party in Britain or the United States can do. The elections were a caricature, with only a little more real freedom of expression than exists in a communist state. In the elections in January 1950, the Wafd was at the height of its power. Even so, only fifteen per cent. of the electorate in Cairo cast their votes. It was a rich party and a party of rich men, many of whom had grown fat at the expense of the state.

The King might have been able to halt the deterioration, but his reputation and authority were at a low ebb. His second marriage brought him no popularity, and his absence for three and a half months, on what was judged to be an unedifying holiday by the Mediterranean, led to personal attacks upon him in the press in terms unbelievable a year before.

Increasingly plagued by its internal troubles, the Wafd chose the remedy of history; it sought out foreign quarrels. Even so, it might have ridden the storm, had it remained in control of the forces it let loose. The Wafd made hardly any attempt to do so. For months past, Egyptian Ministers had been privately assuring the Labour Government, which was then in power in Britain, that they were sincere in wishing to negotiate a new Anglo-Egyptian agreement. When that Government produced its proposals for the revision of the treaty, the Wafd rejected them out of hand.

The evacuation of the British management and staff from Abadan and the loss of the refinery had its immediate consequence. The press in Egypt did not hesitate to draw a lesson from Musaddiq's 'firm stand', as it was proclaimed. This proved to their satisfaction that the British would yield to a campaign of threats and violence.

In October, Nahas Pasha, to deafening plaudits, denounced the Anglo-Egyptian Treaty, which had still five years to run. Even before this, terrorist activity had been growing, especially in the canal zone. It now multiplied, encouraged by a violently extremist press, which on this scale was a new phenomenon in Egyptian life.

The position I had to face in Egypt was more forbidding than anything which was happening in Persia. I was convinced that there the situation had been made worse by some unimaginative mishandling, which I believed could be remedied. In Egypt the outlook was much darker; almost everything seemed rotten in the state. Food prices were rising sharply and income tax had been increased upon all but those best able to pay. 'Liberation squads' were occupied extorting subscriptions, but thousands who had left work with the British forces found none elsewhere. Many of these had given up their employment with regret, intimidation was rife. Contact between communities in the canal zone had virtually ceased. The Labour Government had just ordered reinforcements to the zone, where the military commitment was already a heavy one.

On taking over, I caused a note to be delivered by our Ambassador in Cairo informing the Egyptian Government that we intended to uphold our treaty rights. The text of this note should be recalled, for its first paragraph was consistently applied by us to later events. Failure by the world to heed this truth is, in my judgment, the chief cause of the deterioration in international relations. Bad practices have been indulged and they have grown and multiplied:

> The Anglo-Egyptian Treaty of friendship and alliance of 1936 contains no provision for unilateral denunciation at any time. If the principle were accepted that one party to such a treaty were entitled to denounce that treaty unilaterally, no reliance could be placed on any international agreement, and the whole basis and structure of international relations would cease to exist.
>
> The action of the Egyptian Government in repudiating this treaty is therefore illegal and without validity, and entirely contrary to the principles of the Charter of the United Nations, paragraph 3 of the preamble to which expressly states that one of the main purposes of the organization is 'to establish conditions under

which justice and respect for the obligations arising from treaties and other sources of international law can be maintained'.

His Majesty's Government are willing, as were their predecessors, to enter into negotiation at any time for a revision of the treaty of 1936, under the procedure set forth in Articles 8 and 16 of that treaty. Meanwhile they regard the treaty and the condominium agreements of 1899 as remaining in force, and intend fully to maintain their rights under those instruments.

In addition they hold the Egyptian Government responsible for any breach of the peace and any damage to life or property that may result from their purported abrogation of those instruments.

The United Nations were due to hold their annual General Assembly within a few days of my return to the Foreign Office. The meeting was in Paris and I decided to use this occasion to display Western unity in Middle Eastern affairs. I intended to anticipate criticism from Arab states against the Middle Eastern defence plan of our predecessors and I prepared a text accordingly. After discussion with our allies, I abandoned my draft and agreed to work upon an American text.

This became a document of some importance. It set out our intentions, and the advantages in equipment and unity which went with them. In a four-power statement agreed by the United States, France, Turkey and ourselves, we explained that the Middle East command would be an integrated allied command. All states which joined would be individual and equal. Any facilities which they granted to the command would be the subject of specific agreement. 'A continuing objective of the Middle East command', we said, 'is to reduce such deficiencies as exist at present in organization and capacity for defence in a vitally important area.' As a result, the part played by countries in the area would increase in peacetime. Equally important to them, the part played by countries not in the area would decrease proportionately. These were reasonable explanations, but they did not suffice.

Patiently as the four Governments had worked for this proposal, it never really had a chance. The Syrian reaction was characteristic. The Prime Minister, Khaled el Azm, who had shown courage in supporting the Middle East command, had fallen. The Syrian President was backing him and he might have returned, but his Cabinet was against him. The Syrian representative at U.N. to whom I commended the defence proposals, replied in terms expressive of much Arab opinion, then and since. 'The people of Syria', he said, 'are by no means opposed to the Anglo-Saxon countries, nor do they have strong anti-Soviet feelings; they have, in fact, very little feeling at all about the Soviet Union. The threat of aggression to them is not from Russia, but from Israel.' When Syria learns that this is a mistaken view, it is unlikely that she will be in a position to use her knowledge. The Egyptian Government having recalled Amr Pasha, their friendly and experienced Ambassador in London, I used the occasion of this Assembly meeting for a direct talk with the Egyptian Foreign Minister, Salah ed-Din.

I complained of the attacks on Egyptian members of our Embassy in Cairo and on British forces in the canal zone. In both cases the Egyptian authorities had shown themselves to be openly hostile. I deplored the present state of Anglo-Egyptian relations. If they were to improve these incidents must cease. When this had been brought about, I recommended the four-power proposals as a fair basis for a settlement. My report continued:

> The Minister agreed that the incidents were regrettable. He then spoke on familiar terms about the impossibility of Egypt accepting British or any other foreign 'occupation' and said that the Egyptian Government had rejected the four-power proposals after close study had shown them to differ little from the earlier and equally rejected proposals of April.
>
> I said I could not accept the Minister's view of the four-power proposals, which had been worked out most carefully with the object of meeting as far as possible Egyptian requirements. I then enumerated the specific advantages which the proposals offered to Egypt. I was confident that the points of difference could be ironed out if only the proposals could be discussed. I made it quite plain that we could not meet the Egyptian demand for evacuation and that it was no good the Egyptian Minister expecting it.
>
> After further discussion the Minister said he would report our conversation to his Government, putting to them the suggestion that efforts should now be made to bring incidents to an end (as regards which I said we had already done our part by excluding our forces from Port Said, Suez, and Ismailia), and that thereafter both sides should consider the four-power proposals without commitment. I said I was ready to contemplate talks either in London or Cairo. The Minister said he was proposing to return to Cairo in a month. No mention was made of the Sudan. I cannot tell whether

anything will come out of this talk. I gave nothing away and the Minister seemed in a more reasonable mood than I had anticipated. We agreed that the press should be told simply that we had had a general exchange of views on Anglo-Egyptian relations.

Although I had not discussed the Sudan with the Egyptian Foreign Minister, I was aware of Egyptian activities in that country and of their purpose, the unity of the two countries under the Egyptian crown. If this was what the Sudanese wanted, which I doubted, there was no cause for us to stand in the way, but I was definitely not prepared to allow the Egyptians to bounce the Sudanese into a union which was not to their liking. We had done well by the Sudan. The country was admirably administered by a small Civil Service of the highest quality. We intended that the Sudan should have early self-government, but it must be free to make its own decisions about its future.

I thought it desirable to state this plainly, publicly and soon. On my return from Paris, I made an announcement to the House of Commons, having first secured its approval by my colleagues. In the course of this I said:

> In view of the uncertainty caused in the Sudan and elsewhere by the Egyptian Government's unilateral action in purporting to abrogate the 1936 treaty of alliance and the two condominium agreements of 1899, His Majesty's Government find it necessary to reaffirm that they regard the Governor-General and the present Sudan Government as fully responsible for continuing the administration of the Sudan.
>
> His Majesty's Government are glad to note that the Sudan has for some time been, and is now, moving rapidly in the direction of self-government. In their view this progress can and should continue on the lines already laid down. . . . His Majesty's Government are glad to know that a constitution providing for self-government may be completed and in operation by the end of 1952.
>
> Having attained self-government, it will be for the Sudanese people to choose their own future status and relationship with the United Kingdom and with Egypt.

The Governor-General reported that this statement was welcomed all over the Sudan and went far to counter the sentiment that, Egypt having revoked the condominium agreement, the Sudan should automatically be released from foreign tutelage of any sort. Many Sudanese were shrewd enough to observe that Egypt's clamour for the Sudan's freedom was not disinterested. There was an Egyptian price.

The United States Government were, however, uneasy about the Sudan and the effect of Egyptian propaganda moves, as my record shows:

> When the United States Ambassador came to see me this morning he said he had been instructed to speak to me about the Sudan.
>
> The State Department had been rather troubled by the Egyptian Foreign Minister's challenge about a plebiscite in the Sudan. They thought that perhaps we should make some reply, or at least make plain our reasons for not acceding to this request. I replied that I had considered the matter carefully, and my own strong present view was that Salah ed-Din's proposal should be left alone. It did not cause any great stir in the world. I should prefer to let it die. It was, of course, quite impracticable, and was a mere propaganda move. Discussion about it would really be playing the Egyptian game. The Ambassador, who seemed already aware of our point of view, said he understood that we would therefore prefer the Americans not to talk about it either. I said 'Yes' and he appeared to accept this conclusion.

Despite Mr. Gifford's understanding we continued to be urged by the United States Government to recognize King Farouk as King of the Sudan. A few days later the American Ambassador came to see me again to renew this suggestion, which was to be part of a 'package deal'. I repeated that we could not yield on the Sudan.

This Egyptian move advocating the acceptance of King Farouk as King of the Sudan, subject to ratification by the Sudanese, was astute. Endorsement by us of such a title, even provisionally, would be taken by many in the Sudan to mean that we were no longer interested in the matter, and that we acknowledged the King of Egypt as the future ruler of the country. They would conclude that it was no use their resisting this decision and they would vote for the King of Egypt. This would not be a true expression of Sudanese opinion. The Pakistani High Commissioner also drew my attention to this danger.

It was unfortunate that the British and American points of view about the Sudan at this time were known to be out of line. In an interview after his return, the Egyptian Ambassador warned me that the American Ambassador in Cairo, Mr. Caffery, 'was not wholly behind us over the question of the Sudan'. This hardly surprised me, but I was determined that there should be no misunderstanding of where the United Kingdom Government stood. Accordingly I concluded a despatch, in which I later instructed Sir Ralph Stevenson, our Ambassador in Cairo, to open discussions with a new Egyptian Government, with these words:

> It must be quite clear that sincerely as Her Majesty's Government wish for agreement with Egypt on the future of the Sudan, they neither can nor will make a bargain with Egypt over the heads of the Sudanese, in return for strategic concessions in the canal zone.

In the last week of January 1952, the Prime Minister was sailing the Atlantic on a return journey from the United States and I was in charge in his absence. There had been a bloody affray in the canal zone on January 25th, between our forces and two Egyptian police posts, with heavy casualties to the Egyptians. The next day demonstrations took place in Cairo, in the dust and confusion of which small gangs of men appeared suddenly in a number of places in the centre of the city and began systematically firing buildings. All eye-witness accounts agreed that these gangs were very well organized; they worked on a carefully prepared plan and carried with them lists of their targets. They had battering rams, rags soaked in kerosene and all the paraphernalia of arson. A number of British-owned buildings were set on fire, as well as cinemas, restaurants, cafés and department stores. Some of these were owned by British subjects, but not all. Nevertheless, the violence was in the main anti-British. The most tragic occurrence was at the Turf Club, where the Canadian Trade Commissioner and nine British subjects were killed, most of them murdered by the mob.

It is impossible to determine how far the Government were implicated in all this. The Minister of the Interior, Serag ed-Din, probably knew what was intended. Outside the Turf Club, forty police were usually stationed because of repeated threats. That morning they had been reduced to four.

The material damage in central Cairo was later estimated to amount to three or four million pounds to British interests alone. The fire brigades had been prevented from working and much of their equipment had been destroyed. Had there been any wind that day, most of Cairo east of the Nile would have burnt out. The army was called in and arrived at the centre of the city in the late afternoon, whereupon the gangs melted away, leaving only the mob which was easily dealt with.

The destructive work of the day was caused by two different elements, the organized gangs which destroyed specific objectives, and the mob which followed in their wake like jackals after the larger beasts of prey. The gangs showed extraordinary efficiency and discipline. Several organizations are thought to have played a part. The Peace Movement, a semi-communist body, was one of these. The Socialist Party, led by Ahmed Hussein, was also under suspicion, and some members of the Muslim Brotherhood may have had a hand. I think it probable that an expert communist organizer, perhaps a member of the Peace Movement, controlled the business, which had a definite revolutionary flavour.

While Cairo blazed, messages began to come through from the Embassy to the Foreign Office and on the teleprinter from our military headquarters in the canal zone to the War Office. A plan had been worked out under which our forces would intervene in Cairo and Alexandria to protect the lives and property of British subjects, including Maltese. However, during this Saturday, a message arrived from the British command in Egypt expressing concern at the resistance shown in the recent fighting at the police post. Serious doubts were expressed as to whether the forces available from the canal zone would be enough for the tasks allotted them under the plan. Most of my senior Cabinet colleagues were away from London that Saturday. The Lord Chancellor, Lord Simonds, was at hand and I asked him to come round to my flat in Carlton Gardens. I told him of the position and showed him a message I was sending to our Commander, saying that if instructed to intervene he must do so, whatever the risks. The Lord Chancellor firmly agreed.

The belief that we had the forces and the conviction that we were prepared to use them were powerful arguments in prodding the Egyptian army to quell the riots. Whether at the order of King or Government, this military action saved Cairo. The fear that our forces were arriving also exerted an influence the next day, when, after prolonged discussions at the Palace, the King dismissed Nahas Pasha and called upon Ali Maher to form a Government. Though so recently all-conquering, the Wafd never returned to power. It had been the fleshy body of Egyptian politics since 1920. The Wafd had destroyed itself by its excesses and almost destroyed Egypt by its example.

The country was teetering on the edge of anarchy. Ali Maher was old, skilled and cunning, but he had an almost impossible task. Much of Cairo was still smouldering, so was the Wafd, with its agents among the King's company. Ali Maher only lasted five weeks. His success was that he restored order, stopped the radio excesses, called off the 'liberation squads' and reduced the cost of living. His was the first Government for years to do anything for the poor of Egypt, no mean record. He promised to arraign the Wafd for their corruption, but he put it off from day to day. His brother had been assassinated and he did not want to share his fate.

Ali Maher served his country well, yet the King was wise to make a change. With Hilali Pasha, who was vigorous and sincere, at its head and Ali Maher's two strongest Ministers to help him at the Treasury and the Interior, the new Government had a fair chance to survive, particularly if our negotiations for a treaty could make progress. Here we were back in the public opinion dilemma which the Wafd had created. We could not make the concessions which the Wafd had demanded because some were at the expense of another country. It was difficult for Hilali to take less. We had, therefore, to find a new approach and sufficient cover to satisfy opinion while we went to work.

At the end of March, the United States Government pressed us to hasten our discussions with Egypt. 'Our information', they told us, 'leads us to believe that as each day passes without definite progress towards resolving outstanding issues, the eventual survival of the present Government is placed increasingly in jeopardy.' An immediate start on the withdrawal of our forces from Egypt was urged upon us. The United States Ambassador in London was understanding, as usual, and admitted that there was perhaps something of the cloister about the study which he presented on behalf of his Government.

I was concerned at the implication of this American proposal for the Sudan. It included British recognition of the title 'King of the Sudan' for the Egyptian King. As I had explained several times before, any such recognition, except by agreement with the Sudanese, which was not likely to be forthcoming, would be regarded in the Sudan as a betrayal. I expressed to the Ambassador the hope that Mr. Caffery would not continue to think that it was impossible to reach an agreement with the Egyptians without recognition by us of the title.

In my written reply to this United States document, I also explained the problem of the redeployment of our forces in the Middle East. Gaza had been examined and rejected as a possible alternative station. Other areas had other limitations. 'All this', I wrote, 'does not make it easier for us to agree to a large and immediate withdrawal of troops from the canal zone, while continuing to prepare for the defence of the Middle East against outside aggression.' While I set out our difficulties to the United States Government, who were naturally impatient, I was trying to find a solution of Egyptian-Sudanese relations which would not be a breach of our engagement to the Sudan. I called home the Governor-General, Sir Robert Howe, and our Ambassador in Cairo, Sir Ralph Stevenson, and held a number of meetings with them and my Foreign Office advisers. As a result of these consultations we evolved the following formula, which the Governor-General was authorized to put to the Executive Council in Khartoum, while our Ambassador in Cairo approached the Egyptian Government:

> The Egyptian Government having declared that His Majesty King Farouk holds the title of King of Egypt and the Sudan, Her Majesty's Government re-affirm that they would accept either the unity of Egypt and the Sudan under the Egyptian Crown or any other status for the Sudan, provided that it resulted from the exercise of the right of the Sudanese people freely to decide their future status, which right is recognized and accepted by both Governments. Her Majesty's Government realize that there are differences of opinion between the two Governments as to the question of the King's title during the interim period before self-determination. They therefore also declare that they are ready to enter into immediate consultation with the Sudanese in regard to this matter, in order to ascertain whether any solution is possible, agreeable to the Sudanese and consistent with the pledges given by Her Majesty's Government to them.

I had some hopes that our statement would bring about joint discussions between the Egyptians and the Sudanese. I was ready to encourage these, especially with Hilali's Government, but I was not prepared to dragoon the Sudanese against their better judgment.

The Governor-General reported that the immediate reaction of the Sudanese members of his Council was one of caution and suspicion. They felt that there must be a catch somewhere, and the psychological effect of the reference to King Farouk's title of 'King of the Sudan' in the opening sentence was evident. Some of them raised the question which the Governor-General had anticipated. Would Her Majesty's Government, after consultation, insist on recognition of the title, even if the Sudanese were opposed to it? Clearly we could not do this.

The Egyptian Ambassador in London, Amr Pasha, continued to work for agreement, and was able to report some progress at the Cairo end of the line. I told him that if relations continued to improve, we could make a start with some deliveries of military equipment, at least for training purposes.

Direct discussions between Egypt and the Sudan made little progress. Throughout May and June, at meetings and in despatches, American pressure was heavy upon us to put pressure on the Sudanese. At one of these discussions I had to say bluntly that we could not keep the Egyptian Government alive by feeding the Sudanese to them.

Early in June, Mr. Byroade visited London after a tour of the Middle East made on behalf of the American State Department. He suggested that some really authoritative figure might visit the Sudan, and so explain matters to the Sudanese that they would be prepared to acquiesce in the title.

The business could not, however, be settled so simply. The Sudanese desire for independence was deep and real; so was their suspicion of the Egyptians. By the end of the month it was clear that the Sudanese were not prepared to accept King Farouk's claim to be their King. While the visit of the Sudanese delegation to Cairo had, for the first time, injected some realism into relations between Egypt and the Sudan, no Egyptian Government dared to reach an agreement with us without some satisfaction on the Sudan, which the Sudanese were not prepared to give. When the Wafd Government had denounced their treaty with us, they had also abrogated the condominium agreement by which our two countries held joint responsibility in the Sudan. That was not the fault of the present Egyptian Government, who wanted to regain the position the Wafd had thrown away. We were ready to help them as far as we could do so, without being false to our own engagement to the Sudan.

The position was usefully discussed at meetings with Mr. Acheson at the Foreign Office at the end of June, which both the Governor-General of the Sudan and our Ambassador in Cairo attended. The United States Ambassador in London and Mr. Acheson's Middle Eastern advisers came with him. We explained the deadlock in our negotiations with Egypt over the question of the recognition of King Farouk's title. Sir Sayed Abdul Rahman el Mahdi was not prepared to accept that claim. As one of the two principal leaders in the Sudan, and chief of the largest political party, the Sayed's representative had been in Cairo and failed to agree with his hosts. On the other hand we wished to help the present Egyptian Government. It was my hope that we might be able to handle together the programme of constitutional development for the Sudan. Accordingly, I proposed to invite the Egyptians to discuss with us a draft statute submitted by the Governor-General for the self-government of the country.

I explained that while the Sudanese were against the King's title, they did recognize the need for close relations with Egypt. I thought that my method would take account of these realities, and enable Egypt and ourselves to help the Sudan's political development. The first Sudanese Parliament would be elected in the autumn. It could pronounce on the King's title, and, though it might not be anxious to do so, we were ready to give encouragement. By promoting direct talks between the Egyptians and Sudanese, we thought we had opened a back door which might help us to get round the question of the King's title. I was proposing to open another door by enabling the Egyptians to associate themselves with the last stages of constitutional development in the Sudan.

Our American guests accepted these plans as useful, but they continued to hover round the title, and thought we should talk to the Sudanese and impress upon them the importance of agreement with Egypt.

We had scarcely dispersed, when bad news came out of Egypt. Hilali's government was firm and honest. I thought it the best the country had known for years. It was making ready to arraign those who had waxed on previous systems of graft. The Wafd leaders were to be indicted. It was also reported that the Finance Minister intended to press the Government's claims against Abboud Pasha, for unpaid taxes amounting to several millions of Egyptian pounds. Abboud was a man of immense riches, the source of some of whose fortune was known to the Wafd. Into this morass Hilali resolved to move. I admired his courage, but in a state rotted by bribery and sodden with favouritism, the path of the reformer is slippery and full of peril.

Threatened with these unpleasant exposures, Abboud took action at the Palace, paying large sums of money in Swiss francs to two of its less creditable but influential hangers-on, Elias Andraos Pasha and Kerim Tabet Pasha. These two worthies were to engineer Hilali's downfall. The Prime Minister soon found himself entangled in a financial and political mesh, characteristic of Egypt. The combination of Abboud Pasha, who feared he might have to pay taxes, and ex-Wafdist Ministers, who saw themselves being indicted for corruption, overthrew Hilali Pasha.

This palace intrigue was damaging to the country and to the King. Hafiz Afifi Pasha, his senior adviser, had tried to save King Farouk from the consequences of his own acts. Seeing clearly the dangers, this loyal servant did everything he could to persuade Hilali to carry on. He failed, and the Prime Minister's resignation marked the beginning of the end of royal rule in Egypt.

A confused and decaying interlude followed, in which small men had their way. Sirry Pasha was sent for by the King to form a Government. He was an unimpressive personality with little following, and there was no rush to serve. The faithful Hafiz Afifi was at work meanwhile attempting to secure the appointment of a Prime Minister of repute and some integrity. He was still trying to save the reputation of the King. On his pleading, Bahi ed-Din Barakat Pasha was sent for to form a Government. He could have met the needs of the hour but King Farouk's evil star was now guiding him. Barakat Pasha had been at work only a few hours, when the King changed his mind and summoned Sirry Pasha once again, in the middle of the night of July 1st-2nd. This time he formed a Government of underlings and the unknown, the inclusion of Kerim Tabet Pasha being a sinister warning. There were to be no more attempts to root out corruption. Egypt was back in its dirty financial groove.

I thought that these events heralded the return of the Wafd, and so it seemed to many in Egypt. Pictures were shown of the former Prime Minister, Nahas Pasha, in his silk dressing-gown welcoming back his most discreditable colleague, Serag ed-Din, who had been under restraint for corruption and his alleged part in the Cairo riots.

The affairs of Egypt were now sharply set upon a downward course. The intriguers were triumphant, and honest men hid their heads. They would be lucky if they did not find themselves in prison. The King knew well enough that the British Government deplored and resented the fall of Hilali, but this did not trouble him. He felt no need to take account of us. He thought that he could always prevent Britain taking strong action in Egypt by appealing to the United States and working on their Ambassador's fears of a revolution. He also thought that if a revolution occurred, British forces would in the last resort come to his rescue. In this he was mistaken. Although we had a plan for intervention, should a crisis threaten British lives, we had decided that it could only be brought into action by a Ministerial decision. It would be wrong to place heavy political responsibility on the Commander-in-Chief.

Our Chargé d'Affaires in Cairo commented, in a despatch, that it was necessary to make an end to the practice of Egypt playing on American fears and on the vanity of the United States Ambassador in Cairo. The King must be urged to restore to power men of proven character and resolute in action. As a result of this message, I instructed a senior member of the Foreign Office to see the United States Ambassador and put the position clearly before him. He gave Mr. Gifford our information and told him that we knew that the United States Ambassador in Cairo, Mr. Caffery, had had talks with Abboud Pasha and Kerim Tabet before the recent change of Government in Egypt. We did not suppose that Mr. Caffery had told these men that the United States would favour a change of Government leading to the return of the Wafd, but the fact that he had talked to them had been widely misinterpreted in Egypt.

As usual, Mr. Gifford was most helpful and did everything he could to bring our policies into line. Unfortunately he was only partly successful. He could only agree that Egyptian opinion knew of the divergencies between our two Governments. In particular, Egypt was aware of Mr. Caffery's insistence on the importance of the King's dual title, Egypt and the Sudan. The Foreign Office representative commented to the Ambassador: 'It was unfortunate that the United States Government found such difficulty generally in the Middle East in giving Her Majesty's Government support in the only way in which the Oriental understood the word.' Egyptians, and King Farouk in particular, he said, must be made to realize that they could not rely on driving a wedge between us and the Americans.

These differences were also known in the Sudan, where, in an interview Sir Sayed Abdul Rahman expressed a hope that constitutional progress in the Sudan would not be held up, despite American pressure on Her Majesty's Government to yield to Egyptian demands.

The rottenness and inefficiency of the new administration in Egypt were soon apparent. Sirry Pasha's Government lasted barely three weeks, the monarchy a few days more. The new Prime Minister took over the portfolios of War and Marine, as well as a number of other offices. The King appointed one of his favourites, General Hussein Sirry Amer, to the committee of the Officers Club, the epitome of the military life of Egypt. The General was most unpopular and suspected of murdering a fellow officer. When the King's appointment was rejected, he retaliated by dismissing the committee. The Prime Minister was troubled that discipline might collapse, and said as much in a letter to our Embassy asking for the release of British war material. On July 20th it became known that the Prime Minister had submitted his resignation as a result of a difference with the King over the appointment of a new Minister of War.

The Prime Minister had proposed to appoint General Neguib, thinking that his popularity with junior officers would help. The King would not agree and once again proposed General Hussein Sirry Amer for yet another appointment. It is likely that the decision to attempt the military revolution was taken during this Cabinet crisis. Meanwhile, the King had become frightened by the growing unpopularity of his actions and, stimulated by his fears, he called upon Hilali Pasha to form a second Government. This time Hilali rightly laid down certain conditions before accepting. These were that the purge of corrupters should continue; that the electoral laws should be amended; that elections should be held when he himself thought it advisable; that martial law should continue, but only against those accused of taking part in the burning of Cairo; most important of all, that there should be no interference by 'irresponsibles', the Palace hangers-on.

King Farouk had been scared by the disapproval of the Sirry Pasha Government all over Egypt, as well as abroad, and by unrest in the army, which was symptomatic of the general discontent. Year by year, after 1948, the army brooded over its ignominious defeats by the Israelis. Without much difficulty the young officers persuaded themselves that the fault was not theirs. A scapegoat must be found. They had been let down by the Palace and its minions and by corruption in high places. This was the motive power which led to the King's downfall and the establishment of military rule.

King Farouk sent for Hilali Pasha too late, the army was already on the move. The King and the diplomatic corps were at this time in Alexandria. During the night of July 22nd–23rd a group of dissident officers took over control in Cairo. The police obeyed their orders.

In the early hours of the morning the conspirators moved on Abbassia barracks, and by 7 a.m. it was clear that all army units in the capital supported General Neguib. The revolt had been entirely successful. This tactical victory was no doubt facilitated by the absence of the King and Ministers from Cairo, as was the custom during the summer months.

From 8 a.m. onwards, the King was frequently on the telephone to the United States Ambassador. He repeated, each time more clearly, that only foreign intervention could save him and his dynasty. He did not ask explicitly for British military action, but the implication was obvious. I had frequently indicated to our Embassy that British forces would not intervene to keep King Farouk on his throne. Our Chargé d'Affaires had this in mind and gave no encouraging reply to Mr. Caffery's messages.

I thought it necessary that we should at once make our position clear to General Neguib, and I instructed our Embassy in Cairo to send Mr. Hamilton★ to see Neguib at once and to tell him that, while we had no wish to intervene in internal affairs in Egypt, we should not hesitate to do so if we thought it necessary to protect British lives. For this reason we had issued instructions to our forces which would bring them to a state of readiness. We had noted General Neguib's statement that the Egyptian army would be responsible for the protection of foreign lives and property, and we sincerely hoped that no intervention by British forces would therefore be necessary. The military preparations which we were making were in no way directed against Egyptian armed forces and every effort would be made by us to avoid the possibility of any incident.

A reply came back promptly:

> Action duly taken 2300 hours today. General thanked Assistant Military Attaché and myself for delivery of message and repeated his assurance regarding protection foreign lives. In so far as possible to gauge in short time, headquarters seemed both calm and confident.

General Neguib had good reasons for his confidence. Meanwhile, in Alexandria, Hilali's Government despatched Maraghi Pasha, a man of firmness and resolution, to Cairo to talk matters over with the General. Before the Government's emissary could arrive, General Neguib demanded the appointment of Ali Maher Pasha as Prime Minister and the King yielded. He also insisted on the dismissal of a number of the

★ Counsellor at Her Majesty's Embassy in Cairo and a man of much experience in Egyptian affairs.

King's favourites, including Kerim Tabet and Elias Andraos, the two men who bore the chief responsibility for the fall of Hilali's first Government; the second had only lasted a few hours. Ali Maher's Government was not impressive, but he himself retained most of the important offices. I did not consider that this could be more than an interim arrangement.

Alexandria was entered by General Neguib on July 25th. He was accompanied by a force of troops, tanks and artillery. There was little enthusiasm, and uncertainty brooded on the scene. A number of senior officers from the army and the police were arrested by Neguib in Cairo and, on the following day, in Alexandria.

Early the next morning, aircraft flew low over the royal palaces, and armoured units and tanks broke into their gardens. There was very little firing.

The King had continued in close contact throughout these days with the United States Ambassador and made a last appeal to him for help. No help was forthcoming, and the King accepted General Neguib's demands that he should abdicate before noon and leave the country that evening. At the appointed hour of six o'clock, a little group composed of the Prime Minister, the American Ambassador, some officers of the Palace guard and domestic servants, saw the King and his family leave Egyptian soil. Neguib and his followers arrived too late for any parting, a mishap which appeared to annoy the General. All reports agreed that there was little excitement and that the Royal departure did not stir the nation.

It was a misfortune for King Farouk that he succeeded to the throne so young. He had been entered as a cadet at Woolwich just before his father died and a toughening training might have added strength to his intelligence and character to his nimble wits. Back in Cairo as a King, with one or two sage advisers amid a flock of toadies and panders, he found it too easy to drift with the tide. The outcome was unhappy for him and disastrous for his country. With a discredited monarchy and despised political parties, all was made ready for a military dictatorship, which was later to fall under aggressive leadership with baleful consequences.

At this stage, General Neguib's revolt was accepted rather than acclaimed. The revolution had one immediate and unfortunate consequence for the relations between our two countries. The Egyptian Ambassador, Amr Pasha, a patriot and a man of courage who was prepared to take risks in the real interests of our two countries, was succeeded by Mahmoud Fawzi.

Once the General was installed, numerous arrests followed of public men, deserving and undeserving. Loyal servants of Egypt were imprisoned, including the ex-Prime Minister Hilali, Maraghi and Hafiz Afifi. A number of prominent Wafdists shared their fate and better deserved it.

A new wind began to blow in Egypt and I had now to decide on our attitude to the revolutionary leaders. General Neguib posed many problems. I knew that he was partly Sudanese and had been educated at Gordon College in Khartoum. Men spoke well of him, his honesty and his intentions. He had fought bravely in the Israeli war and been wounded. His powers of leadership were more doubtful and I was disturbed to notice that in his earlier meetings with our Ambassador or our Chargé d'Affaires, he was never alone and did not appear to lead his side. There were risks in any course. General Neguib was at least a better bet than either King or Wafd. He must be given his chance to cleanse the Egyptian stable. As the King had embarked on his launch to leave his country, he observed tartly to Ali Maher that his Premiership would not last long. The prophecy was soon fulfilled, and within six weeks Neguib had taken over in fact as well as in name.

Her Majesty's Government had first to test the new Egyptian Government in negotiation, beginning, as usual, with the vexed question of the Sudan. The abdication of the King had at least removed the significance of one of the most troublesome Egyptian demands, that of his dual title. I would normally have given the new Government time to settle down before making any approaches, but I had to act promptly because of our joint responsibilities in the Sudan. A draft statute, which was to be its constitution, had been prepared for that country. By November 8th, when the new Sudanese Parliament was due to meet, it had to be determined.

I had to make plain our own attitude at least a month before, and preferred to do so in harmony with General Neguib, if I could. Accordingly, I addressed a comprehensive despatch to our Ambassador in Cairo in which I set out our plan. I explained that I wanted agreement with Egypt, but that I could not on this account delay the elections in the Sudan indefinitely, nor hold up the constitution. The new Egyptian Government must be aware of the feelings of the Sudanese. Sayed Abdul Rahman's representative had been in discussion in Cairo. The Sayed had intended to follow this up with a personal visit, but he cancelled it on learning of the military revolt in Egypt. After the Sudanese constitution had been brought into force there would be an interim period, under the arrangements we had agreed, before the Sudanese determined their future. I wanted the Egyptian Government to be associated with us during that time. I asked our Ambassador to put all this to Neguib.

Meanwhile, Sir Sayed Abdul Rahman el Mahdi came to see me in London and I had some memorable discussions with this remarkable man, whose father had led a religious movement which had swept the Sudan and driven out Egyptians and British. We had returned by force, but the administration which followed had cared for the welfare of the Sudanese, and the people knew that. I was not surprised when the Sayed, criticizing condominium rule as anomalous, added that trouble had only been avoided by the wisdom of British officials in the Sudan. We discussed the inevitable difficulties which beset the first steps in democratic government in the Sudan, when the elections ought to be held and how long they should take. The Sayed was concerned that his country should, from the outset, be guided by a responsible Parliament from which the Sudanese Cabinet could be drawn. He wanted more direct elections and a time limit for self-determination, not later than the end of 1953. I said that the date was a matter for the new Sudanese Parliament. If they decided as he proposed, I would have no objection, provided that they were ready for it. I enjoyed his visit and respected his personality and the directness of his approach.

The 'National Front' also came to see me. They did not want elections or self-government followed by self-determination. They wanted a plebiscite at once to decide the future of the Sudan. I could not agree with them, but they were told that if all parties in the new Sudanese Parliament wanted a plebiscite, they could hold one. In the event, as I expected, they did no such thing. On October 22nd I announced in Parliament that Her Majesty's Government had given their consent to action by the Governor-General to bring the self-government statute into force.

★   ★   ★   ★   ★

The autumn brought an important and welcome change. Greece and Turkey became allies in N.A.T.O., with strategic consequences which affected our Middle Eastern deployment. I was particularly delighted at this new relationship with Turkey. I had always deplored the hostilities with that country in the first world war and their legacy. One of my first speeches in Parliament was in 1924 in support of the

Treaty of Lausanne, which made peace between us. I admired the peasant toughness of the Turk and knew him for a loyal friend.

At this time I sent a despatch to our Ambassador in Cairo which included the following observations on the situation as I saw it then:

> While I do not expect the new Egyptian Government to show any marked friendliness towards us, they do seem to be approaching Anglo-Egyptian problems in a more practical way and this is at last beginning to show results.
>
> The new regime in Egypt is not, however, the only change influencing our attitude to Egypt on defence problems. Other major factors are:
>
> (a) the entry of Turkey into the Middle Eastern picture as a firm ally;
>
> (b) the possibility that financial considerations may make necessary the reduction of the forces which we are able to maintain in the Middle East in peacetime; and that the forces deployed in the Middle East in the first six months of war may be smaller than previously envisaged;
>
> (c) the steps taken towards the setting up of a Middle East defence organization: this is now designed in the first instance as a planning organization and references in my despatch No. 65 to a supreme allied commander and a Middle East command are therefore no longer appropriate. If, however, further progress is to be made with setting up an organization on these lines, the solution of Anglo-Egyptian problems should fit in with the form of the organization.
>
> These considerations, and particularly the first two, have made it necessary to review in detail our whole strategy in the Middle East. This review is now proceeding, and it may well emerge that a base in Egypt, although desirable, is no longer absolutely essential to our interests. Hitherto the basis of our policy towards Egypt has been the advice which we have received that it is essential to maintain in peacetime the Egypt base if the Middle East is to be successfully defended in war. If this advice is to be modified—and I must emphasize that it has not yet been modified—we may find it easier to come to terms with Egypt.

Early in December Her Majesty's Government decided in principle to transfer the joint headquarters in the Middle East to Cyprus. They authorized the expenditure of up to half a million pounds on preparatory work. This predictive decision was welcomed by Turkey. Cyprus as an air base was within range of the Persian Gulf, but the island unfortunately had no natural harbour. The cost of building one would have been very high. We did not do so and were to pay dearly for that omission.

On the last day of the year I had a talk with the Turkish Ambassador who was urging me to conclude an agreement with the present Egyptian Government. I explained that I was having a great deal of difficulty. General Neguib was by no means easy to negotiate with and his speeches were a constant irritant to us. If he really wanted to work with us, he must stop threatening. The Ambassador replied that I would understand General Neguib's internal difficulties. I said I thought I did, and hoped our Turkish friends would continue to impress upon him that he must go some way to meet us.

As I reflected at the end of the year upon our responsibilities in this part of the world, I thought that there had been some improvement in politics, but the economic situation in Egypt was bad and growing worse. This had already dimmed much of the popularity of the new military rulers. It could have more serious consequences in the New Year.

★　　★　　★　　★　　★

Sudanese affairs had undergone a sea change in the autumn of 1952. The Egyptian Government could no longer make the claim that the King of Egypt was King of Sudan; by an act of statesmanship General Neguib dropped that claim to the unity of Egypt and the Sudan. This was, of course, extremely welcome to the Sudanese, whose political parties made a number of agreements with the Government of Egypt in the next few weeks.

Britain also negotiated with the Egyptian Government in these new conditions. The agreement which we reached expressly recognized the right of the Sudanese people to self-determination and to its effective exercise at the right time with the necessary safeguards. The problem of the South, and of the replacement of British officials in the Sudan service by Sudanese, presented considerably difficulties, but on the whole the arrangements made were acceptable. Two commissions were to be set up, one to assist the Governor-General in the exercise of certain of his powers. This would consist of a Pakistani as chairman and two Sudanese, proposed by ourselves and the Egyptian Government in agreement, and approved by the Sudanese Parliament. The second was an electoral commission which would supervise the preparations and conduct the elections. This would have seven members, three Sudanese, appointed by the Governor-General, one British, one Egyptian, one American and one Indian, who was to be chairman. In the event, both these commissions did their work quite well.

I was anxious that Her Majesty's Government should endorse this agreement without delay. The Sudanese had been led to expect self-government by the end of 1952. It would be much easier to defend the agreement we had now negotiated with the Egyptians, which included reasonable provision for replacing British officials and for safeguarding the southern provinces, than to accept the much less satisfactory agreements which the Egyptians had negotiated with the Sudanese political parties behind our backs. The Sudanese elections ought to be held before the rainy season began, and this would be impossible unless the preliminary arrangements were completed by the end of February.

The Government discussed the agreement, but some felt that there was misunderstanding and uncertainty about it in the House of Commons. I therefore undertook to explain the agreement to a meeting of Government supporters that evening. My colleagues accepted that if I were satisfied that I could command enough support, they would then authorize the conclusion of the agreement. At my request, the final decision was to be taken that night after I had addressed the meeting.

I had no doubt which was our right course. If we delayed, made difficulties and refused to conclude the agreement, the Sudanese would put the chief blame upon us for the inevitable postponement of the elections and any other political difficulties which might result. The Egyptians would no doubt try to mount an anti-British campaign, but that campaign was less likely to be successful with the Sudanese if we maintained a consistent attitude. In the autumn of 1951, I had publicly pledged the Government, without dissent in Parliament, to self-government for the Sudan. To go back or hesitate now would be to play into the hands of the Egyptians and to cause dismay and despair among our friends in the Sudan. Admittedly the choice was between difficulties, as so often happens in foreign affairs, but the wise course, to go ahead with the agreements, was also the one that we were in duty bound to follow. I felt sure that if we held steadily to our decision, the violence of the Egyptian campaign to induce the Sudanese to align their future with Egypt would, in time, produce its own reaction. Egypt and the Sudan had many reasons for living on friendly terms and we had no wish that they should not do so. But if the Egyptians were going to bribe or bully the Sudanese into unity they would soon, I believed, be taught a sharp lesson. However events worked out, it must be to our advantage to pursue a consistent course. I explained the position to the Conservative Members of Parliament and was thought to have dispelled many of their doubts and anxieties. The Government endorsed my proposal late that evening and I made a statement in Parliament the next day. I should have had to resign if I had not got my way.

This was one of the rare occasions when I differed from Sir Winston Churchill on a matter of foreign policy. As he remarked on another occasion, you could put each of us in a separate room, put any questions of foreign policy to us, and nine times out of ten we would give the same answer. This was certainly true and I think that Sir Winston was influenced on this occasion by his own memories of the Sudan many years before. Also he probably felt, as I did, that the agreement could have been greatly improved upon.

The aftermath proved the Government's decision to have been correct. While the pro-Egyptian parties gained a narrow victory at the polls, they did not remain united for long. Dissensions broke out among them and exasperation at Egyptian interference increased steadily, with the result that, within a year or two, the Sudan was firmly set upon its independent course. Whether or not the Sudan and Egypt come closer together in the future, the Sudan has been given every opportunity to evolve its national life as it wills. We could not ensure more than this.

Eighteen months later I commented to the House of Commons:

> We want to have friendship ourselves both with Egypt and the Sudan, but we trust that all concerned will give to the Sudan a real opportunity to decide its own national life and future. All the reports we have had for the last few months show that there is an increasing determination in the Sudan to do just that. Beyond that, we have no claim which it would be within our rights to make.

Early in the New Year of 1953 I gave much time to setting out in the clearest terms, our requirements in Egypt, the offer we proposed to make to the Egyptian Government and the part which we hoped that the United States Government would play. After a number of discussions with my colleagues, I set down the ideas which I thought a general settlement should include:

1. A phased withdrawal of British troops from Egypt.

2. Maintenance of a military base in the canal zone in peace under conditions which would enable us and our allies to have immediate use of it in war.

3. An Anglo-Egyptian organization for the air defence of Egypt.

4. Egypt's participation in a Middle East defence organization.

5. A programme of military and economic assistance to Egypt by the United Kingdom and the United States.

All these proposals I considered to be interdependent and I wrote:

We must be sure that the base will be readily available in a future war. Middle East defence organization must be more than a paper plan and Egypt must prove that she intends to back it. If France and other maritime nations are to be satisfied that free passage of the canal will continue, we must show that some satisfactory alternative for protection by British troops has been provided. The United States must be closely associated with Middle East defence organization.

Here was an early indication of the canal problem which would vex us so much in the future.

In January the Prime Minister paid a visit to the United States and saw the President-elect. During his discussions with Mr. Eisenhower, he emphasized the importance we attached to full sympathy and support from the United States during our negotiations with Egypt. We were not asking them, he explained, to give us any military help in Egypt at present. We had ample forces of our own there.

The Government considered my proposals in the light of the Prime Ministers' discussions in the United States and of the negotiations I had been holding with the State Department. I had already had a number of exchanges through diplomatic channels with the United States Government, which encouraged me to think that they would agree with us. Two days later, they did so. All seemed to be going well. A week after this, however, the Prime Minister told me that while the

President accepted our proposals, he wanted to discuss with me, when I came to Washington, the question of sending a United States military representative. This arose from a suggestion by the Prime Minister that in negotiations of this character, which were so largely military, the Ambassadors should be double-banked by military representation. I welcomed this, for Neguib was also a soldier; General Slim was to be our representative.

Throughout my stay I kept in the closest touch with the Prime Minister. When negotiating for my country abroad I have often found it useful to receive a current commentary from those at home as I went along, and I have tried to provide it for others who are in the same position. In discussion with a foreign power one is sometimes drawn almost insensibly toward their point of view. Even on minor points this can add up to a considerable shift of emphasis. While, therefore, a negotiator is entitled to a fair latitude, it can help him to be reminded of his point of departure. It may be irritating to have one's elbow jogged too much; it is much worse to feel that what one is trying to do is not understood. In all the years that Sir Winston Churchill and I worked together, it was this comprehension at the end of the wire that was most remarkable. I suppose that it was in part the result of our lifetimes' experience of world affairs.

On the day of my arrival in Washington I had a conversation with the President at which Mr. Dulles and our Ambassador were present. The following is the text of my personal message to the Prime Minister that night, retailing the part of our conversation which dealt with Egypt:

> The President agreed with me that it was essential to maintain the base in Egypt and that if we were to evacuate the canal zone before making a Middle Eastern defence arrangement we should be exposing ourselves to Egyptian blackmail. In contrast to Dulles, he was clear and firm on this point. I put it to him strongly that Egypt was the key to Middle East defence but that if we were to secure a satisfactory agreement, we must act together. I pressed him repeatedly to send a military adviser to Cairo to work with Slim. He seemed finally to agree with this. His difficulty was to find a suitable officer. But he said that he would consider the possibility of sending General Hull (the Deputy Chief of Staff and an entirely suitable man) accompanied by a personal message to Neguib stressing the importance which he attached to the setting up of an

effective defence organization in the Middle East and the securing of a base on the canal.

Towards the end of the conversation I expressed my anxiety to try to reach an agreed policy with him on the Middle East during this visit. The President thought that this would be possible and asked me to go over the ground with Mr. Dulles, preparatory to a further talk with him on Friday, March 6th. I shall do this, and shall hope to make progress. The prospects in regard to Egypt seem fairly hopeful but I foresee the greatest difficulty in regard to Persia.

The President could not have been more friendly and said that he wanted to have more than one further talk with me while I was here.

On March 6th I had a long discussion with Mr. Dulles and his advisers under six different headings, one of which was Egypt. In the course of this exchange we reached agreement on a formula to cover our negotiations, which I would refer to the Government at home and he to the President.

We followed this up in a conversation with the President later the same day. At this meeting, the President said he was prepared to make General Hull available to assist the United States Ambassador in Cairo for a period of about six weeks, provided the terms of reference were agreed. General Hull would be available from March 9th. But there was a preliminary point; he was not willing to gate-crash the negotiation and the Egyptians would have to invite the Americans to participate. They had at present no basis for intervention. I observed that the Egyptian army would have to be equipped largely from American resources and that the Egyptians had already asked to be supplied with arms. There was a direct relationship between the arming of the Egyptians and defence arrangements in the Middle East. The President admitted this, but maintained his view that the Egyptians must assent to United States participation in the talks. Subject to this he would accept the terms of reference which Mr. Dulles and I had proposed. I undertook to report the position we had reached to my colleagues.

Our original proposal contained a number of choices known as Case 'A', Case 'B' and Case 'C'. In all three schemes the canal zone would be handed over to Egypt. In Case 'A', up to seven thousand British servicemen would run the existing depots and installations; in Case 'B', this would be done by the Egyptians under our supervision;

in Case 'C', our rôle would be restricted to one of periodical inspection. It was estimated that 'A' would enable us to put the base on a war footing immediately, but that under 'B' and 'C' delays of sixty and ninety days would be inevitable. Case 'A' contained the terms of settlement which we all wished to see. The Government in London had not agreed to go beyond this, though the United States Government had been fully informed of the other courses.

Overnight a telegram arrived from the Foreign Office stressing the importance of preserving, in any text agreed with the Americans, a suitable reference to the package proposal and suggesting that an additional paragraph should be included in the agreement to the following effect:

> The United States and the United Kingdom Governments will propose to the Egyptian Government a general settlement comprising:
>   (a) the maintenance of the canal zone base in peace with a view to its immediate reactivation in the event of war;
>   (b) an arrangement for the air defence of Egypt;
>   (c) a phased withdrawal of British armed forces from Egyptian territory;
>   (d) the participation of Egypt in a Middle East defence organization; and
>   (e) a programme of military and economic assistance to Egypt.
> The representatives will indicate that if British forces are to be withdrawn from the canal zone, it is imperative that alternative arrangements be made at the same time for the defence of the Middle East as a whole. It is for this reason that all the items comprising the proposed general settlement should be treated as interdependent.

On March 9th I again saw the President and reported to the Prime Minister on the outcome:

> I had a good talk with the President on Egypt. He spoke very fully about the necessity of having a workable base in Egypt. He wants to get a base which is workable in peacetime (Case 'A') and will strive for this. If we cannot get it, then we must have a base which can be reactivated as soon as possible after the outbreak of

war and in no event in more than two months. In the second case he spoke firmly of the necessity of keeping certain installations and depots under British technical supervision and control. But our two soldiers in his opinion should be allowed to judge the technical conditions which are necessary to achieve this objective, and he thinks that they should have latitude to make modifications in the optimum plan which they both agree.

I read to the President the 'package' proposals, and he thought they were good, but in paragraph (a) he would speak of the 'earliest possible' rather than the 'immediate' reactivation of the base on the understanding recorded in the preceding paragraph of this telegram.

I can assure you that both the President and Bedell Smith are perfectly clear about the issues involved and on what is required for an operational base in Egypt.

The President said he would send a personal message to Neguib by General Hull who has already begun work setting out his position and interest in these defence negotiations.

I concluded my visit with a further message to the Prime Minister:

My telegram [just quoted] was read out by Her Majesty's Ambassador to Mr. Bedell Smith on the conclusion of our meetings this morning. He agreed that this accurately set out the position we had reached. If, as I devoutly hope, these arrangements are acceptable, the next step is the joint approach by the two Ambassadors to the Egyptian Government of which Caffery has already been warned.

I am leaving for New York in an hour and you will no doubt send the necessary instructions to Her Majesty's Ambassador, Cairo, repeating to Washington, so that this joint step can be taken as soon as possible.

Hull is ready to start and, the moment the Ambassadors give the all clear, will fly direct to Cairo by special aircraft.

Americans at one time suggested that conversations should start without waiting for Hull's arrival. I deprecated this because of my mistrust of Caffery which they understand and, while acutely conscious of the time factor, they have agreed to wait for Hull.

Our communiqué said little, as is usual with such documents. On the flight to New York, where I was to speak to the Foreign Policy

Association that night, I thought with satisfaction on the outcome.

When I got home, I was able to tell my colleagues that as a result of my discussions in Washington full agreement had been reached on Egyptian negotiations. Unfortunately, an unexpected hitch was to derail these carefully prepared plans. The Egyptians rejected the idea that the Americans should participate, and the President had made Egyptian acceptance a condition for taking part. The Egyptian argument for their refusal was that an agreement must first be reached on evacuating British troops from Egypt. Middle East defence as a whole could be considered afterwards. We were not prepared to discuss our exodus in isolation. There was, in consequence, no basis on which to begin the negotiation.

I have given a detailed account of these exchanges because of their importance, and because they were characteristic of so much diplomacy then and later. If we had been able to bring about joint Anglo-American negotiations with Egypt at this stage, as the Prime Minister and I both wished to do, the future position in the Middle East would have worked out differently. It was unfortunate that the United States Government and, in particular, their Ambassador in Cairo, were not prepared to put any pressure upon the Egyptians to bring this about. In view of the help, financial and other, which the United States had given and was proposing to give to Egypt, it would, in my judgment, have been possible for them to make a firm request to attend without being accused of gate-crashing. However, it was impossible to persuade the Americans to make any further effort to attend the meeting. The Egyptians were left to act as they wished and they preferred to divide both the discussions and the allies.

On my return to Britain, my attention was soon drawn to a pending delivery of arms from the United States to Egypt. I asked the United States Ambassador to come to see me and told him that I wanted to be quite clear where we were in respect of United States delivery of arms for Egypt. As I understood it, while the Americans had made a general offer of arms to the Egyptian Government, they did not contemplate the delivery of any lethal weapons while the political situation in Egypt and relations with us remained disturbed. The Ambassador said that this was also his understanding of the position, though he had heard nothing on the subject lately. He had always taken the view, and expressed it, that the Americans could not supply weapons to Egypt which might be used to kill British troops. I thanked the Ambassador and said that he would remember that this was a topic on which I had made strong representations to Mr. Dulles. In view of the difficulties which we were now encountering in opening our negotiations, I would send him a brief memorandum of our views. I said that I would be grateful if he would transmit this to the State Department and make sure that there was no doubt on the subject.

Meanwhile, Mr. Selwyn Lloyd, the Minister of State at the Foreign Office, on his way back from the Sudan, had some conversations in Cairo with both General Neguib and Colonel Nasser, who was becoming a rival leader on the Revolutionary Council. To the former he said that, in the present situation, the delivery of more jet aircraft was impossible. The present attacks on the British administration in the Sudan and upon Her Majesty's Government were such as to make it exceedingly difficult to carry out the agreement. Towards the end of this discussion, General Neguib repeated that he did not want any Egyptians to interfere with the course of the Sudanese elections and that he promised to stop them going. The Minister of State asked General Neguib whether he could quote him on this point. The General replied that he could and Mr. Lloyd wrote on a piece of paper these words, with Egyptian agreement: 'General Neguib affirmed that it was not the desire of the Egyptian Government to interfere with the complete freedom of the elections in the Sudan.' I have no doubt that Neguib intended these words to be observed. His personal position in the Sudan was strong and he may have known that extraneous Egyptian activities would not help him there. Others in Egypt thought and acted differently.

★　　★　　★　　★　　★

Illness laid me aside from any further participation in Egyptian discussions during the next six months, during which time sinister portents began to appear. General Neguib was not in good health and his authority weakened. His policies had been restrained and civilized, but they did not always prevail against the will of Colonel Nasser and other officers of the Council for the Revolutionary Command. Outside opposition was being progressively smothered. The Wafd counted for less, which was no bad thing, and Gestapo methods for more, which was ominous. The Council declared a republic and seized the royal family's property without compensation, contrary, it was rumoured, to the wishes of both General Neguib and Colonel Nasser. Neguib's own period of restraint was not far off.

At this time, negotiations between the British and Egyptian Governments were being held intermittently and both sides moved nearer agreement. Cairo admitted that the canal base need not be only Egyptian, while London suggested reducing the numbers of British technicians to be stationed there. We made no better progress on my return in October, 'availability' and the status of our technicians held up agreement. The first was the more important issue. The Egyptians accepted our use of the base if an Arab country were attacked, while we held that we must be able to return to it if Iran or Turkey were involved. By the end of October this deadlock had made further negotiations useless.

On the other hand there were signs that the Egyptians wanted a settlement and that their rejection of our proposals was only a tactical move. The Egyptian press was abusive over the Sudan elections, but silent about the defence negotiations; the raids on the canal zone were rarer and weaker than in the past. The Egyptian Government could afford to wait for the results of the Sudan elections, which were to be held in November. Their candidates would be handicapped if Egypt were simultaneously running an anti-British campaign in the Sudan, and negotiating for friendly Anglo-Egyptian relations in Cairo. If they won the elections they would be in a stronger position.

At the end of November, the Sudanese National Unionist Party, supported by the Egyptians and aided by their opponents' divisions, gained a small over-all majority. Although the N.U.P. included extremist groups like the Ashigga, I doubted if the majority of the party would work for union with Egypt. I thought it more likely that the victory would encourage the Egyptian Government to take some hostile action against us. They could renew their attacks on our forces, victimize British subjects, or even make a pact with Russia. Many of our own supporters in the Commons held strong views on the future of the base; they wanted the Government to break off negotiations completely. I was not impressed by their arguments and still hoped for an agreement with the Egyptian Government. If we failed, we should be confronted with the choice of several undoubted evils:

First to stay on indefinitely in the canal zone, despite Egyptian hostility and attempts to remove us by international action;

Second to announce that we should liquidate the base, evacuate the canal zone and deploy elsewhere in the Middle East the forces which we considered necessary, making it clear that we would do so in our own time, but aiming to complete the operation by December 1956;

Third to state that we were prepared to revise the 1936 treaty, and as agreement with the Egyptians upon revision was impossible, we were prepared to go to arbitration upon it in accordance with the treaty.

The first course, advocated by a minority of the Conservative Party, had many disadvantages, political, military and economic. It would ensure complete hostility from Egypt and a deterioration of our relations with other Arab powers. Friendly states like Iraq and Pakistan were at that time anxious that we should come to terms with Egypt. Ambitious plans for a militant dictatorship and for an Egyptian hegemony were then unknown. General Neguib did not harbour them. If Egypt invoked international authority, the verdict was likely to be against us. The attacks on our base would be intensified: we would be unable to find any Egyptian labour; our water supply, by the Sweet Water Canal, might be cut off, or the filter plants sabotaged. Without these plants the water was undrinkable. So many troops would be tied down in the canal zone that we should be unable to meet any crisis elsewhere.

If we chose the second course, we would abandon our position in Egypt without securing any alternative base. The effect upon our authority throughout the Middle East would be damaging.

If the Egyptians refused arbitration, the choice of the third course would improve our position in any quarrel. It would be defensible to our friends and allies, and it would allow us to redeploy our forces in our own time. It was clear that this plan was the lesser evil, but it was equally plain that a successful treaty was our best chance. My colleagues shared this view. If we were forced to redeploy our troops, a base in Turkey would allow us to cover Egypt and the northern frontier of Iraq. Gaza was ruled out by the absence of a harbour and of fresh water supplies.

Anglo-American differences about Egyptian policy persisted. In a report home on the year our Ambassador in Cairo commented that American policy in general seemed to be conditioned by a belief that Egypt was still the victim of British 'colonialism', and as such deserving of American sympathy. It also appeared to be influenced by a desire to reach a quick solution almost at any cost and by a pathetic belief that, once agreement was reached, all would be well. These considerations, combined with a horror of unpopularity and fear of losing their influence with the new regime, particularly on the part of the United States Embassy in Cairo and also an apparent disinclination by the United States Government to take second place even in an area where primary responsibility was not theirs, resulted in the Americans, at least locally, withholding the wholehearted support which their partner in N.A.T.O. had the right to expect and which would have been of great, if not decisive, influence on our negotiations. Inevitably the Egyptians exploited the equivocal American attitude.

The instability of the Egyptian Government showed itself in the first months of 1954. On January 12th, the Revolutionary Council dissolved the Muslim Brotherhood after a clash between their respective supporters at Cairo University. The Brotherhood had been a religious, political and social organization, with a private army of over 10,000 men. Although it had taken no part in the original revolt, which put the officers in power, it had, at times, played an important rôle in keeping them in that position. The Brotherhood's demands for a law based on the Qurân and for a purifying of the country's morality reached far further than the Revolutionary Council's tentative plans for reform. Their political ambition, their claim for treatment as an equal force with the C.R.C., and their request for a veto over legislation, led to frequent quarrels and intrigues on both sides. From our point of view the outcome was satisfactory. Although El Hodeibi, the Supreme Guide of the Brotherhood, had been anxious for friendly relations with us, the majority of his followers were set against any settlement acceptable to us until after evacuation was complete, and many of the worst terrorists and rioters were members.

At the end of February, a more serious clash threatened to split the army junta, which had ruled Egypt for the last eighteen months. Throughout this period General Neguib's position had been anomalous. President, Prime Minister and Chairman of the C.R.C., his popularity in the Sudan was immense. The local boy who had made good was Egypt's best chance of union. But as the leader of a successful revolution in his own country his position was remarkably weak. In spite of his imposing titles, his actual power was scarcely greater than that of any other member of the junta.

The formal inauguration of the Sudan Parliament, to which he was invited, gave General Neguib an opportunity to increase his authority at home. During his attempts to do so, he made a tactical resignation, which he must have thought safe at a time when his presence in Khartoum would soon be essential to Egyptian interests. He had miscalculated. His resignation was unanimously accepted and Colonel Nasser was appointed Premier and Chairman of the C.R.C. Reaction in Egypt was immediate and violent. Although the civilian population was puzzled, passive and, at the most, disapproving, the cavalry immediately came out in support of General Neguib. Colonel Nasser and General Amer, the Commander-in-Chief, were forced to choose between conciliation and civil war, with the certain loss of the Sudan. They yielded and invited Neguib to return on February 27th, only two days after his resignation.

The effect of these events on Sudanese opinion was to leave the General as the only member of the Egyptian Government with any following in the Sudan. Major Salem was pointedly ignored when he arrived on March 1st for the re-opening of Parliament. More serious, he and the General were greeted in Khartoum by anti-Egyptian riots organized by the Ansar. These developed into a violent battle with the police, who mostly belonged to the rival Khatmiya sect. Over thirty people were killed, including the British Commandant of the Khartoum police, and several hundred injured.

In Egypt, the return of General Neguib to Cairo had left every issue undecided. Any prospect of an understanding between him and Colonel Nasser was soon dispelled. Neguib was anxious to check the army extremists, but he had failed to build up his own power. The General had never contemplated dictatorship and on March 8th, on his initiative, the abolition of press censorship was announced and a constituent assembly promised for July. On March 25th, the C.R.C. voted its own dissolution to take place in July and allowed the immediate re-establishment of political parties.

The press revelled in their new freedom, General Neguib and the junta being attacked in terms which the newspapers would not have dared to use a few weeks before. The students in Cairo University demonstrated in favour of a return to constitutional life. But their efforts were dwarfed by an impressive strike organized by the C.R.C. in protest against its own dissolution, a truly Egyptian twist to events, which succeeded. Under this self-imposed pressure the C.R.C. was able, on March 29th, to postpone its liberal measures. This decision was followed on April 5th by the announcement of the need to purge the press, restore discipline among the students, eliminate the politically corrupt from public life and 'safeguard the Revolution' by law.

Although General Neguib lost none of his positions during these intrigues, Colonel Nasser emerged from them with the full support of the army. The reversal of General Neguib's reforms was followed by the systematic destruction of opposition to the C.R.C. All Ministers who had held office under the royal government since 1942 were deprived of their political rights for ten years. This trend was intensified when illness forced General Neguib to ask Colonel Nasser to form a

Cabinet. Arrests of cavalry officers and civilians followed, on charges of plotting to restore a parliamentary government. Two leading newspaper owners were imprisoned for ten and fifteen years, their papers placed under Government control.

In October a member of the Muslim Brotherhood attempted to assassinate Colonel Nasser during the latter's speech at Alexandria. His shot missed and his failure gave Nasser the opportunity to attack El Hodeibi and General Neguib, the two most serious obstacles in his path. At the trial of the assassin, the General was accused of allowing his jealousy of Nasser to make him a tool in the hands of the Brotherhood. The Supreme Guide and four hundred followers were arrested. Shortly afterwards Neguib was deposed, but he was never brought to trial. He is still under restraint.* Uncompromising laws against subversive activity and harsh sentences on El Hodeibi and his followers left the C.R.C. supreme in power.

*　　*　　*　　*　　*

During this turmoil our negotiations followed a troubled course. In the summer of 1953, the Egyptians had said that they would not let us use the base if Turkey or Iran were threatened with attack. In the autumn they had rejected a formula which would have made the United Nations an arbiter in the decision. Six months later they modified this position and said that they would be willing to let us re-enter the base, if Turkey were threatened with aggression. I thought this an important concession because of Turkey's geographical position and because she was our ally in N.A.T.O. Noting this sign of grace, Her Majesty's Government decided to persist in negotiation.

Meanwhile relations were growing closer between Turkey and Pakistan. I encouraged this development and helped it all I could. Noting this tendency in the northern tier, it seemed to me worthwhile making another effort to bring about military talks with the United States on the whole Middle East. When Mr. Byroade, Assistant Secretary of State, passed through London on his way home from a conference of American Heads of Missions at Istanbul, I was glad to learn that he favoured such exchanges. Hitherto the Americans had held out against involving themselves in anything of the kind. I was all the more anxious to bring about discussions, because the State Department was once again canvassing economic aid to Egypt, as a sweetener, pending the conclusion of our negotiations.

* August 1959.

An opportunity shortly presented itself for an Anglo-American meeting. The Prime Minister and I paid a visit to Washington late in June 1954, when Egyptian negotiations were again a principal topic. The Americans agreed to use their economic help as an incentive to induce the Egyptians to make and keep an agreement on acceptable terms. This was to be understood by all concerned, but not blatantly expressed. The United States Government also undertook at this meeting to support in public the principle of freedom of transit through the Suez Canal, which we and the Egyptians were to reaffirm. We plunged back into the cauldron of negotiation.

Many influences were at work on Anglo-Egyptian relations that summer, the most powerful was self-interest. Time and modern needs were bringing changes. The Suez Canal remained of supreme importance, the base was yearly less so. The tangled mass of workshops and railways in an area the size of Wales was cumbersome and dependent upon Egyptian labour. It did not seem likely that in this nuclear age we should ever need a base on the past scale. Smaller bases, redeployment and dispersal would serve our purpose better. The Minister of Defence, Lord Alexander, favoured agreement, so did the Secretary of State for War, Mr. Antony Head, and most military opinion. A treaty seemed to them a method of resolving an outdated commitment. Service in the canal zone was also a poor recruiting agent.

Politically there were hazards either way. Apart from pressure from the United States, our friends in the Arab world were eager for agreement. The new administration in Egypt was admittedly a question mark and General Neguib's fall had inked it in. It seemed, however, free of some of the vices of the Wafd and showed no signs as yet of those wider ambitions of empire which Colonel Nasser was later to proclaim and pursue. On balance the agreement seemed to our advantage and worth a trial.

The Government having taken this decision, Mr. Head was chosen to lead our delegation in Cairo and did so admirably. In a few days he established heads of agreement which covered the future of the base. This included its organization and services in peace and the facilities needed to place it on a war footing, including the use of Egyptian ports. There were also over-flying and landing facilities for the R.A.F. Her Majesty's forces would be completely withdrawn from Egyptian territory within a period of twenty months from the signature of the agreement. Both parties would uphold the 1888 Convention guaranteeing freedom of navigation of the canal.

Later discussions in Cairo elaborated these arrangements, Mr. Nutting representing Her Majesty's Government. Signatures were affixed on October 19th, 1954.

This agreement was a declaration of convenience for Britain and Egypt. Neither country wanted the existing state of affairs to continue. The agreement's most serious weakness was not recognized by many at the time. Egypt still proclaimed herself at war with Israel and there was nothing in the clauses to limit or restrain future Egyptian ambitions, except a reaffirmation of the freedom of the canal. Nor were there any evident reasons for insisting on this. The hope was rather that Anglo-American co-operation, strengthened by the agreement, could work more effectively for improved relations between Israel and the Arab states. During the next twelve months our two Governments plodded steadily after schemes to that end. I did not then foresee the extent of Egyptian expansionist aims over other Arab states, nor the growing menace which Egyptian words and acts, such as the *fedayeen* raids, would later bring upon Israel. It is probable that the absence of British forces from the zone, however circumscribed they had been, facilitated aggressive Egyptian activities, both overt and covert, against her neighbours. Even so, the 1936 treaty did not give us a right to a base in Egypt, nor to the large forces we maintained there. Under that treaty, no British troops could have been on the canal in the autumn of 1956, for by then it would have expired.

BOOK TWO

Prime Minister

I

ON BECOMING PRIME MINISTER
April 1955

Sir Winston Churchill resigns – My objectives as Prime Minister – Soviet ambitions – Property-owning democracy – Contrasts with the U.S.A. – The timing of the hand-over – The office of Prime Minister – For and against an early election – My tribute to Sir Winston – Date of the election decided – Cabinet changes – The Foreign Office and the House of Lords – My colleagues – The new Cabinet

No two men have ever changed guard more smoothly. In these words Sir Winston Churchill afterwards described his resignation from the office of Prime Minister and my summons from Her Majesty to succeed him. Here was a movement which, on personal as well as political grounds, called for delicacy in execution. It was not made easier by Sir Winston's stature, nor by the fact that I had been so long his second in command. Churchill's resignation from the active political scene was, by any measurement, a world event. My own reflections were mixed.

In my early years in Parliament, my main interest had lain in overseas affairs, foreign and imperial. My ambition never rose beyond service in the Foreign Office or the Colonial Office, which then dealt with all matters concerning the Commonwealth and Empire.

For the first forty years of my life fortune favoured me. I had achieved more than I had expected when I became Foreign Secretary in 1935. When I resigned in 1938, I never thought to hold office again. This was not because I felt I had forfeited the nation's confidence; I have never felt that. At every important point in my career, I have had a better public than press. The people have understood when the newspapers have belaboured. The reason for my pessimistic thoughts in 1938 was that I knew my view to be a minority one in the party, and the hierarchy was powerful. I did not feel willing to change my party, so active politics seemed over. Unfortunately I was wrong, for war brought me back.

Though I knew that I had figured high in opinion polls for Prime Minister, before and after my resignation in 1938, I had never seriously given that office a thought. The first time I had cause to do so was in December 1940, when the death of Lord Lothian, our Ambassador in Washington, led to changes in the Government. Mr. Churchill then told me firmly that, in his judgment, I must succeed him if he were incapacitated from any cause during the war and on that account I must become a member of the War Cabinet. I was then Secretary of State for War, a post not in the War Cabinet. Despite this, my inclination was to stay with the Army, for I loved the work there and it seemed to me what mattered most. I knew the Prime Minister, who was also Minister of Defence, and at that time the leading soldiers did not. I thought that here was scope for me in the rough times that lay ahead. For once, the Foreign Office had little appeal, at a period when we had only exiled governments as allies and little opportunity for diplomacy.

At this point Lord Halifax, then Foreign Secretary, came over to see me at the War Office to talk over who was to go as our Ambassador to Washington. In his opinion there were only two choices, himself and myself. Which was it to be? The Foreign Secretary was very pleasant about it, but I thought that he hoped it would be me. I was embarrassed, for I loathed the idea of leaving the centre of events just then. I explained myself as best I could. Fortunately I knew that the Prime Minister did not want me to go either, and Lord Halifax was the most understanding of men. He went to the United States to do excellent work as our Ambassador. I went back to the Foreign Office and into the War Cabinet.

In June 1942 Mr. Churchill gave more authority to his decision about me in a formal submission to the King, at His Majesty's request. The long era as crown prince was established, a position not necessarily enviable in politics.

*　*　*　*　*

Perhaps this experience helped to dampen my exhilaration when the time came to succeed, on April 6th. Yet I was clear what I wanted to do. Abroad, I foresaw a growing communist ambition and wished the free world to find a closer unity in every continent to meet it. At home, I believed that a property-owning democracy could be encouraged to grow and that it fitted the national character as Socialism did not.

I thought that the attitude of mind was as important as the action, if we were to break out from the endless pursuit of wages after prices before we had priced ourselves out of world markets. I was really troubled with this aspect of our future. We had not, like the United States, an immense home market on which to rest, and our ability to negotiate with the other great market which must be expected to loom up, composed of a group of European countries, depended upon the kind of showing we could make in confident efficiency. That was true whether we joined it, as seemed unlikely, or made terms with it, as seemed essential. To bargain effectively, we had to have something to give, or they something to fear, which came back again to efficiency and the spirit in industry, a sense of thrusting well-being and no more nationalization. All this I intended to preach and work out over the years. It would take time, but I could make a start in the general election campaign.

I expressed my views about a property-owning democracy more fully at the Party Conference held at Bournemouth later in the year. After speaking of measures taken to assist industry and, in particular, our export trade, I said:

> The Government can only create the conditions. It is industry which must create the wealth. British industry has been doing powerful work. Men and management alike deserve praise for the increase in production which has been won. The figures I have just given show it. We ought not to forget that the greater part of industry has been running with smoothness and good will.
>
> As you know, I have personally had talks in the last few months with the leading employers and trade unionists, representatives of all sections of industry. Our invaluable Minister of Labour is following up this matter, and we hope that the discussions which are now going on will lead to constructive ideas and action.
>
> We also welcome the steps which have been taken in the last few months by the T.U.C. In this field of industrial relations I am particularly anxious to see the growth of what I call 'partnership in industry', and I use the word 'partnership', as the Minister of Labour did yesterday, in its widest sense. I

include in it joint consultation, the giving of full information to employees about the affairs of the companies in which they work, and also profit sharing in a number of forms, particularly when it offers opportunities for employees to hold shares, and so acquire a real stake in the enterprise in which they work.

Now I would ask every firm in this country to consider carefully and urgently whether they cannot introduce further measures to promote the sense of partnership of which I speak.

In this and in other ways I believe that we can, over the years, bring greater peace throughout industry and at the same time we shall do something more than that. We shall make work a more satisfying part of life and thereby raise the whole quality of our free society.

These words, and especially the last two paragraphs, express the core of my faith in domestic politics. I felt that there was something awry in popular thought about profits. The man who makes money can be an asset to the community and he is not always a miscreant, or even greedy. Sometimes I think that the American outlook on these matters is more wholesome than ours. In the United States, they respect a man who has worked from the bottom to the top in industry and they do not envy him, they hope to be like him. Even if a man displays money rather too blatantly, he is not condemned outright. We may think wealth is too much admired in the United States; with us, gaining it can be too much despised. This may be due to the concentration of wealth in too few hands in this country in the past. But the remedy for that, I felt, was not for the State to take it all, but for those in industry, whatever their status, to get more of it.

The successful company in my eyes is the one that can increase output and sell it at margins which give rising profits, from which all engaged in the industry benefit, because they are shareholders too. I like the account I read recently of a truck driver who retired after forty-four years with Sears, Roebuck & Company and withdrew $289,000 under their profit-sharing plan. He had deposited just under $6,000 from wages, the rest was capital gains and the company's yearly contribution from net income, plus dividends and interest. Admittedly this is exceptional, but not utterly so. Employees retiring from this same firm in 1958 with twenty to twenty-five years' service withdrew an average of $36,695, after deposits over the years of $3,593. That is something I would like to see happening at home, together with a conviction that to make profits is not a crime but a necessity, for the State as much as for the shareholders. In any such scheme it is important that as many grades of workers as possible be included.

*   *   *   *   *

Earlier conversations between Sir Winston and myself had fixed the approximate date of the hand-over as the spring of 1955, and before I left for the Bangkok Conference at the end of January, we had agreed that my journey home would have to be speeded. I was sorry to have to do this, for I had looked forward to longer visits to Rangoon, Delhi and Baghdad. On the other hand, I realized that the new Prime Minister would need to give answers to a number of pressing questions. I was determined not to be drawn into doing this until I had assumed office and had had an opportunity to take my bearings from that position. Though I had sat for many years in Cabinets and presided over them on a number of occasions, I knew how different the stage would look to me when I had the principal responsibility.

A Prime Minister is still nominally *primus inter pares*, but in fact his authority is stronger than that. The right to choose his colleagues, to ask for a dissolution of Parliament and, if he is a Conservative, to appoint the chairman of the party organization, add up to a formidable total of power. Some of the responsibility for consultation overseas must also be his. Every Foreign Secretary, however individual or influential he may be, knows how much it strengthens him to discuss his problems with a colleague of experience. Many scores of times after a prolonged examination together of the draft of a telegram or a speech I have heard Sir Winston say, 'Two heads are better than one'; not the kind of phrase popularly associated with him. Then there are telegrams to colleagues in the Commonwealth, often from Prime Minister to Prime Minister and therefore calling for personal scrutiny. In financial and economic business, so infinitely more strenuous and perplexing in these years than before the war, a Chancellor of the Exchequer is wise if he shares his burdens to some extent with the Prime Minister; clearly he cannot share them with the whole Cabinet.

I have sat in Cabinets or attended them under four Prime Ministers, MacDonald, Baldwin, Chamberlain and Churchill. I thought Baldwin's method of frequent consultation alone with each of his principal colleagues was good and I followed it. His failing lay in not always supporting the result with sufficient authority, but that is another matter. My colleagues knew that I was always available to each one of them and we saved the Cabinet some extra stress of business that way.

The most important question I had to decide soon was whether I should ask Her Majesty for the dissolution of Parliament and a general election. The arguments for and against were nicely balanced. There is, of course, no obligation upon a new Prime Minister to seek a dissolution, so long as he commands a majority in the House of Commons. The country has no love for general elections, and if public opinion judges appeal to the country to be uncalled for, it is likely to resent it. The instinctive dislike would be sharpened if the election were judged to be a snap one, in order to gain advantage from a certain disarray in the ranks of the Opposition.

On the international scene, I was much concerned with the dangers of conflict in the Far East. Quemoy and the off-shore islands were then presenting their first threat to peace. Nobody could wish to be electioneering in the event of war. As against this, we had hopes of organizing during the summer a meeting between the four Heads of Government, the United States, France, Soviet Russia and ourselves. If such a meeting was possible, I wished to play a part in it. It was tempting for a new Prime Minister to postpone the hazards of the poll at least until he had made an effort to use such a meeting to better the chances of world peace.

Finally, there was the memory that summer elections had not, in the past, been fortunate for the Conservative Party. The habit of early summer holidays would probably cost us a seat or two. Some of us could recall the general election of 1929 when, after four years of, as we thought, successful administration of the nation's affairs, our party was incontinently flung from office. On the other hand, in 1955 employment was at a very high level, the balance of payments for once was giving no trouble and electorally, so far as one could judge, the tide appeared to be with us.

I knew that the margin was pretty narrow; a small percentage either way would decide. The Conservatives had never had a majority among the electors since 1935. In 1951 the Labour Party won more votes than ourselves and our allies, although chance gave us a majority of 17 seats on a minority of the total poll. This might not happen again and I did not much want it to; my aim was a clear majority of votes as well as seats. I wanted to feel that I had the country's support for the work I wished to do. Nothing but the verdict of the nation at the polls could really give me that.

Before I had finally to determine these issues, I must first meet Parliament as Prime Minister and pay the traditional tribute to my predecessor. I have always found a parliamentary speech to be an ordeal. Thirty years' practice in addressing the House has never cured me of this sentiment. Above all, I have a dislike for the set speech and, if I have to speak at all, prefer to wind up a debate rather than open it. Too much self-confidence is not a parliamentary gift from the gods. I recall Arthur Balfour's answer to an ardent young Member who asked his advice on addressing the House: 'Speak often, speak at length, and you will soon enjoy that contempt for your audience which only a bore commands.'

On this occasion I was very conscious that the House, which had in late years heard me so often on foreign affairs, would be applying another scale of values in my new office. In the event, members were kindly in their welcome and Mr. Attlee's opening, as Leader of the Opposition, eased my task.

Tributes to Sir Winston Churchill are difficult to frame for those who know him well, not because there is so little to say, but because there is so much. On this occasion I made my first reference to our sixteen years of intimate political work together:

Although my right hon. Friend has perhaps the widest and most varied interests in life of any man we are likely to know— and that is true—I still think that his great passion was the political life and that he brought to the service of it a most complete vision. No man I have ever known could make one understand the range of a problem and, at the same time, go straight to its core. I believe that in statesmanship that will be the attribute which many who know him would place first among his many gifts.

Apart from these things, in spirit there was the magnanimity, most agreeable of virtues; and, let us be frank about it, not one which we politicians find it always easy to practise, although we should all like to do so. In part, perhaps, this was easier with him, because I think he always thought of problems not in abstract terms but in human values; and that was one of the things which endeared him to all this House.

Finally, as has been so well said, there was the humour—the humour based in the incomparable command of the English language, which was so often our delight, not least at Question Time. I am sure that my right hon. Friend will be deeply moved

271

by the things which right hon. and hon. Gentlemen have said of him this afternoon, for he loves this House—loves it in companionship and in conflict.

With the passage of days the likelihood that the general election might be regarded as unwarranted grew less. Public opinion appeared to be more reconciled to the possibility. I became convinced that, if we were to continue to hold office with such a narrow majority as seventeen without an appeal to the country, we should be living in an election atmosphere until that event took place. This was thoroughly unhealthy and I decided to ask the Queen for a dissolution and the country for a mandate. I had an audience of Her Majesty on the afternoon of April 15th, 1955, and that night I announced the dissolution to the nation. I chose the briefest terms:

> The announcement I want to make to you tonight is an important one and I thought that I should give it to you myself.
> The Parliament elected in 1951 is now in its fourth year. It is, therefore, not surprising that with a change of Prime Minister there should be expectation of a general election. Uncertainty at home and abroad about the political future is bad for our influence in world affairs, bad for trade, and unsettling in many ways. I believe that it is better to face this issue now.
> Accordingly I have asked Her Majesty the Queen to grant a dissolution of Parliament on May 6th, and Her Majesty has been pleased to signify her acceptance of my recommendation. Between now and then we shall invite both Houses of Parliament to deal with essential financial and other business. Polling will take place on May 26th. The advance notice which I am giving is in accordance with the practice of recent years and will give all concerned time to make preparations for the election.
> The new Parliament will be summoned on Tuesday, June 7th, when first business will be the election of the Speaker and the swearing-in of members. Her Majesty has graciously intimated her intention to open the new Parliament on Tuesday, June 14th.

Among the distractions of the hour was the London newspaper strike, thought by some to be a reason against holding an election. I decided that to ask for a dissolution and announce it when no newspapers were being printed in the capital, and there might be none for some weeks to debate the controversial issues, was a risk which must be taken. I thought, too, that the decision might influence the contestants to come to terms.

I decided not to make a major overhaul of the Government until after the general election. Ministers were accustomed to their offices, and I wished the administration to run smoothly in the weeks that must intervene before we went to the country. One position of outstanding importance had, however, to be filled at once, the Foreign Office. There was one man who was exceptionally experienced and qualified for the post, Lord Salisbury.

During the period in 1953 when Sir Winston and I were both ill, Lord Salisbury had conducted the affairs of the Foreign Office with authority. He had been my Under-Secretary when I took over the Foreign Office in 1935 and we had worked together at intervals ever since. His ministerial experience exceeded that of any of my Cabinet colleagues. As Dominions Secretary in the later stages of the war, he had access to the War Cabinet, of which Lord Woolton and I were the only two surviving members in my administration. Apart from strong ties of personal friendship, I had the greatest admiration for his mind and character.

Against all this, I had to set the very serious difficulties which must arise if the Foreign Secretary were to be a member of the House of Lords in present times. The House of Commons would never take an important statement on foreign affairs from a junior Minister. A member of the Cabinet would therefore have to be the spokesman of the Foreign Office in the House of Commons on all major issues. This could only be the Prime Minister. Mr. Chamberlain had found it necessary to resort to this procedure in 1938, and the relative importance of the two Houses has tilted in favour of the Commons since that date. I would have had to be principal Foreign Office spokesman in the House of Commons myself, a heavy additional load upon any Prime Minister. I was most reluctant to undertake it for other reasons besides physical ones.

I had serious doubts whether such a system could work any longer. There is a certain difference of view and of emphasis in the discussion of international affairs between the two Houses. The House of Lords debate foreign affairs with more reserve and more responsibility; on the other hand their discussions can be more academic. I was sure that there was a danger of misunderstanding if foreign policy statements, or an important part of them, were made in the upper House, and if the main debates were held there. On the other hand, neither the Foreign Secretary nor I would find it tolerable if the more important speeches on foreign affairs were made by the Prime Minister in a House to which the Foreign Secretary did not belong. The conclusion was inescapable. I felt it impossible to ask a member of the House of Lords to be Foreign Secretary.

The consequences of this conclusion should be faced. It applies with greater force to the Prime Ministership. No member of the House of Lords can expect to hold that office at the present time. Nor can he be Chancellor of the Exchequer, since the upper House has no say in money matters. One who is born to an hereditary peerage cannot therefore hold the three highest offices in the State, however well he may be fitted for each or all of them. In these conditions the corollary should be accepted; such a member of the House of Lords should be entitled to stand for the House of Commons, on condition that he renounces his membership of the upper House.

Having reluctantly decided that I could not offer this post to Lord Salisbury, I was sure that Mr. Macmillan should be my choice. I felt that his active and fertile mind would team well with the high quality of Foreign Office leadership under Sir Ivone Kirkpatrick, which he was to inherit. Mr. Macmillan entered Parliament in 1924, having been, like myself, a survivor of the first world war and one of those whom our elders used to call 'the missing generation'. He first joined a Cabinet in 1951 as Minister of Housing, and brilliantly fulfilled a programme which I had considered over-ambitious when it was announced. Mr. Macmillan had not set the target, he reached it. His period as Minister of Defence was shorter and seemed less happy. Sir Winston, whatever his head ordained, never accepted in his heart the position of a Minister of Defence divorced from his own authority. In impatient moments he would sometimes murmur that the post did not exist.

To succeed Mr. Macmillan at the Ministry of Defence, I selected Mr. Selwyn Lloyd, who had gained knowledge of defence problems as Minister of Supply. Mr. Lloyd's experience of Parliament was comparatively short. His service in the war years had earned him rapid promotion and he had held staff appointments. There was no dispute about his abilities, and he soon won the respect of his colleagues and of the Service departments by his handling of a new responsibility.

Commonwealth Relations was the other major department where I considered a change desirable. I had been Secretary of State in this Ministry and I had visited most of the Dominions on many occasions. I was sure that this department needed a comparatively young man who could lead it for many years and get to know intimately the principal Ministers in all the Commonwealth countries. After considering possible candidates, I selected Lord Home. He has developed, as I was sure he would, into an understanding head of his department and a constant colleague.

Every Cabinet needs its counsellors, men of stable opinion who can be relied upon to give sound judgment and hold to it. They are probably not those who talk most, but they are steadfast and indispensable in building the team. One of these in my Cabinet was Gwilym Lloyd-George. The Home Office is not a glittering department, but it is easy to make mistakes there, and issues can arise which call for moral courage. Mr. Lloyd-George is devoted to his father's memory and has inherited some of his gifts of statesmanship, though he is modest in displaying them. He owes still more to his mother, many of whose wonderful qualities of loyalty and character are his too. I thought most highly of him.

The Cabinet was now a balanced team, well qualified to go into the election. This was its composition:

Prime Minister	Sir Anthony Eden
Lord President of the Council	Lord Salisbury
Foreign Secretary	Mr. Macmillan
Chancellor of the Exchequer	Mr. Butler
Lord Privy Seal and Leader of the House of Commons	Mr. Crookshank
Lord Chancellor	Lord Kilmuir
Minister of Defence	Mr. Selwyn Lloyd
Home Secretary	Mr. Lloyd-George
Colonial Secretary	Mr. Lennox-Boyd
Secretary for Commonwealth Relations	Lord Home
Secretary of State for Scotland	Mr. Stuart
Minister of Labour	Sir Walter Monckton
President of the Board of Trade	Mr. Thorneycroft
Minister of Housing and Local Government	Mr. Sandys
Chancellor of the Duchy of Lancaster	Lord Woolton
Minister of Education	Sir David Eccles
Minister of Agriculture	Mr. Heathcoat Amory
Minister of Pensions	Mr. Peake

II

THE FIRST THREE MONTHS
April – June 1955

Financial and economic problems – Mr. Butler lowers income tax – A successful Budget – Opposition criticism – My reply – My experience of general elections – Lord Woolton's able management – Television – Meetings at Glasgow and Birmingham – A conclusive victory – The newspaper strike – Trouble in the docks – Inter-union differences – A.S.L.E.F. cease work – Emergency measures – My broadcast to the nation – End of the strikes – Some thoughts on labour relations

Before we went to the polls, the Budget was due.

During the years which I spent in the Cabinet before the war, I never once heard mention of the problem of gold and dollar reserves. These were ample for any purpose, immediate or conceivable. Even after the first world war our investments overseas brought in a comfortable income. An adverse trade balance was disagreeable but not dangerous. The banker of the sterling area was at ease, at least in this respect.

The second world war changed all this. Behind the transient economic situation the problem of the balance of payments obtruded continuously; exasperating, monotonous and inescapable. Between 1939 and 1945 production had multiplied at home, but all this and much more had gone to prosecute the war. The total effort had been at a prodigious total cost. After 1945 the banker was for ever stretching an inadequate blanket over some uncovered limb.

During our three and a half years of Conservative government we had had our full share of financial and economic problems. Mr. Butler had battled well against inflation at home and a perpetually shifting balance of payments with the rest of the world. All Budgets since 1951 had been designed to offer a stronger incentive to work, releasing the country's economy and encouraging expansion of production and better living standards. These aims were not difficult to declare, they were harder to fulfil. They required a nice calculation in the use of the financial machinery at our disposal and a constant watch on the elements influencing world trade.

The Chancellor's flexible monetary policies had helped to maintain a steady general advance. The economy was expanding and prosperity growing, but set-backs were sudden, sharp, and disagreeably frequent. I had felt uneasy in the autumn of 1954 at some signs and portents. The Prime Minister accordingly called a number of his principal colleagues together for an informal discussion. Here I found that my concern was not generally shared, the Treasury taking a more confident view.

In February the economy had started to slide. The cost of imports rose dangerously with the inevitable accompaniment of a drain on our gold and dollar reserves. The Chancellor took precautionary action, the Bank Rate was raised and all forms of credits restricted, including hire purchase transactions. These measures, known as the 'credit squeeze', were disagreeable and painful, but they had their immediate effect. By April the economy had stiffened and Mr. Butler felt able to take a further step forward in our policy of incentive. On the facts then before him, he was fully justified. The surplus for the year available to him for reductions of taxation was about £280 million. He decided to give away less than half of it. This seemed prudent in any year and restrained in an election year.

The Chancellor considered how best to use this sum to help the national economy. The burden of direct taxation lies heavy on British industry and the British people. To read the balance sheet of a successful company, which exports perhaps half its products, and to find it handing over half its profits to the Exchequer, ought not to please anyone in this country. Our strongest competitors do not bear a comparable weight. Our main Budget proposal was to lower the rate of income tax by 6d. in the £. Nearly one-third of this benefit went to industry. Personal, married, and children's tax-free allowances were raised, which had the effect of exempting nearly 2,500,000 people from the need to pay income tax. There was a risk in adding to the amount of money available for private spending. The Government proposed to meet it by offering fresh opportunities and encouragement for personal savings, which were showing a promising upward trend.

I thought then that we were not sufficiently imaginative in our savings projects and I returned to this topic many times in the next two years.

The Budget proposals derived from a conviction that heavy direct taxation petrifies effort. The danger that it will stifle a spirit of enterprise can be greater than any which may arise from increasing the public's purchasing power. There were many calls to cut indirect taxes, as there always are at Budget time. Mr. Butler knew of the extra hardship caused by some of these levies, particularly the purchase tax. He was also conscious of the dangers involved in openly stimulating consumption, and of the inconsistency of doing so at a time of restricted credit. He decided that indirect taxes must stand, with one exception. The textile industries of Lancashire and Northern Ireland were experiencing particular difficulties. To help them, Mr. Butler halved the purchase tax on all cotton and allied goods.

Such were the financial proposals placed before Parliament and the long-term considerations on which we based them. They seemed to me to strike a fair balance. When I consider the surplus at the Chancellor's disposal, I am astonished at his moderation. During the election campaign which followed, the Budget was battered about. There was little logic in this, since the concessions the Opposition advocated would have cost much more, a phenomenon not unknown in politics. As I said in the House of Commons on a later occasion, 'Sometimes it was called an electioneering Budget and sometimes it was called a robbing-the-poor Budget. I confess that how it can be both at the same time beats me.'

*　　*　　*　　*　　*

I do not lack experience of the hustings. Besides fighting ten general elections, I can boast one record that is not likely to be beaten. I spoke at every by-election from 1946 to 1951 and we never gained one. But I got to know quite a lot of people and what they thought, which is useful for a Foreign Secretary.

Politicians are of two categories, those who enjoy elections and those who endure them. I belong to the second category. Perhaps the least disagreeable of my contests was the first, in County Durham. I was on home ground and the miners were pleasantly tolerant of my beliefs, though they never dreamt of voting for them. Joe Batey, who defeated me there, became a friend for our joint political lives and attended the ceremony in Durham at which I was made a freeman of the city, more than twenty years later. Next ranked my first contest in Warwickshire, where I was flattered to find large audiences who both listened and agreed. The 1951 election was the stiffest ordeal of all. I had a very heavy speaking programme all over the country and, in addition, made the important closing broadcast and the only television appearance for the party. I entered the campaign very fit and was completely exhausted at the finish.

I found the general election of 1955, when I was leader, less exacting than rowing number seven in the boat. Central Office was well organized and staffed. Lord Woolton was a wise and urbane chairman who did not make the mistake of interfering too much in detail himself. He had a brilliant gift for choosing men and, having chosen them, left them to do their work, which they did admirably.

I do not think that we made a political mistake in the campaign, except, perhaps, that we put an insufficient weight of speakers into the eastern counties. This was an accident. When Lord Woolton and I had discussed the campaign he had generously undertaken to go there himself. Laryngitis silenced this intention.

The political case we had to present was a strong one. It rested on the prosperous condition of the country and three years of achievement by the Government. I knew that if we were to improve our position, I must in particular get my message to the better skilled industrial worker, who could be expected to benefit most from the kind of society we wanted to create. I think that we succeeded.

In international affairs I rested on our record. In my election address four-fifths of the space was devoted to home politics, for it was on these questions that the electors wanted to know my views. I gave them this programme:

To encourage savings and investment so as to build up the production power of our own land and of the countries of the Commonwealth and Empire;

To modernize and re-equip our railways;

To reconstruct and develop our road system;

To press ahead with the building of more houses and more schools and the first new hospital building programme since before the war;

To renew with determination our pre-war onslaught on slum clearance;

To provide another million new school places in the next five years and to improve existing school buildings and equipment;

To ensure that local authorities are strong and well equipped to carry out this progressive social policy in the best interests of their communities;

To strengthen personal freedom and to appoint a special committee on administrative law to ensure that justice is done by the State in its dealings with individuals.

And this summing up of our deeds and faith:

We have strengthened the influence of Great Britain in world affairs.

We have played our part in bringing two major wars to an end and in building unity in the West.

At home:

Earnings are higher;
Savings are higher;
Taxes are lower;
Pensions and social benefits have been increased;
A million new homes have been built;
Rationing is a thing of the past;
There is variety and abundance in the shops.
There is more hope, more choice, more freedom for all.

Our task is not complete. Much remains to do. I ask you to renew our mandate to work for peace abroad and the creation of a property-owning democracy at home.

I devoted only three lines to our opponents, it being my conviction that the British people soon wearies of strictures upon the other party. After all, it can do that pretty well for itself.

I had some difficult decisions to take about my personal part in the campaign. I attached first importance to television as a medium and, after discussion with Lord Woolton and Mr. Mark Chapman-Walker, his brilliant assistant in propaganda matters, we made our first selection. I would appear with some of my colleagues and meet a panel of editors of newspapers who would ask us questions of which we had not been advised in advance. The result was fairly successful, though both questions and answers were apt to go on too long.

We had one other period on television. How was that to be used?

I knew what I wanted to do, but I was not sure that I dared. This was to speak direct to the British people for fifteen minutes without company and without script. This sounds simple enough now, but at that time nothing of the kind had ever been attempted, and if it were a flop the consequences on our electoral fortunes could be serious. The Opposition were not risking a lone appearance by any of their leaders. Encouraged by Mr. Chapman-Walker, I made the attempt.

The Opposition did not, I think, make good use of their television time. I watched them as far as I could, despite the calls of the campaign, for it is a useful part of one's own preparations to see one's opponents perform. Giving radio and television first preference, I reduced the number of public meetings in comparison with my programme in 1951, though I carried out a number of tours to different parts of the country. Some days are sharp in my memory. There was Glasgow where we were greeted by a wonderful meeting at St. Andrew's Hall. After it was over, I asked its organizers whether it was a ticket meeting and they replied, yes, that was the tradition in Glasgow. A tradition that probably dated from rowdier times. The next day I addressed some half dozen outdoor meetings throughout the city. These were largely attended and I could not have been treated with more courtesy and friendliness. As my wife and I drove from one meeting to another the townsfolk turned out to greet us. At factory gates there would be a group of workmen to wave and cheer. I knew, though, that this was just Scottish good manners and that they could go back and vote against our party the next evening.

We had a remarkable meeting at Birmingham. When I was asked if I would speak there, I agreed, provided it was not at the town hall. My reason for this was that the town hall meetings, where accommodation is limited, are apt to be gatherings of the faithful, which, however admirable or even exhilarating, can play no part in deciding an election. I had expected, as a result of my reply, that I would be asked to address several meetings in different parts of the city as I had done at previous elections. However, this time the organizers had done much better. Thinking that they were meeting my wishes, they organized a meeting in the Rag Market, where it is possible to accommodate an audience of 10,000 or more, standing. The Rag Market had been a popular place for Joseph Chamberlain in his Radical days. It had never been used for Conservative or Unionist meetings. Mr. Attlee had been there a night or two before and had been welcomed, I was told, by an audience of about 2,000. There was some uncertainty as to how our meeting would go, but as it turned out it was the best of the campaign. I shall always remember that great crowd, its vitality, its humour and its youth. The Market was packed and there were overflows into the street. As we drove away, I could not help being moved by the welcome of these crowds.

My wife immensely eased the burden of the campaign. While she has no love of politics, or perhaps because of this, she was a firm if sympathetic critic. More important still, she understood how to limit the strain by reducing the number of personal engagements outside the meeting halls and so, on the whole, I got through in better physical shape than I had expected.

After Birmingham, I had little doubt of the outcome. The last night was to be in my own constituency, the only time in the campaign spent among those whom I had represented for more than thirty years, in all the weathers of my political fortunes and their national safety. This was a relaxed evening among friends. The next day I motored round the polling stations, ending up, shortly before the poll closed, in a ward in Leamington where many who worked in the Lockheed factory lived. It was a ward with a Labour majority in the municipal elections. As we had expected the Opposition to poll less well nationally than in the general election of 1951, I anticipated that the poll here might be relatively light. I was taken aback to find it about 80 per cent., and as I drove away with my wife I remarked, 'It seems as though all our calculations may be wrong. If Labour has polled heavily in this ward and done the same in the country, maybe they will be back after all.'

My forebodings were not justified. I heard the first few results, which showed increased majorities, and then went round to my own count, which was quickly concluded, and gave me a majority increased by more than 4,000. This was larger than I had ever expected. Having thanked my supporters in Warwick and Leamington, we listened for a while to the results in the town hall. When I heard that we had won Watford, a result I had been advised by Lord Woolton to look out for, I felt confident of our national majority. I went back to Kenilworth, where we were spending the night, and retired to bed to listen agreeably to the results.

As my wife and I motored to London on the morning of May 27th some later results were coming through on the wireless. I looked forward to reading the rest at leisure in the evening papers when I reached London, but they were never to leave my in-tray. From the moment of my arrival in Downing Street a series of strikes took all my attention. No time was left to savour victory. A few moments at party headquarters to thank Lord Woolton and a happy staff was all I could allow myself. When the new House of Commons met, we held 345 seats and had improved our majority from 17 in the old House to 60 in the new. We had gained 49·8 per cent. of all votes cast in the election, compared with Labour's 46·3 per cent. and the Liberals' 2·2 per cent.

★   ★   ★   ★   ★

I have already mentioned the newspaper strike, which began before I became the Prime Minister and in some degree muted the opening weeks of the election campaign. Eventually a return to work was arranged and the London press resumed publication on April 21st, encouraged perhaps by my announcement of the general election. The nation endured this period of deprivation with a stoical calm.

Other strikes were threatening. They concerned the railways and the docks, where the trouble had been coming to a head for some time. The dock strike was solely an inter-union conflict. It was less in the public eye than the railway dispute, but it caused the country more damage.

Its origins were simple. The large Transport and General Workers' Union had been built up by Ernest Bevin and Arthur Deakin and had included almost all British dockers among its members. In some parts of the country it was losing the loyalty of its men. A separate union, the National Amalgamated Stevedores and Dockers, had gained a considerable following in the London docks, particularly since the war. It was now extending its activities into the north country, especially Hull, Merseyside and Manchester. It was not recognized there as a negotiating body and the Transport and General Workers' Union strongly opposed its intrusion. Despite this, the stevedores' union won over about ten thousand members from its larger rival. For this offence it was expelled from membership of the Trades Union Congress.

On May 23rd the stevedores struck with a demand for representation on all negotiating bodies, both national and local. Some eighteen thousand men ceased work in English ports. The strike lasted six weeks and caused about one-third of the shipping using these ports to be delayed or lie idle. Merseyside was the area hardest hit.

No wage claim was involved and in these circumstances a Government has no authority to employ conciliation. At the same time the threat to national prosperity was urgent. The Minister of Labour, Sir Walter Monckton, and I met representatives of the Trades Union Congress before and after the strikes began. We discussed both this and the railway dispute with them. Sir Walter was zealous in his consultations, but it took time to get the parties to come to terms. At length the Trades Union Congress agreed to re-admit the stevedores' union to membership and its own disputes committee took the problem in hand. After considerable negotiation the strike came to an end on July 4th.

The railway strike coincided with the dock strike. Recent awards by the Railway Staff National Tribunal had raised wage rates throughout the industry and reduced the differentials paid to footplatemen. The sums involved were small, but the footplatemen's union, the Associated Society of Locomotive Engineers and Firemen, was intent on preventing any shrinking of differentials. About three-quarters of the footplatemen in the country belonged to this union. The rest were members of the National Union of Railwaymen, which included all kinds of railway workers, unskilled as well as skilled.

The locomotive union felt that its larger rival had gained an advantage at its expense, and believed it was fighting for the rewards of skill. It took an abrupt decision to strike as from May 1st, but urgent negotiations gained a respite of four weeks. All this took place during the general election campaign, and the Minister of Labour and I were exchanging frequent messages as I moved about the country. Determined to keep himself available to give impartial guidance, Sir Walter Monckton, with my agreement, took virtually no part in election activities. But despite his efforts, and those of his officers, a settlement could not be reached. The strike of locomotive men began at midnight on May 28th, little more than forty-eight hours after the polling booths had closed. I gave a broadcast to the nation the next evening, with an account of these events:

> One of the major difficulties has been the absence of common ground between the two unions: without this the Transport Commission couldn't know the full size of the bill which they, and all their customers, would be asked to meet.
>
> The Minister was unable to get the unions to establish a common front on which the Transport Commission could deal with them. Then Sir Walter Monckton suggested that a Board of

Conciliation should be set up. This would have helped in the conduct of the negotiations, and it might also have created the kind of atmosphere in which a settlement could have been reached. The locomotive men rejected this suggestion.

Yesterday, again with the help of T.U.C. representatives, another series of attempts was made to find a way out. These also failed.

You will see from what I have said that although this is a dispute between the Associated Society and the Transport Commission, the difficulties in the way of settling it have mainly been brought about by the differing points of view of the two unions involved. That is why the Minister of Labour has sought and received so much help from the T.U.C. The prospects for peace in this great industry would be transformed if only these two unions would talk and work together. . . .

I had previously set up a Ministerial Committee on Emergencies under the chairmanship of the Home Secretary, Mr. Lloyd-George, to make any preparations that might be necessary. This committee remained in being throughout the strikes and, at my direction and that of the Cabinet, took action to relieve the breakdown in transport and the stoppage at the docks. On May 31st an emergency was officially proclaimed. This gave the Government the power to make any regulations necessary for 'securing the essentials of life to the community'.

At the same time the Minister of Transport, Mr. Boyd-Carpenter, kept me informed by daily reports of the position on the railways, where seven thousand trains a day were running, about one-sixth of the normal service.

I broadcast a second time on June 5th:

I am not going to leave you in any doubt about the deadly seriousness of what is happening to our country. There is little unemployment, as yet. But you cannot stop most of the trains in a land like ours without soon bringing some factories to a halt. . . . We can all understand that grievances must arise from time to time about the rates of pay and that there are rivalries between unions. But it is not right to give vent to them at such a cost to the country. Every hour that these strikes last we are slipping behind in the race with our foreign competitors. If we go on like this we shall smash up our hard-earned prosperity. So far from raising our standard of living we shall lower it and that applies to every one of us, railwaymen and dockers included.

I have sympathy with men who want to keep the differential standard they have worked for in a world drab with uniformity, but I thought these inter-union rows rough and unfair on the public. Negotiations continued for another week, intensive, searching, and informal. The strike came to an end on June 14th and comparative peace reigned in the railways for the rest of the year.

These details are not unimportant. Trade Unionism in Britain is as conservative as many other institutions. It is also generally respected, though there are times when its internal differences goad a tolerant public to exasperation. The British people will generally accept and understand a dispute concerned with rates of pay and standards of life. They resent being penalized for a frontier dispute or battle for authority between unions. In that summer they certainly felt that they had the chief grievance and were being needlessly exploited. These two strikes and other smaller ones which took place at this time gave them just cause, though they proved nothing like so formidable as those in the year which followed my resignation, the worst since the General Strike of 1926. I knew that our national record in industrial disputes was good when compared with our principal rivals in the free world, but I feared that the nation might drift into sharp antagonisms if no attempt was made to clear the issues and guide opinion. The danger of a widespread renewal of strikes was real.

I discussed the situation with Sir Walter Monckton and one or two senior colleagues and decided upon a general review of industrial relations. The talks which I had held at 10 Downing Street during the strikes had made some things clear. The trade union leaders saw the dangers and they were concerned at the indiscipline among some union members, which was aimed in part at them. If the Government could strengthen their hand, they would welcome it, but they did not want any fresh legislation. I had not much faith in this either.

The employers were much concerned to avoid action which would precipitate a collision with the unions. The climate for agreement was therefore pretty good. I wanted to use it to determine policy in advance of the next round of trouble. There were too many unofficial strikes; the question was whether these should be made illegal. Both sides of industry were opposed to this and I shared their doubts as to whether legislation would be effective. Everybody would be in a worse position if it were not. We canvassed the proposal that a secret ballot should be made compulsory before any union took strike action. This had many supporters, but it would be difficult to supervise and would not prevent unofficial strikes. We also considered means of extending the existing system of arbitration, but these could hardly be made effective without a general independent inquiry into industrial relations, a slow business and no immediate solution.

I thought that the most promising of the remedies was to revive what was called a 'period of reflection'. This would involve legislation and would mean that, by law, twenty-one days would have to go by between a union's decision and the beginning of a strike. The compulsory pause would allow time for tempers to cool and for every method of conciliation to be tried. The procedure had existed during the war and was continued until 1951, when the Labour Government abolished it. The limitation of this procedure in practice is that it has delayed official strikes without affecting unofficial ones, which can be more damaging. On this account it is not popular with the trade union leaders. I thought we should publicly encourage the period of reflection without at once making it legally compulsory. In this form it was acceptable to the T.U.C. and I still think the idea worth pursuing. The nation also has a position in these affairs. It suffers at best discomfort, at worst heavy loss from these disputes and is entitled to reasonable reassurance. Here is one that could be given.

III

DIPLOMATIC PREPARATIONS
March – July 1955

The Paris Agreements – My paper on Russia – Preliminary discussions with Americans and French – A limited agenda – The Austrian Treaty – A flexible time-table – My plans for Germany – A visit from Dr. Adenauer – His views

Towards the end of March 1955, our hopes were centred on the ratification of the Paris Agreements. This would finally complete the union of the West and bring into being the Western European partnership, which I had been working on since my journey round the capitals in the previous September. With the memory of the fate of the European Defence Community in our minds we could not be sure what would happen in Paris, but I was confident that if the agreements were ratified, free Europe would be given a fresh impetus and would regain much of its authority in the world.

The Russians kept repeating their vehement objections to the agreements, but I did not set much store by this. I was sure that, once ratified, they would pass into history and be accepted with that realism which is part of communist practice. As a consequence, my thoughts ranged wider and I began to consider afresh the possibility of a four-power meeting. Independently, the French had the same idea and the French Prime Minister, M. Edgar Faure, expressed it in a public speech on March 25th. The French Government also suggested privately to us that meetings of officials should be held to work out methods. We agreed and proposed that they should begin in London in mid-April between officials of the French, United States and United Kingdom Governments, and that there should be a later meeting, probably in Paris, at which the West German Government would also be represented. This could be followed by talks between Western Foreign Secretaries.

I had circulated a paper to my colleagues towards the end of March, setting out my views on talks with Soviet Russia. I argued that this was the right moment at which to prepare for discussions with the Soviet Union. I thought it unlikely that with the passage of time our relative position would improve. On the contrary, I thought that once saturation in thermo-nuclear weapons was reached, the relative military strength of the West would decline. The ratification of the Paris Agreements might represent a high point of Western political cohesion. In accordance with the methods I had advocated over so many years, I thought it important that this meeting of the four powers, at whatever level it was held, should aim at some definite, even if limited result. I was not hopeful that a general discussion of the hydrogen bomb, or disarmament, or the Far East, would get us anywhere. But I did want to see whether the conference could achieve something in Europe. The agenda I proposed was: (1) Austria, Germany and European Security. (2) Study of ways and means to deal with all other issues outstanding between East and West. If we made progress with (1) we could embark upon (2) with a better chance of success.

I proposed to begin with the discussion of the Austrian situation, for here our position was best. At Berlin the allies had offered to sign the Austrian Treaty with the Soviet texts of all the disagreed articles. They should keep on pressing this. If the Russians were ready to conclude a treaty on such terms, the allies might further agree to consider the military and political neutralization of Austria. On March 26th Her Majesty's Government publicly welcomed M. Faure's speech. We were ready to join in proposing negotiations with the Soviet Government.

The discussions between the Western allies, to prepare a meeting with the Soviets, went smoothly, principally in Paris. On May 10th the three Western Governments invited Russia to join with us in an effort to remove the sources of conflict. We said that we realized that these problems could not be solved in a single meeting, nor hastily, in view of their complexity and importance, and suggested that they should be approached in two stages. First, by a meeting of the Heads of Government, accompanied by their Foreign Secretaries, for an exchange of views. In the limited time for which the Heads of Government were able to meet, they could not undertake to agree upon substantive answers to the major difficulties facing the world. Such a meeting should rather provide a new impetus and establish new methods. The Heads of Government would prepare and order the next stage, in which the problems would be examined in detail. We also proposed that the Foreign Secretaries should come together shortly in advance of the Heads of Government to assist them in their work. If the Soviet Union agreed to an early meeting, we suggested that the Foreign Secretaries who were soon to meet in Vienna should first discuss these ideas there.

Events had moved rapidly on the Austrian question. Early in April the Soviet Government had summoned an Austrian delegation to Moscow and, after some discussion, announced their willingness to sign the Austrian State Treaty and to withdraw their occupation forces, in return for an Austrian declaration of neutrality. The Russians made some important concessions in the economic clauses of the treaty, including the renunciation of their claim to the Austrian oilfields and refineries. It is possible that they hoped by this apparent leniency to make a favourable impression upon Federal Germany, with which they were about to open diplomatic relations. The Austrian Treaty was signed on May 15th and the last of the occupying forces withdrew during the following months.

The efforts of the Western powers at the Berlin Conference, where Austria had been last discussed, had been closely co-ordinated and well worked out. Despite some difficult periods, we managed always to keep in line. Yet at the time the exercise appeared to be without reward. In fact this was not so. The Soviets had overplayed their hand in their treatment of Austria. Sympathy for the Austrian position was almost universal wherever even the bare facts were known. I do not suggest that this was decisive in bringing the Soviets to modify their policies towards Austria; I do not think it was, but I am sure that it had an influence. By this time, the Russians were anxious to present a reasonable countenance to the world. Its expression could not seem sincere, even to those most ready to smile back, while Austria was occupied by foreign troops and the Western offer to accept the Soviet terms was ignored. Here we see the long-term good effects of Western unity, firmness and reasonableness, quite as important in their way as the examples of failure to give determined support to each other at critical times, which we were later to experience.

In Vienna, Mr. Molotov agreed with the three Western Foreign Secretaries that a meeting of the Heads of Government would help to ease the tension. The purpose of the meeting would be to lay down methods of work, and it was to be regarded as the beginning of a sequence of conferences. The Russians formally accepted our joint invitation to the talks on May 26th. They were to be held at Geneva in July. I hoped that we could follow up our Austrian success there, at least we must make the attempt.

After the general election in the United Kingdom was over, I had an opportunity to resume preparations for the talks. I explained to my Western colleagues the importance I attached to our not being tied down to a rigid time-table. I told them that, in my experience, it was informal contacts with the Russians which were the more useful. This was especially true if, for internal reasons or otherwise, the Soviets were more disposed for serious discussion of our differences than they had been at any time since the war. I did not add what was also in my mind, that our proceedings at Yalta had suffered from being rushed at the close, President Roosevelt having committed himself to a fixed date. He had arranged a meeting with King Ibn Saud for mid-February 1945, on the cruiser *Quincy* in the Suez Canal, presumably in order to bring us up against decisions. It was not really a good plan, because we had to scamper at the finish. It is sometimes wise to order a train for departure, but one must have control of the train. I wanted the West to be sure of that control this time.

I would have been happier if it had been possible to arrange a preliminary meeting of the three Western Heads of Government before we went to Geneva. I thought this would be helpful to ourselves and educative for the Russians. It would be good for them to see how close was our accord in advance of the meeting. I tried to fix this in London. M. Faure was willing, but the President could not get away.

I made one further point to President Eisenhower and M. Faure before we met. I looked upon this conference of Heads of Government as the first of a series. If all went well the plan should unroll. Therefore we could not exclude the possibility of a further summit meeting at some later date.

The more detailed preparations were made at the official level in Washington. I thought that these were committing us to too meticulous a programme, dividing up the topics which each Head of Government should raise. I did not think that we should be staging a play, but ought to allow each other plenty of room for manœuvre to make use of such indications as there were of changes in Soviet policy. For instance, we should try to build on the Austrian agreement and acknowledge that some progress had been made. This seemed to me more useful than to talk to Marshal Bulganin as if he were Stalin. He might be, or Mr. Khrushchev might be, but until it was proved it would be better to leave ourselves free as to methods. Towards the end of May the Americans became more hopeful about our meeting. Their Secretary of State assured the German Chancellor of his confidence that the talks would lead to the unification of Germany.

During the weeks before the conference we spent many hours trying to work out possible schemes to serve our dual purpose. This was to reunify Germany, while giving Russia all the assurances we could that the consequences of this event would be no threat to her. Every negotiator always has some weakness in his position. I felt, however, that we would be stronger at Geneva than in any previous negotiation with the Russians, including the Berlin Conference. We ought not to forget that. We should keep the initiative by having a plan of our own, and not allow ourselves to be drawn unnecessarily into the discussion of Russian plans. These were likely to have only one purpose; to delay German unity. It might be that Russia was not in fact so interested in the neutralization of Germany as was often supposed. It might be that her principal interest was to maintain her authority in Eastern Germany, as being essential to her defensive position, or ultimately, from that base, to spread communism into West Germany. There were indications that Moscow was professing to believe in a general acceptance of a divided Germany. I was convinced that there was no such acquiescence amongst the Germans and it was highly dangerous for the Russians to pretend that there was.

Our ideas began to take shape. I had in mind a collective proposal which would include at least three ingredients. The first, a demilitarized strip in Europe. I did not believe that the Russians at Geneva would be ready to make broad concessions in Germany, but I thought that they might agree to step back a little if given a positive reassurance. A modest proposal was more likely to lead to results than a far-flung plan which would lead to endless negotiation. In discussions with my colleagues and the Chiefs of Staff in June, I put forward a suggestion for the demilitarization of a comparatively narrow strip on both sides of the Iron Curtain. This certainly would have involved the military planners at N.A.T.O. in some withdrawal of their advanced bases in central Europe. But I thought that this would be worthwhile if Russian and Russian-sponsored forces could be persuaded to retire many miles to the east, and if the Soviet Government would then agree to free elections in Germany and to progress on German unity. In the general field of discussion an agreement with the Russians, even upon a narrow segment of Europe, would help. The second ingredient of my collective proposal would be a limitation of armaments within specified areas of Europe, and the third a European security pact. These limitations would not imply equality, nor would there be any thinning out of our forces in Western Germany. They would, however, be subject to the ceiling imposed by the Paris Agreements, and, if the Russians agreed, to a common system of control. I wanted to try out such a system with the Russians taking part in it. Control was the key to so many matters, including nuclear tests. The Russians were suspicious of control. This was part of their national character and not just to be ascribed to communism. I felt that if a system of international control could be established, even on a limited scale, the dragon might be found to be not so very dangerous after all. When the great powers have accepted a system of international control in some sphere and begun to work it, we may emerge from the cold war. Until they do, we shall be rival armed camps dividing the world and endangering peace.

It was likely that the Western allies would agree to put forward again the Eden Plan for Germany, which I had proposed on their behalf at the Berlin Conference, but I did not feel that this in itself would be enough. We should follow it up by giving some indication of our further proposals on the lines I have just described. While it was unwise to be too rigid in our preparations and in allotting tasks between us, it was desirable that our first statements at the conference should be related to the moves we subsequently intended to make. For instance, I might say in my opening remarks that we had proposals to make about a progressive advance towards the limitation of forces in Germany. If we had a clear plan of our own we could hope to succeed in steering the conference to work upon it.

Dr. Adenauer, the Chancellor of Federal Germany, paid me a visit at Chequers at my invitation, on June 19th. I was glad of the opportunity to talk to him before the conference opened. He had recently told us of a tentative German plan for demilitarized areas in Europe, which bore some likeness to my own thoughts. We had a discussion in which we found our ideas very much in accord.

I always enjoyed a talk about world affairs with the German Chancellor. We sat in the Long Library that summer afternoon, looking out over the countryside, and took a prowl together round Europe. Dr. Adenauer is clear and forceful, and never allows his purpose to become confused. He understands the full reality of the communist challenge, that it is something much more than a left-wing movement, and he reacts against it with all the conviction of a European and a

Catholic from the Rhineland. But, in my many conversations with him, I never knew him deal with his problems in exaggerated terms.

The Soviets had recently recognized the Federal German Government and had invited its Chancellor to go to Moscow. We discussed this state of affairs. Dr. Adenauer understood that he must go and was fully prepared to do so, but he had no illusions about Soviet intentions. The Western European Union had just been created, and he and I had played a leading part in bringing it about. The Russians had made no secret of their dislike of this association, and still more of Germany's entry into N.A.T.O; as always, the Kremlin wished to divide the West. The Chancellor thought that he should accept the invitation to Moscow now, but not make the visit until after our Geneva meeting.

I outlined our collective proposal to the Chancellor and he seemed to like it. He spoke of the importance of showing at Geneva that the Western powers wanted the unification of Germany and that they had practical suggestions to make. We must also show that we wanted disarmament; in sponsoring the idea of a demilitarized area, he considered that we were taking a great step to bring this about. The Chancellor held that, in these conditions, the Soviets had no good reason to be afraid of reunification. If Germany were united, a great deal of German energy would for a long time be absorbed in bringing the Eastern zone back into prosperity. Conditions there, he emphasized, were deplorably bad. The Chancellor agreed with me that we could not expect either quick or easy success in our discussions with the Russians. He believed, as I did, that if the conference held out no serious prospects of immediate agreement, then a series of meetings with the Russians should be kept going, in the hope of making gradual progress.

Finally, we spoke of our two countries. The Chancellor said he rejoiced at the good relations between us. He had always felt that Germany had taken the wrong road at the end of the nineteenth century. I agreed; the consequences of that tragic decision will still stretch far into the future. European civilization has almost destroyed itself. Almost but not quite; there is enough potential strength among the Western allies to withstand the communist hordes. I am not so sure that there is enough leadership, where the strength lies, to discern and point the danger.

IV

THE SUMMIT
July 1955

I talk to President Eisenhower and M. Faure – Our agreement –
First plenary session – Russian objections to a united
Germany – Characters of Marshal Bulganin and Mr. Khrushchev
– Our discussion at dinner – Russian memories – A proposed
non-aggression pact – Disarmament – The order of the agenda –
A compromise – Final speeches – I invite the Russian leaders to
England – Hospitality at the conference – The off-shore islands
– Russian and American views – A verdict on the conference –
I return to England

The Foreign Secretaries of the three Western powers met in Paris
on July 15th to put the finishing touches to the preparations for
the Geneva meeting. It had been arranged that after the opening
discussion, the Heads of Government should meet in the afternoons
and the Foreign Secretaries in the mornings. As a result of our work, we
hoped to agree upon the subjects and terms of reference for the Foreign
Secretaries at their later meeting in the autumn. I wanted to preserve
freedom in our arrangements.

We flew to Geneva on the afternoon of Saturday, July 16th. My wife
and I returned to the house which had been lent to us by its owner,
M. Pictet, during the Indo-China Conference. Le Reposoir was a
pleasant blend of French and Swiss architecture of the eighteenth
century, a graceful home which we enjoyed. Next morning M. Faure
and I joined Mr. Eisenhower for an informal meeting at his villa,
where we discussed the statements we would make at the opening of the
conference. They were to be published; the further development of
our ideas was to take place in private.

I told the President and M. Faure that I considered German unification by far the most important of the questions to be discussed at the conference. The Russians would not be anxious to spend time on this. But the right tactics for the Western powers were to insist on discussing it and to put forward proposals which the Russians would find difficult to reject. These tactics would be advantageous from the point of view of public opinion in Germany, and they were also the most likely to produce results. The pressure for an Austrian settlement, which the Western powers had brought to bear on the Russians at the Berlin Conference, had in the end borne fruit. Similar pressure now might have the same result in respect of Germany. It was in the Russian interest to delay a settlement in Germany. They doubtless thought that they might get a settlement more favourable to themselves if they waited until Dr. Adenauer retired, or until the patience of the West Germans became exhausted. If we could make some practical progress at Geneva towards the unification of Germany, the conference would be a success for the Western powers.

The French Prime Minister, while agreeing with my suggestions, told us that he had a number of positive proposals to make on security and disarmament as well as on Germany. He was anxious to develop these at an early stage. The President felt that it was preferable to arrive at precise formulas gradually.

With slightly differing attitudes on tactics, but in substantial agreement, we prepared for the five days that lay ahead. The first full meeting was held on Monday morning in the Council Chamber of the Palais des Nations. The President, being a Head of State as well as Head of Government, took the chair on the first day; after this we took it in turns. Mr. Eisenhower opened the proceedings and indicated some of the subjects which we had all agreed to discuss. First was the problem of unifying Germany and forming an all-German Government based on free elections. In the interest of enduring peace, said the President, our solution should take account of the legitimate security interests of all concerned. That is why we insisted that a united Germany be entitled to its choice to exercise its inherent right of collective self-defence. By the same token we were willing to take account of the legitimate security interests of the Soviet Union. The Paris Agreements contained many provisions which served this purpose. We were quite ready to consider further reciprocal safeguards which were reasonable, practical and compatible with the security of all concerned.

On a broader plane, the President said, there was the problem of respecting the right of peoples to choose the form of government under which they would live, and of restoring sovereign rights and self-government to those who had been deprived of them. The American people held strongly that certain peoples of eastern Europe, many with a long and proud record of national existence, had not yet been given the benefit of this pledge of our United Nations wartime declaration, reinforced by other wartime agreements. 'We are here', the President said, 'to launch fresh negotiations under conditions of good augury.'

M. Faure followed with a more detailed survey of the problems before us. 'The people of the world', he said, 'hoped that our meeting might put an end to the period of history known as the cold war. Our aim must be to create a European security system which would include a unified Germany and which would take into account the legitimate anxieties of other powers.'

I said that the purpose of our meeting was to deal with the problems and differences between us, mainly in the context of Europe. Chief among them was the unity of Germany. Within the limits of our Western zone we had done all we could to unify Germany. We had broken down the barriers between our zones. Quite apart from the larger issues of German unity, it would mark a real advance if, pending our negotiations for German unity, the Soviet Government felt able to relax the physical restrictions which now aggravated the division of Germany and prevented contact between Germans in the East and West. On the wider issue, I said that our aim was to ensure that the unification of Germany and her freedom to associate with countries of her choice should not involve any threat to anybody. There were, no doubt, many ways of doing this. I would give some examples, consisting partly of actions and partly of assurances. I took the assurances first. We would be prepared, I said, to be parties to a security pact of which those round the table and a united Germany would be members. By its terms each country could declare itself ready to go to the assistance of the victim of aggression, whoever it might be. There were many forms which such a pact might take. We would be ready to examine them and to set out our views about them.

Secondly, we would be ready to discuss and try to reach agreement as to the total of forces and armaments on each side in Germany and the countries neighbouring Germany. To do this it would be necessary to join in a system of reciprocal control to supervise the arrangements effectively. All those represented at the conference would, we hoped, be partners in this, together with a united Germany. I also suggested that we should examine the possibility of a demilitarized zone between East and West, as a further reassurance.

When Marshal Bulganin's turn came, he spoke in terms reminiscent of Mr. Molotov at the Berlin Conference in 1954. His emphasis was on security, not on German unity. He declared that the Soviet Government believed that 'our eventual objective should be to have no foreign troops remaining on the territories of the States of Europe. Their withdrawal', he maintained, 'would remove one of the principal, if not the primary, sources of the present distrust in international relations.' He considered that the rearming of West Germany and its integration into the military groupings of the Western powers was the main obstacle to reunification. Marshal Bulganin refused to discuss the problem of free government in the communist satellite states, which the President had raised. He also referred to the problems of the Far East, about which we later had private talks, and China's representation in the United Nations.

The following morning, the Foreign Secretaries met to prepare an agenda. Four topics raised in our opening speeches had been common ground for discussion. These were: the reunification of Germany, European security, disarmament, and the development of contacts between East and West. It was agreed that these items should be submitted to us for further examination. Mr. Molotov wished to inscribe on the agenda three further points: the termination of the cold war, the encouragement of neutrality among the states of Europe and the problems of the Far East. After some exchanges, it was left to the Heads of Government to decide whether these questions should be added to the list. They did not add them.

Marshal Bulganin made the Soviet position still clearer at our next meeting that afternoon. He put his points with courtesy but force. He declared that Russia could not be expected to agree to a united Germany entering the military groupings of the Western powers, and that the conditions which would permit the reunification of Germany had not yet matured. Nor was he attracted by the proposed system of security which I had outlined. The security of the Soviet Union, he maintained, could not depend on guarantees provided by particular states. He wanted a system of collective security which would include the whole of Europe. The rest of us at once recognized that this scheme would take so long as to postpone the unification of Germany indefinitely.

In the course of his reply, President Eisenhower described the true purposes of N.A.T.O., as he had known them when he was first Commander-in-Chief of its forces. These were purely defensive and the treaties which bound the N.A.T.O. countries together, including West Germany, provided against aggression by any one of them, either among themselves or against anyone else.

M. Faure pleaded the dangers of delay. Referring to the creation of a new security pact to include the whole of Europe, he said we must be able to measure approximately the time which it would take. If we could not do that, there was a risk of postponing the matter indefinitely. And that led to a refusal of reunification.

I pursued the same theme when I spoke. A general European pact, as Marshal Bulganin had proposed, would take years to work out. Many of the countries of Europe had divergent views on these matters and very different interests. A limited security system, embracing the four powers present at the conference and a united Germany, was a more practical basis from which to start. I did not exclude the addition of other powers as the negotiations developed. I urged, as I had before, that we must try, in any plan for German unification, to agree upon the total armed strength to be stationed in Germany and the neighbouring countries. Such an agreement would give us the first opportunity to practise a system of international supervision amongst ourselves. That would be very important and it might help to increase confidence between us.

At the conclusion of this discussion, it was agreed that the Foreign Secretaries should continue their work on the German question, as they had wished. Upon my insistence, it was laid down that the Heads of Government might revert to the matter at any time during the conference. I felt that we had far from finished with this topic.

★　　★　　★　　★　　★

During my several wartime visits to Moscow, Marshal Bulganin and Mr. Khrushchev were not prominent and we never had any discussion together. The two men made a remarkable contrast. Bulganin was the more mellow and smooth and polished. He gave the impression of having been one of the professional classes rather than a military man. He might be cast for the family doctor in a novel by Turgenev, his favourite author. He could be sharp enough on occasion, but the general impression was poised and patient, rather than thrusting.

Mr. Khrushchev was vigorous, downright and stubborn, but prepared to laugh. A forceful personality, always ready to go over to the attack. At this time, Bulganin did by far the greater part of the talking, but even so, the authority of Khrushchev could always be felt when the two men were together. He is perceptive and a man who knows his power; he could even overestimate it.

After the discussion at the second conference session was over, Bulganin came up to me and admitted the reality of our divergence and the seriousness of the German question. He said he thought that I understood their position. I said I did understand that they did not want to see East Germany join West Germany in N.A.T.O. On the other hand, how could we devise a security arrangement which satisfied him and allowed Germany to take her own decision, as any country must be able to do? He agreed that this was the heart of the problem and made various complimentary remarks as to how I could resolve it. I indicated that I felt the prospects were not bright after the day's discussions. We agreed to continue to examine the topic that night after the dinner which we were giving to the Soviet leaders. I drove back to my villa reflecting that if this should prove to be so, at least our evening would be more useful than that of our French and American friends, whom the Russians had left without any serious talk, immediately after the coffee.

The Foreign Secretary and I, with Sir Norman Brook, Secretary to the Cabinet, Sir Ivone Kirkpatrick, Permanent Under-Secretary at the Foreign Office, and Sir William Hayter, our Ambassador in Moscow, welcomed our Soviet guests to dinner that evening. Marshal Bulganin and Mr. Khrushchev, with Mr. Molotov, Marshal Zhukov and Mr. Malik, Soviet Ambassador in London, made up the party. During dinner I sat between Bulganin and Khrushchev and had a forthcoming talk with the former, who appeared to wish to give an account of his preoccupations. After some preliminary conversation about the war years, Bulganin plunged into the problem of Germany. He explained, on familiar lines, how real were Soviet fears of a German recovery. Almost every family in Soviet Russia, including his own, had suffered some personal loss. I replied that we in Britain also had no reason to feel tenderly to the Germans after the experience of two wars. But we had to look to the future and, whatever the fear of Germany had been, I could not believe that in this nuclear age Germany could really be a formidable danger to Russia. Bulganin, however, would not altogether accept this. He admitted that the Germans might not be able to make hydrogen bombs, but after all they could be given them.

We had some talk about these new weapons and their possible

consequences for the world. I was troubled about too wide a dispersal of knowledge of how to make the bomb. Bulganin maintained that the problem for the present and for some time to come was one which only concerned the United States, Russia and ourselves. He did not foresee a future when the smaller powers would be able to make the bomb. I argued that, whatever the Soviet fears of Germany, we were all agreed that at some time Germany must be united, and my suggestions had been based on a desire to meet what I well understood to be Russian fears. Bulganin said he thought that some of our suggestions were important. We discussed the possibility of reaching some agreement about forces and armaments in Germany and neighbouring countries, together with a form of supervision to control them. He thought this worth examining, but said that he had not given detailed thought to it. I advised him to give it consideration. We also discussed the security pact and I told him I thought it a pretty hopeless proposition to try to create a pact for all Europe. How, for instance, could Tito and Franco be accommodated together? He laughed and said that perhaps this was not necessary; maybe the Soviets cast their nets too wide. Perhaps it would be possible to form some pact between us which covered at least a part of Europe.

In later discussions that evening, in which Mr. Khrushchev took part, the suggestion was made that the N.A.T.O. powers should maintain their organization and the Warsaw powers theirs. All these should join the European pact, with the addition of some other countries. They gladly accepted that these should include the United States and Canada. After we had discussed these matters for some time, Bulganin said that he wanted to say something to me which he had said to nobody else. It was really not possible for his Government to return to Moscow from this conference, having agreed to the immediate unification of Germany. They were a united Government and reasonably solidly based in the country, but this was something that Russia would not accept and if they were to agree to it, neither the army nor the people would understand, and this was no time to weaken the Government. The people would say that this was something Stalin would have never agreed to. On this he simply could not meet us.

As I reflected upon our conversation later that night, I felt that there was a genuine streak in what I had been told. The West, and in particular the United States, has never clearly understood the terrible significance of the German invasion for Russia. A nation of eighty million had invaded a nation of one hundred and sixty million, devastated its western provinces and almost reached its capital. The Russian people could never forget this. They had no Atlantic between them and Germany, not even a Channel. They would not run such risks again. In much that is false in the stream of comment which flows from the Soviets, there is one cry that is real. It is that of a nation which has nearly bled to death, not for the first time in Russian history. The Napoleonic war, the first world war, both tolled the same experience. Russians have long memories, they would be feckless not to take precautions.

On the occasion of one of my visits to Moscow towards the end of the war, when I was arranging to fly home, Stalin asked me the evening before I left which way I proposed to fly. I said I was going down to Tehran and that I would much like to fly over Stalingrad if that could be arranged. He replied that certainly it could, and permission was given for my aeroplane to do so. We flew round and round the city at a moderate height, though it was not really a city that we flew over. It was more than this, an area of factories, something like Tyneside at home, covering many miles in length. All this had been fought over, bombed, shelled, until its broken masonry and twisted steel girders gave the impression from above of two giants having played spillikins with the devastation they had created. In a long experience of war I have never seen anything like it for an impression of vehement destructive force. Villages and towns in Flanders were more completely wiped out; Stalingrad gave the fiercer impression of the struggle of man against man.

★　　★　　★　　★　　★

Now the debate in the conference surged around Germany. The Soviets liked to present their argument in terms of European security. which is certainly how they instinctively viewed it. They wished this to be discussed in advance of Germany and to be dealt with in advance of German unity. Their objective was either an indefinite continuation of the division of Germany or, possibly, some German reunion which extracted West Germany out of its association with the West. Even the latter would hardly have satisfied them, except in conditions which would have given a communist Government in East Germany virtual control. The dilemma in which the Soviets found themselves, and still do, on this issue, is inescapable. They know that the great majority of Germans, in whatever part of Germany they now live, are antagonistic to communism and all that it stands for. This feeling is strong in the Eastern zone. A remarkable feature of post-war Europe has been the tenacity and courage with which these East Germans behind the Iron Curtain have held to their faith. A generation has now grown up which has known nothing but Russian communist rule through its German puppets. Outside contacts are few and rare. There is a constant flow of refugees which deprives the East of some of the toughest and youngest of its population. Yet the sentiments of the masses do not change. Union with their own country, freedom from the last vestige of Moscow rule, are what they yearn for.

If this is accepted, nobody should be surprised at the constant argument about which is the cart and which is the horse in European affairs. Does the union of Germany come first and bring security, or must security be established by some wide European pact before any kind of unity within Germany can be contemplated? These discussions were not about arid diplomatic points, they would decide the future life of Germany and they dominated the conference table and our discussions outside it.

I suggested that it might be worth studying the possibility of a simultaneous approach to a security pact and to German unity. If the pact were not too wide in scope, and its negotiation were a comparatively simple matter, the two moves could go forward together. At this session I happened to be in the chair and at the end of the discussion I proposed that the Foreign Secretaries should draft instructions in this sense, which we could then approve. If they were able to do this, the instructions could form a later directive for their own meeting. I did not expect that they would succeed immediately, but this was the work which had to be done. The draft proposed by the Western powers was unacceptable to Mr. Molotov, and the Foreign Secretaries asked for a further day.

The Soviets chose this moment to produce their plan for a non-aggression treaty between the members of N.A.T.O. and the states of the Warsaw Pact. They tabled it in full conference. This proposal contained the disadvantages of which we had already spoken, it called for agreement between some twenty-five to thirty governments and it would take a long time to realize. Meanwhile, of course, Germany would remain divided. The Russians further asked that this proposal should be at once referred to the Foreign Secretaries without our having an opportunity to discuss it first in the conference. I did not like this for two reasons. I wanted the Foreign Secretaries to concentrate on the intricate subject already remitted to them in the form we had agreed.

This was the important issue of the conference and I did not want them, or ourselves, taken too far away from it. I saw dangers of confusion and delay if they had also to debate the new Russian proposal which the Heads of Government had not even discussed. After some exchanges, it was agreed that the matter should be referred to the Foreign Secretaries in the light of the considerations I had advanced. This was the best I could get and it was not enough.

The conference was rolling in an uneasy swell as we approached the third item on our agenda, disarmament. Here the President sprang a surprise. He put forward a plan by which the four powers would exchange blueprints of their military establishments and offer one another facilities for reconnaissance by aerial photography. This was intended as a step towards a general system for the inspection of armaments. It was to be a means of creating confidence, thereby leading to the reduction of arms.

Later when we met together in the buffet, the Russians, in conversation with me, poured scorn on this idea. I said that it was new to me, which was true, but that it was well worth further examination. There ought to be a welcome amongst us all for new ideas. These buffet meetings, which the Americans had initiated, were supposed to lead to informal discussions. They did not give any important results, because there were too many people about for any free or serious exchange of opinion.

Meanwhile, at the conference table, I had put forward another of the proposals we had been working on. I had already told the French and Americans about it. This, I now informed the conference, was aimed at reducing tension in the area which most acutely concerned us all, where the forces of East and West faced each other. My idea was that we should work out a simple plan for the joint inspection of the forces actually confronting one another in Europe. Over a specified area to be agreed between us, extending for a fixed depth on either side of the line now dividing east and west Europe, there should be supervision by inspecting teams appointed by the military commands on both sides. I considered this a practical proposal which could easily be extended outwards from the centre of the area in which it was launched. This scheme could be a useful one, and a start might be made with international inspection this way. No harm could result and confidence might be gained.

The draft of a directive for the Foreign Secretaries on disarmament presented no difficulties. The questions of German unity and European security continued to be much more stubborn. The Foreign Secretaries had agreed that the Russian draft treaty between N.A.T.O. and the countries of the Warsaw Pact should be one of the subjects for further study at their next meeting, which was arranged for October. They were still at odds about the terms in which the first two problems should be set out and they could not agree upon the order in which Germany, security and disarmament should be listed. These matters were considered by the Heads of Government in the privacy of a restricted session of only four a side. We soon reached agreement on those points which concerned disarmament and further consultation with representatives of the two Germanies. But the order of the agenda remained in dispute.

I suggested that the Foreign Secretaries should take the four subjects in the order in which they had been discussed at our conference, with German unity first. The Russians wanted to put it in the third place. This was no mere point of procedure, but one of substance. I had good reason to distrust a rigid agenda. At the Potsdam Conference an agenda had been drawn up which had, as its first two items, the Italian Peace Treaty and the Austrian Peace Treaty. For two years thereafter the Russians had refused to discuss Austria until the Italian Treaty had been concluded. If we met Russian wishes now, we must expect that they would insist on postponing the German problem until after agreement had been reached on both security and disarmament. The main subject which we had assembled to consider at Geneva would be shelved indefinitely.

We returned to this point of contention again and again, and discussed many possibilities of compromise. As German unity was so closely related to European security, I urged that the two items should be studied in parallel. Marshal Bulganin held to the view that Germany could not be united until after a European security pact had been concluded, but he advanced some way towards our position. He was willing to merge the two subjects in a single paragraph of the directive, so long as security was mentioned first.

We adjourned while a fresh draft was prepared. When we resumed we reached agreement, after some modification of the compromise before us. In accepting it, the Western powers declared that they could not contemplate the breakdown of the conference on a point which world opinion would consider to be procedural, even though in fact it was not. This directive was the best we could get and it was good enough, if the will to work it was there.

Our meetings concluded with the issue of the directive and with public speeches on the evening of July 23rd. The President was in the chair and in accordance with our practice, the country on the left, France, spoke first. I came next and gave the following summing-up for my country:

Ten years ago the war in Europe was brought to an end. Now at last we have made a start with the work which we might have hoped to begin in 1945. What we have now agreed makes it possible to get to grips with the twin problems of the unity of Germany and the security of Europe. No one expects that it will be easy to settle every detail of these complicated issues. But there is now a better chance than we have known at any time since the war to get to work on practical proposals to solve the differences which have divided Europe all these years. If we can continue our work together in the spirit of this meeting, what is hopeful promise today should become solid performance as events unfold.

It was then the turn of the Russians, who could not resist the opportunity of a public session and delivered a propaganda speech. This made a disagreeable impression, for which I was not altogether sorry; it would prevent any over-optimistic assessment of the position. Mr. Eisenhower spoke last and adapted his text skilfully to meet this Soviet behaviour, but he looked somewhat rueful, and I sympathized with him.

Even so, the Geneva Conference taught some lessons, which were powerfully to affect the course of events in the next few years. Each country present learnt that no country attending wanted war and each understood why. The Russians realized, as we did, that this situation had been created by the deterrent power of thermo-nuclear weapons. Accordingly, they were determined to keep a free hand to develop these weapons as far and as fast as their country's very considerable resources would take them. They had resolved to hold the most up-to-date weapons; this decided their attitude to control, which they feared might hamper them. In the minds of the men who commanded power in the world, the lessons of the conference might result in a reduced risk of total destruction to the human race. A less comfortable conclusion could also be drawn. The communist powers would continue to prosecute their purpose by every means. To do this, they would work in areas, and by methods, including the use of conventional weapons, which they believed would not entail retaliation by nuclear weapons. Here I felt was the likely pattern of future events.

On July 22nd, the Soviet delegation gave a dinner for me. Afterwards Marshal Bulganin drew me out on to the terrace, which overlooked the garden of the small villa they occupied. He began to speak of a visit by me to Moscow. He said that it had been many years since I was last there, in the war, and now conditions were greatly changed. I could be sure that the Russian people would give me a great welcome. I thanked Marshal Bulganin for his invitation and explained, as I had done before, that I had already paid many visits to Russia and that my work at home could hardly allow of another journey at present. I added that if anyone was to do any travelling, it was really the turn of the Russians to visit us. The Marshal smiled and replied that he accepted this. Stalin had never liked to travel. He himself had no similar feelings on the subject, neither had Mr. Khrushchev. They probably would be going abroad and would like to come to London. I said that this would certainly be welcome to me and to my colleagues.

I thought that it would be useful to renew the contacts we had established at Geneva. In London we could have thorough discussions at our leisure on the many problems that troubled the world. I would also like to give our visitors a chance to see something of the country. It was a mistake to suppose that all Britain was to be found in London. Marshal Bulganin responded readily to all this and, with Mr. Khrushchev, who had joined us during the conversation, expressing the same sentiments, the matter was soon arranged.

I had expected that something of this kind might happen during my visit to Geneva. It had seemed prudent to sound one or two of my colleagues in London in advance. I had no doubt, therefore, that this decision would be welcome to the Cabinet, as it was later to Parliament. I told Mr. Eisenhower at once of these developments and the same reaction was understanding.

For those of us who had been familiar with the long, black, bullet-proof cars of the Russians, it was a surprise to note the turn-out of the new Soviet leaders. They seemed to take pride in the minimum of display, and drove to and fro in an open car, with the smallest of police escorts. This was, no doubt, intended to show a fair similarity to the habit of French and British Prime Ministers. It was in some contrast to the President of the United States, who, alone among us, was a Head of State. He had to endure the road-sweeping tactics of the Secret Service, which seemed a little out of proportion in the scale of democratic Switzerland.

At times, this new-found Soviet enthusiasm for free and easy methods led to some discomfort. In the later afternoon of the final day of the conference, I went round to see the Russian leaders, in company with Sir Harold Caccia, then a Deputy Under-Secretary of State at the Foreign Office. Mr. Macmillan was to meet me there and we were to talk over the Geneva accords affecting Indo-China, negotiated a year before. On my arrival, I saw a large number of photographers of various nationalities by the front door. I paid little attention and walked through into the garden where Marshal Bulganin and Mr. Khrushchev and others were standing. I had hardly shaken hands, when the earth shook with the trampling of a herd of buffaloes and the photographers broke through from all directions. Our small island was soon almost overwhelmed. One over-excited photographer jabbed me furiously in the back, crying, 'Get out of my way, can't you?' I did not oblige. Eventually, perplexed by this display of western manners, the Russian leaders contrived to shepherd their guests into the house.

At a conference like this, it is usual for private discussions to be the most worthwhile. We entertained each other informally and made working occasions of the meals. Apart from attending a dinner given by our Swiss hosts, the President was firm in taking all his meals at home. He had brought his own Filipinos to cook for him and they had brought their frozen steaks from the United States. M. Faure was a convivial host and regaled us with *vin jaune* from the Jura nearby. This was his own country and he took a justifiable pride in its local wine, which is pleasantly refreshing when drunk on the spot.

Our formal meetings were concerned with Europe, our private anxieties with the Far East. I soon learnt that the other delegations at the conference thought there was no immediate danger of war in Europe. It was equally clear that all were deeply concerned at the situation in the Far East, especially that of the off-shore islands of Quemoy and the Matsus. The United States might declare that they owed nothing to Chiang Kai-shek, but he was necessary to the defence of Formosa, or so at least the Americans believed, and Formosa formed part of the United States Pacific defences. No Chinese Government could be expected to accept this, though they might tolerate it under repeated protests. The Formosans themselves would probably prefer to lead their own lives, without either Chiang or Peking to dominate them.

The off-shore islands were in a different category. They had always been part of China, and were garrisoned and defended by Chiang

308

Kai-shek. No great power could seriously want to fight about them, yet they could be a cause of war, just the same. They were never mentioned at the conference table, but they were the world's flash point in the summer of 1955. I am convinced that the Geneva Conference damped their explosive force, for the time being at least.

Clearly this was not a topic likely to yield to direct United States and Soviet talks, but I had no inhibitions about taking a hand in it myself. After a detailed conversation alone with the President, I was absolutely convinced of American sincerity. The Americans knew that they had a bear by the tail. I soon found that the Soviet leaders shared my concern at the danger, while persistently upholding their ally's standpoint. In one of our informal discussions Mr. Khrushchev commented that the Chinese had been very patient; he did not think that the Russians would have been so patient. I replied that he underestimated his own statesmanship. The position of Quemoy and the Matsus was very difficult for the Americans and for everybody concerned. The Americans might wish their ally to take steps he was not prepared to take. We were not always able to get our friends to do what we wanted. The Russians appeared to accept this, but they were clearly still anxious about the Far Eastern situation.

As these informal exchanges proceeded, I felt increasingly convinced that all the member powers wished to avoid conflict in the area. This, I believed, also applied to the Chinese Government of Peking, though, as the Russians commented, 'The master of the house is absent.' I thought that it might even suit the Chinese Communists to have Chiang's forces on the off-shore islands. They constituted a constant grievance with which most of world opinion would sympathize. The islands were militarily vulnerable and could be harassed or bombarded by conventional weapons at any time, when Chiang would have to evacuate or supply them. The former would be a humiliation, the latter costly in supplies and perhaps in life. On the other hand, if Chiang were soon to evacuate Quemoy and the Matsus, as he had Tachen, then the Chinese Communist case against Chiang and the United States would be much weaker, politically and militarily. World opinion would not feel about Formosa, with its chequered history and so recently Japanese, as it did about small islands in the mouths of Chinese harbours and rivers. Militarily, the Chinese Communists could do little that was effective to threaten Formosa, so long as it was part of the United States defensive chain. To get there, they would have to swim or fly against a formidable fortress a hundred miles away. Therefore, from the American point of view, the position in Formosa would be stronger without the commitment of the off-shore islands.

It seemed to me that here was an occasion where time was on the side of peace. Already in Formosa the army was changing its character. It was becoming composed more and more of young Formosans, who did not want to return to the mainland. As that development continued, the off-shore islands would matter less. In the talks I held, I did everything I could to persuade those present, and absent, of the peaceful intentions of the other side.

On the evening when I dined with the Russians, Marshal Bulganin and Mr. Khrushchev spoke of the position in the Far East. Marshal Zhukov was also present, but he took no part in the conversation. My hosts said that they had been greatly impressed by what they had seen during their visit to China. The new leaders there were men to be reckoned with. Both Mao Tse-tung and Chou En-lai were strong characters, men of balanced judgment, who were unlikely to take hasty or ill-considered action. The regime was firmly established; much material progress was being made and, in ten years or so, China would be a strong modern state. Meanwhile, their revolution was young. It was natural, therefore, that they should resent Chiang's occupation of Quemoy and the Matsus so near their coastline, and the United States protection of Chiang in Formosa. It was natural, too, that they should wish to take China's seat in the United Nations. On that point the Russians claimed that they certainly had right on their side.

I said that President Eisenhower was doing his best to steady public opinion in the United States on the subject of Quemoy and the Matsus. The Russians should, however, recognize his difficulties. This was a subject on which emotions ran high in the United States. Our own interests in China had been mainly commercial. We had traded there for a long time, and over the years had earned a good return for what we had invested. The Americans, during the war and since, had poured money into China, and the average American now felt that the Chinese had bitten the hand that fed them. As a result, the Americans were specially sensitive about the present situation. The President was trying, in spite of this, to calm things down. If he were given more time, all might yet be well. Were the Chinese prepared to be equally patient?

Mr. Khrushchev said that traditionally the Chinese were a patient people. He believed that they would not take any rash action at the present time. It was to be hoped, however, that some fruitful result would come from the meetings which were to be held in Geneva between two ambassadors appointed by the United States and China. I said that these discussions should help. Though they would begin with such questions as release of prisoners, they might well broaden out to cover some of the more substantial issues.

The Geneva meeting was worthwhile if only for the discreet improvement it brought about in the Formosa Strait. By the end of the conference, the Foreign Secretary and I were convinced that all present would have been sincerely happy to see the off-shore islands sunk under the sea. All this seemed to justify the comment I made to the House of Commons on my return: 'Geneva has given this simple message to the whole world: it has reduced the dangers of war.'

★　　★　　★　　★　　★

The day following our return, my wife and I drove to Winchester, where my regiment was celebrating its two hundredth anniversary. The King's Royal Rifle Corps (60th Rifles) began life on the American continent in the mid-eighteenth century, under the title of the Royal American Regiment. Swift in movement and dark green in uniform, it was formed to aid and cover the more cumbrous manœuvres of the traditional red-coats, against the French and their Red Indian allies. The American connection has existed ever since. When, in the second world war, a number of young Americans volunteered to join the British Army before Pearl Harbour, it was natural that the 60th should be their choice. They served bravely in the North African campaign, some staying with the regiment throughout the war. It was moving to meet a number of the survivors once again, on this afternoon of memories in a perfect English setting.

The Queen, our Colonel-in-Chief, took the salute. The drill movements to the note of the bugle and the double past made a dashing and unusual spectacle in which I took pride. Later that afternoon I had an audience of Her Majesty at the Deanery in Winchester, and reported on the Geneva meeting and the projected Russian visit. As my wife and I drove back through the city to our cottage near Salisbury, the citizens gave us a splendid greeting, the countryside was fresh and green in the evening light. These interludes are rare in the life of a Prime Minister.

V

THE PLAGUES OF PROSPERITY
July 1955 – July 1956

*The balance of payments – Further credit squeeze – My minute
to the Chancellor – Defence – Housing – The Rent Acts – Food
subsidies – Increased purchase tax – My views on savings – The
autumn Budget – Reconstruction of the Cabinet – Cost of living
– My speech at Bradford – The White Paper on Full Employment
– Mr. Macmillan's Budget – Premium bonds – My minute on
price stability – M.P.s' salaries – I oppose a rise – A brighter
economic prospect*

A few weeks after the general election, our economy began to
feel twinges at its most sensitive point, the balance of payments.
The 'credit squeeze' was helping to check home demand but
it could only be long-term in its effects. In the meanwhile, increases
in wages agreed earlier in the year were influencing prices. More
directly harmful were the strikes from May to July, and especially
the dock strike. They held up our exports and held down the rate of
industrial output.

The damage these events did to our balance of payments showed
itself as the weeks went by, though it was not popular to point it out.
As a result, the economy of Britain, though extremely vigorous, was
getting out of balance again. I had to determine whether this condition was temporary and would right itself, or whether the Government should take further measures. That was the decision which
faced us in July, when preparations were far advanced for the meeting
of Heads of Government at Geneva. The figures and forecasts indicated where the strain lay. World trade was rapidly expanding, yet
Britain, in common with some other countries of Western Europe, was
scarcely balancing its payments. We were not gaining the substantial
surplus we should need in the coming autumn months, always

unfavourable to us. We were consuming too much of our increased production and exporting too little.

If this was the best we could do in favourable circumstances, the outlook was grim should world trade suffer a setback. The tendency was still for rising costs to swallow economies which had been carefully planned and painfully made in every field of government expenditure. In one of my minutes to the Chancellor of the Exchequer I remarked that we had to run very hard to stay where we were.

Nobody likes restriction, but clearly there had to be a further tightening of the 'credit squeeze' and I agreed to this before I left for Geneva. Mr. Butler announced in the House on July 25th that the banks had been officially requested to reduce their advances to customers. Local authorities were asked to hold back their schemes for capital expenditure and the rates at which they could borrow from the Public Works Loans Board were raised. The boards of the nationalized industries were urged to slow down on their programmes of development and re-equipment. The terms of hire purchase were stiffened.

These July decisions were comparatively mild and were patiently received. I was, however, concerned as to whether they would prove enough. Throughout August and September a detailed examination was carried out at the instance of the Cabinet, and once again the holidays of Ministers were harshly cut about.

By the end of August our gold and dollar reserves were falling by over $100 million a month. The country was plainly attempting to do too much with the limited resources at its disposal. Britain was trying to build houses, schools, hospitals, factories and office blocks, which were all needed, and at the same time sustain the heavy burdens of defence and National Service. We were maintaining the essential health, welfare and educational systems, to which all parties were committed, while attempting to re-equip industry, both nationalized and private, on the extensive scale which had been planned and was necessary if our competition was to remain effective. Even if all this allowed of no easy and agreeable answer, we had to protect the future.

The development of nuclear power was essential to the future of our industry and to our national life, but it was expensive. Soon after the war, when on a private visit to the United States, I had, through the kindness of President Truman, an opportunity for a discussion with a leading official dealing with atomic matters. He told me that he expected that we should lead the United States in the development of atomic power for civil use. He added that this was as it should be, because the United States, with its valuable resources of oil and gas, had less urgent need of this new source of power.

I was insistent that the atomic energy programme must not be hampered. We had established a lead in nuclear power and we must keep it, for development could be expected to result in more power at a cheapening price. In all the discussions that followed I maintained this position. The cuts we had to determine did not have to be large. Small but sharp economies here and there would serve our purpose, but where everything is desirable, what is to be sacrificed? We had to act decisively and ahead of trouble without creating an atmosphere of crisis. Any changes made must be fair and seen to be so, we had to have a balanced plan. It was to this that Ministers addressed themselves during the holiday months of August and September.

I had a number of talks with the Chancellor of the Exchequer, outside the Cabinet as well as in it. After one of these conversations I sent him on August 30th a minute which read as follows:

> I have been thinking over our talks yesterday. I hope they were useful. They have convinced me that we must put the battle against inflation before anything else. After all, if we win out, the other problems, for example the gold and dollar reserves, will take care of themselves.
>
> Therefore I think we should approach our problem mainly from this angle. With this in mind I will press the Services hard, because to release more men is to fight inflation. But oughtn't we to consider all matters, for example the price of bacon, from this angle, and the price of bread, too. In this train of thought I feel that it would be quite wrong to raise the purchase tax, but arguable that we should lower it. We have to make up our minds what is our main objective and go for it. The danger is for the Government to try to do too many things in policies, as the nation is trying to do in activities.
>
> These are just thoughts which I send you because I am sure after yesterday that we shall not get either side in industry to move first. If we on the other hand could take a series of steps aimed at reducing the cost of living we should have a right to speak to both of them and the nation will back us up. Can we work these out?

To be effective our action against inflation had to curb both government and private spending. In each it must restrain both consumption and investment. The largest single item in government expenditure was defence. I had ordered a general examination of this, but it must take time to get results. A shortage of manpower was one of the principal elements at that time in the country's inflationary pattern. The only contribution which could immediately be made by the Service departments was to speed the reduction in the armed forces to swell the ranks of civilian labour. This we did.

We could not hope to get all we needed from defence alone. Next in importance was expenditure on housing and on the investment programme of the nationalized industries. I had discussions with the National Coal Board, which convinced me that their plans could not be cut down without a further loss of coal output. As it was, our purchases of foreign coal had risen by no less than 875 per cent. during the first seven months of 1955, compared with the same period of the year before. This hardly seemed the moment to risk reducing our potential coal production. The other principal nationalized industries, electricity, gas and the railways, were all engaged on long-term plans. It was agreed that these would have to be slowed down.

We had faithfully fulfilled our election promise to build 300,000 new houses a year. We had been doing this for more than two years and the greater part of the total was subsidized housing, built by local authorities. Altogether, 1,500,000 new houses had been built since 1951, plus a million more since the war. I considered that the programme must be adjusted to take account of our changing needs. The work of slum-clearance must be speeded up and the special needs of the new towns and of the mining communities provided for, while some reduction was effected in the total of houses built. Local authorities were spending £400 million a year on subsidized housing, more than two-thirds of their budgets. The Government scaled down plans for subsidized housing by about 15 per cent. and reduced the general exchequer subsidy on each new house from £22 to £10. We also stiffened the terms on which the local authorities could secure loans.

As a result of this, we estimated that new houses would henceforth be built at the rate of 250,000 a year. I thought this about right, in the light of conflicting demands. The problem of housing, however, was inevitably complicated by the series of Rent Control Acts which applied to existing property. The working of these acts was acknowledged by all to be out of date, but no Government had yet dared to tackle the explosive task of dealing with them. We decided that this duty could no longer be ignored and put in hand the studies which resulted in the Rent Bill one year later.

The purchase tax was brought in during the war as a special measure and has remained to scourge us. It had also, I suspect, a vogue as a means of dealing with 'an excessive spending capacity'. We reluctantly decided to raise this tax by one-fifth on all ranges of goods and to include pots and pans, amongst others, which had previously been exempt. These decisions were thought economically right at the time, they were certainly politically odious and cut across our party's philosophy. It is difficult to advocate a property-owning democracy to the tune of 'Your kettles will cost you more'. In spite of which dichotomy I felt that the British people would accept the necessity for these disagreeable penalties, if they could be seen to be fairly applied. Everything turned on this condition. We spent many hours of discussion and the Chancellor many days of wearisome travail, trying to get the balance right.

In our modern form of society in Britain, the effect of the high level of income tax and surtax is to tip the balance further in favour of the man who has capital. It was only fair that the man with capital, as well as the wage earner and salaried man, should be brought within the scope of our proposals. Accordingly, the tax on distributed profits was increased to the extent of 5 per cent.

My constant concern in the discussion of these financial matters was to find new schemes to encourage saving. I worried successive Chancellors by a repeated return to this theme. This time a new issue of defence bonds was offered, at a slightly higher rate of interest. I should have liked to go further and propose an increase in the income tax reliefs on savings, either on life assurance premiums or by increasing the capital sums that could be invested in national savings, or both. There was also much to be said for making saving certificates free of death duty. Although the level of saving at this time was fairly encouraging, it was only so by comparison with the low level of earlier years. I felt it important to try to find new schemes of saving with a more attractive flavour. There might be savings loans of a more speculative kind for colonial and Commonwealth development, which would bring into the national savings net the investor who was willing to run risks. Or savings certificates could be issued with interest linked to the cost of living. The complexities of administering any such schemes were immense and could not be quickly resolved. The Treasury were studying the report of a Commission on Taxation which raised many problems. They wished to consider this before making any new departures. Our next main move on savings was therefore delayed, to my regret, until April of the following year.

The Chancellor of the Exchequer presented his proposals to the House of Commons in a Budget on October 26th. It had a rough reception from the Opposition, but Mr. Butler made a brilliant speech in reply to the taunts thrown at him. The two main points which I made later in the debate are, I think, still true. Credit restrictions imposed in February and July had not worked as we had expected, because our prosperous economy was expanding so fast. In successive budgets we had given incentives to invest. This was sound policy, but investment, like rearmament, is a programme slow to get under way. In the first year or two the results do not show, in the third year they are suddenly spread abroad. Everybody in the House knew this, for as we travelled about the country during the general election we had all seen it with our own eyes. Some action to check this expansion must be taken, or the competition between companies for material and labour would bring our industries to chaos. We took that action. It was, on the face of it, an exaggeration to pretend that Mr. Butler's proposals, though disagreeable, were either harsh or cruel.

★   ★   ★   ★   ★

As the year 1955 neared its close, I considered that some major changes in the Government were necessary. I write 'necessary' because changes in a well-balanced team are not in themselves welcome to a Prime Minister or to his colleagues, if they are working well together. There will always be some pressure for change in a healthy party, younger men thrusting from below. This tendency is both normal and wholesome. A Prime Minister must take account of it, but he has to be on his guard that it does not cause him to jettison good men too soon.

Mr. Butler had been at the Treasury for four strenuous years. All the higher offices of State are heavy going in times like these. Pressure is most unremitting at the Foreign Office and the Treasury. Both of these offices are more exacting in their demands than that of Prime Minister, except in times of crisis. It was clear to me that Mr. Butler ought, in fairness, to have a break, and I think that he felt so too. It would also be a good thing for him to have some wider Parliamentary experience. I felt that he would lead the House of Commons well. The Chief Whip, Mr. Patrick Buchan-Hepburn, shared my view.

I had therefore to find a new Chancellor of the Exchequer. The choice seemed to me to lie between Mr. Macmillan from the Foreign Office and Mr. Heathcoat Amory from the Ministry of Agriculture. Mr. Heathcoat Amory had but recently entered the Cabinet and at that time hardly possessed the authority for so senior an office. Also, he was doing very well in Agriculture. After much thought I decided to ask my two colleagues in the House of Commons, Mr. Butler and Mr. Macmillan, to accept changes which would give the former the leadership of the House and the latter the Treasury. This decision meant that I had to lose the services of Mr. Crookshank, which I much regretted, for his Parliamentary experience and independence of mind, and for his loyalty.

The need to transfer Mr. Macmillan from the Foreign Office to the Treasury left me with a problem at the Foreign Office. Mr. Selwyn Lloyd was clearly a strong candidate. He had been a successful Minister of State and had handled vexing problems at the United Nations with a skill which had won him general applause in that critical assembly. He was a good Minister of Defence, but there was no other candidate in the House of Commons who had comparable experience of the Foreign Office. I decided to offer him that post. It took him time to handle Parliament as successfully as he dealt with his colleagues. But the House of Commons can be a cruel assembly. I remember Mr. Baldwin once attempting to comfort me during a comparatively rough passage in debate with the comment: 'The House can be merciless. The Tories nearly killed Haldane.' As a negotiator, Mr. Selwyn Lloyd is clear, firm and consistent. As a chairman of an international conference he can pilot an uncertain assembly with confidence through all kinds of weather.

Lord Monckton has a brilliant mind, weighted by a humane conscience, and is the most loyal of friends. He had now spent a number of persevering years at the Ministry of Labour, which had tried his health highly, and he several times expressed to me his desire for transfer to some less exacting office. He is the best of co-ordinators and has never lost interest in Service matters since his brave military career in the first world war. I thought that the Ministry of Defence which, for all its urgent tasks, normally does not carry a heavy Parliamentary charge, would fit him admirably and he welcomed the change.

The Ministry of Labour is a key post in a Conservative administration; a good appointment to that office can smooth relations with industry, a bad or indifferent one will soon rouse as many quills of trouble as on the fretful porcupine. The Ministry is also a useful training ground for a possible future Prime Minister. Having ruled out Mr. Heathcoat Amory because I did not wish to disturb his work at the Ministry of Agriculture, I thought this an opportunity to give one of our younger men his chance, if I could be sure he had the qualifications.

My choice was Mr. Iain Macleod, who had proved himself as Minister of Health; he has done very well.

I announced these and other changes on December 22nd. The composition of the Cabinet now was:

Prime Minister	Sir Anthony Eden
Lord President	Lord Salisbury
Foreign Secretary	Mr. Selwyn Lloyd
Chancellor of the Exchequer	Mr. Macmillan
Lord Privy Seal and Leader of the House of Commons	Mr. Butler
Lord Chancellor	Lord Kilmuir
Minister of Defence	Sir Walter Monckton
Home Secretary	Mr. Lloyd-George
Colonial Secretary	Mr. Lennox-Boyd
Secretary for Commonwealth Relations	Lord Home
Secretary of State for Scotland	Mr. Stuart
Minister of Labour	Mr. Macleod
President of the Board of Trade	Mr. Thorneycroft
Minister of Housing and Local Government	Mr. Sandys
Chancellor of the Duchy of Lancaster	Lord Selkirk
Minister of Education	Sir David Eccles
Minister of Agriculture	Mr. Heathcoat Amory
Minister of Works	Mr. Buchan-Hepburn

★   ★   ★   ★   ★

One day in December Mr. Attlee came to tell me of his decision to retire from the leadership of the Opposition. I was sorry to hear of this on all counts, national and personal. He had led the Labour Party since the retirement of George Lansbury, twenty years before. It seemed to me like the end of an epoch, and I told Mr. Attlee so. In the war years we had grown to know each other well, though my relations with him were not so close as they became with Mr. Bevin, when the latter was Foreign Secretary. Mr. Attlee is a man with whom it is easy to be friendly, but difficult to be intimate. For the time being, his decision had to remain confidential between us, but he agreed that I should tell the Queen and make the formal submission for an earldom.

Attlee's modesty in expression conceals a firmness of purpose. Though not imaginative, he sees more clearly than most the limits of

319

his action and never strays beyond them. He is infinitely patient and I often marvelled during the war years at his perseverance in doodling during evening Cabinets, which I sometimes found exasperatingly drawn out. It was not in his nature to do so, but if he had to, he could snap and bite with the best. I trusted him completely as a colleague and respected him as an opponent.

I have thought Attlee's opinions to the left of those commonly attributed to him. He has suggested that a Prime Minister should be left of centre, quoting Stanley Baldwin's dictum. But I think he has misunderstood that statesman's meaning. Baldwin had in mind that a Conservative Prime Minister should be left of centre. Thus placed, he could influence the floating vote to his left. By the same token, Baldwin would, I think, have placed a Socialist Prime Minister right of centre.

Naturally I was curious about the succession. There seemed to be one man whose gifts and experience in politics raised him above any possible competition. Mr. Herbert Morrison had behind him a considerable career by any standards. His leadership for many years of the Labour majority on the London County Council had given him an exceptional grasp of the problems of local government. He had been a Minister in earlier Labour Governments and had carried doughtily his administrative responsibilities during the war. When the Labour Party won the general election of 1945, he led the House well and seemed to us in Opposition a formidable and ingenious opponent, upon whom the Government were ready enough to rely. All this should have weighed more heavily in the scales than a comparatively unhappy period at the Foreign Office. But there was something else, or at least we in the Opposition believed that there was something else. Mr. Attlee did not appear to look favourably on Mr. Morrison as his successor. Whether this affected the outcome or not, the final result of the voting gave Mr. Gaitskell the first place and Mr. Morrison the last. I had no doubt that this was a national misfortune.

I was unable to establish with Mr. Gaitskell the political and personal relations which I had enjoyed with all his predecessors. This was one of my failures, but curiously enough in all my years of political life I had not met anyone with his cast of mind and approach to problems. We never seemed able to get on terms.

*   *   *   *   *

On taking over as Prime Minister, I had given much thought to industrial relations, the course of which I had already watched for so

many years in Cabinet. I was sure that we needed a prolonged educational campaign on the broad subject of wages and prices. During the
summer of 1955, a committee I set up was preparing a White Paper to
analyse the causes of discontent and unrest in industry. Inflation was
first among them.

The purpose of this paper was to provide the background for a new
approach to stabilize prices and prevent a perpetual upward spiral in
wage claims and in the cost of living. Its publication was to be accompanied by a popular exposition of the theme, and by a series of talks
with both sides of industry. The White Paper had a long and difficult
birth. The circumstances which had originally prompted it were
modified. In the country at large the rash of strikes had died away and
during the autumn we became less immediately concerned with labour
relations than with action against inflation. The course of events which
led to the autumn Budget underlined this. The White Paper had now
to give first place to the fight against rising prices.

At the end of the year I expressed my views on the general economic
situation to the new Chancellor of the Exchequer in a minute of
December 27th:

> Here are some notes on topics which I have discussed before
> with your predecessor and with you when you were still at the
> Foreign Office. I do not feel, however, that time has altered the
> necessity for some measures of this kind.
>
> Savings. I suspect that one of the most painful contrasts between
> our economy and the American at the present time is how little
> relatively our people save. This is no doubt in part due to the con-
> tinuing fall in the value of money. But whatever the reason, I am
> sure that a remedy must be found for this if our economy is to be
> firmly established again. I believe that the British people could
> still be induced to join in a big savings campaign to wipe up sur-
> plus spending power if it were attractive and had an element of
> real capital gain in it. It might be possible to link this in some way
> with the future value of real money. I do not think this suggestion
> is so alarming as it sounds, because it is surely true that the more our
> people save, the stronger the pound will be. Moreover saving, by
> reducing demand on goods, would directly help against inflation.
> Personally I very much prefer saving to taxation for 'mopping
> up surplus purchasing power'. I put this as our number one need.
>
> It seems to me that our excessive spending as a nation is due, as

Woolton pointed out some time ago, to the fact that both Government and industrialists have been captivated by the idea of an 'expanding economy'. We are right to expand, but now we have done it so that we are bursting at the seams.

In this connection I am still troubled about building. Our two heavy import bills are for coal and for steel. I presume that building is responsible for some of the latter. I do not mean houses. I think the action we have taken there is just right. Factory building will be affected by the credit squeeze, but office building still seems to leap ahead. This last cannot be so urgent. If we could find some way of checking office building without re-imposing control this would help us to reduce our imports.

As to this question of imports, I should be most reluctant to contemplate any return to licensing and Government control as I am sure you would be. Is it not, however, possible to get something of the same results by other methods? Cannot the banks, for instance, be given some indication from time to time that such and such materials are those for the import of which we should be most reluctant to see money advanced. If something of this kind were practicable I should much prefer it to import control.

And now the question of the cost of living. The most disturbing feature of our economy is that the Americans' cost of living and that of many other countries has remained about stable over the last four years, while ours has climbed steadily, and of late sharply.

I do not believe that we can persuade the people of this country that the Government is tackling the cost of living by putting on more taxes, e.g., purchase tax, which would raise the cost of living and cause a scramble for the goods before they are taxed. Is there not some other way in which we could make a more evident frontal attack which would enlist their sympathy and support? That is what I had in mind when I suggested a reduction in the beer duty this autumn. I accepted that it was not appropriate then but I think that it would be appropriate in the future and it would take (is it two points?) off the cost-of-living index. There are other measures of this kind that could be taken in the Budget to reduce the cost of living.

Now, the trade unions do understand that if our costs go on rising we shall inevitably price ourselves out of world markets and they will be the first to suffer. Therefore they will always lend a sympathetic ear to any doctrine aimed at avoiding this danger. If in addition to the measures I have suggested we could call for restraint in dividends and expenditure generally, and produce an attractive savings programme, we should have a fair chance of enlisting their help in trying to keep wages steady over the next few years. We have simply got to do this somehow. Hence my suggestion of a preliminary private talk with them on Monday.

I have not troubled you with detailed topics in this note which is long enough already, but I am still unconvinced that further reductions are impossible in some of the Civil Service figures, e.g., the Admiralty and War Office staff are much above those of the R.A.F. I discussed this with Selwyn Lloyd while he was still at the Ministry of Defence. But these are matters of detail in relation to the wider matters I have tried to set down in this crude fashion.

★   ★   ★   ★   ★

Before my visit to the United States in January 1956 for discussions with President Eisenhower, I went to Yorkshire to give the country an account of what we were doing. I am always glad of a chance to speak to a north country meeting, particularly if I have a difficult case to make. Perhaps this is because I am a north countryman myself. I have found audiences there suspicious of sensationalism and patient with hard argument. In the north they are not easily swayed by the fashion of the hour and they attach as much authority to a man's character as to his words. They are staunchly loyal to those they trust. Bradford was therefore a good choice for what I had to say and, as so often in my life, I found direct contact with the people a stimulus and a corrective.

The main theme of my speech was that, while we all wanted full employment and steady prices, we had not yet succeeded in combining the two. Industrial investment was going up by leaps and bounds, twice as much factory building had been approved during the past twelve months as in 1951. 'But here', I said, 'we come to the plagues of prosperity. Our victories are threatened. We have overstretched ourselves. It is this surge of confidence and expansion, healthy enough in itself, which has produced the unfamiliar problems with which we are now grappling. The danger is not of depression and stagnation, but of launching out on new efforts in too many directions at once. We still favour expansion, but it must be balanced and restrained. We don't want a blown up economy; we want a steadily developing economy.'

I described the action the Government was taking to make economies in the branches of expenditure under its control, including cuts
in defence and in the number of civil servants. But ours was a positive
programme. We had extensive plans for harnessing nuclear energy
and for developing technical education. Britain could not afford to
fall behind in the world-wide scientific revolution now taking place.

Concerning the immediate problems of industrial relations and the
critical connection between wages and prices, I spoke of the conversations which the Minister of Labour and I had already held and intended
to continue with employers and trade unionists, on how to reach
some level of stability. 'The creation of a sense of partnership in
industry', I said, 'has long been my aim. Many firms both great
and small are working in their own way towards it. We all want
an increase in our standard of living. We can get it if everyone
makes a vigorous effort to put production up, and if we are prepared
to think of the community as a whole.

'Some industries, some sectors of the economy, are bound to increase production more quickly than others. The engineer can do this;
it is not so easy for the bus driver. If those engaged in these industries,
where production is being vigorously increased, will take the wider
view, they will allow part of the benefits of their higher production to
be passed on to the community, which includes themselves, in the
form of lower prices. A number of firms have set a helpful example.
They have taken a decision to hold their prices stable, some for six
months, some for a year. This is a practical example of how to fight
rising prices. The best way in which the benefits of higher production
can reach the whole community is by lower prices. This means that
increased profits should be passed on in the form of lower prices,
rather than of increased dividends.'

In conclusion I said: 'The battle against inflation is on. If the
weapons we are using now do not suffice, we shall not hesitate to use
others. What is tantalising in all this is that if once our balance of payments could be put right and our reserves built up there is hardly any
limit to our future. There are the countries of the Commonwealth
eager to use our help, our technical skills and experience.'

The White Paper, which bore the title of the Economic Implications of Full Employment, was eventually issued in March 1956,
immediately before the Budget of that year. It was favourably received
by the press and the public. The main theme echoed my Bradford
speech and reviewed the decade which had passed since the end of the

war. Unemployment had not been a problem. It had averaged 1½ per cent. of the total labour force since 1945, compared with 10 per cent. before the war. Total output had risen by 3 per cent. fairly regularly year by year. But this was counterbalanced by the startling increase in prices. In nine years they had risen by no less than 50 per cent. The main fact at home was sharp and clear: the cost of wages, salaries, profits was rising much faster than the value of output, and a halt, or at least a scaling down in the annual rise, was essential for the country's health.

Over the decade of 1945–55 output had risen by 30 per cent., but the combined incomes of those who produced it had gone up by 90 per cent. Wages and salaries were by far the biggest item in this bill. The purpose of the White Paper was not to appeal for restraint in making wage claims and fixing margins of profit, but to show the need for it. The Government followed this impartial survey of British economic life by consultations with both sides of industry to persuade them to recognize the reality of the problem and get them to act in line.

★   ★   ★   ★   ★

Mr. Macmillan, as the new Chancellor, now introduced the Budget of 1956. Low savings and high government spending had long been two of the country's main weaknesses. The emphasis of this Budget was on saving, and in two directions. The Government proposed to cut expenditure by £100 million, that was its contribution. More savings had to be coaxed from those of the public who were ready to invest but needed a spur.

New and more rewarding issues of defence bonds and savings certificates were announced, but the innovation which caught popular attention was the premium bond scheme. This offered its partakers tax-free prizes. These proposals were akin to my own minutes to the Treasury over the past six months. There was an element of lottery in the premium bonds which drew denunciation from stern critics and mockery from more frivolous spirits. I agreed with the Chancellor that it was a good plan to attract into public funds a part of the large sums annually spent by those who like to play with chance. It may be that the prizes are not yet large enough or that there are not enough of them for the attraction to be as broadly popular as it could be made.

In my minutes to the Chancellor, I reverted to the White Paper, for I had every intention of taking action upon it. I wrote to him in April:

Of course, I have never thought that we could or should achieve a standstill or freeze on wages or prices. On the other hand, short of taking deflationary measures to a length which is politically not tolerable, I do not see how we can hope to limit wage claims by removing pressure on the labour market. Surely the bulk of wage demands springs from the traditional and annual reaction of the unions to the upward creep of prices, rather than the competitive bidding for labour by individual firms.

If I am right we should do all that we can to discourage wage demands both by explaining that the true interest of the community lies in price stability and also by doing what we can to keep prices stable where they are in our control.

By 'what we can' I do not mean the indiscriminate subsidizing of losses in the nationalized industries. But the postponement of price increases, where increasing efficiency gives grounds for this, may well make it worth while to put some temporary burden on the Exchequer now and again. I am sure that it would be dangerous to do nothing about the inevitability of price increases, over the rest of the year. We should then find pressure building up for another round of wage increases, which would in turn mean higher prices, and so on. I do not see how we could hope to wait for a few months and then draw the line.

Budget decisions, by which the bread and milk subsidies were removed, would probably add about one point to the cost-of-living index; wage claims, already agreed to, would add another. On the basis of this rise of two points, I was determined to make an effort to stabilize the position during the spring and summer.

There was one field in which I felt considerable personal difficulty, so did the Government. This was in the House of Commons, where there was strong pressure for a rise in Members' salaries. I sympathized with the financial hardships which many Members were experiencing, but I did not see how we could convincingly appeal to the country for wage restraint and at the same time vote ourselves an increase in pay. The Opposition raised the question on a motion to which I replied:

I do not deny that some increase in the salary of Members would be justified now if there were not certain special considerations, but in the Government's view there are special considerations, and they govern this question.

As the result of a number of measures, some of which Mr. Gaitskell has acclaimed, we have now reached a position where we may hope that, with continued restraint on all sides, we may achieve a greater stability in prices. This is something we all want to see. This is something from which we shall all benefit. Last month there was stability. It will be interesting to see—we do not yet know—the figure this month. . . .

I need not tell the House after that, that an increase here at this time in the full glare of publicity, in which we have to live as Members of Parliament, whether we like it or whether we do not, cannot but have its effect at once on other sections of the community, at a time when we are urging restraint. . . . We are in this special position and we must not be the ones to set the spiral working again.

My colleagues were in full agreement with this decision, but it did not smooth the working of the House of Commons. I had not been long gone, in 1957, when this was adjusted, to the natural accompaniment of laudatory speeches.

During the early summer I had a number of meetings with the representatives of the employers, the T.U.C. and the nationalized industries. Mr. Macmillan, Mr. Butler and the Minister of Labour, Mr. Macleod, attended these. We made encouraging progress, and at the end of July we had a heartening report to issue. Retail prices were steady; exports for the first six months of the year had gone up; the balance of payments showed a surplus of £100 million. The Government had set an example by reducing the estimates of its expenditure by £75 million. Industrialists and labour leaders were showing a welcome understanding of the need to break the spiral of costs and prices. The outlook was better than it had been for a long time.

I felt rewarded by the result of our initiatives over the past fifteen months. The Government published a statement registering the progress we had made, and counselling further effort. We added a note of caution: 'Apart from the possible effects of a major disturbance in international relations, the future of the general price level now lies largely in our own hands.'

These words were written late in July. On the 26th Nasser proclaimed the nationalization of the Suez Canal. An international crisis was at once upon our maritime nation, darkening the whole prospect before us, economic as well as political, commercial as well as diplomatic.

VI

VISIT TO WASHINGTON
February 1956

Failure of the Foreign Secretaries' conference – Middle Eastern dangers – Israel and Egypt – King Saud – The Russian visit to India – Problems of the Far East – Mr. Selwyn Lloyd and I go to Washington – Our discussions there – A warning on China – We discuss the Tripartite Declaration – American dislike of our policy towards Buraimi – Our common attitude to Colonel Nasser – America and the Baghdad Pact – Divergent views on Chinese trade – I address Congress – Canadian help and understanding

For some time I had been trying to arrange a visit to the United States in the early summer of 1956. Harvard University having offered me a degree, I looked forward to accepting this honour. However, it soon emerged that, with other inescapable plans for the summer, including the overriding claims of the Commonwealth Conference at the end of June, there was no hope of carrying out my intention. In correspondence with our Ambassador at Washington, Sir Roger Makins, I had reconciled myself to the postponement of the visit.

Then came bad news. The four-power meeting of the Foreign Secretaries at Geneva, which lasted for three weeks in October and November 1955, brought us no pleasant surprises. The Soviet attitude, which the Foreign Secretary had reported as fairly flexible at the beginning of the conference, became rigid after the return of Mr. Molotov, who had been to Moscow for consultation. It is not easy even now to assess the reasons for this. They may have been in part internal. In the war, when I was trying to explain to Stalin the uncertainties of electoral majorities in the Western democracies, he listened in silence and then commented, 'We have a public opinion, too, but it expresses itself differently. I have seen three revolutions in my lifetime.' Or the reason may have been unrest in some of the satellite countries, encouraged by the apparent greater freedom of policy in Moscow. It was not possible to celebrate the death of Stalin and of his policies, without hungry sheep in these lands looking up and hoping to be fed. They could hardly be expected to understand that for them this was all words.

Whatever the reasons for this rigidity, it was there and it would have been of no use to attempt further meetings, at least until we saw what was to be the outcome of the Soviet leaders' visit to this country, supposing that they made it. I thought a lot about this visit and how we could best turn it to good purpose. It seemed to me that the Soviet attitude was well described by the able United States Ambassador in Moscow, Mr. Bohlen, as 'peace at no price'. This meant that while the Soviet Union was quite prepared to see some relaxation of tension, at any rate in Europe, it had no intention of making any concessions concerning the unity of Germany or her relations with the West. The Foreign Secretaries' conference showed clearly that this was true. The question was whether the Russians had other thoughts in mind.

The Soviet Union had now secured, and so had we, a situation of a certain equilibrium in the Far East, so that there the dangers were less than they had been six months before. Much the same could be said of Europe. Here there was no expectation of any heightening of tension and nothing immediately to be gained from it for the Soviets. The same was not true of the Middle East. There were indications that Soviet thoughts were turning in that direction. They were not likely to put out any hostages to fortune or run any uncalculated risks. The Berlin airlift had taught that lesson. But if they saw the opportunity of advancing without danger, they would not hesitate to take it. I thought that a useful purpose for our meeting with the Soviet Ministers would be to make plain to them that we would have to take forceful action against any interference with our vital interests in the Middle East.

Meanwhile, I turned my mind to the possibility of taking some new initiative in Middle Eastern affairs. I discussed this with the Foreign Secretary and he with our American allies. It seemed to us that there was scope for a joint move of the kind we had made when the Trieste situation had been so taut. On September 27th, Nasser announced in a speech that Egypt had concluded an agreement with Czechoslovakia for the supply of arms. This injected a new element of danger into a situation already delicate. Nasser was vague in public about the details, but our information, subsequently confirmed, was that the arrangement provided for the despatch to Cairo in considerable quantities of MIG fighters, Ilyushin jet bombers, Joseph Stalin Mark III tanks, Czech T.34 tanks and other heavy equipment. In the following February the Egyptian Government released photographs of some of these Soviet supplied armaments arrayed on the frontiers of Israel.

It seemed to me in the autumn of 1955, when deliveries from the Soviet bloc began, that unless some positive action were taken, the situation must grow steadily more dangerous. There were risks in any initiative. There had been at Trieste, but the method of Trieste seemed to be the only one by which negotiations might be set going again. At present it was deadlock everywhere, and that must mean growing danger everywhere. In the Prime Minister's annual speech at the Guildhall on November 9th, I attempted to break out of the ring. I said that we had tried for a long time past to find common ground for some kind of settlement. I thought the time had come when the acute dangers of the situation forced us to try again. I suggested that if some arrangement could be reached between Israel and her Arab neighbours about their boundaries, the United States and Britain, and perhaps other powers also, would be prepared to give a formal guarantee to both sides. I said that an attempt should be made to bridge the gap between existing positions. In this way, confidence and security might at last be restored in this part of the Middle East. I added that Her Majesty's Government, and myself personally, were available to render any service in this cause.

Some probing questions in Parliament followed, but I had been deliberately inexplicit in my remarks, wishing to open up discussions if I could, even by shock tactics. Careful and prolonged negotiation would then be required. Though the response from public opinion at home was steady and reasonable, I now think that once Russian arms had begun to flow into Egypt in such formidable quantities, it was unwise to raise the issue of frontiers. At any rate, the attempt failed, despite helpful supporting words from the United States.

On November 16th, the Foreign Secretaries' meeting at Geneva ended in a stalemate. Most papers in the United States agreed about the 'flat failure of the Foreign Secretaries' conference'. I wrote on the telegram which reported this: 'I should go to the United States at the end of January. Private Secretary please speak.' I telegraphed to our Ambassador accordingly and he thought my proposal well-timed. After a friendly response from Washington, and with an improvement in the President's health, arrangements for the meeting went ahead.

Little that was good had emerged on the world scene in recent months. Mr. Molotov had been wholly negative at Geneva, and the results of the second Geneva Conference set back any prospect of achieving the unity of Germany. Public opinion in Germany had borne this disappointment calmly, largely owing to the lead given by Dr. Adenauer.

More immediately dangerous was the Middle Eastern situation in view of the threat poised by Soviet strategy. This was the main topic which I wished to discuss in the United States. Soviet arms continued to flow into Egypt from Czechoslovakia, and Moscow was showing an increasing determination to intrude into Middle Eastern affairs. This was traditional Soviet policy, making itself felt at a time of growing Soviet confidence. The consequences could be very grave.

There was first the effect upon Israel, which must become increasingly uneasy as supplies of arms were delivered to Egypt. It was natural enough that we should wish to avoid an arms race between the Arab states and Israel, and think its consequences dangerous. This could not comfort Israel much, if, as a result, she was placed at an increasing disadvantage with Egypt. The situation might to some extent be mended by reaffirming the Tripartite Declaration of 1950 in which Britain, France and the United States had undertaken to prevent violations of the armistice lines between Israel and the Arabs. I considered that if this were to serve its purpose, the signatories must also make the necessary preparations to give it effect, showing the world that they were doing so, otherwise they were not likely to be believed. We had to try for this. Meanwhile, both France and Canada were discussing the despatch of fighter aircraft for Israel's defence. I did not consider that this could be discouraged, in view of the fast bombers reaching Egypt from Russia. A month later we agreed to deliver six Meteors to Israel, and the French followed this with the delivery in May of some new Mystères, which had the height and speed to deal with the Russian bombers already supplied to Egypt. These supplies had American agreement.

There were also the larger problems of the area. We had to make yet another effort to resolve our admitted differences. The policies being pursued by King Saud were the most pernicious of these. He was making continuous attempts to undermine his neighbours on the Persian Gulf and in Oman. Widespread and lavish bribery was directed against the British position in the Middle East. As a result, an absolute monarch of a medieval State was playing the Soviet game. The fact that he was doing so with money paid him by American oil companies did not ease the situation.

The Baghdad Pact was proving a firm stabilizer. It would have been helpful if the United States had shown more friendliness towards it and I thought it urgent that we should review all this in Washington. The visit of Marshal Bulganin and Mr. Khrushchev to India and Burma had not helped us. Western leadership had been put on the defensive by the anti-colonial manifesto they had flourished there. It was necessary that we and the United States should draw closer together on this prickly topic and find words to express a common philosophy. As I telegraphed to Washington ahead of our arrival: 'I am not suggesting anything as grandiloquent as the Atlantic Charter, but something which shows that, both materially and in true values, the West has its own message to give.'

Then there was the Far Eastern scene. We had to test the endurance of the agreements made at Geneva. S.E.A.T.O's health had to be examined and reported on. We must raise the question of trade with communist China and reduce the forbidden exports in the China List, as it was called. Malaya was suffering from the effects of these restrictions. Malaya could sell rubber to Russia and Russia could resell it to China, but direct sale from Malaya to China was forbidden. This was damaging to Malaya's interests and inexplicable to her leaders or her people, who were rapidly approaching independence.

An agenda, to include these and other matters, was discussed and agreed through the Ambassadors. We held several meetings at Downing Street to evolve our detailed plans. No serious difficulties presented themselves in these preparations and our Ambassador in Washington reported the President's determination to give all the time his doctors would allow to our conversations. And so, accompanied by the United States Ambassador in London, Mr. Winthrop Aldrich, always a helpful personality in our work, and Mr. Selwyn Lloyd, I sailed in the *Queen Elizabeth* on January 25th.

We flew down from New York to Washington in the remarkable comfort of the President's aeroplane, the *Columbine*. I now understood how men heavily burdened with responsibility could find relief in long aeroplane journeys and arrive fresher than when they left. Admirably fitted up to resemble the office, the drawing-room and the bedroom, the aircraft was so completely silent that work could go ahead undisturbed by the discomforts of ordinary air travel or by the inevitable interruptions of official life.

On arrival the Foreign Secretary and I attended an informal luncheon with the President and the Secretary of State, with only the Ambassador, Sir Roger Makins, and one or two others present. Here the United States views on China and the United Nations were at once vigorously expressed to us. It was evident that any move to get China into the United Nations would now meet with strong American opposition. If the Peking Government were admitted, the United States Government might be expected to resign from the organization, when the problem of the United Nations headquarters would also arise. A move to get China into the United Nations now would, in the view of our hosts, be fatal.

Nor would they accept that these remarks were limited in application to an election year. There was no hope of changing the feeling in the United States or Congress 'in the proximate future'. I pointed out, as I often had before, that a good case could be made in the opposite sense; there was now a truce in the Far East, and the United Nations was a universal organization in which one must expect to have unpleasant people. But I made no impression. Fortunately, as the United Nations was not sitting, there was no immediate need for a decision on this troublesome issue.

In the afternoon of the first day, we began with Middle Eastern topics. Of the general course of our discussions I telegraphed that evening to Mr. Butler, who was presiding over the Cabinet in my absence: 'Work generally plods on, with no more than expected difficulties.' These expected difficulties were two-fold. First, we were anxious to put teeth into the Tripartite Declaration of 1950. By this we meant that we should not only declare our determination to prevent violations of the Arab-Israeli frontier and consult together how to do so on the military level, but actually be seen to be making preparatory moves to enable us to act. Nothing less, I was convinced, would give any real confidence. The Americans, though sympathetic in general terms, laid stress on their constitutional difficulties, which, they said, prevented them from giving commitments to use force without Congressional approval. They could not even concentrate forces as a precaution. We were only able to speak of 'increased dangers' in the Middle East and of our readiness to discuss how we might deal with them. We could not declare with France that we were prepared to act and demonstrate the truth of this by joint movements of our forces.

One evening at the Tehran Conference in 1943, when in a restricted circle of the leaders of the three countries, Harry Hopkins teased Mr. Churchill and myself about British constitutional practices. 'We have a little more experience of the British than you have, Marshal Stalin,' Mr. Hopkins remarked. 'Would you like to know how the constitution works?' 'I would,' said Stalin. 'It depends', said Mr. Hopkins, 'rather on the result that they want to get. If the British want to agree quickly, they manage it all right. If, however, they are not so sure, or they want a delay, they will tell you they have to consult the Dominions and that until they have the answers from all of them, they cannot give you a clear reply. It really works quite well.' I wondered to myself whether Mr. Hopkins' analysis of our alleged practices might not fit that of his own country in relation to Congress just then.

The second matter concerned our relations with Saudi Arabia. Here we went over familiar ground. The United States argued that we should first attempt direct negotiations with Saudi Arabia, whatever might follow subsequently. I had no objection to trying this once again, but I could not feel sanguine about the result, unless the United States Government put considerable pressure upon the Saudis. At this time, I pointed out, Saudi money was being used not only against us but against Iraq. President Chamoun of the Lebanon had given a warning against the evil influence of the Saudi money all over the Middle East. Saud was also attacking the Baghdad Pact.

One glimpse of American thinking we found highly disturbing. The President told us that we had to take account of world opinion. People in general, he maintained, were very ignorant about Muscat and Buraimi, and tended to think that the whole Arabian peninsula belonged, or ought to belong, to King Saud. Naturally we contested this, which took no account of the continuous expansion of Saudi claims ever since 1935. It also ignored the Yemen and Muscat, the independent sheikhdoms in the Persian Gulf, and ourselves in Aden. It certainly showed the dangers of over-simplification.

During the Suez crisis, I learnt that the United States Government had regarded our action, during the autumn of 1955, in furthering the reoccupation of Buraimi by the Sultan of Muscat and the Sheikh of Abu Dhabi as an act of aggression. This opinion was expressed to two of our closest friends and allies, Australia and the Netherlands, but not to us. There was no warrant for any such charge. When our Dutch friends asked Mr. Dulles who had ever suggested that there was any aggression by the United Kingdom at Buraimi, Mr. Dulles replied,

'Public opinion in Saudi Arabia.' He left himself open to the Dutch rejoinder that there was no such thing.

Buraimi had not in modern history formed part of Saudi territory, although Wahabi raiders occasionally swooped upon it from the Nejd in the first half of the last century. Neither on the map nor by any evidence had Buraimi been Saudi for at least a hundred years, until that country's forces recently bribed their way in. It was perhaps arguable whether the Sultan or the Sheikh had suzerainty. All these two rulers had done was to reoccupy their own territory.

However, there is no doubt that this topic was a more troublesome one under the surface than I realized during my connection with it at the Foreign Office and as Prime Minister. In Washington at the time we felt that we had made some progress. The Americans appeared to accept our view that further efforts should be made with the Saudis to induce them to divert their excessive oil revenues to more profitable purposes. They told us that they would consider what could be done to promote investment in roads, hospitals and other activities more beneficial to the Saudi people and to ourselves than bribery. This was on the lines sponsored by Britain in Iraq and Kuwait for years past.

Anglo-American policies towards Egypt, on the other hand, were at this time closely in accord. I sent a message to London after our first session: 'We agreed that the future of our policy in the Middle East depended to a considerable extent on Nasser. If he showed himself willing to co-operate with us, we should reciprocate. The Americans thought that the present talks about the Aswan Dam with Mr. Black might indicate his state of mind. If his attitude on this and other matters was that he would not co-operate, we would both have to reconsider our policy towards him.' We were both concerned at the violent attack which Nasser had just made on Nuri es-Said, the Prime Minister of Iraq. Nor could we overlook his vicious campaign against General Glubb and the loyalty of the Arab Legion.

As for the Baghdad Pact, while the Americans would not join it, they were prepared to give it 'moral support'. They also discussed with us a number of practical methods for helping individual members of the pact. These included the delivery to Iraq of tanks for their armoured division, for which they had been asking for a while, and the support of Pakistan against the demands which Afghanistan was making against her, as I thought, unreasonably. I felt that we had a responsibility in this because Pakistan was the inheritor of the Indian Empire's frontier in the area.

In recent years the United States has sometimes failed to put its weight behind its friends, in the hope of being popular with their foes. The practical consequences of this uncertain diplomacy are illustrated by United States treatment of the Baghdad Pact. Having played a leading part to inspire the project, the United States Government held back while Britain joined it, alone of the Western powers. Worse still, they tried to take credit for this attitude in capitals like Cairo, which were hostile to the pact. Then, by a series of hesitant steps they drew nearer the pact, sending an observer and spending money, but still not joining it. An ounce of membership would have been worth all the havering and saved a ton of trouble later on.

A strong power, rich in resources, once it determines its goal, has a fair chance to reach it, if it holds to its purpose. A devious course is disastrous. It is a borrower and lender in diplomacy and loses both itself and friend. Nobody credited the involved pretexts produced by the United States Government for not joining the Baghdad Pact; they were members, when they wanted to be, of N.A.T.O. and S.E.A.T.O. The repeated hesitations perplexed and harassed our friends in Turkey and Iraq, Iran and Pakistan. They strengthened Russian and Egyptian will to destroy the pact and overthrow the Governments which supported it. The irony of the business is that in March 1959 the United States made separate defence agreements with Iran, Pakistan and Turkey which, for Iran at least, was more difficult of acceptance than membership of the Baghdad Pact had been.

★　　★　　★　　★　　★

On the second day the greater part of my time was spent agreeably in talks with the President alone, free from the formality which attaches to any conference. Despite our admitted differences, I felt that our discussions had brought us closer together. The unanimous impression of our delegation was that the President himself seemed remarkably well and contributed fully to our deliberations.

We also spent some time in conference on the Declaration of Washington. The President had taken considerable pains over this. We tried to put its thought into a form which would be useful in other lands than our own. I telegraphed to London explaining this, adding about the conference: 'We are emphasizing that there is solid agreement between the two countries over the major part of the field. We have had the courage to admit our differences where they exist.'

Europe was one of the most important areas of agreement. We

were at one in our approach to the German problem. The United States Government were prepared to give full support to our claim that Germany should continue to make a contribution towards the cost of British forces in that country. We were not so completely in agreement in our attitude towards two new schemes for economic integration in Europe, the proposals resulting from the Messina Conference which foreshadowed a common market, and the project for a European atomic energy authority. The United States Government entertained for these proposals the same enthusiasm as they had shown towards the ill-fated European Defence Community. The Canadian Government, on the other hand, were much more alive to the risk that these associations could lead to a high tariff group in Europe.

I now think that the six-power community is of undoubted benefit to the world, though I hope that it will not remain indefinitely six-power. The seven-power free trade area which the United Kingdom and other countries are creating, is a reply to the six which is, no doubt, meant to have consequences. If it should lead to a wider European free trade area, that would be better, but it would not, in my judgment, be enough. Both for economic and for political reasons, the necessary solution is a wide area of trade agreements which comprises the British Commonwealth and Europe. In vitality and variety this has almost limitless possibilities and would be an effective counterpart to the communist bloc and to the United States. Of course, it will be difficult to realize, but so is anything that is worth while.

We recorded the divergence of view, noted on several previous occasions, about the admission of the Peking Government to the United Nations. These same sentiments dominated American policy towards the China List. Account had to be taken, we were told, of the psychological effect which any weakening of the United States position might have in reducing the confidence of other countries in the stability of the United States policy. On the other hand, the Americans agreed that it was not in the interests of the free world to deprive nations such as Japan and Indonesia of the means of earning their own livelihood.

Our concern was not so much for ourselves, as for some of our colonies and other members of the Commonwealth. Ceylon, at that time one of the most steadfastly anti-communist countries, had acted in defiance of the United Nations and made substantial shipments of rubber to China. We felt that a start must be made at once in revising the list of forbidden items. We finally agreed that the controls 'should continue and should be reviewed now and periodically as to their scope in the light of changing conditions, so that they may best serve the interests of the free world.' 'Now' was the operative word. The President, in particular, was understanding and was prepared to give weight to our arguments. Even so, it was many months before any results were seen, and in the end we had to take a decision on our own account to prevent Malaya's position being made intolerable.

On personal grounds I had enjoyed the visit and the opportunity it had given me to meet many friends again, both in the Administration and outside it. Probably I over-valued the political results, as one is apt to do at a time of contact with close allies. Both sides are ready to stretch their true meaning. Even if the outcome of the talks had been more meagre, it was necessary to hold them. The Soviet leaders were to visit us in the spring and it was right, as well as important for our negotiating position, that the President and I should meet in advance of that event.

Congress had often welcomed me on earlier visits to Washington. On one occasion I remember watching the proceedings in the Senate from the floor. The Senate then adjourning, I stood beside the Vice-President and was introduced to the Senators present as they filed past. I thought this a very pleasant compliment to pay a visitor. I have sat on the floor of Australian and Canadian Parliaments also. I have often thought it unfortunate that we cannot reciprocate in kind, because our rules do not allow of visitors on the floor of the House itself. The best we can do is to invite a guest to speak to Members in one of our committee rooms, which, as a compliment, does not compare with the invitation to speak to the Senate and to the House of Representatives in their own Chamber and under their own Vice-President or Speaker. I did this on the last day of my visit to Washington, when I said:

Wars in the past have often begun because one power or combination of powers has believed its force sufficient to win and hold some overwhelming advantage. This has dazzled the eyes and enticed the minds of conquerors down the ages. Sometimes their ambition has brought them victory. It can never do so in this nuclear age, when oblivion confronts aggressor and victim alike.

Brought to a halt in Europe, Soviet expansion now feels its way south and probes in other lands. There is nothing particularly new in this. You can read it all in Russian imperialist history. But the emphasis has changed, and the symbol and method, too.

This is a struggle for men's minds, once expressed in these regions in conflicting faiths, but now in rival ideologies. From the Kremlin streams forth into the lands of what we call the Middle East, and into all Asia, a mixture of blandishment and threat, offers of arms and menaces to individuals, all couched in terms of fierce hostility for Western ideals.

In the face of this, what answer should the West give? We do not intend to base our policies on the revival of old threats or the creation of new ones. We know that we can neither hold communism nor beat it back by force of arms alone.

We invite nations to share our free way of life. We neither compel them to join our company, nor hold them by force once they have done so. That is the difference between our approach to the rights of nations and the communist denial of them.

The contrast cannot, we think, be more sharply shown than in our Commonwealth community. Its older members—Canada, Australia, New Zealand and South Africa—have for generations played their free and individual parts in world affairs and made their distinctive contributions. More lately they have been joined by the new partners in Asia—India, Pakistan and Ceylon.

But I would not like you to think that the process has stopped there, or can do so. It is a continuing development. Everywhere through our Commonwealth and Empire nations are growing up. This places a heavy responsibility upon the parent. He has to be sure that patience is shown, that guidance is given, that experience is passed—as a warning but not as a command.

At this very moment Her Majesty the Queen is in Nigeria, where dwell more than thirty millions of her people with elected legislators and African Ministers, and the spontaneous enthusiasm of her welcome will have shown how the people really feel.

I have painted you this scene because you will see how different it is from the view of a Soviet leader who recently told us that he could not understand why people should go into other countries except to pump out their wealth and resources.

My visit to Ottawa was helpful, restful and enjoyable. I stayed at Government House with my old friend, Vincent Massey, the Governor-General. For me there was always a sense of relaxed homecoming in Canada, with the added touch of spontaneous and generous Canadian hospitality. Even the hardest tasks, like speech-making, are made as easy as can be. At the invitation of the Prime Minister, Mr. St. Laurent, the Foreign Secretary and I attended the Cabinet, as I had done on a few occasions before. I gave them a full account of our discussions in Washington which they seemed to consider as useful as we could have hoped for. The two Prime Ministers and Foreign Secretaries had some further discussions alone, which were helpful to us. Once again I spoke to the Canadian Parliament, which is an impressive and at first almost a daunting ceremony for the visitor, but the warmth of welcome and the response of the audience soon changes all that. This, my last official visit, I enjoyed most of all. Little did I foresee that in just over a year I should be back again as the Governor-General's guest and as a private citizen recovering from a major surgical operation.

In the last twenty years I have visited Canada more often than any country overseas except our immediate neighbour, France, travelling from coast to coast across the land with its contrasts of vigorous life and its varied beauty. Canada will always have my affection and gratitude for the kindness shown to my son Simon, and to thousands of other young men in the Royal Air Force, who came to do their training there in the second world war. Simon was at Edmonton and Winnipeg, after some preliminary training in Ontario. Everywhere he and his friends were made welcome in Canadian homes. This was the recurring theme of his letters from a land which he loved and to which he hoped to return.

VII

JORDAN
March 1956

Jordan and the Baghdad Pact – Saudi Arabian intrigues – Nuri es-Said's anxiety – Military help to Jordan – Field Marshal Templer visits Amman – Nasser's offer to subsidize Jordan – A Russian move – Riots in Jordan – Attitude of Iraq – We warn Saudi Arabia – King Hussein dismisses General Glubb – The King's explanations – My interview with General Glubb – Views of the Ambassador – We withdraw British officers – Diplomacy and Parliament – An embarrassing debate – Signs of improvement

It would be tedious to describe the dealings with many countries which make up the diplomatic history of this period. Nor was I, as Prime Minister, concerned with the details. To give an account of the character of the work we had to do, I have chosen one example for full treatment. Jordan was a country for which we had special responsibility; we had brought it into being.

Early in November 1955, our Ambassador, Mr. Duke, reported a conversation with King Hussein. The Jordanian Government was ready to join the Baghdad Pact, the King said, provided it received 'the necessary backing' from us. A court Minister spoke in the same sense and General Glubb reported like information to the War Office. All these sources agreed that this was a moment of opportunity. If the Jordanian Government did not act now, it would waver indefinitely.

At the same time, I was anxious, as were our informants, about possible internal reactions fermented by Egyptian propaganda and Saudi money. To meet this danger, I felt sure that we should draw up an agreement, showing what we planned to do, so that all Jordanians could see the definite and tangible gains which justified them joining the Baghdad Pact.

Our Ambassador had the same thought. He took the view that it was no use waiting for practical proposals from the Jordanian Government. We must make an offer, which they could quote publicly, of the help we would give them, both in treaty revision and in the supply of armaments, if they joined the pact. He suggested that the Foreign Secretary, then Mr. Macmillan, should call briefly at Amman on his way back from Baghdad, where he was to attend a meeting of the Baghdad Pact powers.

There was talk of early delivery of fighter aircraft, as a free gift. The Foreign Office were enthusiastic to do this and I had no objection in principle. Before agreeing I minuted the Foreign Secretary: 'I would like to be satisfied that the balance between Israel and the Arab states is not upset by this gift.' Account had to be taken of the recent Czecho-slovak supplies of war material to Egypt.

The President of the Lebanon, Mr. Chamoun, had already let us know that he was worried by developments. He asked for economic aid and for arms in order to safeguard his country. The Lebanon had for many years been very friendly to us and had been a moderating influence in the Middle East. I was naturally anxious that we should do all we could to help its President to resist the strong pressure which was now being brought to bear on him to join the Syrian-Egyptian Pact. Mr. Macmillan was then in Geneva for the meeting of Foreign Secretaries which was to follow up the summit conference and on October 26th I had already telegraphed to him, asking him to take up with Mr. Dulles the possibility that the United States might give some economic aid to the Lebanon. In the course of November we were able ourselves to offer President Chamoun some quantities of military equipment, with which he was much pleased.

Mr. Macmillan was encouraged by his meeting at Baghdad and judged this to be the moment to get some other Arab states to join the pact. Iraq felt isolated as the only Arab present. The first new member, he considered, should be Jordan.

The situation in the Middle East was being rapidly undermined and corrupted by Saudi money. This, the Foreign Secretary reported, emerged most clearly from all he had learnt in Baghdad and again in Beirut. The agents of King Saud, their pockets bulging with gold, were co-operating everywhere with the communists against Western interests. In accordance with their practice, the United States Government were treating the payments by the Arabian-American Oil Company to Saudi Arabia as a purely commercial transaction. Unlike ourselves, they did not feel any responsibility for ensuring that these oil revenues were wisely invested. King Saud, at liberty to spend his money as he wished, chose palaces for his family at home and subversion for his policy abroad, in Jordan, the Lebanon and Iraq. American, that is A.R.A.M.C.O., money was being spent on a lavish scale to abet communism in the Middle East.

In November 1955 Nuri es-Said made a special plea at the Baghdad Conference, directed particularly to the American observer, to find means of stopping, even for six months, the payments by A.R.A.M.C.O. to the Saudis. If this could happen, he thought that the whole situation would change in Syria, the Lebanon, Jordan and even in Egypt. Objectives which now seemed impossible, including an Arab-Israeli settlement, would become possible. All this was true enough, but I knew the difficulties of stirring the United States Government to action where King Saud was concerned.

Meanwhile, Her Majesty's Government had further considered the question of fighter aircraft for Jordan and had decided to offer ten Vampires. King Hussein was delighted. We acted quickly and, despite our financial cares at home, we made ready a substantial gift of military equipment. We also prepared the text of an agreement to replace the Anglo-Jordanian Treaty. This was to be negotiated as soon as Jordan had acceded to the Baghdad Pact. While in the Middle East, the Foreign Secretary had the idea that the C.I.G.S., Sir Gerald Templer, should fly out to discuss these proposals in Amman. The Jordanian Prime Minister, Said el-Mufti, welcomed the visit. He was impressed by the status of the messenger and gratified by the speed with which Her Majesty's Government were acting.

The C.I.G.S. was in Jordan from December 6th to 14th. He told the Jordanian Government what we could do. We could equip and maintain additional units of the Arab Legion, including two infantry battalions with seventeen-pounder guns, three-inch mortars and the usual small arms. A medium artillery regiment would be armed and trained with eighteen 5·5-inch guns. We would re-equip an armoured car regiment with Comet tanks. All this would result in increasing the strength of the Arab Legion to one infantry division and approximately one new-style armoured division. Apart from the military help, we would enter into immediate negotiations to replace the Anglo-Jordanian Treaty by a special agreement. The Prime Minister thought that our proposals were acceptable and so did the Minister of Defence. The view of the King was described by the C.I.G.S. as 'encouraging'.

However, His Majesty was greatly exercised by the subversive propaganda of the Saudis. He felt there was a danger that, if Jordan acceded to the pact immediately, it might result in his Government losing control of public opinion. I had exactly the same concern. This was the only passage I marked in a two-page telegram which arrived from our Ambassador on December 9th. The Jordanian Prime Minister was thinking particularly about the west bank of the River Jordan, where most of the Palestinian refugees from Israel existed miserably. The only way of influencing opinion there was through the press and that could only be done with money. The Egyptians and Saudis, he told us, were already spending freely. We could counter this, because the press would be content with less money if it came from the Jordanian Government; patriotism at a price.

While the Jordanian Cabinet as a whole liked these proposals, the C.I.G.S. reported that the Israeli problem dominated the minds of some members to the exclusion of all else. They feared that to join the pact would divert attention from Israel and incur the hostility of Egypt. The dissident Ministers believed that they had public support behind them, which was probably true of the refugees on the west bank.

In any event, these four Ministers resigned, the general belief being that they had been bribed by the Egyptian Government. The Prime Minister was replaced for a while by Hazza Majali, the Deputy Prime Minister and Minister of the Interior, who was a firmer character. Even so the new Prime Minister thought it unwise for the C.I.G.S. to remain in Jordan while the new Government was being formed. Sir Gerald Templer accordingly returned home, though he agreed with the Prime Minister to take up the task again if the new Jordanian Government were in a position to continue negotiations. Neither Hazza Majali nor his successors felt able to do this.

There were clearly risks in sending a personality of the standing of Sir Gerald Templer to Amman to negotiate this agreement. On the other hand, his personal authority gave him an excellent chance of success. His visit certainly increased support for the Baghdad Pact with the King and some of his Ministers.

At the end of the year, the first six of the Vampire jets were handed over in the presence of the King at Amman. This made everyone happy for a while. All the same, after what had occurred, I considered that we should not continue to press Jordan to enter the Baghdad Pact at this time, and I so minuted on Foreign Office telegrams. I felt it important to show that, in spite of what had happened, we were still good friends to Jordan. I agreed with the view which the King had expressed to our Ambassador, that in time the question of Jordan joining the Baghdad Pact could come up again. If we pressed matters too sharply, we might spoil all.

Early in the New Year, rioting broke out in Jordan. 'The Voice of the Arabs' from Cairo was active and effective in inciting violence. As our Chargé d'Affaires remarked to the Prime Minister, 'There were plenty of good instructors in Cairo and, no doubt, some had found their way to Amman.' He also warned the Prime Minister that Egyptian interference was highly dangerous for Jordan, quite apart from the Baghdad Pact question. Egypt had long been creating trouble for Jordan on her frontier with Israel. This was a twisty way of entangling a neighbour.

By January 9th the position had grown worse and the insecurity of British women and children in the country was worrying. A new Prime Minister, Samir Rifai, was struggling to form a Government. Our representative telegraphed that we should consider the immediate despatch of a sufficient body of British troops to Amman, at least two brigades. In the face of the deteriorating situation which Egypt was creating and the threat of mob law, the King thought of asking for Iraqi troops to be flown in. The Legion was fully extended. He asked us to transmit a message in this sense to Baghdad. At once there were yelps of concern from Cairo. Colonel Nasser would regard such an event as a British plot and might, as a result, turn totally against us. It seemed to me that he was already working against us as hard as he could. We decided to deliver the message in Baghdad as requested.

Baghdad reacted resolutely to King Hussein's appeal. If Iraqi help was to be sent, it must be in sufficient quantities to make success certain. At the same time, Nuri es-Said saw the political realities clearly. He emphasized that any action in Jordan would not really get to the root of the trouble, which was Egypt. He said: 'The Americans would be well advised to bring the sternest possible pressure on Egypt to cease her activities in Jordan.' He also suggested that we 'should make it clear to Egypt that, if she persisted, we would no longer consider the protection afforded by the Tripartite Declaration as applying to Egypt.' In proposing this, Nuri was only anticipating the boast soon to be made by the Egyptian press that the Tripartite Declaration did not apply to Egypt.

The next day we decided to fly two battalions of the Parachute Brigade and a battalion of Highland Light Infantry to Cyprus at once. The wing of the R.A.F. Regiment at Habbaniya was alerted to fly to

Amman and the armoured regiment at Aqaba to move nearer to Amman. We made a number of other preliminary arrangements to enable us to protect British subjects in Jerusalem and elsewhere, should the need arise.

The Foreign Secretary, now Mr. Selwyn Lloyd, sent a firm message to Colonel Nasser, through our Ambassador in Cairo. He denied that there were any grounds for the suspicions which Colonel Nasser had declared he harboured, that Britain wished to isolate Egypt in order to re-establish a position of dominance over her and was promoting a defensive pact between the Sudan and Ethiopia. The Ambassador was to add that he found Her Majesty's Government anxious to work for an improvement in relations between Egypt and Iraq, this being in their view the surest way of repairing the divisions in the Arab world and countering the efforts now being made to subvert the area in the interests of international communism. But the Ambassador was also to make it plain that our future relationship must depend on Egypt ceasing to be so hostile. In particular, Egypt was inciting the people of Jordan to civil war and to attacks on her British ally. Finally, the Foreign Secretary referred to the Egyptian wireless campaign, about which the Ambassador was instructed to press for immediate action.

Meanwhile, stirring up sand in troubled deserts, a Saudi Arabian force, fifteen hundred to two thousand strong, with armoured cars and a few guns, had arrived in the Hovuk area south of Jordan's southern frontier. The Saudis were recruiting there and in the Qaf area, which is not far east of Amman, and recruits were being offered the fantastic pay, by local standards, of £25 a month. Saudi aircraft had delivered weapons and military equipment. This was an Arab Legion report on which both we and King Hussein felt we could rely.

Accordingly, Her Majesty's Government thought it wise to tell the Saudi Government that we were aware of these movements and to inquire of them what their purpose was. We also left them in no doubt that, if these forces committed an act of aggression against Jordan, we should fulfil our obligations to help Jordan under the Anglo-Jordanian Treaty of 1948. This action was salutary and the Saudis drew back.

At this time Egypt was attempting to smuggle bombs and other material into Iraq to create disturbance. In their country, so the Iraqi Government told us, Egypt and Saudi Arabia were being blamed for events in Jordan and the weakening of a sister Arab state. Saudi activities at this time had certainly become intolerable. As King Hussein described them: 'They are using their money to try to corrupt the people of Jordan, while at the same time they are building up military forces and stores on the southern border of the country.'

Colonel Nasser gave assurances to our Ambassador, in reply to the Foreign Secretary's message, that propaganda against ourselves and Jordan would be stopped at once. Two days later the Iraqi Government were reporting that they could observe no diminution of propaganda by Egypt. I minuted on the same day that there appeared to be no decrease. In fact, for a while the Egyptian radio reduced its attacks on Jordan and the United Kingdom and shifted their direction towards Iraq. They soon began again and by February 15th were in full blast against General Glubb, the commander of the Arab Legion. However, the general situation had quietened a little by the end of the month and Mr. Selwyn Lloyd set out on a Middle Eastern tour.

Soon after mid-day on March 1st, the Prime Minister of Jordan sent for our Ambassador at Amman. The Prime Minister told him that the King had come to his office about noon that day and produced an order, written in the King's own hand and signed by him, for the immediate dismissal of General Glubb and his principal adjutants and for the transfer of numerous Arab officers throughout the Legion. The King said that he would await the intimation of the Government's compliance with his order and departed, leaving the Head of the Royal Diwan at the Prime Minister's office. The Prime Minister immediately summoned the other Ministers and, according to his account, put before them the alternative courses of action, one of which would have to be taken at once. These were: to comply with the King's orders; to ignore them; to remonstrate with the King and be prepared to resign, or be dismissed, if he could not be persuaded to change his mind.

General Glubb had had a long conversation with the King only the day before. It was entirely friendly and the General had no suspicion of what was impending. The Prime Minister now told him that he must leave early the next morning.

Our Ambassador was received by King Hussein late that evening. When he asked the King why he had taken this sudden and drastic action against General Glubb and other British officers, King Hussein began by referring to long-standing and cordial relations between Jordan and Great Britain. He asserted that he wished to retain those relations on the same footing. The Ambassador interjected that he seemed to have delivered a sharp blow at them. The King replied that he thought it would not prove to be so in the long run. He went on to complain about grave deficiencies which he alleged he had discovered in equipment and stores, particularly for the Arab Legion. He also said that there was serious discontent among the officers, which had now been remedied by new postings to positions they were fitted to hold. He added that he had also been 'fighting Egyptian propaganda attacks on Glubb but "from the other side" (presumably from Glubb) there had been no co-operation.' He had felt bound to do what he considered essential for the preservation and honour of the kingdom.

King Hussein had only recently expressed his confidence in General Glubb, both in London and Amman, and there was no excuse for dismissing him suddenly like a pilfering servant. I thought at the time, and I am convinced now, that part of the King's sentiment towards Glubb was based on jealousy of a younger man for an older one long established in a position of authority in the country. It would seem that his action against Glubb, however unfortunate its manner, had been the result of a personal dislike which had grown to something of a phobia. The King admitted to the Ambassador that he had been upset by constant articles in the press, even in England, representing General Glubb as everything that mattered in Jordan. The *coup* against Glubb was no sudden brainstorm; it was planned carefully for weeks beforehand. It was extraordinary that the General failed to hear about it at any time before its execution.

The Prime Minister of Jordan was very apologetic but could avail nothing. Whether he was really in ignorance of General Glubb's impending dismissal or not, he should have had an inkling, for he was close to the King. Some thought that Saudi money was active in ministerial circles. In any event it was meanly done, and King Hussein's explanation, that he had to act in this sudden way in order to avoid trouble in the Legion, did not excuse him. Messages reported that the mobs were cheering the King and Colonel Nasser in one breath. This was the measure of the false position into which the King had got himself. Clearly he could not continue in this close association without being gobbled up, and the process would not take long either.

The King had without doubt been encouraged in this deed by some of those around him, particularly by his A.D.C., Lieutenant-Colonel Ali Abu Nuwar, whom he was soon to make Chief of Staff. This was the officer who later intrigued against his master in favour of Colonel Nasser's policies and had to flee to Egyptian asylum. It is now clear that his influence at the time of General Glubb's dismissal was used to weaken the King's position.

The Foreign Secretary being away on his travels, the emergency telegrams fell to me to deal with. I sent an immediate message to the Ambassador that evening, endorsing what he had said to the Prime Minister and instructing him to speak to the King in the same terms. This the Ambassador did later that night. The King maintained that he was doing the right thing, which would prove in the long run to be in the best interests of Great Britain, as well as of Jordan. He certainly did not wish to lose the services of British officers other than those who had been dismissed. I sent a personal message to King Hussein that evening. After discussion with some of my senior colleagues, I also sent instructions to our Ambassador to see the King as soon as possible and give him a message from me. I gave him discretion to speak to the Prime Minister in the same sense if he thought it useful. I explained that Ministers had met in London that morning to discuss events in Jordan and that, on the information so far received, these were wholly inexplicable to us. The King had said that he wished to maintain friendly relations with us, but he should recognize that his action was a severe blow to confidence on which good relations were based. I asked that positive action should be taken to remedy the situation and that His Majesty should make a public statement confirming the remaining officers in their posts and expressing his confidence in them, as proof of the value he attached to our friendship and to the treaty.

I next sent a message to General Glubb, who had arrived in Cyprus from Jordan. One of the factors which helped me to handle this most difficult situation was the attitude of the General himself. It would have been only human to feel resentment against King Hussein and even the country which he had served so faithfully and so long. This was at no time his sentiment. I asked him to come to see me at Chequers as soon as he arrived, and we had a long talk together. His advice was clear and constant. We should make allowance for the young King and for the feelings which he might have towards an older man in authority. We should be patient with Jordan and do what we could to mend the damage. I felt admiration for this man and his opinion supported me in carrying through the policies which I thought right. The incident was none the less damaging to British authority.

Britain's national interest was to maintain the independence of Jordan, which was an outpost of Iraq. It was not to our advantage to drive King Hussein to extreme courses. These views were shared by our Ambassador, who handled the whole situation with firmness and calm. I determined to encourage contact with Iraq, where a more experienced Royal Family might explain to King Hussein wiser politics and more subtle methods. The right solution, at some later date, might be for the two countries to come together, but the time was not ripe for that.

In a telegram four days after the event, Mr. Duke gave us some further reflections. He wondered if our regard for General Glubb's great personal qualities and services to Jordan, and resentment at the ignoble manner of his dismissal, had not led us to take a more tragic view than was justified of this upset for Anglo-Jordanian relations. King Hussein, the Prime Minister of Jordan and the Minister of Economics, with all of whom he had discussed this sudden tempest, repeatedly stressed that the action taken was directed against General Glubb personally, and that they did not want to mar the close and friendly relations between Jordan and Great Britain. The Government, it was reported, had been threatened that if they refused to remove General Glubb, a group of officers was ready to bring troops into Amman and remove him by force. These threats may have been real. It was, the Ambassador thought, because the Jordanians feared what they believed Glubb could and might do to defend himself, that they had adopted this summary method of getting rid of him.

This may also have been the reason why the King did not take any of the repeated opportunities he was offered, both in Amman and London, to discuss his anxieties with us. If it was, I considered that we ought not to allow indignation at General Glubb's treatment to make us declare too hastily that the whole basis of mutual confidence and friendship had been destroyed.

Despite these considerations, I felt that our officers who held executive commands in the Jordanian Army were in an impossible position. After what had happened, they could not be expected to exercise responsibility without authority, and Her Majesty's Government asked that such officers should be relieved of their commands. The Jordanians expressed surprise and concern at this proposal and asked that we should reconsider it, pointing out the need for coolness and prudence in handling our relations. We sent this reply:

Please inform Jordan Prime Minister that my request was made after four full days of careful consideration and that for the reasons already stated I must maintain it.

If he should revert to his unfortunately worded request for coolness and prudence, you might appropriately point out that after the events of March 1st, an injunction to show coolness and prudence comes very strangely from Jordan.

At this juncture, Colonel Nasser made a move to add to King Hussein's difficulties. The Egyptian, Saudi Arabian and Syrian Governments had recently held discussions together. Nasser announced that, as a result of these, the three countries were prepared to replace all Her Majesty's Government's assistance to Jordan by an annual subvention of £20 million sterling. Although both we and the King realized that Egypt was not in the least likely to make any payment, and that Syria was in no position to do so, the offer had its propaganda value. The Egyptian press described this fickle gesture of financial aid as a 'new dawn' in the Arab world. It was certainly a false dawn, for the cash was never paid.

A graver warning followed. The Soviet Minister in Cairo called upon the Jordanian Chargé d'Affaires. He announced that he was authorized by his Government to offer Jordan any financial or military aid the country might need, with a view to establishing good relations. The Soviet Minister went on to inquire what the reaction of Jordan might be to the offer of assistance from Egypt, Saudi Arabia and Syria, to replace the money which Jordan had hitherto been receiving from Great Britain. This conversation confirmed Jordan's suspicion that Russia was behind the manœuvres of the three Arab states to replace British assistance. It was not only with those states that Jordan now had to contend but with the whole weight of Soviet power.

I had no doubt that, if King Hussein threw in his lot with Egypt and Saudi Arabia, they would soon unseat him. Having driven the Hashemite family from the throne of Jordan, they would turn next on the Hashemite monarchy of Iraq. I was sure that this would be understood in Baghdad, and a move from that quarter seemed most likely to be effective now.

A conversation between our Ambassador and King Hussein on March 6th, a week before Nasser's financial offer, was the first indication that our analysis might be right. The King had spoken with great earnestness and the Ambassador believed him to be sincere. His Majesty said that he hoped for closer and stronger ties than ever with Britain, now that this one man, who had been the focus of suspicion of the British, had been removed. He continued, 'We do not want to be left a prey to the Saudis or Egypt or the Russians, some of whom are only too anxious to come in and benefit by the situation. We want to stick to our old friends.'

Though this tolerant restraint might be the right line for Britain to take internationally, it was about as difficult a hand to play in Parliament as could well be imagined. A debate was at once demanded by the Opposition and, following the practice of recent years, could not be refused. A Government has little real choice nowadays in determining these debates, whatever the consequences of the speeches which will be delivered. There was a time when the fixing of a foreign affairs debate was related to concern for British interests abroad. Speeches were even sometimes couched in moderate terms so as not to increase the difficulties of Her Majesty's Ministers. I remember an occasion in the 'twenties, in a debate on a Middle Eastern issue connected with Iraq. The Leader of the Opposition, Mr. Ramsay MacDonald, being unable to endorse the action of the Government, but unwilling to embarrass them, briefly stated his party's grounds for objection and led his followers from the House. There may be occasions when this is a proper course to pursue, but such restraints have long since gone by the board. It is as much a free-for-all in foreign as in domestic affairs and never mind the consequences abroad.

Our general policy in the Middle East was founded on the need to protect British interests in Iraq and the Persian Gulf. The main threat to these interests was the growing influence of Nasser with his anti-Western ideology and collusion with Soviet Russia, especially in arms supply. I was in detailed consultation with the Government of Iraq, which fully understood the dangers, but I did not think it right as yet to give an account of this in Parliament. Nor could I make an announcement in the debate on the future of our relations with Jordan. I was in the unhappy situation of having to meet a House of Commons critical on the Opposition benches and anxious on our own, knowing that I ought to say as little as possible. To make matters more difficult, I had no time to prepare the speech I must make, and it is always difficult to say nothing convincingly. Discussions with the Minister of Defence, and arrangements for the protection or evacuation of British families in Jordan, had to be carried through before I could go into the House.

The speech which I made in the debate was regarded as one of the worst in my career. I have no doubt that it was, from the parliamentary point of view. I got well lectured in the House of Commons. My friends were embarrassed and my critics exultant. There was general comment that I had cut so poor a figure on a subject with which I must be familiar. But as diplomacy, the speech served its purpose. It broke no bridges with Jordan. Had I, as it would have been easy to do, roundly blamed the King, this would have won me cheers. Had I announced that we would pay no more subsidy, many would have been pleased. As it was, I forecast no action. It was an occasion for doing nothing. As a result of doing nothing, we were able gradually to pick up the pieces and to mend our relations with Jordan, which recovered well over the next few years.

The Jordanians now began to be worried at the turn of events. Sir Alexander Kirkbride, who happened to be at Amman on his way to Jerusalem, reported in this sense. Sir Alexander had for more than twenty years held official appointments in Jordan and had at all times been a close friend of King Abdullah. The Jordanians, he told us, had come to realize that if Her Majesty's Government withdrew their support, it was only a question of time before the Kingdom of Jordan disintegrated. They had no illusions as to the selfishness of the Arab states who were offering to replace our assistance.

My main purpose was to try to draw Iraq and Jordan closer together. The best way to start the process was by a meeting between the two Hashemite kings, and this I set about to encourage. Baghdad was watching events closely and understood well enough that our standing in the Middle East was doubly involved. Judgment was suspended until it was seen more clearly how events developed and how we handled them. If the upshot of the whole business was that Jordan became a satellite of Egypt, the United Kingdom's influence would be shattered. If, however, the result was that Jordan and Iraq became partners under our encouragement, the policy of co-operation with Britain would be consolidated.

So, for the time being, it turned out. The meeting of the two Kings went off well. Both sides were pleased with their discussion. I was all the more encouraged by this, since King Hussein had only a few days before refused a meeting with three Arab Heads of State in Cairo. The mending had begun.

VIII

BULGANIN AND KHRUSHCHEV IN BRITAIN
April 1956

The invitation stands – The agenda – Arrival of Marshal Bulganin and Mr. Khrushchev – A quiet dinner at Claridge's – Official talks begin – Russian aims in the Middle East – Formosa – Trade – I accept invitation to return the visit – The Labour Party's dinner – The Russian view on armaments – Diplomacy and personal contacts – Reflections on Russian policy – My minute to the Foreign Secretary – Necessity for new approach – A retrograde proposal from Washington

In December 1955 Marshal Bulganin and Mr. Khrushchev made an extensive visit to India and Burma, where they indulged themselves in abusive rhetoric of the colonial system, ignoring their own extensive empire over subject peoples from Samarkand to Hungary. One example by Mr. Khrushchev at Taunggyi in the Shan State will suffice: 'We say, however: The colonialists stayed in your country in order to rob your people, to take the last piece of bread away from them.' The contrast between Delhi and Rangoon, which enjoyed full freedom in every respect, and Bokhara and Bucharest, which were farther than ever from anything of the kind, did not daunt the visitors. The violence of their language drew a demurrer from the Burmese. It was obvious that the direct references to Britain must cause offence in this country and make many doubt the value of a visit from the Soviet leaders in such circumstances. It also seemed clear that Marshal Bulganin and Mr. Khrushchev were, for the present, more interested in making friends and influencing people in Asia than in Europe.

On their return to Moscow, both leaders addressed the Supreme Soviet in the last days of the year. Marshal Bulganin made a speech which was acceptable in tone and content. Mr. Khrushchev, on the other hand, let himself go in extravagant hyperbole of abuse against the West, obviously enjoying himself as he delivered his more extreme passages. This further called in question the visit to Britain. Naturally I weighed all these considerations carefully and discussed them with my principal colleagues. It seemed to me that we had invited the Soviet leaders to Britain not because it suited them to come, but because it suited us to receive them, and I thought, on balance, that the visit would be to our advantage. The violence of Mr. Khrushchev's speech showed the depth of his ignorance of our country and I did not think this a reason to deny him the chance of informing himself. We decided that the visit should stand, unless, of course, the Russians themselves gave any indication of wishing to cry it off, which so far they had not done. So we entered 1956.

At the same time, we thought it useful to point out to the Soviet Government that this series of utterances seemed to have been deliberately calculated to cause tension and to do harm to Anglo-Soviet relations, and to ask them their intentions. Moscow seemed somewhat taken aback by these representations and hastened to make it plain that the Soviet Government still wished to improve Anglo-Soviet relations and that their references had been to the past. Our Ambassador, Sir William Hayter, considered that our comments had probably been salutary and we proceeded with our arrangements for the visit.

The Foreign Office prepared a detailed agenda for the talks which, while it included a number of points of importance, seemed to me too tightly packed with items for our purpose. I was anxious that the discussions should take place in an informal atmosphere and that they should range over the whole field of international affairs. I proposed that it should be understood that either side could raise any subject. Accordingly, I suggested that the agenda should be framed in the most general terms:

1. Anglo-Soviet relations
2. Review of world affairs including:
   (a) European situation
   (b) Middle Eastern situation
   (c) Far Eastern situation
   (d) Disarmament (taking account of the state of discussion in the United Nations disarmament sub-committee).

The Russians shared our views about the nature of the talks and agreed to the agenda. Meanwhile arrangements for the programme were concluded despite occasional flurries about detailed items. These caused fewer difficulties than I had expected. Members of Parliament were full of suggestions, both as to places the Soviet Ministers should visit and topics we should discuss. I declined, however, to give any account of the agenda in advance, or to vary the arrangements for our guests in order to meet Parliamentary criticism.

The Russian leaders arrived on April 18th. Lord Reading, who was in charge of the programme, reported to me at the end of the first twenty-four hours that, since their arrival, the Russians had not made the slightest attempt either to criticize it or to change the details. Indeed Marshal Bulganin began his first conversation by expressing regret for all the trouble the arrangements had given and thanking us warmly for everything that had been done.

The journey of the Soviet leaders, the greetings at Victoria Station and the drive to Claridge's Hotel passed off without incident. At this time and throughout the visit, wherever the Russians went, the behaviour of the crowds could not have been better had we tried to arrange it, as no doubt our guests assumed that we had. There were usually large numbers on the route, most of them curious rather than demonstrative. When there was any demonstration it was inclined to cancel itself out. If there was booing, some cheered. If there was cheering there might be some booing. In general the welcome was polite, but restrained. I noticed that in their comments on their journeys throughout the country, the Soviet leaders and their party were impressed as much by the housing as by anything else. They liked our houses and our gardens. 'Neat' and 'tidy' were words they often used about them.

Finding that our guests were not tired and that they would welcome a talk that first evening, the Foreign Secretary, Lord Reading and I, together with Sir William Hayter, joined their party for a quiet dinner at Claridge's. We talked informally together for some time on a wide variety of topics from the origins of the second world war to modern broadcasting. This was a useful prelude to the conversations which opened the next day. It gave us a chance to get on terms.

When in discussion with Russians I have not found difficulty in putting an opposing point of view. They are on the whole good listeners, certainly better than other representatives of dictatorial powers I have had to deal with. On the other hand, there is little to be gained by trying to take debating points off them in terms of parliamentary argument. They do not understand the purpose of this kind of dialectic and they are apt to resent it. The best diplomacy is that which gets its own way, but leaves the other side reasonably satisfied. It is often good diplomacy to resist a score.

★　　★　　★　　★　　★

Official talks took place at Downing Street and made a considerable call upon the endurance of our visitors. We considered topics concerning all parts of the world and our conversations went to the root of the matter. They were the longest international discussions between two powers in which I have ever taken part. As the Soviet representatives came into the Cabinet room at Downing Street to take their places opposite us at the third or fourth of our meetings, Mr. Khrushchev remarked, 'See how well trained we are, we file in like horses into their stalls.'

It was about colonial affairs that argument was the toughest and, at times, the roughest. The Russians thought that we had in mind their speeches in India and Burma and maintained that a question of principle was at stake. They would criticize any country which followed a policy of colonialism. We retorted that we were proud of what we had done and were doing in the Commonwealth and Empire to bring their peoples towards self-government. It was a continuous process; Malaya, the Gold Coast and Nigeria were present examples. We said that we had nothing to hide, but if our friendship was to grow, it must have a basis of understanding. The Russians conceded that the British must be given their due, but held tight to their principle. After much debate, I felt that even on this subject, where all communists show the most stubbornly closed minds, we had at least paraded what were to our guests new arguments and they had listened to them.

Throughout their history the appeal of the warm-water port has always been strong for the Russians. Istanbul, though frequently coveted, could never meet this need. It only admits to the Mediterranean, another enclosed sea, both ends of which were at one time controlled by Britain. The attraction of the Persian Gulf to the Russians has always lain as much in the outlet it would give to the wider oceans as in the oil itself, perhaps more. The leaders of the Revolution have emphasized the importance of making their gains in the East. They understood that in Europe they would come up against a civilization strongly based upon respect for individual man. There would be weaker barriers if they turned towards the East. As Zinoviev declared in

1925, 'The road to world revolution lies through the East, rather than through the West.'

The Soviets have always realized the strategic importance of Iraq. Control of that country's economy would also give command of a considerable oil production. This would be a useful weapon in the economic tactics which the Soviets are now employing against the free world. In November 1940, Ribbentrop and Molotov were negotiating a four-power pact in Berlin. In the course of the discussions, Ribbentrop spoke discursively of 'the great changes which will take place throughout the world after the war' and 'the new ordering of affairs in the British Empire, finally reaching the Persian Gulf and the Arabian Sea.' Molotov, so Schmidt, the official German interpreter, tells us*, sat opposite him with an impenetrable expression. The Russian made no reference to these hints while in Berlin. Only after his return to Moscow did a telegram arrive from the German Ambassador stating that Molotov agreed with the proposals regarding the four-power pact, 'subject to the condition that the territory south of Batum and Baku in the general direction of the Persian Gulf was recognized as a focal point of Soviet aims.' The purposes of Soviet policy have not greatly changed since that date.

When we discussed the Middle East in London, I told the Russians that the uninterrupted supply of oil was literally vital to our economy. They showed an understanding of our interest and appeared to be willing to meet it. I said I thought I must be absolutely blunt about the oil, because we would fight for it. Mr. Khrushchev replied that I would hardly find sympathy with the Soviet Government if I said I was prepared to start a war. They, for their part, would only resort to war if an attack were made on them or on the Warsaw Pact countries.

Later in the talks Mr. Khrushchev reverted to this topic and to my statement, as he put it, that I was prepared to fight a war in that part of the world. He said that it was close to the Soviet frontiers. If my statement was intended as a threat they must reject it. I repeated that what I had said was that we could not live without oil and that we had no intention of being strangled to death. We were not threatening anybody. Later events showed that the Russians heeded this warning and understood our position pretty well. When troubles came, their opening moves were prudent.

As to the Middle East arms limitation, the Russians maintained,

* *Hitler's Interpreter*, by Dr. Paul Schmidt, ed. R. H. C. Steed (Heinemann, 1951).

with some justice, that the problem did not concern our two countries alone, nor did they wish to take any initiative in the matter themselves, though they were ready to hear any proposals others might have to make. We both understood that the Middle East was the area where our differences of policy were most likely to become acute. These discussions did something to put that danger at a further remove.

We did not shirk the topics on which we disagreed. For instance, the Soviet representatives made their outspoken criticisms of the Baghdad Pact. I was left with the conviction that, if we could make it plain and public that no further military bases would be established, by ourselves or by the United States, in the countries of the Middle East which were members of the pact, it could bring quite an important measure of reassurance. If properly defined, such an arrangement need not interfere with the defensive purposes of the pact.

It was in our interest to give priority to economic activities under the Baghdad Pact. Russian infiltration was more to be feared than Russian invasion. To meet this, increasing prosperity in the area was the most effective weapon, though inevitably taking time to forge. The more emphasis we could put on it, the more hope there was that gradually the Soviets would come to regard the pact for what it was, an expression of mutual help in an area of common interest and not a menace hovering over the oilfields of Baku. A short while before, threats had been uttered by the Soviets at the consequences to Europe of building some alternative organization to the European Defence Community. In fact, the Western European Union had come to be endured if not accepted, so in time might the Baghdad Pact.

On disarmament, the Soviet leaders told us, in confidence and in advance, of action they proposed to take later in the reduction of conventional weapons. On the Far East, we both noted with relief that the tension in the Formosa Channel was less acute though not resolved. The Soviets had a warning to give of the danger of allowing the situation to drag on indefinitely.

Next, the Russians marshalled their objections to strategic controls upon trade. They maintained that these had not, in fact, done serious injury to the Soviet Union. On the contrary, they said, they had compelled them to manufacture or build for themselves where they would otherwise have been content to import. For example, after the export of tankers by Denmark had been forbidden, Russia had built her own tankers and she was now exporting them. This did not prevent the Soviet leaders from expressing their resentment at the controls. We had to explain that these were not matters for ourselves alone and that there was considerable scope for increased trade outside them.

Some progress was made with the hardy biennial so grimly described as 'cultural exchanges'. We made it plain to our guests that there could not be an improvement in this aspect of Anglo-Soviet relations, if they continued to use for this purpose organizations in our country which were controlled by communists. The Soviet leaders took the point and some improvement followed their return to Moscow.

The subjects on which we failed to agree were more numerous. We recorded bluntly in our official statement that we had not reached an understanding on the means to achieve peace and security in Europe. All the same, I was sure that the Soviet leaders now had a clearer understanding of the views and considerations underlying our policies. Marshal Bulganin and Mr. Khrushchev pressed me to make a return visit to the Soviet Union. I accepted this invitation, although I could not then fix a definite date.

One incident during their visit made a marked impression on the Soviet leaders. The Labour Party's dinner to them in the House of Commons had ended in a rumpus. Mr. Khrushchev was indignant at what he regarded as the discourteous treatment meted out to him, and next day expressed himself vigorously to those with whom he spoke. This included the Foreign Secretary and myself. I did not encourage Mr. Khrushchev to elaborate his views to me. I have never attacked the Government of my own country when abroad, however sharply I disagreed with their policies. By the same token, when in the Government I was not eager to hear criticism of the Opposition by foreigners. Both these are habits to which politicians might with advantage revert, though they do not appear likely to do so. The Americans nowadays observe these restraints better than we. In my own mind, I was pretty sure that one of the factors which had led to such an unhappy meeting was the Labour leaders' underestimation of the knowledge and ability of their Soviet guests. The last thing that men of Mr. Khrushchev's temperament and background can endure is anything in the nature of intellectual patronage.

The truth was that these men had a remarkable fund of knowledge, not only of the Soviet Union's special problems but also of the world's weak points. In our prolonged talks at Number 10, I found Marshal Bulganin and Mr. Khrushchev perfectly capable of upholding their end of the discussion on any subject. They did this without briefs or detailed guidance from any of their advisers. I have spent my whole life conducting international affairs and I viewed this performance with respect. It will be tragic for us, and it may be fatal, to underestimate these men and their knowledge.

One of the topics which Mr. Khrushchev and I discussed from time to time was the immense burden imposed upon our countries by the effect of the rapid progress of science on the production of armaments. No sooner is a weapon invented and put into mass production, than it is outdated by some later invention. I found Khrushchev more alive to this problem than I had expected, in view of the control over finance that a dictatorship exercises. After a dinner at Number 10, he told Sir Winston Churchill, who was a guest, how we had all been spending money on increasing the speed of aircraft, but now the whole emphasis had switched to guided missiles and a great deal of the previous effort was wasted. He said that he and Marshal Bulganin had come to Britain in one of their newest cruisers, but already it was practically a museum piece. Probably its future rôle would be to act as a super-yacht for such ceremonial occasions, but he could not visualize surface ships engaging in duels at ranges of hundreds of miles. He added that this must be a matter of regret for Sir Winston as a former head of the Navy, but the march of time was inexorable.

I like to exchange ideas with intelligent men who can express the mind and thought of foreign countries, whether in politics or the arts. Now that politics are over for me, I look forward to the last most of all. As a result of ten days spent together in almost constant contact, I felt that I knew these Russians as no volumes of despatches could have revealed them to me. I found their characters, especially Mr. Khrushchev's, deeply intriguing. I am sorry that, for diverse reasons, I am unlikely to meet either of them again. My wife and I had found entertaining Marshal Bulganin and Mr. Khrushchev for the week-end at Chequers easy and interesting. The Russians rose early, about six o'clock in the morning. Probably western European food and drink were not much to their taste, for they ate little and drank less. Marshal Bulganin was urbane and discreet, while Mr. Khrushchev was more outspoken. We tried to bring something of family life into the stay. Mr. Khrushchev's son came down, driven by my son, Nicholas. Each spoke a few words of the other's language and they talked together of motor cars, the traffic jams impressing the Russian.

The diplomatic discussions at Chequers were attended by only four a side, the Foreign Secretary, Mr. Butler and Sir Ivone Kirkpatrick being with me. These talks were the least inhibited and the most useful of the series.

At the end of the visit, as I watched the last coaches of the train sweep out of Victoria Station I breathed a sigh of relief. This was in no sense personal, for our guests had been at great pains to be considerate to us. It was only when the visit was well launched that I realized the variety of risks I had run in staging it. However, all that was behind us, and it remained to realize the results.

There is dispute about the place of personal contacts in modern diplomacy. Every prime minister or foreign secretary is apt to consider himself better qualified than most to make contacts with leading foreign statesmen. This failing has caused some people to hold firmly the contrary view, that there should be no contacts between foreign governments except through diplomatic channels. However natural in the leisured eighteenth century, this practice is not sufficient now. Castlereagh was wise to change it. An age that reaches for the moon can hardly refuse to make direct contact with its earthly neighbours. Travel is accepted as educative and to have personal contact with foreign statesmen is to travel in the mind. I have found it an advantage to know the man to whom I was addressing a communication through ambassadors. When one has cantered many miles, it is good to take a jump from time to time. Direct international contacts are the fences of diplomatic life.

I pondered over my return journey to Moscow, which I thought might be scheduled for the month of May the next year. I hoped it would mark a further stage towards confidence, and that it might carry me into some parts of the Soviet Union I had never visited, perhaps even to Bokhara and Samarkand, of which I had read so much in the Persian writers during my years at Oxford.

Back at Number 10, I had to decide what our policy should now be. The present Soviet rulers had as much confidence as their predecessors in the ultimate triumph of communism. They were unshakeably determined. The methods they would employ might be different from those of Stalin and they might be harder to meet. Many influences had served to bring about this change, including the power of the nuclear deterrent as a major influence against world war. We had to consider the adjustments needed in our policies to cope with a new situation, for a new situation it undoubtedly was. We were moving from a period of fixed positions to a period of some flexibility. In military terms, Khrushchev had stopped preparing for the last war and was modifying the plans for the war that might have been, if no nuclear deterrent had existed. All this set formidable problems for us. We had entered the nuclear field, we were making the hydrogen bomb, yet neither in Europe nor in the Middle East could these entirely replace conventional forces, which were still insufficiently mobile. Our over-burdened economy had somehow to meet these various demands, at a time when every new weapon cost twice as much as its predecessor.

In a month or two's time, the Commonwealth Conference of Prime Ministers would present an opportunity to examine these consequences. Meanwhile we had to look again at our own plans. On April 30th I sent a minute to the Foreign Secretary and a number of my colleagues.

> Now that the Russian visit is over, it is necessary to review our policy. There are a number of points to be looked at. Our main weapons of resistance to Soviet encroachment have hitherto been military. But do they meet the needs of the present time? I do not believe that the Russians have any plans at present for military aggression in the West. On the other hand, are we prepared with other weapons to meet the new challenge? This seems to me to be the major issue of foreign policy. It will not be dealt with merely by Dulles' new thoughts for N.A.T.O., whatever they may be. But it is bound up with a review of our defence policy and it may be better to handle it in that connection. We must discuss this before you leave for N.A.T.O.

I further told the Foreign Secretary that we would meet our senior colleagues the next day to discuss this and Anglo-Soviet relations, including trade, the Middle East and disarmament. I considered that these questions were all urgent and that we must not lose the impetus.

There was one factor in the situation which had certainly influenced the new Soviet leaders. Western solidarity had been created by Stalin's policies. It was the military threat to the West, expressed in immensely superior Soviet military power and in the attempt to blockade Berlin, which brought N.A.T.O. into being. As the menace of major war receded, the existing basis of Western cohesion against Soviet encroachment might be weakened. We should need to adjust our policy with more speed if we were to maintain the solidarity of the free world to meet the new challenge from the Soviet Union. In foreign policy it looked as though we should lay more emphasis in future on economic propaganda weapons and less on military strength.

These considerations I discussed with the Foreign Secretary and with the Minister of Defence before their departure for N.A.T.O. They agreed to place them in the forefront of the forthcoming discussions. It was evident to us all that adjustments would have to be made within N.A.T.O. to meet the new situation, but it was important to avoid any premature dismantling of the military foundations of the alliance. We wished to justify the necessary changes for technical military reasons as much as for political ones. Both were real.

At this moment a trade proposal came from the United States Government which could only be regarded as a sharp step backwards. At our meeting in Washington in January, the United States Government had undertaken, at the instance of the President, to examine relaxations of the existing restrictions on trade with China 'now'. In the months that followed we had done everything we could to get some fulfilment of this undertaking. The position was not made any easier by the fact that our agreement to such action had been publicly announced in Washington, with the result that Parliament clamoured week by week for some results.

A few days after the Russians had left, the long-awaited American reply arrived. This suggested that, in return for small relaxations in the existing restrictions on trade with China, we should agree to reinstate the prohibition on the export of copper wire to the Soviet Union. There were no strong strategic arguments in favour of this action, nor could we accept that copper wire was of direct military importance. It would be most embarrassing for us to reinstate the prohibition, for our increased exports of copper wire were a principal ingredient of the recent expansion in Anglo-Soviet trade. Politically, we could hardly be expected to agree to the imposition of this further restriction on trade with the Soviet bloc so soon after we had agreed, in the talks with the Soviet leaders, to work for an expansion of trade.

For all these reasons, my colleagues and I agreed that the American suggestion must be rejected. It had first reached me in a message from the President. I was disturbed, not only because of the new restriction proposed on Russian trade, but because we were still making no progress to help the industries of Malaya and Hong Kong, which depended so much on Far Eastern markets. The existing restrictions were creating very serious difficulties for them. In particular, Malaya must be freed of all conditions governing her trade in rubber.

After consultations with one or two of my colleagues, we agreed that I should reply to the President warning him of our concern, and that the Foreign Secretary should take up these matters with the American Secretary of State at N.A.T.O. within the next few days. Progress in reducing restrictions on China trade continued wretchedly slow, until the seizure of the Suez Canal engulfed this and much else besides.

One event, which occurred during the visit of the Russian leaders, gave rise to much subsequent comment and criticism. This was the death of Commander Crabb. Two days after the Russians had left, the Admiralty announced that the Commander, a frogman of the Royal Navy, 'did not return from a test dive which took place in connection with trials of certain under-water apparatus in Stokes Bay in the Portsmouth area, about a week ago.' On May 4th we received a note from Moscow stating that a frogman had been seen swimming near two Russian destroyers in Portsmouth Harbour, and demanding an explanation. As Mr. Selwyn Lloyd was away, it fell to me to answer the note. We acknowledged the fact that Commander Crabb had approached the Russian warships without permission and expressed our regret and apologies. On May 9th, the same day that I sent our answer to Moscow, a Labour M.P., Mr. John Dugdale, asked a question in the House about Commander Crabb. I had given very careful consideration to my reply, for the episode raised a difficult question of consitutional propriety. It is customary for Ministers to take formal responsibility for all the actions of their subordinates, but in this particular instance where the action in question had never been authorized by any Minister and was indeed quite unknown to us until after the event, a different course seemed right. It was highly undesirable that the Russian leaders should believe that while they were our guests on a friendly visit we had connived at espionage against the ships in which they had travelled. I replied to Mr. Dugdale as follows:

> It would not be in the public interest to disclose the circumstances in which Commander Crabb is presumed to have met his death.
>
> While it is the practice for Ministers to accept responsibility I think it is necessary, in the special circumstances of the case, to make it clear that what was done was done without the authority or the knowledge of Her Majesty's Ministers. Appropriate disciplinary steps are being taken.

Beyond this I refused, and still refuse, to be drawn. The Opposition professed themselves dissatisfied and insisted upon a debate, which took place on May 14th. In my reply to Mr. Gaitskell I pointed out that there was ample precedent for a Government refusing to disclose matters on which, in its opinion, publicity would be damaging to the national interest. I instanced the Labour Government's own success in concealing for many years their expenditure on the atomic bomb. I ended:

But in this business I do not rest only on the national interest. The national interest is of first importance to us in the House of Commons, but there is also in this business a very important international interest, and I confess that all I care for is that the outcome of our discussions with the Soviet leaders should in truth prove to be, as I have said, the beginning of a beginning. I intend to safeguard that possibility at all costs. I believe that that is also in the mind of the Soviet leaders, and it is for that reason that I deplore this debate and will say no more.

When Mr. Gaitskell pressed the matter to a division, the Government had a majority of eighty-seven, about thirty higher than the usual figure. This suggests that some members of the Opposition may have shared my views on the imprudence of holding a debate on such a subject at such a time.

IX

DEFENCE
1955 – 56

*The Prime Minister and defence – My personal experiences –
Labour and the atom bomb – Construction of the H-bomb –
New strategic situation – Dangers of Soviet infiltration – Cost of
our defences – My telegram to President Eisenhower – National
Service – Reduction in numbers – Central organization of
defence – Commonwealth Conference – Strategy and economic
aid – Thermo-nuclear weapons – H-bomb tests – My rationing
proposals – Franco-British disarmament plan*

Defence is very much a Prime Minister's special subject. He
presides over the meetings of the Defence Committee which are
attended by the Chiefs of Staff. He may, on occasion, hold
informal meetings with the Minister of Defence and the Chiefs of
Staff, or with these and the Service Ministers as well. The Prime Minister is ultimately responsible for all important decisions on defence.
That is how it should be.

In the first world war, I learnt one side of the problem as a serving
soldier and, for over a year, as a brigade-major in the field, an exacting
but fascinating job. A great part of my life as a Minister has been mixed
up with defence questions. In my first years in the Cabinet, before the
war, the state of our defences and successive rearmament projects were
constantly a subject of discussion, and generally one of disappointment.

In the second world war, from the moment when Mr. Churchill
took over in the spring of 1940, I was closely concerned with its military
conduct, first as Secretary of State for War, then as a member of the
War Cabinet and of the more restricted Defence Committee. In the
years of Opposition and after my return to the Foreign Office in 1951,
problems of defence were always intermingled with my work. Defence

367

and foreign policy had to be considered together and they formed the
chief topic of conversation between Sir Winston Churchill and myself
in sixteen years.

I was not entirely content with our defence position as I found it. As
not infrequently happens in these matters, the distemper was easier to
diagnose than to remedy. We were trying to do too many things for
our resources, with consequent strains and shortcomings.

After the war, the Labour Government had made the atomic bomb
in secret, ingeniously concealing the large sums expended from public
and parliamentary gaze. They were certainly right to make the bomb,
and they may have been wise to conceal the fact from their followers.
We, in our turn, decided to make the hydrogen bomb in 1952, and so
reported to Parliament. When I became Prime Minister, our first
hydrogen bomb test was still more than a year away, but its influence
on our defence problems was growing. Our scientists were doing
brilliant work in nuclear development of every kind. The relationship
between the military side of our nuclear programme and its industrial
counterpart had also to be considered. The lead we held must be kept.

I felt confident that men like Sir William Penney would be as successful with the hydrogen bomb as they had been with the atomic. If so,
we should soon be one of the three powers in the world possessed of
this most powerful nuclear deterrent. We were building a strategic
air force, and we were at work on rockets and ballistic missiles.

It was likely that in a year or two we should have in our own hands
the deterrent authority of formidable weapons. We should possess the
quills of the porcupine and they would be deadly against any power.
I believed that to own and control a stock of hydrogen and atomic
bombs in these islands, and the means to deliver them, would increase
the security of the population against sudden attack. It could also influence the ambitions of others. This is what I meant by deterrent
power.

One consequence of the evolution from the atomic to the hydrogen
bomb was to diminish the advantage of physically larger countries.
All became equally vulnerable. I had been acutely conscious in the
atomic age of our unenviable position in a small and crowded island,
but if continents, and not merely small islands, were doomed to
destruction, all was equal in the grim reckoning.

My conversations with the Soviet leaders, from 1954 onwards, convinced me that they had clearly estimated the strategic changes created
by nuclear weapons. World conflict meant mutual destruction, which

they did not intend to provoke. This I first sensed in our discussion over Indo-China at Geneva in 1954. It was not paraded, but it was felt. After Mr. Khrushchev's visit in 1956, I knew that the Russians were busy applying the new lessons. We had to do so in a situation made more difficult by our limited resources.

Immediately after the war, Soviet Russia and its satellites had enjoyed the advantage of possessing conventional weapons and the men to handle them, in numbers far superior to any that the Western powers could muster. Democracies always relax after a war; dictatorships do not, because they can keep their people at duty. In 1955 the N.A.T.O. powers possessed a compelling answer in the nuclear bomb, even though it was not theirs alone. Broadly speaking, the Russians were matching us, device for device and explosion for explosion, but at least the bomb was the deterrent to superior conventional forces in Europe. Within a few years a stage of saturation would be reached, when both Eastern and Western groups of powers would have enough nuclear weapons to obliterate each other. Then surely each would be prudent to avoid the use of weapons which carried the certainty of annihilation.

If the number of nuclear powers remained restricted, the dangers of global war might then recede. Even so, precautions would be necessary against the threat which remained, the use of conventional weapons on a limited scale. This was a method well suited to communist tactics. There would be a temptation to think that the reluctance to use nuclear weapons created an opportunity to make experiments in a new type of aggression without risk. What had been attempted in Berlin and achieved in Indo-China might be attempted again elsewhere. A series of conflicts where local pressure was applied might bring gains for the great power which instigated or encouraged them, while protesting bland innocence. However the expression changes, it remains the Soviet purpose to destroy the capitalist world.

Our negotiations with the Russians had led to some easing of tension but not to a general relaxation, and I did not see how they could do so in the circumstances of the existing balance of power. Our defence policy, as we set it forth in a statement in February 1956, was consequently based on the assumption that Soviet aims remained the same: the overthrow of capitalism and the support of revolutionary forces everywhere. We had to accept that Soviet policy would use coexistence as a screen for fresh prodding offensives, which did not carry major risks of world conflict. Europe was the least promising theatre and it would be easier to turn the flank of N.A.T.O. than to breach its front. The Middle East and South-East Asia offered opportunities which the Soviets would try to exploit.

In some of these regions the Western powers had made defensive engagements with countries situated there. We had to uphold these. Alone among the allies of the United States, we were making nuclear bombs and building air power to deliver them. We had our garrison obligations to N.A.T.O. which we were fulfilling in Germany at the cost of foreign exchange. Some reduction might be negotiated, but a commitment would remain. We had to guard our overseas territories, still considerable, and sustain the Baghdad Pact and S.E.A.T.O. We had to be prepared for limited war, at the same time we had to be ready to adapt our forces to global war, if, against probability, one should overtake us.

The extent and cost of these defence preparations were formidable and ever-increasing. Soon after the general election of 1955 I decided that we must make economies in the defence programmes without sacrificing the power to strike back at any aggressor. The Minister of Defence, Mr. Selwyn Lloyd, reported to me in July that, unless existing programmes were revised, the cost of defence would rise during the next four years from £1,527 million in 1955 to £1,929 million in 1959. The economy of the country could not be expected to stand this mounting strain. We had to call a halt in defence expenditure and hold it over a period of years. After discussion with me, Mr. Lloyd, with my approval, put in hand a series of studies for a revision of programmes. I believed that we should run the least military risk by making some cuts in the forces and equipment designed for use in global warfare and, more particularly, in those contributed by the United Kingdom to N.A.T.O.

As is not unusual in the history of the armed forces, there was some difficulty in reconciling the Treasury's view of what could be afforded with the Service estimates of what was essential. I called for a further examination of programmes, and we reached our decisions. In the Royal Navy, we reduced the plans for the active and reserve fleets, scaled down the capacity of some overseas bases and cut expenditure on war reserves. In the Army, the strength but not the fighting power of units was reduced, also the size of the strategic reserve. In the Royal Air Force, a small reduction was ordered in the medium bomber force and larger ones in Fighter and Coastal Commands. We examined our programme for guided weapons and selected those we thought would best meet our defensive needs over the years. Fortunately they are turning out well.

By these means the defence estimate was cut down to £1,535 million for 1956-57, with proportionate reductions for later years, which was a financially satisfactory improvement. The cost of defence was not all that concerned me. We needed something better than the annual exchanges between the Treasury and the fighting Services. I I felt that a thorough re-examination of our long-term needs was required, and in the early summer of 1956 I asked Lord Salisbury, Mr. Macmillan, Mr. Selwyn Lloyd, Sir Walter Monckton and Mr. Butler to discuss with me the revision of our policies. We had before us a paper prepared by officials on the future of Britain in world affairs. This paper considered our objectives in the light of the transformation of the world brought about by the existence of the hydrogen bomb. It also recognized that since the war the United Kingdom had attempted too much in too many spheres of defence, which had contributed to the economic crisis which every administration had suffered since 1945.

Before the meetings began, I set out the following pointers:

> In our studies of future policy we must bear in mind that:
>
> (1) The main threat to our position and influence in the world is now political and economic rather than military; and our policies should be adapted to meet that changed situation. Effort must be transferred from military preparations to the maintenance and improvement of our political and economic position.
>
> (2) The period of foreign aid is ending and we must now cut our coat according to the cloth. There is not much cloth. We have to find means of increasing by £400 million a year the credit side of our balance of payments.
>
> (3) In our defence programmes generally we are doing too much to guard against the least likely risk, viz. the risk of major war; and we are spending too much on forces of types which are no longer of primary importance.

It was upon these assumptions that discussions were based. They went at a formidable pace, as can be seen from the following time-table:

Week beginning July 9th
   1. National Service
   2. Home defence

Week beginning July 16th
  1. New strategy for N.A.T.O.—Chiefs of Staff appreciation
  2. Bombers
  3. Fighters—air defence
Week beginning July 23rd
  1. Royal Navy
  2. Forces for limited war and internal security
  3. Military facilities in Middle East and Far East
  4. Non-military measures in Middle East
  5. Non-military measures in South-East Asia
  6. Antarctica
  7. Relief grants to local authorities for civil defence
  8. Economic objectives in relation to world affairs
Week beginning July 30th
  1. Research and development
  2. Medium-range ballistic missile
  3. Africa
  4. Review of N.A.T.O. reappraisal
  5. Round-up and conclusion.

These examinations had important consequences. The most immediately significant result was the reappraisal of N.A.T.O's strategy and of the doctrine of reliance upon the nuclear deterrent. The following passage from a telegram which I sent to President Eisenhower on July 18th expressed the concept on which our main defence policy was in future to be based:

> The political need to maintain the solidarity of the European countries is as strong as ever. For this purpose, even if for no other, it would still be important that some United States and British forces should remain on the ground in Europe under N.A.T.O. command.
>
> The military purposes for which those forces are now required are, however, different from those on which the military policy of N.A.T.O. was first framed. It was originally designed to meet the threat of a Soviet land invasion, and its pattern was established before the advent of the nuclear weapon. Today, the situation is changing. It is on the thermo-nuclear bomb and atomic weapons that we now rely, not only to deter aggression, but to deal with aggression if it should be launched. A 'shield' of conventional

forces is still required; but it is no longer our principal military protection. Need it be capable of fighting a major land battle? Its primary military function seems now to be to deal with any local infiltration, to prevent external intimidation and to enable aggression to be identified as such. It may be that it should also be capable of imposing some delay on the progress of a Soviet land invasion until the full impact is felt of the thermo-nuclear retaliation which would be launched against the Soviet Union.

★　★　★　★　★

This re-examination created an opportunity to reduce the strength of the armed forces. I had long wished to bring National Service to an end. A large proportion of our forces had to be ready to travel to distant theatres of war and it was uneconomic that they should be composed largely of National Servicemen, admirably though these carried out their duties. Apart from the new demands which nuclear warfare imposed upon us, I wished to meet the needs of the armed Services by volunteers who would engage for longer terms of service than eighteen months or two years. I was not, however, prepared to give an undertaking to bring National Service to an end until I was certain that we had the necessary voluntary enlistment. It would be harmful to the State to announce the end of National Service, then fail to reach our target of volunteers and revert to some form of call-up once again. This was why, when the Opposition began to canvass the possibility of abolishing National Service at the general election, I reacted sharply and refused to give any commitment. These were the words I used at a meeting at Rugby, as soon as I learnt of the temptations which were being offered to the electorate:

> Everybody wants to reduce the period of National Service. If we make progress with Soviet Russia I hope that some reduction will be possible. But it would be criminal folly to weaken ourselves before the negotiations begin. I would rather say bluntly, 'Lose every vote in this general election rather than take a step which would imperil our negotiations with Russia.'

I announced in October 1955 that over the next two and a half years the strength of the Services would be reduced from 800,000 to 700,000. If we were to get the volunteers, pay must be improved. The Minister of Defence, the Chancellor of the Exchequer and I discussed this, and in the following February the Minister inaugurated a new pay code. It was based on the principle that the longer the service the higher the pay, not only in the later stages but from the start.

As a result of the revision of policy in July 1956, which I have described, I was able to set out the principles which should underlie further defence planning and issue a general directive upon manpower. We were to depend on smaller forces, equipped with weapons fully up to date. The total number of officers and men serving in the three arms of warfare would be reduced to about 445,000, made up of Navy 90,000, Army 200,000 and Air Force 155,000. My aim was to get down to these figures by April 1960; a year later was the outside limit. An important requirement was that as many as possible of these men should be fighting men, and that the long tail of auxiliaries needed for the supply and service of a modern striking force should be made up more and more from civilian labour.

It was the expressed intention of this directive that we should not become entirely dependent on the United States for supplies of atomic weapons, warheads or fissile material.

There remained the problem of mobility. I was not satisfied that our forces had the mobility required for prompt action in a limited war overseas. We had the power to deliver a formidable initial blow by bombing, but our capacity to follow it up was weak. We needed to be able to transport armed forces by air in effective numbers. When we made our review of defence measures in 1955, the movement of reinforcements was still heavily dependent on sea-transport. Accordingly we placed orders for a number of Comet and Britannia aircraft. Unhappily such programmes take years to realize, and the Government of the day are heavily committed by the decisions of their predecessors.

I decided to strengthen the central machinery of defence. The Minister of Defence was advised jointly by the three Chiefs of Staff, each responsible for his own Service and reflecting the views of his own department. Hitherto, the officer most senior in rank had acted as chairman of the joint Chiefs of Staff. I thought there would be an advantage in appointing a permanent chairman, in addition to the three Chiefs of Staff, who would represent their collective views to the Minister. He could also take some of the burden off the Chiefs of Staff and attend the many meetings of international defence organizations, which called for much time, energy and devotion. This would improve co-ordination between the three Services at the highest level, while it could not seriously impair the responsibility of the three Chiefs of Staff to their respective Ministers. I decided to recommend this new appointment to the Queen. The Royal Air Force must play an increasingly important part in our military scheme of things in the future, and it seemed to me appropriate that an officer of that service should be the first to hold the new post. Marshal of the Royal Air Force Sir William Dickson was appointed.

At the same time I announced an increase in the powers of the Minister of Defence. His duty was to see that the composition and balance of forces within the three Services gave effect to strategic policy laid down by the Defence Committee of the Cabinet. He was to concern himself with the content of Service programmes as well as with their cost. Some Ministers of Defence in the past had found themselves acting as co-ordinators, rather than as directors of policy. The danger here was that decisions taken would be based upon the lowest common denominator of compromise, which is agreement by weakness. The fresh powers which the Minister was given in October 1955, comprised overseas as well as home defence, and all matters affecting more than one Service.

I discussed the question of further powers with the new Minister of Defence in October 1956, not a very easy moment for an overhaul of machinery. Mr. Head was satisfied that his existing powers were sufficient for his immediate needs, though we contemplated some amendment in the functions of the Ministry of Supply. We agreed that a further overhaul of the Ministry of Defence might be necessary later.

★　　★　　★　　★　　★

At the end of June a meeting of the Commonwealth Prime Ministers was due to take place in London. I had attended many such meetings before as Foreign Secretary and I enjoyed the plain-spoken and informal atmosphere in which all questions were discussed. The success of these conferences brings its own problem for the future. It is questionable whether we can still keep them intimate, as membership of the Commonwealth grows larger and year by year the numbers swell, yet it is in their intimacy and in the confidential character of the discussions that their value lies.

In 1956 ten Prime Ministers were present. The previous meeting had been held eighteen months before, when the main problem had been the impact of nuclear weapons upon international problems. Since then, the political significance of the hydrogen bomb had been generally accepted. I proposed now to confer with my Commonwealth colleagues on the new situation.

There was no change in the Soviet purpose, but we had to discuss the modified tactics which Moscow was likely to pursue. The conviction now shared by the United States and the Soviets, that neither would start a nuclear war, had to be weighed and its consequences too. At the same time, the Soviets wished to be more favourably regarded, especially by uncommitted states like India, and to undo the effect of Stalin's policies, which had been to set the world against them. Though they showed no disposition to make concessions, they were willing to discuss international questions patiently without confusing them with communist propaganda. In Russia itself, and in satellite countries, there were reports of some relaxation of restrictions, though no one could tell whether these would go further or prove to be just a passing phase.

Whatever the tactics, I had no doubt that the Soviets would continue to try to divide the democracies, and that the offer of competitive co-existence was designed to this end. Their promises of economic aid to other countries were cold, political calculations. I felt we should counter them by giving more emphasis to the economic aid which the Commonwealth was providing without conditions, for instance under the Colombo Plan. One of the topics discussed during my recent visit to Canada had been how to improve the presentation of the economic help we were giving to other countries. The Canadians were alive to this issue. They had themselves given considerable aid to India. They felt, as we did, that the Russians got much credit for doing little, we got little credit for doing much. The Canadians and ourselves both realized that the Russians intended to use the economic weapon increasingly to spread disarray in the West. We saw in advance that they would employ their surplus of raw materials to make things difficult in the markets of the free world. I looked forward to discussing these matters with my Commonwealth colleagues.

Our Commonwealth meeting lasted a week and many problems besides relations with Russia were discussed, expecially those in the Far and Middle East. Russia, however, was our most important theme. In the statement issued at the end of the conference we said:

> This meeting has been held at a significant stage in the development of international relations. A new element has been introduced by the growing recognition of the devastating power of thermo-nuclear weapons. Other developments of importance

376

have taken place in the world, including changes in the Soviet Union. . . . A progressive improvement in the relations between the Soviet Union and the other great powers would help to remove the fear of war and serve the interests of world peace. The Governments of the Commonwealth countries will persevere in the search for just and lasting settlements of outstanding international problems.

The value of Commonwealth conferences is not to be measured in terms of communiqués. It lies in the sharing of views. I felt that after our meeting, the United Kingdom Government could with renewed confidence take up the many international problems which faced them. Among the most important questions discussed at the conference was the control of thermo-nuclear weapons. This subject was becoming pressing as more weapons were tested by explosion. The United States and Russia were already carrying out tests; Britain was shortly to do so and in time other countries might be expected to follow. On June 7th, 1956, I announced in the House of Commons that, early in the following year, the United Kingdom would carry out a number of tests of the hydrogen bomb, which had now been in production for eighteen months. The tests were to take place in a remote part of the Pacific. The Royal Air Force and the scientific authorities conducting them were to be based on Christmas Island. Aid and ancillary support had been promised by Her Majesty's Governments in Australia and New Zealand.

It had always been implicit in the United Kingdom's decision to make hydrogen bombs that they would be tested. But the Government were fully aware of the possible dangers to human health arising from radio-active fall-out from a series of nuclear explosions. In fact, the tests which we proposed to undertake would be high air-bursts, which would not involve any heavy local fall-out. Nevertheless, the effects of radiation, especially if tests continued and multiplied, called for expert study. At the Government's request, the Medical Research Council drew up a report on this subject. They concluded that no detectable increase in ill-effects was to be expected from the present level of tests. But if the level of test explosions grew higher, and if larger numbers of thermo-nuclear weapons were used, we could 'within the lifetime of some now living be approaching levels at which ill-effects might be produced in a small proportion of the population.' This was a cautious but definite warning and I was not prepared to ignore it. The obvious course was to try to limit tests by international agreement.

As long before as December 1955, I had told the House of Commons that the Government were prepared to discuss methods of regulating and limiting test explosions, though we could not undertake to place the United Kingdom in a permanent position of inferiority in relation to other powers, by ourselves unilaterally foregoing tests. In June and July 1956, I reiterated my desire in answer to various questions in the House 'to seize every opportunity to put a policy of limitation of tests into effect'. There are many problems in trying to do so. Our scientific advisers at the time were by no means certain that a reliable system for detecting nuclear tests could be established, which would reveal any that might be attempted in secret. Moreover, as I said in the House of Commons, a limitation or a ban on testing alone did not rule out the accumulation of stockpiles of untested nuclear weapons in all countries capable of making them.

We needed a comprehensive plan by which a limitation, and perhaps eventually a ban, on nuclear tests would be linked with a limitation, and eventually a ban, on the manufacture of nuclear weapons. This would entail a global system of inspection and control to which all nations must conform. It would need to extend to conventional weapons and forces also, since in this field the Russians were greatly superior to the West.

A new comprehensive disarmament plan had been drawn up by the French and British Governments early in 1956. The Foreign Secretary had taken a direct personal interest in this and had kept me informed of his thought. The plan was, and remains, the most practical and fair of any so far devised. It was discussed by a sub-committee of the United Nations Disarmament Commission at a conference held in Lancaster House in March and April. In spite of strenuous efforts, no agreement was reached with the Russian representative on the commission. The Russian Government were pursuing their own series of nuclear tests, which continued throughout the year and on into 1957. Yet their disarmament proposals, which comprised an elaborate plan for the reduction of conventional weapons, made no provision then for the control of nuclear arms or tests. They stuck rigidly to their plan, which even in its positive features was not acceptable to us. It made no concessions to the need for a thorough system of international control and inspection, in the air as well as on land.

The general problem of disarmament had been referred by the

378

Lancaster House Conference to future meetings of the United Nations Commission. Her Majesty's Government had some hope that a modification of the original Anglo-French plan might yield a basis for agreement. But everyone who has taken part in disarmament talks knows only too well how technicalities frequently confound the issue and delay conclusions. Our proposal for a limitation of nuclear tests under a system of control and inspection was undoubtedly the most urgent item. Rather than allow it to become tangled in lengthy discussions on other points, I was prepared to follow it separately. As I told the House of Commons on July 12th, we should prefer the Anglo-French plan, with its wide scope, to be adopted in its entirety. But if progress was not made, we would be quite ready to consider other methods. We could deal with the nuclear limitation scheme in some other way by itself.

I repeated this pledge on July 23rd in a debate on foreign affairs. Plans now went forward to draw up a scheme of international control for the limitation of tests. On December 20th I announced that we were working on proposals to that end, Lord Salisbury, as Lord President of the Council, being the Minister directly concerned.

After I had resigned, the Prime Minister decided with the Americans at the Bermuda Conference in March 1957 that the proposals which I had in mind would not work. The argument against them was that if a deliberate attempt were made to run a test explosion in such a way as to avoid detection, it would almost certainly be successful. This was disappointing, but I do not think that we should abandon attempts to improve our means of detection. Our project had more significance than appears superficially, because it would be necessary to establish a system of international supervision to check its working. This is capital to any progress in international confidence and here was an excellent occasion on which to attempt it. Ration the number of explosions at a low figure for a year or two and check by international supervision that all concerned remain within their figure. If some were prepared to offer zero, so much the better. This acceptance of supervision is a modest request to make, yet if it were endorsed, it might be found to open perspectives to more ambitious schemes of supervision which have so far eluded international agreement. It could mark a beginning. One step at a time remains a good maxim in world affairs; we should try again.

There seems also a certain futility in continuing attempts to perfect these weapons. Once the powers have enough bombs or missiles to blow each other to pieces there seems small advantage in piling on the agony. If the world is to die, it matters little whether it does so by clean bombs or dirty ones. There remains the problem of those who have made no bomb and have a mind to do so, France for instance. The plan I outlined could be used to meet their needs and limit the consequences.

X

COLONIALISM AND MALTA
1955 – 56

*Colonial self-government – Faults of omission – Fiji – Two
Colonial Secretaries –Malta and Cyprus – Mr. Mintoff favours
integration – He becomes Prime Minister – I propose a round-
table conference – It recommends presence of Maltese M.P.s at
Westminster – Mr. Mintoff's referendum – We decide to fulfil
the conference's report – Difficulties over economic assistance –
An economic commission – Some reflections on island colonies*

In 1955, large British colonial territories were moving towards
responsible government. This trend has been continuous for some
time, its pace sharpening after the second world war. Within these
two years, 1955–57, the results were both chequered and expansive.
Malaya advanced with steady confidence towards self-government,
while Singapore was in uneasy ferment. The British West Indian
islands, some of them with Parliaments centuries old, were feeling
their way to federation, soon to be realized. In Africa, the position was
less certain. The Gold Coast was in the political lead, naming itself
Ghana. I was doubtful of a truly democratic development there;
Nigeria showed better promise of stability and tolerance.

A responsible choice faces any colonial power. Many will impatiently
ignore it, but it is none the less real in terms of human liberty and
suffering. The clamour for independence is general and widely supported. In many British colonial territories the doctrines of democracy
and government by parliamentary majorities, fairly elected from between contending parties, have been preached and practised over a
number of years. The rights of the individual and of minorities, respect
for *habeas corpus*, the equality of all before the law, have been taught
and apparently accepted. As a result, some understanding of the

workings of a free parliamentary democracy has been implanted. It is impossible to be sure how deep the roots have struck, but it is possible that they are sometimes shallow. When this is so, the result of granting self-government may be not parliamentary rule by the people, but dictatorship by a caucus or by one man; not the protection of minorities, but their suppression; not equality before the law, but arrest on political grounds, imprisonment, or deportation. Then, in the name of independence, tyranny returns. Political growth in the world to-day is not towards parliamentary government, but away from it, which makes it all the more necessary that the system should be well founded if it is to survive.

These reflections are not written to urge that the practice of colonial powers leading their territories towards self-government should be modified. That is neither desirable nor possible, but it is important that some of the illusions which accompany this process should be dispelled. In terms of the happiness, welfare and security of the great mass of the population, a hurried end of colonial administration may yield bitter fruit.

Colonial history has dark pages in its record, but in this century the faults have been mainly of omission, serious enough in their consequences. One example, though small in itself, made a deep impression upon me. Thirty-five years ago I made my first voyage across the Pacific from Vancouver to Auckland. We touched at Fiji and I was happily impressed by all I saw. The Fijians were a thriving, cheerful community, with apparently no regrets for the action of their last King in entrusting his people to the care of Queen Victoria. Their loyalty had recently been displayed in the first world war; it was to be repeated. There was an Indian minority, but it was small, and further immigration had been stopped in 1917. I returned to Fiji in 1957. In the interval the Indian population, which grows far faster than the Fijian, had come to outnumber the Fijians, who are thus a minority on their own islands. I was assured that the relations between the three races were happy; the British being the third. Maybe so, but this was not fulfilling the spirit of trust reposed in the Crown. It is unthinkable that, if the British Cabinet had been aware of the position in earlier years, they would not have called a halt to immigration before it was too late. This was a sin of omission on a small scale; there have been others. They influenced me firmly to oppose proposals by the Colonial Office for Chinese immigration from refugee-packed Hong Kong to North Borneo and Sarawak. I admitted the overcrowding in

Hong Kong and the scanty population in the other territories, but we were responsible for their future and we should not make it Chinese.

On our party's return to office in 1951 the post of Colonial Secretary had special significance. Whoever held that office would have to guide and influence hopes and ambitions in every continent. Mr. Oliver Lyttelton, now Lord Chandos, did this work brilliantly and selflessly. He charted the course for the Conservative administration in colonial affairs. His robust strength of character and disarming wit were as welcome to his colleagues in peace as they had been to the War Cabinet in which we had sat together. I was deeply grieved when he left us, in the summer of 1954, to take up a leading appointment in industry, and I have missed his counsel at every turn. He was a grand colleague in an emergency and a true friend at all times.

His successor may be said to have chosen himself. Mr. Lennox-Boyd has given his whole life to the study of colonial problems and colonial territories and today commands unrivalled knowledge and experience. He has held the Colonial Office with distinction and acclaim in a period of endless harassment. Colony after colony, inspired or infected by the universal bacillus of nationalism, has tried to run before it could walk. With patient care and parental indulgence, the Colonial Secretary has led their first footsteps. His guiding hand has always been there, unobtrusively. If all his charges have not grown up with the code of conduct in which he had instructed them, that is not the fault of their patient guardian. Mr. Lennox-Boyd's success is due to his real affection for the colonies and to an infinite capacity for taking pains. It has also been due to a cheerful willingness to discard, where need be, the conventions of Whitehall.

$$\star \quad \star \quad \star \quad \star \quad \star$$

In the Mediterranean, two island colonies, Malta and Cyprus, raised vexing difficulties. Malta presented a constant problem with its small size and ancient lineage, barren territory and natural pride. This fortress, battered through the years of war, had won affection and regard. A European people with a civilization older than our own, the Maltese were sensitive to anything in the nature of colonial status. At the time of the coronation of Queen Elizabeth, their Prime Minister, Dr. Borg Olivier, asked that he should be accorded what he described as his 'rightful place alongside other Prime Ministers of the Commonwealth' in the coronation ceremonies. This difficulty was tactfully resolved by Mr. Oliver Lyttelton, on whose advice the Prime Minister of Malta was accorded treatment identical with that of the Prime Minister of Southern Rhodesia. It was explained to him that this was done in recognition of Malta's unique position in having been awarded the George Cross for gallantry in the war. It was not to be taken as implying a willingness to entertain his constitutional claims.

Malta's economy has depended on expenditure by our Mediterranean forces. Its population, now 320,000, grows fast. Emigration to the Commonwealth, and in particular to Australia, has helped at both ends; the Maltese are excellent citizens in these new lands. But some enterprise from outside is necessary if its people are all to find employment. Even so, the island is too small to become a truly self-governing member of the Commonwealth comparable with such a country as New Zealand. How then is the constitutional difficulty to be handled? A number of proposals were canvassed and much time was spent by the Colonial Secretary, Mr. Lennox-Boyd, in seeking a solution. A status similar to that of the Isle of Man or the Channel Islands was advocated. This would have put Malta under the Privy Council and made the Home Secretary responsible for her affairs. I thought this a good solution. Unhappily, it was not accepted by Malta.

Small islands are alike in nothing but their marked individuality. They are problem children with strongly contrasting characteristics. Cyprus and Malta, both bristling with difficulties, could hardly be more different. Cyprus, an island with mineral as well as agricultural resources, has no particular economic need of our air base or of the work it brings, or even of the money spent by the troops in quieter times. If the island can enjoy stable conditions, it will soon add a rich tourist traffic to its many resources. I have travelled many lands and have seen no lovelier natural setting.

In the autumn of 1954, the Prime Minister of Malta, Dr. Olivier, prompted by the notification of an increase in the strength of the United States Naval Air Squadrons in the island, declared that his Government intended to press at an early date for full self-government for Malta within the Commonwealth. He no doubt considered that Malta should have a voice in such decisions, involving a foreign power. In the following year various possibilities for resolving the problem of Maltese constitutional development were considered. The most helpful was that a conference should be held with the representatives of Maltese political parties to discuss the subject. Such a conference would be presided over by a Minister from the Colonial Office and could reach practical conclusions. The United Kingdom Government wryly accepted that, whatever course was followed, an increased financial burden must be expected to fall upon them.

In February 1955, Mr. Mintoff, hitherto the Opposition leader, won the election in Malta on a policy of integration with the United Kingdom. In June the Maltese party leaders came to London to see what effect could be given to their wishes. They had made a close study of the representation of Hawaii and Puerto Rico in Congress up to that time, and of the practice of colonial representation in the French Parliament. Neither system appeared to be working to the entire satisfaction of their beneficiaries. Some Maltese were encouraged to support representation in Parliament at Westminster because they felt that the island could not take the normal road of constitutional development to full Commonwealth membership. Her Majesty's Government also wanted to meet the wishes of a colony which asked for closer association with the United Kingdom. The demand had not always been that way.

There were other considerations, too. If Malta were now to be given representation at Westminster, several of the smaller colonies like Bermuda, the Bahamas, Mauritius and Cyprus might ask for the same. Many experienced parliamentarians had doubts whether the House of Commons should contain small groups of members from overseas who would not be mainly interested in the government of the United Kingdom. While some put forward the special circumstances of Malta, others argued that the chief purpose behind the constitutional demands of the Maltese Government was economic integration. They wanted to raise the standard of living on the island and safeguard it against an uncertain future. If this were the demand, we ought to meet it on the economic level, rather than create a constitutional precedent which might have unhappy consequences.

The Colonial Secretary and I tried to hack a way through this thicket, helped by frequent consultations with the Lord Chancellor, Lord Kilmuir, and others of our senior colleagues, and finally with the Cabinet. We decided that these constitutional questions would only grow more troublesome, and perhaps dangerous, the longer they were delayed. We should try to settle them now. The best method of doing this was by a conference, modelled on the round-table conference which had considered Indian reforms between the wars. I announced the Government's intentions in the following statement to Parliament on July 6th:

In the discussions which he has been holding with my right hon.

Friend the Colonial Secretary, the Maltese Prime Minister has put forward proposals for a closer association between Malta and the United Kingdom. Her Majesty's Government welcome this initiative. They feel sure that in all parts of the House there will be a sympathetic response to the suggestion that the two peoples should draw more closely together.

The administrative, financial and constitutional aspects of these proposals are closely linked. The administrative and financial aspects are at present under discussion with the Maltese Government delegation. On the constitutional side, there is included a proposal that Malta, while retaining its own Legislative Assembly, should, in the future, be represented in the Parliament at Westminster. The Government feel that all sections of political opinion in Parliament should have an opportunity to consider, and express their views upon, a new constitutional development of such importance.

They therefore propose to convene a round-table conference, comprising representatives of all the political parties at Westminster, to consider constitutional questions arising from these proposals. This conference will meet during the summer recess. It will call into consultation representatives of the political parties in the Legislative Assembly of Malta. Her Majesty's Government believe that by this procedure of practical co-operation between the two Parliaments this imaginative proposal can be considered in a way that accords with its constitutional importance and with the interests of both peoples.

The proposals received a welcome in all parts of the House and Mr. Mintoff sent me a letter of thanks in enthusiastic terms. Arrangements for the conference went ahead rapidly. The Chancellor of the Exchequer, Mr. Butler, who was in charge while I was at Geneva for the Summit Conference, consulted me about the terms of reference and the chairmanship. Fortunately the Lord Chancellor, Lord Kilmuir, was prepared to give his experience and patient guidance to this work. On July 28th, I announced the membership of the conference, which included, on the Conservative side, Mr. Walter Elliot, Mr. John Maclay, Lord Perth and five others; on the Labour side, Mr. Attlee, Mr. Bevan, Mr. James Griffiths and four others; for the Liberals, Mr. Clement Davies.

The conference, which first met in September, worked expeditiously in London and visited Malta. Lord Kilmuir kept me informed of its proceedings. After some six weeks, he reported the majority of the conference as favouring representation at Westminster. He thought that none of the alternative proposals seemed likely to attract majority support in the island. We needed that support to ensure our defence interests.

The Lord Chancellor submitted the report of the conference to me on December 9th. It was laid before Parliament and published a week later. In its examination of the constitutional changes the report stated:

> The offer of representation at Westminster would be a recognition by the people of the United Kingdom that the people of Malta should enjoy equality of status. Common membership of the Parliament at Westminster . . . would make this equality manifest and meet the realities of the situation. However, it is for the Maltese people themselves to determine and to demonstrate clearly and unmistakably whether the proposals of the Maltese Government do indeed correspond to their own wishes.

The report then recommended that, having regard to the basis on which the separate parts of the United Kingdom were represented in Parliament and the size of the Maltese electorate, there should be three Maltese representatives at Westminster. These should be elected in exactly the same way and under the same electoral laws as Members from the United Kingdom.

The Leader of the House, now Mr. Butler, in announcing the publication of the report to Parliament, observed:

> The Government will consider the report with all speed, but no action will be taken until the House has had the opportunity of debating the report after Christmas, thus enabling the Government to take full account of the views of hon. Members in this important constitutional question.

Mr. Mintoff decided to go ahead at once with his campaign for the referendum. He planned that the voting should take place in February, before Lent, and would not heed earnest advice to give more time for the Maltese people to consider these matters. There followed an argument as to the terms in which the referendum should be made. My concern was to ensure that the proposals, and their economic aspects in particular, should not be put more favourably to the electors than the facts warranted. In the end this was fairly reasonably met.

The result of the referendum was declared on February 14th. It showed 67,607 Yes, 20,177 No, and 2,559 votes not valid, of a total electoral register of 152,823. The number of people voting Yes corresponded closely to the total Labour vote at the last election, which was 68,447. The outcome was probably as good, from Mr. Mintoff's point of view, as he expected, but nearly half the electorate had not voted. A question which could never be resolved was how many of the large number who abstained must be regarded as having been deterred by the strong advice given by the Church. The Roman Catholic Church in Malta certainly considered that Mr. Mintoff had aggravated the situation by rushing his referendum and by his hostile reception of their moderate pastoral letter on the subject.

The Governor, Sir Robert Laycock, rightly felt that he must do all he could to halt the split now widening between Government and Church. If integration was to be really acceptable to the Maltese population, both sides would have to work for a reconciliation. Sir Robert wished to come home for consultation on possible action; he managed to patch up a spiky truce for the period of his absence. The Colonial Secretary being absent on duty in Cyprus, I saw Sir Robert Laycock at Number 10, on February 27th, and telegraphed our conclusions to Lennox-Boyd. I endorsed a provisional plan which the Governor had made to see the Pope. I also asked the Colonial Secretary to visit Malta on his way back from Cyprus, even though the Governor would not by then have returned. I told him that I would make the necessary arrangements in Parliament for the postponement of his statement on Cyprus. His visit proved helpful.

These tensions on the island had their consequences at home, where a number of Government supporters in Parliament showed increasing reluctance to accept Maltese representation at Westminster. There were suggestions that any discussion of the report should be delayed. I felt that this was unacceptable. If, after more than three months, we adjourned for Easter without having even a preliminary discussion of the round-table report, we should subsequently be blamed, and rightly, for any further deterioration of the situation in Malta.

In the debate which followed, on March 26th, the Colonial Secretary made it plain that the Government favoured the recommendations put forward by the conference. We had given the House a full opportunity to express itself before announcing our intentions, and I now felt that continuing delay did not help. The fence would not become any easier to jump by taking a longer look at it. I therefore authorized the Colonial Secretary to declare, when winding-up the debate, that we would make our decisions known within a few days. Two days later I announced our intention to proceed with legislation giving effect to the recommendations of the round-table conference. I added one condition: that the part of the Bill which concerned the representation of Malta in the House of Commons would be brought into operation only if and when the Maltese people had shown their desire for it in a general election. The Prime Minister of Malta had said that he would request the Governor to grant a dissolution. Mr. Mintoff was in London for these discussions and when I made the announcement he wrote to me to express his thanks. I replied:

I am glad that you feel my colleagues and I are giving friendly and sympathetic handling to Malta's problems. This is indeed no more than the truth and, like you, I hope that our decisions will prove to be the right ones. The ties which bind the people of Malta and the people of the United Kingdom are strong and I believe that they will grow even closer.

For a while the chances improved of reaching agreement between the Government and the ecclesiastical authorities in Malta. I was grateful for that, but the general calm did not last long. Towards the end of June, the Prime Minister of Malta was again in London, this time to ask for economic assistance at the rate of £7 million in the coming financial year. It had been assumed throughout the proceedings of the round-table conference, so the Lord Chancellor and the Colonial Secretary maintained, that Malta's need would not exceed a level of between £4 million and £5 million a year. United Kingdom help to Malta had already been steeply rising at the rate of about £1 million a year. Mr. Mintoff's latest proposal would have doubled the rate of increase. This was a wide gap to close. The Cabinet did not consider that it could meet Mr. Mintoff's demand and he was informed accordingly.

The Prime Minister of Malta then wrote to me and I saw him the next day, in company with the Colonial Secretary. Mintoff argued his case, but I explained that the United Kingdom Government must adhere to the level of aid forecast in the report. I told him that my wife and I hoped to spend a holiday in Malta in August, and that we were greatly looking forward to this. I hoped that all would be serene by then. Mintoff seemed to share my wish, but other events destroyed our plan.

After the Prime Minister's return to Malta, protracted discussions took place with the Governor. Sir Robert showed full understanding of the Maltese position throughout. He was Mr. Mintoff's advocate to a remarkable extent. The next move came on June 25th, when the Prime Minster made a statement in the Legislative Assembly attempting to place on the United Kingdom the obligation of deciding, before the end of the week, to accept a commitment to vote funds for total assistance of £7 million for the year.

The Colonial Secretary explained to Parliament on June 29th that he could not recommend acceptance of this demand. As a means of resolving the deadlock, he had proposed to Mr. Mintoff an arrangement for an agreed budget to be drawn up on the basis of eighteen months, from April 1955. Our contribution would be fixed at £7½ million. At the same time, we would appoint an economic commission to report on the matter, in the light of the recommendations of the round-table conference. He hoped that, with the proposal in mind, the Maltese Prime Minister and his colleagues would seriously reflect on their position. Sharp altercations followed in the House of Commons, mainly about the extent to which the round-table conference had intended to give guidance on expenditure.

The Governor continued his efforts undaunted and in the early hours of June 30th we received a characteristic telegram: 'Crisis temporarily averted by last minute negotiations stop emergency telegram follows.' Three weeks later the Colonial Secretary informed me that there were still difficulties, though negotiations were making progress. These discussions took place during the critical days following on Nasser's seizure of the Suez Canal.

The next source of trouble was Mintoff's interference with Malta Rediffusion, which provided the island's broadcasting service. At this time British civilians were being evacuated from Egypt by flying-boats which landed at Malta. The air authorities asked Rediffusion to broadcast warnings to fishermen to keep out of the flying boats' path at certain hours of the day. Mr. Mintoff considered this an affront and temporarily closed down Rediffusion. It was an impatient act which the circumstances did not justify.

Soon after, I received a letter of complaint from the Prime Minister, the greater part of which appeared simultaneously in the press. I sent him a reply in terms of general reassurance and told him that we were trying to meet his grievances by appointing an economic commission. I declined to enter into the detailed points he raised. A further letter from Mr. Mintoff to me followed a week later. I was saved from having to enter into more argument at this stage by his acceptance of an invitation to come to London early in September.

In the meantime, we had been able to make progress with the economic commission with the help of Sir George Schuster, an eminent banker and public servant, who gave his time and services. The Prime Minister of Malta had asked that he should be made available. In his letter to the Colonial Secretary, Sir George kindly wrote: 'I am interested in Malta and also it will give me pleasure that I may perhaps be some help to you and, above all, to our Prime Minister, who seems to me to have had rather a load of undeserved troubles recently, to put it mildly.'

This time, effort was rewarded. After Mr. Mintoff's arrival in London the dispute between the Maltese Government and Rediffusion was composed. The membership of the economic commission was agreed and temporary financial arrangements made to cover the period until it reported. 'A spirit of friendly understanding', said the published statement, contributed to the success of the talks. Much patience shown by the Colonial Secretary over many months had played a part, too.

I saw the Maltese Prime Minister on September 7th and gave him some account of the negotiations which had taken place in London and elsewhere since Nasser's action in seizing the canal. We also made arrangements for keeping him informed about future developments. We discussed the defence of Malta together and the pay and pensions of the Maltese who might be called upon to serve in the event of hostilities. We followed up these matters later and, at the Prime Minister's request, sent out some Hunter fighter aircraft to Malta, as we had done to Cyprus, even though Malta was at the extreme range of Colonel Nasser's Russian bombers. The Colonial Secretary sent me a note later that evening to tell me that Mr. Mintoff had just been round to see him 'beaming with pleasure at his interview'.

$$\star \quad \star \quad \star \quad \star \quad \star$$

I have given this account of my dealings with Malta at some length, because it is typical of the relations between us and the small communities which are part of our former colonial empire. What I have here set down about Malta is not remarkable, nor is it even complete. There is something to be learnt from this story all the same. Small island communities are as intensely national as their land-bound counterparts, perhaps more so, and have a better chance of survival in character. This makes them more complicated and sensitive to handle.

I remember once at Geneva before the war, discussing with a foreign statesman of experience the future of the Baltic States. We spoke of Latvia, Estonia and Lithuania, not long since created by the terms of the peace treaty. My friend praised their way of life, then shook his head sadly. '*Malheureusement,*' he said, '*ce ne sont pas des états viables.*'

The United Nations today is steeped in anti-colonial prejudice. Colonialism is a subject on which it will neither hear reason nor act reasonably. Soviet Russia can take into her Moloch jaws the free Baltic countries and much else besides. Nobody, it seems, considers that act colonial grab. Soviet Russia may stretch forth into central Asia, into lands which have never known communism or Soviet rule before. So long as the whole is part of some great land mass, nobody considers this colonialism. Soviet Russia has by far the greatest colonial possessions on earth. Yet it leads the attack on others, where the links that unite the colonies and the home country are the sea lanes of the world.

Malta joined Britain voluntarily in a dark hour of the struggle with Napoleon. Other island territories have had their association with us for a hundred years and more. I would like to see this continue and each to preserve its individual character. How is it to be done? These islands are not large enough to be on their own and yet they have, as part of their heritage, a tenacious determination to be free. This presents no difficulties within their own territories. Most have had their own Parliaments and ruled themselves since the seventeenth century, but the larger questions of defence and foreign policy persist. These small communities can hardly be directly represented at frequent Commonwealth conferences with the larger countries, yet they must have some sense of being in active partnership with the United Kingdom. This has to be expressed in a fashion which will be satisfactory to them and yet make practical sense in the modern political world.

I would like to see a new departure contrived to meet their particular circumstances. Some islands are now technically under the Privy Council, a body which rarely meets. It might be well if, to all islands not at present federated, were given the opportunity to be represented on some more active council. They could meet, discuss, exchange and decide certain aspects of policy. It is true that these island communities are, many of them, separated by thousands of miles of ocean, though this matters less every year. It might be that, at the start, the meetings of the council would not be frequent and the issues discussed not of the first importance. The idea would have to be allowed to grow. On all subjects, not only political ones, opinions could be exchanged with advantage, once the habit was formed. This way of doing business could be developed. Maltese membership of the House of Commons could have been a solution and I thought it the best at hand. Whether it is finally accepted or not, we should attempt a practical working method to give these islands the life, opportunity, and association for which they crave.

XI

CYPRUS
1955 – 56

My visit to Cyprus in 1941 – Its past history – E.O.K.A. and Enosis – Attitude of Turkish-Cypriots – Greece and U.N. – The Government's plan for a constitution – Talks in London with Greeks and Turks proposed – An economic development plan – Terrorism and emergency measures–London Conference – Sir John Harding as Governor – His negotiations with Archbishop Makarios – Declaration of October 20th – Turkish concern - The Archbishop's negative – Helpful efforts of U.S. Consul – Debate in the House of Commons – Paralysis in Athens – More demands by the Archbishop – Mr. Lennox-Boyd flies to Cyprus - Our offers refused – We resolve to deport the Archbishop – Lord Radcliffe's constitution for Cyprus – Sir John Harding's courage – World opinion and Cyprus

The only time I visited Cyprus was in the spring of 1941. I met the Turkish Foreign Minister there, when Hitler's invasion of the Balkans was imminent. The news of the visit spread in the island and when we had finished our talks the Governor, Sir William Battershill, suggested that Mr. Sarajoğlu and I should drive through Nicosia on our way to the airport. He thought that the people should be given a chance to express their feelings. They certainly did. Every vantage point and every housetop was packed with cheering Greeks and Turks, the Greeks shouting to the Turks to come into the war. In the main square the throng was so thick that it brought our open car to a standstill. I began to be worried, there was only a handful of police and I felt responsible for Mr. Sarajoğlu's safety. The noise was terrific; suddenly a spout of warm blood gushed from in front of the open car and spattered the windscreen. I thought that the murdering had begun, but it turned out to be a sheep, sacrificed by a Turk in honour of his Foreign Minister.

When I told Mr. Churchill of my experience, he gave me the story of his first visit to Cyprus. This was in the early years of the century, when Mr. Churchill was a young Minister at the Colonial Office. As he approached the island in a destroyer, he was impressed to see a large crowd assembled on the shore to greet him with flags and banners. He thought this splendid, for he had not dared to hope that his re-nown had spread so fast and so far. He commented upon this to the captain. 'Wait till you get nearer,' was the reply. This was Mr. Church-ill's first experience of an Enosis demonstration. I, or any other British Minister, approaching Cyprus in like conditions in 1955 would have fared much worse.

Cyprus has not been easy to govern, ever since Britain acquired it by lease in 1878. Disraeli's purpose then was to establish a base from which Britain could support Turkey against a Russian attack. More than one attempt has been made at establishing representative institutions since the island became British by Order-in-Council in 1914. These have all failed. Successive Greek Governments tried to raise the issue of Enosis, or the union of Cyprus with Greece. The Labour Government in Britain, during its years of office after the war, stead-fastly refused to discuss the subject. The Conservative Government which succeeded them maintained the same attitude.

Cyprus has never belonged to Greece, though nine hundred years ago it formed part of the Byzantine Empire, from which it was severed by King Richard I of England in the twelfth century. By the middle of the twentieth century, the population of the island numbered half a million. The Greek proportion was swollen as a result of the welcome given to Greek refugees from Turkey after the Graeco-Turkish war of 1920-22. They now number over 400,000 as against less than 100,000 Turks.

Early in 1955, the British authorities in Cyprus began to have to deal not with demonstrations by crowds, but with terrorism led by a few. Some two or three hundred members of an organization, known by its initials as E.O.K.A., had taken to violence, shooting at British security forces and planting bombs. E.O.K.A. was acting not in the name of independence, which is common form in colonial agitations, but in the name of Enosis. E.O.K.A. received direct support from Greece in money, arms, organization and propaganda. Greek-speaking Cypriots were awed by E.O.K.A. terrorists and subject to bombardment by Athens radio. Our Ambassador's repeated protests to the Greek Government against this practice were in vain. The ethnarchy, headed by Archbishop Makarios, which had much influence upon opinion in the island, openly preached in favour of Enosis.

The Turkish-speaking Cypriots were strongly opposed to union with Greece. In early 1955 their passions were not yet inflamed, for the Turk is slow to anger, but once roused, he is implacable. Graeco-Turkish racial conflict on the island was a far greater danger than anything E.O.K.A. terrorism could contrive. The British Government had to try to suppress terrorism before it led to widespread racial conflict, and to seek a political solution which would give the people of Cyprus as a whole scope to govern themselves. Communist Cypriots fished in these troubled waters.

The action which the British Government could take was circumscribed by international considerations. First came the strategic value of the island. Our military advisers regarded it as an essential staging point for the maintenance of our position in the Middle East, including the Persian Gulf. There must be some security of tenure. It was not then thought enough to lease certain sites on the island from some future administration on whose policies we could not depend.

The Turks, in 1955, wished to see the *status quo* preserved in Cyprus. They had always made it plain that they could not contemplate the union of the island with Greece. I knew that they regarded Cyprus as the last of their off-shore islands and were convinced that its ownership by Greece would menace their safety. This was quite apart from the position of the Turkish minority in Cyprus. Collaboration between Turkey and Greece was important to N.A.T.O. and could not be maintained if Enosis were granted.

Another complication was the position at the United Nations, where the Greeks were virulently pursuing their campaign. They had once before inscribed the question of Cyprus on the agenda of the General Assembly and managed to get it discussed, though no resolution was passed. They were now likely to try again. I expected that the Greek argument would excite some sympathy in the United Nations. It could be represented that the Greeks were simply urging the right of self-determination for the people of Cyprus. Britain had already granted this right to some 500 million people and was continuing to grant it to other colonial territories. It would be urged that Cyprus should have the same treatment. Yet I was sure of what would happen, if a Greek resolution on these lines secured a majority. It would stir up further agitation in Greece, lead to rioting in Cyprus and exacerbate Graeco-Turkish relations.

On all grounds, I thought it right to make a new effort to persuade the people of Cyprus to accept a liberal instalment of self-government. Even if we could not grant self-determination, we ought to be able to show the Cypriots that the self-government we offered was an important stage towards it. A successful constitutional advance now would lessen tension in the island and perhaps make further progress possible.

The Colonial Secretary and I were in agreement upon this. We each circulated our views a day or two before I took over as Prime Minister. One of my first actions then was to ask Lord Salisbury, Mr. Macmillan and Mr. Lennox-Boyd to work out with me the most promising means of establishing self-government.

We discussed plans for a constitution. Cyprus would have an assembly with an elected majority. It would be led by a Cypriot Chief Minister and enjoy full powers over all subjects except defence, foreign affairs and security. These would be reserved for the Governor. A proportion of seats in the assembly would be allotted to the Turkish minority. The main problem was not, however, to devise a constitution, but to secure the co-operation of Cypriots in working it. To do this, we had to carry with us some goodwill from Greece and Turkey. Our best chance of winning this was to invite Greek and Turkish representatives to London and work for agreement there. This we decided to do and I think rightly, because, as events were to show, no plan could succeed without the concurrence of both countries.

We had some difficulty in formulating the terms in which our new move should be presented. It was necessary to work out in advance the proposals we should lay before the Greek and Turkish Governments, but we could not confine discussion to constitutional matters, for these were only part of the problem. Accordingly, when Mr. Macmillan issued the invitations at the end of June, he emphasized the common interests of the three Governments in the political and defence problems of the eastern Mediterranean as a whole. Cyprus was to be considered in this broader context.

I read the Foreign Secretary's communication to the House of Commons on June 30th, adding: 'Our intention is that there should be no fixed agenda, and that the discussions should range widely over all the questions involved . . . without prior commitment by any party.' This initiative was well received by the House and I was questioned chiefly on how soon the conference would take place. Obviously it could not be held until later in the summer, after the four-power talks at Geneva. If the Greek and Turkish responses were favourable, the Foreign Secretary intended to discuss arrangements with their representatives at the Strasbourg meeting of N.A.T.O., fixed for the following week.

Our proposal had a fair international reception at Strasbourg. The Turkish Government were favourable but the Greeks took longer to accept. Their Government were not strong and the Prime Minister, Field-Marshal Papagos, was a sick man. Their Ministers spoke, in self-excuse as they often did, of having to appease the fanatical elements in their country who felt deeply about Cyprus. They wished us to advance the date of the meeting earlier than we conveniently could, and threatened to appeal to the United Nations meanwhile. In reply, we urged them to await the result of the conference. Still raising difficulties, they none the less accepted. By a curious process of logic, they even brought themselves to declare that if we had taken earlier this initiative which they were so reluctant to accept, many unfortunate occurrences would have been avoided in relations between our two countries.

The way was now prepared for a meeting in August. I had been giving some thought to the sequel. On July 1st, I wrote to the Colonial Secretary:

I think it is very important that if our plans for a conference with the Greeks and Turks on Cyprus turn out as we hope, we should be prepared to formulate as soon as possible a long-term development plan for the colony. This would give the Cypriots something to look forward to and might even have some effect over the years on their attitude towards the British connection. If the offer of a liberal constitution is to be made after the conference, it would be good if the development plan could be made public at the same time. Education, it seems to me, is particularly important. There might be much to be gained by the provision of an institution of university status, linked with our own universities, which would help to wean the Cypriots away from the cultural attraction of Athens.

A development plan was shortly produced, costing some £38 million, and a scheme was drawn up for a new teachers' training college. I asked to be kept informed of the progress of these projects.

The Colonial Secretary paid a flying visit to Cyprus ahead of the London meeting to discuss these and other administrative questions with the Governor, Sir Robert Armitage, and his Executive Council. It had to be decided whether the Governor should proclaim a state of emergency, under which he would have special powers to detain terrorists indefinitely, even when specific criminal charges could not be brought against them. Her Majesty's Government were reluctant to do this on the eve of the conference with the Greeks and Turks, especially as the situation in Cyprus had become quieter after the acceptance of our invitation. Instead, the Governor was to be authorized to enact a special law of detention which he could put into effect against members of E.O.K.A. The Colonial Secretary discussed this with him and the proposed law was made.

At the same time, we arranged to strengthen the security and intelligence departments of the Government of Cyprus. These were bearing a dangerous burden and needed the reinforcement of experienced officers from other colonies and from Britain.

While in the island, the Colonial Secretary had an interview with Archbishop Makarios and reported him as entirely non-committal. The Archbishop repaired immediately afterwards to Athens, where he brought every pressure he could to bear upon the Greek Government to inscribe the Cyprus issue upon the agenda of the United Nations, before the London Conference opened. He did not hesitate to make strong statements in Athens itself, which could only embarrass the Greek Government if they wished to find a solution. It was clear that Archbishop Makarios was out to make as much difficulty as possible. This he did in private and in public.

On July 16th at a press conference, he said:

> We unhesitatingly believe that the convocation of a conference constitutes a trap and a means of delay, with the purpose of undermining Greece's appeal to the United Nations, and of entangling the matter in complicated patterns, whence it will not be easy for it to be extricated.
>
> The Cyprus question does not constitute a political issue between Britain on the one hand and Greece and Turkey on the other. The Cyprus issue is purely a question of self-determination and concerns the British Government and the Cypriot people only, and it can be extended so as to concern the Greek Government, whenever the latter, in interpreting the feelings of the Greek and

especially the Cypriot people, acts as the people's mandatory for the safeguarding of the island's right of self-determination.

The Turkish press meanwhile declared that if the Greek-Cypriots on the island were given enough autonomy to enable them to establish Greek rule there, the Turkish alliance with Britain and Greece would have no more than paper value. The Turkish newspapers had hitherto been more outspoken than the Turkish Government, which had behaved with restraint. It was as well, I wrote on a telegram at the time, that they should speak out, because it was the truth that the Turks would never let the Greeks have Cyprus.

The opening of the London Conference was fixed for August 29th, a little later than we had originally intended. The Colonial Secretary was due to make a tour of the Far East, where the future of Malaya and Singapore was being discussed, and would not be back until early September. Mr. Macmillan set forth in his speech the historical and strategic reasons for the British administration of Cyprus. He did not put forward our proposals for the future at this stage, but said he would disclose them after the Greek and Turkish representatives had stated their views. We knew how wide the difference of opinion was between the Greeks and Turks, but the world did not. Too many thought our troubles due to old-fashioned British colonialism. By securing a precise definition of these differences we hoped to show the true nature of the problem. The exact terms of our proposals for the future could then be presented.

The Greek Foreign Minister, Mr. Stephanopoulos, spoke next. He demanded the right of self-determination for Cyprus. Although he disowned Enosis as a policy, he went on to detail the safeguards which the Greek Government would give the Turkish minority in Cyprus. The Turkish Foreign Minister, Mr. Zorlu, as we had foreseen, spoke against self-determination and also against self-government as an immediate prospect. He hinted that any change in the status of Cyprus would amount to a revision of the Treaty of Lausanne and open the way to Turkish counter-claims against Greece in Thrace and the Dodecanese. Both Governments agreed that their views should be set forth, together with those of Britain, in a joint communiqué, which helped to make clear to uninformed opinion that Cyprus was not purely an Anglo-Greek dispute. It was also a gain that at the conference the Greeks abandoned their pressure for union at once and an immediate plebiscite.

The moment had now come to present our constitutional plans. Before the Foreign Secretary did so, I saw both the Greek and Turkish Foreign Ministers separately. I urged upon them the necessity for a solution of the Cyprus problem and asked them, in their own interests, to consider our plans very carefully. The Cyprus problem has always been an international one and I hoped that the three powers concerned would be able to work out a solution on the basis of our proposals. I suggested that the conference should be adjourned, if need be, to allow the delegates the necessary time to go home and consult their Governments.

In Cyprus itself, bomb outrages continued and the Government took precautions. Extra naval forces were provided to prevent arms smuggling from Greece and military reinforcements were despatched. Additional police officers were transferred to duty in Cyprus from other colonies.

In London, the Greek and Turkish delegations studied our proposals and maintained their positions for and against self-determination. The conference was obliged to record that it could not agree on the future international status of Cyprus. Confronted by this deadlock, Her Majesty's Government proposed that a three-power committee should be set up in London to examine our constitutional plans in detail and consider a system of guarantees to the Cypriot communities. We were prepared to reconvene the conference itself when the new constitution came into operation. We hoped that elected representatives of the people of Cyprus could then be associated with it. Upon this the conference dispersed. As it did so, riots broke out in Istanbul and Izmir, directed against the Greeks. The strength of the Turkish feeling was beginning to declare itself.

At this point, the United States Government, without any previous consultation with us, took two initiatives. They made representations to the Turks on the subject of the anti-Greek riots, and expressed in Athens their gratification at the 'calmness' of the Greeks. Her Majesty's Government feared that this attitude would further encourage the Greeks to raise the Cyprus issue at the United Nations, and to have it discussed there on a keynote of Turkish misbehaviour. We pointed out that it was the Greeks who had started the trouble, and that it would go on until their agitation stopped. One thing which would help to make them stop would be a rebuff by a clear majority at the United Nations. To secure this, we needed active American support.

We reminded the United States Government that the United Nations had themselves decided in 1954 not to discuss Cyprus any further for the time being. It was even more inappropriate to do so in 1955. If the Greeks were encouraged to appeal to the United Nations, it would only make them and the Turks more rigid in their attitudes and inflame the situation in the island. On these grounds we asked for American support at the United Nations. After much argument, we obtained it. The Greek motion was rejected by a majority of the General Committee of the Assembly and subsequently by the Assembly itself.

I was convinced that the Cyprus problem would only be resolved between the three Governments, British, Greek and Turkish. The best hope of reconciling our views was by diplomacy and confidential talks. We had set this in train by the conference and we intended to persevere with this method, using much the same technique as I had employed over Trieste. At the same time we would go ahead with our constitutional plans. With such a programme in mind I began to consider the Governorship of the island. Intelligent and faithful service was being given by the present incumbent, Sir Robert Armitage, but the position seemed to call for a rare blend of military and diplomatic qualities. I thought I knew the man, but he was outside the Colonial Service; I resolved to talk the matter over with the Colonial Secretary.

As I expected, I found him understanding of my concern and ready to agree to the appointment I had in mind: Field-Marshal Sir John Harding, the Chief of the Imperial General Staff, whose term was shortly to come to an end. None the less, I had some hesitation in asking Sir John, not because I had any doubts as to his suitability for the post, but because I knew that he had made plans for his retirement and that what I had to propose would sadly interfere with them. I knew also that he was so unselfish a man that, if he thought it his duty to accept, no personal considerations, financial or otherwise, would stand in his way for a moment. I asked him and he accepted.

The new Governor set about his task with vigour and enterprise in the political field, as well as in matters of security. As soon as he arrived in the island, in early October, he held a series of meetings with Archbishop Makarios. He informed the Colonial Secretary and myself of their course, in detail. The Field-Marshal soon determined that the alternatives confronting the island were sharp. Either he would reach a basis of co-operation with the Archbishop, or a full-scale conflict would break out. He made patient and ingenious efforts to reach agreement with the Archbishop and took immediate precautions against a conflict.

In these conversations the Governor set the problem of Cyprus in its international context. He described the London proposals and asked for the co-operation of the Archbishop to make possible the constitutional advance and the development plans which would follow them. These would include an elected Cypriot Assembly, responsible for all internal matters of government. The Governor urged the Archbishop to defer for the time being the question of self-determination. We could not give way on this issue, but we were prepared to discuss it with Cypriot representatives at a reconvened conference, once self-government had come into existence.

This was more than half a loaf, but the Archbishop took his stand on self-determination and would not budge. He required an immediate pledge which would recognize it as a right, and as an indispensable basis for the solution of the Cyprus question. It also became plain as the talks went on, that he wished to exclude the Turkish Government, and possibly even the Greek Government, from future constitutional discussions. We could not agree to these conditions. The Governor in Nicosia and the Government in London both tried to devise a formula on self-determination, which the Archbishop would accept. But he stuck fast to his original demand that the right of self-determination must be recognized before he would co-operate in self-government. On this the talks ground to a halt.

Even so, the Governor wisely took care to keep open his channels of contact with the Archbishop. I was glad of this, because I thought at the time that what divided us could be quite small. In this I was over-optimistic, believing, as I put it in a minute to Lord Lloyd, the Under-Secretary for the Colonies: 'What we have offered to Cyprus goes so far to meet Cypriot wishes as to embarrass the Archbishop in refusing it.' I thought we should consider whether to have another round with him and tried to devise a basis for it. I had, however, exaggerated the Archbishop's capacity to be embarrassed.

My colleagues and I exchanged opinions with Field-Marshal Harding on the wording which was to express our new attempt. We agreed with him, on October 20th, the following statement on behalf of Her Majesty's Government:

> It is not their position that the principle of self-determination can never be applicable to Cyprus. It is their position that it is not now a practical proposition both on account of the present strategic importance of the island and on account of the consequences

on relations between N.A.T.O. powers in the eastern Mediterranean.

Her Majesty's Government have offered a wide measure of self-government now. If the people of Cyprus will participate in the constitutional development, Her Majesty's Government will be prepared to discuss the future of the island with representatives of the people of Cyprus when sufficient progress has been made and self-government has proved itself a workable proposition capable of safeguarding the interests of all elements of the people of Cyprus.

In view of the considerations set out in paragraph one, Her Majesty's Government consider that the Greek and Turkish Governments should also be associated with these discussions by whatever method seems most appropriate.

Mr. Macmillan intended to see what he could do with this presentation of our position, in discussion with the Greek and Turkish Foreign Ministers at a meeting of the N.A.T.O. powers. We wanted the Governor's views as to when and how to re-open talks with Archbishop Makarios. Sir John returned to London for consultations on November 1st, when we again went over the argument, but did not change the substance of our statement. The Governor expressed the view that any approach to the Archbishop should be coupled with a demand that he make an unequivocal denunciation of violence. We agreed with this.

I considered it capital that we should carry the Turks with us in any new move. We had now to convince them that our purpose was not to abandon our interests or theirs in Cyprus, but to find a solution which would meet Western defence needs in the eastern Mediterranean. I sent a message to the Turkish Prime Minister, Mr. Menderes, asking for his understanding.

I had met Mr. Menderes on a number of occasions and held discussions with him in London while I was Foreign Secretary. Plans had been made for me to pay an official return visit to Turkey, when I had to undergo my first emergency operation in April 1953. I respected his vigorous abilities and had known his country and his predecessors for many years. I realized how much I was asking and was not surprised when the Turkish Government were perturbed and their reply was involved and stiff. We took it to mean an unwilling acceptance of our plans.

We had in fact gone to Turkey's limit to find a basis for co-operation with Greek-speaking Cypriots on a plan for self-government. We could not afford to take Turkish friendship and understanding for granted; we held their confidence and we must keep it. Any failure on our part to do so would be grave for us. It would also reduce Graeco-Turkish relations to the level existing between the Arab states and Israel. If this were ever to come about, an area of sharp antagonisms and deadly hatreds would separate us from the Middle East.

Mr. Macmillan used the opportunity of the meeting of the Baghdad Pact that autumn to convey a friendly message from me to the Turkish Prime Minister. They had useful and reassuring discussions. The Governor met the Archbishop, who had been in Athens on November 21st, and laid our proposals before him with a remarkable command of argument. The Archbishop was obdurate. He said that our proposals meant a refusal of self-determination and were therefore unacceptable. He made it clear that no progress could be made by discussing them.

We were now confronted with the grim reality of the Cyprus position as created by the Archbishop's demands. The Cyprus dispute could never be settled until the importance of the Turkish position was understood and accepted. This meant that Enosis must be ruled out as a solution, for whether one was for it or against it, Turkey would never accept that answer. Therefore the solution must be an international one, in which the Greek and Turkish Governments would agree, and must imply the abandonment of Enosis. At this time neither Greeks, nor Americans, nor U.N.O. would take the Turkish position seriously enough for this to be possible against the Archbishop's opposition.

Our Ambassador at Athens, Sir Charles Peake, informed the new Greek Foreign Minister, Mr. Theotokis, of Archbishop Makarios' outright rejection of our proposal. The Foreign Minister was 'very shaken' by the news and had not expected the Archbishop to break off the conversations so abruptly. He said that his Government had considered our formula a constructive advance. He did not, however, feel that the Greek Government were in a sufficiently strong position to take any constructive action, or to put pressure on the Archbishop. The Ambassador, who was courageous and wise, wrestled manfully with the Greeks, encouraging them to try to persuade the Archbishop to heed the proposals we had put to him. When Sir Charles telegraphed that he thought the only resource remaining was a message from myself to the Greek Prime Minister, Mr. Karamanlis, I responded in the following terms:

I am glad to hear from Her Majesty's Ambassador that you think that our statement on Cyprus is constructive.

It is a sincere proof of the determination of Her Majesty's Government to make their full contribution towards finding a way out of this deplorable dispute. We gave it most careful consideration and have taken full account of your views and difficulties. We feel that we have done our utmost, consistent with our obligations and weighty defence responsibilities, to meet your position and that of the ethnarchy.

I feel that with your co-operation we have what may well be a real chance to find an amicable settlement. If this is missed, no one can foresee the consequences and the harm which will result to our common Western cause.

I appeal to Your Excellency to take a bold initiative and recommend our statement to the Archbishop. I believe that if you would do this, there would still be a chance of persuading the ethnarchy not to reject our offer. It would then be possible for Cyprus to take the first steps towards a happier future and for us to restore the friendly relations which have been traditional between our countries and which are indispensable to the whole enterprise of Western defence.

The United States Government backed the initiative, both in Athens and in Cyprus. All this diplomatic activity was unpublished, and meanwhile press criticism of our alleged inaction was growing at home. This had to be endured, since explanations were impossible, without prejudice to the work we were doing. Whatever the consequence on the home front or in Parliament, I was determined that we should make no statement until it was quite clear that we could not gain the Archbishop's co-operation. The United States Government were so informed. The United States Consul, Mr. Courtney, called on Archbishop Makarios and told him that the United States Government viewed our formula very favourably. They felt strongly that it should be accepted and they would be extremely distressed if it were finally rejected.

Mr. Courtney, whose attitude throughout was consistently helpful, told the Governor that he encountered the same arguments and evasions as the Governor had, at his meeting with the Archbishop a few days before. In reply to a suggestion that he might be well advised to consult the Greek Government, the Archbishop told the United States Consul that he had not done so because he considered it unnecessary. He was already assured of their full support. The United States Consul was clearly very disappointed. The Greek Government were told of this interview, but it was clear to me that the Archbishop felt absolute confidence that he could maintain his extreme position. He felt that the Greek Government, even if they wished to, would not dare to act in a moderating sense, the more so as a general election was impending. He was right, for the Greek Government believed that Archbishop Makarios was beginning to rouse opposition against them, and they feared this.

The point which the negotiations had now reached was typical of Cypriot politics. We had worked out a plan which would have broken the deadlock. The Americans were helpful and willing, the Turks were reluctant but willing, the Greeks were timid but willing, the Archbishop was neither willing nor reluctant, he held all in check. At the same time, the murders and ambushes were stepped up by E.O.K.A. in Cyprus. The Governor felt compelled to ask for wider powers and we to grant them. Meanwhile the Greek Government were still wrestling with their conscience and begging us to say nothing of our offer, and we were being lambasted at home for our inactivity.

The United States Government instructed their Consul in Cyprus to return to the charge. He made no progress in a second talk with the Archbishop. When the question of a further reference to the United Nations came up, the Consul emphasized to the Archbishop that, if he rejected our formula, he would get even less support than in the past for his case in the United Nations. The Archbishop replied that reference to the United Nations had made Cyprus a world problem and that the organization would continue to be a useful platform for his purpose. Events proved the Archbishop right.

I continued to try to persuade the Greek Prime Minister. This was the position until December 4th. Then, as so often happens, a new voice was heard from the American side. Their Ambassador in Athens began to see matters rather differently. He thought that Archbishop Makarios was a prisoner of the extremists and that it was important to extract him from that position. Accordingly, the Archbishop was to be helped, and the way to help him was for us to make further modifications in the formula which we had already put forward and which the United States Government had strongly approved.

On the next day the House of Commons debated Cyprus, when the Foreign Secretary and the Colonial Secretary gave an account of the position. Immediately afterwards the ethnarchy made its most intransigent statement to date. After the usual demands, they said: 'Our claim can be realized only by securing all those factors which will make the exercise of self-determination in the island easy and quick.' 'Easy' and 'quick' were new words in the situation. On them the Governor commented: 'The Archbishop has raised his sights. He has directly raised the time factor, which he had glossed over in his previous proposals to me.'

After a fortnight, the Greek Government responded to my approach with a reply of many pages and we made a modest amendment to our statement to meet one of their criticisms. This now read as follows:

> Her Majesty's Government adhere to the principles embodied in the Charter of the United Nations, the Potomac Charter and the Pacific Charter, to which they have subscribed. It is not therefore their position that the principle of self-determination can never be applicable to Cyprus. It is their position that it is not now a practical proposition both on account of the present strategic situation and on account of the consequences on relations between N.A.T.O. powers in the eastern Mediterranean.
>
> Her Majesty's Government have offered a wide measure of self-government now. If the people of Cyprus will participate in the constitutional development, it is the intention of Her Majesty's Government to work for a final solution consistent with the treaty obligations and strategic interests of Her Majesty's Government and its allies, which will satisfy the wishes of the people of Cyprus.
>
> Her Majesty's Government will be prepared to discuss the future of the island with representatives of the people of Cyprus when self-government has proved itself a workable proposition and capable of safeguarding the interests of all sections of the community.

This was surely as fair as human ingenuity could contrive. Even read after this lapse of time, I feel that our statement should have made agreement possible, if all had wanted agreement. Still the Greek Government could not make up their mind. On December 10th, Sir Charles Peake telegraphed: 'It is very frustrating that after all this endless talking and arguing, I have so far been unable to shake the Greek Government out of the moral paralysis which has descended upon them.' That was true enough, and the paralysis was aggravated by fear of the Archbishop.

Sir John Harding did not endorse the new American view that the Archbishop was a prisoner of the extremists. He considered that the Archbishop could still carry the great majority of the Greek-Cypriot people with him in any settlement he might accept. The Governor wrote: 'I suspect that he knows this very well and admits it to himself. But he will not hesitate to use pressure from the extremists to justify intransigence on his own part and to frighten the Greek Government.' I am sure that this was a true judgment.

I was always on the watch to see that we did not get into the position of approving a form of words which would divide us from the Turks. In the second half of December, the Foreign Secretary attended a N.A.T.O. meeting in Paris. There he had some discussion with the Greek Foreign Secretary, who, in his turn, produced a text on which I commented:

> I do not suppose that the Americans will be tempted to look at the text in your telegram [which contained the Greek text], but it would, I imagine, be completely unacceptable to the Turks. It is not our strategic interests only which have to be safeguarded, but the joint working of N.A.T.O. in the eastern Mediterranean.

Two days later our Ambassador in Ankara was also warning us that any further juggling with the statement would produce an explosion there. Despite the Greek Government's protests of a wish to help, the Athens radio, under direct Government supervision, continued to do everything in its power to inflame the situation and to encourage acts of terrorism. By December 23rd, Sir Charles Peake felt it unlikely that we should get any more favourable response from the Greek Government. We should not, he advised, delay the execution of our policy any longer.

The Governor persevered. He had a further meeting with the Archbishop on January 27th and a little progress was recorded. Sir John had asked the Archbishop's co-operation in the proposed constitutional development, and in the restoration of law and order. The Archbishop held a series of meetings with representatives of Cypriot nationalist organizations before replying. There was concern both in Athens and Ankara when the facts of these exchanges became known. The Greek Government were shortly to take part in the general election and were most anxious that the terms of our offer should not be known before this. The Turkish Government were sceptical as to whether any constitutional arrangements, which could be agreed with the Archbishop, would effectively safeguard the interests of the Turkish community.

The exchanges between the Archbishop and the Governor continued until the middle of February and were fully reported to me during my visit to North America. They culminated in a further series of demands for concessions by the Archbishop. The Governor and Her Majesty's Government agreed that these should be rejected, the Colonial Secretary remarking that it certainly looked as if, when we resolved one doubt in the Archbishop's mind, he raised another. Typical of this was a new demand for an amnesty for terrorists, suddenly raised by the Archbishop at this stage. We were not prepared to sign anything about an amnesty in advance of an undertaking to cease fire and evidence that violence had in fact ceased. The Governor was firm on this point and so were we.

Exchanges continued between the Governor and the Archbishop, on the subject of the constitution and on the proposal for an amnesty. Towards the end of February, the Governor suggested that it would help him if the Colonial Secretary could fly out. Mr. Lennox-Boyd was eager to do this and, with my assent, flew to Cyprus early on February 26th. Before his departure, I sent him the following minute:

> You may like to have these few thoughts as you set out on your journey. I find myself closely in agreement with Sir John Harding's recommendation in his telegram, that the time has now come when we should make plain to our own people and to the world what are the series of offers that we have made to the Archbishop, culminating in our present propositions over the whole field.
>
> It is fair to recall that we began with the request that we should make plain our position on self-determination. This we did in the much discussed formula, asking only of the Archbishop that he should declare for his part, separately, that he would seek to call off violence, if we made plain our declaration. Instead, we were asked a series of questions about the constitution by the Archbishop. These we have answered to the fullest extent possible, as shown in the telegrams. Finally, the question of amnesty is raised and here, too, Sir John Harding's proposals seem to me, and would, I believe, seem to the world, a fair response to a new demand.
>
> Now the time has come to explain to the world where we are heading, unless you and Sir John Harding think it undesirable, recapitulating once more to the Archbishop what our position is.

Even at this stage we are placing no time limit on our offer. We are only informing the world of proposals we have already put before the Archbishop, so far without affirmative response.

There remains the important consideration of the Turkish position both on the island and internationally. It seems to me that we have gone as far, in concessions to Makarios, as it is reasonable to expect the Turks to accept at this stage. We all know that they are not happy. There is always the danger that, if they become convinced that a process of yielding on our part is to be continuous, the tension both internationally and, I should have thought, locally, would become very dangerous. In any event, we have shown the Turks in all good faith certain statements in connection with the constitution, which the Archbishop has also seen. We cannot modify those statements in any important particular.

I know that you will express to the Governor my unbounded confidence in him and my sense of admiration for the patience and courage he has shown throughout these wearying months. If during your talks there are any considerations you want to put to the Cabinet, do not hesitate to tell me. My own instinct in this business now is that we should let the world know what we have offered and see how the medicine works.

Full discussions followed with the Archbishop but the gap could not be bridged. There were still differences on the amnesty, on public security and on the definition of 'an elected majority'. At one time I told the Colonial Secretary that if he felt it necessary, I would go out to Cyprus myself. He said that he would like me to do so, if the remaining differences were only constitutional. Unhappily, they were not. Five months of discussion had come to naught. The Archbishop insisted that the proposed amnesty should be extended to cover those involved in crimes of violence against the person, or the illegal possession of arms, ammunition or explosives. Secondly, he made the demand that in advance of any recommendation by the Constitutional Commissioner, the principle of a Greek-Cypriot majority should be accepted. And thirdly, he was unwilling to agree that the time for transferring responsibility for internal security should be left to the discretion of the Governor. This last was decisive; we could not agree that the security of the island should depend on the Archbishop's timing.

The Colonial Secretary informed us on his return that, at the end of the discussions, there was little room for doubt that the Archbishop had not wished to reach an agreement. The full correspondence was published in a White Paper. The Colonial Secretary made a statement in the House of Commons on March 5th. He read out the final version of the formula on self-government, as proposed to the Archbishop, and described the painstaking negotiations which had followed and ended in deadlock. In reply to a question he added: 'The Government's view has been put forward . . . over the last five months. We have made a series of concessions to the Archbishop's point of view. I must confess with distress, that as soon as one obstacle is out of the way another one, unheard of until a week or two before, rears its head.' We knew that there were Greeks who had had an opportunity to follow the negotiations of the last month and who shared our view of the Archbishop's tactics and intentions.

Evidence had reached us that the Archbishop had close links with the terrorist organization and had encouraged plans for bringing ammunition and explosives into the island. His colleague, the Bishop of Kyrenia, was even more deeply implicated. The Governor had the power to deport those responsible for disorder and disaffection. We had asked him to take no action against the two bishops without reference to us. In early March, Sir John considered that the disturbed situation demanded their removal for the time being to some place of refuge where they could do no harm.

My colleagues and I in London examined the alternative course of simply expelling the two priests from the island. No doubt that would have been more acceptable to international opinion, but it would have left them at large to stir up trouble for the Government of Cyprus, from Athens and elsewhere. We decided that the interests of order and security justified their despatch to the Seychelles and we authorized the deportations on March 6th. These were carried out on March 9th. I said in the House of Commons on March 14th: 'I submit to the House that, having been told that order could not be restored while the Archbishop was in the island, we had no choice but to fulfil our responsibilities or abdicate our authority, and we chose the former. It was not an agreeable decision.' With the departure of the bishops, the military operations against E.O.K.A. made good headway. Sir John Harding reported in April: 'Under the surface of Enotist solidarity the Greek–Cypriot people have considerable doubts and reservations about Enosis even in their present inflamed state.'

The Government now concentrated on the action necessary to

prepare a working plan for self-government. Fortunately, we were able to enlist the help of Lord Radcliffe, for he was an authority to command respect in all unprejudiced minds. He visited Cyprus and the work of constitution-making was got under way. Even though it was unlikely that we could get enough co-operation to work our scheme at present, that day might come later. It was prudent to have a scheme examined and tested, at home and in Cyprus.

Constitutional plans for Cyprus, and the examination of ways and means to promote international agreement on the island's future, continued for several months. Lord Salisbury gave his experienced help to the Ministers most immediately concerned. It is work of this kind, of which the public hears nothing, which takes the heaviest toll on the strength and time of Cabinet Ministers and high officials. I attended their discussions whenever I could, and the views of our Ambassadors in Ankara and Athens, as well as of Sir Roger Makins at Washington, were constantly helpful.

All this involved more work for the Governor. In addition to the daily risks he was running, he had to bear the harassment of painful decisions in hanging terrorists. His rifleman servant had found a bomb under his bed. None of this weakened Sir John Harding's spirit, but I was concerned that his willingness should not be overstrained. I wrote across a telegram from him to the Colonial Secretary, which outlined his proposed activities on a visit to London, 'He must not work too hard.'

Sir John Harding, on his return to London on June 3rd, 1956, gave an account of recent developments at a meeting with myself and some of my colleagues. The operations against the terrorists had won some success recently. Our troops had carried out a wide sweep in the Paphos mountains, which had led to the destruction of two of the six or seven gangs of hard-core terrorists. The leaders of two of the other gangs had also been taken and there had been useful hauls of arms, clothing and food.

I recalled an earlier suggestion which had attracted me when it was made by the Foreign and Colonial Secretaries. This was to work out a plan whereby the Greek and Turkish Governments could be associated with our administration in Cyprus. I was reminded that such a possibility had been put forward during the tripartite talks in London and had not been well received. It was thought unlikely that any such arrangement would prevent continued Enosis agitation in Cyprus and in Greece. However, it became useful later as the basis for the plan used in 1958 which brought international agreement.

I felt concerned at this time at the little understanding in world opinion of the fervour of Turkish emotion about Cyprus. I regarded our alliance with Turkey as the first consideration in our policy in that part of the world. When our discussions with the Governor were concluded, I made some comments upon this in a message to President Eisenhower:

> Though the Turks say less than the Greeks, it does not mean that they feel less, and their anxiety about their future has put them into a highly excitable state. They are violently determined against Enosis. There is also a considerable population of Turkish-Cypriots in Turkey itself which plays its part in moulding Turkish opinion. I believe they number a quarter of a million or more. If anything in the nature of widespread communal disturbances were to break out, this would put a heavy and most disagreeable task upon our forces which would have to try to keep the parties apart and restore order.

The different assessments which could be made on the relative importance of the Greek and Turkish views was shown by the American reception of the constitutional proposals we had prepared. These brought a sharp reaction from the Turks. On the other hand, the United States Government declined to support the proposals on the grounds that they were insufficiently favourable to the Greeks.

The United States Government were not yet prepared to accept the importance and reality of the Turkish interest. An American official commented ironically, in reply to our explanations, that his Government were well aware of the Turkish interest, but that there was no Turkish lobby in the United States. By the same token, American support of a plan did not impress the Turks, since they took the view that the Americans would be the first to advocate that it be whittled down, as the pressure of the election campaign increased.

In view of these reactions, the Government determined to pursue their efforts, but not to make a public statement that summer. Discussions continued and on December 19th Lord Radcliffe's constitutional proposals were announced in the House of Commons and in Cyprus. They offered almost complete self-government, but were rejected by the Greeks. They may yet play a part in the future life of the island.

★　★　★　★　★

In geography and in tactical considerations, the Turks have the stronger claim in Cyprus; in race and language, the Greeks; in strategy, the British, so long as their industrial life depends on oil supplies from the Persian Gulf. Progress in self-government could not be made until these claims were reconciled, and one of two methods had to be chosen. Greeks and Turks could be associated with the British in control of the island, or the island could be partitioned. The first course we proposed on two occasions. Partition also had its advocates, especially in Turkey, and we agreed in December that it must be included among the eventual options before the Cypriot people. It has proved a supportable device in larger territories such as Korea and Indo-China, but I regarded it as the last refuge of baffled statesmanship.

The problem could only be solved if Greeks and Turks would really come together and meet each others' points of view. For two years they did not do so. Shortly after I left office, the Cypriot bishops were released from deportation, without any word from them condemning the use of force by terrorists. The worst period of terrorism followed in 1958, with racial feeling between Greeks and Turks at its height. Murder extended to civilians and even to the wives of soldiers on their shopping errands. But the Greek mind is flexible. In the course of time, the Greeks and the Archbishop decided that they could abandon Enosis, and the Turks then forsook the notion of partition. Progress could at last be made. In February 1959 the Greeks and the Turks reached an agreement at Zürich, which was endorsed in London, upon the establishment of a Republic of Cyprus within the Commonwealth. This held a promise of realizing some of the ideas I had entertained for the future of the vexed island. The value of the compromise will depend upon the spirit in which it is worked and upon acceptable arrangements for our military bases.

BOOK THREE

Suez

I

THEFT
July 19th – August 2nd, 1956

The Aswan Dam – Nasser seeks a loan – Egyptian-Soviet intrigues – Anglo-American misgivings – Mr. Dulles calls off the loan – Visit of the King of Iraq – The canal is seized – Implications of Nasser's action – Meeting with M. Pineau – The Government's decision – My telegram informing Mr. Eisenhower – Financial and economic measures – Reflections on dictators – Proposal for a conference of maritime powers – Talks with M. Pineau and Mr. Murphy – Mr. Dulles flies to London – Character and views of M. Pineau – Mr. Dulles' declared sympathy with our aims – Canal dues – General agreement in the House of Commons

When the July days came our thoughts turned to holiday plans. The year before they had not worked out, but this time my wife and I had firm hopes of three weeks rest in August. We both longed above all things for hot sunshine and seas in which to bathe. The Governor of Malta, Sir Robert Laycock, had most kindly found for us one of the loveliest villas in the island, by the sea. We began to count the days.

All through the summer Middle Eastern problems had continued to plague us. In particular, the conduct of Egypt over the project for building the Aswan Dam made things increasingly difficult. In 1955 the Egyptian Government came forward with an ambitious scheme to improve the irrigation of the Nile Valley and develop hydro-electricity. To do this they planned to build a new high dam, three miles long, across the river a few miles south of the existing dam at Aswan. Her Majesty's Government were prepared to help. We knew of Egypt's needs, her growing population and falling standard of living. But this scheme raised many problems, among them the division of the Nile waters between the Sudan and Egypt, upon which the two countries were not agreed. It also raised intricate questions of finance. The total cost over a period of sixteen years was estimated at $1,300 million. Large sums in foreign exchange were involved, which Egypt could certainly not meet out of her own resources. Her balance of payments was precarious.

British, French and German firms were involved in a consortium for carrying out the project. The Governments of all three countries were willing to back their contractors with financial aid. To help meet the considerable risks, we enlisted the aid of the United States Government and of the World Bank. A plan was devised, involving the participation of us all, which was expensive but workable. The initial Anglo-American grant towards the cost was to be $70 million, of which our share was to be $14 million, and the World Bank agreed to lend $200 million.

The Soviet Government then made tempting overtures for the contract. They offered to build the high dam on terms which were uneconomic and all the more attractive for being so. I did not want to see Soviet influence expand in Africa, and in November 1955 we discussed the threat of this with the United States Government and determined to persist.

In the new year of 1956, agreement had nearly been reached with the Egyptians. Then they began to raise more and more difficulties over the terms suggested by the World Bank for the issue of a loan. Every effort was made by Her Majesty's Government and our allies to make these terms acceptable to Egypt, and the World Bank did its share. However, head in air as a result of Soviet promises, Egypt declared in January that the guarantees required for such a large outlay of international money amounted to a demand for 'the control of the Egyptian economy'. These guarantees were not drastic; a promise that the Egyptians would give the dam priority over other projects, that contracts would be awarded on a competitive basis and that aid from communist sources would be refused.

As the months passed a growing proportion of Egyptian revenues was directed to meeting payments for arms from behind the Iron Curtain. We were disturbed at this mortgaging of the country's economy. Appeals and remonstrances to Colonel Nasser on this account were met by evasions or counter-complaints against Israel. The Egyptian financial position deteriorated and it became more and more doubtful whether the Egyptian Government would be able to cover its part of the inevitable expenditure for the dam project.

The more uncertain the Egyptian contribution, the greater our lia-
bility loomed. There was a point beyond which we could not go in
financing this venture. There was not only a limit to what we could
afford, we had also to take account of the position of our allies, notably
Iraq, who had their own needs. Already at the beginning of the year the
Iraqi Government were complaining that the Egyptians had done better
out of the West by bullying than they had by co-operating. The Iraqis
had got £3 million and a few tanks; the Egyptians seemed about to
get the Aswan Dam. If there was to be charity, then friendly Arab
countries had the right to apply. They could hardly be expected to
view with enthusiasm the advance of large sums for an Egyptian
project, while that country was becoming ever more closely linked with
Soviet Russia and while Egyptian propaganda was viciously attacking
both them and us.

Throughout that summer we had increasing evidence, from secret
sources and otherwise, of the activity of Egyptian agents in all Middle
Eastern lands. In Libya, the Egyptian Military Attaché had been busy
trying to undermine the authority of the King and substitute an
administration more subservient to Nasser. He was sent home. There
were similar activities in the Lebanon, where President Chamoun's
refusal to display anti-Western fanaticism won him Nasser's unrelenting
hostility. In Jordan, there were plots against the King, the extent of
which the Jordan Government revealed many months later. In Iraq,
there were intrigues and attempted assassinations; again a military
attaché had to be sent back to Egypt. In the Sudan, subversion was
active, aided by the inflated staff of the Soviet mission. Throughout the
Middle East the 'Voice of the Arabs' from Cairo was blaring out
hostility to the West and to the lackeys of imperialism, as our friends
were called. In the same breath, more money was being demanded for
the scheme to build the dam.

The Foreign Secretary, Mr. Selwyn Lloyd, set to work to exchange
views on this state of affairs with the United States Government, and
found that the State Department shared both our doubts for the present
and our apprehension for the future of the scheme. Consultation continued between a number of my colleagues, in which the Chancellor
of the Exchequer, the Foreign Secretary and I took a leading part. In
mid-July, after the most careful canvassing of all the arguments, the
Government came to the conclusion that they could not go on with a
project likely to become increasingly onerous in finance and unsatisfactory in practice.

I would have preferred to play this long and not to have forced the issue. There was no need to hurry. Unhappily things did not work out that way. The Egyptian Government no doubt sensed Western reluctance to promise ever larger sums for the scheme, when they were themselves jeopardizing their own contribution. They tried to clinch the business on their own terms. The Egyptian Finance Minister, Dr. Kaissouny, arrived in Washington and had a series of interviews with the International Bank and with the State Department. On July 19th, for reasons connected with the Senate's attitude to foreign aid and the critical climate towards neutralism then prevalent in Washington, Mr. Dulles felt obliged to tell the Egyptian Ambassador that the deal was off. We were informed but not consulted and so had no prior opportunity for criticism or comment. As a result of this decision the loan from the World Bank was also cancelled, for the two transactions were interdependent.

We were sorry that the matter was carried through so abruptly, because it gave our two countries no chance to concert either timing or methods, though these were quite as important as the substance. At this moment Colonel Nasser was in Brioni at a meeting with Marshal Tito and Mr. Nehru, and the news was wounding to his pride.

*　*　*　*　*

In July, the King of Iraq, with his uncle, who had recently been Prince Regent, and Nuri es-Said, the veteran Prime Minister who had been a personal friend of mine for thirty years, were paying a state visit to London. Nasser was then campaigning vehemently against Iraq. During the ceremonies and discussions the King impressed everyone with his sincerity and natural charm. He was familiar with the development plans upon which his Government had embarked and eager to speed them. He seemed to me the best type of young ruler, caring for his people, modest in his living and direct in his approach. As I listened to his speech at the dinner given in his honour at Buckingham Palace, my mind went back to my first meeting with his grandfather, founder of Iraq and of his dynasty, who had ridden with Lawrence and been our ally in the first world war. Faisal I would have been proud of his grandson that evening.

I had a conversation with Nuri es-Said after dinner at Buckingham Palace. I found him deafer, but as resolute as ever and without illusions. We spoke of the past and of our first meeting in Baghdad in 1925 and of the personalities, British and Iraqi, in his country at that time; of

General Jafar and the King, of Sir Francis Humphreys and Miss Gertrude Bell. Then of the present; Nuri es-Said was coldly aware of the menace to him and to the work he was doing for his country, of Nasser and his virulent brand of demagogy. He knew that Iraq's development board and all its works were a race against time. Once the people saw the results of these projects and benefited from them, they would understand and they would not let them go. But this would take time, and whether they had time enough would depend upon the support we and the Americans gave Iraq. He spoke warmly of the work of our Ambassador, Sir Michael Wright. As I listened I felt, as so often before, admiration for this man, who was such a tough and resilient fighter in politics and in war, and my heart warmed to him. I knew how active and unscrupulous were Nasser's agents and that the Iraqi was an obstacle to the Egyptian's schemes of empire. There had been at least one recent plot against Nuri es-Said's life, but I knew, too, the young King's popularity, especially among the tribes. I little thought that this was the last intimate talk we were to hold together.

Two years later King Faisal was massacred in Baghdad with his uncle and relations, men, women and children, ministers and friends, in conditions of exceptional barbarity, even by modern standards. The nearest parallel in my lifetime was the murder in 1903 of King Alexander and Queen Draga in Belgrade who were flung from the windows of their palace to the street below. When they tried to hold on to the window's edge, their hands were hacked away. Then, a thrill of horror ran through Europe. The Baghdad massacre was more degrading and more widespread. The naked bodies of the former Regent and of Nuri es-Said were dragged through the streets of Baghdad amid scenes of unmentionable beastliness. A British officer was shot within the Embassy. Three Americans were torn to pieces by the mob, with faint protest by their Government. Within a few days the free nations of the West recognized the Government which had endorsed, if it had not sanctioned, the gruesome deeds. In London, only the initiative of friends, which included Ministers, working against ecclesiastical difficulties, organized a small service in memory of these national figures whose friendship proved faithful unto death. This did not seem enough to mark our country's respect and gratitude.

★   ★   ★   ★   ★

On the night of July 26th, the King and other Iraqi leaders were dining with me at Downing Street. While we were at dinner, one of my Private Secretaries came in with the news that Nasser had seized the Suez Canal and forcibly taken over all the properties of the company which had administered it under international agreement. In a speech at Alexandria he had declared that Egypt herself would find the funds with which to build the Aswan Dam. The means lay ready to hand. He would seize the canal and draw upon its revenues for the capital he needed.

I told my guests. They saw clearly that here was an event which changed all perspectives, and understood at once how much would depend upon the resolution with which the act of defiance was met. Our party broke up early, its social purpose now out of joint. Mr. Selwyn Lloyd, Lord Salisbury and Lord Home were dining with me, and we adjourned to the Cabinet room to discuss our course of action. The Lord Chancellor and the Chiefs of Staff also joined us. I had no doubt how Nasser's deed would be read, from Agadir to Karachi. This was a seizure of Western property in reply to the action of the United States Government. On its outcome would depend whose authority would prevail.

We decided to invite the French Ambassador, M. Chauvel, and the United States Chargé d'Affaires, Mr. Foster, to take part in our consultation. When they arrived I told them what we knew. In our judgment the economic life of Western Europe was threatened with disruption by the Egyptian seizure of the canal. Here was an issue of the first importance, in which an international agreement was at stake. We ought immediately to concert steps between our three Governments. The French and American representatives were given the terms of a statement I proposed to make in the House of Commons next morning. They undertook to ask their Governments to take similar action. Telegrams were despatched in the early hours of the morning to our Embassies in Paris and Washington informing them of this step.

On the morning of July 27th, in the House of Commons, I answered a Private Notice question put by the Leader of the Opposition. I said:

The unilateral decision of the Egyptian Government to expropriate the Suez Canal Company, without notice and in breach of the Concession agreements, affects the rights and interests of many nations. Her Majesty's Government are consulting other Governments immediately concerned with regard to the serious situation thus created. The consultations will cover both the effect of this arbitrary action upon the operation of the Suez Canal and also the wider questions which it raises.

Mr. Gaitskell declared that: 'On this side of the House we deeply deplore this high-handed and totally unjustifiable step by the Egyptian Government.' At that moment, as the House understood, I could say no more about the exchanges we had initiated less than twelve hours earlier.

I then discussed the situation with my colleagues and with the Chiefs of Staff. We had seen the text of Colonel Nasser's speech, which was a vehement nationalistic manifesto and a catalogue of supposed grievances:

> This, O citizens, is the battle in which we are now involved. It is a battle against imperialism and the methods and tactics of imperialism, and a battle against Israel, the vanguard of imperialism. . . . As I told you, Arab nationalism has been set on fire from the Atlantic Ocean to the Persian Gulf. Arab nationalism feels its existence, its structure and strength.

This was the context in which Nasser chose to set his action. Egypt, he claimed, had forced Britain to evacuate the canal zone base. She had applied to Britain for arms for use against Israel and been refused. Russia, on the other hand, had supplied her needs without attaching conditions. When Egypt had appealed for financial aid with which to build the Aswan Dam, the World Bank had sought to impose conditions which would have subjected the Egyptian economy to Western tutelage. The American offer of funds had been withdrawn for the political reason that Egypt was opposed to the Baghdad Pact. The canal would therefore now be nationalized in retaliation, and also because the Canal Company had usurped the rights of the Egyptian people.

As we debated the action we should take, we were aware of Nasser's intentions to milk the revenues of the canal and divert them to the finance of his high dam. He was, in fact, taking over the money of an international company and intending to use it for his own internal purposes. He soon gave an earnest of his methods. The branch of the Ottoman Bank in Cairo was ordered to hand over the balance of the Suez Canal Company's account which it held. Five million Egyptian pounds thus passed into Colonel Nasser's hands. As I wrote in one of my telegrams despatched that day, a man with Colonel Nasser's record could not be allowed 'to have his thumb on our windpipe'.

The Government considered the situation fully that Friday morning and decided that they could not allow Nasser to seize control of the canal in defiance of international agreements. The canal was an international asset and had been recognized as such ever since the Convention of 1888. In recent years its importance had been greatly increased by the development of the Middle Eastern oilfields and by the dependence of Western Europe on them for a large part of its oil supplies. In 1955, 14,666 ships passed through the canal. Three-quarters of them belonged to N.A.T.O. countries and nearly one-third were British. The Government determined that our essential interests in this area must be safeguarded, if necessary by military action, and that the needful preparations must be made. Failure to keep the canal international would inevitably lead to the loss one by one of all our interests and assets in the Middle East, and even if Her Majesty's Government had to act alone they could not stop short of using force to protect their position. This was our recorded opinion, which I still hold.

The Government had at this stage to consider both matters of principle and immediate practical steps. We took a number of decisions which were to guide our course through the next three months. We resolved that, in the first instance, President Eisenhower should be invited to send a representative to London to discuss the situation and align a joint policy with the Foreign Secretary and the French Foreign Minister. M. Pineau was, by a previous arrangement, due to arrive in England on the following Sunday, July 29th.

The Government foresaw that some friends, especially in the Commonwealth, might urge us to refer the problem of Suez at once to the Security Council of the United Nations. Though we favoured using every method of conciliation, we were not convinced that it was wise to begin by a reference to the Security Council. The precedents were discouraging. During the past four years Egypt had flagrantly disregarded the Security Council's resolution that Israeli ships should have freedom of passage through the canal. The Russians, who were the armers and backers of Colonel Nasser, had the power of veto in the Council, and would not hesitate to use it. They could nullify any resolution taken by a majority of the Security Council. When discussions opened between the three powers, the Americans and French agreed with us that reference to the Security Council at this stage would be a mistake.

The next question the Government faced was the crucial one. Should we be prepared in the last resort to use force to dislodge Colonel Nasser from the canal? It was our intention first to bring the maximum political pressure to bear upon him. The means would be worked out in the tripartite talks of the next few days. Economic weapons were also at our disposal and the Chancellor of the Exchequer had prepared financial measures which were to come into operation at midnight that night. But economic and political pressures alone might not succeed in checking Nasser and re-establishing international control over the canal. From the start we had to prepare to back our remonstrances with military action. The Chiefs of Staff were instructed to get ready a plan and a time-table for an operation designed to occupy and secure the canal, should other methods fail. We hoped to count upon the participation of the French in any expedition which was mounted. We expected that the United States would at least be neutral. But if assistance were not forthcoming from our friends, we had to be in a position to take action alone. I informed the President of this decision in the telegram I sent him on the evening of July 27th. The Commonwealth Prime Ministers were also informed through their High Commissioners in London. In my telegram to Mr. Eisenhower I said:

> This morning I have reviewed the whole position with my Cabinet colleagues and Chiefs of Staff. We are all agreed that we cannot afford to allow Nasser to seize control of the canal in this way, in defiance of international agreements. If we take a firm stand over this now we shall have the support of all the maritime powers. If we do not, our influence and yours throughout the Middle East will, we are convinced, be finally destroyed.
>
> The immediate threat is to the oil supplies to Western Europe, a great part of which flows through the canal. . . . If the canal were closed we should have to ask you to help us by reducing the amount which you draw from the pipeline terminals in the eastern Mediterranean and possibly by sending us supplementary supplies for a time from your side of the world.
>
> It is, however, the outlook for the longer term which is more threatening. The canal is an international asset and facility, which is vital to the free world. The maritime powers cannot afford to allow Egypt to expropriate it and to exploit it by using the revenues for her own internal purposes irrespective of the interests of the canal and of the canal users. . . .

We should not allow ourselves to become involved in legal quibbles about the rights of the Egyptian Government to nationalize what is technically an Egyptian company, or in financial arguments about their capacity to pay the compensation which they have offered. I feel sure that we should take issue with Nasser on the broader international grounds.

As we see it we are unlikely to attain our objective by economic pressures alone. I gather that Egypt is not due to receive any further aid from you. No large payments from her sterling balances here are due before January. We ought in the first instance to bring the maximum political pressure to bear on Egypt. For this, apart from our own action, we should invoke the support of all the interested powers. My colleagues and I are convinced that we must be ready, in the last resort, to use force to bring Nasser to his senses. For our part we are prepared to do so. I have this morning instructed our Chiefs of Staff to prepare a military plan accordingly.

However, the first step must be for you and us and France to exchange views, align our policies and concert together how we can best bring the maximum pressure to bear on the Egyptian Government.

The recent behaviour of the Egyptian Government did not give us confidence that in the long term they would manage the canal with a full sense of international obligations. If they won sole control, further pressure must be expected in time, on Israel and others. We were convinced that the answer to Nasser must take account of the modern trend towards internationalism and away from nationalism. Our object must be to undo his action and to place the management of the canal firmly in international custody. The Suez Canal Company doubted the technical capacity of the Egyptians to widen and deepen the canal and accommodate the larger oil tankers and heavy traffic of the future. The Commonwealth Governments were informed of these reflections.

★　　★　　★　　★　　★

During our deliberations on that Friday, a number of decisions were taken and put into effect. The Bank of England and the commercial banks were given authority to block the current Egyptian sterling balances held in London. The funds and assets of the Suez Canal

Company in London were protected against Egyptian expropriation. The export of arms and military materials to Egypt was banned. Four Egyptian destroyers, at that time in the harbours of the United Kingdom and Malta, were to have their sailings delayed by every means short of physical interference. Our own shipping position was to be examined, with a view to any requisitioning which might be necessary for a military operation. The Foreign Office was to warn British subjects resident in Egypt of likely developments.

A formal note of protest against the seizure of the canal was delivered to the Egyptian Government. Later that night the Egyptians sent back our note with an unsigned slip attached, which read: 'Returned to British Embassy.'

We estimated that the United Kingdom had reserves of oil which would last for six weeks, and that the other countries of Western Europe owned comparatively smaller stocks. The continuing supply of fuel, which was a vital source of power to the economy of Britain, was now subject to Colonel Nasser's whim. The oilfields of the Middle East were then producing about 145 million tons a year. Nearly 70 million tons of oil had passed through the Suez Canal in 1955, almost all of it destined for Western Europe. Another 40 million tons of oil reached the ports of the Levant by pipelines running through the territories of Egypt's then allies, Syria and Saudi Arabia.

More than half of Britain's annual imports of oil came through the canal. At any time the Egyptians might decide to interfere with its passage. They might also prompt their allies to cut the pipelines. We had to gauge the implications of bringing oil from the Persian Gulf by the long haul around the Cape of Good Hope.

A criticism was subsequently made that we and the French, as the powers principally concerned, should have reacted at once and forcibly reoccupied the canal. The argument runs, especially in the United States, that if we had done so there could have been little complaint. There are two answers to this.

The first answer is political. As signatories of the Charter of the United Nations, we were bound first to seek redress by peaceful means. Though we were conscious of the Soviet veto and of the weakness of the United Nations as an executive body, we knew that we must at some time take the issue to the Security Council. We might even be able to prod them into action. To accept this did not mean abandoning the use of force as a last resort. This was always the position of Her Majesty's Government and of the French Government at all stages of the dispute.

We made it clear repeatedly, in public and in private, from the first day to the last.

The second is military. Unless the action could have been carried through exclusively by airborne troops, there was no alternative to an expedition from Malta. Unless we could fly all the forces needed, they had to swim. The nearest place from which to swim was Malta, a thousand miles away. Cyprus has no sufficient harbour for landing-craft or transports. There is no escape from these logistics. We had nothing like enough airborne troops for an operation of this kind. The French had more, but together we could not have mustered a full division with artillery support. The follow-up would have taken several weeks to organize, even with the most brilliant improvisation.

The invasion of Sicily from North Africa took six weeks to prepare in the midst of the second world war. True, action against Egyptians is not militarily comparable with action against Germans, as I was constantly urging. On the other hand, our resources in the Mediterranean at this time were not comparable with those of the British and United States forces at the height of their power.

Earlier that summer my family and I had been watching the Trooping the Colour on Horse Guards' Parade. As we walked back across Downing Street garden, I asked my son what he thought of it. He replied, 'I should be happier if they were paratroopers.' It may be a fair criticism that after the Berlin airlift and the threat to the West which had to be met there, our military plans had been too closely concentrated on the defence of free Europe by land, sea and air against Soviet attack. Between 1947 and 1956, preparations for airborne action on an important scale had not been made. I was not satisfied and earlier in July the Government had taken the decision to create a reserve in England which would be mobile by air. There had not been time to give effect to this. Neither the aeroplanes nor the men could be conjured up overnight. They could only have been made ready over the years.

★   ★   ★   ★   ★

Modern dictatorships are not all of a type. The example that comes most readily to mind is also the most dangerous, the dictator who has a streak of paranoia. He sees himself as a conqueror on behalf of his people, dominating a large part of the world. He feeds the mob with demagogy, the mob feeds him with power; it is a mutual indulgence. His megalomania need not exclude a quick, subtle or scheming mind, nor a personality which gulls interviewers. He may attract the devotion of large numbers of his countrymen and echo their patriotic aspirations in his frantic oratory. He may even command brilliant gifts of statesmanship. Evil lies in the use he makes of them.

All dictatorships are repressive governments, intolerant of opposition, but in degrees that vary widely. There is the redemptive type of dictator, whose rule is comparatively mild and beneficial. A nation, through war or other calamity, meets disaster. The call is for a man who, by his qualities and experience, can lead the people and redeem their fortunes within their own land. Mustapha Kemal in Turkey was one of these, during and after the Graeco-Turkish war of 1920-22. Dr. Salazar in Portugal is another example, restoring his country's economy after recurrent crises in the early 'twenties.

Communist states fall into another category; they are totalitarian in the sense that they have neither the spirit nor the machinery of democracy. They are one-party states, but those who rule in communist countries, though they may have seized power, only wield it for a spell. The communist dictators are working for a cause, world domination by communism, not necessarily to be realized in their lifetime. Communist rulers are the primitive and ruthless priests of a modern religion, more skilful and more cautious than the megalomaniacal dictator, who is compelled to achieve power and fulfil his ambitions before he dies.

It is important to reduce the stature of the megalomaniacal dictator at an early stage. A check to Hitler when he moved to reoccupy the Rhineland would not have destroyed him, but it would have made him pause. The world would then have had time to assess the truth, and the Germans occasion to question themselves. This process would have been altogether salutary. 'Though your enemy be an ant,' runs the Turkish proverb, 'imagine that he is an elephant.' Nowadays it is considered immoral to recognize an enemy. Some say that Nasser is no Hitler or Mussolini. Allowing for a difference in scale, I am not so sure. He has followed Hitler's pattern, even to concentration camps and the propagation of *Mein Kampf* among his officers.* He has understood and used the Goebbels pattern of propaganda in all its lying ruthlessness. Egypt's strategic position increases the threat to others from any aggressive militant dictatorship there.

* A number of Arabic translations of Hitler's *Mein Kampf* were found by the Israeli army in the possession of Egyptian officers after the Sinai campaign. These were not a standard issue, but the quantity of copies showed that the book had a highly popular appeal.

If any dictatorial government has it in mind to pursue an aggressive policy, it will do well to label itself 'Socialist' from the start. Hitler was the first to understand the value of this camouflage. Despite the world's experience of German National Socialism, there is still a tendency to regard even a Government like Nasser's as Socialist and therefore as having a left-wing colouring. I have observed with amazement how national leaders in other countries, who hold left-wing views, have thought that they had more affinity with, for example, Colonel Nasser in Egypt than with Nuri es-Said in Iraq. The administration of Iraq under Nuri was infinitely more progressive and mindful of its people's welfare than the Egyptian. Three-quarters of Iraq's revenues from oil were devoted to public works, irrigation, electrification and improved living conditions. Only Kuwait, in a much smaller area, has attempted anything comparable. The poverty of the Egyptians further deepened when Colonel Nasser forced out General Neguib; arms before bread.

★　　★　　★　　★　　★

On Saturday morning, July 28th, there was a meeting of the ministerial group which had been set up on the previous day to keep in contact with the situation on behalf of the Cabinet. They had to work out plans day by day to put our policy into effect. Six of my colleagues, in addition to myself, were permanent members of this group and other ministers frequently joined in our deliberations. The Chiefs of Staff were in attendance when required. In the months ahead we held many meetings and the Cabinet were kept in touch with our work. That morning I told my colleagues of a message I had received from President Eisenhower, who was anxious that the largest possible number of maritime nations affected by the seizure of the canal should be brought quickly into consultation. He was sending Mr. Murphy of the State Department to represent the United States in talks with M. Pineau and the Foreign Secretary. Mr. Dulles at that moment was touring South America. He was in Peru.

At the beginning of the crisis the Americans appeared to wish to isolate Egypt among the nations of the world, and to bring the moral pressure of combined opinion to bear upon Colonel Nasser. This was an acceptable intention, but it took no account of the probability that Nasser would show himself impervious to moral pressure. In practice it was to mean conferences and resolutions, but no action. The result was words. Some suspicion of this difference in our approach was already beginning to appear in reports we were receiving of initial reactions in Washington. It became more pronounced during the consultations of the following week, though we had hopes of bridging it. For the time being we assumed that the American attitude, in the absence of the Secretary of State, was one of prudence rather than divergence.

Her Majesty's Government agreed to summon a conference of maritime powers. Its composition and its timing were the problems now to be considered. We favoured restricting representation to the six or ten powers who were the principal users of the canal in terms of tonnage and trade. It would be a matter for discussion with M. Pineau and Mr. Murphy whether an Anglo-French note should be immediately presented to Egypt. A tripartite note was greatly to be preferred, but American participation in such a step was doubtful. The alternative would be to delay diplomatic action until after the conference had met, and then to make a move on behalf of as many of the maritime powers as would associate themselves with us. In that event, if we got no satisfactory reply from Egypt, we must be ready for the possibility of having to back our joint requirements by military action.

That Saturday afternoon my wife and I motored to Broad Chalke. The cottage there was a haven. My wife had bought it several years before we married. It lies in the fields at the lane's end; its western windows overlook Gainsborough scenery in the Ebble Valley, its eastern gives on to downland. The garden is small, but cleverly laid out and large enough for us to plan and battle in. It is a frost pocket and the soil is chalk and stony and not too amenable. None of this mattered, for scenery, setting and friends outdid all. Forty-eight hours at the cottage were worth a week's holiday to me.

Throughout Sunday in Wiltshire I was in frequent touch with the Foreign Secretary, who was opening his conversations with M. Pineau and Mr. Murphy in London. In the evening I returned to London, for I had a statement to make in the House of Commons next day. After Questions on Monday, July 30th, I told the House of the financial measures we had put into effect to freeze the Egyptian sterling balances and safeguard the assets of the Canal Company. I announced that conversations had begun with M. Pineau and Mr. Murphy, and that we were in close touch with the Governments of the Commonwealth countries. Within the next few days, and before the House rose for the summer recess, I hoped to make a further statement. Should the House wish to debate the subject, I was agreeable, but we would need to consider the world-wide repercussions of anything that was said. Our position was clear and I defined it in these words:

No arrangements for the future of this great international waterway could be acceptable to Her Majesty's Government which would leave it in the unfettered control of a single power which could, as recent events have shown, exploit it purely for purposes of national policy.

This often quoted statement of our aims was acclaimed, no one in the House dissented. Our aims were not fulfilled.

★   ★   ★   ★   ★

Meanwhile, talks were continuing in London between the Foreign Secretary, M. Pineau and Mr. Murphy. They made slow progress. All agreed that the operation of the canal must be placed under international authority, but there were differences as to the best means to adopt. Our Ambassador in Washington had already reported to us that he had found the State Department cool and hesitant about taking urgent action. The Department gave the impression of wishing to stand aloof from the dispute with Egypt. Its officials were much concerned about the effects of any possible action on American public opinion, especially if there were an interruption in the passage of oil tankers through the canal. No doubt the impending American election also cast its shadow.

Mr. Murphy, on his arrival in London, soon made plain that his approach was a legal one. He wished to invoke the Convention of Constantinople, signed in 1888. This document guaranteed for all time the international character of the canal, irrespective of any particular concession from the rulers of Egypt to the Suez Canal Company. The Convention was an important element in our case, but it was by no means the whole story. Moreover, the Russians had signed it, but the United States had not. This was likely to land us in vexing problems if we were to base our action on the Convention alone. The Americans were not in favour of referring the problem to the United Nations at this stage, but they thought that a special agency of the United Nations should be entrusted with the control of the canal. We agreed that any canal authority which might be set up should work in association with the United Nations.

On August 1st Mr. Dulles arrived in London. He advanced much the same view as his assistants and advisers, but with new arguments.

He showed that he and his department had other grounds for their insistence upon taking action under the Constantinople Convention. If military measures became unavoidable, the President would need the authority of Congress for any American commitment. In the eyes of Dulles and Murphy it was therefore essential that the legal basis of our joint proceedings should be unimpeachable. I found it encouraging that the United States Government should be thinking in the context of military action at all.

There was another preoccupation in American minds which was gradually revealed as the talks progressed. It was a very proper one. The Americans were nervous about the Panama Canal. They were anxious to emphasize that the problem of Suez was of a totally different order from any dispute that might arise in connection with Panama. Suez was an international matter, as the Constantinople Convention went to prove. The Panama Canal, on the contrary, was a private affair, regulated by a treaty between the Governments of the United States and the Panamanian Republic only. According to this agreement, the zone through which the Panama Canal ran was leased in perpetuity to the United States. It was thus an American and not an international waterway. The United States Government were determined to keep it so. They wished to distinguish forthrightly between their privileged position on the isthmus of Panama and the international complexities of Suez.

No such hesitations disturbed the French. M. Pineau was a man of independent mind who could argue clearly, even vehemently, for his cause. He had had considerable ministerial experience and was apt to be impatient of diplomatic detail, which was no bad thing. We always found him a vigorous but loyal colleague, unwilling to dupe himself or others and stalwart in critical hours.

Pineau now declared that his Government were unanimous in desiring urgent and decisive action. The Suez Canal had been built by the French. Moreover, the repercussions of Nasser's action touched France closely in another and vital sphere. From the first, Pineau emphasized the effects that it would have in Algeria and upon the entire French position in North Africa. If Egypt were allowed to succeed in grabbing the canal, the Algerian nationalists would take fresh heart. They would also look to Egypt for backing, which they would certainly receive, both in arms and clamour. France could not permit this threat to develop. We agreed with M. Pineau's forecast and supported his views. He proved himself a true prophet. The Americans were less receptive, in part because their inveterate distrust of 'colonialism' left them basically out of sympathy with French problems in North Africa.

M. Pineau had another grievance. Nasser had described his action as retaliation for the refusal to finance the Aswan Dam. The United States had a responsibility for this decision and should not, Pineau felt, disinterest itself from the consequences. Murphy and Dulles both maintained that Nasser's action was not retaliatory and had long been in his mind. They did not convince Pineau.

The French attitude to the crisis was far nearer to ours than the American, though French interests in Asia and Africa differed in kind and in degree from ours. The French had a war on their hands in North Africa which was being inflamed, and to some extent supplied, by Cairo. They had opposed the Baghdad Pact, though M. Mollet had loyally refrained from criticizing it since his visit to me at Chequers earlier in the year, when we had done good work in aligning our policies.

While the United Kingdom had far-reaching treaty engagements with Jordan, France's relations with Israel were very close. There was national sympathy in France for a small country seeking to maintain itself in the face of a trade boycott and the hostility of larger neighbours. Our divergencies could be reconciled by diplomacy and events, but at this time they had not been.

At an early stage in their discussions, the three Foreign Secretaries agreed that the Arab-Israeli dispute should be treated as a separate matter from the future of the canal. Israel had suffered for five years from the Egyptian refusal to obey the United Nations resolution to give free passage through the canal. Her shipping had been unjustly barred from using it. The Security Council resolution of September 1st, 1951, was specific. It found that the Egyptian action was 'inconsistent with the objectives of a peaceful settlement between the parties and the establishment of a permanent peace in Palestine set forth in the armistice agreement.' Israel was also the frequent victim of Egyptian armed raids. Though this was all too true, to associate Israel's problems with those arising from the nationalization of the canal would, at this time, have tangled them to Nasser's advantage. If we were to get action, we had to keep the issues crisp.

Mr. Dulles brought with him a message from the President, who was emphatic upon the importance of negotiation. The President did not rule out the use of force. He recognized the transcendent worth of the canal to the free world and the possibility that the eventual use of force might become necessary in order to protect international rights. But he felt that every possibility of peaceful settlement must be exhausted before this was done.

At his first meeting with the other Foreign Secretaries on August 1st, Mr. Dulles summed up his views as follows:

> (1) It was intolerable that the canal should be under the domination of any single country without any international control;
>
> (2) We should use the 1888 Convention as a basis for discussion in order to avoid complications with the Panama Canal;
>
> (3) Force was the last method to be tried, but the United States did not exclude the use of force if all other methods failed;
>
> (4) We should mobilize world opinion in favour of international operation of the canal;
>
> (5) We should attempt to get our tripartite views accepted by at least a two-thirds majority of the conference that was to be called.

In further discussion at this meeting on the 1st, Mr. Dulles said:

> A way had to be found to make Nasser disgorge what he was attempting to swallow. . . . We must make a genuine effort to bring world opinion to favour the international operation of the canal. . . . It should be possible to create a world opinion so adverse to Nasser that he would be isolated. Then if a military operation had to be undertaken it would be more apt to succeed and have less grave repercussions than if it had been undertaken precipitately.

Dulles had several conversations with the Foreign Secretary, and one at Downing Street with both of us, in addition to the three-power meetings. We were encouraged by his statements. He agreed emphatically that the seizure of a great international waterway was intolerable. This was still more so when the single nation that set out to dominate the canal was Egypt. Nasser must be made, as Mr. Dulles put it to me, 'to disgorge'. These were forthright words. They rang in my ears for months.

I did not wish to conceal anything from Mr. Dulles and I told him that the United States Naval Attaché had been asking for information about our military preparations. I said that we were quite ready to give this, but that I wanted first to make sure that the United States Government really wished to have it. Mr. Dulles replied that the United States Government perfectly well understood the purpose of our preparations and he thought that they had had a good effect. It was preferable that the United States Government should not seek detailed information.

I felt a great sense of relief that evening. Every allowance had to be made for a different approach between us and the Americans, and for a differing sense of urgency. But if Nasser had in the end 'to disgorge', the result would be plain for all to see. Theft would not have paid off, a breach of agreement would not have been endured, a wholesome lesson would have been taught in respect for the sanctity of agreements. The United States, we were told by Mr. Dulles, did not exclude the use of force if all other methods failed, but there must be genuine efforts first to reach a settlement by negotiation. Mr. Eisenhower believed that our countries could marshal world opinion in support of a conciliatory but firm position, and that an international conference of canal users would have, at the least, a profound educational effect throughout the world. Such was also my hope. But I did not wish to lose momentum, or to allow discussions to drag on from conference to conference.

The three Governments were now committed to summon an international conference. Britain and France would have preferred it to meet as soon as possible; Dulles favoured several weeks of preparation. In the end we compromised and August 16th was the date fixed. We also compromised on membership. We accepted the American request that invitations should be sent to the eight signatories of the Constantinople Convention, Russia included. The Americans agreed that invitations should likewise be sent to the sixteen principal users of the canal, selected in terms of tonnage and trade. These twenty-four countries were listed in the statement issued at the close of the consultations on the evening of August 2nd.

One further difficult question aroused much discussion at these three-power meetings. It concerned the payment of canal dues in the weeks ahead. Most British shipowners paid their dues into the account of the Suez Canal Company in London; the French paid in Paris. A number of other countries, including the United States, were in the habit of paying in Egypt. Normally 55 per cent. of the dues were annually collected in London, 35 per cent. in Egypt and 10 per cent. in Paris. We wished British shipowners to continue to pay the legitimate Canal Company in London until such time as a new international authority was established. If the new Egyptian authority attempted to exact payments, we might have to instruct British shipowners to re-route their ships by the Cape. The French and ourselves intended that as little money as possible from ships passing through the canal should find its way into Egyptian hands. On this we found it hard to secure American co-operation. Mr. Dulles could not say how the United States ship-owners would react to any advice given them. Moreover, the American Government had no power to give instructions to the numerous American-owned ships, registered in Panama, Liberia and elsewhere, and flying the flags of those countries. Our talks on this point were inconclusive and the problems of dues remained to perplex us for many a long day and night.

★   ★   ★   ★   ★

Some agreement was won at these London talks. A positive statement containing precise proposals was issued on behalf of the three powers. This first defined the deed:

> The present action involves far more than a simple act of nationalization. It involves the arbitrary and unilateral seizure by one nation of an international agency which has the responsibility to maintain and to operate the Suez Canal so that all the signatories to, and beneficiaries of, the treaty of 1888 can effectively enjoy the use of an international waterway upon which the economy, commerce, and security of much of the world depends.

The Convention of 1888 had guaranteed these benefits 'for all the world . . . and for all time'. The statement recalled that as recently as October 1954 Egypt had renewed her undertakings to uphold the Convention. 'The action taken by the Egyptian Government', the three powers declared, 'threatens the freedom and security of the canal.' This made it necessary that the signatories to the Convention, and all other nations entitled to enjoy its benefits, should take steps to safeguard their rights. In consequence, 'operating arrangements under an international system' should be restored. Respect would be shown for legitimate Egyptian interests. Finally, the three powers formally convened a conference of the twenty-four nations principally concerned with the use of the canal.

In the event, all except Egypt and Greece accepted our invitations and attended. Three days later the proposals of the three powers on the purposes and functions of an international authority were despatched for the invited nations to consider.

Some hours before the statement of August 2nd was issued I opened a debate on the Suez Canal in the House of Commons. I was not yet able to quote the three-power statement, which was still being drafted. But I emphasized once more:

> . . . the freedom and security of transit through the canal can only be effectively secured by an international authority. It is upon this that we must insist. It is upon this we are working in negotiation at this moment with other powers deeply concerned.

I outlined the history of the Constantinople Convention, and also of the concessionary agreements between Egypt and the Canal Company. The agreements had been last endorsed by Nasser's Government only six weeks before. 'These undertakings', I said, 'are now torn up, and one can have no confidence in the word of a man who does that.' The Leader of the Opposition and the large majority of speakers in the debate on both sides of the House were at that time in general agreement. The House did not seem to be divided on party lines. Mr. Herbert Morrison, a former Foreign Secretary, wished us luck in solving this problem. He said: 'I ask the Government not to be too nervous, because if they are too nervous we shall begin to evolve a situation in which countries can set themselves up against international practice, international morals and international interests, and, in that case, we are not helping the peace of the world.' Other Opposition speakers echoed this theme with variations of their own. Mr. Gaitskell said of Nasser's attitude: 'It is all very familiar. It is exactly the same that we encountered from Mussolini and Hitler in those years before the war.' He added, 'I believe we were right to react sharply to this move.'

To one Socialist peer who was listening, these comments seemed more warlike than mine. Lord Stansgate, who observed the events of that day from the Gallery of our House, reported on them as follows to his own House an hour or two later: 'I went to another place this morning and I can correctly and sincerely say that I found much more reason, common sense and conviction in the Prime Minister's speech than there was in the rather heady wine which was produced by my own Front Bench.'

During my speech I announced the precautionary measures we were taking to strengthen our position in the eastern Mediterranean. These included the movement from Britain of a number of Navy, Army and Air Force units, and the calling up of about twenty thousand Army reservists. The concentration had its effect upon Colonel Nasser. He did not interfere with our ships, nor try to compel them to pay to his nationalized authority. He recognized what the consequences would be if he attempted to do so. The memory of the massacres in Cairo in 1952 was also fresh in my mind. Such a tragedy might recur, and there were some 13,000 British subjects still in Egypt. We had to be able to protect them.

At this period there was a general conviction throughout the country that Nasser must not be allowed to get away with his theft and that we would be fully justified in taking forcible steps to prevent him. *The Times* on August 1st, the day before the Parliamentary debate just described, contained a leading article whose opening paragraphs deserve quotation:

When the Commons take up Suez tomorrow there is one thing they can be sure of. It must be their guiding thought. If Nasser is allowed to get away with his *coup* all the British and other Western interests in the Middle East will crumble. The modern world has suffered many acts, like Hitler's march into the Rhineland or the Stalinist overthrow of freedom in Czechoslovakia, which were claimed to be assertions of domestic sovereignty. They were, in fact, hinges of history. Nasser's seizure of the Canal Company is another such turning point. Quibbling over whether or not he was 'legally entitled' to make the grab will delight the finicky and comfort the fainthearted, but entirely misses the real issues.

The first is quite simple. Freedom of passage through the Suez Canal, in peace or war, is a prime Western interest. That freedom can be assured only if the canal is in friendly and trustworthy hands. Nasser's grab and his accompanying speeches give final proof that he is both unfriendly and untrustworthy. The second issue is no less obvious. The great oil works and fields of the Middle East are one of the main foundations of Britain's and Western Europe's industry and security. Anyone who thinks that a victory for Nasser would not encourage other extremist demands against the oilfields—and against strategic bases—should confine himself to tiddleywinks or blind man's buff. The third issue is wider still. There can be no stability and confidence in the world so long as agreements can be scrapped with impunity.

II

EIGHTEEN POWERS
August 2nd – August 23rd

Nasser's abusive speech – Arab nationalism – The Russian attitude to the conference – Views of Mr. Nehru – Problem of the reservists – National unity and the Left – Firmer attitude in Washington – My broadcast – Mr. Menzies – The conference meets – Decision in favour of international control – Indian Government dissents – Mr. Menzies agrees to help

A fortnight went by before the conference of twenty-two powers opened in London. This period was filled with diplomatic activity and with the mounting of our military precautions. Reactions at home and abroad were generally favourable to the idea and purpose of the conference, except in one quarter. Egypt took up a rigid position, after consultation with the Russians. The contacts between the two countries were close. We learnt from Colonel Nasser that Russia proposed to attend the London Conference, some time before our Ambassador in Moscow was so informed.

The Egyptian Government called the London Conference imperialistic. International authority was the same thing as colonialism, they said. Such perversion of the ordinary terms of language is common to dictatorships and in this, as in other matters, Nasser was following the example of his European predecessors. At the same time the Egyptians professed their belief in freedom and mutual respect. What they meant by 'mutual respect' we soon found out. Their Foreign Minister informed the United States Ambassador that if their plans and actions were not accepted by the rest of the world, there would be 'great disturbance' throughout Africa and the Middle East.

A few days before the conference was due to start, Nasser made a speech of the abusive kind to which we were by now accustomed. He accused the free world of 'imperialism and the bloodsucking of peoples'. The proposed internationalization of the canal he described as a 'conspiracy'. He went on once more to invoke the Arab world against the West: 'One day after the nationalization of the Suez Canal, voices in the Arab world began to say: "This is not called the Suez Canal, it is called the Arabs' Canal." Arab nationalism began to appear in its full shape and in its best form. Support for Egypt began to pour in from the kings and leaders of the Arabs.' This was not fact, but wishful thinking. According to our information, the Governments of several Arab States were alarmed that Nasser might be allowed to get away with his pillage. If a sharp check were not administered to him now, his wishful thoughts might largely be fulfilled, at the expense of the independence of Middle Eastern and African peoples.

A Nigerian Chief of the Muslim faith was at this time passing through Cairo, where an attempt was made to persuade him to sign a paper for publication endorsing Nasser's seizure of the canal. To the Chief's credit, he not only refused, he tore the paper up. What would his attitude be if Nasser were allowed by the world to seize his spoil and keep it? The policy of plunder would have been seen to pay off.

In Moscow, meanwhile, Mr. Shepilov, the Foreign Minister, had some conversations with our Ambassador. I was fairly satisfied with these. The Soviet Government recognized our special interests in the Middle East. Marshal Bulganin and Mr. Khrushchev had evidently recalled our conversations at Downing Street earlier in the year. The Russians may also have remembered that not many years before, during negotiations over the passage from the Black Sea to the Ægean, they had demanded international control of Suez. They did not oppose the holding of a conference, but they raised some demur about its composition, its place and its timing. The Russians wanted to delay it until the end of August, they would prefer it to be held in Cairo and they wished us to invite some twenty further countries, many of them in the Soviet orbit and others under Nasser's influence. As I had expected, they did not fail to point out that the United States had not signed the Convention of 1888 and ought not to be one of the inviting powers. They expressed concern at our military precautions, though not in terms suggesting that they were unduly worried. Having registered all these points, they accepted our invitation.

It was clear to us that they would attend the conference as watchdogs for Nasser, making use of any opportunity which might arise to widen divergences among the powers.

When Egypt first seized the canal, the Indian Government showed some embarrassment, no doubt accentuated by the fact that Mr. Nehru had been the guest of Colonel Nasser in Cairo only a few days before. With the passage of time the Indians embarked actively upon a policy which, they assured us, was an attempt to reach a compromise between two points of view. In effect, their policy really meant that Nasser must be appeased. Their representatives in Cairo, and the aviatory Mr. Krishna Menon, kept in constant touch with the Egyptian Government and freely offered advice to Her Majesty's Government. The Indians did not believe in setting up an international authority with more than advisory powers. This would have been entirely ineffective in giving any kind of guarantee to the users of the canal.

★   ★   ★   ★   ★

On August 8th, I broadcast to the country:

The alternatives are now clear to see. If we all join together to create an international system for the canal and spend its revenues as they should be spent, to develop it rapidly, that can bring growing prosperity to East and West alike, the countries that produce the oil and the countries which buy it. There will then be wealth for all to share, including Egypt. There is no question of denying her a fair deal, or a just return. But if anyone is going to snatch and grab and try to pocket what really belongs to the world, the result will be impoverishment for all, and a refusal by some countries at least to lead their life at such a hazard. Meanwhile, we have too much at risk not to take precautions. We have done so. That is the meaning of the movements by land, sea and air of which you have heard in the last few days.

We do not seek a solution by force, but by the broadest possible international agreement. That is why we have called the conference. We shall do all we can to help its work, but this I must make plain. We cannot agree that an act of plunder which threatens the livelihood of many nations shall be allowed to succeed. And we must make sure that the life of the great trading nations of the world cannot, in the future, be strangled at any moment by some interruption to the free passage of the canal.

Meanwhile, public opinion in our own country held steadier than appeared from press reports. Left-wing and doubtful-minded journals saw in the possible use of force a handy stick with which to beat the Government. From early August onwards they did not hesitate to employ it. Left-wing Governments, if they are firm in the discharge of their responsibilities in international affairs, can always count on national support. Right-wing Governments cannot always do so. It was perhaps fortunate that it was a Labour Government which had to expose Soviet behaviour after the war and break the blockade of Berlin by the airlift.

One of our difficulties was the problem of the reservists. These men were indispensable if our forces were to be immediately ready for use. They were, most of them, taken from important work in civil life. The service which they had to be ready to give was often tedious and entailed much waiting about, as is always the lot of those who serve in the armed forces. Most of the reservists bore up cheerfully and without complaint. A few became restive and some newspapers made use of this to fan every incident and exaggerate every discontent.

On August 13th the Opposition Shadow Cabinet issued a statement. The retreat then began amid a clatter of excuses. The most contradictory of these maintained that forcible action was certainly justified if it had the sanction of the United Nations. From the first the Soviet Government made it plain that it would give diplomatic support to the Egyptians. This meant that Moscow would run no risks, but would take every political pot-shot from behind cover. The use of the veto in the Security Council was the easiest of these, for it was an exercise which never gave the Kremlin the slightest embarrassment. Apparently the Soviet veto was at Nasser's disposal, as in fact it proved to be when the eighteen-power proposals came before the Security Council two months later. Nor would any initiative in the General Assembly meet with success in the face of Afro-Asian extremists supported by the Soviets. Therefore the condition of United Nations approval for the use of force by Britain and France was equivalent to denying its use.

Not all those who advocated forcible action, subject to this limitation, understood what they were saying to Nasser, but some did. Those who did would more fairly have expressed their attitude by declaring 'forcible action will not be possible, because it cannot be employed without the sanction of the United Nations and in view of the Soviet use of the veto that sanction cannot be expected'. This would have been an honest attitude, the implications of which ought to be considered, for it inhibits action by the free nations while permitting the use of force to the communist powers, who accept no limitations by the United Nations on their actions, as the treatment of Hungary showed.

It is pardonable not to see the danger. It is excusable to see it and declare it and do nothing effective about it on moral grounds. It is unpardonable to see it and make a pretence of meeting it by methods one knows in one's heart to be totally ineffective.

Despite all this, in August 1956 the nation understood the issues at stake and the instability of opinion was very much less than it was pictured to be. But there can be no question that what was believed to be the deep division in the country created difficulties for our diplomacy almost from the start. Doubt about British national unity had its repercussions in the United States. It was constantly quoted to us by American negotiators and helped to weaken American resolution.

Following my usual custom, I maintained my hopes of American support, and had written to Mr. Eisenhower on August 5th after the three-power talks, expressing the belief that we could now 'display to Nasser and to the world a united front between our two countries and the French.' I added that 'we must prepare to meet the eventuality that Nasser would refuse to accept the outcome of the conference.' The President let me know that he had a great deal of sympathy with our line of thought. Our Ambassador in Washington, Sir Roger Makins, assured us at this time that the Administration completely accepted the impossibility of leaving the control of the Suez Canal in the hands of a man like Nasser. Though they would strain every nerve to bring about a settlement by negotiation, they realized that in the last resort force might have to be used and they understood the necessity for the military precautions which we and the French were taking. The Ambassador thought that there would be a deep division of opinion in the United States on the use of force and that the political problems which it would raise in an election year would be appalling. Nasser could hardly have chosen a better time for his action in terms of American domestic politics. Even so, the Ambassador reported, the President and Mr. Dulles were showing firmness, and the attitude of the Administration was becoming more robust. There was talk in Washington of calling a special session of Congress in order to give the President emergency powers. The State Department was working out the details of a proposal for an international authority. Consultations were going forward on oil supplies, should passage through the canal be stopped.

Our relations with the French throughout this period were very good. The task of co-ordinating our policy and our precautions went forward steadily day by day. At the same time, we sought to reach agreement with them over a variety of problems in the Middle East, where there had been some sharp differences in our outlook since 1918.

★　★　★　★　★

In the days before the London Conference met, Mr. Menzies, the Prime Minister of Australia, joined us. When the Suez crisis began, he had been in the United States and was about to pay a visit to Japan and the Far East. The gravity of events was not lost upon him and he cancelled his tour. When he told me of his decision, I at once invited him to join us in London and take part in our councils. He generously consented to do so. We could not have had a wiser or more forthright colleague.

I had first met Bob Menzies in 1935 when he was Attorney-General and I came to know him well in the dark days of 1941, perhaps the worst period of the second world war. I had come back from the Middle East, where I had taken a prominent part in difficult decisions about the Greek campaign. Events have since proved that our decisions were right, but at the time they were much criticized. Since Australia made a generous contribution to the military operation, it was inevitable that some of the blame should fall, albeit unjustly, upon Mr. Menzies, who was the Commonwealth Prime Minister. He was himself in London during part of the time when the decisions were taken. I admired his courage then for endorsing what he believed to be right. He stood by it, even when he was involved in some obloquy at home, and lost a general election.

I remember that when I arrived back in London from Cairo and attended my first Cabinet, I found Menzies sitting next to me. He passed a note, 'This is the strangest Cabinet I ever sat in. Since you have been away I have only heard one voice. Do none of them ever speak up?' I explained to him afterwards how the technique worked. The War Cabinet did not wish to be immersed in the details of military operations. Whatever the Prime Minister had to say on these topics, which sometimes filled the greater part of our discussions, was not usually commented upon then, because it was the Defence Committee which handled those affairs.

Later I had been Menzies' guest in Australia when he was Leader of the Opposition and I was also out of office. Our friendship had grown through the years and I felt a deep affection both for him and his charming family. Menzies shows his legal training in the lucidity of his mind and a penetrating intelligence. His statesmanship is something more. He has an instinct for great affairs and he cannot tolerate humbug.

When Menzies came to London at this critical time, I gained an immense reinforcement from his knowledge and experience. 'It is lonely at the top', as Stanley Baldwin used to say. There are political colleagues with whom one has been through the toughest experiences. This was true of Lord Salisbury, and also of Oliver Lyttelton, who was a member of the War Cabinet and the Defence Committee for long periods during my service there. It was true more especially of my relations with Sir Winston Churchill. Now, at this sharp testing time for myself, it was good to be able to sit down and assess the problems with Mr. Menzies. We had been through this kind of thing together before.

At this period I had a strange interlude with the British Broadcasting Corporation. In conversation with Menzies, a day or two after his arrival, I asked him if he would comment publicly on the situation, preferably in a television broadcast. He replied that he would do anything he could to help. I said I had no doubt that this would be very welcome and passed on the information to the B.B.C. A little while later I learnt, almost by accident, that Mr. Menzies had not been asked to speak. I made inquiry why this was so. I was told that as I had already appeared and, I think, some other speaker who shared my point of view, it was felt that if Mr. Menzies were to be asked to speak, someone who clearly disagreed, Mr. Emrys Hughes was the name mentioned, should be put on the air to balance the presentation of views. I thought that this attitude was insulting to a Commonwealth Prime Minister, whatever his politics, and Mr. Menzies was invited to speak on television, which he did admirably.

During these weeks I took one night off, our wedding anniversary. On that evening my wife and I went to see *Romanoff and Juliet* and enjoyed its wit. When we returned to Downing Street, we found a group of students of varied nationalities vociferating in the wake of two Members of Parliament. Their boos drowned the cheers of supporters, and we ate our supper to a noise like a palace revolution. Strange wedding bells, but it seemed a fitting epilogue to our play.

★   ★   ★   ★   ★

A week before the London Conference was due to begin, most of the powers had accepted our invitations. I wanted two results from the conference. First, that it should reach agreement by a large majority on the international control of the canal. Secondly, that it should decide upon the steps to take to effect this. I wished to secure a declaration from the conference that, if Egypt rejected its recommendations for international control, the powers using the canal would refuse to pay their transit dues to the Egyptian company. A firm sanction would then be at our command. At present, Nasser was still getting about 35 per cent. of the dues, most of this from American sources. I wanted the nations to proclaim their intention of paying their dues into a blocked account, to be held, perhaps by the World Bank, until an international authority was in operation.

We realized that some delegates at the conference might press for the early reference of the issue to the United Nations. I could sympathize with this line of thought, but I knew that it was not well-founded, having taken a leading part myself in working out the terms of the United Nations Charter at San Francisco. This was a type of emergency which had been allowed for at the time. Article 33 of the Charter did not demand that every international dispute should be taken to the Security Council or the General Assembly. It stated:

> The parties to any dispute, the continuance of which is likely to endanger the maintenance of international peace and security, shall, first of all, seek a solution by negotiation, inquiry, mediation, conciliation, arbitration, judicial settlement, resort to regional agencies or arrangements, or other peaceful means of their own choice.

Setting up a regional agency was exactly the purpose of the conference. A link between it and the United Nations could be worked out later.

★　　★　　★　　★　　★

The conference held its first session on August 16th at Lancaster House, attracting considerable attention from the holiday crowds always in London during that month. After I had briefly opened the proceedings with a warning that all had a common interest in the sanctity of agreements, the Foreign Secretary took the chair. The Americans were at first doubtful whether he, or any representative of the three powers, should do so. They found the majority of delegates content that the host country should preside.

Mr. Selwyn Lloyd handled the proceedings of the London Conference with skill and despatch. He also had a number of private conversations with the Foreign Secretaries of all the powers and their advisers. In the course of these, we were quickly assured of the support of at least two-thirds of the members of the conference, Australia and New Zealand being wholly with us. The maritime powers of Europe, with some reserve on the part of Spain, were all in favour of re-asserting international control over the canal. The powers of the Baghdad Pact who were present, Iran, Pakistan and Turkey, thought the same. They held that we must bring Nasser to accept the rule of law. If we failed to do so, we should pile up fresh difficulties for the future. They thought it possible that, for political ends, Colonel Nasser would interfere with their trade and shipping.

There was general alarm at the Egyptian threat to freedom of navigation. Portugal, for instance, was perturbed about her communications with Goa. The Netherlands feared for their East Indian commerce. The Dutch were particularly indignant that only the Indonesians had been sent a special message by the United States, urging them to attend the conference. Their leaders had recently received a public blessing from Mr. Dulles in Djakarta, yet only a while before, Indonesia had repudiated her debts to the Netherlands. The Dutch had forebodings that, encouraged by Nasser's action, Indonesia would next confiscate the assets of Dutch companies.

So it proved. A year later Indonesia made a brazen attempt to blackmail the Netherlands into abandoning its sovereignty over New Guinea. They seized shipping plying between the islands. They confiscated Dutch properties wholesale and compelled thousands of Netherlands citizens, who had never known any other home, to flee as refugees. No compensation of any kind was paid to these companies or to those who worked for them; no action was taken by the United Nations. After all, the Netherlands was only a colonial power. Cynically, the Indonesian Government remarked that compensation would only be paid when the Netherlands had abandoned Western New Guinea. So the pattern of pillage spread.

At the conference some of the powers, and particularly those of the Baghdad Pact, wished to emphasize Egyptian sovereignty over the canal, at the same time asserting the need for international control. They had national problems of their own in mind, which we understood. The question of sovereignty, we told them, was not a matter of absolutes. The British Government had sovereign rights in Uganda, at the headwaters of the Nile. We should not think our sovereignty infringed if, to reassure Egypt and the Sudan, we waived our right to divert the waters of the river. It was no inroad on Egyptian sovereignty to ask for international control of passage through the canal in exchange for a fair financial return. At the conference we were able to meet the Pakistani, Iranian and Turkish point of view by accepting their amendments.

By August 22nd the business of the conference was all but formally completed. Mr. Dulles had opened the proceedings in a speech presenting the three-power conclusions. These were later embodied in a draft declaration which asserted the principle of international control, recognized the sovereign rights of Egypt, guaranteed her a fair return for the use of the canal, and proposed the negotiation of a new convention. Under the new convention the operation of the canal would be entrusted to a board:

> The members of the board, in addition to Egypt, would be other states chosen in a manner to be agreed upon from among the states parties to the convention with due regard to use, pattern of trade and geographical distribution; the composition of the board to be such as to assure that its responsibilities would be discharged solely with a view to achieving the best possible operating results without political motivation in favour of, or in prejudice against, any user of the canal.

Provisions were to be laid down in the convention for the arbitration of disputes, for sanctions in case of violation and for some form of association with the United Nations. This declaration was perfectly satisfactory to us and it was reassuring that the Americans presented it. If its terms had been maintained, all would have been well.

Eighteen nations* subscribed to this declaration, though Spain made a minor reservation. India, Soviet Russia, Indonesia and Ceylon supported a proposal for a purely advisory international board which would enjoy no powers of control. We were sorry that India was out of step with the majority of the conference, which represented more than 95 per cent. of the tonnage passing through the canal. In an attempt to persuade the Indian delegation to come nearer to us, we asked them whether they could endorse the principles upon which eighteen of the powers had agreed, even though they reserved their position as to the methods to give effect to them. This they felt unable to do.

Meanwhile, Her Majesty's Government had decided upon the action

* The eighteen nations were: Australia, Denmark, Ethiopia, France, Federal Germany, Iran, Italy, Japan, the Netherlands, New Zealand, Norway, Pakistan, Portugal, Spain, Sweden, Turkey, United Kingdom, United States.

which must follow. The declaration of the conference should be put before the Egyptian Government by a small committee. If Colonel Nasser accepted it as a basis, negotiations would follow. If not, we must reserve our position. My desire was to send a small, strong, and highly representative committee to Cairo, determined to reach a quick conclusion. At my appeal and that of the conference, Mr. Menzies undertook the leadership. He did so despite political inconvenience at home, the Australian Parliament being due to debate the Budget on August 30th. I telegraphed to Sir Arthur Fadden, the Deputy Prime Minister in Canberra, to say:

> The Commonwealth of Australia will be rendering a signal service to the solution of this vexed problem if you and your colleagues can spare your Prime Minister for a few more days to give his personal help. . . . The experience and counsel brought to our proceedings by Mr. Menzies during these anxious days has proved quite invaluable.

Sir Arthur agreed to our request.

On August 23rd the Declaration of the London Conference was published. Mr. Menzies was appointed by the eighteen powers to convey their proposals to the Egyptian Government accompanied by the representatives of Ethiopia, Iran, Sweden and the United States. The first three countries were represented by their Foreign Secretaries, and the United States by Mr. Loy Henderson, in whom we had confidence, although we were sorry that Mr. Dulles could not attend himself. Thus the five continents were associated in this new mission.

A few days later I telegraphed to the President:

> This is a message to thank you for all the help Foster has given. Though I could not be at the conference myself, I heard praise on all sides for the outstanding quality of his speeches and his constructive leadership. He will tell you how things have gone. It was, I think, a remarkable achievement to unite eighteen nations on an agreed statement of this clarity and force.
>
> Before he left, Foster spoke to me of the destructive efforts of the Russians at the conference. I have been giving some thought to this and I would like to give you my conclusions.
>
> I have no doubt that the Bear is using Nasser, with or without his knowledge, to further his immediate aims. These are, I think, first to dislodge the West from the Middle East, and second to get a foothold in Africa so as to dominate that continent in turn. In

this connection I have seen a reliable report from someone who was present at the lunch which Shepilov gave for the Arab Ambassadors. There the Soviet claim was that they 'only wanted to see Arab unity in Asia and Africa and the abolition of all foreign bases and exploitation. An agreed unified Arab nation must take its rightful place in the world.'

This policy is clearly aimed at Wheelus Field and Habbaniya as well as at our Middle East oil supplies. Meanwhile the communist bloc continue their economic and political blandishments towards the African countries which are already independent. Soon they will have a wider field for subversion as our colonies, particularly in the West, achieve self-government. All this makes me more than ever sure that Nasser must not be allowed to get away with it this time. We have many friends in the Middle East and in Africa and others who are shrewd enough to know where the plans of a Nasser or a Musaddiq would lead them. But they will not be strong enough to stand against the power of the mobs if Nasser wins again. The firmer the front we show together, the greater the chance that Nasser will give way without the need for any resort to force. That is why we were grateful for your policy and Foster's expression of it at the conference. It is also one of the reasons why we have to continue our military preparations in conjunction with our French allies.

We have been examining what other action could be taken if Nasser refuses to negotiate on the basis of the London Conference. There is the question of the dues. The Dutch and the Germans have already indicated that they will give support in this respect. The Dutch may even be taking action in the next few days. Then there is the question of currency and economic action. We are studying these with your people and the French in London and will be sending our comments soon. It looks as though we shall have a few days until Nasser gives Menzies his final reply. After that we should be in a position to act swiftly. Selwyn Lloyd is telegraphing to Foster about tactics, particularly in relation to United Nations.

Meanwhile I thought I should set out some of our reflections on the dangerous situation which still confronts us. It is certainly the most hazardous that our country has known since 1940.

I was so glad to see such excellent photographic testimony of your growing health and abounding energy. That is the very best news for us all.

III

THE MENZIES MISSION
August 23rd – September 9th

*Meeting with Nasser fixed – Question of Security Council –
Economic pressure – Oil supplies – Problem of using force – We
resolve to appeal to U.N., if Menzies Mission fails – Issue raised
with N.A.T.O. – M. Spaak's warning – Our draft resolution
for Security Council – 'Ganging-up' – Mr. Dulles proposes
Users' Club – My letter to Mr. Eisenhower – The Canal
Company's staff – Failure of the Mission – Mr. Menzies' letter*

Mr. Menzies' committee spent some time in London preparing their case and arranging their meeting with Colonel Nasser. Every consideration was shown for Egyptian convenience. A meeting was eventually fixed for September 3rd in Cairo, and the interchanges there lasted six days. Little more than a fortnight passed between the declaration of the eighteen powers and the completion of Mr. Menzies' mission, but it was a critical fortnight in the development of the Suez crisis.

The United Kingdom Government had to determine what action to take if Nasser turned down the proposals of the eighteen powers. The United States was not in agreement with France and ourselves on the nature of this action and its timing. We wished to refer the issue to the Security Council, if Nasser declared his unwillingness to negotiate. We also desired as many powers as possible to exert financial and economic pressure upon Egypt. The United States discouraged us in both these initiatives.

While Mr. Dulles was still in London we had again urged upon him the importance of denying the canal dues to Nasser. Each year some 55 per cent. of the dues were paid by British and French ships, and these were already being withheld from Egypt. American-owned ships were the third largest payers. After them came the ships of Italy, the Netherlands and Norway. The Dutch, Norwegians and Germans were willing to take steps in line with our policy. Mr. Dulles was not forthcoming. He sidestepped the point by telling us much that we already knew about the disadvantages of sailing round the Cape and the undesirability of petrol rationing.

On dues, the United States Government never agreed to effective action. This made it impossible to put pressure upon Nasser by a means which was ready to hand, depriving him of the revenue of the canal he had seized, until a new settlement was made.

The United States Government were not helpful about other forms of financial restraint. The French and ourselves had blocked all Egyptian sterling and franc accounts a month before. The United States had merely frozen the dollar balances of the Egyptian Government and the National Bank of Egypt, as they stood on July 31st. New receipts in these accounts were not affected, nor were privately owned dollar accounts. This meant that maximum pressure was not being exerted on Egyptian finance and commerce.

Our policy was to persuade as many powers as we could, and especially the United States, to take the same action as we had done. A number of them were already in line. Dulles, however, felt that he had first to pave the way with the American public for any further steps. In the event, no paving was ever done. On his return to Washington, Dulles spoke to our Ambassador of keeping a number of alternatives in view. In principle, he was in favour of economic measures, but all he could promise was that the United States Government should prepare to take them. In fact, they never took them.

While the United States was in a hesitant mood, we had to face the dilemma of our oil supplies. All would be well if the Americans continued to uphold the declaration which Menzies was taking to Cairo, and played their part in getting it accepted by Egypt, but time was not on our side. To allow discussions to drag on was more likely to diminish than increase the chances of a satisfactory settlement. Her Majesty's Government accepted that every diplomatic method must be employed and exhausted, and shown to be exhausted, before resorting to military action. We were agreed that we should put our case to the United Nations. The Security Council had to be given a full and genuine opportunity to debate the situation. On the other hand, means had to be found to prevent the endless circumlocution and eventual disregard which usually befell resolutions coming before the Council.

There was always a danger that the passage of time and the multiplication of talk would weaken the resolve of the eighteen powers. The risk of letting Nasser keep his prize might in the end be greater than the risk of using force. The question was, how long we could pursue diplomatic methods and economic sanctions, which very likely would not succeed, before the possibility of military action slipped from our grasp. Winter was approaching, when action would be more difficult and other plans would be called for. On August 28th French forces took up their stations in Cyprus. In a few weeks we should be poised to strike, if we had to strike. It would be very costly to keep up this position indefinitely.

During these days in late August, the Government discussed the wisdom of taking the issue to the United Nations. There was no binding obligation to do so at this stage, for the Charter of the United Nations itself allows latitude. The threat to peace in 1948 at Berlin was not referred to the United Nations until some months after the Russian blockade and the answering airlift began. Nothing happened then but talk.

There were risks in going to the United Nations. All kinds of suggestions might be put forward at the Security Council for solving our differences with Egypt which would only prolong them. The State Department had so far shown itself against any such step on our part. One of Mr. Dulles' advisers described the Security Council to us as a quicksand. Once in it, one did not know how deep it would prove, or whether one would ever get out. Pineau had remarked that the power possessed by the United Nations was one of 'suspensive action'. All this was true but, as signatories to the Charter, we had undertaken not to resort to military action without first going to the United Nations. We were pledged and we intended to keep our word. The questions before us were when and in what form we should do so.

We thought that advantage lay in an early appeal. It was important to take the initiative before Egypt or any other power did so. Our concentration of forces in the Mediterranean might be used as a pretext against us. On the other hand, it would be unwise to go to the Security Council before Mr. Menzies' committee had elicited a reply from Nasser. We must not weaken the committee's position by giving the impression that the ground was being cut from under its feet, or that we expected its proposals to be rejected by the Egyptian Government. Nor should we give Nasser the pretext to withhold his answer until the Security Council had considered the matter. There was still a chance that the Egyptians might accept outright, or at least with qualifications which would not rule out further negotiations.

The Government decided on August 28th to go to the United Nations, only after we had heard from Mr. Menzies. This in turn had its parliamentary consequences. I wished to summon Parliament from the summer recess at the earliest possible moment, but it was desirable to give Members something concrete to debate. Parliament is not at its best when asked to discuss general situations; it is wiser, if possible, to give solid fare. We agreed, after consulting Mr. Menzies while he was in Cairo, that Parliament should be called together immediately after his return. The report of his committee would then be available for debate.

The form of our appeal to the Security Council was our next problem. A possible course was to introduce a resolution seeking support for the principles of the eighteen-power declaration and inviting Egypt to accept them. France and Australia, as members of the Council, would certainly join with us in this. The United States could hardly do otherwise in view of its leading part in drafting and sponsoring the declaration. A resolution would in all likelihood evoke a Russian veto, but we hoped it would be possible to show that a large majority in the Security Council endorsed the London proposals. There were other risks besides the Russian veto. During the Council's debates some amendments might be moved by one of the less friendly powers, in an attempt to shackle our freedom of action. If we had the firm co-operation of the United States, such amendments would probably fail to pass. These were the Government's conclusions and the Foreign Secretary was authorized, on August 28th, to convey them to Mr. Dulles and enlist his aid.

At the same time I wanted to give the countries of free Europe a chance to consider together the situation which faced us all. It was these countries which had most to lose if the Egyptian Government were not checked. It was they who would become dependent for the security of their oil supplies upon the decisions of one man. I suggested that we should raise the matter at N.A.T.O. This would accord with the broader political character which we wished that organization to assume. It was decided that the Foreign Secretary should deliver a report to the council of N.A.T.O. on the discussions at the London Conference.

This he did on September 5th. He found a vigorous ally in the

Netherlands Foreign Minister, M. Luns, who urged that the North Atlantic powers should refuse to recognize the seizure of the canal, withhold dues from the new authority and join in a reference to the Security Council. The Canadian Foreign Minister, Mr. Lester Pearson, endorsed these views. Though he was averse to military sanctions, he did not exclude them in the last resort. Mr. Selwyn Lloyd considered that the meeting of the council had been a success and that its discussions of Suez would have a useful influence.

M. Spaak, the Foreign Minister of Belgium, who had been paying a visit to the Congo in August, came back to Europe fully alerted to the danger of Colonel Nasser's *coup*. It would have ramifications throughout Africa, not only in the north but deep in the central tropics. M. Spaak was firm on the importance of re-establishing international control over the Suez waterway, but he was convinced that the question was even larger than this. If the Western powers quailed, he foresaw a long series of retreats before them, in Africa and the Middle East. He strongly favoured enlisting the support of the North Atlantic Treaty powers, and declared himself haunted by the mistakes committed at the outset of the Hitler period. He feared that they might now be repeated. So did I.

Our information tallied with M. Spaak's. We had received reports from West and East Africa, Somaliland and Aden. Taken singly, these might not be alarming, but in sum they foreshadowed widespread unrest in the Muslim world. We knew that the Egyptian Government were laying plans for a revolutionary upheaval in Iraq. There was also an underlying threat to the Government of Iran. The Foreign Secretary and I were much encouraged by M. Spaak's determination that this menace must be faced, even if the United States were not squarely behind us. Belgium, he told us, would agree to pay her canal dues into a blocked account, and she would be at one with us in any proceedings at the United Nations. He was as good as his word.

★　★　★　★　★

The course of the Suez Canal crisis was decided by the American attitude to it. If the United States Government had approached this issue in the spirit of an ally, they would have done everything in their power, short of the use of force, to support the nations whose economic security depended upon the freedom of passage through the Suez Canal. They would have closely planned their policies with their allies and held stoutly to the decisions arrived at. They would have insisted on restoring international authority in order to insulate the canal from the politics of any one country. It is now clear that this was never the attitude of the United States Government. Rather did they try to gain time, coast along over difficulties as they arose and improvise policies, each following on the failure of its immediate predecessor. None of these was geared to the long-term purpose of serving a joint cause.

The reality of the issue was clearly put by a communist, M. Djilas, in his remarkable book, *The New Class*★. He saw the struggle for what it was: 'a dispute between Egyptian nationalism and world trade, which, by a coincidence, happened to be represented by the old colonial powers of Britain and France.'

Unhappily for the future of Asia and Africa, no such clarity of vision advantaged the Administration in Washington. The old spoor of colonialism confused the trail.

★　★　★　★　★

At the end of August we began to receive American views on our proposed approach to the United Nations. Dulles agreed in general that the Security Council should be consulted before any decision was taken on military action, but he expressed a number of doubts. He drew attention to technical difficulties. On August 29th he asked whether our problem in the language of the Charter was a 'dispute' or a 'situation'. If the former, he said we might be faced with a considerable adverse vote, and if the latter, we could not, under the procedure we had suggested, ask the Council for any effective resolution. We met Dulles on this point by choosing a different procedure, but we did not satisfy his doubts.

The Government decided that they must make their position clear beyond question. Accordingly we sent to Washington the next day the terms of the draft resolution which we proposed to submit. This found 'that a threat to peace exists', and, in the name of the United Nations, invited Egypt to negotiate on the basis of the eighteen-power proposals. We pointed out that we could go forward with this resolution only after we had got a clear answer from Egypt on the proposals of the Menzies mission.

Mr. Dulles at first sight liked our draft, but he was preoccupied with counting heads in the Security Council and worried by the question of the number of votes on which we could depend. He

★ Thames and Hudson, 1957.

declared that we could naturally rely upon the support of the United States at the Council, on the understanding that our move was an honest attempt to reach a solution and not 'a device for obtaining cover'. Mr. Dulles thought that our proposition implied the possible use of force. The United States did not necessarily want to be committed to this. We could not ourselves see any signs of this implication in our draft, which was as follows:

Draft Security Council Resolution

Recognizing that the arbitrary and unilateral action of the Government of Egypt in relation to the operation of the Suez Canal has disturbed the *status quo* and has created a situation which may endanger the free and open passage of shipping through the canal, without distinction of flag, as laid down by the Suez Canal Convention of 1888, and has thus given rise to a threat to the peace;

Noting that a conference to discuss this situation was called in London on August 16th, 1956, and that eighteen of the twenty-two states attending that conference, who between them represent over 95 per cent. of the user interest in the canal, put forward proposals to the Egyptian Government;

Regretting the refusal of the Egyptian Government to negotiate on the basis of the above-mentioned proposals, which appear to offer means for a just and equitable solution;

Considering that such refusal constitutes an aggravation of the situation;

Recalling the Egyptian Government's failure to comply with the Security Council's resolution of September 1st, 1951:

1. Finds that a threat to the peace exists;

2. Reminds the Government of Egypt of its continuing obligation, under Article 25 of the Charter, to accept and carry out the above-mentioned resolution;

3. Reaffirms the principle of the freedom of navigation of the Suez Canal in accordance with the Suez Canal Convention of 1888;

4. Considers it essential that, in order to guarantee this principle, the canal should be operated on the basis of the above-mentioned five-power proposals;*

* Those carried to Cairo by Mr. Menzies' mission on behalf of the eighteen powers.

5. Calls on the Government of Egypt to negotiate on the basis of these proposals.

In further discussions, the American officials questioned the time-table which we had in mind. They did not think that a week of debate would be sufficient. If a lot of amendments were tabled, it would take much hard work in the lobbies to dispose of them. In London we were well aware of this characteristic defect in the United Nations' machinery, hence our determination to try to speed it up. But the Americans were particularly anxious to avoid creating the impression of what they called railroading tactics. They also did not want us to add Belgium, or any other power which had not been represented at the London Conference, to our list of sponsors. Belgium was a member of the Security Council and in our view nothing was more natural than to call on the support of our friends, but the Americans considered that this looked like 'ganging-up'.

This term ganging-up requires some explanation. It has a melancholy history. I think that I first heard it in connection with the Yalta Conference. There it was interpreted as meaning that we and the United States must not get too close together for fear of arousing the suspicions of the Russians whom we were to meet. It certainly was an obstacle in the way of close understanding at the highest level, though Mr. Stettinius, then Secretary of State, did not share a love for this phrase. Neither at Yalta nor later at San Francisco did he ever use it or lean upon it. However, it plagued our discussions at Yalta, where the conference would have had better results for the world had it not prevailed.

Negotiators with the United States from many of the Western powers have since become more accustomed to this unhappy frame of mind, though I have never heard the phrase used when representa-tions were made to induce them to align their policies with those of the United States. Nobody suggested, for instance, that acquiescence by Britain and France in the repeated refusal to admit communist China to the United Nations was in any sense ganging-up.

★   ★   ★   ★   ★

So, for a few days, matters rested on the issue of the appeal to the United Nations. Our draft resolution was in the hands of the United States. The French had approved it, the Americans held back. The next move came unexpectedly. Mr. Dulles returned on September 4th from a week-end holiday on Duck Island, Lake Ontario, with some fresh thoughts. He now declared that we did not need a new convention with Egypt, though this was precisely what had been asked for by the eighteen powers in the London proposals, which he had himself put forward.

Mr. Dulles told our Ambassador that he regarded our position as a weak one judicially. Although we were not infringing Egyptian sovereignty by asking them to accept a new treaty, we were threatening force if they refused. This implied, he said, that we did not possess adequate rights under existing treaties and needed to acquire them. But, in fact, the Convention of 1888 gave us all the rights we required.

He suggested that the users should club together, hire the pilots, organize navigation, and themselves manage the canal. This might be inconvenient, but it was quite feasible and would probably lead in time to some settlement with Egypt. If we could show that, in the event of Nasser refusing our proposals, we had an alternative to war, we would be in a far stronger position. The Convention gave Nasser no right to make a profit out of the operation of the canal. He would now see the money vanishing from his grasp and this, so Dulles argued, would deflate him more effectively than the threat or use of force. By thus relying on the rights which we possessed under the Convention, rather than asserting fresh ones, we would be much better placed in regard to the United Nations.

This account was amplified next day at the State Department when Her Majesty's Minister was told that, in the opinion of the United States Government, the users, including the United States, should issue an announcement rehearsing their rights and declaring their intention to set up a new organization. They must define exactly what it would do, and make clear that all ships passing through the canal would have to use the services of this organization.

Such was the first exposition of the idea of a Users' Club, which was to deflect the course of events. It marked a turning point. As reported, we thought this a promising plan, but we were doubtful of its legal basis. Our advice in London was that though the Convention imposed obligations on Egypt, there was nothing in it which gave the users any such rights as Dulles claimed. The signatories of the Convention could make certain that it was observed only by diplomatic and economic pressure and in the last resort by force. Moreover, we were faced with the same difficulty as at the summoning of the London Conference. There were far more user nations than there were surviving signatories of the Convention.

On September 6th we had news from Mr. Menzies that his mission was near deadlock. We decided to pursue our appeal to the United Nations, at the same time exploring the meaning of Mr. Dulles' latest idea. The Government regarded resort to the Security Council as a further attempt to persuade Egypt to accept a solution on the lines agreed at the London Conference. We suggested to the United States that our representative at the United Nations should deliver a message to the President of the Security Council requesting him to summon a meeting. The French Government agreed with this course of action. We knew that the Egyptian Government wanted to prolong the palavers while they strengthened their hold on the canal. Admittedly our move at the United Nations would give them still further time. However, Mr. Dulles' Users' Club, we hoped, would provide a method of denying Egypt any profit from her act of nationalization, until a settlement was reached.

Canal transit dues, the Foreign Secretary insisted in his communications with Washington, must be paid to the Users' Club. This was the key to the whole business. Meanwhile Nasser must not get the dues. The body proposed by the United States Government, he told them, might for the time being fulfil most of the functions of the international authority proposed by the London Conference. I reflected that the United States would be fully committed to take part in it.

I still believed that the United States Government held firmly to their determination that Nasser must be made 'to disgorge'. This being so, I considered that they must be allowed as free a hand as possible in selecting methods. The Users' Club could be the American choice. It was true that the club would take some time to constitute. We therefore proposed to make our approach to the United Nations at once while Mr. Dulles' ideas were still being clarified. In the event, we were frustrated and the Users' Club assumed a different form from that which we had been led to expect.

In the meantime I had received a disquieting message from Mr. Eisenhower on September 3rd. Hitherto he and his officials had always given us to understand that the United States would not take exception to the use of force, if all peaceful means of settlement had been exhausted. The fact that we had taken military precautions had, furthermore, been approved from time to time. Now the President told me that American public opinion flatly rejected force. He admitted that the procedures of negotiation on which we were then engaged would probably not give Nasser the setback he deserved. But he advised that we should sharply separate the question of the canal from our general policy towards the Egyptian dictatorship and the menace under which Africa and the Middle East lay. The latter he considered a long-term problem.

I found this most disturbing. I felt that we had to deal with the canal not only for its own importance, but because Nasser's seizure of it affected the whole position in the Middle East and Africa. The canal was not a problem that could be isolated from the many other manifestations of Arab nationalism and Egyptian ambition.

I replied to the President on September 6th in a message on which I had spent much care:

> Thank you for your message and writing thus frankly.
>
> There is no doubt as to where we are agreed and have been agreed from the very beginning, namely that we should do everything we can to get a peaceful settlement. It is in this spirit that we favoured calling the twenty-two power conference and that we have worked in the closest co-operation with you about this business since. There has never been any question of our suddenly or without further provocation resorting to arms, while these processes were at work. In any event, as your own wide knowledge would confirm, we could not have done this without extensive preparation lasting several weeks.
>
> This question of precautions has troubled me considerably and still does. I have not forgotten the riots and murders in Cairo in 1952, for I was in charge here at the time when Winston was on the high seas on his way back from the United States.
>
> We are both agreed that we must give the Suez committee every chance to fulfil their mission. This is our firm resolve. If the committee and subsequent negotiations succeed in getting Nasser's agreement to the London proposals of the eighteen powers, there will be no call for force. But if the committee fails, we must have some immediate alternative which will show that Nasser is not going to get his way. In this connection we are attracted by Foster's suggestion, if I understand it rightly, for the running of the canal by the users in virtue of their rights under the 1888 Convention. We heard about this from our Embassy in Washington yesterday. I think that we could go along with this, provided that the intention was made clear by both of us immediately the Menzies mission finishes its work. But unless we can

proceed with this, or something very like it, what should the next step be?

You suggest that this is where we diverge. If that is so I think that the divergence springs from a difference in our assessment of Nasser's plans and intentions. May I set out our view of the position.

In the nineteen-thirties Hitler established his position by a series of carefully planned movements. These began with the occupation of the Rhineland and were followed by successive acts of aggression against Austria, Czechoslovakia, Poland, and the West. His actions were tolerated and excused by the majority of the population of Western Europe. It was argued either that Hitler had committed no act of aggression against anyone, or that he was entitled to do what he liked in his own territory, or that it was impossible to prove that he had any ulterior designs, or that the Covenant of the League of Nations did not entitle us to use force and that it would be wiser to wait until he did commit an act of aggression.

In more recent years Russia has attempted similar tactics. The blockade of Berlin was to have been the opening move in a campaign designed at least to deprive the Western powers of their whole position in Germany. On this occasion we fortunately reacted at once with the result that the Russian design was never unfolded. But I am sure that you would agree that it would be wrong to infer from this circumstance that no Russian design existed.

Similarly the seizure of the Suez Canal is, we are convinced, the opening gambit in a planned campaign designed by Nasser to expel all Western influence and interests from Arab countries. He believes that if he can get away with this, and if he can successfully defy eighteen nations, his prestige in Arabia will be so great that he will be able to mount revolutions of young officers in Saudi Arabia, Jordan, Syria and Iraq. (We know that he is already preparing a revolution in Iraq, which is the most stable and progressive.) These new Governments will in effect be Egyptian satellites if not Russian ones. They will have to place their united oil resources under the control of a united Arabia led by Egypt and under Russian influence. When that moment comes Nasser can deny oil to Western Europe and we here shall all be at his mercy.

There are some who doubt whether Saudi Arabia, Iraq and

Kuwait will be prepared even for a time to sacrifice their oil revenues for the sake of Nasser's ambitions. But if we place ourselves in their position I think the dangers are clear. If Nasser says to them, ' I have nationalized the Suez Canal. I have successfully defied eighteen powerful nations including the United States, I have defied the whole of the United Nations in the matter of the Israel blockade, I have expropriated all Western property. Trust me and withhold oil from Western Europe. Within six months or a year, the Continent of Europe will be on its knees before you.' Will the Arabs not be prepared to follow this lead? Can we rely on them to be more sensible than were the Germans? Even if the Arabs eventually fall apart again as they did after the early Caliphs, the damage will have been done meanwhile.

In short we are convinced that if Nasser is allowed to defy the eighteen nations it will be a matter of months before revolution breaks out in the oil-bearing countries and the West is wholly deprived of Middle Eastern oil. In this belief we are fortified by the advice of friendly leaders in the Middle East.

The Iraqis are the most insistent in their warnings; both Nuri and the Crown Prince have spoken to us several times of the consequences of Nasser succeeding in his grab. They would be swept away.

[I then gave the President an account of three other warnings which we had received, each from a different Middle Eastern country: as the authors of these warnings are still alive, I do not propose to make their names public.]

The difference which separates us today [my message continued] appears to be a difference of assessment of Nasser's plans and intentions and of the consequences in the Middle East of military action against him.

You may feel that even if we are right it would be better to wait until Nasser has unmistakably unveiled his intentions. But this was the argument which prevailed in 1936 and which we both rejected in 1948. Admittedly there are risks in the use of force against Egypt now. It is, however, clear that military intervention designed to reverse Nasser's revolutions in the whole continent would be a much more costly and difficult undertaking. I am very troubled, as it is, that if we do not reach a conclusion either way about the canal very soon one or other of these eastern lands may be toppled at any moment by Nasser's revolutionary movements.

I agree with you that prolonged military operations as well as the denial of Middle East oil would place an immense strain on the economy of Western Europe. I can assure you that we are conscious of the burdens and perils attending military intervention. But if our assessment is correct, and if the only alternative is to allow Nasser's plans quietly to develop until this country and all Western Europe are held to ransom by Egypt acting at Russia's behest it seems to us that our duty is plain. We have many times led Europe in the fight for freedom. It would be an ignoble end to our long history if we accepted to perish by degrees.

★   ★   ★   ★   ★

Syria was one of the lands we were watching. Communist agitation was active there. The neighbouring Lebanon was small, but stoutly led by its President, Mr. Chamoun, whom I knew personally. Libya was another country where Nasser's agents were busy, and in Jordan elections were due whose outcome might result in closer association between that country and Egypt.

While we exchanged messages with Washington, we kept our eyes on Cairo. Our Ambassador held many conversations with Egyptian Ministers before Mr. Menzies arrived. He reminded them that only a few months earlier they had been speaking of an enlarged canal as a further link to strengthen relations between Egypt and the West. They had then told him that they would do nothing to infringe the rights of the old company. They had now changed all that. The Egyptians made no excuses; they waited to see what would happen.

Egypt was not seriously hit by the economic measures which a number of countries, including France and ourselves, had taken. Nasser was getting help from communist countries, from uncommitted states and from India. Such sufferings as Egypt had so far experienced were falling upon the opponents of the dictatorship. This confirmed my scepticism about the effect of economic sanctions. It strengthened the need for speed in our diplomacy and in any possible military sequel.

The problem of the Suez Canal Company's staff gave us much trouble. Many of the pilots had wished to quit the service as soon as the canal had been nationalized, even though the Egyptian Government threatened to imprison them if they did not continue at work. The French and British Governments urged them to stay at their posts, first until the end of the London Conference and then until Mr. Menzies' mission was finished.

Despite our efforts, about sixty pilots had either left Egypt or failed to return from leave by early September. Only two-thirds of the original number were still on duty. A Swede who had made good his escape, declared:

> I have no intention of going back to Suez so long as the canal is under Egyptian administration, and the same applies to my sixty colleagues who are at present in Europe. . . . I have no confidence in the Egyptians. I was there during the days of terror in 1952. For my part I hope no sea-captains get caught on Nasser's hook.

Colonel Nasser himself told the American Ambassador at this time that if the pilots left, he would get others from elsewhere, if necessary from Russia. This he did. The replacements, drawn from many lands, did their job much better than the company or we had been led to expect.

★   ★   ★   ★   ★

Mr. Menzies and his committee had arrived in Cairo on September 3rd. His plan was to keep discussions with the Egyptians short. He presented Colonel Nasser with an *aide-mémoire* describing the London proposals, and explaining to him the spirit in which he and his colleagues were approaching their task. He kept the conversations strictly to the point in his determination to get an answer within a week. Mr. Menzies' *aide-mémoire* was cogent. In it he said:

> The nations for whom we speak . . . have a clear belief that, if the canal is to be maintained and developed as a waterway open to the use of vessels of all nations, it should be detached from politics, and the management of its operations should be placed on such a basis as to secure the maximum of international confidence and co-operation. . . . There is a long history of friendly relations with Egypt. . . . We have all welcomed Egypt's attainment of complete self-government and we would desire that anything done or proposed now should be regarded as containing no derogation from Egypt's sovereignty and national dignity. These two points of view were indeed clearly illustrated by the whole temper and tone of the discussions at the London Conference.

Mr. Menzies conducted his talks with customary candour and lack of cant. He said that his mission was to expound the London proposals and that he was not empowered to consider alternatives. His committee showed unity and gave him firm support. During the first talks with Nasser, Menzies felt that he had made a considerable impression. At their conclusion, in a private interview, Menzies warned Nasser that he would be mistaken if he supposed that the London Conference had ruled out the use of force. It had not addressed itself to that question. But France and Britain took a very serious view of the situation and had taken the precautions of which he was aware.

Nasser did not contest this, and Menzies left the meeting with some confidence, believing that the Egyptian Prime Minister had taken his warning to heart. Perhaps he had, but at this moment a stroke of bad luck befell us. Overnight came a statement from Mr. Eisenhower. He said, at a press conference: 'We are determined to exhaust every possible, every feasible method of peaceful settlement.' This was well enough, then he added in answer to a question asking him what he would do if Egypt refused the London proposals: 'I am still very hopeful that the London proposals will be accepted; but the position of the United States is not to give up, even if we do run into obstacles.' This sentence gave encouragement to Nasser, who did not need much, to raise those obstacles. The Egyptians began to feel it safe to say no. Such was the impression gained by Mr. Menzies.

Thinking aloud about the next move is a dangerous practice. It almost inevitably destroys the chances of success for the present move. It is also a process which causes acute embarrassment to friends. Often in these weeks we longed for the crisp 'No comment', so firm an ally of American diplomacy in the past. Alas, it never came.

This was not the first occasion upon which we had suffered from episodes of this kind. Already, while Mr. Menzies was on his way to Egypt, Mr. Dulles, in answer to a question from the press, had said that the canal was not of primary importance to the United States. No doubt he hoped thus to reassure American opinion; he also reassured Nasser.

Two days were spent by Nasser in reflection on the eighteen-power proposals and on the impression he had derived from the United States. Then he said no. He said that the idea of insulating the canal from politics was unreal, it could never be sundered from Egypt's political life. He also talked of sovereignty and declared several times that an international authority would mean 'the restoration of collective colonialism'.

All the members of the committee responded promptly to the taunt of colonialism. The Ethiopian, Iranian, and Swedish members were outspoken in rejecting it as ridiculous. Mr. Henderson joined them by pointing to the anti-colonial record of the United States. The Egyptians put forward no counter-proposals to Mr. Menzies and his committee. They confined themselves to vague generalities. There was nothing to be gained by discussing these and Mr. Menzies held firmly to the position that he was not authorized to do so. He carried his colleagues with him.

The committee's next step was to agree upon the terms of a letter to Nasser, recounting the course of the conversations and drawing attention to the principle of international authority on which these had broken down. The letter stressed the sovereign position which Egypt would continue to hold under the London proposals. It stated:

> Our discussions have been conducted in an atmosphere of courteous frankness and responsibility. But they have, in our opinion, disclosed deep differences of approach and principle which it seems clear that no repetition of debate can affect. . . . The whole essence of what we have put forward is (to use a homely illustration) that, Egypt's position as the landlord of the canal being completely accepted, she should proceed by international agreement to install a tenant so constituted that the future of the canal would be satisfactory both to its owners and to those many nations who use it. We believe, as we have pointed out, that it cannot seriously be maintained that when a landlord grants a lease of premises that lease derogates from his ownership. . . . Indeed, as the 'tenant' in this analogy would be a body which includes Egypt herself, the position of Egypt would be even stronger.

The committee finished their work on September 9th. They then dispersed and Mr. Menzies flew back to Australia by way of London and Washington. On arrival in Melbourne, he sent me the following personal letter:

> You have about as difficult a task over Suez as mortal man ever had. I am sorry that we have not been able to get it solved for you in Cairo. Our report and, in particular, our *aide-mémoire* to Nasser

will give a pretty fair picture of the arguments that we were using and of those we encountered. There are some aspects of this matter, however, which no committee could officially mention but which I would like to put down for your personal assistance.

Egypt is not only a dictatorship but it has all the earmarks of a police state. The tapping of telephone lines, the installation of microphones, the creation of a vast body of security police— all these things are accepted as commonplace.

I was told that Nasser was a man of great personal charm who might beguile me into believing something foreign to my own thought. This is not so. He is in some ways quite a likeable fellow but so far from being charming he is rather *gauche*, with some irritating mannerisms, such as rolling his eyes up to the ceiling when he is talking to you and producing a quick, quite evanescent grin when he can think of nothing else to do. I would say that he was a man of considerable but immature intelligence. He lacks training or experience in many of the things he is dealing with and is, therefore, awkward with them. He will occasionally use rather blustering expressions, but drops them very quickly if he finds them challenged in a good-humoured way. His logic does not travel very far; that is to say, he will produce a perfectly accurate major premise and sometimes an accurate minor premise, but his deduction will be astonishing. I will give you a powerful example of this which I think you might usefully have in mind. I will put it in the form of a substantially verbatim account of one passage in one of the arguments which I had with him.

NASSER: You say in your proposals that you are 'concerned by the grave situation regarding the Suez Canal'. I agree that there is. But who created it? We didn't create it, for all we did was to nationalize the Suez Canal Company and this was a matter which we had a perfect legal right to do. Therefore that action of ours could not have created the grave situation. It was the subsequent threats of Great Britain and France which created the grave situation.

MENZIES: But don't you see that the critical atmosphere in the world began at the very moment that you nationalized? It was that announcement which brought me back from America to the United Kingdom. It was that announcement

471

which took Dulles from the United States to London. It was that announcement which brought the representatives of twenty-two nations to London. What you are overlooking is that the actual thing you did was to repudiate (and I use that expression because plain language will be appreciated) a concession which had twelve years to run.

NASSER: But how could anybody complain about that, if it was within our power?

MENZIES: I don't concede it was within your power. In fact I think it was not. But can't you see that if your attitude is that merely because it was within your power you can repudiate a contract binding upon you, this, in one hit, destroys the confidence that the world has in your contractual word?

NASSER: I don't understand this. The concession would have expired in twelve years anyhow and then I suppose the same uproar would have occurred, if you are right.

MENZIES: Not at all. If you had not interfered with the concession, I have no doubt that the company itself would have quite soon begun negotiations with you for some future organization for the canal. But those negotiations would have been conducted in an atmosphere which was not one of crisis, and sensible and fair conclusions might well have been arrived at without the heated exchanges on such matters as 'sovereignty'.

NASSER: But this ignores the fact that we had the right to do what we did, and if we have the right to do something we can't understand how people can take exception to it.

This will explain the kind of logical mess which exists in his mind. It is just as if one said that, as the Parliament of the United Kingdom has power to pass any laws it thinks fit to pass, nobody should ever be at liberty to complain about its law, to resent it, to seek to alter it.

With frightful reiteration he kept coming back to the slogans. Our proposal was 'collective colonialism' which we were seeking to enforce; he constantly came back to 'sovereignty'; to our desire for the 'domination' of the canal; to our proposed 'seizure' of the canal. I exhausted my energy and almost wore out my patience in explaining to him that he was surely underestimating his own significance as the political head of Egypt. What we were seeking was *an agreement*; and any scheme for the actual control and management of the operations of the canal, while leaving Egypt's sovereign rights untouched, was the kind of working arrangement which was an exercise of sovercignty and not a derogation from it, and could be described as 'domination' or 'seizure' only if he made his agreement under actual duress.

I pointed out that many countries in the world had willingly granted concessions to foreign enterprises to explore and develop national resources, and that so far from thinking that these represented foreign domination, the nations granting such concessions granted them willingly because they were convinced that their own resources and position would be thereby strengthened. To this he replied that he saw no analogy, because the grantees of these concessions remain entirely subject to national law (and, therefore, no doubt could have their concessions revoked at will).

Mr. Menzies had not won success, though he had deserved it. Thanks to his efforts, and those of his committee, the difference which was revealed was on clearly defined issues.

IV

THE USERS' CLUB
September 10th – 17th

Illegality of Nasser's seizure – American doubts – Mr. Dulles discourages appeal to Security Council – We confer with French Ministers on September 10th – Their loyalty and understanding – Details of Users' Club – Its possibilities – American proposals on oil supplies – Our doubts about the Users' Club – Our decision – Debate in the House of Commons – Criticism of Users' Club – Effect of Mr. Dulles' statement – I wind up the debate – Nasser rejects the Users' Club – A letter from Marshal Bulganin – My reply

On September 7th, when Mr. Menzies' talks in Cairo broke down, we informed Washington that we might, within twenty-four hours, wish to announce our decision to go to the Security Council. News of our plans had already begun to appear in the press, though in garbled form. At the same time, our ambassadors and high commissioners accredited to the eighteen powers were asked to take action on the refusal we now expected from Egypt. We wished as many governments as possible to state publicly that they did not consider the nationalization of the canal to be valid, that they did not recognize the new Egyptian authority and that they would deny it transit dues.

There was a strong legal argument to advance, based upon the close link between the Convention of 1888 and the Concession to the Canal Company. The Concession was the earlier and had been granted in 1856 by the Khedive of Egypt, with a life of ninety-nine years after the opening of the canal to navigation. It was not due to terminate until 1968. The Sultan of Turkey in 1866 had issued an Imperial Firman sanctioning the Khedive's concession. The Convention of 1888 had

474

set out to 'guarantee at all times and for all powers the free use of the Suez Maritime Canal and thus to complete the system under which navigation of this canal had been placed' by the Imperial Firman.

It was implicit in the Convention that the operation of the canal should not be entrusted to any single power. The canal had an international character, commonly assumed in the various agreements made between the Canal Company and the Egyptian Government. Egypt had never hitherto dissented from this view. Moreover, as a member of the United Nations, she had undertaken 'to establish conditions under which justice and respect for obligations arising from treaties and other sources of international law can be maintained.' By nationalization, by peremptorily ending the concession, the Egyptian Government had destroyed all assurance that the rights guaranteed by the Convention to users of the canal would continue to be enjoyed. Nasser had himself stated that he intended to use the canal revenues to build the Aswan Dam. This was clearly illegal.

Here were good grounds for our stand, in terms of law, which we wished to proclaim formally and in public. The United States Government, however, now took a different view, although at the first London Conference they had expressed no such doubts. They questioned our basis in law. They were opposed to any immediate pronouncement. They also let us know that they would not join in sponsoring the draft Franco-British resolution to the Security Council. What is more, they would not even support it. As Mr. Dulles expressed it to our Ambassador on September 7th, 'he would find it very difficult to go along with the operation in its present form.' He accused us of trying to enlist the aid of the Security Council to force a new treaty on Egypt which would bestow new rights on the users of the canal. In fact, we simply wished to reaffirm old rights and make certain that they would be observed.

The French and ourselves were determined that an appeal to the United Nations must be firmly based on two conditions. First, that the United States and our two countries should agree in advance not to accept any solution which fell short of the eighteen-power proposals. Secondly, that together we should resist any move by less friendly powers to limit our freedom of action. The United States Government now told us that they could not be bound in advance by either of these conditions. This was extraordinary, since the United States Government had themselves tabled the proposals which the eighteen powers had endorsed.

Mr. Dulles urged us, for the time being, merely to inform the Security Council of the situation by letter and ask for no action. One of the French leaders described this procedure contemptuously as 'leaving a visiting card'. He saw no harm in it, but no good either. Given the lack of American support for a stronger move, we were obliged to adopt it. Even then, the United States Government declined to add their signature to our letter. We were told that they did not wish to create an identity of interest, which might prove embarrassing to the French and ourselves.

We found the American response to our proposals disappointing and the Foreign Secretary said so. Our two countries, he told the United States Government on September 8th, seemed farther apart in their thinking than at any time since the crisis began.

Mr. Lloyd expressed his grave anxiety at the present state of our consultations and urged the absolute necessity for effective action. Delay would be disastrous for a number of reasons. Every day Nasser was strengthening his hold on the canal. The Western powers would lose face unless they could react clearly and speedily to his rejection of the eighteen-power proposals, which now seemed certain. Meanwhile the friendly Arab states were in great and ever-increasing peril.

Her Majesty's Government, Mr. Selwyn Lloyd said, did not believe that the canal issue could be separated from the general Egyptian menace to the friendly governments of the Muslim world. At that moment, the Foreign Secretary told Washington, we could not make out where the United States stood. They had poured cold water on our suggestions without so far putting forward any alternative.

Such was the position until September 10th. That day we were concerting our ideas with the French Prime Minister and Foreign Minister, who had come to London. I was to have many other meetings with M. Mollet in the next few weeks. I always found him, as on this occasion, cool, resolute and reasonable. His convictions were firmly held but argued with calm. He understood that others could differ from him in equal good faith. We had met before we each became Prime Minister, but I had not known him as intimately as other leading French political figures. The times we lived through together were tense and tough. Our association could have been very difficult; it was not. I have never enjoyed more completely loyal understanding with any man. In the hours of strain there was never a harsh word, a reproach or a recrimination between us.

We knew that we were approaching a situation in which there was no good course, though some were less bad than others. We were eager for a solution by negotiation, even when we were least hopeful of one. Whatever the cost, we were determined not just to drift. Those who have held high responsibility know how enervating that temptation is, and the higher the responsibility the more persuasive it becomes. We both felt this many times, but we knew that to yield to it was to make disaster certain, and in the worst conditions. We also knew that if we took positive action at any time in these months, it would make us many enemies.

It is in the nature of things that those who clamour for strong action are often the first to condemn it when it is taken. This they do on the specious pretext that the intention is right, but the circumstances or the execution are wrong. They excuse themselves by demanding a perfection into which events are not malleable. We knew, too, that one of the consequences of action is that no one can finally determine what would have been the consequences of inaction. The immediate results can be criticized, the worse results that would have befallen can be ignored or shrugged off.

All these things we knew and something else as well. A Minister's final responsibility is to his own convictions, sharpened by his own experience.

While M. Mollet and M. Pineau were with us, the latest formulation of Mr. Dulles' thought on the proposed Users' Club arrived. We at once turned our minds to this and studied it together. The telegrams which reached us showed that the United States Government had now worked out their scheme in some detail. They also made plain that they regarded the scheme as the answer to our immediate requirements.

The American draft, describing the purposes of the club, emphasized co-operation between users and its legal and historical justification. 'It has become appropriate and necessary', the draft ran, 'that the Governments of the users should organize as among themselves for the most effective possible enjoyment of the rights of passage given by the 1888 Convention.' These were unexceptionable words, so long as action was taken at once. The proposed association would 'promote safe, orderly, efficient and economical transit of member-controlled vessels' through the canal. Membership would include, it was hoped, all the eighteen powers and such others as might qualify by virtue of their pattern of trade and tonnage. The club would have its headquarters in Rome and be governed by an elected executive group. In the first instance, this body might consist of nations which had been represented on Mr. Menzies' committee. This was agreeable to us, provided that the principal users of the canal, the French and ourselves, were added to the group.

The association was to appoint an administrator to supervise the passage of its members' ships. He was to co-operate with Egypt, in so far as co-operation was forthcoming, on matters of pilotage, scheduling, signalling and the manipulation of bridges. Full use was to be made of the pilots and technical staff of the old Suez Canal Company, and all those still at their posts were to be encouraged to remain there. Not much time was left, since most of the pilots and staff were at the end of their tether and eager for release, unless they could transfer their services to the Users' Club at once.

If Egypt made difficulties, the administrator was to carry out his task from two ships stationed at either end of the canal, which would serve as his marshalling centres. He was to collect dues from all ships convoyed under the auspices of the club, at rates to be determined by it, without profit to any member. Egypt was to be compensated for the facilities she afforded, but the main purpose of collecting dues was to defray the expenses of the association.

Despite the various practical drawbacks which were evident in it, even as outlined to us, this appeared to the United Kingdom Government to be a possible interim scheme. We proposed only a few modifications. We urged that the Users' Club should set up immediately a separate bank account, into which dues would be paid. We also asked the United States to take steps to see that all American-owned ships, whatever flag they flew, should comply. We were to be disappointed on both points.

The French Ministers viewed the plan with misgiving from the start. They did not particularly mind the delay in appealing to the Security Council, since public opinion in France had little confidence anyway in the efficacy of the United Nations. But they were concerned at Mr. Dulles' general procrastination in dealing with the canal, and they suspected that the Users' Club was a device to prevent Britain and France bringing matters to a head with Nasser. M. Pineau frankly regarded further talk with the United States Government about the Users' Club as a waste of time. We were ourselves perturbed at the extent to which successive American modifications had already watered down the original plan. On the other hand it was now presented to us by Mr. Dulles in one of the messages we received that day as something that 'Egypt would like much less' than the eighteen-power proposals which Nasser had rejected, Dulles' argument being that the Egyptians, having refused these, could not expect such good terms again. The plan would also provide a means of withholding the canal dues. Both these were capital considerations for us and without them we would not have contemplated the scheme. Above all, it provided a means of working with the United States. I was prepared to lean over backwards to achieve this.

For these reasons, and with the reluctant agreement of the French Ministers, we accepted the Users' Club. We tried to make it work in the weeks that followed, only to find that the vital assurances on which the offer rested did not exist in substance at all. Her Majesty's Government fell in with the idea in order to keep unity with the United States. It was to lose us unity in the House of Commons. The paradox was that the United States Government made this lack of unity at home an increasing reproach against us.

Putting Mr. Dulles' plan into effect was to be accompanied, he told us, by two further prongs of attack. One prong was provided by the financial measures which the French and ourselves had already taken, but in respect of which the United States continued to lag behind. The other prong was the re-routing of oil traffic. The object of this, in American eyes, was to decrease our dependence upon the canal. Much thought had been given to this proposal by the State Department, in conjunction with the American oil companies. It was an ambitious plan and meant sending round the Cape of Good Hope about half the one and a half million barrels of oil a day which usually passed through the canal. The other half of the normal Western consumption of canal-borne oil was to be obtained from expanded production in the Gulf of Mexico and the Caribbean.

The plan had two unwelcome implications for us. First, friendly countries in the Middle East would have to be asked, while this emergency lasted, to cut back their oil production, though their stability largely depended on its revenues. Secondly, Britain would have to spend many dollars to replace her supplies by Gulf and Caribbean oil. Even if we were granted a loan from the Export-Import Bank to finance this oil transaction, as had been promised, that loan would eventually have to be repaid in dollars and with interest. Since we and the French were not paying dues to Nasser, and did not intend to do so, to send our oil round the Cape would injure us more than Nasser. The Cabinet decided against this project as an immediate means of pressure upon Egypt.

Our meeting with the French Ministers in London was concluded on September 11th. In the next forty-eight hours a sheaf of telegrams passed between ourselves, Washington and Paris, which seemed to clarify the Users' Club idea. The form and the actual words in which it should be announced were carefully agreed between us.

The President was asked at a press conference on September 11th whether the United States would back France and Britain, should these countries be obliged to resort to force. He replied by a reference to his constitutional powers as United States Commander-in-Chief:

> I don't know exactly what you mean by backing them. As you know, this country will not go to war ever while I am occupying my present post unless the Congress is called into session and Congress declares such a war. And the only exception to that would be in the case of unexpected and unwarranted attack on this nation, where self-defence itself would dictate some quick response while you call Congress into action.

A fair comment on this statement in the international context of the time was made by a correspondent at Mr. Dulles' conference two days later. He asked the Secretary of State: 'With the United States announcing in advance that it will not use force, and Soviet Russia backing Egypt with its propaganda, does not that leave all the trump cards in Nasser's hands?'

The decision whether to endorse the American users' plan was one of the most crucial we had to face during the whole Suez crisis. Its consequences were far-reaching. If we had told the United States Government that we did not consider the Users' Club a workable proposition and that we preferred to go direct to the Security Council in support of the kind of resolution we had already shown them and they had declined to approve, we would I suppose have forfeited, for the time being at least, something of their good will. On the other hand, we would have avoided the long and dismal trail of negotiation in which we became involved in an effort to set up this Users' Club. I have to bear a large part of the responsibility for this decision myself. A number of my colleagues were uneasy, some because they doubted whether the scheme could be made to work, others because they doubted whether the United States Government were in earnest in the assurances they had given and would see the scheme through. Disturbed as I had been by some recent events, I was still in a temper to endorse an American initiative which had a hope of success, and take a chance upon it. Close co-operation with the United States had been a guiding principle throughout my political life. On this account I had differed gravely from Mr. Chamberlain in 1938, and later, during the war, had accepted decisions which, on a cold calculation, I would not have endorsed.

I believed in our common interest and I had no thought of abandoning this conviction now. If the benefit of the doubt had to be given, I would give it. The Government took their decision on the evening of September 11th, my colleagues concurring with varying degrees of confidence.

Looking back over the run of events, I think that I probably underestimated the parliamentary consequences of the action I was going to advocate in the House of Commons. If I did, it was because I was eager to maintain an Anglo-American front on this issue of respect for agreements, which must decide all our futures. On another count, I now think that this decision on the Users' Club may have been wrong. The future of the canal was, among the great powers, primarily our concern and that of the French; American interest was secondary. We might have done better to adhere to our own plan, refusing to be side-tracked from it, even by the new ideas of a powerful ally, however strongly urged upon us. The United States might or might not have given us full support at the United Nations. But we would have been acting in fulfilment of our conviction and would at least have been spared a disastrous chapter of disillusion.

The next morning I was busy with the speech I was to make in the House in a few hours' time, when the Foreign Secretary asked to see me. He told me that he had had a night of indifferent sleep, during which he had turned over and over again in his mind this question of the Users' Club. Should we go ahead, or should we not? On reflection he had come to the conclusion that we had better not. He felt convinced that the scheme was not really workable. He had come round to tell me so and to ask me whether I had had the same reflections. I was naturally a good deal shaken by the view now expressed by the Foreign Secretary. I put aside the notes for the speech and we talked the matter over. Eventually we decided, with a full consciousness of the risks we were taking, that we should go on with the policy which the Cabinet had decided upon the night before.

On September 12th I opened the Suez debate in the House of Commons. As I took my seat the Chief Whip, Mr. Heath, murmured to me, 'There will be no division if you announce that you are going immediately to the United Nations.' This, in view of our acceptance of the Users' Club, I could not do. I reminded the House that our last debate five weeks earlier:

> ... had revealed a remarkable measure of unanimity of opinion in the House and in the country. . . . There was wide acceptance of the proposition that to prevent any interference with the free use of the canal, and to maintain the efficiency of its operation, the canal should be placed under an international system designed to secure the rights of the users. There was also acceptance of the view that the precautionary military measures taken by the Government had been justified. . . . Nothing which the Government have done since that debate took place has in any way changed the policy which the Foreign Secretary and I described in our speeches on that occasion.

Having rehearsed the arguments for restoring an international character to the canal, I then gave an account of the London Conference, the Menzies mission and the Egyptian rejection of the offer which it carried. Mr. Menzies was himself in the gallery.

I told the House that we had informed the President of the Security Council of the situation and we certainly did not exclude referring the dispute to the United Nations, if it became necessary. But we were setting up immediately a Canal Users' Association, which I then described, concluding in the exact words agreed with the United States and French Governments:

> I must make it clear that if the Egyptian Government should seek to interfere with the operations of the association, or refuse to extend to it the essential minimum of co-operation, then that Government will once more be in breach of the Convention of 1888. In that event, Her Majesty's Government and others concerned will be free to take such further steps as seem to be required either through the United Nations, or by other means for the assertion of their rights.

I was at once interrupted with a request to explain the meaning of these words. This I declined to do, the words having been deliberately chosen by the three powers.

Sir Robert Boothby wound up the debate on that evening in words which expressed my own thoughts. He said:

We went through all this in the nineteen-thirties, and it was not much fun. Shameless appeasement does not really pay . . . .

As I listened to the Prime Minister this afternoon, I thought of what Nasser had been saying about what he was going to do to establish an Arab Empire from Morocco to the Persian Gulf, and how he was going to eliminate Israel altogether. That is all in his speeches, and in a horrible little book called *A Philosophy of Revolution*, which is like a potted edition of *Mein Kampf*. As I heard the Prime Minister speaking, I said to myself, 'Well, thank goodness, at any rate we shall not have to go through all that again', and we shall not.

Though there were some difficult moments on the first day of the debate and some encouraging shouts of 'provocation' and 'resign', all went reasonably well. On the morning of the following day, M. Mollet made his parallel statement in Paris in the agreed terms. This aroused no critical comment. Mr. Dulles did the same in Washington, but in answer to questions afterwards, he made a remark which caught world-wide attention and entirely submerged the identity of our original statements. 'We do not intend', he said, 'to shoot our way through. It may be we have the right to do it but we don't intend to do it as far as the United States is concerned.' The alternative for the United States, he admitted, was to 'send our vessels round the Cape'. On being asked whether there was a conflict between British and American views on this point, Mr. Dulles replied:

I think that each nation has to decide for itself what action it will have to take to defend and if possible realize its rights which it believes it has as a matter of treaty. I do not recall just exactly what Sir Anthony Eden said on this point. I did not get the impression that there was any undertaking or pledge given by him to shoot their way through the canal.

It would be hard to imagine a statement more likely to cause the maximum allied disunity and disarray. The Americans having themselves volunteered that the new arrangements would be less acceptable to the Egyptians than the eighteen-power proposals, Mr. Dulles proceeded to make plain at this juncture that the United States did not intend to use force, even though it had the right to do so. The words were an advertisement to Nasser that he could reject the project with impunity. We had never been told that a statement of this kind was to accompany the announcement of the Users' Club. Had we known that they were to be used as an accompaniment to the American announcement, we would never have endorsed it. To us, the emphasis had been that the Egyptians, having rejected reasonable eighteen-power proposals, could not expect to do as well. To the public, the emphasis now was that, whatever happened, the Egyptians had nothing to fear. The Users' Club was an American project to which we had conformed. We were all three in agreement, even to the actual words of the announcement. Yet here was the spokesman of the United States saying that each nation must decide for itself and expressing himself as unable to recall what the spokesman of a principal ally had said. Such cynicism towards allies destroys true partnership. It leaves only the choice of parting, or a master and vassal relationship in foreign policy.

In the House I had, in fact, said nothing to suggest that we would shoot our way through. I had used the formula agreed with the United States Government, which M. Mollet had also used, that we would seek our rights 'through the United Nations or by any other means'. This left the course of future action deliberately vague so as to strengthen pressure on behalf of the Users' Club. The whole purpose of the Users' Club had been, by a display of unity in association with the United States, to avoid having recourse to force. American torpedoing of their own plan on the first day of launching it, left no alternative but to use force or acquiesce in Nasser's triumph.

Mr. Dulles' words, as headlined in the press, helped to create a considerable storm on the second day of our debate. This was not allayed by the speech of a former Conservative Attorney-General, Sir Lionel Heald, in which he maintained that force could not be used unless we first went to the United Nations. I was asked to say that the Government endorsed this. I could not do so. I could not foretell what emergency might arise, as had occurred in Korea and was to occur later in the Lebanon and Jordan. Moreover, the French had asked us not to undertake publicly that we would go to the United Nations at this moment, just as the Users' Club was being formed. They felt, quite rightly, that the Egyptian Government would then be able to ignore the club, arguing that, as we were going to the United Nations, they would make their case there. Nor could I explain that we were taking account of the United States wishes in deferring our approach to the United Nations.

In our Parliament, the Government spokesman on foreign affairs is often hampered by being unable to tell the whole story of the reasons for the policy he advocates publicly in debate. This is a greater embarrassment in Britain, for instance, than in the United States, where neither the President nor the Secretary of State is called upon publicly to explain his attitude to Congress. It is true that they have to face press conferences from time to time, but these are neither so closely reasoned nor have as much authority as debate in Parliament.

In France the use of all-party committees reduces the embarrassment, for though there may be leakages, there is no official reporting and more information can be given. This also applies to the powerful Foreign Affairs Committee of the United States Senate.

In my winding-up speech, amidst much interruption, I said:

> I want to deal with the question: would Her Majesty's Government give a pledge not to use force except after reference to the Security Council? If such a pledge or guarantee is to be absolute, then neither I nor any British Minister standing at this Box could give it. No one can possibly tell what will be Colonel Nasser's action, either in the canal or in Egypt.
>
> Nevertheless, I will give this reply, which is as far as any Government can go: it would certainly be our intention, if circumstances allowed, or in other words, except in an emergency, to refer a matter of that kind to the Security Council.

The Government hoped they had proved the strength of their case, while retaining essential powers and doing what they could to hold the alliance together. In the division we had a majority of 70, which was satisfactory.

The *Star* newspaper, generally liberal in its views, printed a leading article on the evening of the 12th approving the Users' Club. 'Unless Nasser is quite regardless of his country's interest,' it said, 'and is merely a power-crazed dictator, he must surely agree to negotiate on the basis of this Western plan.' However, members of the Opposition in the debate, while endorsing the broad aims of the plan, denounced some important aspects of it as provocative. They insisted that it would be a provocation towards Egypt for the Users' Association to employ its own pilots and to collect its own dues. They did not explain what effective purpose the club would serve if it did not do this.

Our own shipowners, whom the Minister of Transport frequently consulted, took the practical view that the club would be of no value unless it actively managed the transit of the canal, as Mr. Dulles' original proposal had provided.

We applied ourselves now to the next immediate step. There was a danger that shipping would pile up at either end of the canal because the pilots could no longer be held at their posts under the Egyptian authority. The users' agency must begin its work with all speed, otherwise it would lose its customers. Some would divert their ships around the Cape, while others might be tempted to reach a compromise with Nasser. The British shipping industry urged us to ask the United States to request Egypt for minimum facilities forthwith on behalf of the agency. This approach would be made in the spirit of the 1888 Convention and on the basis of the agency's willingness to co-operate with Egypt.

Any hopes we entertained of this suggestion were at once destroyed by the Egyptian reaction to the users' plan. Colonel Nasser made a speech on September 15th in which he accused the eighteen powers of 'international thuggery and imperialism'. He declared that 'not only the Egyptian Government but also the whole of the Egyptian people will resist any attempt on the part of any nation or group of nations to have an international body exercise Egypt's sovereign rights.' He described the Users' Association as an 'association for waging war', and flatly announced that he would resist force with force. After the assurances volunteered by Mr. Dulles, this bravado was both safe and popular.

The association for waging war was meanwhile being peacefully prepared. Invitations had been sent out on September 14th to the eighteen powers for another meeting in London to consider the report of the Menzies mission, to take note of the Egyptian memorandum of refusal and to discuss arrangements for the Users' Club. Thus the stage was set for the second London Conference.

★   ★   ★   ★   ★

While we were debating our policy at Westminster and concerting plans for the Users' Club, the Russians, who had for some time been silent on the subject of Suez, made a new move. Marshal Bulganin wrote me a long letter. He went out of his way to deny reports that the Soviet Government were inciting Egypt. Far from it, he maintained, Russia was eager to contribute to a peaceful settlement with due regard to the interests of all the states concerned. Nevertheless, Russia stood by Egypt's side. How could the Soviet Union, Marshal Bulganin asked, not treat favourably Egypt's position when she was defending her sovereignty and her national territory? He then accused France and Britain of threatening Egypt's inalienable rights with the use of force and spoke of official declarations of the readiness of Britain and France, on the pretext of defending their interests, to lead their forces on to Egyptian territory and infringe Egypt's territorial integrity and inviolability.

I pointed out in my reply to Moscow on September 17th that no such declarations had ever been made. On the contrary, we had publicly stated many times that our aim was to seek a peaceful solution. I told the Soviet Premier of the successive steps we had taken to secure this. As to our military measures, which he criticized, I added:

> I must tell you frankly that these precautionary military measures are fully justified by the circumstances. In the first place the ruler of Egypt is a militarist who glories in the fact. In his book, for example, he says 'Throughout my life I have had faith in militarism'. Secondly, Colonel Nasser not only preaches militarism but employs it. Thus the premises of the Universal Suez Canal Company were occupied by troops, its assets were forcibly seized and the foreign employees of the company were threatened. This act of force which has created a state of tension in the Middle East has not yet evoked any expression of disapproval on the part of the Soviet Government.

Finally I reminded Marshal Bulganin:

> In 1946 the Soviet Government proclaimed their support for the international control of the canal. That is what we seek and it is of course fully consistent both with Egypt's sovereignty and with the Charter of the United Nations.

A fortnight went by before Marshal Bulganin wrote again. By then he had critical views to express on the Users' Association. So had we, but from a different standpoint.

V

THE UNITED NATIONS
September 19th – October 13th

*American reluctance to withhold dues – Users' Association set up –
Indian opinion – Deterioration of our position in the Middle East –
France and United Kingdom decide to appeal to Security
Council – Mr. Macmillan's visit to Washington – Mr. Menzies'
speech – Mr. Selwyn Lloyd and I meet French Ministers in Paris –
Some thoughts on U.N.O. – Anglo-French decisions announced –
Marshal Bulganin's objections – My telegram to President
Eisenhower – America and 'colonialism' – Users' Association
meets – Mr. Krishna Menon's views – Mr. Dulles and Mr.
Selwyn Lloyd – The Security Council – Russia uses the veto*

The second London Conference was convened to meet on September 19th with the Foreign Secretary once again in the chair. In
the meantime, the Egyptians were handling the traffic of ships
through the canal by various expedients. The remaining pilots of the old
company were working overtime and new ones were being recruited
from all over the world. Russia, Yugoslavia and the United States
were among the contributors. An early breakdown in the operation
of the canal, which had been one of our fears, was not now expected
by our shipping advisers. This in its turn had certain consequences.

One of the main purposes of the Users' Club in its original form
had been to convoy the ships of its members through the canal if the
Egyptians refused or proved unable to do so. The second contingency
was now unlikely to arise. Should this modify the object of the club,
and if so, how? Obviously it was all the more important that the
agency should now withhold the dues from Egypt until a general
settlement was reached, and that this should be set forth clearly and
accepted by as many maritime powers as possible. The British draft

declaration, which was to be considered at the conference, therefore firmly proposed that the Users' Association should:

> . . . hold in trust the surplus revenues accruing from the pay-
> ment of canal dues to the association as a fund for allocation in
> accordance with such permanent arrangements as may be made
> for the operation of the Suez Canal.

The French were equally strong on this point and judged the issue with admirable clarity. They held that we must persuade the countries, representing at least 80 per cent. of the traffic passing through the canal, either to join the new association or at least to deny dues to Egypt. This was the only sure weapon, short of force, which we could bring to bear on Colonel Nasser. If we did not use it effectively, the world would clearly see that he had got away with his prize. All the consequences in Asia and Africa, forecast by ourselves and the French two months earlier, would begin to come to pass.

The American delegation at the second London Conference were less precise in their expressions. Mr. Dulles in his opening speech stated:

> Membership of the association would not involve the assump-
> tion by any member of any obligation. It would however be
> hoped that members of the association would voluntarily take such
> action with respect to their ships and the payment of canal dues
> as would facilitate the work of the association and build up its
> prestige and authority, and consequently its ability to serve.

This was a further weakening of the Users' Club. An organization towards which members had no obligations could hardly be expected to show greater firmness than the eighteen-power proposals. Yet this was the basis on which the Users' Club had been traded to us.

After debate, the conference issued a statement on September 21st reaffirming its belief in the reasonableness of the eighteen-power proposals as presented to Egypt by Mr. Menzies' committee. These, it declared, 'still offer a fair basis for a peaceful solution of the Suez Canal problem'. It also published a declaration proposing the setting up of the Canal Users' Association, to which Governments repre-sented at the conference were invited to adhere.

In the main, this document followed the lines already agreed upon in three-power talks between Britain, France and the United States. But the British draft had been considerably modified in the course of negotiation. The clause defining the purpose of the Suez Canal Users' Association on dues now read as follows:

> . . . to receive, hold and disburse the revenues accruing from dues and other sums which any user of the canal may pay to the association without prejudice to existing rights, pending a final settlement.

There were pitfalls in this which later became apparent. The words 'may pay' did not commit the subscribing countries to withholding dues from Egypt. Moreover, the word 'disburse' would allow the association to hand over to Egypt any proportion it chose of the dues it collected.

At the time, we accepted the assurances given us by the United States delegation. They declared their Government ready to take action to prevent payment to Egypt. They could not, however, compel their shipowners to pay to the new association. Nor, we acknowledged, could we. But Britain and other countries were already denying dues to Egypt, whereas the United States was not. It was agreed that once the association had been constituted, had set up a separate bank account, and made some interim arrangement with the former Canal Company, the voluntary consent of ship-owners to pay to the Users' Club, and the Users' Club only, should be sought and obtained. The shipowners were likely to work closely together so long as there was no discrimination between them.

This was the best that our delegation, and those who thought like us, could get at the second London Conference. The declaration was undoubtedly marked by some ambiguity and it had a cool, though not unfavourable, public reception. The results could be made effective if the machinery of the association was established at once and set to work in the way that the French and ourselves wanted, for which we thought we had United States' backing. It became clear to us only gradually that the American conception of the association was now evolving so fast that it would end as an agency for collecting dues for Nasser. Perhaps this was not clear to the United States delegation themselves at the time.

★   ★   ★   ★   ★

From the start, the Suez crisis was never a problem between Egypt and two, or even three, powers only; it concerned a very large part of the world. We realized that the repercussions of the crisis ranged wide and we naturally took heed of the advice offered.

The Indian Government, for instance, were constantly urging a negotiated settlement upon us. As we repeatedly explained to them, this was what we were seeking. This had been our aim in Korea, in Indo-China, in Trieste and in Iran, and we had gained it in all cases, sometimes with Indian help. We had no need to be ashamed of our record. Our difficulty now was that there could be no negotiation with Egypt unless there were some basis on which to negotiate. Mr. Menzies' committee had carried their fair proposals to Cairo, but Nasser had turned them down. Still we perservered in pursuit of an international solution, hence the Canal Users' Club. Meanwhile, Mr. Krishna Menon made a number of journeys between Cairo, London and eventually New York. Her Majesty's Government considered fully and at length all suggestions put to them by India, but Delhi did not then share our view of the importance of keeping international agreements in the interest of all nations, or of the need to restore them when broken.

The Egyptian Government showed no readiness to compromise, though they had at first been apprehensive of the Users' Association. They feared for a while that it might be really effective. Reassured on this point, they were content to stand pat.

Our information from the Middle East at this time confirmed the gloomy views we had been forming in London about the effects of the second London Conference. We had telegraphed for reports. Opinion in Cairo, we were told, had been encouraged to think that Nasser had succeeded, that the affair was practically over and that the threat of sanctions by the Western powers no longer existed. From elsewhere in the Middle East we learnt that the second London Conference had given an impression of far less firmness and unanimity than the first. Several Arab leaders were still perturbed by Nasser's declarations against the West and by his co-operation with Russia, and they were beginning to fear that time might be on his side. They mistrusted the forces that he represented, and the ambitions he entertained to enhance Egypt's position at the expense of her neighbours. If Nasser could not be obliged to accept some form of international control of the canal, he would have won the game.

The negotiations at the second London Conference, like those of the first, were handled exclusively by the Foreign Secretary, and he did all a man could do. He saw me often and we talked over the situation, but I took no part in the detailed work of the conference. An attempt to do so could only have led to confusion. I did meet the principal delegates informally from time to time, often at Number 10, or with the Foreign Secretary at his house in Carlton Gardens. On one of these occasions, Mr. Dulles told us that Mr. Gaitskell had asked to see him, and Mr. Dulles inquired whether we had any objection to his doing so. I replied that we certainly had none.

It had always been a principle with me, since I became Foreign Secretary in 1935, to encourage meetings between foreign visitors and the Opposition or other leading figures in our country. I thought this useful on many counts and in no sense embarrassing to the Government. Any good embassy has contacts with the leading political figures in a free country, and the Government does itself no harm by encouraging what is likely to happen anyway. I used to invite Mr. Churchill, when he was out of office before the war, to meet visitors when they came to London. He told me long afterwards how much he had valued this, and I have no doubt that he did my visitors good too.

On an informal occasion Mr. Dulles spoke several times of the state of public opinion in Britain, which he maintained was not in support of the Government's policies over Suez. In the end I had to contest this myself. I still believe that American opinion underestimated the firm sentiments of our country at that time, and that this underestimate had a debilitating influence on their policies.

The United States Government were still reluctant to approach the United Nations and we tried to meet them on this for a while longer. But the closing stage of the London Conference brought increasing pressure upon us to go to the Security Council. This was publicly voiced at the last meeting; privately the pressure became even stronger. Several representatives of the eighteen powers emphasized to the Foreign Secretary that it would be easier for them to join the Users' Association if an appeal to the United Nations were under way at the same time. This was repeatedly put to me at a luncheon which I gave on the last day to the leading delegates of New Zealand, Iran, Norway and Portugal, the Foreign Secretary being also present. They wanted us to help them to help us. My colleagues and I felt that they were right. The indifferent outcome of the conference lent support to the pressure for further action by us. Finally the repercussions in the Middle East showed that if we waited longer our position would slip. Therefore, even though the United States still favoured delay, we felt we could no longer hold our hand.

The French were now ready for United Nations action, so was our own public opinion, and there was some danger that the Russians might anticipate us at the Security Council. Our plan was to inaugurate the Users' Association in London on October 1st and to ask for a debate at the Council on October 3rd, a full ten days after the conclusion of the London Conference. We held up our move for a day, so that Mr. Dulles might be informed in advance. He expressed himself unhappy at our timing, but he did not seek to dissuade us. The United States Government, however, would not sponsor our letter to the President of the Security Council, which we despatched on September 23rd, requesting that the Suez problem be placed on the Council's agenda. This was therefore an Anglo-French document.

The Chancellor of the Exchequer, Mr. Harold Macmillan, at this time paid a visit to Washington. He found the American attitude reassuring in a number of respects. He reported that the United States Government definitely undertook to make it unlawful for their ships to pay canal dues to Egypt. This was an important decision of principle if it were carried out, but, to have any real effect, American-owned ships flying the flags of Panama and Liberia must be included. Mr. Macmillan also told us that the American Administration was prepared to use its influence on these countries, but was doubtful of their co-operation, especially in the case of Panama, which the United States regarded as virtually lined up with Egypt. I was sure from past experience that, if the Americans had the will, they would find a way. The Chancellor of the Exchequer said that he found Washington confident that six months of economic pressure upon Nasser would accomplish all we wanted. On this point I was less sanguine, especially as nearly two months had passed since the canal had been seized and user nations were still as far as ever from applying any effective pressure, economic or otherwise.

Mr. Dulles now returned to a more resolute line about the use of force. In a television interview he said:

> I do believe that peace and justice and international law are two sides of the coin, and you can't always count on nations not using

force unless there is some alternative which conforms to international peace and justice.

On September 25th, Mr. Menzies, speaking in the Australian House of Representatives, surveyed the history of the Suez crisis in lucid and forcible language. In his conclusion he summed up the alternatives which faced us:

First: Negotiation for a peaceful settlement by means of an honourable agreement. So far, we have tried this without success. Our failure, let me repeat and emphasize, has not been due to any unfairness or illiberality on our side, but to a dictatorial intransigence on the other. Should we continue to negotiate on a watered down basis in a spirit which says that any agreement is better than none? I cannot imagine anything more calculated to strengthen Colonel Nasser's hand or weaken our own.

Second: Putting on of pressure by a co-operative effort on the part of user nations. Colonel Nasser must be brought to understand that his course of action is unprofitable to his country and to his people and that he is abandoning the substance for the shadow. This is one of the great merits of the Users' Association now established by the second London Conference. The more canal revenue is diverted from the Egyptian Government the less will the Egyptian people believe that it pays to repudiate.

Third: Should the United Nations, by reason of veto, prove unable to direct any active course of positive action, we may find ourselves confronted by a choice which we cannot avoid making. I state this choice in stark terms:

(a) We can organize a full-blooded programme of economic sanctions against Egypt, or

(b) We can use force to restore international control of the canal, or

(c) We can have further negotiations, provided we do not abandon vital principles, or

(d) We can 'call it a day', leave Egypt in command of the canal, and resign ourselves to the total collapse of our position and interests in the Middle East with all the implications for the economic strength and the industrial prosperity of the nations whose well being is vital to ours.

This, I believe, is a realistic analysis of the position.

It has been for me an astonishing experience to find that there are people who reject force out of hand, reject economic action on the ground that it is provocative and so, being opposed to action of either kind, are prepared to accept new tyranny with regret, perhaps, but without resistance. Such an attitude is so inconsistent with the vigorous tradition of our race that I cannot believe it commands any genuine and informed public support.

★   ★   ★   ★   ★

On September 26th the Foreign Secretary and I flew to Paris to consult the French Government. M. Mollet and M. Pineau were firm in their belief that we must stand by the eighteen-power proposals and resolutely oppose negotiation on any other grounds.

At this moment the United Nations was buzzing with projects for negotiating committees, some based on Indian proposals for compromise, others arising from attempts by Russia and her satellites to weaken the Western position, and still others from the readiness of the United Nations Secretariat to devise means of negotiation at any price, whatever the cost to the sanctity of international agreements.

The United Nations was founded as a means to an end, to keep the peace. Armed conflict will not be avoided unless international agreements are respected. The chief purpose of the United Nations should be to uphold these engagements. We sought the best method by which the Security Council could do this. The League of Nations always set much store by the preservation of international agreements. There is less taste for this in the present United Nations, because some of the newly created states among its members still feel expansive. They have not yet understood that the rule of law is important to them as to others.

The United Nations is built round the Security Council, which should be its Cabinet, and the Assembly, which should be its forum for general discussion. These were to be its executive and debating components. The abuse of the veto in the Council has restricted the opportunities of the greater powers to exercise diplomatic leadership. As a result, totalitarian states can hope to get away with illegal acts, especially if they raise a clamour of anti-colonialism. Two standards of conduct are being evolved. One for the free nations who wish to be law-abiding. The other for communist powers who see no incongruity in denying the authority of the United Nations to influence their own actions, while noisily demanding sanctions against others. Satan rebuking sin is a modest moralist beside them.

At our meeting in Paris, the French and ourselves were agreed that we must not allow our case to be submerged or manœuvred into a backwater at the United Nations. I wanted to reassure our allies that we would not abandon our main objective, to remove the canal from the control of a single Government or man, and to secure enforceable guarantees for efficient navigation and maintenance. The French were sceptical about the United Nations and more sceptical still about the Users' Club, which had been even less well received by their public opinion than by ours. They felt that the American Administration was not fulfilling its promises, that some of the utterances of the President and Mr. Dulles would make the Russians believe that they could back Nasser with impunity, that the delay was allowing Nasser to build up an ever stronger position, thanks to a continuous supply of Russian arms. Finally, there was a danger of the whole Middle East coming under the dominance not so much of Egypt as of Russia. For all these reasons the French favoured action at an early date.

I had much sympathy with their views, but I was sure that we must first have recourse to the United Nations and do our best there. The Foreign Secretary and I undertook, however, that, if the Security Council showed itself incapable of maintaining international agreements, Britain would not stand aside and allow them to be flouted. If necessary we would be prepared to use whatever steps, including force, might be needed to re-establish respect for these obligations. The French Ministers agreed, though with some reluctance, to try out all the resources of the Security Council, on the strict understanding that there should be no abandonment of the original proposals approved by the eighteen powers. This was an attitude with which we were ourselves in full agreement. We issued the following statement at the end of our meeting:

The primary purpose of this meeting, the importance of which has been greatly increased by the latest international developments, was to strengthen Franco-British solidarity in every respect. This result was fully achieved.

In particular the Ministers defined their common position in the United Nations as a result of the recent British decision to place the question of the Suez Canal before the Security Council.

They were fully agreed on the line to be followed by them in the forthcoming debate.

The Ministers expressed their determination to continue, in respect of any further developments, the close co-operation which has characterized the policy of the two Governments since the beginning of the Suez Canal crisis.

The Ministers then reviewed the course of the relationship between France and the United Kingdom in recent years, and reaffirmed the identity of aim and community of interests of the British and French peoples. To this end they agreed on further studies designed to eliminate such minor points as may be outstanding between the two countries.

Finally they recalled the action taken by both countries since the war to strengthen political, military and economic co-operation between the nations of Western Europe. They agreed to pursue this policy and to study, in the European organizations to which they belong or by other means, the new forms which it might take.

They expressed their determination to ensure that constructive results should flow from these initiatives.

Further ministerial meetings between the two countries will be arranged as may be necessary.

On leaving Le Bourget, I added these words :

We have during these two days had some very useful talks, in the course of which we have established a common Franco-British policy on many points. In particular, we have agreed upon a common action in the United Nations during the forthcoming debates . . . .

This crisis, or rather the *coup de force* of Nasser, has not only endangered the economic interests of many nations, but has constituted an attack on the traditional respect of treaties, and gnawed at the very basis of international confidence. This was a lesson before the war, and is also one today. It is our duty to work together, French and English, to find a just solution to the present difficulties.

On my return to London, I received a further long letter from Marshal Bulganin, who now objected to every action upon the Suez problem that the maritime powers had ever proposed or taken. The future of the canal was of little practical concern to Russia, but the Soviet Government saw an opportunity to fish in troubled waters and fish they did. This letter prompted me to telegraph President Eisenhower:

> You can be sure that we are fully alive to the wider dangers of the Middle East situation. They can be summed up in one word—Russia . . . .
>
> There is no doubt in our minds that Nasser, whether he likes it or not, is now effectively in Russian hands, just as Mussolini was in Hitler's. It would be as ineffective to show weakness to Nasser now in order to placate him as it was to show weakness to Mussolini. The only result was and would be to bring the two together.
>
> No doubt your people will have told you of the accumulating evidence of Egyptian plots in Libya, Saudi Arabia and Iraq. At any moment any of these may be touched off unless we can prove to the Middle East that Nasser is losing. That is why we are so concerned to do everything we can to make the Users' Club an effective instrument. If your ships under the Panamanian and Liberian flags would follow the example of those under your flag that would greatly help.
>
> I feel sure that anything which you can say or do to show firmness to Nasser at this time will help the peace by giving the Russians pause. As usual I send you my thoughts in this frank way.

This message was despatched to the President on October 1st. The next day a damaging statement came from Mr. Dulles at a press conference. This, however unintentionally, was likely to make Nasser believe that if he held fast, the United States would fall apart from France and Britain over the seizure of the canal.

> The United States [the Secretary of State said] cannot be expected to identify itself 100 per cent. either with the colonial powers or the powers uniquely concerned with the problem of getting independence as rapidly and as fully as possible. There were, I admit, differences of approach by the three nations to the Suez dispute, which perhaps arise from fundamental concepts. For while we stand together, and I hope we shall always stand together in treaty relations covering the North Atlantic, any

areas encroaching in some form or manner on the problem of so-called colonialism, find the United States playing a somewhat independent role. The shift from colonialism to independence will be going on for another fifty years, and I believe that the task of the United Nations is to try to see that this process moves forward in a constructive, evolutionary way, and does not come to a halt or go forward through violent, revolutionary processes which would be destructive of much good.

He then spoke of the Users' Association:

> There is talk about teeth being pulled out of the plan, but I know of no teeth: there were no teeth in it, so far as I am aware.

The representatives of the Users' Association countries were then assembled in London confidently awaiting the United States decision to pay the canal dues to their organization. These were the teeth. Mr. Dulles' statement was in conflict with the users' understanding of the United States Government's intentions. Our representative on the committee, Lord John Hope, reported exasperation and dismay in their ranks. The dispute over Nasser's seizure of the canal had, of course, nothing to do with colonialism, but was concerned with international rights. If the United States had to defend their treaty rights in the Panama Canal, they would not regard such action as colonialism, neither would I. Yet their rights in Panama are those of one nation, not of many nations, as at Suez.

★　★　★　★　★

It would be foolish to pretend that Mr. Dulles' remarks on colonialism did not represent his feelings and those of many of his countrymen. These sentiments certainly played their part in the reaction of some Americans to the Anglo-French intervention at Suez. It is worth while to probe deeper into the causes for the frequent divergences on colonialism, which have presented a continuing problem in Anglo-American relations and still do so, despite official denials.

With the passage of nearly two centuries since 1776, this issue should vex us less. George III has much to answer for. But it is too easy an explanation merely to take refuge in that monarch's mistaken judgments. Britain has had her share of responsibility for the instinctive American reaction to any question of colonialism. What is disturbing is its tendency to reappear at any critical moment in the relations of the United States with one of her Western allies. I have no doubt that in part these sentiments are due to a difference of approach to the general problem of relationship with what are often called 'dependent peoples'. The United Kingdom has, for a century or more and in an increasing degree, applied herself to the trustee conception of her responsibilities towards colonial territories. As a result, we have for years past fostered and admired the growth of countries which were once colonies and have since become partners in the Commonwealth. Great nations like Canada and Australia, countries growing apace like New Zealand and the Union of South Africa, are the earliest examples. More have followed.

At the Peace Conference after the first world war, there was a characteristic tussle, from which Mr. Lloyd George emerged victorious, to secure a fair representation for the Dominions. Later, during the inter-war years, when the League of Nations was in the heyday of its power, these Commonwealth countries were prominent. One of them was always a member of the Council of the League of Nations which, unlike the Security Council, was regularly manned by the Foreign Secretaries of the countries composing it. As a result, the British Foreign Secretary of the day experienced a continuing and most helpful contact. I enjoyed working very closely in those years with men like Stanley Bruce, of Australia, who had been Prime Minister of his country, and William Jordan, of New Zealand.

Our personal relations were so happy in our countries' friendship that they occasioned comment which was sometimes envious. The states of the Little Entente, which were active at Geneva, did not always find their relations with their ally France quite so easy. I remember in particular one luncheon at which both M. Titulescu, the brilliant Foreign Minister of Roumania, and the French Foreign Minister of the day, were present among others. While Stanley Bruce and I were having some friendly exchanges across the table, M. Titulescu, who had been crossed in some argument with his French colleague earlier in the day, galvanized the assembled company with a sudden exclamation: '*Moi, je veux être dominion*'.

The United States point of view on trusteeship tends to differ from our own. In their judgment, there is nothing wrong in expending large sums of capital in the development of a country and deriving much gain from the process, the American companies or individuals accepting no responsibility for the administration of the country. This point of view is strongly held and there can be no doubt than in many parts of the world the results are satisfactory, both to the countries concerned and to the United States. On the other hand, this practice can also have unexpected consequences which seem less laudable. It remains a fact that two of the more backward countries in the Middle East and in Africa, Saudi Arabia and Liberia, are also two where American interests play a conspicuously large part.

Much of the sparring between the United States and Great Britain on colonial issues could certainly be removed if more was understood of the record of this country in the colonial sphere, especially since the beginning of the century. But the orderly development of self-government in an important territory, like Malaya or Nigeria, is not sensational news ; a riot in Cyprus is. As a consequence, understanding grows slowly.

★　★　★　★　★

On October 1st the Foreign Secretary presided over the inaugural meeting of the Users' Association in London. Then, at long last, all was set for an approach to the Security Council of the United Nations. Mr. Selwyn Lloyd flew over to New York to state our case. Throughout this period he worked closely and effectively with his French colleague, M. Pineau, and with the Australian representative on the Security Council, Dr. Walker. M. Spaak also lent valuable aid. We were, in fact, fortunate in the composition of the Council at this time. Australia, Belgium, Cuba, Iran, Peru and Yugoslavia were the elected representatives. Except for Yugoslavia, which took a line akin to that of Moscow, this was as friendly a membership as we could wish. Nevertheless, we had our anxieties.

The Foreign Secretary and M. Pineau made clear in their preliminary consultations with other representatives that they were determined to hold fast to the eighteen-power proposals as a basis for any negotiation with Egypt. Between the declared position of the eighteen users of the canal and Nasser's refusal of any international authority, there was no place for committees of mediation. The issues were clear cut, a decisive pronouncement was called for. From the outset, however, there had been in all countries those who were not prepared to see this dispute for what it was, the denial of an international engagement, recently reaffirmed by the Egyptian Government, and the seizure by force of international property. They preferred to look upon it as the expression of a nationalist mood in a country recently emancipated, for which, therefore, benevolent allowances must be made.

This was broadly the Indian view. The Government of that country looked to the West for repeated concessions and found no difficulty in urging this course, while refusing the slightest concession to Pakistan over Kashmir. The Indian Government were canvassing their scheme, which they now put in writing, for attaching an international advisory body, which would only have vague powers of supervision, to the Egyptian nationalized canal authority. Mr. Menon had found ears in Cairo ready to listen to such a proposal, naturally enough, for this meant that any effective international element was eliminated. It might be that the Indians had sincerely convinced themselves that Nasser would not accept the eighteen-power proposals. Certainly the Indian Government had not supported them, but this did not seem a sufficient reason why all eighteen powers should, in deference, abandon their position. We had already considered Mr. Menon's ideas in London and found no substance in them. Thanks to the staunchness of the principal users of the canal, he now failed to sway the deliberations of the Security Council, but his activities caused a continuing superficial flurry.

Meanwhile, in New York Mr. Selwyn Lloyd had found the United States Secretary of State in a cordial frame of mind. It is true that Mr. Dulles had once more alluded to the 'suddenness' of the Anglo-French decision to have recourse to the Security Council, but he had seemed convinced by Mr. Lloyd's assurance that this move was indeed a genuine effort to reach a settlement on the part of France and Britain. He also appeared to accept our argument that time was running out and that there was every need for decision.

At international conferences rumours, ill-founded and otherwise, are apt to find their way into the press. This is all the more likely to happen when great cities are chosen as their setting. It is one of the reasons why Geneva would have been a better headquarters for the United Nations than New York. The newspapers in New York now reported that the American delegation were openly talking of 'rifts' between themselves and their French and British colleagues. It was also written that the United States was thinking of accepting the Indian proposals. The Foreign Secretary took this up direct with the Secretary of State.

Mr. Dulles strongly denied having given any support to ideas of compromise, or having taken any part in putting these rumours about.

He declared that he was with Britain on every point, except the use of force. Even force he did not rule out as an ultimate resort, and he once more recognized our right to maintain the threat of using it. Nevertheless, he felt that to employ force in the immediate future would be a mistake, since in his view Nasser's position was deteriorating. There seemed no grounds for this last estimate.

Direct talks with the Egyptian Foreign Minister, Dr. Fawzi, began on October 9th. They were conducted with firmness and patience by the French and British Foreign Secretaries. The Egyptian counterproposals offered vague hopes for negotiation, but as the days went by they lost what little precision they had. In particular the Egyptians accepted no international authority and they offered no effective sanction for any breach of the principle of free navigation.

Meanwhile, a number of developments were serving, at least in appearance, to weaken the position of the eighteen powers in Egyptian minds. There were delays in setting up the Canal Users' Association for effective work. Fifteen members had so far joined, but no administrator had yet been appointed. As late as October 10th, the American representative in London was still without authority to open a bank account into which canal dues could be paid. It had not even been firmly laid down and accepted that dues must be paid to the association. Unless the association had the power to withhold dues from Egypt, it would possess no safeguard against Egyptian interference with its members' ships. There was still a disturbing lack of unanimity within the Users' Club as to how dues should be apportioned; how much for the maintenance and development of the canal, how much in compensation to the Suez Canal Company and how much for payments to the Egyptian Government. The United States was inclining to the view that a considerable part of the dues ought to be paid to Egypt. We had never been willing to agree to this in advance of the settlement and felt growing exasperation at the constant whittling away of our position.

After ten days of discussion at the United Nations, a vote was now due in the Security Council. The resolution before the Council was substantially the one which we had agreed with the French and the United States. By skill and hard work, various weaker or vaguer alternative resolutions had been set aside, yet the outcome gave us only partial satisfaction. It confirmed our standpoint, but it brought us no nearer the solution we sought. The resolution under debate on October 13th consisted of two parts, the first part of which was passed unanimously. This laid down six principles by which it was agreed that any settlement of the Suez question must abide. At my suggestion these principles, which largely coincided with those outlined by Mr. Dulles in his speech at the first London Conference, had now been renamed 'requirements'. They ran as follows:

1. There should be free and open transit through the canal without discrimination, overt or covert.
2. The sovereignty of Egypt should be respected.
3. The operation of the canal should be insulated from the politics of any country.
4. The manner of fixing tolls and charges should be decided by agreement between Egypt and the users.
5. A fair proportion of the dues should be allotted to development.
6. In case of disputes, unresolved affairs between the Suez Canal Company and the Egyptian Government should be settled by arbitration.

The second part of the resolution declared that the proposals of the eighteen powers corresponded to these requirements and invited the Egyptian Government to put forward its proposals to give effect to them. It requested the Governments of Egypt, France and the United Kingdom to continue their interchanges. It also laid down that in the meantime the canal should offer free passage to all shipping. Thus we hoped to open a way for a test case on the banning of Israeli ships. It further declared that the Users' Association should receive the dues payable by the ships of its members, and that the association and the Egyptian nationalized authority should co-operate to ensure the satisfactory management of the canal. This part of the resolution was what mattered to us; it obtained nine votes. There were two against, the Soviet Foreign Secretary, Mr. Shepilov, and the Yugoslav representative. Mr. Shepilov's vote was a veto and so the operative part of the resolution was killed.

This was as far as our appeal to the United Nations took us. We were left with six principles, and principles are aimless unless translated into action. The Soviets having vetoed the part of the resolution which set out the action to be taken, no method was left for harnessing the principles. They just flapped in the air. Nor had a time limit been set to the interchanges expected of the French, British and Egyptian

Governments. The way was open to endless procrastination by Egypt. Worse, it also lay open to her to renew her aggressive designs in other fields.

These discussions bowed out the practical proposals of the eighteen powers, which were our minimum requirement for the security of the canal. They were never allowed the limelight again. Though the Americans had been the first advocates of these proposals, the Administration showed no concern at their defeat by the communist veto. Beaming through rose-coloured spectacles, they acclaimed the six principles in their place. I soon learnt that the Soviet Government regarded the proceedings at the United Nations as a victory for Egypt and for them. In this they were undoubtedly right. I was not surprised when messages from our friends in the Middle East showed dismay at Nasser's swelling success.

It was clear enough to me where we were. The powers at the London Conference had worked out, with care and forethought, a scheme which would have made the Suez Canal part of an international system giving security for all. The United States had put its whole authority behind the scheme and her Secretary of State had introduced the proposals himself before the London Conference. Now all this was dead. It was of no use to fool ourselves on that account. We had been strung along over many months of negotiation from pretext to pretext, from device to device, and from contrivance to contrivance. At each stage in this weary pilgrimage we had seen our position weakened. Now we had gone to the United Nations itself. It was not at our wish that we had been so late to make an appeal there. Here was the result. Two communist powers, Yugoslavia and Soviet Russia, had voted against the only practical scheme in existence for the creation of an international system for the Suez Canal. As a consequence of the Soviet veto, the free world had recoiled, some with reluctance and some with relief. There was no one in that room at the United Nations, at the conclusion of the vote, who supposed for an instant that any life was left in the work of the London Conference. The Soviets had had their way and no amount of soothing optimism could conceal the truth.

Yet the notion gained currency that the Security Council had prepared the terms for a peaceful and just settlement of the dispute. Those who wished to assure themselves that the easy path is also the wise one, pointed to the six principles, which all the members of the Council had endorsed. Six principles, when it had taken us three months of negotiation to carry practical working proposals for the future of the canal to the United Nations, only to have them smothered. At the end of that time we were to rejoice at being offered six principles in their place. The truth was starkly clear to me. Plunder had paid off.

Perhaps the most disturbing feature of all these discussions was the utter indifference shown by the United Nations to the international aspects of the crisis. The Suez Canal was the greatest international waterway in the world and had been internationally owned and administered. The founders of the United Nations believed that they were building an international order. It might be thought that one of the first duties of that order would be to protect the international organizations which already existed in the world, and to promote others. The guardian of internationalism might have been expected to defend this successful experiment. Nothing of the kind. From the start to the end of the business, not one single syllable of censure or regret was uttered by the United Nations, or on its behalf either by the Security Council or by the General Assembly, at the seizure of a great international waterway by force. It is inevitable that there will be a reckoning for this moral backsliding.

VI

PRELUDE
October 13th – 23rd

My speech to Conservative Conference at Llandudno – Meeting with MM. Mollet and Pineau – Course of our discussions – We decide to stand by eighteen-power proposals – Our despondency about the Users' Club – Danger of an Israeli attack on Jordan – Our joint communiqué – The fedayeen – Nasser's threats to Israel – Russian arms supplies to Egypt – The two world wars – Arab joint command established – Ministerial changes – Steadfast attitude of my colleagues

On October 12th, towards the end of the proceedings at the Security Council, I travelled to Llandudno to address the public meeting which, by tradition, closes the Conservative Party Conference. As not infrequently happens, there had been gloomy forebodings in the press about the state of the party. These had not been fulfilled and the conference had shown itself vigorous and united. I found its members more lively and enthusiastic than they had been a year before in the wake of victory. I also found them in agreement with our foreign policy. Lord Salisbury, who was to have spoken during the foreign policy discussion, was unfortunately not well enough to come to the conference and take part. His speech was delivered for him by Mr. Anthony Nutting and warmly acclaimed.

Early on the morning of October 13th, the day of my speech, a message came through from the Foreign Secretary in New York, telling me of an optimistic statement made by the President of the United States in a television interview the day before. He had said that progress on the Suez Canal dispute had been 'most gratifying' and that it looked as though 'a very great crisis is behind us'. This confidence was ill-timed, for on the next night Soviet Russia vetoed the operative part of the resolution at the Security Council, thus denying the eighteen-power proposals and those of the Users' Association, which the United States Government had themselves sponsored. The Foreign Secretary was much concerned at this American attitude, which was remote from reality and would fortify the Egyptian position still further. We had hoped, at the least, for a grave statement about the serious position threatening at the Security Council and an exhortation to the United Nations to give effect to the agreed views of the eighteen powers.

The difference in time between London and New York created a constant problem during these negotiations, the morning in Wales was still night in New York. The Foreign Secretary had got to bed late after a strenuous day and I was most reluctant to wake him. Yet I had to speak at 2 p.m. our time, only 9 a.m. in New York. I left him to sleep as long as I could and, a little over an hour before I had to begin my speech, telephoned to him about the situation. We both wished to avoid an open divergence and I told him of my intention to seize on the least optimistic of the President's phrases, underline it, and point out once again that force could not be excluded. We also agreed that he should speak plainly to the United States Government, expressing our concern at the consequences for us of these repeated and unjustified flights of hopeful fancy. I spent luncheon rewriting my speech and glumly reflecting on the disturbing precedent which had been set for the future.

In my speech I gave an account of the Suez crisis and of the position as it then stood. I first warned the delegates not to indulge in hasty or over-optimistic judgment. I continued:

President Eisenhower in his press conference on Thursday is reported to have said that you must have peace with justice, or it is not peace. I agree with those words. We should all take them as our text. That is why we have always said that with us force is the last resort, but it cannot be excluded. Therefore, we have refused to say that in no circumstances would we ever use force. No responsible Government could ever give such a pledge.

When we drove to the overflow meetings, it took my wife and me quite a while to make our way through the cheering throngs. I came back to London encouraged by the loyalty of the conference. The testing time for our policy was at hand. The veto fell that night.

When the Foreign Secretary returned from New York, my colleagues and I talked things over. There had been a suggestion at the United Nations for a meeting between representatives of French and Egyptian Governments and ourselves at Geneva. There was never any hope that the Egyptians would agree to this on the basis of the eighteen-power proposals, or on any that restored international control over the canal. Perhaps we could have found a pretext for going to Geneva. We might even have persuaded the French to come along too and negotiate with Nasser an agreement of sorts about the canal. It might have been dressed up to look fairly reasonable, even though I knew that it did not mean much. This was in fact approximately what happened when the Americans were later entrusted with the task, after I had resigned.

It might be said that such a policy would have led to postponing the crunch with Nasser, and would have been advantageous to us. I did not believe this and, not believing it, I could not pursue such a course. I could not return from Geneva with a piece of paper and commend it to the House of Commons, when I knew it had no real value. This would have lulled people at a time when I thought they should be alerted. It would have reassured the world about a dictator whose intentions were, I was sure, predatory. Those who did not wish to face unpleasant realities would have been encouraged, and by an agreement which I had brought about and commended. Such action would have been false to everything I had learnt in thirty years of foreign policy. Nor would it have insulated the canal from the control of one man. If we did not ensure this we were laying up certain trouble for the future, first with Israeli commerce, later with that of others.

I had been through so much of this before. I had not been willing to commend to Parliament an agreement with Mussolini which I had not believed would be fulfilled. Having resigned rather than do this twenty years ago, in the lesser responsibility of a Foreign Secretary, I was not prepared to reach and proclaim another agreement as a step to peace, when I did not believe that it was any such thing. As I said two years later in a speech at Leamington:

In external affairs a democratic state has to be on its guard against certain dangers. The most insidious of these is to take the easy way, and to put off decision. Drift is the demon of democracy. Democracies should rather consider, in any step they take in world affairs, whether what they do will serve only to relax tension for a while, or whether it is in the true interest of lasting peace. That is the difference between appeasement and peace.

The Government agreed that they must await the proposals which the Egyptian Government had been told to produce, though with little expectation that they would provide a basis for discussion. The Security Council was no sooner over than the Egyptians began to plead excuses against even the principles which they had accepted. The Government decided meanwhile to align their views with the French Government who were their partners in these talks. It was all the more necessary to do so, because the Middle Eastern scene began to look threatening again; the immediate consequence of weakness.

★　★　★　★　★

The Foreign Secretary and I flew to Paris on October 16th to see M. Mollet and M. Pineau. There was no lack of material for discussion, little of it encouraging. We had to deal with three principal topics. The first was the state of general negotiations about the future of the canal. We had to assess the position as it was left after the Security Council meeting and the conversations in which M. Pineau and Mr. Selwyn Lloyd had taken part with the Secretary-General and the Egyptian Foreign Minister. The second was the progress, if such it could be called, of the Users' Club and what our next step should be. In the third place we had to pool our information and consider the action we must take in the light of developments in the Middle East itself and, in particular, the growing menace of hostility by Egypt against Israel. The moment that the Security Council acquiesced in the Russian veto, and relieved Colonel Nasser of any anxiety at the United Nations, tension began to grow in the area again. The *fedayeen* raids on Israel were started up afresh.

We began with a discussion of the position at the United Nations. We felt that the proceedings of the Security Council had decided nothing, the Soviet veto having crushed the effective part of them. We agreed that the general principles which had been endorsed were impeccable, but they had been accepted because they were not a serious commitment. When it came to detailed action like the eighteen-power proposals, all was held up.

We and the French reviewed alternatives. The more we examined these the more we came back to the proposals, which seemed to us to improve in usefulness when set against the confusion of the present situation. We decided we must stand by them. As regards the tactics to employ in negotiation, these were reasonably clear. The Egyptians had been instructed by the Security Council to produce proposals to conform to the six principles. They had not yet done so. There-fore the ball was firmly in their court. We would examine what they might put forward and use as our criterion the extent to which they approached the eighteen-power proposals on which the nations who used the canal were agreed.

The next point which we discussed was the Users' Club. Here was much disappointment. Communications had been exchanged only the day before between Mr. Dulles and the Foreign Secretary; their mes-sages had, in fact, crossed. The general American complaint was that we were concerned with the punitive character of the Users' Club proposals, whereas the United States Government regarded them as a means of co-operating with Egypt. This was not how they had been originally described to us. Our cause for disappointment was more particular. We saw the Users' Club being increasingly organized as an agency to forward dues to Egypt. There was a danger of absurdity in this. At that time 60 per cent. of the canal dues were being denied to Nasser by the ships of Britain, France and others who had followed our lead. From what Mr. Dulles had told the Foreign Secretary, it appeared that nine-tenths of this 60 per cent. was to be handed over to Egypt when the Users' Club was in force. The only gain to the users would be that they would retain one-tenth of the 3 per cent. of canal dues paid by ships flying the American flag. Nasser would have every reason to be grateful to the Users' Club if he could so much increase his proportion of dues. But all hope of Egyptian agreement to the eighteen-power proposals, or anything like them, would be dead.

The American assurance, on which the whole of this discussion began, was that Nasser could not expect anything so good, having rejected the proposals of the eighteen powers. He was now to be paid infinitely more than anything he had been offered before. Both the French and ourselves felt that we could not continue with proposals of this character. The French in particular were without illusions and clearly had no confidence in American support for our negotiations.

Finally, at our meeting we discussed the situation in the Middle East, its dangers and what we could do. The line-up between Jordan, Egypt and Syria was becoming ever closer. There were reports of the establish-ment of a joint command under Egyptian direction, which in fact soon came into existence. Cairo radio blared with increasing vehemence against Israel, menacing her with destruction. Unless Israel was pre-pared just to sit and wait until it suited her enemies to strangle and finally destroy her, it was clear that before long she would have to take some counter-action, at least to put an end to the *fedayeen* raids. If directed against Jordan, from which some of the *fedayeen* raids were said to be mounted under Egyptian leadership, then the position for us would be terrible indeed. We had a treaty obligation to defend Jordan. The Jordanians had no effective air force, our fighter squadrons provided their only protection. Already there had nearly been an incident when, in some counter-raid, an Israeli aircraft had for the first time been engaged. Our help had been called for and our aircraft were on the point of going up, when a wise and rapid exchange of cautionary messages on the spot avoided catastrophe.

Nevertheless, the danger was there. If an attack were launched against Jordan, the Israelis would be using their French Mystères, the delivery of a number of these having previously been agreed by the United States, France and ourselves, the three partners to the Tripartite Declaration. The Royal Air Force would be in action for Jordan, the United States would be on the sidelines. This was a nightmare which could only too easily come true; Jordan calling for support from Nasser and ourselves, Nasser calling for support from Russia, France lined up with Israel on the other side.

As long ago as January, our Ambassador had warned Jordan that Egyptian interference was highly dangerous for her. Egypt was manœuvring to embroil Jordan with Israel. If Israel were to act against one of her encircling enemies, the choice lay between Jordan and Egypt. Syria was insufficiently important. Jordan had provided the one effective Arab military force, the Arab Legion, in the fighting of 1948-9. Despite the large supplies of Soviet equipment which the Egyptians had received, the Legion was probably still the most formidable military formation which Israel's neighbours could put into the field. It might be thought imprudent to act against Egypt while leaving the Legion intact. As against this, Egypt was the political source and inspiration of the threat to Israel. It was the Cairo radio which blared out the daily hatred and the incitement to kill. It was Nasser who had thought out the horror of the *fedayeen*. In the event, Israel found the answer by keeping her best troops in position to cover the front against Jordan, while using less experienced forces for the incursion into Sinai. They proved brilliantly equal to the call upon them.

My colleagues and I were acutely aware of the consequence of action by Israel against Jordan, which we had to do all in our power to avert. Our relations with Israel were not close or intimate, there were constant arguments about the supply of arms. Therefore, at this meeting in Paris, we asked the French Ministers to do everything they could to make clear to Israel that an attack on Jordan would have to be resisted by us. This they undertook to do. It was not only our own treaty engagements which concerned us, but the effect upon Iraq of events in Jordan. To fail to carry out our engagement would be the end of our position in the Middle East, to have to carry it out would be disastrous to Western unity. No dilemma could be more difficult. If Israel were to break out against Egypt and not against Jordan, this dilemma would not arise. For this reason, if there were to be a break-out it was better from our point of view that it should be against Egypt. On the other hand, if the break out were against Egypt, then there would be other worries, for example the safety of the canal. We discussed these matters in all their political and military aspects. In common prudence we had to consider what our action should be, for our two countries were, as we knew, the only powers to have effective military forces at our command in the area. During recent months we had been mounting our military preparations to deal with any interference or other act by Nasser against our ships or our people. Now Nasser's policies were provoking Israel beyond endurance and this also we had to prepare for.

We four Ministers, M. Mollet and I, M. Pineau and Mr. Lloyd, after talking for an hour or so, dined together. After dinner we adjourned to another room where our advisers were waiting and in due course started to draw up our communiqué. It is an old maxim of conferences that if you do not want to waste time at the end, you should start drafting the communiqué at the beginning, or even have it ready in advance. We broke this excellent rule, with the result that we sat later than we need have done.

> As agreed at the last meeting [we announced] between the French and British Ministers in Paris on September 25th, a meeting was held today at the Hôtel Matignon between Sir Anthony Eden and Mr. Selwyn Lloyd on the one hand, and Monsieur Guy Mollet and Monsieur Christian Pineau on the other.
>
> They examined the situation resulting from the recent votes in the Security Council on the Anglo-French resolution.
>
> They resolved to adhere to the requirements set out in the first part of the resolution and unanimously approved, and noted with regret that these were already being questioned in certain Egyptian quarters.

As regards the implementation of these requirements they also resolved to stand by the second part of the resolution, which received nine votes but was vetoed by the Soviet Union. According to the resolution, the eighteen-power proposals, including the international operation of the canal, should constitute the basis for a settlement, unless the Egyptian Government produce other proposals for a system meeting the requirements and affording equivalent guarantees to the users.

The two Governments are ready to consider together any proposals of this nature.

They also had a general exchange of views on the other problems of the Middle East and decided to maintain constant contact on these questions in the spirit of the closest Anglo-French friendship.

On October 18th at a meeting with our Cabinet colleagues in London, the Foreign Secretary and I went over the ground which we had covered in our discussions in Paris. We reported the exchanges of views which we had had with French Ministers on the stage which the negotiations had reached in the Security Council, and the direction in which the Users' Club proposals were developing. We described the increasing tension in the Middle East, with the growing danger that Israel, under provocation from Egypt, would make some military move. The position was indeed serious, but at this stage Her Majesty's Government decided they must await the proposals they had been told to expect from the Egyptians.

★　★　★　★　★

The clouds were lowering and menacing in October 1956. The storm could not be far ahead. No record of events at that time can be true which does not take account of this.

One set of circumstances might have countered this rising tension. Britain, France and the United States had signed an agreement in 1950, declaring that they would prevent any violation of the armistice lines in Palestine, either by Israel or by the Arab States. If the signatories of this agreement had not only declared their intention to fulfil it, but had taken military precautions together publicly, to make action effective, then there might have been sufficient comfort in such preparations to give confidence to Israel. I had made this proposal when I was in Washington in January. It had not been possible to agree upon it. Ever since I had been increasingly concerned at what the outcome must be.

I had seen so many of these situations before, deteriorating rapidly, even menacingly, yet there being no new element to seize and use, and nobody prepared to inject one. Trieste had been such another a year or two back. Then we and the Americans had intruded the new ingredient and it had flashed and flared in our faces. We had been much blamed at the time and for a while it looked as if we had only made matters worse. But we had not, we had made everyone realize the reality of the dangers Europe was running. The alternative to composition was collision, which meant war; composition was to be preferred. It might be necessary to treat the Middle Eastern menace by the same methods.

★   ★   ★   ★   ★

Nasser's seizure of power from General Neguib brought with it a new essay in frightfulness against Israel, the *fedayeen* commando raids directed against the civil life of the nation in the night hours. 'Wait and see,' he said, 'soon will be proven to you the strength and will of our nation. Egypt will grind you to the dust.' These raids began in the spring of 1955 and for some months Cairo disclaimed responsibility. Then, on August 31st, an official communiqué informed the world of this new military technique: 'Egypt has decided to despatch her heroes, the disciples of Pharaoh and the sons of Islam, and they will clean the land of Palestine.' And then again, on September 2nd, Cairo broadcast: 'The forces of the Egyptian *fedayeen* moved towards Israel, approached her capital and caused heavy casualties along the border between Gaza and Tel Aviv.'

In the spring of 1956 the campaign grew more furious and more dangerous. The United Nations attempted to negotiate a cease-fire which was promptly broken by Egypt. On May 15th Cairo radio announced: 'The war is not now confined to attacks along the border, but has reached the heart of Israel and places which were believed to be safe from danger. The quiet reigning in the villages and towns remote from the armistice lines has turned to terror.' Israeli casualties were heavy and war drew nearer.

The seizure of the Suez Canal in July brought a marked relaxation of raids across the Israeli frontier, a fair indication of where the guilt lay. After the Security Council had pronounced in October, and diplomatic discussions of seemingly unlimited duration had begun, the danger signals were out again. The *fedayeen* resumed their activities with increased intensity. The main recruiting area and headquarters were in the Gaza strip. Later the raiders began to operate from Syria and Jordan as well, sometimes under the command of Egyptian officers, sometimes under the supervision of the Egyptian Military Attaché.

In the last days of October the Egyptians declared that it was they who would choose time and place for the final assault, that it was for Israel to wait passively the moment of their selection. Months before this, General Burns, the head of the United Nations Truce Supervisory Organization, had written to the Foreign Minister of Israel, 'I consider that if Egypt has ordered these *fedayeen* raids, she has now put herself in the position of the aggressor.'

All evidence pointed one way. Egypt was gathering her allies, piling up Soviet arms and enlisting Soviet technical help, sharpening her propaganda and intensifying her raids. The risks entailed in the seizure of the canal having been safely negotiated, all was being got ready for the next objective. When later the Israeli armies captured El Arish, they found huge supplies of equipment, stores and petrol which could only have been assembled in such a forward position for an imminent offensive. Was Israel to wait for it, and if so, how long? Her country and her cities were vulnerable, especially to air attack. Egypt was strong in modern Russian bombers and growing stronger. Egypt had fifty, Israel had none.

Syria as well as Egypt was now receiving a steady flow of arms, equipment and technicians from behind the Iron Curtain. In the past fifteen months Egypt had been supplied with equipment to the value of £150 million. Syria had been given arms to the value of £20 million. There were a thousand technicians and instructors from the Soviet bloc in Egypt. However unskilled those who received it were, the cumulative effect of so much communist aid and instruction must in time increase their offensive power. It certainly raised Egyptian confidence; so had Western failure to obtain any concession from Nasser in the negotiations over the canal. The dread began to grow in the Middle East that nothing could check the swelling authority of the Egyptian dictator. Warning after warning came from friendly Arab states of the consequences of allowing this fear to become a conviction.

★   ★   ★   ★   ★

We are all marked to some extent by the stamp of our generation, mine is that of the assassination in Sarajevo and all that flowed from it. I was on the river at Eton being coached near an elbow in the Thames we called 'sandbanks', when I heard the news. Is it imagination, or did

I really feel that for a moment our young world stood still in something like fear, before it resumed its course? My tutor was gloomy when I got back to rafts. I was seventeen a few days before and, for the first and last time in my life, I kept a regular diary. I have it still, with its school entries and the careful day-to-day account, mainly gleaned from the newspapers, of events as they grew in ugly shape.

The Archduke was murdered on June 28th, the Austrian ultimatum was delivered on July 23rd, Europe was at war less than a fortnight later. In the last days the Foreign Office was strenuously active though hobbled most dangerously, as France and Russia repeatedly protested, by an inability to tell what we would do, because we did not know. The Foreign Secretary did all he could at that late hour. Sir Horace Rumbold, one of the best Ambassadors this country has ever had, and counsellor in Berlin at the time, was a stout defender of our official action. Yet he wrote * :

> The Entente statesmen had shown the maximum of good will, resource and patience. Events had been too much for them, however, and they had always been a lap behind in the march of events.

Therein lies the tragedy. It is impossible to read the record now and not feel that we had a responsibility for being always a lap behind. A month passed between the murder of the Archduke and the despatch of the Austrian ultimatum to Serbia. In that time we made no move. We hoped that the emergency could be localized, as between Austria and Serbia; we had no authority to intervene. How could it be localized except by Austria being left to deal with Serbia as she wished? How could Slav stand quiet while Teuton seized Belgrade? Even the wary Stalin rumbled when a like threat menaced Yugoslavia in 1941.

We should have learnt the Russian mood in those long weeks in 1914 and warned Vienna of the dangers of asking too much, and done so in advance of the publicly stated demand, from which retreat was so difficult. If this was not an earlier example of 'a little country far away', there was certainly a wishful hope that we might not be involved, with all the debilitating consequences. Stranger still, even after the Austrian ultimatum, we addressed all our wise projects for restraint *via* Berlin, not using the direct channel also, even in the last emergency. The post office was sluggish in delivery and not always accurate, as might have been foreseen. Always a lap behind, that fatal lap.

* *The War Crisis in Berlin* (Constable, 1940), p. 287.

When the 'thirties came the problem was the same under another guise. In our country some thought that methods of diplomacy which were suitable when dealing with democracies controlled by free parliaments could not be applied without reserve to militant dictatorships. These dictatorships were not subject to the restraints of an elected chamber. Their word alone did not suffice, because it need not be kept. Therefore precautions must be taken. Others took a different view. They thought it important not to build up suspicion of the dictators or in the minds of the dictators. They thought that they must be met as honourable men and dealt with as such, and that the papers they signed and the assurances they gave must be accepted as having a validity comparable to those signed by elected governments. Not only must this be the form in which negotiations with them were conducted, but it must be the spirit and the faith.

As a consequence of all this, the dictators themselves were led to underestimate the temper of the people with whom they had to deal, on account of their experience in dealing with the leaders. Success in a number of adventures involving the breaking of agreements in Abyssinia, in the Rhineland, in Austria, in Czechoslovakia, in Albania, had persuaded Hitler and Mussolini that the democracies had not the will to resist, that they could now march with the certitude of success from signpost to signpost along the road which led to world dominion. They were deceived. The second world war resulted.

★　　★　　★　　★　　★

As my colleagues and I surveyed the scene in these autumn months of 1956, we were determined that the like should not come again. We had seen how insidious was the excuse, how difficult the action. There might be other mistakes, there would not be that one. Drift spelt certain disaster for the West's authority and meant an Arab-Israeli war, fought under conditions most perilous for the peace of the whole area. Intervention by the Western powers, with all its risks, was clearly to be preferred. Nasser was well aware of this and guarded all the more carefully against a direct provocation. He was not ready for that, yet. It would not be good to act only at the time of his choosing. Unchecked over Suez, he set to work upon the next projects, needful to realize his proclaimed ambitions of Empire. These were to increase his supply of armaments from communist sources, to undermine those Arab leaders who were in his way, and to tighten the noose around Israel, whose destruction in his own time was his declared objective.

In existing circumstances it was idle to hope for effective action by the United States or the United Nations. Left to itself, the United Nations would never move, as its melancholy record in Middle Eastern events clearly showed. If led or goaded by others, it might do so.

Meanwhile, pro-Nasser parties had won the election in Jordan. This was immediately followed by the establishment on October 23rd of a joint command between Egypt, Jordan and Syria, under Egypt's leadership. Israel could not depend upon the United Nations coming to her aid in time, or expect that Nasser would not carry out his threats against her. The first was too nebulous a hope, the second too careless. The world knew that approval by the United Nations of action by the United States in Korea was an accident, due to Soviet absence from the Security Council and the non-application of the veto. The Soviets were not absent now. In the dispute over the canal we had seen the eighteen-power proposals vetoed and no action follow, except an invitation to talk over principles instead. Israel could not await the culmination of her enemies' preparations on a scale she knew she could not equal. No government of a small, free nation could rest on such frail hope. Some may doubt the wisdom of Israel's action, none can deny her courage nor the provocation offered her. For my part, if the responsibility had been mine as the head of the Israeli Government, I hope that I would have taken just such action as Israel took.

★ ★ ★ ★ ★

As was to be expected, the strain of these months on the Ministers who had to bear the principal directing and administrative responsibilities was very heavy. When I had appointed Sir Walter Monckton to the Ministry of Defence, I had admittedly not foreseen anything of this kind and I was made anxious by the effect upon his health, which was clearly suffering. I was therefore not surprised when he felt compelled to ask for his release. I was loath to lose his advice in the Cabinet and he readily agreed to stay as Paymaster-General.

In deciding upon his successor, I had no doubt that Antony Head was the man for the job. Earlier in the life of the Government I had suggested to him that he might take an office outside the Service Ministries. I did this, not because I was critical of the work he was doing, but because I thought that, from the point of view of his own career, he would be wise to gain some experience in a civil department. He preferred to remain with the Army, where his life and loyalty had always lain. In the hazards of political selection it is always pleasing when a Minister grows to fill his responsibilities. I have never known any man do this so naturally and completely as did Antony Head. I have no doubt that he would have proved to be the best Minister of Defence this country has had since the close of the war, had he been continued in office after I resigned. Mr. John Hare succeeded Mr. Head at the War Office. These appointments, which had been decided before my visit to Paris, were announced on the evening of October 18th.

I had interviews with a number of colleagues individually, during the weeks which passed after the seizure of the canal. There was no friction of any kind between us. When we were in council, no marked divergences were revealed. I have been a member of many Governments in times of nominal peace. I have not known one more united on an issue of the first importance. There were, of course, shades of opinion, but these did not obtrude. The points of view ranged from that of the Minister who fervently informed Mr. Dulles at the United States Embassy that we would go through with the business, even if it meant 'pawning the pictures in the National Gallery', through those who were quietly determined, to the more cautious characters who, whether from conviction or loyalty, were there all the same.

This calm passage during a period of many months was probably due to our having talked over the situation fully in its earliest phases. We had grown to know each other's minds; every senior member of the Government realized this and remembered the mood in which we had taken our first decisions. The others were their consequence.

VII

THE CRUNCH
October 23rd – 31st

*Hungarian rebellion – Israel mobilizes and moves into Egypt –
Our reasons for intervention – Anglo-French note to Egypt and
Israel – Question of consulting U.S. and Commonwealth – My
messages to President Eisenhower – My statement to the House –
U.S. resolution in Security Council – The veto – Russian
resolution – Sir Pierson Dixon's warning – 'Uniting for Peace' –
Debate in Parliament – Israel accepts and Egypt rejects – The
military situation and plans – Soviet 'technicians' – Disorder in
the House – Victory for Israeli arms*

For some days after the return of the Foreign Secretary and myself
from Paris, conflicting reports reached us on Israeli intentions. In
the meantime an incident sparked between Egypt and France.
The French had intercepted a ship carrying arms from Egypt to the
Algerian rebels. They withdrew their Ambassador from Cairo in protest and lodged a complaint with the Security Council.

It was now, on October 23rd, that the first reports of disturbances in
Hungary began to come in. They were soon to swell into fearful
tragedy. Here certain historical facts must be recalled. In 1945, when
the principal allies in the war against Hitler were gathered in Yalta, the
future of Europe was decided between them. The Yalta agreements
have often been severely criticized as giving too great an advantage to
Soviet Russia. I have always thought that it was not the agreements
themselves, but Russia's failure to observe them, which led to so much
grief and suffering.

The agreements should be examined in the light of the Hungarian
situation as it developed in the early autumn of 1956. Soviet Russia, by
her own declaration at Yalta, by her own signed statement, can only

station troops in Hungary as a corridor, for so long as she maintains an occupation force in Austria. Once Soviet contingents had been withdrawn from Austria, then Soviet Russia has no right, on her own showing at Yalta, to maintain troops in Hungary. It was my knowledge of this condition which had made me doubt whether the utmost pressure which the West could use would induce Russia to withdraw from Austria. In the event, after the long Berlin Conference, Russian policy underwent a change.

It is quite true that Russia claims to be in Hungary now by virtue of the Warsaw Pact. But the Yalta agreements also declared that the Hungarian Government must be chosen by free election. The Soviet Government broke this stipulation too. The Warsaw Pact was made by an imposed communist Government. In both these respects, and in others, the presence of Soviet troops in Hungary has no shadow of justification.

Agitation against the unpopular communist Government in Budapest had long been growing. The example of Poland, which seemed to be winning some degree of national freedom within the Soviet orbit, provided a further inspiration to the Hungarians. In October, demands were voiced all over the country that Hungary should withdraw from the Warsaw Pact and declare herself neutral, as Austria had done, that free elections should be held and democratic liberties restored and that Russian troops should leave. Russian troops not only stayed, they shot.

Towards the end of the month a new Government was formed by Mr. Imre Nagy, himself a communist who had at one time been expelled from the party. Mr. Nagy drew into his administration representatives of the non-communist parties and attempted to form a coalition Government, pledged to a programme of free elections. This was supported by a widespread nationalist revolutionary movement directed against the presence of Soviet troops and the activities of the communist security police. Events moved towards a climax on October 24th. On that day a column of Russian troops, stationed in Hungary, intervened in Budapest and fired upon a crowd of demonstrators. Worse was to follow. During the previous night fresh Russian forces had been entering Hungary from Roumania.

*   *   *   *   *

On October 25th a report came that Israel was about to mobilize. She did so on the 27th and moved against Egypt on the evening of the

29th. I thought then, and I think now, that the Israelis had justification for their action. It is at least a grim possibility that they would not be a free nation today had they not taken it. The marked victim of the garrotter is not to be condemned if he strikes out before the noose is round his throat.

If we were not prepared to condemn Israel, we could not stand aside and watch events. In an Israeli-Egyptian conflict our military advisers expected the Israelis to win; their quality, intelligent training and dedicated courage outmatching the Egyptian advantage in numbers and equipment. The chief peril to us lay not in the conflict but in its extension by the intervention of other Arab states. The best way to halt that was by intervening ourselves. These considerations decided our course of action.

Ministers had already considered at several meetings the ways in which the situation might develop. These had also been canvassed with the French. On October 25th the Cabinet discussed the specific possibility of conflict between Israel and Egypt and decided in principle how it would react if this occurred. The Governments of France and the United Kingdom should, it considered, at once call on both parties to stop hostilities and withdraw their forces to a distance from either bank of the canal. If one or both failed to comply within a definite period, then British and French forces would intervene as a temporary measure to separate the combatants. To ensure this being effective, they would have to occupy key positions at Port Said, Ismailia and Suez. Our purpose was to safeguard free passage through the canal, if it were threatened with becoming a zone of warfare, and to arrest the spread of fighting in the Middle East.

To realize this we would put into operation the plan for occupation of the Suez Canal zone, prepared by the joint Anglo-French military staff which had been studying the problem since the end of July. An advantage of this course was that we did not need to recast our military preparations. The same plan that had been intended to deal with Nasser's seizure of the canal fitted equally well with our new objective. Critics asked why we landed so far behind the combatant area. The answer is that to land anywhere except as planned would have involved delay and we could not afford delay. We were also limited by shortage of landing craft and had to have the use of a port.

Of course there were dangers in this policy. But there were dangers in any policy which we might have chosen, not least in that of complete inaction. Political decisions, especially when they concern the Middle

East, usually involve a choice of evils. I am convinced that we chose the lesser evil.

It was still necessary to be as certain as possible of the facts. For some time we had been keeping occasional and informal watch on the canal and Egyptian troop movements. We had done this by means of Canberras flying high and often a little way out to sea. There had never been any attempted interference with these flights and we believed them to be unperceived. Late on the evening of the 29th I had a talk with the Minister of Defence and the Chief of the Air Staff. I told them how important it was for us to have information upon which we could depend for certain, as early as possible the next day. A dawn reconnaissance was ordered by four Canberras flying at a great height, thirty to forty thousand feet. They would locate and, if possible, photograph the opposing forces. The Canberras carried out their instructions. Despite their altitude, all four were located and intercepted and some were fired on. All returned safe to base, but one machine was damaged. This interception was a brilliant piece of work by any standards, and when it was reported to me the next day it gave me grim cause for thought. I kept my own counsel. In the later fighting the Egyptian air force was, by contrast, completely ineffective. I do not know the explanation. Maybe the pilots of another nation were flying M.I.G.s that dawn.

On the morning of October 30th the Cabinet were informed that Israeli troops had entered Egyptian territory on the evening of the 29th and during the night had reached a point half way between their frontier and Ismailia. A second Israeli force was reported to be striking towards Suez. Other swift Israeli actions were also unrolling, though we only learnt details of these later. This was the situation the Cabinet had considered five days before.

The Cabinet was sternly conscious of the importance and urgency of the decisions it had to take. Now that the situation had actually arisen, it confirmed its readiness to act as had been decided, subject to the agreement of the French Ministers who were flying to London for consultations. It now considered the actual terms of the note in which this demand was to be addressed to Egypt and Israel; these would be discussed with M. Mollet and M. Pineau on their arrival.

The Cabinet examined the wording of the statement I was to make in the House that afternoon and endorsed it. We also discussed the attitude of the United States. The American Administration was urgently proposing to have Israel branded as an aggressor by the

Security Council. It was unmoved by the history of the dispute or Egypt's aggressive attitude and declared intentions against Israel. Our hope was that the United States would take some account of those events and be watchful of Soviet moves. The Cabinet then approved the terms of a message to President Eisenhower inviting his general support. I sent two telegrams to Washington that day. In the first I said:

> We have never made any secret of our belief that justice entitled us to defend our vital interests against Nasser's designs. But we acted with you in summoning the London Conference, in despatching the abortive Menzies mission and in seeking to establish S.C.U.A. [the Users' Club]. As you know, the Russians regarded the Security Council proceedings as a victory for themselves and Egypt. Nevertheless we continued through the Secretary-General of the United Nations to seek a basis for the continuation of the negotiations.
>
> Egypt has to a large extent brought this attack on herself by insisting that the state of war persists, by defying the Security Council and by declaring her intention to marshal the Arab states for the destruction of Israel. The latest example of Egyptian intentions is the announcement of a joint command between Egypt, Jordan and Syria.
>
> We have earnestly deliberated what we should do in this serious situation. We cannot afford to see the canal closed or to lose the shipping which is daily on passage through it. We have a responsibility for the people in these ships. We feel that decisive action should be taken at once to stop hostilities. We have agreed with you to go to the Security Council and instructions are being sent this moment. Experience however shows that its procedure is unlikely to be either rapid or effective.

My second message was sent after our talks with the French Ministers and the delivery of our jointly agreed notes to the Egyptian Ambassador and the Israeli Chargé d'Affaires. It informed the President of the requests we were making to the belligerents, and continued:

> My first instinct would have been to ask you to associate yourself and your country with the declaration. But I know the constitutional and other difficulties in which you are placed. I think there is a chance that both sides will accept. In any case it would help this

result very much if you found it possible to support what we have done at least in general terms. We are well aware that no real settlement of Middle Eastern problems is possible except through the closest co-operation between our two countries. Our two Governments have tried with the best will in the world all sorts of public and private negotiations through the last two or three years and they have all failed. This seems an opportunity for a fresh start.

. . . Nothing could have prevented this volcano from erupting somewhere, but when the dust settles there may well be a chance for our doing a really constructive piece of work together and thereby strengthening the weakest point in the line against communism.

A message from President Eisenhower crossed my telegrams. He expressed his disquiet upon a number of points, but considered it of the greatest importance that the United Kingdom and the United States should quickly and clearly lay out their present views and intentions before each other, so that they might not in any real crisis be powerless to act in concert because of misunderstanding. That had been my purpose also at the January meeting in Washington, and all through this drawn-out business.

The question of consultation before action with the Commonwealth countries and the United States was one that troubled us greatly. Of course we would have preferred to do this. Whatever the outcome of such consultation, it would have smoothed our path. On the other hand, however sharply pressed, such consultation was not possible within a matter of hours; it must take days at least. Nor was there any chance that all concerned would take precisely the same view of what action must follow the consultation. As a result there would be attempts to modify our proposals, to reach some compromise between several divergent points of view and, before we knew where we were, we would be back at an eighteen-power conference once more. This was the last thing in the world we wanted, because we knew quite well that once palavers began, no effective action would be possible.

The chief danger, especially for us, was that the conflict would spread. A localized war between Israel and Egypt, while troublesome, should not be highly dangerous internationally. The same could not be said of a war which had spread to include Syria and Jordan, with Iraq morally compelled to take a hand too. If this were to happen, the Jordan commitment would raise its head again, not in so acute a form, but alarming enough. Two events could be counted on to encourage Jordan and Syria to inaction, swift Israeli military success and the knowledge that British and French forces were on the way and would be used to localize the dispute. If that restraint was to be effective it must be applied at once. Twenty-four hours might well be too late, forty-eight certainly would.

The choice for us was stark and inescapable, either act at once to bring about the result we sought, the localization of the conflict, or involve ourselves in consultations. This would mean the same inaction as in the last three months. We chose to act.

I can imagine no conditions in which this conflict, so long expected, could have taken place with less risk of wider consequences for the world. Among these conditions Anglo-French presence and action signified most. It may be that our intervention brought the conflict 'prematurely' to an end, to use the adverb which the Leader of the Opposition employed. It is evident that intervention stopped it spreading.

Our consultations with the French Ministers began the moment they. arrived and continued over luncheon. As soon as these had been concluded and all points of action and timing settled, the Foreign Secretary, Mr. Butler, who was Leader of the House, and I saw the leaders of the Opposition. We gave them in advance a copy of the statement I was about to make in the House of Commons.

I thought it my duty to tell the House of the decision we had taken at the earliest moment. This led me into what I now consider was an error in timing. If I had done so two hours later, the Opposition would have been given time to consider the statement I was to make. The Commonwealth and the United States would have had time to reflect upon the messages we had sent them. However, I informed the House at 4.30 p.m. that the French and British Governments were agreed 'that everything should be done to bring hostilities to an end as soon as possible'. I announced the terms of our notes to Israel and Egypt and described the action we proposed to take if those countries did not comply. Our purpose was 'to separate the belligerents and to guarantee freedom of transit through the canal by the ships of all nations.'

I emphasized that if Anglo-French forces were obliged to move into key positions on the canal, this occupation would be temporary. At the same time I told the House that our representative at the United Nations had been instructed to join with the United States in seeking an immediate meeting of the Security Council.

Later in the evening I intervened again in the House:

Naturally, we hope that compliance by both sides with our appeal will enable those two objects to be secured rapidly, and then there would clearly be no need for anything more than token forces to make sure that what was accepted by both sides was, in fact, carried out, and they would, of course, be withdrawn the moment an agreement, a settlement, was arrived at.

I was questioned upon our obligations under the Tripartite Declaration of 1950. I pointed out that the Egyptian Government had never accepted this declaration. They did not regard it as giving rise to contractual duties and they had made it plain that it did not apply to them in the event of conflict with Israel. I added:

In any case, there is nothing in the Tripartite Declaration nor in the Charter of the United Nations which abrogates the right of a Government to take such steps as are essential to protect vital international rights such as are here at stake.

At that very moment the Security Council was meeting in New York. When the House divided about ten o'clock in the evening, giving us a majority of 52, we did not know what the United Nations would decide.

On the night of the 30th I received a further telegram from the President. Mr. Eisenhower had now learnt the terms of our notes to Egypt and Israel. He was deeply concerned at the prospect of drastic action and he expressed the belief that peaceful processes could and should prevail. I was not surprised at this sentiment, but we had no reason at this moment to suppose that the United States would oppose us at the United Nations upon almost every point. The substance of the President's message to me was published in the United States that night. In consequence, I asked him if I could use in the House of Commons the two telegrams I had sent him earlier that day. The President at once agreed, but in fact I did not have to quote from the texts of the telegrams themselves.

Further reports were reaching us from Washington and New York of the reactions of the United States Government. They were unfavourable. Few officials concealed the irritation they felt that we and the French should at last have taken the action which we had long forecast.

All United States opinion did not share this view. The *New York Times*, on November 1st, was critical of our action, but not deceived by Nasser. The newspaper wrote, explaining our attitude:

It would be ridiculous to permit Colonel Nasser to pose before the United Nations or the world as the innocent victim of aggression, or to hold a protecting hand over him. On the contrary, in so far as there is any one man guilty of aggression it is the Egyptian President, for he has waged war against Israel, Britain and France by propaganda, by gun-running, by infiltration of murderous bands, by stirring up rebellion in French North Africa, by seizing the Suez Canal by force, and scrapping a treaty in the same manner in which Hitler marched into the Rhineland, by blocking the canal for Israeli shipping in defiance of United Nations orders—finally, by his whole loudly proclaimed programme of throwing Israel into the sea in alliance with other Arab states and creating an Arab empire under his own hegemony which would expand his influence in concentric circles to all Africa and the whole Muslim world.

Ridiculous or not, this is precisely what happened. The Security Council met on the morning of October 30th and its debates continued throughout the day. From the start, the United States delegation were determined simply to condemn Israeli action in forthright terms, without laying down any principles for a general settlement. They refused to amend the letter summoning the Security Council so that the French and ourselves could also sign it. To denounce and neither to offer nor to accept any constructive suggestions was the core of American policy.

We and the French pointed out that the long history of Israeli-Egyptian relations must be taken into account. We also considered that the Israeli action must be viewed in the light of the Egyptian threat to peace and security in the Middle East. This had been growing alarmingly in the past three years. All our diplomatic efforts in recent months had failed to secure redress for the seizure of the canal.

Our arguments were not heeded. The United States took the lead. Its representatives at the Council meeting put forward a resolution demanding an immediate cease-fire and the withdrawal of Israeli forces behind the armistice lines. The resolution also urged all members to refrain from the use of force, or even threat of force, in the area and to avoid giving any assistance to Israel so long as she did not comply with the resolution.

The object of this move was to take the initiative out of the hands of the French and British Governments and to render our joint summons to Egypt and Israel unnecessary. The United Nations itself possessed no means of securing compliance with the resolutions which it passed. Therefore the effect of the American proposal would have been to condemn Anglo-French initiative, while substituting nothing for it. We urged a short delay at the Security Council, at least until there had been time in New York to consider the text of my statement in London. The Australian and Belgian representatives were understanding and helpful about this. The former added that his Government accepted none of the objections raised to the action undertaken by Britain and France, which he hoped would achieve its objective.

Mr. Cabot Lodge, the American representative, pressed his resolution to a vote with all speed and included in it phrases explicitly directed against Anglo-French action. His only reply to the arguments of the British representative, in public and in private, was to ask the Council to take the vote at once. As a result, Britain used her veto for the first time in her membership of the United Nations. The American resolution secured seven votes, we and the French voted against it, Australia and Belgium abstained.

The Russians then moved a resolution substantially the same as the American draft, but without its most offensive paragraph directed at the French and ourselves. We were willing to abstain on this vote, in the hope of taking some of the heat out of the debate and inducing reflection on the wider issues at stake. It would certainly have been helpful if this had been possible, but here we were up against the difficulties of rapid consultation between the capitals and New York, and the insistence on immediate decisions by the United States delegate. The French delegation were under instructions to use their veto and no time was allowed for further discussion between the Governments. For the sake of solidarity, therefore, we acted together. Tension mounted at the United Nations and our friends among the maritime powers were appalled at the rift which was revealed between us and the United States.

★　　★　　★　　★　　★

During this period Parliament was in almost continuous session for long hours at a stretch. In addition, as military operations developed, I had to hold frequent meetings with the Ministers concerned and the

Chiefs of Staff. It was therefore not possible for the Foreign Secretary to be present at U.N.O. in person. Fortunately this was not as serious a handicap as it might have been, for our representative in New York was Sir Pierson Dixon, one of the ablest diplomatists I have ever known. It was said of him when the period of the Suez crisis was over, 'He went through the whole business without ever missing a trick and without making an enemy.'

I had known Sir Pierson since the days of the war when he was my Principal Private Secretary at the Foreign Office. He figured prominently in many events and in the taking of critical decisions. He has a remarkable sense of diplomacy and played a leading part in the Iranian oil negotiations and those concerning Trieste. There is something of the renaissance in the suppleness of his methods. Though a scholar of repute, there is nothing academic about the thrust of his mind. In this situation I might have been unhappy at leaving an official in such a position, but I was quite sure that if this had to be, no better choice was possible.

Sir Pierson warned the Council that the danger of a major war between Israel and her Arab neighbours had never been so imminent. The Anglo-French intervention was designed to prevent a disastrous conflagration from spreading. We were also exercising our right to defend our vital interests in the canal, which was now threatened by fighting. Our intervention was a temporary measure and in no way aimed at the sovereignty or territorial integrity of Egypt. The Security Council had spent ten years attempting to grapple with the problem of Palestine, to little effect. Owing to persistent Russian opposition, the United Nations had never been equipped with an armed force of its own which would see to it that the resolutions of the Security Council were observed. The absence of such a force had made Anglo-French action essential.

The next move, by the Yugoslav delegation, was fateful in its consequences. Prompted from the sidelines by the Indian representative, Yugoslavia sought to transfer the dispute from the Security Council to a special session of the General Assembly, under the procedure known as 'Uniting for Peace', originally devised at the time of the Korean conflict. In a General Assembly of eighty members, any chance of examining these events dispassionately, or of using them to bring about a Middle Eastern settlement, would be infinitely less than in the smaller Security Council. The authors of the Charter knew what they were about when they charged the Assembly with the power to debate and recommend, and the Council with the power to take decisions. Now the Assembly was to be invited to give orders.

The resolution to give effect to the Yugoslav proposal could be adopted only if it received at least seven votes in the Security Council. As the resolution concerned procedure, it was not subject to the veto. For the purpose of voting, abstentions had the same consequence as votes against. The French and ourselves voted against the resolution. Australia and Belgium abstained. The seven in favour were Nationalist China, Cuba, Iran, Yugoslavia, Peru, the Soviet Union and the United States. The United States vote decided the issue.

★　★　★　★　★

On October 31st the Cabinet decided that, Egypt having rejected the Anglo-French note, the Commander-in-Chief of the Allied Forces should be authorized to put into operation the approved plan. At dusk that evening the attack on the Egyptian air force began.

On the same day I explained in the House of Commons why Her Majesty's Government could not associate themselves at the United Nations with a condemnation of Israel:

> It is not possible to pronounce in this way against one of the parties in the dispute for the action which they have taken, regardless of the cumulative effects that went before. . . . The Security Council resolution simply called upon the Israeli Government to withdraw within their frontiers. That seems to us in all the circumstances that have preceded these events to be a harsh demand, if it is to stand alone. It certainly could not be said to meet in any way the guarantees for Israel's security, which were asked for by several hon. Members in the course of yesterday's debate.

I announced Israel's acceptance of the terms of the Anglo-French note, and Egypt's rejection:

> We have no desire, nor have the French Government, that the military action that we shall have to take should be more than temporary in its duration, but it is our intention that our action to protect the canal and separate the combatants should result in a settlement which will prevent such a situation arising in the future. If we can do that we shall have performed a service not only to this country but to all users of the canal.

Some Members during these debates expressed concern about our relations with the United States. I gave the House the substance of the messages sent to President Eisenhower on the previous day. Apart from the exchanges between the President and myself upon the Middle Eastern problem, my colleagues had held numerous consultations with the American Secretary of State and American Ministers and officials during recent months. We had come to a conclusion which I then stated:

> It is an obvious truth that safety of transit through the canal, though clearly of concern to the United States, is for them not a matter of survival as it is to us and, indeed, to all Europe and many other lands. Indeed, Mr. Dulles himself made this clear on August 28th when he said the United States' economy is not dependent upon the canal. Of course that is true. We must all accept it, and we should not complain about it, but it is equally true that throughout all these months this fact has inevitably influenced the attitude of the United States to these problems, as compared to that of ourselves and France.
>
> If anyone says that on that account we should have held up action until agreement could be reached with the United States as to what to do, I can only say that this would have been to ignore what everyone here and in the United States knows to have been different approaches to some of these vital Middle Eastern questions. They know it. We know it. Of course, we deplore it, but I do not think that it can carry with it this corollary, that we must in all circumstances secure agreement from our American ally before we can act ourselves in what we know to be our own vital interests.

At the outset of the Suez crisis the Chiefs of Staff had been asked to prepare a plan of action for armed intervention against Egypt, should the need arise. The operation proposed had involved a build-up of forces at home and in the Mediterranean over a period of six weeks. Mid-September was the earliest date by which action could be taken.

From mid-September until the end of October our forces had been standing ready. During this period, Ministers had frequently examined the state of our precautions in conjunction with the Chiefs of Staff and with the Commander-in-Chief, Middle East Land Forces, General Sir Charles Keightley, who had been appointed Allied Commander-in-Chief for the operation. After much consideration, a plan had been drawn up, designed to secure our objectives with the utmost speed and the least possible loss of military or civilian life.

One Sunday in October, Sir Winston Churchill invited himself to luncheon at Chequers. On the three-hour journey by car from Chartwell he had dictated a series of queries and suggestions. We had a stimulating discussion which covered almost every eventuality. As he left, he said: 'I must look up and see exactly where Napoleon landed.'

Our planning had been complicated by various factors. The number of parachute troops and carrier aircraft available to us was limited by decisions taken some years before. There was also a crippling shortage of landing craft. The French 10th Airborne Division, allied to our own 16th Independent Parachute Brigade group, went some way to meet the first of our needs. The shortage of landing craft we met as best we could by requisitioning any that could be found, including some which were being used for ferrying commercial vehicles to and from Northern Ireland. Even so, this shortage definitely ruled out certain types of operation. To land on a coast without a deep-water port to facilitate the unloading of heavy equipment and stores, involves the use of a large number of landing ships and craft, particularly tank-landing ships. Shortage of suitable craft constricted us. Our advisers agreed that a deep-water port must be captured.

We also needed a deep-water port at which to embark. Cyprus has none. This meant that a seaborne assault in immediate support of an airborne landing had to be mounted from Malta, which lies more than nine hundred miles from Port Said. This is six days' steaming time. Further support troops to follow up the initial landing would have to be drawn from the United Kingdom, Libya and Algeria. These were inescapable strategic facts which had to be taken into account.

The plan was for an operation which could be launched at short notice, but which could also be held back for some time without loss of efficiency. The first phase was to consist of the elimination of the Egyptian air force, if possible on the ground, by bombing from Cyprus, Malta and Aden, and by fighter attacks from carriers and from Cyprus. We hoped also in this phase to put Cairo radio out of action and to sink as many Egyptian blockships as possible by pin-point bombing, before they took up blocking positions in the canal.

In the second phase, our air assault was to be switched to Egyptian military targets and installations, with the object of destroying the Egyptian capacity for organized defence. It had originally been estimated that these two phases might occupy from ten to fourteen days.

In our discussions of the military plan we had, however, reduced the preliminary period of air bombardment to six days. In the third phase, the airborne drop from Cyprus would be made on Port Said, to be followed within twenty-four hours by the seaborne landing from Malta. It was not possible to be certain that the first two phases, with their strictly limited military targets, would succeed in their purpose. The military commanders had therefore prepared for the possibility of a tough and troublesome battle in the third stage.

There was one element in all these calculations which could not then be ignored, the part that the foreign technicians in Egypt would play. Would they remain technicians or become 'volunteers', most incongruous of communist phrases? It was to be expected that they would give good advice as to initial military dispositions and that their training would have brought about some improvement in the handling of their weapons by the Egyptians. We could not tell if this would be all. We knew what had happened in Korea, how, when the communist forces were being worsted, Chinese 'volunteers' had come to the rescue of the hard-pressed North Koreans. The same technique could be followed in Egypt. Even if this were not done on a considerable scale, the technicians could fly the aeroplanes and maybe man some of the tanks. If so, the nature of the opposition to be overcome would be far greater than that which the Egyptian forces themselves could offer.

There was another element. During September information had reached us of naval reinforcements to Egypt. These were of little account in themselves, but they might be taken as an indication of similar help being given in the air and on the land, where it would be much more serious. Two submarines had sailed for Alexandria under the Polish flag with Russian ratings and Egyptian officers on board. It was probable that an equivalent reinforcement had arrived by air.

In the event, when the Anglo-French intervention took place, the Soviet technicians were withdrawn to Khartoum.

★　★　★　★　★

On November 1st the Minister of Defence, Mr. Antony Head, gave the House details of the first raids on Egyptian airfields. There was much interruption and disorder and the Speaker was obliged to suspend the sitting for half an hour. When the House resumed, the Opposition moved a vote of censure.

In my reply to the debate I made the suggestion that a United Nations force should eventually be associated with the Anglo-French police action. This idea was taken up in the General Assembly the next day by Mr. Lester Pearson and others. I had put it in the following words:

We best avoid great wars by taking even physical action to stop small ones. Everybody knows that the United Nations is not in a position to do that. We and the French have the forces available. We must face the fact that the United Nations is not yet the international equivalent of our own legal system and the rule of law....

Effective action to re-establish peace will make easier an international solution of the many problems which exist in that area. Of course, we do not delegate to ourselves any special position in that respect. On the contrary, we would welcome and look for the participation of many other nations in bringing about a settlement and in upholding it.

Israel and Egypt are locked in conflict in that area. The first and urgent task is to separate these combatants and to stabilize the position. That is our purpose. If the United Nations were then willing to take over the physical task of maintaining peace in that area, no one would be better pleased than we. But police action there must be to separate the belligerents and to prevent a resumption of hostilities.

This was no chance suggestion. I had always thought how much the League of Nations had suffered from lack of an international force to back its decisions. From the first conception of the United Nations, I had, as Foreign Secretary, been an advocate of the creation of such a force. Mr. Stettinius, Mr. Molotov and I discussed this at San Francisco in 1945, but the Russians were cool towards the idea. However, with the support of the French, we carried matters to the point where it was agreed that an international army would be created and placed at the disposal of the United Nations. The organization of this force should have been one of the first tasks of the United Nations in accordance with the terms of the Charter; Articles 43-48 provided for it. Mainly owing to Soviet obstruction, it never came into being.

Mr. Selwyn Lloyd and I, when together at the Foreign Office and later, had been concerned to strengthen the forces at General Burns' disposal against the evident dangers on the borders of Israel and the Arab States. There was little enthusiasm for this suggestion either, and to have proposed a United Nations force in advance of the outbreak of hostilities would have evoked no response. Now, however, there was a chance, not only to create a force, but to use it to bring about a permanent settlement in the Middle East.

In the division which followed, the Government had a majority of 69, but the most important outcome of the debate was that the idea of a United Nations police force had been implanted.

★ ★ ★ ★ ★

Meanwhile, the Israelis in Sinai had won a brilliant series of victories. Their objective was not to acquire territory, it was to forestall aggression. Their intention was to defeat the Egyptian army and to destroy its extensive equipment; to stamp out the nests of *fedayeen* raiders; to open the Gulf of Aqaba to international shipping. Egyptian forces in Sinai numbered some forty-five thousand men and the Israeli numbers were about the same. The Egyptians were better equipped and they held well-sited and well-fortified strongpoints. The Israelis were splendid in their courage and confidence. The mobilization caused no alarm, it even brought relief after the strain and tension and the raids of the last months.

There were four prongs to their attack. The first action at nightfall on October 29th was the dropping of a parachute battalion in the passes of the Mitla mountains forty miles to the east of Suez. This advance guard was speedily reinforced by the rest of the airborne brigade, which travelled overland from the Israeli frontier, a distance of a hundred and thirty miles through the centre of Sinai, taking fortified positions on the way.

Farther north a second task force of two brigades overcame formidable defences outside Abu Aweigla. These had been planned by the Egyptian army's German advisers. The task force then advanced by road to Ismailia on the canal, which they reached in four days.

In the north of the peninsula, near the Mediterranean coast, a third task force stormed the Egyptian bases of Rafa and El Arish. These were strong positions, with highly organized defences, which could have been expected to put up a stout resistance. Each fell within a few hours of a dawn attack. Here the victorious Israelis found workshops, ordnance depots, stores and vast parks of the latest war material covering many square miles of territory. What was all this for?

The Gaza strip was thus sealed off and its surrender followed after a short struggle. Detachments of this northern force then moved westwards in the direction of El Qantara, on the canal. When their

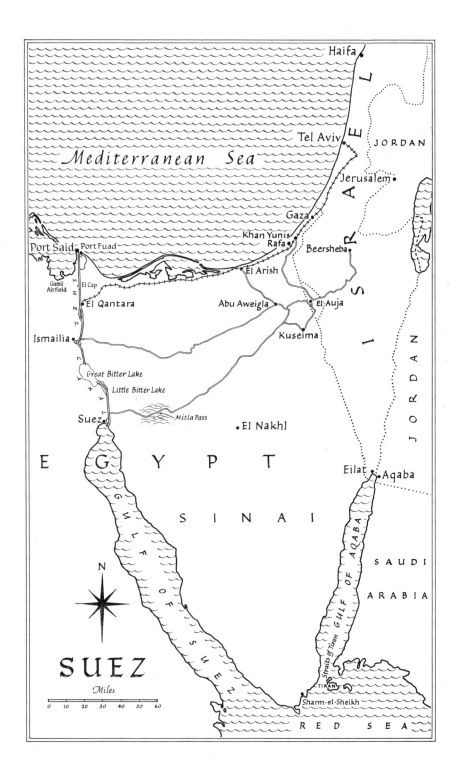

Government accepted the Anglo-French notes, all three of these Israeli forces withdrew from the neighbourhood of the canal.

The fourth Israeli column of one brigade plunged towards the south. It advanced along almost impassable tracks down the west coast of the Gulf of Aqaba and assaulted the fortified position of Sharm-el-Sheikh. The Egyptian Government had spent much money on the defence of this position, which was the key point from which they had been blockading the Israeli port of Eilat on the gulf. Although its commander had two thousand men and was strongly entrenched, he surrendered after a brief fight. Like many Egyptian commanders, he explained that his men were 'no good'.

Thus after five days' struggle, the Israeli army had gained all its main objectives. The Egyptians were everywhere in retreat. Israeli losses were one hundred and eighty killed and four captured. The Egyptians lost one thousand men killed in action and six thousand prisoners; others were killed by the unfriendly Bedouin.

While the Israelis were driving home these victorious thrusts against Egyptian forces with superior equipment, cries for help went out from Cairo, by code, and sometimes even *en clair*, to Amman and to Damascus. These were received with caution and returned with prudence, various pretexts being alleged to cover present inaction and a variety of assurances being offered of support to come. In reality, however, the knowledge that the Allied expedition was on its way and the speed of the Israeli victories, strengthened those in Jordan and in Syria who wisely preferred discretion.

The outcome of this fighting casts an interesting reflection on the Egyptian revolution. Many had supposed that it had some resemblance to comparable upheavals in other lands, notably that of the Young Turks in the first Balkan war. The expectation was that, while the senior officers might still be inefficient, the younger ones at least, brought up in the atmosphere of the revolution, would show themselves brave and determined in battle. The reverse proved to be true. The older officers in some instances fought well, the younger ones were the first to leave the battle. The Egyptian revolution has clearly not affected the quality of leadership in its armed forces. All of which was notched up by watchful neighbours.

VIII

THE FIGHTING
October 31st – November 7th

*General Assembly's meeting – U.S.A. in the lead against us –
Mr. Lester Pearson's intervention – Our attitude – The
Hungarian tragedy – Mr. Nagy's Government – Russian troops
capture Budapest – U.N. failure – Mr. Nehru – British reactions
to Suez intervention – Public opinion swings – Scenes in the
House – Dr. Gilbert Murray – My life during the crisis –
Anglo-French forces approach Port Said – Our parachutists drop –
News of cease-fire at Port Said – Its later reversal – We advance
down the causeway – The decision to halt – Russian attitude –
Marshal Bulganin's threatening letter – My reply – The run on
the pound – Reasons for our decision*

The General Assembly of the United Nations met on the morning
of November 2nd. Sir Pierson Dixon rehearsed the case for our
police action with his customary clarity and vigour. But the
Assembly was in an emotional mood. There was talk of collective
measures against the French and ourselves. Our friends were concerned
lest some rash initiative should lead to a situation in which either the
French and ourselves would have to abandon our purpose or leave
the organization. Such was the frenetic atmosphere prevailing in
New York. In London the Government had no intention of doing
either.

It was not Soviet Russia, or any Arab state, but the Government of
the United States which took the lead in the Assembly against Israel,
France and Britain. Their Secretary of State said he moved the
resolution with a heavy heart. It took no account whatever of events
preceding the action by Israel or France and Britain, nor did it propose
any initiative by the United Nations to mend the dangerous condition

of affairs which had existed in the area for so long. There was no suggestion of going to the root of the matter, or of using the Anglo-French
intervention to good purpose, either to create an effective international
force, or to negotiate a peace settlement for the area and an international
agreement for the canal. There was no attempt to snatch opportunity
out of trouble, which is the stamp of statesmanship. This we had done
when Trieste brought Italy and Yugoslavia to the verge of war, and
when the collapse of E.D.C. endangered the unity of Europe.

The resolution put peace in a strait-jacket. Directed against Anglo-
French intervention as well as the fighting, it declared that all parties
now engaged in hostilities in the Middle East should agree to an
immediate cease-fire; it urged all members to refrain from introducing
military goods into the area and asked the Assembly to remain in
emergency session until the resolution was complied with. Mr. Dulles
recognized that a resolution which merely sought to restore the
status quo before the Israeli attack was neither adequate nor comprehensive. He hoped that the United Nations would strive to bring
about a betterment of the conditions that had led to what he described
as 'this tragedy'. He did not suggest how this could be done.

The Canadian Minister for External Affairs, Mr. Lester Pearson,
explained why he could not vote for the United States resolution. In his
speech he developed the idea, which I had advocated in the House of
Commons the day before, of a United Nations police force. Mr. Pearson felt, as we did, that calling for a cease-fire and a withdrawal of
forces was insufficient unless it were linked with proposals for a permanent settlement of the Israel and Suez problems. He declared that
the resolution should have invited the Secretary-General to work out
a scheme for a United Nations police force which would keep the
peace on the frontiers of Israel. Canada was willing to contribute to
such a force. The Norwegian Foreign Minister and other representatives
were also attracted by this proposal, which they hoped would be
approved.

Had the United States been willing to play a part as balanced as
Canada's, the course of history must have been different, but this was
not to be. The Assembly was in a mood to punish. The hunt was up
after Israel and the 'colonial' powers. Mr. Nixon, Vice-President of the
United States, declared in a speech: ·

For the first time in history we have shown independence of
Anglo-French policies towards Asia and Africa which seemed to us

to reflect the colonial tradition. This declaration of independence has had an electrifying effect throughout the world.

Mr. Dulles' resolution was adopted by the Assembly by 64 votes to 5. Australia, New Zealand and Israel voted with Britain and France. Canada, South Africa, Belgium, Laos, the Netherlands and Portugal abstained.

Her Majesty's Government had no doubt about their reply. We were not prepared to halt our action while the fighting continued. If an international force were created by the United Nations, we were willing, under certain conditions, to hand over to them. The terms of our note were agreed with M. Pineau in the course of the day and approved by the Cabinet that evening.

On November 3rd I announced them to the House of Commons:

> The British and French Governments have given careful consideration to the resolution passed by the General Assembly on November 2nd. They maintain their view that police action must be carried through urgently to stop the hostilities which are now threatening the Suez Canal, to prevent a resumption of these hostilities and to pave the way for a definite settlement of the Arab-Israel war which threatens the legitimate interests of so many countries.
>
> They would most willingly stop military action as soon as the following conditions could be satisfied:
>
> 1. Both the Egyptian and the Israeli Governments agree to accept a United Nations force to keep the peace;
>
> 2. The United Nations decides to constitute and maintain such a force until an Arab-Israeli peace settlement is reached and until satisfactory arrangements have been agreed in regard to the Suez Canal, both agreements to be guaranteed by the United Nations;
>
> 3. In the meantime, until the United Nations force is constituted, both combatants agree to accept forthwith limited detachments of Anglo-French troops to be stationed between combatants.

Our reply to the General Assembly also dealt with the future of the Suez Canal, as Mr. Pearson's speech had done the day before. We did this because we thought that the situation could be used to resolve the principal problems of the region. We defined our position accordingly.

It should have been clear that there would be no peace between Israel and the Arab states, unless the United Nations played an active physical part in the area, nor would there be security for world commerce in the canal unless freedom of passage were accepted as an international obligation. If these were insured by an international force, there would be confidence in the future. The gage which we and the French hoped to win at Port Said and along the canal might be exchanged for effective United Nations control. Financially, such an arrangement could be made attractive to an Egyptian Government bedraggled in authority by humiliating defeats in the field. Here was an occasion which could be used to negotiate an arrangement to ensure the future freedom of the canal for world commerce.

Nearly three years have passed since these events. I am more than ever convinced that an intelligent use of these opportunities would have resulted in an agreement of a lasting character for the Middle East. If Anglo-French action had been followed by the creation of an effective United Nations force, we would have made a reality of our attempts at international order. This would have sobered the whole area, discouraged imperialist ambition and interference in the affairs of other nations by radio and other methods of subversion. Much subsequent tragedy would have been averted, including the massacres in Baghdad.

While the majority of the United Nations was in haste to pillory France and Britain and Israel, not a mouse moved in Arab lands. As Israeli columns lunged victoriously across Sinai, and British and French sailed the Mediterranean, all was still from Morocco to the Persian Gulf. Cairo radio was successfully put out of action after a preliminary warning which avoided casualties.

Forecasts of universal hate for the Europeans who intervened were not borne out either then or later, because many were hesitant and some understood. The West has been as slow to read Nasser's *A Philosophy of Revolution* as it was to read Hitler's *Mein Kampf*, with less excuse because it is shorter and not so turgid. But Eastern rulers had read it, and there were many who knew that, if the Egyptian triumphed unchecked, his prowl to conquest would have wider scope and their turn in Syria, Saudi Arabia and elsewhere must soon follow. Nasser coveted their wealth and their empire, and whether they used their power for schemes of welfare for their people or for their own ends, if he won they would forfeit it.

★ ★ ★ ★ ★

Events in Hungary were now following their ruthless pattern. Real power in the country rested with the Soviet military authorities. They claimed, after the event, that their troops had been asked to restore order under the terms of the Warsaw Pact. The truth was that the Hungarian revolution was moving faster and farther than suited the Russians. They were determined not to let Hungary slip wholly from their grasp, and were fearful of the influence of the Hungarian movement upon other satellite states of eastern Europe. The Hungarian army began to fraternize with demonstrators in the streets. When, on October 30th, Mr. Nagy promised the people of Hungary that he would negotiate for the withdrawal of the Soviet forces, the Russian reaction was immediate. While sporadic fighting had been raging in Budapest, the Russians had built up their strength for a counter-attack.

Two days later, further Russian forces entered Hungary from the Ukraine with their tanks and heavy equipment. Nagy protested against this new Russian invasion. He proclaimed the neutrality of his country, appealed to the United Nations and asked for the aid of the four great powers in protecting Hungarian neutrality. While negotiations were going forward between Soviet and Hungarian officials, Budapest was surrounded by two Soviet divisions and five further Soviet divisions took up positions in the country. On Sunday, November 4th, the Russians attacked the capital and an appalling struggle ensued. There were fifty thousand casualties in Budapest alone.

The back of Hungarian resistance was broken in ten days of fighting. Guerilla warfare continued long after. There was a prolonged strike and demonstrations were frequent for months to come. Several times crowds assembled outside the British Legation, seeking Western sympathy. Our Minister gave them what comfort he could. On one occasion the crowd was surrounded by Russian tanks, their guns trained on the Legation door.

Nagy was kidnapped by the Russians and nothing more was heard of him for eighteen months, when the Russians executed him. Full-dress communist government was reimposed upon Hungary. Before the end of the year some 150,000 refugees had fled the country, and many thousand fighters for freedom had been deported to Russia.

The pitiable failure of the United Nations to influence Hungarian events in the slightest degree lit up that tragedy in flaming colour. I announced from 10 Downing Street on October 28th that in concert with our allies we were referring the Hungarian situation to the United Nations. The Security Council did not dally at the start. It considered the plight of Hungary on that same day. The Western powers indicted the Soviet Union for 'violently repressing the rights of the Hungarian people', but the debate was inconclusive and the Council adjourned.

Five days passed without any further Council meeting upon Hungary, despite repeated attempts by ourselves and others to bring one about. The United States representative was reluctant, and voiced his suspicion that we were urging the Hungarian situation to divert attention from Suez. The United States Government appeared in no hurry to move. Their attitude provided a damaging contrast to the alacrity they were showing in arraigning the French and ourselves.

At length, on the night of November 3rd, the Council met while fresh Russian troops were speeding to Budapest. The Russians for the seventy-ninth time used their veto. Thereupon the issue was transferred to the General Assembly which passed a resolution next day by 50 votes to 8 with 15 abstentions, calling upon the Russian Government to withdraw its forces from Hungary immediately. It also instructed the Secretary-General to visit Hungary and arrange for the entry of United Nations observers. The United Nations was not even treated to the pretence of ceremony, the Secretary-General was refused admission and its observers were never allowed into Hungary. The Russian forces remained and ruled. The General Assembly repeated its request to Russia on November 9th, but to no effect. On that occasion India alone voted with the Soviet bloc.

The Indian reaction was remarkable. Mr. Nehru declared in a speech that whereas in Egypt 'every single thing that had happened was as clear as daylight', he could not follow 'the very confusing situation' in Hungary. He then proceeded to read out the excuses which Marshal Bulganin had sent him for the Russian intervention. These Mr. Nehru described as 'facts'. He displayed the same readiness to accept Russia's explanations as he had Nasser's.

★   ★   ★   ★   ★

The week-end of November 3rd–5th was tense and busy in London. On Sunday, November 4th, a crowd of several thousand assembled in Trafalgar Square to hear Opposition speakers address them upon the slogan of 'Law, not War'. After the meeting a part of the audience attempted to make a demonstration by marching down Whitehall to Downing Street. There were scuffles with the police. Twenty-seven demonstrators were arrested and eight constables were injured. Eventually the crowd expended its energies in marching around the streets of the West End bearing banners abusing the Government. This rowdy demonstration won much notice in the newspapers of the following day. It took place at a time when the public opinion polls showed the nation to be almost evenly divided upon the Government's handling of the Middle Eastern crisis.

My wife was an eye-witness of the Trafalgar Square meeting. She had walked to it from Number 10 and stood on the edge of the crowd. She was wearing a scarf round her head but, in spite of this, onlookers began to recognize her. So many of them took the opportunity to congratulate her that she thought it prudent to return to Downing Street. A day or two later she received a letter from a London bus-driver who had been in the midst of the affair. He wrote of me:

> He's done the only thing possible—my opinion and also that of a great number of fellow bus employees—only a small proportion of London's multitudes—but if a bus driver agrees—he must be right—I personally thank God we've got one man who's not afraid to do the right thing. As regards the rioting of the other evening—as I was on a bus (driving) right in the middle of it—I saw possibly more than most people—Eighty per cent. of the crowd were of foreign extraction so that was no true census of opinion and can be ignored.

During the days which passed after our decision to intervene I had little leisure to learn about any changes in public opinion. However, one's mail bag can give a fair indication. In the first few days after our decision the letters were heavily adverse, at the outset something like eight to one against. With the passage of time, this majority weakened and finally disappeared until, in the later stages and on the day before the cease-fire, the majority was heavily in favour of the action we had taken to the extent of about four to one. The *Daily Express* public opinion poll bears out this impression. Between October 30th and November 5th support for the Government's action rose from $48\frac{1}{2}$ per cent. to $51\frac{1}{2}$ per cent. and opposition dropped from 39 per cent. to 30 per cent. During the next fortnight, until November 21st, the same poll recorded that satisfaction with my leadership of the Government rose from $51\frac{1}{2}$ per cent. to $60\frac{1}{2}$ per cent. and that opposition fell away from 36 per cent. to $30\frac{1}{2}$ per cent.

The little I saw of public demonstrations confirmed this. Every day I drove in the early afternoon across to the House of Commons and, though the way was short, there were usually small crowds on the road. In the early days the booing about equalled the cheering. As time went on, the booing grew fainter and the cheering louder until in the last stages the booing had entirely disappeared; except in the House of Commons.

I have often known noisy interludes in the House, but never such a continuous abuse of the rules of order as during the Suez debates, if by any stretch of courtesy they can be so called. It was impossible to respect or heed the House in such conditions. One ambassador of a foreign power with a regard for democracy was seen to leave the diplomatic gallery almost in tears during one of these displays. Perhaps the most ludicrous scene took place one evening when, as the Speaker left the Chair, the Opposition leaders rose and booed me as I went out. What they hoped to gain by this demonstration I cannot tell.

There is one particular in which the habits of the House of Commons have recently deteriorated. Members wanting to interrupt used to jump to their feet and try to make the Member in possession of the House give way, if he was prepared to do so. This sometimes led to noisy exchanges, but at least the Member who was challenged, and the House, knew who the interrupter was. Now it is a frequent habit of Members to heckle as if they were at a public meeting, shouting insults at a Minister or other speaker while sitting or sprawling. This is a sloppy and not exactly courageous practice which Front Benchers should set an example in shunning. They do not.

One of the letters protesting against the Government's action which appeared in the newspapers at this time came from Oxford University and was signed by a number of professors and heads of colleges. It drew a powerful rejoinder from a number of equally eminent dons, which was published before the cease-fire. They declared that:

> The fact remains that after years of conflicting and often cynical attempts by Russia and other nations to influence, even confuse, political affairs in the Middle East and after the clear and repeated failures of the United Nations to act effectively in the Israeli-Egyptian dispute, a crisis was likely sooner or later to develop when one or more major powers would feel impelled to intervene to prevent a more serious war.

They appealed for 'patient but, if necessary, critical support' of British and French action until the United Nations had itself taken on the task.

Dr. Gilbert Murray headed the list of signatories. This fine scholar, humanist and champion of the League of Nations wrote a further letter to the weekly paper *Time & Tide* of November 10th, 1956. In it he said:

The rather wild confusion into which people have fallen about the Middle East situation is, I think, due to two main causes. First, it is strictly a question of International Law, and our system of International Law is not complete. The U.N. was intended to have a means of enforcing the law; it has no such means. (See Articles 43–48 of the Charter.) Egypt and Israel have been breaking the law for nine years with no correction.

Secondly, the Nasser danger is much more serious and pressing than a local friction consisting of Colonel Nasser's irregular nationalization of the canal and the perpetual war between Egypt and Israel, with which the U.N. has been unable to deal. The real danger was that, if the Nasser movement had been allowed to progress unchecked, we should have been faced by a coalition of all Arab, Muslim, Asiatic, and anti-Western States, led nominally by Egypt but really by Russia; that is, a division of the world in which the enemies of civilization are stronger than its supporters. Such a danger, the Prime Minister saw, must be stopped instantly, and, since the U.N. has no instrument, it must be stopped, however irregularly, by those nations who can act at once.

So much for the immediate present; the next step, of course, is the creation of a police force for the U.N. Happily this has now been done. As soon as a cessation of hostilities has been imposed, that force should proceed to discharge its functions of maintaining the law afterwards. The Russian plan has actually been revealed on November 6th. It is frustrated and indeed shown to be absurd; but we can see now what Russia and Nasser once intended and may possibly still make a desperate attempt to renew.

The Prime Minister's policy may well prove to have been the only road to success.

I mention Dr. Murray's views because they were based upon long reflection on world affairs and a lifetime's devotion to the cause of international peace. The conclusion which he had reached at Oxford was the same as I had formed in Downing Street.

★　　★　　★　　★　　★

The pace was faster and the strain more intense upon the principal members of the Government during these days and nights than at any time during the second world war. It is true that we had held debates then of the first importance, the results of which were sometimes critical, but these had not been frequent. Now they were continuous. They took place virtually every day during the decisive period and lasted throughout the session. This always made it difficult, and often made it impossible, to deal with even the most urgent work while the House was sitting, which was at least from 2.30 p.m. to 10 p.m. and sometimes later. Added to this was the problem of the difference in time. During the war there was hardly any communication by telephone across the Atlantic. For one thing it was not safe, the Germans might listen in, and did. Now all this was changed. It was after midnight, our time, that the United Nations and Washington became most active, both by telegram and telephone. I had always to be available and so had the Foreign Secretary. My excellent staff did all they could to spare me and were organized to be at hand in relays, but frequent interruptions of a night's rest were inescapable.

Robert Allan was my Parliamentary Private Secretary. He was a Member of Parliament with a brilliant war record as a Naval officer. It was his task to keep in touch with the House of Commons and to report to me on moods and sentiment there. He also dealt as far as possible with Members who wanted to see me or get messages to me.

My day ran something like this. While I was shaving, bathing, and dressing, Mr. Allan would report to me and raise any points he wished. Sometimes one of the Private Secretaries would break in with an immediate telegram, or the Chief Whip, Mr. Edward Heath, with whom lay the responsibility for guiding and marshalling our forces in the House of Commons, would arrive with some suggestion or point for decision. Though Mr. Heath's service in Parliament had been short at that time, I have never known a better equipped Chief Whip. A ready smile concealed a firm mind. Downstairs in the Cabinet room at Number 10, where I always worked, as being more convenient than my study on the first floor, the morning was the only time we ever had for the urgent affairs of the nation. Into this period had to be crammed Cabinet sessions, special meetings to deal with the military, financial, economic or diplomatic aspects of the crisis, messages to and from Commonwealth Prime Ministers, consultation with individual colleagues, and a chance to think.

My critics wrote that I was calm under the strain. I felt at ease; there was a reason for this. From the first I was convinced that the course on which we had decided was the only acceptable one in a grim choice of difficulties. I did not expect it to be popular, but my colleagues and I had been grappling with the deteriorating situation for months and we were confident in our course. That makes for calm.

During these days private life ceased to exist. It was useless to fix engagements and unwise to invite guests to meals. Luncheon could be at any hour and dinner was often not eaten until far into the night. My wife somehow adapted our domestic arrangements to meet these unsteady requirements; my digestion took less kindly to them.

As a result of having no country home, except the cottage at Broad Chalke, we had moved our own pictures, furniture and books into Downing Street. I was never more happy at this arrangement than during these heavily charged days and nights. It was a refreshment to escape for a while from the official rooms and be able to reflect in an atmosphere which was part of my own personal life.

I do not have many pictures, for I have never been rich enough to buy much. A watercolour by Dunoyer de Segonzac, 'Le Canotier', which is a sketch for a painting now hanging in one of the national collections in Paris, was the first picture I ever bought. My collection was made for the most part when on holiday in France. I also hung upstairs in Downing Street a number of my father's watercolours, which I like more and more with the passage of years. My admiration of them is not merely filial. On several occasions during the prolonged crisis I found time to sit in my wife's green drawing-room and enjoy the two Derain sanguines, and the Degas bronze of a girl in her bath which Sir Alexander Korda had given us as a wedding present.

★   ★   ★   ★   ★

On the noisy Sunday of November 4th we held two meetings of the committee of Ministers which had kept in constant touch with the situation throughout these anxious months. In the evening a full Cabinet considered the position. Our armada from Malta was nearing Port Said. The Minister of Defence, who had just paid a flying visit to Allied headquarters in Cyprus, reported that Egyptian forces appeared to be withdrawing upon Cairo. The outlook for our action at Port Said was favourable and the Allied commanders believed that they could occupy key positions in the town by immediate parachute drop. This air assault was due to be launched at first light next day. There were good hopes of success without recourse to naval bombardment.

When the Cabinet met, the next stage in military operations lay still some twelve hours in the future. We had to consider two further resolutions which had been adopted by the General Assembly of the United Nations. One had been put forward by Canada and the other by a group of Afro-Asian States prompted by India.

The Canadian resolution asked the Secretary-General to work out a plan within forty-eight hours for the creation of a United Nations force which would secure and supervise the ending of hostilities in the area of the canal. This was welcome to us. Reports reaching us from the United Nations, however, indicated that the purpose and composition of the force might not conform to our ideas. Sir Pierson Dixon was instructed to speak in favour of the Canadian resolution, while making our reservations clear and abstaining on the vote if they were not met.

The Afro-Asian resolution called upon the Secretary-General to arrange a cease-fire within the next twelve hours. A reply had to be sent to Mr. Hammarskjöld before midnight. The Government had a choice of three courses. We could proceed with our action at Port Said, repeating our offer to hand over to the United Nations as soon as an effective force reached the canal. Alternatively, we could postpone the parachute landings for twenty-four hours. This would give Egypt and Israel an opportunity to accept a United Nations force and allow time for the General Assembly to consider whether the Anglo-French forces might be accepted as its advance guard. Thirdly, we could defer all further military action on the grounds that we had in fact put an end to the Israeli-Egyptian conflict.

It was clear to me that a postponement could not be accepted. I was confident that the Commander-in-Chief, if consulted, would urge overwhelming arguments against it, which he properly and promptly did. The political objections were also obvious, once action was halted it could hardly be resumed. Postponement would, in fact, have meant calling off the operation. If we postponed now we should be doing so before we had gained our main physical objective, to insert an impartial force between Egypt and Israel along the canal. There was no United Nations force yet in being to fulfil our aims for us. Unless we persisted, it might never come into existence. The Cabinet was in favour of going forward and shouldering the political risks. It was determined by the news that reached us towards the end of our meeting. Though Israel had accepted a cease-fire in principle, she had not yet agreed to the United Nations force, wishing no doubt for information as to its location, duties and composition. All was still uncertain, there was every reason for proceeding with our action.

I gave an account of our opinion in a telegram to the President, in which I wrote:

> If we draw back now chaos will not be avoided. Everything will go up in flames in the Middle East. You will realize, with all your experience, that we cannot have a military vacuum while a United Nations force is being constituted and is being transported to the spot. That is why we feel we must go on to hold the position until we can hand over responsibility to the United Nations.

★   ★   ★   ★   ★

In the afternoon of November 5th the Minister of Defence announced the airborne assault on Port Said. The Egyptian air force had been destroyed by November 2nd, and the R.A.F. flew virtually without opposition. They took immense trouble to avoid civilian casualties. Egyptian military movements in the canal area were heavily intermingled with civilian traffic of all kinds. Many targets were not attacked by us for this reason. Our pilots reported that Egyptian military crews generally abandoned their vehicles on the appearance of our aircraft, while civilian traffic went on unperturbed. Such was the effect of our broadcast intentions to attack from the air military targets only.

At 8 a.m. on the 5th, some six hundred British parachutists had begun their jump on Gamil airfield to the west of the town, which itself lies on the west bank of the canal entrance. At the same time five hundred French parachutists dropped to the south of Port Said near the waterworks, which they seized, together with an important bridge over the interior basin. Gamil airfield was quickly secured and the British parachute battalion advanced eastwards into the town itself. Continuous support was given by aircraft from the carrier force. At 1.45 p.m. a reinforcing drop of a hundred men with vehicles and heavy equipment was made at Gamil airfield. A further four hundred and sixty French parachutists were dropped on the southern outskirts of Port Fuad, on the east bank of the canal, which they proceeded to occupy. Resistance was offered by the Egyptians during the morning, but at 3 p.m. the local Egyptian commander offered to discuss surrender terms on behalf of the Governor of Port Said. At 3.30 a cease-fire was ordered, while negotiations went forward. About an hour later I gave this news to the House, which was then noisily cross-examining the Foreign Secretary.

I am not sure that I was wise to do so. The effect in the House was instantaneous, the Government's supporters rising to their feet to cheer and wave their order papers and the Opposition being temporarily subdued. By this announcement I told the world of the cease-fire, thus alerting those who would not welcome it and giving them an opportunity of working against it.

At seven o'clock in the evening a further signal arrived stating that the Egyptians had agreed to our terms. Their forces in Port Said had begun to lay down their arms, and their police were co-operating with us in the town. I was immensely relieved. It seemed that our operations had succeeded instantly and at remarkably small cost. An hour and a half later came a very different message. The Governor of Port Said reported that he could not now agree to the terms and that fighting must resume.

Who had caused him to reverse his decision? It is hard to believe that the Governor would have negotiated a cease-fire and then have proceeded to actual surrender without the knowledge of his Government. Nasser must have known during those five hours what was going on in Port Said. I am convinced that this reversal of action was prompted from further afield. We may never be able to prove it, but what is certain and significant is that loudspeaker vans toured Port Said announcing that Russian help was on the way, that London and Paris had been bombed and that the third world war had started. At this moment a menacing letter from Bulganin had been despatched to me, the first word I had received from him since our decision to intervene. Encouraged by the attitude of the United States and the United Nations, the Russians had taken their decision. The Soviet Consul became suddenly active in Port Said, stimulating resistance and promising help. The Russian hat was now in the ring.

When fighting was resumed it took the form of sniping and guerilla tactics in built-up areas. It was during this later period that the town was damaged. The parachute force had done its job swiftly and brilliantly, but it was too small in numbers to complete the capture of the town, now that the truce was off. The assault forces from Malta did so next day, arriving exactly on time. The Royal Marine commandos went ashore at Port Said in the early hours of the morning of November 6th. French commandos and supporting troops landed at Port Fuad. The street fighting which followed was complicated by the fact that most of the Egyptian regular troops had discarded their uniforms and were indistinguishable from civilians, many of whom were also armed.

Some centres of resistance held out until the afternoon, but by dusk organized fighting had ceased. Our forces had started upon an advance to the south and by 5 p.m. had reached El Cap, twenty-three miles down the causeway.

General Keightley had estimated that he could occupy Ismailia by November 8th and Suez by November 12th. As he put it later in his despatch, 'that would have completed the whole operation in twelve days from the start of air operations.' Fighting between Israel and Egypt ceased on November 6th and our plans were therefore never completed. No other Arab state had joined in and the United Nations were scratching together a force to take up positions in the areas of fighting. Our intervention had compelled both these decisions. At 5 p.m. on November 6th the Allied Commander-in-Chief was given orders to cease fire at midnight.

It will be seen from an account of events in London how this fateful decision to cease fire was taken. Throughout the day of November 5th we were being continually pressed to accept a United Nations command in the Suez area, as meeting all our conditions for a cease-fire. This it did not do. A commander without forces could not fill the vacuum. During the night Marshal Bulganin's letter arrived. He had made it public before it reached me and its tone caused scare headlines in some sections of the press. The Soviet Premier declared that the war in Egypt could grow into a third world war. He threatened that Russia would resort to force and asked:

> In what position would Britain have found herself if she herself had been attacked by more powerful states possessing every kind of modern destructive weapon? And there are countries now which need not have sent a navy or air force to the coasts of Britain, but could have used other means, such as a rocket technique. We are filled with determination to use force to crush the aggressors and to restore peace in the East. We hope you will show the necessary prudence and will draw from this the appropriate conclusions.

We drew different conclusions. During the first four days, the Soviets, both at the United Nations and in their wireless statements, remained extremely quiet and restrained. Their first intervention at the Security Council was more moderate than that of the United States and did not condemn Anglo-French action as Mr. Cabot Lodge's resolution had done. Their propaganda was stepped up only some days after it became clear that the United States was in the lead against us at the United Nations. Oblivious of Hungary, the Russians felt they could snarl with the pack.

This period of Soviet reserve was due to a number of causes. The Russians were determined not to risk putting themselves in an exposed position from which they might have to retreat, as over the Berlin blockade. They also recalled the warning I had given to Khrushchev and Bulganin when they came to London, that if need be we would defend our interests in the Middle East by force. Probably they were suspicious that official United States indignation against its allies could not really be as violent as it appeared. From the Soviet angle, it was rather too good to be true. To them it seemed unthinkable that the United States should not be mindful of the interests of its allies as Soviet Russia was prepared to be of hers. There might be a catch in it somewhere and it would be wise to move prudently. Reassured on this point, and encouraged by the failure for several days even to discuss Hungary at the Security Council, the Russians thought they could take on something else. They made a leap for the lead.

We considered that the threats in Marshal Bulganin's note need not be taken literally. I returned him an appropriate reply:

> I have received with deep regret your message of yesterday. The language which you used in it made me think at first that I could only instruct Her Majesty's Ambassador to return it as entirely unacceptable. But the moment is so grave that I feel I must try to answer you with those counsels of reason with which you and I have in the past been able to discuss issues vital for the whole world.

I told Marshal Bulganin that we had virtually achieved our aim of separating the combatants in Egypt and that we welcomed the proposed United Nations force which would take over from us. I then went on:

> If your Government will support proposals for an international force whose functions will be to prevent the resumption of hostilities between Israel and Egypt, to secure the withdrawal of the Israeli forces, to take the necessary measures to remove obstructions and restore traffic through the Suez Canal, and to promote a settlement of the problems of the area, you will be making a contribution to peace which we would welcome.

Our aim is to find a peaceful solution, not to engage in argument

555

with you. But I cannot leave unanswered the baseless accusations in your message. You accuse us of waging war against the national independence of the countries of the Near and Middle East. We have already proved the absurdity of this charge by declaring our willingness that the United Nations should take over the physical task of maintaining peace in the area. . . .

The world knows that in the past three days Soviet forces in Hungary have been ruthlessly crushing the heroic resistance of a truly national movement for independence, a movement which by declaring its neutrality, proved that it offered no threat to the security of the Soviet Union.

At such a time it ill becomes the Soviet Government to speak of the actions of Her Majesty's Government as 'barbaric'. The United Nations have called on your Government to desist from all armed attack on the peoples of Hungary, to withdraw its forces from Hungarian territory, and to accept United Nations observers in Hungary. The world will judge from your reply the sincerity of the words which you have thought fit to use about Her Majesty's Government.

A more formidable threat than Marshal Bulganin's confronted us. A run on the pound, at a speed which threatened disaster to our whole economic position, had developed in the world's financial markets. Two months earlier the Cabinet had considered the financial consequences of taking action at Suez. The cost of the military precautions had been some £12 million. Holding our proposed operation in readiness from mid-September onwards had been costing us about £2 million a month. The operation itself was estimated to cost about £100 million, equivalent to one-sixteenth of the annual cost of the defence programme. The Treasury had felt satisfied that these outlays could be borne without undue stress, though if the canal were blocked and the pipelines were cut indefinitely, our balance of payments would be endangered.

The position was made immediately critical by speculation against sterling, largely in the American market or on American account. Chinese balances were also withdrawn, no doubt for political reasons, and Indian balances reduced. The Chancellor of the Exchequer, Mr. Macmillan, later gave the House the figures. During the first half of the year, the gold and dollar reserves of the United Kingdom had been rising. Some pressure against sterling had been expected in the autumn and allowance had been made for it. This pressure was greatly intensified at the beginning of November. Our reserves fell by $57 million in September, $84 million in October, and $279 million in November. $279 million represented about fifteen per cent. of our total gold and dollar reserves. This was gloomy foreboding and could have been decisive within the next few days.

There were reports at this time of a dissident minority in the Conservative Party in the House of Commons. I was told that if a cease-fire were not announced that day, some of them would not vote with us. I was not influenced by these reports, or by the knowledge that there had been some contacts between one or two members of our party and the Opposition leaders. The overwhelming majority was firmly loyal. There are always weak sisters in any crisis and sometimes they will be found among those who were toughest at the outset of the journey.

Popularly my problem was very different. The country had made up its mind that we were right to start, they would not be so easy to convince that we were right to stop. If I had been playing politics, nothing would have suited me better than a defeat in the House of Commons at this juncture. I had no doubt that failure to assert international authority would result in a sharp deterioration in the Middle East within the next year or two, until intervention became inevitable once again. That would be the moment for me and those who shared my views. But I was not playing politics and I expected to stay in office until that moment came.

None of these considerations determined our decision when we met at 9.45 a.m. on November 6th, although all were in our minds in varying degree. The Chancellor of the Exchequer had rightly been to see the Foreign Secretary about our financial position earlier that day and I knew that it was grim. Another factor weighed even more in my mind, and I am sure in that of my colleagues. We had intervened to divide and, above all, to contain the conflict. The occasion for our intervention was over, the fire was out. Once the fighting had ceased, justification for further intervention ceased with it. I have no doubt that it was on this account more than any other that no suggestion was made by any of my colleagues, either then or in the hours which elapsed before my announcement in the House that evening, that we and the French should continue our intervention.

Our allies accepted this conclusion with understanding loyalty, though they would have liked to see what even a slightly longer period of action might have brought forth.

We knew, of course, that the heaviest pressure had been put upon

Israel during the last forty-eight hours to accept the Assembly's resolution. The United States Government in particular had used every resource at their command, and they were many. There were promises also. President Eisenhower sent a personal appeal to Mr. Ben-Gurion in which he declared that once Israel had withdrawn from Egyptian territory new and energetic steps would be taken to solve the basic problems which had given rise to the present difficulty. It took eighteen months and Egyptian subversion in Lebanon and Jordan to compel any steps at all; the basic problems still remain untouched.

I doubt whether service was rendered to peace by applying this pressure. Nasser's position in Egypt was by this time threatened. Our patrols reported growing panic on the roads back from the Sinai peninsula to Cairo, but the fighting had stopped and we had no justification for going on.

★ ★ ★ ★ ★

We would have taken a second, and maybe a third, look at the problem had we understood what was to come. We were ashore with a sufficient force to hold Port Said. We held a gage. Nasser had received a humiliating defeat in the field and most of his Russian equipment had been captured or destroyed by the Israelis or ourselves. His position was badly shaken. Out of this situation intelligent international statesmanship should, we thought, be able to shape a lasting settlement for the Arab-Israeli conflict and for the future of the canal. We had not understood that, so far from doing this, the United Nations, and in particular the United States, would insist that all the advantages gained must be thrown away before serious negotiation began. This was the most calamitous of all errors. Had we expected it to be perpetrated, our course might have been otherwise, but we could not know. As it seems to me, the major mistakes were made, not before the cease-fire or in that decision, but after it. I did not foresee them.

Happily, by a combination of brilliant courage and firmness, Mr. Ben-Gurion was able to secure for his country one capital advantage, free passage of the Gulf of Aqaba to the port of Eilat, which could transform the economy of Israel and make everything that small country had endured worth while.

Optimists maintain that another forty-eight hours would have seen the occupation of the whole canal and the end of the fighting. That was not our military advice, which reckoned on five days more, and it is likely that the longer period would have been required. Even if fighting by organized units had not lasted long, the practice of the

Egyptian army in Port Said of throwing away uniforms and using guerilla tactics in civilian clothes would in all probability have been repeated. It must have taken a little time to deal with, encouraged as it now was by Russian, and therefore by local communist, support.

In the months after these events I repeatedly read and heard the comment, especially from the United States, even from those in high authority: 'If only you had gone on.' The implication being that, the canal once occupied and the main military operation over, the United States Government would have changed their attitude. I have never seen sufficient reason to accept this comfortable conviction and I do not believe that, if events had reached that point, they would in fact have done so. The United States Government had engaged their authority in the lead against us and would not have been appeased had Anglo-French forces occupied more of the canal or even the whole of it. In all probability they would only have been more indignant.

The factor which must now always remain unknown is the effect of a rapid advance down the canal, and its clearance, upon Nasser's position in Cairo. Militant dictators have more enemies at home than the foreigner ever dreams. It may be that even the Soviet entry into the lists would not have sufficed to save the regime in Cairo, humiliated by defeat and lacking the Voice of Egypt to call disaster victory.

I had seen the chain of failure in the nineteen-thirties from Manchuria to Danzig and had tried in vain to break it. This time we had the opportunity and the responsibility. What we did was only partially effective, but it moved the United Nations to action. It led to later Anglo-American intervention in the Lebanon and Jordan, after the opposition of the United States to our Suez action had been seen to have brought disaster in Iraq. The consequences there may even have taught a little prudence in Cairo. Some of these checks to totalitarian plans may be judged late and feeble, even so they had their impact and their warning message, in revealing contrast to the fatal drift of the nineteen-thirties.

Much of the subsequent controversy over the Suez decision has been about the trees and not about the wood. The main question is whether inertia would have brought better results for the peace of the world than action. I think not. I thought and think that failure to act would have brought the worst of consequences, just as I think the world would have suffered less if Hitler had been resisted on the Rhine, in Austria or in Czechoslovakia, rather than in Poland. This will be for history to determine.

IX

MYOPIA
November 7th, 1956 – January 18th, 1957

*The fighting is over – Casualties – President Eisenhower agrees
to see M. Mollet and myself in Washington – He postpones the
meeting – Clearance of the canal – Nasser is complacent – Egypt
has to modify some demands – We agree to token withdrawal –
My illness – Proceedings in the General Assembly – M. Spaak's
amendment is defeated – His realistic views – Negotiations for
withdrawal – British nationals and property in Egypt – Anglo-
French harmony – My telegram to General Keightley – A
summing up – A visit from Mr. Nehru – Christmas at Chequers –
Illness and Resignation – M. Spaak calls on me – We sail for
New Zealand*

On the morning of November 7th the Anglo-French forces were
firmly in command of Port Said and fighting had stopped,
except for isolated clashes. We had cleared the causeway and
advanced as far as El Cap. The total number of men landed in our
operation was 22,000, of whom 13,500 were British. Our casualties
were sixteen killed and ninety-six wounded and the French ten killed
and thirty-three wounded.

The Egyptians circulated wildly exaggerated stories about their
casualties. The President of the Law Society, Sir Edwin Herbert, later
carried out a thorough investigation into the facts at the request of the
Minister of Defence. His findings upon his mission to Port Said,
published on December 22nd, were that the Egyptians had lost six
hundred and fifty dead and had had nine hundred wounded and
detained in hospital. He also reported that not one bomb had been
dropped on Port Said or its environs, and that the short naval bombardment had been entirely confined to the beaches. He added:

Every possible warning was given by radio to the civil population. Indeed to one like myself, with a long experience of security in war-time, it came as a shock to find that the two overriding considerations in the minds of all concerned were firstly to inform the enemy of our plans and secondly to do him as little damage as possible in the execution of those plans, which I think is a fair summary of the steps taken.

In the afternoon of November 6th President Eisenhower telephoned to me when I was in my room in the House of Commons. He was vigorous and in good spirits. He was delighted by our order to cease fire and commented that we had got what we had set out to do; the fighting was over and had not spread. Mr. Eisenhower was naturally elated by the Presidential election results which had by then come in. I congratulated him and he told me he had increased his majority. This was our first conversation on the new undersea cable. The President commented on its remarkable clarity and encouraged me to keep in touch by this means and telephone to him at any time.

There seemed no doubt at that moment that friendship between our two countries could be quickly reanimated. I sent a telegram to M. Mollet in which I spoke of my confidence that friendship between the three of us was restored and even strengthened. I added that 'as a result of all our efforts we have laid bare the reality of Soviet plans in the Middle East and are physically holding a position which can be decisive for the future.' I was over-optimistic.

The President followed his telephone call with a telegram. It was cordial in tone, but contained some indications of the direction of American thinking which I was perhaps slow to recognize. I did not foresee then that the United States Government would harden against us on almost every point and become harsher after the cease-fire than before. Mr. Eisenhower urged that the United Nations plan for an international force should be immediately carried into effect in order to prevent what he considered to be developments of the greatest gravity in Egypt. By this I took him to mean the possibility of Soviet intervention in some form. I considered that the best guarantee against this was the presence of Anglo-French troops, until the United Nations force had built up sufficient strength on the spot to take over our police duties. In the days ahead we found growing divergence on this issue between the United States and ourselves. On November 6th and 7th this still lay in the future. To avoid giving Russia any excuse for a move, the President strongly recommended that we should consent to the exclusion of contingents from the great powers in the United Nations force. He also affirmed that any attack upon this force would meet with an immediate reaction from all the United Nations. I was glad of this and I thought that there was something to be said for the exclusion of all great powers from the force. I told the President so, but I had to consult my colleagues before decisions were taken.

The Government considered the position. Our object remained, as it had always been, to use this opportunity to secure a solution of Middle Eastern problems. We did not believe in Russian military intervention, but we realized how disastrous it would be if the United States became more intent on making us withdraw our forces than on seeking a comprehensive settlement. In spite of the friendly tone of the President's exchanges with me, we were not sure that his Administration understood the true situation in the area. At lower levels our warnings had been ignored. Our immediate purpose must be to resume close relations with the United States and induce them to recognize the real dangers of Soviet penetration. My colleagues agreed that I should consider the best means of making a further approach.

I thought that there should be an immediate consultation with Mr. Eisenhower and M. Mollet. During luncheon on the 7th I followed the President's suggestion and telephoned to him. The President was receptive. I told him I thought it important that we should meet and have a full discussion on the situation. He agreed and asked me what date I had in mind. I said the sooner the better and suggested that M. Mollet and I might fly over that evening. After a little discussion as to how to make the arrangements, the President authorized me to invite M. Mollet, since communication between us was quicker, and to tell him that a confirmatory invitation from the President would follow. I did this and M. Mollet, like the good colleague he was, at once accepted, although at no little inconvenience to his own plans.

About an hour later the President telephoned to me and said he wanted to be clear that I was not making the journey just to argue about the United Nations resolutions. I said certainly not, and that I did not even know what those resolutions might be at the present time. The purpose of our visit would be for much wider discussion on the whole Middle Eastern scene, and on what action we could take together about it. The President said he was glad of that, because it would be awkward if we were to argue about United Nations resolutions and then not agree. I assured him that was not my purpose.

Later he telephoned again and said that he would be much taken up in the days ahead in consultations with the leaders of Congress. He had come to the conclusion, therefore, that M. Mollet and I should defer our visit, though he did not rule it out for a later date. The conversation took place only a few minutes before I was going down to the House of Commons to announce the visit in the agreed terms.

Later that evening I sent the President a telegram in which I said:

> I do hope that it will be possible for us to meet in the very near future. I should feel much more confident about the decisions and actions which we shall have to take in the short term if we had first reached some common understanding about the attitude which we each intended to take towards a long-term settlement of the outstanding issues in the Middle East. I have for a long time felt that some at least of our troubles there have derived from the lack of a clear understanding between our two countries, ever since the end of the war, on policy in the Middle East. And I doubt whether we shall ever be able to secure stability there unless we are working towards common objectives.

After a reference to Soviet intentions and to the Swiss President's invitation to another Geneva meeting, I concluded:

> On matters such as this it is difficult to come to considered conclusions by correspondence. I would feel much happier if we had been able to meet and talk them over soon. It was with these grave issues in mind that I suggested this morning that I might come out to Washington at once. I still hope that it may be possible for us to meet within the next few days, as soon as your immediate preoccupations are over.

The President replied agreeing to a meeting at an early date, but he held that the United Nations resolutions must first be carried out. This meant that the Anglo-French forces should be withdrawn from Egypt without delay. Mr. Eisenhower now considered that the ground would be favourable for a meeting only when this had been done. Thus we and the French were squarely asked to give up the gage we had won, before concerting with the United States any common policy for the Middle East.

★   ★   ★   ★   ★

563

In our discussions in London we had to determine our attitude to two resolutions which lay before the Assembly. One, sponsored by Afro-Asian powers, called for the immediate withdrawal of the Anglo-French forces. We could not agree to this. The other resolution was put forward by the Argentine. This accepted the Secretary-General's plan for the United Nations force and dealt with the separation of combatants and the withdrawal of Israeli units. It also allowed us to remain at Port Said while the United Nations force was built up. We decided to vote for this resolution, though it did not express concern for the future of the canal or for a final Arab-Israeli settlement.

Both resolutions were passed by the General Assembly. The Afro-Asian one had been amended to require us to withdraw in accordance with the earlier resolutions of the United Nations on the subject. However, we determined to keep our troops on the spot until the international force was there in strength. Our Commander-in-Chief was meanwhile authorized to open staff conversations with General Burns, the United Nations commander-designate, and to agree with him a plan for the orderly and effective transfer of responsibility.

We were now committed to the withdrawal of our forces from the canal, but not by any particular date. We had to avoid a vacuum between our departure and the arrival of a sufficient United Nations force. A phased withdrawal was the way to do this, timed to coincide with the building up of international contingents along the canal.

There were many complications and dangers. There was the possibility that the cease-fire might be broken, our troops and patrols were being frequently sniped at. Only their admirable steadiness prevented ugly incidents. Cairo radio, back on the air again, was inciting the population of Port Said to make trouble, thereby increasing the likelihood of demonstrations and rioting. We knew that the Russian Consul visited the Egyptian Governor of the town, who at once assumed a stiffer attitude to the Allied commanders. The Consul was busy spreading inflammatory publicity against us; in these conditions we could not agree to dribble out our forces.

A further problem was the urgent need to clear the canal. The Egyptians had sunk twenty-one blockships in the harbour of Port Said. We got to work at once with our salvage equipment, which we had assembled in advance for just this purpose, and began removing these obstructions and also those in the short stretch of the canal under our control. In the rest of the waterway the Egyptians were busy sinking ships. By far the greater part of this obstruction to the canal was done after the fighting was over, when politically and physically it was safe to do so. By the time the Egyptians had finished, they had sunk thirty-two ships in the canal, while their propaganda was busy blaming Allied bombing for their own act of sabotage.

The French and ourselves at once sought authority from the United Nations to clear the whole of the canal with the equipment which we, and we only, had at our disposal. Both countries were willing to place their salvage teams under United Nations control. Technically, France and Britain had the means to carry out this task far more quickly than anyone else. We wanted to get on with it at once. All the more so because the United States showed no signs of readiness to assist France and Britain with oil supplies from the western hemisphere.

The Egyptian Government took instant advantage of this situation, and from a position of weakness were once again allowed to seize a position of strength. They declared that they would not contemplate the clearance of the canal until after the Anglo-French forces had gone. Nor would they even then agree to the use of Anglo-French salvage teams by the United Nations. There was no guarantee that they might not carry their opposition further and refuse clearance until after the United Nations force also had come and gone. Under this Egyptian pressure the United Nations gave way. Even before Mr. Hammarskjöld paid his visit to Cairo on November 16th, he had largely accepted the Egyptian point of view. He informed us that no arrangements could be made about either the clearance or the future administration of the canal until we had withdrawn.

At this juncture the Foreign Secretary flew to New York where he remained for ten days, struggling to inject some sense of values. His efforts were largely in vain. The President a few days earlier had granted a friendly interview to our new Ambassador, Sir Harold Caccia, when he presented his credentials. Mr. Eisenhower said he had differed sharply with us on tactics, but he shared my views on Colonel Nasser. He agreed that the urgent task ahead was to work out a settlement of both the Suez and the Arab-Israeli problems. These were promising words, but the President's attitude was not reflected in the actions of his Administration. Mr. Dulles at this time was ill and the authorities in charge of the State Department during his absence were aggressively negative when the Foreign Secretary urged our views upon them. In the possession of Port Said and the Israeli occupation of Sinai, we held strong bargaining counters. Before we agreed to relinquish them, we must ensure that the canal was promptly cleared and that a general settlement of the problems of the area was under negotiation. Soviet designs for penetrating the Middle East had gone much further than the United States believed. Russia regarded Cairo as a future Soviet outpost, and communist sympathizers were busy throughout the area, notably in Syria and Iraq. As Nuri es-Said was to say in 1958, a few days before he was murdered: 'All this shows that unless Nasser is checked, events in the Middle East will continue on a large scale in favour of Russia.'

When the Foreign Secretary used these arguments, he was met with expressions of moral disapproval of our action in Egypt and with the reply that we must first withdraw before anything could be attempted. The United States officials refused to co-operate at any level of policy-making. They declared that Britain, France and the United States must not appear to be conspiring together behind the back of the United Nations. Their only reaction to reports of Russian infiltration in the Middle East was to press us to remove our forces more quickly.

We could not help contrasting the American attitude now with our own attitude at the time of the Guatemala campaign. In that country the United States had encouraged the overthrow of a communist-influenced Government, which it considered a menace to the peace of central America. We had understood their action there and done what we could not to hamper them in the Security Council. They were now behaving in a precisely contrary manner towards us. When this point was put to the United States officials, they had no answer.

It might have been thought that, however much angered, the United States Government would wish to get the best possible results out of the situation for the future of Western Europe, whose economic security was at stake. This was not so. The attitude was rather that the President had been slighted because the Allies had acted without permission. The Allies must pay for it, and pay they did. The many warnings, both public and private, which had been given by the Allies over the waiting months did not help to assuage official American opinion. On the contrary, they irritated it. If an individual has been warned by his friend that the friend will take some action, and has not heeded the warning, and his friend then takes action, the individual is likely to feel sore. His own error of judgment only increases his exasperation. So it can be with countries.

In London, the Government considered practical steps. They were determined that arrangements for clearing the canal should be made before ordering more than a token withdrawal of Allied forces. They also wished to ensure that negotiations about the future administration of the canal should begin before the withdrawal was complete. They were prepared to recall Allied troops unit by unit as the United Nations moved in, but a definite time-table for the clearance of the canal had to be worked out at the same time. A guarantee that this time-table would be put in operation effectively was necessary before any withdrawal was made. The Government were confident that they enjoyed the support of public opinion in laying down these conditions. The Foreign Secretary was asked to make these minimum conditions clear to Mr. Hammarskjöld, who was about to set off for Cairo.

At the United Nations the outlook was darkening. The Egyptian Government were seeking to become the arbiters of the composition and functions of the international force. Having themselves sabotaged the canal, they were now saying that our salvage corps should take no part in the work of clearing it. Nasser was attempting to dictate terms as if he were a victor, while the Soviets were replacing the war material he had lost in the field.

The President had indefinitely postponed consultation with M. Mollet and myself. He did not receive the Foreign Secretary in Washington, nor the Australian Foreign Minister, Mr. Casey, who was the bearer of a message from the Australian Prime Minister. The United States Administration seemed to be dominated at this time by one thought only, to harry their allies. Mr. Dulles, who was still recovering from an operation, deplored to the Foreign Secretary that we had not managed to bring Nasser down and declared that he must be prevented from getting away with it. The actions of the United States Government had exactly the opposite result.

Hammarskjöld, on his visit to Cairo, found Nasser extremely complacent, as well he might be. The Egyptians were putting out much propaganda about the likelihood of riots in Port Said if the Anglo-French forces remained there for many more days. It was propaganda which found willing listeners among the delegates at the General Assembly in New York. The Egyptian Government next threatened to expel all British subjects from Egypt. The purpose of this move was also to bring further pressure to bear upon us.

Hammarskjöld returned from Cairo on November 19th to report the results of his discussions with the Egyptian Government. Some active political exchanges ensued in New York, in which the Foreign Secretary and his French colleague tried to secure results which were prudent and effective. They avoided a number of dangers. Egypt attempted to get a veto on the composition of an international force. This was refused, as was also the power which she demanded to determine where that force should be stationed. Egypt had wished to confine it to the Arab-Israeli armistice lines of 1949. The Egyptians also claimed that the United Nations force would have no further function once the Anglo-French and Israeli troops had left their soil. This was not accepted; it was decided that the force should not be withdrawn until the General Assembly resolved that its functions had been fulfilled.

The General Assembly was now due to meet in full session on November 23rd. The British and French Governments had to take a decision upon the question of withdrawal. We had already agreed to admit into Port Said an advance party of a hundred Danes and Norwegians. We had promised landing and transit facilities to the Yugoslav contingent, which was on its way by sea. We were prepared to supply the United Nations with such vehicles and stores as they might need and they had undertaken to build up a force of four thousand by December 1st.

On these terms the Cabinet decided to make a token withdrawal of one battalion of the Royal West Kent Regiment. They were not prepared to do more than this, until the debate in the General Assembly showed whether the United Nations would in fact carry out the responsibilities which it had assumed.

$$\star \quad \star \quad \star \quad \star \quad \star$$

One Friday afternoon early in October, I had set out to drive down to Chequers with a private secretary and called on my way to see my wife, who was in University College Hospital. I had only been in the room a few moments when I suddenly felt chilled to the bone. My wife assured me that the room was the normal temperature. In a few minutes a severe ague fell upon me and I was put to bed, somewhat ignominiously, in a neighbouring room. I did not know much more after that for a while, but I was told later that my temperature had risen to 106°. I spent the week-end at the hospital and I left on the Monday much refreshed by my rest. This refreshment was probably deceptive, for it is a common feature of these fevers and is apt to be followed by recurrent bouts of weakness. So it proved for me. But at the time I recovered well enough to carry on with my work.

In early November Lord Evans, who was taking care of me medically, began to be anxious at my state of health. Although the fever had not come back, there was no doubt that the bout had weakened me and he became concerned that it might be an indication of a return of my previous bile duct trouble. As against this, the pressure under which I had been working, day and night, for so long a time might have been held to account for the exhaustion from which I was certainly suffering. I had not had even a week-end off for many months. In this uncertainty, Lord Evans felt that I must somehow obtain a respite from my work, even for a short time, as a result of which we would be better able to tell whether my present state of health was only a passing phase, or indicated something more serious. Accordingly, and after consultation with my principal colleagues, I acquiesced in a decision to go for a few weeks to Jamaica. I flew there on November 23rd. Kind friends, Mr. and Mrs. Ian Fleming, lent us a peaceful retreat at Golden Eye. I arranged to be kept in touch with urgent decisions by cable and, though I was not present at the Cabinet whose conclusions I have just recorded, I approved them myself before I left for Jamaica. While I was away the Lord Privy Seal, Mr. Butler, presided at Cabinet meetings. He and his colleagues kept me informed and we exchanged opinions on the decisions they took.

★   ★   ★   ★   ★

Before the meeting of the General Assembly, President Eisenhower once more proclaimed in public that he wished to strengthen the Anglo-American alliance. Armed with this authority, the Foreign Secretary and our Ambassador in Washington both renewed their exchanges with high American officials. We were allies in N.A.T.O. and in S.E.A.T.O., the present Soviet threat was directed at the Middle East, which lay between the spheres of these two pacts. We could hardly be allies in two parts of the world and not in a third. These efforts got us nowhere. One senior American authority frankly declared that it was not possible at this stage for the Administration to talk to Her Majesty's Government. We were accused of 'stalling' on the resolutions of the United Nations and we were taxed with having created the 'black-out' between our countries.

When the General Assembly met it approved the steps taken by the Secretary-General towards clearing the canal and it agreed to his definition of the functions of the United Nations force. The Soviet bloc alone voted against this resolution, which passed by 65 to 9. The next resolution before the Assembly was one of the Afro-Asian kind which regretted that Anglo-French forces were still in Port Said and told us to withdraw forthwith. Mr. Shepilov made a speech in which he accused us of having no intention of withdrawing. Choosing to forget his own country's actions in Hungary, he launched a cynical attack upon Anglo-French 'aggression'.

Mr. Lester Pearson, who spoke next, drily described the Soviet Foreign Minister's remarks as 'a verbal aggression upon truth'. Canada, Mr. Pearson said, believed that as Britain and France were already complying with the wishes of the United Nations, the present resolution was unnecessary. He urged the Assembly to apply itself to practical matters.

M. Spaak, as an experienced diplomatist, saw the opportunity which this situation created and seized it. He moved a friendly amendment to this resolution which omitted the call for immediate withdrawal, took note of the action which we and the French were already taking, and underlined the rôle of the United Nations forces. Had this amendment been carried, the negotiating position of the United Nations would have been immeasurably strengthened. There would have been a real opportunity to initiate negotiation on the wider issues of the Arab-Israeli dispute while some of the cards were still in the hands of the West. Equally, it would have been possible to treat the future of the canal as it should have been treated, a great international issue affecting the lives of many nations as closely as that of Egypt. At one time it seemed that this amendment might be carried. Had the United States put its full weight behind it, it certainly would have been. Even so, the amendment secured 23 votes, there were 37 against it and 18 abstentions, including the United States.

The countries which supported M. Spaak's amendment were Australia, Belgium, Brazil, Canada, China, Cuba, Denmark, the Dominican Republic, France, Iceland, Israel, Italy, Luxembourg, the Netherlands, New Zealand, Norway, Peru, Portugal, Sweden, Thailand, Turkey, South Africa and the United Kingdom.

Thus the Assembly rejected the advice of M. Spaak and Mr. Pearson. Delegates knew that the United States proposed once more to vote against us, which it did. The Afro-Asian resolution was passed by 63 votes to 5 with no less than 10 abstentions. The defence offered by the United States Government for their vote was that they were the prisoners of their own policy and had no choice. This vote caused much resentment in Britain, for it was cast when we were complying with United Nations resolutions.

M. Spaak soon afterwards gave his views upon the United Nations to the public. I print them here because I agree with them. In an article for the magazine *Foreign Affairs* called 'The West in Disarray', he wrote:

In the present United Nations set-up, which is not what its founders wished and hoped it would be, everything short of war is allowed. Treaties may be violated, promises can be broken, a nation is licensed to menace its neighbour or to perpetrate any sort of trick on it, just as long as there is no actual war. The attitude of Egypt during the last few months is a case in point. While Egypt denied transit through the Suez Canal to Israeli ships, sent death commandos on to Israeli soil, violated the Treaty of Constantinople, sent arms to be used against the French in Algeria and made preparations to attack its neighbour, the United Nations was powerless to intervene. Such intervention would not come within the scope of the Charter as at present interpreted. But let Israel in desperation send troops into the Sinai peninsula and let Anglo-French forces land at Port Said, and they are sure to be condemned. Meanwhile, those who were looking on impassively at the brutal repression of the revolt in Hungary could not find words harsh enough to damn them. . . .

The spectacle which Soviet Russia and the satellite countries have presented in the course of debate in the present Assembly is indeed profoundly shocking. They become passionate defenders of the General Assembly's recommendations every time that Egypt is in question, but they treat all resolutions concerning Hungary like dead letters. This attitude is so immoral that the very authority of the Assembly becomes deeply affected by it. Under such conditions it is impossible to believe that peace can be maintained and international justice assured.

In the days which followed the vote in the Assembly, no opening showed itself for negotiation on the important issues, of which this dispute was the expression. They remained to trouble the future and did so very soon. The United States Administration continued obstinately silent, so the Foreign Secretary and his French colleague returned home. The Arab-Israeli problem remained unsolved. The canal was handed back to the control of one man, who was picked up, dusted down and put in full authority again. At the time of writing* Israeli

* August, 1959.

merchant cargoes, on voyage in the ships of other nations, are being refused passage through the canal. The United Nations takes no action at this violation of the rights of nations in an international waterway. Western Europe would be naive indeed to expect free passage of the canal at any time of emergency, unless it has the power to compel it, which it is not likely to have again.

The careless view has been taken that the events of Suez constituted a success for the United Nations. Unhappily this was not so. There is still no known instance of effective action by the United Nations when the two great powers of the world have been in opposition. The United States and Soviet Russia joined together in the General Assembly to issue their instructions on Suez. They were obeyed, but the fact that the United States and Russia were together did not mean that they were right. They could hardly both be so. The Russians are still in Hungary as the Egyptians are in sole command of the canal.

Distance may dim perspective, it should not distort it. The United States could not have taken up so legalistic an attitude if the security of its own continent had been at stake.

★   ★   ★   ★   ★

The British and French Governments were under heavy pressure at the United Nations to name at once a date for the withdrawal of their forces. In this the United States Government took a leading part. The Secretary of the Treasury, Mr. Humphrey, telephoned to Mr. Butler and made it clear that the United States would not extend help or support to Britain until after a definite statement on withdrawal had been made. In a further message he conveyed that the American Administration meant by this the announcement of an early date for such withdrawal.

This was unacceptable to us. Neither the French Government nor ourselves were willing to fix a definite date and announce it in public until certain conditions had been fulfilled. The immediate necessity was to secure precise assurances from the Secretary-General of the United Nations, before we handed over our responsibilities in Port Said to the United Nations contingents.

By persistent argument, we made some headway. It was accepted that the United Nations force should be built up to a competent size, though it did not in the end contain the Canadian contingent for which we hoped and which was made ready. The United Nations accepted responsibility for clearing the canal as quickly as possible. Surveying and diving operations were to begin before the Allied withdrawal. On the other hand, no use was ever made of our offer to place Anglo-French salvage resources at the disposal of the United Nations. Our salvage fleet was working with high efficiency and success in Port Said harbour and clearing the entrance to the canal. If full use had been made of it, the canal could have been opened many weeks sooner. The delay was due to fear of offending Nasser.

We insisted that there must be no discrimination by the Egyptian authorities against British and French shipping when the canal re-opened, and this we secured. It was agreed that negotiations upon the future of the canal should be resumed on the basis of the six principles unanimously approved by the Security Council. This was cold comfort for the canal users. I urged that we should stand upon the eighteen-power proposals. The United States had played a large part in formu-lating them and the fact that they had been vetoed by the communist powers did not seem sufficient reason to drop them. The French Government shared my opinion and our Government's statement on December 3rd reiterated this. It was not welcome to Mr. Hammar-skjöld, who was now committed by his conversations with the Egyptians to regarding the eighteen-power proposals as superseded. We held that only something equivalent would provide acceptable guarantees for freedom of passage through the canal. This should have been the basis for further negotiation.

Though they had only received partial satisfaction on some points, the British and French Governments reluctantly agreed to resume the withdrawal of their troops. These negotiations had committed the United Nations force more seriously and on a larger scale in the area of the canal. They had also alerted United States opinion, if not yet the Government, to the combined dangers presented by growing Soviet penetration and intensified Arab nationalism. We refused, how-ever, to name in public a specific date for final withdrawal. This would have given the signal for further demonstrations and disturbances in Port Said. On our insistence, the phasing was arranged between the Allied Commander-in-Chief and the United Nations Commander, in the light of transport problems and the needs for preserving public order on the spot. After discussion with the French Government, we fixed December 22nd as the final day for embarkation.

During the closing weeks of the Anglo-French occupation, the Egyptians did all they could to stir up incidents and present them to the world as the result of Allied provocation. In spite of the cease-fire agreements, they attempted ambushes, Allied patrols were fired upon and grenades thrown at military vehicles. Arms were smuggled into Port Said and a virulent propaganda campaign was directed at its inhabitants inciting them against Allied authorities. These Egyptian activities were of a pattern with the *fedayeen* raids against Israel and they caused further casualties on both sides. During this tense period, Allied officers and men conducted themselves with remarkable coolness and forbearance. Their commander in Port Said, General Stockwell, protested several times to the United Nations Commander against Egyptian actions, but with little effect.

I returned from Jamaica on December 14th. During my absence I had a courteous exchange of messages with the President, an exchange which brought us no nearer a meeting of Heads of Government, urgent as this was. I was feeling much stronger and had no suspicion of the advice the doctors were to have to give me in January.

At London Airport, where many of my colleagues met me, I made a statement summing up the position and prospects at the moment:

There is now, I am sure from my own post-bag as well as other evidence, a growing understanding in Canada, and also in the United States, about the action which Britain and France were compelled to take in the Middle East. I am sure that this will go on increasing.

The formation of a United Nations force could be the turning point in the history of the United Nations. Does anyone suppose that there would have been a United Nations force but for British and French action? Of course not.

It is true that it would have been perfectly possible to allow events to drift, to let hostilities spread and develop, to allow the Moscow-Cairo axis to perfect its plans. All this would have given us much less immediate anxiety than we have had to bear. It would have been easy to do nothing. It always is for any Government and it would have been popular in some quarters. It would have been easy, but it would have been fatal, just as it was fatal in the years between the wars.

Everybody knows now what the Soviets were planning and preparing to do in the Middle East. Russia supplied arms in such quantities, as has now been revealed, because she knew the Egyptian dictator's ambitions suited her own book.

The aim was just this—more satellites, but this time in the

Middle East. I am convinced, more convinced than I have been about anything in all my public life, that we were right, my colleagues and I, in the judgments and decisions we took, and that history will prove it so.

Of the next steps I said:

It seems to us two things are essential. The canal must be cleared by all available means, and without further delay. Its future must be settled, and permanently. Every country concerned must take a fresh look, and make a new effort to solve the problems that have beset the Middle East for far too long.

Soon after my return, my wife and I lunched alone with Sir Winston and Lady Churchill. We had a full discussion and at the end of it, Sir Winston summed up his judgment on the situation: 'What a magnificent position to fight back from.'

We now found the United States Government more helpful on two matters, the support of sterling and the supply of oil. Other problems arose, however, in connection with the canal area which complicated our plan of withdrawal, and on these they maintained a rigid attitude. The Foreign Secretary explained these difficulties to Mr. Dulles at a meeting in Paris on December 14th. We wished to find solutions for them before our troops finally left. Dulles reacted as if we were seeking an indefinite suspension of our withdrawal, which was not so. He stated that he could not release us from our obligation to withdraw, since to do so would be 'in some sense a breach of faith on the part of the Administration with Congress and United States public opinion.' He maintained that our action had caused revulsion throughout the United States. This was strong language and at variance with the reports of our own representatives, who considered that the sharp feelings displayed at the time in Washington had not really represented American opinion.

The Foreign Secretary told Dulles that we were concerned with the future of British nationals and their property in Egypt. About 10,000 were involved, many of them Cypriots and Maltese. By the middle of December 2,500 had already been driven out by direct or indirect means. About 3,500 French nationals had suffered likewise. Much British and French property had also been seized by the Government. The threat of general expulsion was now hanging over all the remaining British and French subjects in Egypt. By contrast, Egyptian nationals in Britain had not been molested.

We brought strong diplomatic pressure to bear at the United Nations and a general expulsion did not take place. We were also trying to settle upon some system of arbitration, either through the United Nations or directly with the Egyptians, to consider the claims and counter-claims for compensation, which would shortly arise. These included the value of the seized British and French property in Egypt, the cost of clearing the canal and a just assessment of the damage done during the fighting. When we withdrew, the argument was still going on.

Another controversy had a happier outcome. The Egyptians interned some four hundred and fifty British civilian employees of the contractors in charge of the Suez Canal base. They had been engaged to work there under the 1954 agreement with Egypt and we were determined not to leave them interned. On our side we held some two hundred and fifty Egyptians, mostly prisoners of war. An exchange was arranged and took place on the day before final embarkation.

Throughout the seven weeks of these operations, brief, inconclusive and exasperating as they were, Anglo-French co-operation at every level worked with unbroken harmony. A sense of mutual respect grew between the forces serving together. The gallantry of the paratroopers of both nations, the swift and careful execution of the air operation, the smooth timing of the naval landings and the operations which followed, each of these showed work together of a pattern rarely seen between two nations. There was no recrimination, political or military, either then or later. Our French allies showed wonderful generosity. They accepted our command in all the military fields. It would have been only human, when the task was completed, to blame us for not having found some swifter way. There was nothing of the kind. To the sincere respect which British soldiers, sailors and airmen brought back from their joint enterprise, should be added the gratitude of the British people for this understanding by their loyal neighbour.

As our forces were on the way home just before Christmas, I sent a signal to General Keightley:

It is hard to imagine a more thankless task than has been yours and that of those who have served under you in these recent weeks. I have greatly admired the patience and discipline which all ranks of all three Services have shown throughout this period, and now that the main task is completed I should like to send congratulations and gratitude. I am confident that as history unrolls your efforts will have been shown not to have been in vain.

★   ★   ★   ★   ★

Suez was a short-term emergency operation which succeeded, and an attempt to halt a long-term deterioration, whose outcome is still uncertain. A clash between Israel and Egypt was inevitable, given Nasser's declared intentions. Whenever this took place, it could bring grave danger to the general peace. It was far better that it should not happen at a moment of Egypt's choosing, and the explosion could not have occurred in circumstances less damaging, given the speedy action of Britain and France. On balance the world stood to gain by the fact that the conflict took place then and not some months later, when the consequences in relation to world events might have been infinitely graver.

We were not successful in our wider objective; we did not bring about Arab-Israeli peace or restore international control over the canal. It is true that some successes were gained. The military weakness of the Egyptian forces was exposed and duly noted, in particular by neighbours. This had important consequences. From the day of Egyptian defeat in the Sinai desert the chances of a Nasser empire were scotched, not killed. Even so, the Sudan did not hesitate to resist the grasping demands which Nasser later made upon her northern boundary. It is unlikely that Nasser or any other Arab leader will readily undertake a war of extermination against Israel in the immediate future, without support from outside. As against this, Nasser remains ruler of Egypt, his ambition still dangerous. The canal is under his control, Syria has become a part of his empire. Our intervention at least closed the chapter of complacency about the situation in the Middle East. It led to the Eisenhower Doctrine and from that to Anglo-American intervention in the following summer in Jordan and the Lebanon. It helped to show that the West was not prepared to leave the area wide open for infiltration and subversion by others. But these were only partial gains. The uneasy equipose still continues.

A year and a half after these events, an army mutiny in Iraq murdered the King and Crown Prince, Nuri es-Said and their families and many more. Though instigated by Nasser's resourceful and unscrupulous propaganda, this event has not benefited him. The Governments of the Lebanon and Jordan, knowing themselves threatened by Nasser's subversive tactics in their own countries, asked for help from the West. The United Nations observers on the spot denied that there was subversive activity by Nasser in either country. The Secretary-General, Mr. Hammarskjöld, supported his observers. Ignoring this myopic testimony, the United States landed forces in the Lebanon and the United Kingdom flew troops into Jordan, without prior reference to the United Nations. This action was necessary if the right to live of these two small countries was to be preserved; it was unquestionably against the terms of the Charter as interpreted at the time of our intervention at Port Said. Since the United Nations observers were already on the spot and proclaiming that the motives for Anglo-American intervention did not exist, it was rather more heinous.

The intervention succeeded in its limited purpose, the immediate rescue of the Lebanon and Jordan, though probably the more effective deterrent was the conviction that Israel would fight if the United Arab Republic took over Jordan. Egypt now knew beyond argument what Israeli fighting meant.

No attempt was made to redeem Iraq or to halt the deterioration in the Middle East. With communist influence and authority in Iraq, the Russian dream of access to the Persian Gulf draws nearer. These developments will not be checked by support for Nasser in the rôle of an anti-communist dictator. To attempt this would be as useless as it was to seek to use Mussolini against Hitler and would result in the final annihilation of the friends of the West. The position has a certain analogy with that which existed in Iran in 1951, when I returned to the Foreign Office. I was under strong pressure then from the United States to make terms with Musaddiq, communism being regarded as the only alternative. I did not believe that and refused to accept such a policy, preferring to bide our time and await an opportunity to do business with a more responsible authority. I felt sure that this would come. It will come also in the Arab lands, if patience is shown and opportunity and encouragement is given to those, and they are many, who believe that the future of this world must not be placed either in the hands of a militant dictator or of a communist tyranny.

Whatever the transient phenomena of the visits and meetings of statesmen the danger of world conflict does not recede; at best it is held. The period when the deterrent of nuclear power held the world in awe is fading. The wider manufacture and ownership of nuclear weapons spreads familiarity and with it an instinctive drift and carelessness. Nor are we entitled to remonstrate with others for making the weapons we have made. The numbers within the circle will grow and it has as yet no rules.

The United Nations has not been able to meet the need, because the charter has not been fulfilled. The abuse of the veto has nullified the effectiveness of the Security Council, while the failure to create an international force has deprived the United Nations of any backing for its authority. More serious is the attitude shown by that organization to international engagements in recent years. There has been an increasing tendency to condone breaches of international agreement. In order to obtain a temporary easement, it lays up further trouble later on. Up to February 1959, Israeli cargoes had freedom of passage through the Suez Canal. Since that date the Egyptian Government have blocked the passage of ships carrying Israeli goods, and when the captain of a Danish ship declined to yield, his ship was held and its cargo impounded. There was no attempt, even by the Egyptian press, to pretend that these cargoes were strategic. They complained that it was Israel's purpose 'to increase trade with the Afro-Asian countries and develop its economy'. No purpose could be more legitimate. Attempts by the Egyptian Government to halt it are contrary to every engagement given both under the Convention of 1888 and the Charter of the United Nations, to say nothing of the many assurances by Egypt and the United States in the last two years. On February 20th, 1957, President Eisenhower said to the American people: 'We should not assume that, if Israel withdraws, Egypt will prevent Israeli shipping from using the Suez Canal or the Gulf of Aqaba. If, unhappily, Egypt does hereafter violate the armistice agreement or other international obligations, then this should be dealt with firmly by the society of nations.'

In the event there has been no more than a whimper from the United Nations. This attitude on the part of a world organization which should be the custodian of international agreement creates difficulties for Israel, but its consequences will be infinitely graver for all of us, for on this precedent the verdict of history cannot be challenged. To take the easy way, to put off decisions, to fail even to record a protest when international undertakings are broken on which the ink is scarcely dry, can only lead one way. It is all so much more difficult to do later on, and so we come full circle. The insidious appeal of appeasement leads to a deadly reckoning.

There is much that is unreal and unco-ordinated in the present Western position. The rivalry in Arabia has now serious consequences.

The United States supplies weapons of war to Saudi Arabia, which gives encouragement and power to rebel pretenders against the Sultan of Muscat. We, as in treaty bound, help the ruler defend his territories. Nasser backs the rebels by any means to hand. All this is costing British and Arabian life in the fighting, and diplomatic damage in Western disarray.

Few things are more important now than Western policy towards Africa. But the Western leaders do not even meet together on this subject, nor has there been effective discussion of it through the diplomatic channel. There is too little understanding of how closely France's position concerns the security of the Western nations. General de Gaulle's new plans for Algeria are characteristically courageous and far-reaching. They should receive steadfast support.

A strong argument can be made for a Marshall plan for Africa with all free Western countries contributing to it as much as they can and will. Russia could be invited to join and expert administration would be needed and technical advice. Both could be provided and help given to projects and not to countries. Such a plan could influence Africa. The present multiplication of individual efforts does not.

A danger to the free world lies in the incompleteness of its alliances. In Europe N.A.T.O., and in South-East Asia S.E.A.T.O., are both fulfilling after a fashion the purpose for which they were originally created. At least there is no vacuum there. But in the vital intervening continents of central and western Asia and Africa, there is no common policy, plan or propaganda. Alliances cannot be limited geographically in a cold war which is global. The West has a common faith and a common philosophy; it must express both, in thought and action everywhere and always. The interests of allies cannot be regarded as vital in one area and expendable in another, without danger to the whole structure of the alliance. There must be the same unity of purpose and action in a cold war as in a hot. Failure to observe this obligation has resulted in great gains to the communist powers in these post-war years.

There are remedies for this state of affairs, but they are difficult to accept and apply. They involve understanding among the European powers with overseas responsibilities about the aims and limitations of their policies. They involve an examination in the United States of the realities of present-day colonialism and a determined effort by both groups to align their policies. If this is not done, the Western alliance will continue to weaken until it parts at the seams.

★　★　★　★　★

I have been blessed with a tough constitution which has served me well through more than thirty years of politics, nearly twenty in office and ten as Foreign Secretary.

At nineteen I was adjutant of my battalion, and a brigade-major at twenty. When my brigadier drew up a report after more than a year of service with him, I can recall one phrase: 'He is possessed of staying power which his appearance does not suggest.' I did not think the phrase particularly complimentary at the time, but it was true enough.

Even so, the three operations I underwent in 1953 had taken their toll and there was always some uncertainty as to whether or not the condition so brilliantly dealt with by the American surgeon, Dr. Cattell, would return. There had been one or two warnings over the past year, but slight enough, I felt, to be ignored. More serious was the high fever, which had struck me down when visiting my wife in hospital.

We spent a quiet Christmas at Chequers with the family. On Christmas Eve, Mr. Nehru broke his journey in England on his return from a visit to the United States. He motored down to Chequers to see me, accompanied by his sister, Mrs. Pandit, who has made so many friends in this country as India's High Commissioner. Inevitably we were each a little constrained, but I have always felt a sincere liking for Mr. Nehru personally, which differences on policy could not affect. I like to think that he had the same feelings towards me, and our friendship was certainly unimpaired.

Lord Cherwell came over from Oxford to spend Christmas Day with us, firm in supporting our action and deploring the American attitude. It was the last time we were to see this generous and loyal friend; he died a few months later. I had found refreshment in his penetrating if sometimes acid analysis of events. Often critical, he was always true.

After Christmas, while we were still at Chequers, there was some recurrence of fever. This troubled us enough to seek Lord Evans' advice. After an examination, he advised me to come up to London as soon as possible when I could see him with one or other of the specialists who were familiar with this complaint. He did not disguise from me that the bouts of fever might be on their way back. This was grim news for me and it requires some little explanation.

If a man is told that he is suffering from heart trouble or from cancer and is doing some vital work, he may well decide that he can and will go on with it as long as his powers do not fail. Mine was a more difficult decision, for the truth was that these fever attacks, if they began to return at all frequently, were in themselves so weakening that nobody could suffer from them and at the same time do a good day's work, let alone a night's work. A Prime Minister's job in this country, if it is conscientiously discharged, can begin at eight-thirty in the morning and may end at one or two the next morning. There is no possibility of carrying through with work of this responsibility under any recurring disability. After talking over the situation unhappily with my wife, I decided to go to London early in the New Year. I eased off in the work as much as I could, but there was no improvement and the fever lingered.

When Lord Evans saw me in London he repeated his opinion that the indications of a return of my old complaint were serious and that I must expect them to become more frequent. It was impossible to tell how rapidly they would do this, whether there would be several attacks of fever in the next month or two, compelling me to lay down my work then, or whether the intervals would be longer, or shorter, but what was certain in his judgment was that the attacks would continue and increase in intensity. It was only natural that I should feel, in those early days of January, that this was just the time when I wanted to go on. There were difficulties and differences in the Conservative Party, but I was sure that the aftermath of Suez would justify our policy and do so soon. The United States was showing signs of taking action to meet a Middle Eastern situation now threatening to their interests. I was more confident than in 1938 as to how, unhappily, the position would unfold. Further intervention would be inevitable in some part of the Middle East, certainly by ourselves and possibly by the Americans. I wanted to be there when that happened.

We agreed to have a second opinion, that of Sir Gordon Gordon-Taylor, most respected and experienced of surgeons, who forcefully confirmed Lord Evans' opinion. On the following day, we asked for a third opinion, Dr. Thomas Hunt. He took the same view. After this firm and cumulative advice, I knew that I had no choice. If I had to hand in my resignation, I wished to do so at once, so as to give my successor the best chance to appoint his colleagues and take up his responsibilities before meeting Parliament. I asked two of my closest friends, Lord Salisbury and Lord Scarbrough, to see me separately, one from within my political circle and the other from outside it. Both saw Lord Evans, heard the medical opinions and were convinced that the decision must be taken. I felt it unfair to present the Queen with the facts of this situation without any kind of previous warning. I decided to ask Her Majesty whether she would receive my wife and myself at Sandringham. There was nothing exceptional in this, for I had often in earlier years been to Sandringham at this season, most recently as Foreign Secretary a few weeks before the death of King George VI.

We travelled to Sandringham on January 8th. In the evening before dinner I had an audience of Her Majesty, when I told her of the medical opinion and of my conviction that this could not be ignored without detriment to her service. The Queen said that in the circumstances she would go to London later the next day, and it was agreed that I should tender my resignation at Buckingham Palace on the following evening.

The next morning, on my return to London, I summoned one or two of my principal colleagues, among them Mr. Butler and Mr. Macmillan, and I told them the facts. At 5 p.m. I held my last Cabinet. I told them of the medical opinion and of my decision, for which most were entirely unprepared. I think that we were all affected by the personal side of this event, which I tried to make as short as I could. Thus, after twenty-two years, my periods of Cabinet office were ended. With Lord Salisbury I had worked in politics for half a lifetime, with others for lesser periods. While I was changing my clothes to go to the Palace, Antony Head came to see me. He was sad at my decision. The moment seemed to him such a bad one for a change, just as the Americans appeared to be evolving towards a new policy. In fact, the Eisenhower Doctrine for the Middle East was announced a few weeks later. I thanked Antony Head and told him that I agreed with him entirely and I should be only too glad to stay, but that it would not be fair upon my colleagues or the country. Unhappily there was nothing to be done about it.

I then sent for the principal Ministers outside the Cabinet. These partings were painful, but none so much as the final duty which awaited me. I felt respect and devotion for the Sovereign I served. I drove to Buckingham Palace and submitted my resignation to Her Majesty.

The next few days and nights we spent at Chequers. M. Spaak came to England to see the Foreign Secretary at this time, in accordance with plans previously made. He asked to come to see me at Chequers from London Airport, before seeing any of my colleagues. I was grateful for this action by an old friend, whose opinions I had so often found penetrating and courageous. We had been through so much together in the past, Hitler's occupation of the Rhineland, the developing menace of the dictators, my first resignation and the war, when M. Spaak joined us with the Belgian Government in exile, that we understood events and each other more easily than could those who had not shared this experience. He was the last European statesman I saw at Chequers.

Among the messages which reached me was one from Mr. Sidney Holland, the Prime Minister of New Zealand, inviting us to spend the winter in that lovely country. I had been to New Zealand twice before and had often wished to stay there longer. The invitation made a strong appeal to us both. There were doubts on medical grounds, but there was at least a chance that the fevers might not become more frequent and that an improvement in general health, which the voyage would give, would strengthen me to meet them if they did. The risk seemed worth taking and we accepted.

On January 18th we sailed from Tilbury. I gave my final message:

> The difference between the West and Egypt has not been colonialism—it is the difference between democracies and a dictatorship. The British people, with their instinctive good sense, have understood that. I am sure they will always understand.

Friends came to see us off, at dockside, on board ship and at the locks. At one of these, my wife and I were looking casually over the side when a tall figure came running through the fog. It was my kind friend, Lord Bracken, who had missed us at our sailing and headed us off this way to say good-bye.

We dropped down the river on a cold, misty winter's afternoon. Ships called to us and wirelessed their greetings as we passed. They continued to do so all across the Atlantic and across the Pacific into Auckland harbour.

A message from the Captain told us that the cadets of the training ship *Worcester* had asked to be allowed to man ship and speed us on our way. We came up on deck to see them. Their cheers were the last sound I heard in England. We went below.

INDEX

Abadan, loss of, 9, 198; cessation of shipments of oil from, 194; British staff leaves, 195; question of sending Americans to, 213; effect, on Egypt, of British evacuation of, 225-6

Abboud Pasha, 236-8

Abdul Rahman el Mahdi, Sir Sayed, 236, 238, 242-3

Abdullah, King of Jordan, 353

Abu Aweigla, 537

Abu Dhabi, Sheikh of, 334-5

Acheson, Dean, 200; presents disarmament proposals, 9; and Korea, 16-22; encourages Japanese recognition of Nationalist China, 19-20; and E.D.C., 31, 35, 40-1; agrees on timing of four-power conference, 45; in Bonn, 46; in Paris for signing of tripartite declaration, 47; discusses help for France in Indo-China, 82-4; discusses Iranian oil problem, 198, 200-2, 204; discusses Egypt and Sudan, 235-6

Aden, 334, 458, 534

Adenauer, Dr. K. (later Chancellor), visits London, 41; politically weak position of, 46, 146; seeks four-power conference, 53; author talks with, before Berlin Conference, 56-7; seeks close British association, 56, 157; Molotov on, 66-7; and alternatives to E.D.C., 150, 154-7, 162; doubtful about nine-power conference, 152; Benelux appreciation of, 153; author visits, 154, 156; Dulles' unexpected visit to, 158-9; Dulles on doubts of, 162, 164; at London Conference, 167; negotiates with Mendès France over Saar, 170; visits author before Summit Conference, 293-4; invited to Moscow, 294; mentioned, 34, 63, 331

Afghanistan, 335

Africa, self-government in colonies of,

381; reaction in, to seizure of Suez Canal, 435-6, 442-3, 458; Russia seeks influence over, 420, 453; no concerted Western policy on, 580; need of 'Marshall plan' for, 580

Afro-Asian: nationalism, 8; resolutions on Suez crisis, 557, 564, 569-70; trade with Israel, 579

Aldrich, Winthrop, U.S. Ambassador at London, 92, 213, 332

Alexander, King of Yugoslavia, 107

Alexander, Field-Marshal Lord, 21, 260

Alexandria, protection of British lives and property in, 232; Farouk in, at time of military revolt, 239; Neguib enters, 241; attempt on Nasser's life in, 259

Alfhem, S.S., 134

Algeria, Egyptian help to nationalists in, 435-6, 521, 571; de Gaulle's plans for, 480

Ali Abu Nuwar, Lieut.-Colonel, 348

Ali Maher Pasha, 232-3, 240-2

Allan, Robert, 549

Allen, Denis, 95, 104, 118, 125

Amer, Maj.-General Abdel Hakim, 258

Amini, Dr. Ali, Iranian Finance Minister, 219

Amman, 343-6

Amory, Rt. Hon. D. Heathcoat, 275, 317-19

Amr Pasha, Egyptian Ambassador at London, 228, 230, 235, 241

Anglo-American relations: causes of friction, 98-9, 119; differences over Indo-China, 104-6, 107, 111-14, 119-120, 127; threatened by search of ships for arms, 135; importance of maintaining accord, 138, 480-1; differences over Iranian question, 198-203, 208, 212; Musaddiq plays off, 202, 204; differences over Egypt and Sudan, 230-1,